T0297773

Foundations of
Quantum
Programming

Foundations of Quantum Programming

Mingsheng Ying

University of Technology Sydney and Tsinghua University

AMSTERDAM • BOSTON • HEIDELBERG • LONDON
NEW YORK • OXFORD • PARIS • SAN DIEGO
SAN FRANCISCO • SINGAPORE • SYDNEY • TOKYO
Morgan Kaufmann is an imprint of Elsevier

Morgan Kaufmann is an imprint of Elsevier
50 Hampshire Street, 5th Floor, Cambridge, MA 02139, USA

Notices
Knowledge and best practice in this field are constantly changing. As new research and experience
broaden our understanding, changes in research methods, professional practices, or medical treatment
may become necessary.

Practitioners and researchers must always rely on their own experience and knowledge in evaluating and
using any information, methods, compounds, or experiments described herein. In using such information
or methods they should be mindful of their own safety and the safety of others, including parties for
whom they have a professional responsibility.

To the fullest extent of the law, neither the Publisher nor the authors, contributors, or editors, assume any
liability for any injury and/or damage to persons or property as a matter of products liability, negligence
or otherwise, or from any use or operation of any methods, products, instructions, or ideas contained in
the material herein.

British Library Cataloguing in Publication Data
A catalogue record for this book is available from the British Library

Library of Congress Cataloging-in-Publication Data
A catalog record for this book is available from the Library of Congress

ISBN: 978-0-12-802306-8

For information on all Morgan Kaufmann publications,
visit our website at https://www.elsevier.com/

Working together
to grow libraries in
developing countries

www.elsevier.com • www.bookaid.org

Publisher: Todd Green
Acquisition Editor: Todd Green
Editorial Project Manager: Lindsay Lawrence
Production Project Manager: Punithavathy Govindaradjane
Designer: Greg Harris

Typeset by SPi Global, India

Contents

viii   Contents

Preface

Quantum computers promise dramatic advantages over current computers. Governments and industries around the globe are now investing large amounts of money with the expectation of building practical quantum computers. Recent rapid physical experimental progress has made people widely expect that large-scalable and functional quantum computer *hardware* will be built within 10–20 years. However, to realize the super-power of quantum computing, quantum hardware is obviously not enough, and quantum *software* must also play a key role. The software development techniques used today cannot be applied to quantum computers. Essential differences between the nature of the classical world and that of the quantum world mean that new technologies are required to program quantum computers.

Research on quantum programming started as early as 1996, and rich results have been presented at various conferences or reported in various journals in the last 20 years. On the other hand, quantum programming is still a premature subject, with its knowledge base being highly fragmentary and disconnected. This book is intended to provide a systematic and detailed exposition of the subject of quantum programming.

Since quantum programming is still an area under development, the book does not focus on specific quantum programming languages or techniques, which I believe will undergo major changes in the future. Instead, the emphasis is placed on the foundational concepts, methods and mathematical tools that can be widely used for various languages and techniques. Starting from a basic knowledge of quantum mechanics and quantum computation, the book carefully introduces various quantum program constructs and a chain of quantum programming models that can effectively exploit the unique power of quantum computers. Furthermore, semantics, logics, and verification and analysis techniques of quantum programs are systematically discussed.

With the huge investment and rapid progress in quantum computing technology, I believe that within 10 years more and more researchers will enter the exciting field of quantum programming. They will need a reference book as the starting point of their research. Also, a course on quantum programming will be taught at more and more universities. Teachers and students will need a textbook. So, I decided to write this book with the two-fold aim:

 (i) providing a basis for further research in the area; and
(ii) serving as a textbook for a graduate or advanced undergraduate level course.

Quantum programming is a highly interdisciplinary subject. A newcomer and, in particular, a student is usually frustrated with the requisite knowledge from many different subjects. I have tried to keep the book as self-contained as possible, with details being explicitly presented so that it is accessible to the programming languages community.

Writing this book gave me an opportunity to systemize my views on quantum programming. On the other hand, topics included in this book were selected and the materials were organized according to my own understanding of this subject, and several important topics were omitted in the main body of the book due to my limited knowledge about them. As a remedy, some brief discussions about these topics are provided in the prospects chapter at the end of the book.

Acknowledgments

This book has been developed through my research in the last 15 years at the Quantum Computation and Quantum Information Group of the State Key Laboratory of Intelligent Technology and Systems, Tsinghua University and the Quantum Computation Laboratory of the Centre for Quantum Computation and Intelligent Systems, University of Technology Sydney. I have enjoyed very much collaborations and discussions with my colleagues and students there. I would like to thank all of them.

I am particularly indebted to Ichiro Hasuo (University of Tokyo) and Yuan Feng (University of Technology Sydney) who patiently read the draft of this book and kindly provided invaluable comments and suggestions. I am very grateful to the anonymous reviewers for the book proposal; their suggestions were very helpful for the structure of the book. I also would like to sincerely thank Steve Elliot, Punithavathy Govindaradjane, Amy Invernizzi, and Lindsay Lawrence, my editors and project managers at Morgan Kaufmann.

Special thanks go to the Centre for Quantum Computation and Intelligent Systems, Faculty of Engineering and Information Technology, University of Technology Sydney for giving me the freedom to pursue my thoughts.

My research on quantum programming has been supported by the Australian Research Council, the National Natural Science Foundation of China, and the Overseas Team Program of the Academy of Mathematics and Systems Science, Chinese Academy of Sciences. All of them are gratefully acknowledged.

Introduction and preliminaries

Introduction

"The challenge [of quantum software engineering] is to rework and extend the whole of classical software engineering into the quantum domain so that programmers can manipulate quantum programs with the same ease and confidence that they manipulate today's classical programs."

excerpt from the 2004 report *Grand Challenges in Computing Research* [120].

Quantum programming is the study of how to program future quantum computers. This subject mainly addresses the following two problems:

- How can programming methodologies and technologies developed for current computers be extended for quantum computers?
- What kinds of new programming methodologies and technologies can effectively exploit the unique power of quantum computing?

Many technologies that have been very successful in traditional programming will be broken when used to program a quantum computer, due to the weird nature of quantum systems (e.g., no cloning of quantum data, entanglement between quantum processes, and non-commutativity of observables which are all assertions about program variables). Even more important and difficult is to discover programming paradigms, models and abstractions that can properly exploit the unique power of quantum computing – *quantum parallelism* – but cannot be sourced from knowledge of traditional programming.

1.1 BRIEF HISTORY OF QUANTUM PROGRAMMING RESEARCH

The earliest proposal for quantum programming was made by Knill in 1996 [139]. He introduced the Quantum Random Access Machine (QRAM) model and proposed a set of conventions for writing quantum pseudo-code. In the 20 years since then, research on quantum programming has been continuously conducted, mainly in the following directions.

1.1.1 DESIGN OF QUANTUM PROGRAMMING LANGUAGES

Early research on quantum programming focused on the design of quantum programming languages. Several high-level quantum programming languages have been defined in the later 1990s and early 2000s; for example, the first quantum programming language, QCL, was designed by Ömer [177], who also implemented a simulator for this language. A quantum programming language in the style of Dijkstra's guarded-command language, qGCL, was proposed by Sanders and Zuliani [191,241]. A quantum extension of C++ was proposed by Bettelli et al. [39], and implemented in the form of a C++ library. The first quantum language of the functional programming paradigm, QPL, was defined by Selinger [194] based on the idea of classical control and quantum data. A quantum functional programming language QML with quantum control flows was introduced by Altenkirch and Grattage [14]. Tafliovich and Hehner [208,209] defined a quantum extension of a predicative programming language that supports the program development technique in which each programming step is proven correct when it is made.

Recently, two general-purpose, scalable quantum programming languages, Quipper and Scaffold, with compilers, were developed by Green et al. [106] and Abhari et al. [3], respectively. A domain-specific quantum programming language, QuaFL, was developed by Lapets et al. [150]. A quantum software architecture LIQUi|>, together with a quantum programming language embedded in F#, was designed and implemented by Wecker and Svore [215].

1.1.2 SEMANTICS OF QUANTUM PROGRAMMING LANGUAGES

Formal semantics of a programming language give a rigorous mathematical description of the meaning of this language, to enable a precise and deep understanding of the essence of the language beneath its syntax. The operational or denotational semantics of some quantum programming languages were already provided when they were defined; for example, qGCL, QPL and QML.

Two approaches to predicate transformer semantics of quantum programs have been proposed. The first was adopted by Sanders and Zuliani [191] in designing qGCL, where quantum computation is reduced to probabilistic computation by the observation (measurement) procedure, and thus predicate transformer semantics developed for probabilistic programs can be applied to quantum programs. The second was introduced by D'Hondt and Panangaden [70], where a quantum predicate is defined to be a physical observable represented by a Hermitian operator with eigenvalues within the unit interval. Quantum predicate transformer semantics was further developed in [225] with a special class of quantum predicates, namely projection operators. Focusing on projective predicates allows the use of rich mathematical methods developed in Birkhoff-von Neumann quantum logic [42] to establish various healthiness conditions of quantum programs.

Semantic techniques for quantum computation have also been investigated in some abstract, language-independent ways. Abramsky and Coeck [5] proposed a category-theoretic formulation of the basic postulates of quantum mechanics, which can be used to give an elegant description of quantum programs and communication protocols such as teleportation.

Recent progress includes: Hasuo and Hoshino [115] found a semantic model of a functional quantum programming language with recursion via Girard's Geometry of Interaction [101], categorically formulated by Abramsky, Haghverdi and Scott [7]. Pagani, Selinger and Valiron [178] discovered a denotational semantics for a functional quantum programming language with recursion and an infinite data type using constructions from quantitative semantics of linear logic. Jacobs [123] proposed a categorical axiomatization of block constructs in quantum programming. Staton [206] presented an algebraic semantic framework for equational reasoning about quantum programs.

1.1.3 VERIFICATION AND ANALYSIS OF QUANTUM PROGRAMS

Human intuition is much better adapted to the classical world than the quantum world. This fact implies that programmers will commit many more faults in designing programs for quantum computers than in programming classical computers. Thus, it is crucial to develop verification techniques for quantum programs. Baltag and Smets [30] presented a dynamic logic formalism of information flows in quantum systems. Brunet and Jorrand [50] introduced a way of applying Birkhoff-von Neumann quantum logic in reasoning about quantum programs. Chadha, Mateus and Sernadas [52] proposed a proof system of the Floyd-Hoare style for reasoning about imperative quantum programs in which only bounded iterations are allowed. Some useful proof rules for reasoning about quantum programs were proposed by Feng et al. [82] for purely quantum programs. A Floyd-Hoare logic for both partial and total correctness of quantum programs with (relative) completeness was developed in [221].

Program analysis techniques are very useful in the implementation and optimization of programs. Termination analysis of quantum programs was initiated in [227], where a measurement-based quantum loop with a unitary transformation as the loop body was considered. Termination of a more general quantum loop with a quantum operation as the loop body was studied in [234] using the semantic model of quantum Markov chains. It was also shown in [234] that the Sharir-Pnueli-Hart method for proving properties of probabilistic programs [202] can be elegantly generalized to quantum programs by exploiting the Schrödinger-Heisenberg duality between quantum states and observables. This line of research has been continued in [152,153,235,236,238] where termination of nondeterministic and concurrent quantum programs was investigated based on reachability analysis of quantum Markov decision processes. Another line of research in quantum program analysis was initiated by Jorrand and Perdrix [129] who showed how abstract interpretation techniques can be used in quantum programs.

1.2 APPROACHES TO QUANTUM PROGRAMMING

Naturally, research on quantum programming started from extending traditional programming models, methodologies and technologies into the quantum realm. As stated in Section 1.1, both imperative and functional programming have been generalized for quantum computing, and various semantic models, verification and analysis techniques for classical programs have also been adapted to quantum programming.

The ultimate goal of quantum programming is to fully exploit the power of quantum computers. It has been well understood that the advantage of quantum computers over current computers comes from quantum parallelism – *superposition of quantum states* – and its derivatives such as entanglement. So, a key issue in quantum programming is how to incorporate quantum parallelism into traditional programming models. In my opinion, this issue can be properly addressed in the following two paradigms of superposition.

1.2.1 SUPERPOSITION-OF-DATA – QUANTUM PROGRAMS WITH CLASSICAL CONTROL

The main idea of the *superposition-of-data paradigm* is to introduce new program constructs needed to manipulate quantum data, e.g., unitary transformations, quantum measurements. However, the control flows of quantum programs in such a paradigm are similar to those of classical programs. For example, in classical programming, a basic program construct that can be used to define the control flow of a program is the conditional (**if** ... **then** ... **else** ... **fi**) statement, or more generally the case statement:

$$\mathbf{if} \ (\Box i \cdot G_i \rightarrow P_i) \ \mathbf{fi} \tag{1.1}$$

where for each i, the subprogram P_i is guarded by the Boolean expression G_i, and P_i will be executed only when G_i is true. A natural quantum extension of statement (1.1) is the measurement-based case statement:

$$\mathbf{if} \ (\Box i \cdot M[q] = m_i \rightarrow P_i) \ \mathbf{fi} \tag{1.2}$$

where q is a quantum variable and M a measurement performed on q with possible outcomes $m_1, \ldots, m_n$, and for each i, P_i is a (quantum) subprogram. This statement selects a command according to the outcome of measurement M: if the outcome is m_i, then the corresponding command P_i will be executed. It can be appropriately called *classical case statement in quantum programming* because the selection of commands in it is based on classical information – the outcomes of a quantum measurement. Then other language mechanisms used to specify the control flow of quantum programs, e.g., loop and recursion, can be defined based on this case statement.

The programming paradigm defined here is called the superposition-of-data paradigm because the data input to and computed by these programs are quantum data – superposition of data, but programs themselves are not allowed to be superposed. This paradigm can be even more clearly characterized by Selinger's slogan "quantum data, classical control" [194] because the data flows of the programs are quantum, but their control flows are still classical.

The majority of existing research on quantum programming has been carried out in the superposition-of-data paradigm, dealing with quantum programs with classical control.

1.2.2 SUPERPOSITION-OF-PROGRAMS – QUANTUM PROGRAMS WITH QUANTUM CONTROL

Inspired by the construction of quantum walks [9,19], it was observed in [232,233] that there is a fundamentally different way to define a case statement in quantum programming – *quantum case statement* governed by a quantum "coin":

$$\mathbf{qif}[c] \ (\square i \cdot |i\rangle \rightarrow P_i) \ \mathbf{fiq} \tag{1.3}$$

where $\{|i\rangle\}$ is an orthonormal basis of the state Hilbert space of an *external* "coin" system c, and the selection of subprograms P_i's is made according to the basis states $|i\rangle$ of the "coin" space that *can be superposed* and thus is quantum information rather than classical information. Furthermore, we can define a *quantum choice*:

$$[C]\left(\bigoplus_i |i\rangle \rightarrow P_i\right) \overset{\triangle}{=} C[c]; \mathbf{qif}[c] \ (\square i \cdot |i\rangle \rightarrow P_i) \ \mathbf{fiq} \tag{1.4}$$

Intuitively, quantum choice (1.4) runs a "coin-tossing" program C to create a superposition of the execution paths of subprograms $P_1, \ldots, P_n$, followed by a quantum case statement. During the execution of the quantum case statement, each P_i is running along its own path within the whole superposition of execution paths of $P_1, \ldots, P_n$. Based on this kind of quantum case statement and quantum choice, some new quantum program constructs such as quantum recursion can be defined.

This approach to quantum programming can be termed the *superposition-of-programs paradigm*. It is clear from the definitions of quantum case statement and quantum choice that the control flow of a quantum program in the superposition-of-program paradigm is inherently quantum. So, this paradigm can also be characterized by the slogan "quantum data, quantum control"[1].

I have to admit that this paradigm is still in a very early stage of development, and a series of fundamental problems are not well understood. On the other hand, I believe that it introduces a new way of thinking about quantum programming that can help a programmer to further exploit the unique power of quantum computing.

---

[1]The slogan "quantum data, quantum control" was used in [14] and in a series of its continuations to describe a class of quantum programs for which the design idea is very different from that introduced here.

1.3 STRUCTURE OF THE BOOK

This book is a systematic exposition of the theoretical foundations of quantum programming, organized along the line *from superposition-of-data to superposition-of-programs*. The book focuses on imperative quantum programming, but most ideas and techniques introduced in this book can also be generalized to functional quantum programming.

The book is divided into four parts:

- Part I consists of this introductory chapter and Chapter 2, Preliminaries. The prerequisites for reading this book are knowledge of quantum mechanics and quantum computation and reasonable familiarity with the theory of programming languages. All prerequisites for quantum mechanics and quantum computation are provided in Chapter 2. For theory of programming languages, I suggest the reader consult the standard textbooks, e.g., [21,158,162,200].
- Part II studies quantum programs with classical control in the superposition-of-data paradigm. This part contains three chapters. Chapter 3 carefully introduces the syntax and the operational and denotational semantics of quantum programs with classical control (case statement, loop and recursion). Chapter 4 presents a logical foundation for reasoning about correctness of quantum programs with classical control. Chapter 5 develops a series of mathematical tools and algorithmic techniques for analysis of quantum programs with classical control.
- Part III studies quantum programs with quantum control in the superposition-of-programs paradigm. This part consists of two chapters. Chapter 6 defines quantum case statement and quantum choice and their semantics, and establishes a set of algebraic laws for reasoning about quantum programs with the constructs of quantum case statement and quantum choice. Chapter 7 illustrates how recursion with quantum control can be naturally defined using quantum case statement and quantum choice. It further defines the semantics of this kind of quantum recursion with second quantization – a mathematical framework for dealing with quantum systems where the number of particles may vary.
- Part IV consists of a single chapter designed to give a brief introduction to several important topics from quantum programming that have been omitted in the main body of the book and to point out several directions for future research.

The dependencies of chapters are shown in Figure 1.1.

- ***Reading the Book***: From Figure 1.1, we can see that the book is designed to be read along the following three paths:
  - *Path 1*: Chapter 2 → Chapter 3 → Chapter 4. This path is for the reader who is mainly interested in logic for quantum programs.
  - *Path 2*: Chapter 2 → Chapter 3 → Chapter 5. This path is for the reader who is interested in analysis of quantum programs.
  - *Path 3*: Chapter 2 → Chapter 3 → Chapter 6 → Chapter 7. This path is for the reader who would like to learn the basic quantum program constructs in

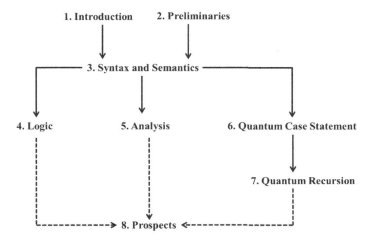

FIGURE 1.1

Dependencies of chapters.

not only the superposition-of-data but also the superposition-of-programs paradigms.

Of course, only a thorough reading from the beginning to the end of the book can give the reader a full picture of the subject of quantum programming.

- ***Teaching from the Book***: A short course on the basics of quantum programming can be taught based on Chapters 2 and 3. Furthermore, Parts I and II of this book can be used for a one- or two-semester advanced undergraduate or graduate course. A one-semester course can cover one of the first two paths described previously. Since the theory of quantum programming with quantum control (in the superposition-of-programs paradigm) is still at an early stage of its development, it is better to use Chapters 6 and 7 as discussion materials for a series of seminars rather than for a course.
- ***Exercises***: The proofs of some lemmas and propositions are left as exercises. They are usually not difficult. The reader is encouraged to try all of them in order to solidify understanding of the related materials.
- ***Research Problems***: A couple of problems for future research are proposed at the end of each chapter in Parts II and III.
- ***Bibliographic Notes***: The last sections of Chapters 2 through 7 are bibliographic notes, where citations and references are given, and recommendations for further reading are provided. The complete bibliography is provided in a separate section at the end of the book, containing the alphabetized list of both cited references and those recommended for further reading.
- ***Errors***: I would appreciate receiving any comments and suggestions about this book. In particular, if you find any errors in the book, please email them to: Mingsheng.Ying@uts.edu.au or yingmsh@tsinghua.edu.cn.

Preliminaries

2

This chapter introduces the basic concepts and notations from quantum mechanics and quantum computation used throughout the book.

- Of course, quantum programming theory is built based on quantum mechanics. So, Section 2.1 introduces the Hilbert space formalism of quantum mechanics, which is exactly the mathematical knowledge base of this book.
- Quantum circuits are introduced in Section 2.2. Historically, several major quantum algorithms appeared before any quantum programming language was defined. So, quantum circuits usually serve as the computational model in which quantum algorithms are described.
- Section 2.3 introduces several basic quantum algorithms. The aim of this section is to provide examples for quantum programming rather than a systematic exposition of quantum algorithms. Thus, I decided not to include more sophisticated quantum algorithms.

In order to allow the reader to enter the core of this book – quantum programming – as quickly as possible, I tried to make this chapter minimal. Thus, the materials in this chapter are presented very briefly. Total newcomers to quantum computation can start with this chapter, but at the same time I suggest that they read the corresponding parts of Chapters 2, 4, 5, 6 and 8 of book [174] for more detailed explanations and examples of the notions introduced in this chapter. On the other hand, for the reader who is familiar with these materials from a standard textbook such as [174], I suggest moving directly to the next chapter, using this chapter only for fixing notations.

2.1 QUANTUM MECHANICS

Quantum mechanics is a fundamental physics subject that studies phenomena at the atomic and subatomic scales. A general formalism of quantum mechanics can be elucidated based on several basic postulates. We choose to introduce the basic postulates of quantum mechanics by presenting the mathematical framework in which these postulates can be properly formulated. The physics interpretations of these postulates are only very briefly discussed. I hope this provides the reader a short cut towards a grasp of quantum programming.

2.1.1 HILBERT SPACES

A Hilbert space usually serves as the state space of a quantum system. It is defined based on the notion of vector space. We write $\mathbb{C}$ for the set of complex numbers. For each complex number $\lambda = a + bi \in \mathbb{C}$, its conjugate is $\lambda^* = a - bi$. We adopt the Dirac notation which is standard in quantum mechanics: $|\varphi\rangle, |\psi\rangle, \ldots$ stands for vectors.

Definition 2.1.1. *A (complex) vector space is a nonempty set $\mathcal{H}$ together with two operations:*

- *vector addition $+ : \mathcal{H} \times \mathcal{H} \to \mathcal{H}$*
- *scalar multiplication $\cdot : \mathbb{C} \times \mathcal{H} \to \mathcal{H}$*

satisfying the following conditions:

(i) *$+$ is commutative: $|\varphi\rangle + |\psi\rangle = |\psi\rangle + |\varphi\rangle$ for any $|\varphi\rangle, |\psi\rangle \in \mathcal{H}$.*
(ii) *$+$ is associative: $|\varphi\rangle + (|\psi\rangle + |\chi\rangle) = (|\varphi\rangle + |\psi\rangle) + |\chi\rangle$ for any $|\varphi\rangle, |\psi\rangle, |\chi\rangle \in \mathcal{H}$.*
(iii) *$+$ has the zero element 0, called the zero vector, such that $0 + |\varphi\rangle = |\varphi\rangle$ for any $|\varphi\rangle \in \mathcal{H}$.*
(iv) *each $|\varphi\rangle \in \mathcal{H}$ has its negative vector $-|\varphi\rangle$ such that $|\varphi\rangle + (-|\varphi\rangle) = 0$.*
(v) *$1|\varphi\rangle = |\varphi\rangle$ for any $|\varphi\rangle \in \mathcal{H}$.*
(vi) *$\lambda(\mu|\varphi\rangle) = \lambda\mu|\varphi\rangle$ for any $|\varphi\rangle \in \mathcal{H}$ and $\lambda, \mu \in \mathbb{C}$.*
(vii) *$(\lambda + \mu)|\varphi\rangle = \lambda|\varphi\rangle + \mu|\varphi\rangle$ for any $|\varphi\rangle \in \mathcal{H}$ and $\lambda, \mu \in \mathbb{C}$.*
(viii) *$\lambda(|\varphi\rangle + |\psi\rangle) = \lambda|\varphi\rangle + \lambda|\psi\rangle$ for any $|\varphi\rangle, |\psi\rangle \in \mathcal{H}$ and $\lambda \in \mathbb{C}$.*

To define the notion of Hilbert space, we also need the following:

Definition 2.1.2. *An inner product space is a vector space $\mathcal{H}$ equipped with an inner product; that is, a mapping:*

$$\langle \cdot | \cdot \rangle : \mathcal{H} \times \mathcal{H} \to \mathbb{C}$$

satisfying the following properties:

(i) *$\langle \varphi | \varphi \rangle \geq 0$ with equality if and only if $|\varphi\rangle = 0$;*
(ii) *$\langle \varphi | \psi \rangle = \langle \psi | \varphi \rangle^*$;*
(iii) *$\langle \varphi | \lambda_1 \psi_1 + \lambda_2 \psi_2 \rangle = \lambda_1 \langle \varphi | \psi_1 \rangle + \lambda_2 \langle \varphi | \psi_2 \rangle$*

for any $|\varphi\rangle, |\psi\rangle, |\psi_1\rangle, |\psi_2\rangle \in \mathcal{H}$ and for any $\lambda_1, \lambda_2 \in \mathbb{C}$.

For any vectors $|\varphi\rangle, |\psi\rangle \in \mathcal{H}$, the complex number $\langle \varphi | \psi \rangle$ is called the inner product of $|\varphi\rangle$ and $|\psi\rangle$. Sometimes, we write $(|\varphi\rangle, |\psi\rangle)$ for $\langle \varphi | \psi \rangle$. If $\langle \varphi | \psi \rangle = 0$, then we say that $|\varphi\rangle$ and $|\psi\rangle$ are orthogonal and write $|\varphi\rangle \perp |\psi\rangle$. The length of a vector $|\psi\rangle \in \mathcal{H}$ is defined to be

$$||\psi|| = \sqrt{\langle \psi | \psi \rangle}.$$

A vector $|\psi\rangle$ is called a unit vector if $||\psi|| = 1$.

The notion of limit can be defined in terms of the length of a vector.

Definition 2.1.3. *Let $\{|\psi_n\rangle\}$ be a sequence of vectors in $\mathcal{H}$ and $|\psi\rangle \in \mathcal{H}$.*

(i) *If for any $\epsilon > 0$, there exists a positive integer N such that $||\psi_m - \psi_n|| < \epsilon$ for all $m, n \geq N$, then $\{|\psi_n\rangle\}$ is called a Cauchy sequence.*

(ii) *If for any $\epsilon > 0$, there exists a positive integer N such that $||\psi_n - \psi|| < \epsilon$ for all $n \geq N$, then $|\psi\rangle$ is called a limit of $\{|\psi_n\rangle\}$ and we write $|\psi\rangle = \lim_{n\to\infty} |\psi_n\rangle$.*

Now we are ready to present the definition of Hilbert space.

Definition 2.1.4. *A Hilbert space is a complete inner product space: that is, an inner product space in which each Cauchy sequence of vectors has a limit.*

A notion that helps us to understand the structure of a Hilbert space is its basis. In this book, we only consider finite-dimensional or countably infinite-dimensional (separable) Hilbert space.

Definition 2.1.5. *A finite or countably infinite family $\{|\psi_i\rangle\}$ of unit vectors is called an orthonormal basis of $\mathcal{H}$ if*

(i) *$\{|\psi_i\rangle\}$ are pairwise orthogonal: $|\psi_i\rangle \perp |\psi_j\rangle$ for any i, j with $i \neq j$;*

(ii) *$\{|\psi_i\rangle\}$ span the whole space $\mathcal{H}$: each $|\psi\rangle \in \mathcal{H}$ can be written as a linear combination $|\psi\rangle = \sum_i \lambda_i |\psi_i\rangle$ for some $\lambda_i \in \mathbb{C}$ and a finite number of $|\psi_i\rangle$.*

The numbers of vectors in any two orthonormal bases are the same. This is called the dimension of $\mathcal{H}$ and written as $\dim \mathcal{H}$; in particular, if an orthonormal basis contains infinitely many vectors, then $\mathcal{H}$ is infinite-dimensional and we write $\dim \mathcal{H} = \infty$.

Infinite-dimensional Hilbert spaces are required in quantum programming theory only when a data type is infinite, e.g., integers. If it is hard for the reader to understand infinite-dimensional Hilbert spaces and associated concepts (e.g., limits in Definition 2.1.3, closed subspaces in Definition 2.1.6 following), she/he can simply focus on finite-dimensional Hilbert spaces, which are exactly the vector spaces that were learned in elementary linear algebra; in this way, the reader can still grasp an essential part of this book.

Whenever $\mathcal{H}$ is finite-dimensional, say $\dim \mathcal{H} = n$, and we consider a *fixed* orthonormal basis $\{|\psi_1\rangle, |\psi_2\rangle, \ldots, |\psi_n\rangle\}$, then each vector $|\psi\rangle = \sum_{i=1}^{n} \lambda_i |\psi_i\rangle \in \mathcal{H}$ can be represented by the vector in $\mathbb{C}^n$:

$$\begin{pmatrix} \lambda_1 \\ \cdots \\ \lambda_n \end{pmatrix}$$

The notion of subspace is also important for understanding the structure of a Hilbert space.

Definition 2.1.6. *Let $\mathcal{H}$ be a Hilbert space.*

(i) *If $X \subseteq \mathcal{H}$, and for any $|\varphi\rangle, |\psi\rangle \in X$ and $\lambda \in \mathbb{C}$,*
    (a) *$|\varphi\rangle + |\psi\rangle \in X$;*
    (b) *$\lambda|\varphi\rangle \in X$,*
    then X is called a subspace of $\mathcal{H}$.

(ii) *For each $X \subseteq \mathcal{H}$, its closure $\overline{X}$ is the set of limits $\lim_{n\to\infty} |\psi_n\rangle$ of sequences $\{|\psi_n\rangle\}$ in X.*
(iii) *A subspace X of $\mathcal{H}$ is closed if $\overline{X} = X$.*

For any subset $X \subseteq \mathcal{H}$, the space spanned by X:

$$spanX = \left\{ \sum_{i=1}^{n} \lambda_i |\psi_i\rangle : n \geq 0, \lambda_i \in \mathbb{C} \text{ and } |\psi_i\rangle \in X \ (i = 1, \ldots, n) \right\} \tag{2.1}$$

is the smallest subspace of $\mathcal{H}$ containing X. In other words, $spanX$ is the subspace of $\mathcal{H}$ generated by X. Moreover, $\overline{spanX}$ is the closed subspace generated by X.

We defined orthogonality between two vectors previously. It can be further defined between two sets of vectors.

Definition 2.1.7. *Let $\mathcal{H}$ be a Hilbert space.*

(i) *For any $X, Y \subseteq \mathcal{H}$, we say that X and Y are orthogonal, written $X \perp Y$, if $|\varphi\rangle \perp |\psi\rangle$ for all $|\varphi\rangle \in X$ and $|\psi\rangle \in Y$. In particular, we simply write $|\varphi\rangle \perp Y$ if X is the singleton $\{|\varphi\rangle\}$.*
(ii) *The orthocomplement of a closed subspace X of $\mathcal{H}$ is*

$$X^{\perp} = \{|\varphi\rangle \in \mathcal{H} : |\varphi\rangle \perp X\}.$$

The orthocomplement $X^{\perp}$ is also a closed subspace of $\mathcal{H}$, and we have $(X^{\perp})^{\perp} = X$ for every closed subspace X of $\mathcal{H}$.

Definition 2.1.8. *Let $\mathcal{H}$ be a Hilbert space, and let X, Y be two subspaces of $\mathcal{H}$. Then*

$$X \oplus Y = \{|\varphi\rangle + |\psi\rangle : |\varphi\rangle \in X \text{ and } |\psi\rangle \in Y\}$$

is called the sum of X and Y.

This definition can be straightforwardly generalized to the sum $\bigoplus_{i=1}^{n} X_i$ of more than two subspaces X_i of $\mathcal{H}$. In particular, if X_i $(1 \leq i \leq n)$ are orthogonal to each other, then $\bigoplus_{i=1}^{n} X_i$ is called an orthogonal sum.

With the above preparation, we can present:

- **Postulate of quantum mechanics 1:** The state space of a closed (i.e., an isolated) quantum system is represented by a Hilbert space, and a pure state of the system is described by a unit vector in its state space.

A linear combination $|\psi\rangle = \sum_{i=1}^{n} \lambda_i |\psi_i\rangle$ of states $|\psi_1\rangle, \ldots, |\psi_n\rangle$ is often called their *superposition*, and the complex coefficients λ_i are called probability amplitudes.

Example 2.1.1. *A qubit – quantum bit – is the quantum counterpart of a bit. Its state space is the two-dimensional Hilbert space:*

$$\mathcal{H}_2 = \mathbb{C}^2 = \{\alpha|0\rangle + \beta|1\rangle : \alpha, \beta \in \mathbb{C}\}.$$

The inner product in $\mathcal{H}_2$ is defined by

$$(\alpha|0\rangle + \beta|1\rangle, \alpha'|0\rangle + \beta'|1\rangle) = \alpha^*\alpha' + \beta^*\beta'$$

for all $\alpha, \alpha', \beta, \beta' \in \mathbb{C}$. Then $\{|0\rangle, |1\rangle\}$ is an orthonormal basis of $\mathcal{H}_2$, called the computational basis. The vectors $|0\rangle, |1\rangle$ themselves are represented as

$$|0\rangle = \begin{pmatrix} 1 \\ 0 \end{pmatrix}, \quad |1\rangle = \begin{pmatrix} 0 \\ 1 \end{pmatrix}$$

in this basis. A state of a qubit is described by a unit vector $|\psi\rangle = \alpha|0\rangle + \beta|1\rangle$ with $|\alpha|^2 + |\beta|^2 = 1$. The two vectors:

$$|+\rangle = \frac{|0\rangle + |1\rangle}{\sqrt{2}} = \frac{1}{\sqrt{2}}\begin{pmatrix} 1 \\ 1 \end{pmatrix}, \quad |-\rangle = \frac{|0\rangle - |1\rangle}{\sqrt{2}} = \frac{1}{\sqrt{2}}\begin{pmatrix} 1 \\ -1 \end{pmatrix}$$

form another orthonormal basis. Both of them are superpositions of $|0\rangle$ and $|1\rangle$. The two-dimensional Hilbert space $\mathcal{H}_2$ can also be seen as the quantum counterpart of the classical Boolean data type.

Example 2.1.2. *Another Hilbert space often used in this book is the space of square summable sequences:*

$$\mathcal{H}_\infty = \left\{ \sum_{n=-\infty}^{\infty} \alpha_n|n\rangle : \alpha_n \in \mathbb{C} \text{ for all } n \in \mathbb{Z} \text{ and } \sum_{n=-\infty}^{\infty} |\alpha_n|^2 < \infty \right\},$$

where $\mathbb{Z}$ is the set of integers. The inner product in $\mathcal{H}_\infty$ is defined by

$$\left(\sum_{n=-\infty}^{\infty} \alpha_n|n\rangle, \sum_{n=-\infty}^{\infty} \alpha'|n\rangle \right) = \sum_{n=-\infty}^{\infty} \alpha_n^*\alpha_n'$$

for all $\alpha_n, \alpha_n' \in \mathbb{C}$ ($-\infty < n < \infty$). Then $\{|n\rangle : n \in \mathbb{Z}\}$ is an orthonormal basis, and $\mathcal{H}_\infty$ is infinite-dimensional. This Hilbert space can be seen as the quantum counterpart of the classical integer data type.

Exercise 2.1.1. *Verify that the inner products defined in the previous two examples satisfy conditions (i)–(iii) in Definition 2.1.2.*

2.1.2 LINEAR OPERATORS

We studied the static description of a quantum system, namely its state space as a Hilbert space, in the previous subsection. Now we turn to learning how to describe the dynamics of a quantum system. The evolution of and all operations on a quantum system can be depicted by linear operators in its state Hilbert space. So, in this subsection, we study linear operators and their matrix representations.

Definition 2.1.9. *Let $\mathcal{H}$ and $\mathcal{K}$ be Hilbert spaces. A mapping*

$$A : \mathcal{H} \to \mathcal{K}$$

is called an (a linear) operator if it satisfies the following conditions:

(i) $A(|\varphi\rangle + |\psi\rangle) = A|\varphi\rangle + A|\psi\rangle$;

(ii) $A(\lambda|\psi\rangle) = \lambda A|\psi\rangle$

for all $|\varphi\rangle, |\psi\rangle \in \mathcal{H}$ *and* $\lambda \in \mathbb{C}$.

An operator from $\mathcal{H}$ to itself is called an operator in $\mathcal{H}$. The identity operator in $\mathcal{H}$ that maps each vector in $\mathcal{H}$ to itself is denoted $I_{\mathcal{H}}$, and the zero operator in $\mathcal{H}$ that maps every vector in $\mathcal{H}$ to the zero vector is denoted $0_{\mathcal{H}}$. For any vectors $|\varphi\rangle, |\psi\rangle \in \mathcal{H}$, their outer product is the operator $|\varphi\rangle\langle\psi|$ in $\mathcal{H}$ defined by

$$(|\varphi\rangle\langle\psi|)|\chi\rangle = \langle\psi|\chi\rangle|\varphi\rangle$$

for every $|\chi\rangle \in \mathcal{H}$. A class of simple but useful operators are projectors. Let X be a closed subspace of $\mathcal{H}$ and $|\psi\rangle \in \mathcal{H}$. Then there exist uniquely $|\psi_0\rangle \in X$ and $|\psi_1\rangle \in X^{\perp}$ such that

$$|\psi\rangle = |\psi_0\rangle + |\psi_1\rangle.$$

The vector $|\psi_0\rangle$ is called the projection of $|\psi\rangle$ onto X and written $|\psi_0\rangle = P_X|\psi\rangle$.

Definition 2.1.10. *For each closed subspace X of $\mathcal{H}$, the operator*

$$P_X : \mathcal{H} \to X, \quad |\psi\rangle \mapsto P_X|\psi\rangle$$

is called the projector onto X.

Exercise 2.1.2. *Show that $P_X = \sum_i |\psi_i\rangle\langle\psi_i|$ if $\{|\psi_i\rangle\}$ is an orthonormal basis of X.*

Throughout this book, we only consider bounded operators, as defined in the following:

Definition 2.1.11. *An operator A in $\mathcal{H}$ is said to be bounded if there is a constant $C \geq 0$ such that*

$$\||A|\psi\rangle\| \leq C \cdot \|\psi\|$$

for all $|\psi\rangle \in \mathcal{H}$. The norm of A is defined to be the nonnegative number:

$$\|A\| = \inf\{C \geq 0 : \||A|\psi\rangle\| \leq C \cdot \|\psi\| \text{ for all } \psi \in \mathcal{H}\}.$$

We write $\mathcal{L}(\mathcal{H})$ for the set of bounded operators in $\mathcal{H}$.

All operators in a finite-dimensional Hilbert space are bounded.

Various operations of operators are very useful in order to combine several operators to produce a new operator. The addition, scalar multiplication and composition of operators can be defined in a natural way: for any $A, B \in \mathcal{L}(\mathcal{H})$, $\lambda \in \mathbb{C}$ and $|\psi\rangle \in \mathcal{H}$,

$$(A + B)|\psi\rangle = A|\psi\rangle + B|\psi\rangle,$$
$$(\lambda A)|\psi\rangle = \lambda(A|\psi\rangle),$$
$$(BA)|\psi\rangle = B(A|\psi\rangle).$$

Exercise 2.1.3. *Show that $\mathcal{L}(\mathcal{H})$ with addition and scalar multiplication forms a vector space.*

We can also define positivity of an operator as well as an order and a distance between operators.

Definition 2.1.12. *An operator $A \in \mathcal{L}(\mathcal{H})$ is positive if for all states $|\psi\rangle \in \mathcal{H}$, $\langle\psi|A|\psi\rangle$ is a nonnegative real number: $\langle\psi|A|\psi\rangle \geq 0$.*

Definition 2.1.13. *The Löwner order $\sqsubseteq$ is defined as follows: for any $A, B \in \mathcal{L}(\mathcal{H})$, $A \sqsubseteq B$ if and only if $B - A = B + (-1)A$ is positive.*

Definition 2.1.14. *Let $A, B \in \mathcal{L}(\mathcal{H})$. Then their distance is*

$$d(A, B) = \sup_{|\psi\rangle} \||A|\psi\rangle - B|\psi\rangle\| \tag{2.2}$$

where $|\psi\rangle$ traverses all pure states (i.e., unit vectors) in $\mathcal{H}$.

Matrix Representation of Operators:

Operators in a finite-dimensional Hilbert space have a matrix representation, which is very convenient in applications. After reading this part, the reader should have a better understanding of those abstract notions defined previously through a connection from them to the corresponding notions that she/he learned in elementary linear algebra.

If $\{|\psi_i\rangle\}$ is an orthonormal basis of $\mathcal{H}$, then an operator A is uniquely determined by the images $A|\psi_i\rangle$ of the basis vectors $|\psi_i\rangle$ under A. In particular, when $\dim \mathcal{H} = n$ is finite and we consider a *fixed* orthonormal basis $\{|\psi_1\rangle, \ldots, |\psi_n\rangle\}$, A can be represented by the $n \times n$ complex matrix:

$$A = (a_{ij})_{n \times n} = \begin{pmatrix} a_{11} & \cdots & a_{1n} \\ & \cdots & \\ a_{n1} & \cdots & a_{nn} \end{pmatrix}$$

where

$$a_{ij} = \langle\psi_i|A|\psi_j\rangle = (|\psi_i\rangle, A|\psi_j\rangle)$$

for every $i, j = 1, \ldots, n$. Moreover, the image of a vector $|\psi\rangle = \sum_{i=1}^{n} \alpha_i|\psi_i\rangle \in \mathcal{H}$ under operator A is represented by the product of matrix $A = (a_{ij})_{n \times n}$ and vector $|\psi\rangle$:

$$A|\psi\rangle = A\begin{pmatrix} \alpha_1 \\ \cdots \\ \alpha_n \end{pmatrix} = \begin{pmatrix} \beta_1 \\ \cdots \\ \beta_n \end{pmatrix}$$

where $\beta_i = \sum_{j=1}^{n} a_{ij}\alpha_j$ for every $i = 1, \ldots, n$. For example, $I_{\mathcal{H}}$ is the unit matrix, and $0_{\mathcal{H}}$ is the zero matrix. If

$$|\varphi\rangle = \begin{pmatrix} \alpha_1 \\ \cdots \\ \alpha_n \end{pmatrix}, \quad |\psi\rangle = \begin{pmatrix} \beta_1 \\ \cdots \\ \beta_n \end{pmatrix},$$

then their outer product is the matrix $|\varphi\rangle\langle\psi| = (a_{ij})_{n \times n}$ with $a_{ij} = \alpha_i\beta_j^*$ for every $i, j = 1, \ldots, n$. Throughout this book, we do not distinguish an operator in a finite-dimensional Hilbert space from its matrix representation.

Exercise 2.1.4. *Show that in a finite-dimensional Hilbert space, addition, scalar multiplication and composition of operators correspond to addition, scalar multiplication and multiplication of their matrix representations, respectively.*

2.1.3 UNITARY TRANSFORMATIONS

The postulate of quantum mechanics 1 introduced in Subsection 2.1.1 provides the static description of a quantum system. In this subsection, we give a description of the dynamics of a quantum system, with the mathematical tool prepared in the last subsection.

The continuous-time dynamics of a quantum system are given by a differential equation, called the Schrödinger equation. But in quantum computation, we usually consider the discrete-time evolution of a system – a unitary transformation. For any operator $A \in \mathcal{L}(\mathcal{H})$, it turns out that there exists a unique (linear) operator $A^\dagger$ in $\mathcal{H}$ such that

$$(A|\varphi\rangle, |\psi\rangle) = \left(|\varphi\rangle, A^\dagger|\psi\rangle\right)$$

for all $|\varphi\rangle, |\psi\rangle \in \mathcal{H}$. The operator $A^\dagger$ is called the adjoint of A. In particular, if an operator in an n-dimensional Hilbert space is represented by the matrix $A = (a_{ij})_{n\times n}$, then its adjoint is represented by the transpose conjugate of A:

$$A^\dagger = (b_{ij})_{n\times n}$$

with $b_{ij} = a_{ji}^*$ for every $i, j = 1, \ldots, n$.

Definition 2.1.15. *An (bounded) operator $U \in \mathcal{L}(\mathcal{H})$ is called a unitary transformation if the adjoint of U is its inverse:*

$$U^\dagger U = UU^\dagger = I_{\mathcal{H}}.$$

All unitary transformations U preserve the inner product:

$$(U|\varphi\rangle, U|\psi\rangle) = \langle\varphi|\psi\rangle$$

for any $|\varphi\rangle, |\psi\rangle \in \mathcal{H}$. The condition $U^\dagger U = I_{\mathcal{H}}$ is equivalent to $UU^\dagger = I_{\mathcal{H}}$ when $\mathcal{H}$ is finite-dimensional. If $\dim \mathcal{H} = n$, then a unitary operator in $\mathcal{H}$ is represented by an $n \times n$ unitary matrix U; i.e., a matrix U with $U^\dagger U = I_n$, where I_n is the n-dimensional unit matrix.

A useful technique for defining a unitary operator is given in the following:

Lemma 2.1.1. *Suppose that $\mathcal{H}$ is a (finite-dimensional) Hilbert space and $\mathcal{K}$ is a closed subspace of $\mathcal{H}$. If linear operator $U : \mathcal{K} \to \mathcal{H}$ preserves the inner product:*

$$(U|\varphi\rangle, U|\psi\rangle) = \langle\varphi|\psi\rangle$$

for any $|\varphi\rangle, |\psi\rangle \in \mathcal{K}$, then there exists a unitary operator V in $\mathcal{H}$ which extends U; i.e., $V|\psi\rangle = U|\psi\rangle$ for all $|\psi\rangle \in \mathcal{K}$.

Exercise 2.1.5. *Prove Lemma 2.1.1.*

Now we are ready to present:

- **Postulate of quantum mechanics 2:** Suppose that the states of a closed quantum system (i.e., a system without interactions with its environment) at times t_0 and t are $|\psi_0\rangle$ and $|\psi\rangle$, respectively. Then they are related to each other by a unitary operator U which depends only on the times t_0 and t,

$$|\psi\rangle = U|\psi_0\rangle.$$

To help the reader understand this postulate, let us consider two simple examples.

Example 2.1.3. *One frequently used unitary operator on a qubit is the Hadamard transformation in the two-dimensional Hilbert space $\mathcal{H}_2$:*

$$H = \frac{1}{\sqrt{2}} \begin{pmatrix} 1 & 1 \\ 1 & -1 \end{pmatrix}$$

It transforms a qubit in the computational basis states $|0\rangle$ and $|1\rangle$ into their superpositions:

$$H|0\rangle = H\begin{pmatrix} 1 \\ 0 \end{pmatrix} = \frac{1}{\sqrt{2}}\begin{pmatrix} 1 \\ 1 \end{pmatrix} = |+\rangle,$$

$$H|1\rangle = H\begin{pmatrix} 0 \\ 1 \end{pmatrix} = \frac{1}{\sqrt{2}}\begin{pmatrix} 1 \\ -1 \end{pmatrix} = |-\rangle.$$

Example 2.1.4. *Let k be an integer. Then the k-translation operator T_k in the infinite-dimensional Hilbert space $\mathcal{H}_\infty$ is defined by*

$$T_k|n\rangle = |n + k\rangle$$

for all $n \in \mathbb{Z}$. It is easy to verify that T_k is a unitary operator. In particular, we write $T_L = T_{-1}$ and $T_R = T_1$. They move a particle on the line one position to the left and to the right, respectively.

More examples will be seen in Section 2.2, where unitary transformations are used as quantum logic gates in a quantum circuit.

2.1.4 QUANTUM MEASUREMENTS

Now that we understand both the static and dynamic descriptions of a quantum system, observation of a quantum system is carried out through a quantum measurement, which is defined by:

- **Postulate of quantum mechanics 3:** A quantum measurement on a system with state Hilbert space $\mathcal{H}$ is described by a collection $\{M_m\} \subseteq \mathcal{L}(\mathcal{H})$ of operators satisfying the normalization condition:

$$\sum_m M_m^\dagger M_m = I_\mathcal{H}, \tag{2.3}$$

where M_m are called measurement operators, and the index m stands for the measurement outcomes that may occur in the experiment. If the state of a quantum system is $|\psi\rangle$ immediately before the measurement, then for each m, the probability that the result m occurs in the measurement is

$$p(m) = ||M_m|\psi\rangle||^2 = \langle\psi|M_m^\dagger M_m|\psi\rangle \quad \text{(Born rule)}$$

and the state of the system after the measurement with outcome m is

$$|\psi_m\rangle = \frac{M_m|\psi\rangle}{\sqrt{p(m)}}.$$

It is easy to see that the normalization condition (2.3) implies that the probabilities for all outcomes sum up to $\sum_m p(m) = 1$.

The following simple example should help the reader to understand this postulate.

Example 2.1.5. *The measurement of a qubit in the computational basis has two outcomes defined by measurement operators:*

$$M_0 = |0\rangle\langle 0|, \quad M_1 = |1\rangle\langle 1|.$$

If the qubit was in state $|\psi\rangle = \alpha|0\rangle + \beta|1\rangle$ before the measurement, then the probability of obtaining outcome 0 is

$$p(0) = \langle\psi|M_0^\dagger M_0|\psi\rangle = \langle\psi|M_0|\psi\rangle = |\alpha|^2,$$

and in this case the state after the measurement is

$$\frac{M_0|\psi\rangle}{\sqrt{p(0)}} = |0\rangle.$$

Similarly, the probability of outcome 1 is $p(1) = |\beta|^2$ and in this case the state after the measurement is $|1\rangle$.

Projective Measurements:

A specially useful class of measurements is defined in terms of Hermitian operators and their spectral decomposition.

Definition 2.1.16. *An operator $M \in \mathcal{L}(\mathcal{H})$ is said to be Hermitian if it is self-adjoint:*

$$M^\dagger = M.$$

In physics, a Hermitian operator is also called an observable.

It turns out that an operator P is a projector; that is, $P = P_X$ for some closed subspace X of $\mathcal{H}$, if and only if P is Hermitian and $P^2 = P$.

A quantum measurement can be constructed from an observable based on the mathematical concept of spectral decomposition of a Hermitian operator. Due to the limit of space, we only consider spectral decomposition in a finite-dimensional Hilbert space $\mathcal{H}$. (The infinite-dimensional case requires a much heavier mathematical mechanism; see [182], Chapter III.5. In this book, it will be used only in Section 3.6 as a tool for the proof of a technical lemma.)

Definition 2.1.17

(i) *An eigenvector of an operator $A \in \mathcal{L}(\mathcal{H})$ is a non-zero vector $|\psi\rangle \in \mathcal{H}$ such that $A|\psi\rangle = \lambda|\psi\rangle$ for some $\lambda \in \mathbb{C}$, where λ is called the eigenvalue of A corresponding to $|\psi\rangle$.*

(ii) *The set of eigenvalues of A is called the (point) spectrum of A and denoted $spec(A)$.*

(iii) *For each eigenvalue $\lambda \in spec(A)$, the set*

$$\{|\psi\rangle \in \mathcal{H} : A|\psi\rangle = \lambda|\psi\rangle\}$$

is a closed subspace of $\mathcal{H}$ and it is called the eigenspace of A corresponding to λ.

The eigenspaces corresponding to different eigenvalues $\lambda_1 \neq \lambda_2$ are orthogonal. All eigenvalues of an observable (i.e., a Hermitian operator) M are real numbers. Moreover, it has the spectral decomposition:

$$M = \sum_{\lambda \in spec(M)} \lambda P_\lambda$$

where P_λ is the projector onto the eigenspace corresponding to λ. Then it defines a measurement $\{P_\lambda : \lambda \in spec(M)\}$, called a projective measurement because all measurement operators P_λ are projectors. Using the Postulate of quantum mechanics 3 introduced earlier, we obtain: upon measuring a system in state $|\psi\rangle$, the probability of getting result λ is

$$p(\lambda) = \langle\psi|P_\lambda^\dagger P_\lambda|\psi\rangle = \langle\psi|P_\lambda^2|\psi\rangle = \langle\psi|P_\lambda|\psi\rangle \tag{2.4}$$

and in this case the state of the system after the measurement is

$$\frac{P_\lambda|\psi\rangle}{\sqrt{p(\lambda)}}. \tag{2.5}$$

Since all possible outcomes $\lambda \in spec(M)$ are real numbers, we can compute the expectation – average value – of M in state $|\psi\rangle$:

$$\begin{aligned}
\langle M \rangle_\psi &= \sum_{\lambda \in spec(M)} p(\lambda) \cdot \lambda \\
&= \sum_{\lambda \in spec(M)} \lambda \langle\psi|P_\lambda|\psi\rangle \\
&= \langle\psi| \sum_{\lambda \in spec(M)} \lambda P_\lambda |\psi\rangle \\
&= \langle\psi|M|\psi\rangle.
\end{aligned}$$

We observe that, given the state $|\psi\rangle$, probability (2.4) and post-measurement state (2.5) are determined only by the projectors $\{P_\lambda\}$ (rather than M itself). It is easy to see that $\{P_\lambda\}$ is a complete set of orthogonal projectors; that is, a set of operators satisfying the conditions:

(i) $P_\lambda P_\delta = \begin{cases} P_\lambda & \text{if } \lambda = \delta, \\ 0_{\mathcal{H}} & \text{otherwise;} \end{cases}$

(ii) $\sum_\lambda P_\lambda = I_{\mathcal{H}}$.

Sometimes, we simply call a complete set of orthogonal projectors a projective measurement. A special case is the measurement in an orthonormal basis $\{|i\rangle\}$ of the state Hilbert space, where $P_i = |i\rangle\langle i|$ for every i. Example 2.1.5 is such a measurement for a qubit.

2.1.5 TENSOR PRODUCTS OF HILBERT SPACES

Up to now we have only considered a single quantum system. In this section, we further show how a large composite system can be made up of two or more subsystems. The description of a composite system is based on the notion of tensor product. We mainly consider the tensor product of a finite family of Hilbert spaces.

Definition 2.1.18. *Let $\mathcal{H}_i$ be a Hilbert space with $\{|\psi_{ij_i}\rangle\}$ as an orthonormal basis for $i = 1, \ldots, n$. We write $\mathcal{B}$ for the set having elements of the form:*

$$|\psi_{1j_1}, \ldots, \psi_{nj_n}\rangle = |\psi_{1j_1} \otimes \ldots \otimes \psi_{nj_n}\rangle = |\psi_{1j_1}\rangle \otimes \ldots \otimes |\psi_{nj_n}\rangle.$$

Then the tensor product of $\mathcal{H}_i$ ($i = 1, \ldots, n$) is the Hilbert space with $\mathcal{B}$ as an orthonormal basis:

$$\bigotimes_i \mathcal{H}_i = \text{span}\mathcal{B}.$$

It follows from equation (2.1) that each element in $\bigotimes_i \mathcal{H}_i$ can be written in the form of

$$\sum_{j_1, \ldots, j_n} \alpha_{j_1, \ldots, j_n} |\varphi_{1j_1}, \ldots, \varphi_{nj_n}\rangle$$

where $|\varphi_{1j_1}\rangle \in \mathcal{H}_1, \ldots, |\varphi_{nj_n}\rangle \in \mathcal{H}_n$ and $\alpha_{j_1, \ldots, j_n} \in \mathbb{C}$ for all $j_1, \ldots, j_n$. Furthermore, it can be shown by linearity that the choice of basis $\{|\psi_{ij_i}\rangle\}$ of each factor space $\mathcal{H}_i$ is not essential in the previous definition: for example, if $|\varphi_i\rangle = \sum_{j_i} \alpha_{j_i} |\varphi_{ij_i}\rangle \in \mathcal{H}_i$ ($i = 1, \ldots, n$), then

$$|\varphi_1\rangle \otimes \ldots \otimes |\varphi_n\rangle = \sum_{j_1, \ldots, j_n} \alpha_{1j_1} \ldots \alpha_{nj_n} |\varphi_{1j_1}, \ldots, \varphi_{nj_n}\rangle.$$

The vector addition, scalar multiplication and inner product in $\bigotimes_i \mathcal{H}_i$ can be naturally defined based on the fact that $\mathcal{B}$ is an orthonormal basis.

We will need to consider the tensor product of a countably infinite family of Hilbert spaces occasionally in this book. Let $\{\mathcal{H}_i\}$ be a countably infinite family of Hilbert spaces, and let $\{|\psi_{ij_i}\rangle\}$ be an orthonormal basis of $\mathcal{H}_i$ for each i. We write $\mathcal{B}$ for the set of tensor products of basis vectors of all $\mathcal{H}_i$:

$$\mathcal{B} = \left\{ \bigotimes_i |\psi_{ij_i}\rangle \right\}.$$

Then $\mathcal{B}$ is a finite or countably infinite set, and it can be written in the form of a sequence of vectors: $\mathcal{B} = \{|\varphi_n\rangle : n = 0, 1, \ldots\}$. The tensor product of $\{\mathcal{H}_i\}$ can be properly defined to be the Hilbert space with $\mathcal{B}$ as an orthonormal basis:

$$\bigotimes_i \mathcal{H}_i = \left\{ \sum_n \alpha_n |\varphi_n\rangle : \alpha_n \in \mathbb{C} \text{ for all } n \geq 0 \text{ and } \sum_n |\alpha_n|^2 < \infty \right\}.$$

Now we are able to present:

- **Postulate of quantum mechanics 4:** The state space of a composite quantum system is the tensor product of the state spaces of its components.

Suppose that S is a quantum system composed of subsystems $S_1, \ldots, S_n$ with state Hilbert space $\mathcal{H}_1, \ldots, \mathcal{H}_n$. If for each $1 \leq i \leq n$, S_i is in state $|\psi_i\rangle \in \mathcal{H}_i$, then S is in the product state $|\psi_1, \ldots, \psi_n\rangle$. Furthermore, S can be in a superposition (i.e., linear combination) of several product states. One of the most interesting and puzzling phenomenon in quantum mechanics – *entanglement* – occurs in a composite system: a state of the composite system is said to be entangled if it is not a product of states of its component systems. The existence of entanglement is one of the major differences between the classical world and the quantum world.

Example 2.1.6. *The state space of the system of n qubits is:*

$$\mathcal{H}_2^{\otimes n} = \mathbb{C}^{2^n} = \left\{ \sum_{x \in \{0,1\}^n} \alpha_x |x\rangle : \alpha_x \in \mathbb{C} \text{ for all } x \in \{0,1\}^n \right\}.$$

In particular, a two-qubit system can be in a product state such as $|00\rangle, |1\rangle|+\rangle$ but also in an entangled state such as the Bell states or the EPR (Einstein-Podolsky-Rosen) pairs:

$$|\beta_{00}\rangle = \frac{1}{\sqrt{2}}(|00\rangle + |11\rangle), \quad |\beta_{01}\rangle = \frac{1}{\sqrt{2}}(|01\rangle + |10\rangle),$$

$$|\beta_{10}\rangle = \frac{1}{\sqrt{2}}(|00\rangle - |11\rangle), \quad |\beta_{11}\rangle = \frac{1}{\sqrt{2}}(|01\rangle - |10\rangle).$$

Of course, we can talk about (linear) operators, unitary transformations and measurements in the tensor product of Hilbert spaces since it is a Hilbert space too. A special class of operators in the tensor product of Hilbert spaces is defined as follows:

Definition 2.1.19. *Let $A_i \in \mathcal{L}(\mathcal{H}_i)$ for $i = 1, \ldots, n$. Then their tensor product is the operator $\bigotimes_{i=1}^{n} A_i = A_1 \otimes \ldots \otimes A_n \in \mathcal{L}\left(\bigotimes_{i=1}^{n} \mathcal{H}_i\right)$ defined by*

$$(A_1 \otimes \ldots \otimes A_n)|\varphi_1, \ldots, \varphi_n\rangle = A_1|\varphi_1\rangle \otimes \ldots \otimes A_n|\varphi_n\rangle$$

for all $|\varphi_i\rangle \in \mathcal{H}_i$ $(i = 1, \ldots, n)$ together with linearity.

But other operators rather than tensor products are indispensable in quantum computation because they can create entanglement.

Example 2.1.7. *The controlled-NOT or CNOT operator C in the state Hilbert space $\mathcal{H}_2^{\otimes 2} = \mathbb{C}^4$ of a two-qubit system is defined by*

$$C|00\rangle = |00\rangle, \quad C|01\rangle = |01\rangle, \quad C|10\rangle = |11\rangle, \quad C|11\rangle = |10\rangle$$

or equivalently as the 4×4 matrix

$$C = \begin{pmatrix} 1 & 0 & 0 & 0 \\ 0 & 1 & 0 & 0 \\ 0 & 0 & 0 & 1 \\ 0 & 0 & 1 & 0 \end{pmatrix}.$$

It can transform product states into entangled states:

$$C|+\rangle|0\rangle = \beta_{00}, \quad C|+\rangle|1\rangle = \beta_{01}, \quad C|-\rangle|0\rangle = \beta_{10}, \quad C|-\rangle|1\rangle = \beta_{11}.$$

Implementing a General Measurement by a Projective Measurement:

Projective measurements are introduced in subsection 2.1.4 as a special class of quantum measurements. The notion of tensor product enables us to show that an arbitrary quantum measurement can be implemented by a projective measurement together with a unitary transformation if we are allowed to introduce an *ancilla* system. Let $M = \{M_m\}$ be a quantum measurement in Hilbert space $\mathcal{H}$.

- We introduce a new Hilbert space $\mathcal{H}_M = span\{|m\rangle\}$, which is used to record the possible outcomes of M.
- We arbitrarily choose a fixed state $|0\rangle \in \mathcal{H}_M$. Define operator

$$U_M(|0\rangle|\psi\rangle) = \sum_m |m\rangle M_m|\psi\rangle$$

for every $|\psi\rangle \in \mathcal{H}$. It is easy to check that U_M preserves the inner product, and by Lemma 2.1.1 it can be extended to a unitary operator in $\mathcal{H}_M \otimes \mathcal{H}$, which is denoted by U_M too.
- We define a projective measurement $\overline{M} = \{\overline{M}_m\}$ in $\mathcal{H}_M \otimes \mathcal{H}$ with $\overline{M}_m = |m\rangle\langle m| \otimes I_{\mathcal{H}}$ for every m.

Then the measurement M is realized by the projective measurement $\overline{M}$ together with the unitary operator U_M, as shown in the following:

Proposition 2.1.1. *Let* $|\psi\rangle \in \mathcal{H}$ *be a pure state.*

- *When we perform measurement M on* $|\psi\rangle$, *the probability of outcome m is denoted* $p_M(m)$ *and the post-measurement state corresponding to m is* $|\psi_m\rangle$.
- *When we perform measurement* $\overline{M}$ *on* $|\overline{\psi}\rangle = U_M(|0\rangle|\psi\rangle)$, *the probability of outcome m is denoted* $p_{\overline{M}}(m)$ *and the post-measurement state corresponding to m is* $|\overline{\psi}_m\rangle$.

Then for each m, we have: $p_{\overline{M}}(m) = p_M(m)$ *and* $|\overline{\psi}_m\rangle = |m\rangle|\psi_m\rangle$. *A similar result holds when we consider a mixed state in* $\mathcal{H}$ *introduced in the next subsection.*
   Exercise 2.1.6. *Prove Proposition 2.1.1.*

2.1.6 DENSITY OPERATORS

We have already learned all of the four basic postulates of quantum mechanics. But they were only formulated in the case of pure states. In this section, we extend these postulates so that they can be used to deal with mixed states.

Sometimes, the state of a quantum system is not completely known, but we know that it is in one of a number of pure states $|\psi_i\rangle$, with respective probabilities p_i, where $|\psi_i\rangle \in \mathcal{H}$, $p_i \geq 0$ for each i, and $\sum_i p_i = 1$. A convenient notion for coping with this situation is the density operator. We call $\{(|\psi_i\rangle, p_i)\}$ an ensemble of pure states or a mixed state, whose density operator is defined to be

$$\rho = \sum_i p_i |\psi_i\rangle\langle\psi_i|. \tag{2.6}$$

In particular, a pure state $|\psi\rangle$ may be seen as a special mixed state $\{(|\psi\rangle, 1)\}$ and its density operator is $\rho = |\psi\rangle\langle\psi|$.

Density operators can be described in a different but equivalent way.
   Definition 2.1.20. *The trace tr(A) of operator* $A \in \mathcal{L}(\mathcal{H})$ *is defined to be*

$$tr(A) = \sum_i \langle\psi_i|A|\psi_i\rangle$$

where $\{|\psi_i\rangle\}$ *is an orthonormal basis of* $\mathcal{H}$.

It can be shown that $tr(A)$ is independent of the choice of basis $\{|\psi_i\rangle\}$.
   Definition 2.1.21. *A density operator* ρ *in a Hilbert space* $\mathcal{H}$ *is a positive operator (see Definition 2.1.12) with* $tr(\rho) = 1$.

It turns out that for any mixed state $\{(|\psi_i\rangle, p_i)\}$, operator ρ defined by equation (2.6) is a density operator according to Definition 2.1.21. Conversely, for any density operator ρ, there exists a (but not necessarily unique) mixed state $\{(|\psi_i\rangle, p_i)\}$ such that equation (2.6) holds.

The evolution of and a measurement on a quantum system in mixed states can be elegantly formulated in the language of density operators:

- Suppose that the evolution of a closed quantum system from time t_0 to t is described by unitary operator U depending on t_0 and t: $|\psi\rangle = U|\psi_0\rangle$, where

$|\psi_0\rangle, |\psi\rangle$ are the states of the system at times t_0 and t, respectively. If the system is in mixed states ρ_0, ρ at times t_0 and t, respectively, then

$$\rho = U\rho_0 U^\dagger. \tag{2.7}$$

• If the state of a quantum system was ρ immediately before measurement $\{M_m\}$ is performed on it, then the probability that result m occurs is

$$p(m) = tr\left(M_m^\dagger M_m \rho\right), \tag{2.8}$$

and in this case the state of the system after the measurement is

$$\rho_m = \frac{M_m \rho M_m^\dagger}{p(m)}. \tag{2.9}$$

Exercise 2.1.7. *Derive equations (2.7), (2.8) and (2.9) from equation (2.6) and Postulates of quantum mechanics 1 and 2.*

Exercise 2.1.8. *Let M be an observable (a Hermitian operator) and $\{P_\lambda : \lambda \in spec(M)\}$ the projective measurement defined by M. Show that the expectation of M in a mixed state ρ is*

$$\langle M \rangle_\rho = \sum_{\lambda \in spec(M)} p(\lambda) \cdot \lambda = tr(M\rho).$$

Reduced Density Operators:

Postulate of quantum mechanics 4 introduced in the last subsection enables us to construct composite quantum systems. Of course, we can talk about a mixed state of a composite system and its density operator because the state space of the composite system is the tensor product of the state Hilbert spaces of its subsystems, which is a Hilbert space too. Conversely, we often need to characterize the state of a subsystem of a quantum system. However, it is possible that a composite system is in a pure state, but some of its subsystems must be seen as in a mixed state. This phenomenon is another major difference between the classical world and the quantum world. Consequently, a proper description of the state of a subsystem of a composite quantum system can be achieved only after introducing the notion of density operator.

Definition 2.1.22. *Let S and T be quantum systems whose state Hilbert spaces are $\mathcal{H}_S$ and $\mathcal{H}_T$, respectively. The partial trace over system T*

$$tr_T : \mathcal{L}(\mathcal{H}_S \otimes \mathcal{H}_T) \to \mathcal{L}(\mathcal{H}_S)$$

is defined by

$$tr_T(|\varphi\rangle\langle\psi| \otimes |\theta\rangle\langle\zeta|) = \langle\zeta|\theta\rangle \cdot |\varphi\rangle\langle\psi|$$

for all $|\varphi\rangle, |\psi\rangle \in \mathcal{H}_S$ and $|\theta\rangle, |\zeta\rangle \in \mathcal{H}_T$ together with linearity.

Definition 2.1.23. *Let ρ be a density operator in $\mathcal{H}_S \otimes \mathcal{H}_T$. Its reduced density operator for system S is*

$$\rho_S = tr_T(\rho).$$

Intuitively, the reduced density operator ρ_S properly describes the state of subsystem S when the composite system ST is in state ρ. For a more detailed explanation, we refer to [174], Section 2.4.3.

Exercise 2.1.9

(i) *When is the reduced density operator $\rho_A = tr_B(|\psi\rangle\langle\psi|)$ of a pure state $|\psi\rangle$ in $\mathcal{H}_A \otimes \mathcal{H}_B$ not a pure state?*

(ii) *Let ρ be a density operator in $\mathcal{H}_A \otimes \mathcal{H}_B \otimes \mathcal{H}_C$. Does it hold that $tr_C(tr_B(\rho)) = tr_{BC}(\rho)$?*

2.1.7 QUANTUM OPERATIONS

Unitary transformations defined in Section 2.1.3 are suited to describe the dynamics of closed quantum systems. For open quantum systems that interact with the outside world through, for example, measurements, we need the much more general notion of quantum operation to depict their state transformations.

A linear operator in vector space $\mathcal{L}(\mathcal{H})$ – the space of (bounded) operators in a Hilbert space $\mathcal{H}$ – is called a *super-operator* in $\mathcal{H}$. To define a quantum operation, we first introduce the notion of tensor product of super-operators.

Definition 2.1.24. *Let $\mathcal{H}$ and $\mathcal{K}$ be Hilbert spaces. For any super-operator $\mathcal{E}$ in $\mathcal{H}$ and super-operator $\mathcal{F}$ in $\mathcal{K}$, their tensor product $\mathcal{E}\otimes\mathcal{F}$ is the super-operator in $\mathcal{H}\otimes\mathcal{K}$ defined as follows: for each $C \in \mathcal{L}(\mathcal{H} \otimes \mathcal{K})$, we can write:*

$$C = \sum_k \alpha_k(A_k \otimes B_k) \tag{2.10}$$

where $A_k \in \mathcal{L}(\mathcal{H})$ and $B_k \in \mathcal{L}(\mathcal{K})$ for all k. Then we define:

$$(\mathcal{E} \otimes \mathcal{F})(C) = \sum_k \alpha_k(\mathcal{E}(A_k) \otimes \mathcal{F}(B_k)).$$

The linearity of $\mathcal{E}$ and $\mathcal{F}$ guarantees that $\mathcal{E} \otimes \mathcal{F}$ is well-defined: $(\mathcal{E} \otimes \mathcal{F})(C)$ is independent of the choice of A_k and B_k in equation (2.10).

Now we are ready to consider the dynamics of an open quantum system. As a generalization of the Postulate of quantum mechanics 2, suppose that the states of a system at times t_0 and t are ρ and ρ', respectively. Then they must be related to each other by a super-operator $\mathcal{E}$ which depends only on the times t_0 and t,

$$\rho' = \mathcal{E}(\rho).$$

The dynamics between times t_0 and t can be seen as a physical process: ρ is the initial state before the process, and $\rho' = \mathcal{E}(\rho)$ is the final state after the process happens. The following definition identifies those super-operators that are suited to model such a process.

Definition 2.1.25. *A quantum operation in a Hilbert space $\mathcal{H}$ is a super-operator in $\mathcal{H}$ satisfying the following conditions:*

(i) $tr[\mathcal{E}(\rho)] \leq tr(\rho) = 1$ *for each density operator ρ in $\mathcal{H}$;*

(ii) *(Complete positivity) For any extra Hilbert space $\mathcal{H}_R$, $(\mathcal{I}_R \otimes \mathcal{E})(A)$ is positive provided A is a positive operator in $\mathcal{H}_R \otimes \mathcal{H}$, where $\mathcal{I}_R$ is the identity operator in $\mathcal{L}(\mathcal{H}_R)$; that is, $\mathcal{I}_R(A) = A$ for each operator $A \in \mathcal{L}(\mathcal{H}_R)$.*

For an argument that quantum operations are an appropriate mathematical model of state transformation of an open quantum system, we refer to [174], Section 8.2.4. Here are two examples showing how unitary transformations and quantum measurements can be treated as special quantum operations:

Example 2.1.8. *Let U be a unitary transformation in a Hilbert space $\mathcal{H}$. We define:*

$$\mathcal{E}(\rho) = U\rho U^\dagger$$

for every density operator ρ. Then $\mathcal{E}$ is a quantum operation in $\mathcal{H}$.

Example 2.1.9. *Let $M = \{M_m\}$ be a quantum measurement in $\mathcal{H}$.*

(i) *For each m, if for any system state ρ before measurement, we define*

$$\mathcal{E}_m(\rho) = p_m\rho_m = M_m\rho M^\dagger$$

where p_m is the probability of outcome m and ρ_m is the post-measurement state corresponding to m, then $\mathcal{E}_m$ is a quantum operation.

(ii) *For any system state ρ before measurement, the post-measurement state is*

$$\mathcal{E}(\rho) = \sum_m \mathcal{E}_m(\rho) = \sum_m M_m\rho M_m^\dagger$$

whenever the measurement outcomes are ignored. Then $\mathcal{E}$ is a quantum operation.

Quantum operations have been widely used in quantum information theory as a mathematical model of communication channels. In this book, quantum operations are adopted as the main mathematical tool for defining semantics of quantum programs, because a quantum program may contain not only unitary transformations but also quantum measurements in order to read the middle or final computational results, and thus are better treated as an open quantum system.

The abstract definition of quantum operations given here is hard to use in applications. Fortunately, the following theorem offers a helpful insight into a quantum operation as an interaction between the system and an environment as well as calculation convenience in terms of operators rather than super-operators.

Theorem 2.1.1. *The following statements are equivalent:*

(i) *$\mathcal{E}$ is a quantum operation in a Hilbert space $\mathcal{H}$;*

(ii) *(System-environment model) There is an environment system E with state Hilbert space $\mathcal{H}_E$, and a unitary transformation U in $\mathcal{H}_E \otimes \mathcal{H}$ and a projector P onto some closed subspace of $\mathcal{H}_E \otimes \mathcal{H}$ such that*

$$\mathcal{E}(\rho) = tr_E \left[PU(|e_0\rangle\langle e_0| \otimes \rho)U^\dagger P \right]$$

for all density operators ρ in $\mathcal{H}$, where $|e_0\rangle$ is a fixed state in $\mathcal{H}_E$;

(iii) *(Kraus operator-sum representation) There exists a finite or countably infinite set of operators $\{E_i\}$ in $\mathcal{H}$ such that $\sum_i E_i^\dagger E_i \sqsubseteq I$ and*

$$\mathcal{E}(\rho) = \sum_i E_i \rho E_i^\dagger$$

for all density operators ρ in $\mathcal{H}$. In this case, we often write:

$$\mathcal{E} = \sum_i E_i \circ E_i^\dagger.$$

The proof of this theorem is quite involved and omitted here, and the reader can find it in [174], Chapter 8.

2.2 QUANTUM CIRCUITS

A general framework of quantum mechanics was developed in the previous section. From this section on, we consider how to harness the power of quantum systems to do computation. We start from a lower-level model of quantum computers – quantum circuits.

2.2.1 BASIC DEFINITIONS

Digital circuits for classical computation are made from logic gates acting on Boolean variables. Quantum circuits are the quantum counterparts of digital circuits. Roughly speaking, they are made up of quantum (logic) gates, which are modelled by unitary transformations defined in Subsection 2.1.3.

We use $p, q, q_1, q_2, \ldots$ to denote qubit variables. Graphically, they can be thought of as wires in quantum circuits. A sequence $\overline{q}$ of distinct qubit variables is called a quantum register. Sometimes, the order of variables in the register is not essential. Then the register is identified with the set of qubit variables in it. So, we can use set-theoretic notations for registers:

$$p \in \overline{q}, \quad \overline{p} \subseteq \overline{q}, \quad \overline{p} \cap \overline{q}, \quad \overline{p} \cup \overline{q}, \quad \overline{p} \setminus \overline{q}.$$

For each qubit variable q, we write $\mathcal{H}_q$ for its state Hilbert space, which is isomorphic to the two-dimensional $\mathcal{H}_2$ (see Example 2.1.1). Furthermore, for a set $V = \{q_1, \ldots, q_n\}$ of qubit variables or a quantum register $\overline{q} = q_1, \ldots, q_n$, we write:

$$\mathcal{H}_V = \bigotimes_{q \in V} \mathcal{H}_q = \bigotimes_{i=1}^n \mathcal{H}_{q_i} = \mathcal{H}_{\overline{q}}$$

for the state space of the composite system consisting of qubits $q_1, \ldots, q_n$. Obviously, $\mathcal{H}_V$ is 2^n-dimensional. Recall that an integer $0 \leq x < 2^n$ can be represented by a string $x_1 \ldots x_n \in \{0, 1\}^n$ of n bits:

$$x = \sum_{i=1}^{n} x_i \cdot 2^{i-1}.$$

We shall not distinguish integer x from its binary representation. Thus, each pure state in $\mathcal{H}_V$ can be written as

$$|\psi\rangle = \sum_{x=0}^{2^n-1} \alpha_x |x\rangle$$

where $\{|x\rangle\}$ is called the computational basis of $\mathcal{H}_2^{\otimes n}$.

Definition 2.2.1. *For any positive integer n, if U is a $2^n \times 2^n$ unitary matrix, and $\bar{q} = q_1, \ldots, q_n$ is a quantum register, then*

$$G \equiv U[\bar{q}] \ \ or \ G \equiv U[q_1, \ldots, q_n]$$

is called an n-qubit gate and we write $qvar(G) = \{q_1, \ldots, q_n\}$ for the set of (quantum) variables in G.

The gate $G \equiv U[\bar{q}]$ is a unitary transformation in the state Hilbert space $\mathcal{H}_{\bar{q}}$ of $\bar{q}$. We often call unitary matrix U a quantum gate without mentioning the quantum register $\bar{q}$.

Definition 2.2.2. *A quantum circuit is a sequence of quantum gates:*

$$C \equiv G_1 \ldots G_m$$

where $m \geq 1$, and $G_1, \ldots, G_m$ are quantum gates. The set of variables of C is

$$qvar(C) = \bigcup_{i=1}^{m} qvar(G_i).$$

The presentations of quantum gates and quantum circuits in the previous two definitions are somehow similar to the Boolean expressions of classical circuits and convenient for algebraic manipulations. However, they are not illustrative. Indeed, quantum circuits can be represented graphically as is commonly done for classical circuits; the reader can find graphic illustrations of various quantum circuits in Chapter 4 of book [174], and a macro package for drawing quantum circuit diagrams can be found at http://physics.unm.edu/CQuIC//Qcircuit/.

Let us see how a quantum circuit $C \equiv G_1 \ldots G_m$ computes. Suppose that $qvar(C) = \{q_1, \ldots, q_n\}$, and each gate $G_i = U_i[\bar{r}_i]$, where register $\bar{r}_i$ is a subsequence of $\bar{q} = q_1, \ldots, q_n$, and U_i is a unitary transformation in the space $\mathcal{H}_{\bar{r}_i}$.

- If a state $|\psi\rangle \in \mathcal{H}_{qvar(C)}$ is input to the circuit C, then the output is

$$C|\psi\rangle = \overline{U}_m \ldots \overline{U}_1 |\psi\rangle \tag{2.11}$$

where for each i, $\overline{U}_i = U_i \otimes I_i$ is the cylindrical extension of U_i in $\mathcal{H}_C$, and I_i is the identity operator in the space $\mathcal{H}_{\overline{q} \setminus \overline{r}_i}$. Note that the applications of unitary operators $U_1, \ldots, U_m$ in equation (2.11) are in the reverse order of $G_1, \ldots, G_m$ in the circuit C.

- More generally, if $qvar(C) \subsetneq V$ is a set of qubit variables, then each state $|\psi\rangle \in \mathcal{H}_V$ can be written in the form of

$$|\psi\rangle = \sum_i \alpha_i |\varphi_i\rangle |\zeta_i\rangle$$

with $|\varphi_i\rangle \in \mathcal{H}_{qvar(C)}$ and $|\zeta_i\rangle \in \mathcal{H}_{V \setminus qvar(C)}$. Whenever we input $|\psi\rangle$ to the circuit C, the output is

$$C|\psi\rangle = \sum_i \alpha_i (C|\varphi_i\rangle) |\zeta_i\rangle.$$

The linearity of C guarantees that this output is well-defined.

Now we can define equivalence of quantum circuits whenever their outputs are the same upon the same input.

Definition 2.2.3. *Let C_1, C_2 be quantum circuits and $V = qvar(C_1) \cup qvar(C_2)$. If for any $|\psi\rangle \in \mathcal{H}_V$, we have:*

$$C_1|\psi\rangle = C_2|\psi\rangle, \tag{2.12}$$

then C_1 and C_2 are equivalent and we write $C_1 = C_2$.

A classical circuit with n input wires and m output wires is actually a Boolean function

$$f : \{0, 1\}^n \to \{0, 1\}^m.$$

Similarly, a quantum circuit C with $qvar(C) = \{q_1, \ldots, q_n\}$ is always equivalent to a unitary transformation in $\mathcal{H}_{qvar(C)}$ or a $2^n \times 2^n$ unitary matrix. This can be clearly seen from equation (2.11).

Finally, we introduce composition of quantum circuits in order to construct a large quantum circuit from small ones.

Definition 2.2.4. *Let $C_1 \equiv G_1 \ldots G_m$ and $C_2 \equiv H_1 \ldots H_n$ be quantum circuits, where $G_1, \ldots, G_m$ and $H_1, \ldots, H_n$ are quantum gates. Then their composition is the concatenation:*

$$C_1 C_2 \equiv G_1 \ldots G_m H_1 \ldots H_n.$$

Exercise 2.2.1

(i) *Prove that if $C_1 = C_2$ then equation (2.12) holds for any state $|\psi\rangle \in \mathcal{H}_V$ and for any $V \supseteq qvar(C_1) \cup qvar(C_2)$.*

(ii) *Prove that if $C_1 = C_2$ then $CC_1 = CC_2$ and $C_1 C = C_2 C$.*

2.2.2 ONE-QUBIT GATES

After introducing the general definitions of quantum gates and quantum circuits in the last subsection, let us look at some examples in this subsection.

The simplest quantum gates are one-qubit gates. They are represented by 2×2 unitary matrices. One example is the Hadamard gate presented in Example 2.1.3. The following are some other one-qubit gates that are frequently used in quantum computation.

Example 2.2.1

(i) *Global phase shift:*

$$M(\alpha) = e^{i\alpha} I,$$

where α is a real number, and

$$I = \begin{pmatrix} 1 & 0 \\ 0 & 1 \end{pmatrix}$$

is the 2×2 unit matrix.

(ii) *(Relative) phase shift:*

$$P(\alpha) = \begin{pmatrix} 1 & 0 \\ 0 & e^{i\alpha} \end{pmatrix},$$

where α is a real number. In particular, we have:

(a) *Phase gate:*

$$S = P(\pi/2) = \begin{pmatrix} 1 & 0 \\ 0 & i \end{pmatrix}.$$

(b) *$\pi/8$ gate:*

$$T = P(\pi/4) = \begin{pmatrix} 1 & 0 \\ 0 & e^{i\pi/4} \end{pmatrix}.$$

Example 2.2.2. *The Pauli matrices:*

$$\sigma_x = X = \begin{pmatrix} 0 & 1 \\ 1 & 0 \end{pmatrix}, \quad \sigma_y = Y = \begin{pmatrix} 0 & -i \\ i & 0 \end{pmatrix}, \quad \sigma_z = Z = \begin{pmatrix} 1 & 0 \\ 0 & -1 \end{pmatrix}.$$

Obviously, we have $X|0\rangle = |1\rangle$ and $X|1\rangle = |0\rangle$. So, Pauli matrix X is actually the NOT gate.

Example 2.2.3. *Rotations about the $\hat{x}, \hat{y}, \hat{z}$ axes of the Bloch sphere:*

$$R_x(\theta) = \cos\frac{\theta}{2} I - i \sin\frac{\theta}{2} X = \begin{pmatrix} \cos\frac{\theta}{2} & -i\sin\frac{\theta}{2} \\ -i\sin\frac{\theta}{2} & \cos\frac{\theta}{2} \end{pmatrix},$$

$$R_y(\theta) = \cos\frac{\theta}{2} I - i \sin\frac{\theta}{2} Y = \begin{pmatrix} \cos\frac{\theta}{2} & -\sin\frac{\theta}{2} \\ \sin\frac{\theta}{2} & \cos\frac{\theta}{2} \end{pmatrix},$$

$$R_z(\theta) = \cos\frac{\theta}{2} I - i \sin\frac{\theta}{2} Z = \begin{pmatrix} e^{-i\theta/2} & 0 \\ 0 & e^{i\theta/2} \end{pmatrix},$$

where θ is a real number.

The gates in Example 2.2.3 have a nice geometric interpretation: a single qubit state can be represented by a vector in the so-called Bloch sphere. The effect of $R_x(\theta), R_y(\theta), R_z(\theta)$ on this state is to rotate it by angle θ about the x, y, z-axis, respectively, of the Bloch sphere; for details, we refer to [174], Sections 1.3.1 and 4.2. It can be shown that any one-qubit gate can be expressed as a circuit consisting of only rotations and global phase shift.

Exercise 2.2.2. *Prove that all the matrices in the previous three examples are unitary.*

2.2.3 CONTROLLED GATES

One-qubit gates are not enough for any useful quantum computation. In this subsection, we introduce an important class of multiple-qubit gates, namely the controlled gates.

The most frequently used among them is the CNOT operator C defined in Example 2.1.7. Here, we look at it in a different way. Let q_1, q_2 be qubit variables. Then $C[q_1, q_2]$ is a two-qubit gate with q_1 as the control qubit and q_2 as the target qubit. It acts as follows:

$$C[q_1, q_2]|i_1, i_2\rangle = |i_1, i_1 \oplus i_2\rangle$$

for $i_1, i_2 \in \{0, 1\}$, where $\oplus$ is addition modulo 2; that is, if q_1 is set to $|1\rangle$, then q_2 is flipped, otherwise q_2 is left unchanged. As a simple generalization of the CNOT gate, we have:

Example 2.2.4. *Let U be a 2×2 unitary matrix. Then the controlled-U is a two-qubit gate defined by*

$$C(U)[q_1, q_2]|i_1, i_2\rangle = |i_1\rangle U^{i_1}|i_2\rangle$$

for $i_1, i_2 \in \{0, 1\}$. Its matrix representation is

$$C(U) = \begin{pmatrix} I & 0 \\ 0 & U \end{pmatrix}$$

where I is the 2×2 unit matrix. Obviously, $C = C(X)$; that is, CNOT is the controlled-X with X being the Pauli matrix.

Exercise 2.2.3. *SWAP is a two-qubit gate defined by*

$$SWAP[q_1, q_2]|i_1, i_2\rangle = |i_2, i_1\rangle$$

for $i_1, i_2 \in \{0, 1\}$. Intuitively, it swaps the states of two qubits. Show that SWAP can be implemented by three CNOT gates:

$$SWAP[q_1, q_2] = C[q_1, q_2]C[q_2, q_1]C[q_1, q_2].$$

Exercise 2.2.4. *Prove the following properties of controlled gates:*

(i) $C[p, q] = H[q]C(Z)[p, q]H[q]$.
(ii) $C(Z)[p, q] = C(Z)[q, p]$.
(iii) $H[p]H[q]C[p, q]H[p]H[q] = C[q, p]$.

(iv) $C(M(\alpha))[p, q] = P(\alpha)[p]$.
(v) $C[p, q]X[p]C[p, q] = X[p]X[q]$.
(vi) $C[p, q]Y[p]C[p, q] = Y[p]X[q]$.
(vii) $C[p, q]Z[p]C[p, q] = Z[p]$.
(viii) $C[p, q]X[q]C[p, q] = X[q]$.
(ix) $C[p, q]Y[q]C[p, q] = Z[p]Y[q]$.
(x) $C[p, q]Z[q]C[p, q] = Z[p]Z[q]$.
(xi) $C[p, q]T[p] = T[p]C[p, q]$.

All the controlled gates considered previously are two-qubit gates. Actually, we can define a much more general notion of controlled gate.

Definition 2.2.5. *Let* $\overline{p} = p_1, \ldots, p_m$ *and* $\overline{q}$ *be registers with* $\overline{p} \cap \overline{q} = \emptyset$. *If* $G = U[\overline{q}]$ *is a quantum gate, then the controlled circuit* $C^{(\overline{p})}(U)$ *with control qubits* $\overline{p}$ *and target qubits* $\overline{q}$ *is the unitary transformation in the state Hilbert space* $\mathcal{H}_{\overline{p} \cup \overline{q}}$ *defined by*

$$C^{(\overline{p})}(U)|\overline{t}\rangle|\psi\rangle = \begin{cases} |\overline{t}\rangle U|\psi\rangle & \text{if } t_1 = \ldots = t_m = 1, \\ |\overline{t}\rangle|\psi\rangle & \text{otherwise} \end{cases}$$

for any $\overline{t} = t_1 \ldots t_m \in \{0, 1\}^m$ *and* $|\psi\rangle \in \mathcal{H}_{\overline{q}}$.

The following example presents a class of three-qubit controlled gates.

Example 2.2.5. *Let* p_1, p_2, q *be qubit variables and* U *a* 2×2 *unitary matrix. The controlled-controlled-U gate:*

$$C^2(U) = C^{(p_1, p_2)}(U)$$

is the unitary transformation in $\mathcal{H}_{p_1} \otimes \mathcal{H}_{p_2} \otimes \mathcal{H}_q$:

$$C^{(2)}(U)|t_1, t_2, \psi\rangle = \begin{cases} |t_1, t_2, \psi\rangle & \text{if } t_1 = 0 \text{ or } t_2 = 0, \\ |t_1, t_2\rangle U|\psi\rangle & \text{if } t_1 = t_2 = 1 \end{cases}$$

for $t_1, t_2 \in \{0, 1\}$ *and for any* $|\psi\rangle \in \mathcal{H}_q$. *In particular, the controlled-controlled-NOT is called the Toffoli gate.*

The Toffoli gate is universal for classical reversible computation, and it is universal for quantum computation with a little extra help (in the sense defined in Subsection 2.2.5 following). It is also very useful in quantum error-correction.

Exercise 2.2.5. *Prove the following equalities that allow us to combine several controlled gates into a single one:*

(i) $C^{(\overline{p})}(C^{(\overline{q})}(U)) = C^{(\overline{p}, \overline{q})}(U)$.
(ii) $C^{(\overline{p})}(U_1)C^{(\overline{p})}(U_2) = C^{(\overline{p})}(U_1 U_2)$.

2.2.4 QUANTUM MULTIPLEXOR

Controlled gates can be further generalized to multiplexors. In this subsection, we introduce the notion of a quantum multiplexor and its matrix representation.

For classical computation, the simplest multiplexor is a *conditional* described by the "**if** . . . **then** . . . **else** . . ." construction: perform the action specified in the "**then**" clause when the condition after "**if**" is true, and perform the action specified in the "**else**" clause when it is false. The implementation of conditionals may be done by first processing the "**then**" and "**else**" clauses in parallel and then multiplexing the outputs.

Quantum conditional is a quantum analog of classical conditional. It is formed by replacing the condition (Boolean expression) after "**if**" by a qubit; that is, replacing truth values *true* and *false* by the basis states $|1\rangle$ and $|0\rangle$, respectively, of a qubit.

Example 2.2.6. *Let p be a qubit variable and $\bar{q} = q_1, \ldots, q_n$ a quantum register, and let $C_0 = U_0[\bar{q}]$ and $C_1 = U_1[\bar{q}]$ be quantum gates. Then quantum conditional $C_0 \oplus C_1$ is a gate on $1 + n$ qubits $p, \bar{q}$ with the first qubit p as the select qubit and the remaining n qubits $\bar{q}$ as the data qubits, defined by:*

$$(C_0 \oplus C_1)|i\rangle|\psi\rangle = |i\rangle U_i|\psi\rangle$$

for $i \in \{0, 1\}$ and for any $|\psi\rangle \in \mathcal{H}_{\bar{q}}$. Equivalently, it is defined by the matrix:

$$C_0 \oplus C_1 = \left(\begin{array}{cc} U_0 & 0 \\ 0 & U_1 \end{array} \right).$$

The controlled-gate defined in Example 2.2.4 is a special case of quantum conditional: $C(U) = I \oplus U$, where I is the unit matrix.

The essential difference between classical and quantum conditionals is that the select qubit can be not only in the basis states $|0\rangle$ and $|1\rangle$ but also in their superpositions:

$$(C_0 \oplus C_1)(\alpha_0|0\rangle|\psi_0\rangle + \alpha_1|1\rangle|\psi_1\rangle) = \alpha_0|0\rangle U_0|\psi_0\rangle + \alpha_1|1\rangle U_1|\psi_1\rangle$$

for any states $|\psi_0\rangle, |\psi_1\rangle \in \mathcal{H}_{\bar{q}}$ and for any complex numbers α_0, α_1 with $|\alpha_0|^2 + |\alpha_1|^2 = 1$.

A multiplexor is a multi-way generalization of conditional. Roughly speaking, a multiplexor is a switch that passes one of its data inputs through to the output, as a function of a set of select inputs. Similarly, a quantum multiplexor (QMUX for short) is a multi-way generalization of quantum conditional.

Definition 2.2.6. *Let $\bar{p} = p_1, \ldots, p_m$ and $\bar{q} = q_1, \ldots, q_n$ be quantum registers, and for each $x \in \{0, 1\}^m$, let $C_x = U_x[\bar{q}]$ be a quantum gate. Then QMUX*

$$\bigoplus_x C_x$$

is a gate on $m + n$ qubits $\bar{p}, \bar{q}$, having the first m qubits $\bar{p}$ as the select qubits and the remaining n qubits $\bar{q}$ as the data qubits. It preserves any state of the select qubits, and performs a unitary transformation on the data qubits, which is chosen according to the state of the select qubits:

$$\left(\bigoplus_x C_x\right)|t\rangle|\psi\rangle = |t\rangle U_t|\psi\rangle$$

for any $t \in \{0,1\}^m$ and $|\psi\rangle \in \mathcal{H}_{\bar{q}}$.

The matrix representation of the QMUX is a diagonal:

$$\bigoplus_x C_x = \bigoplus_{x=0}^{2^m-1} U_x = \begin{pmatrix} U_0 & & & & \\ & U_1 & & & \\ & & \cdot & & \\ & & & \cdot & \\ & & & & \cdot & \\ & & & & & U_{2^m-1} \end{pmatrix}.$$

Here, we identify an integer $0 \le x < 2^m$ with its binary representation $x \in \{0,1\}^m$. The difference between classical multiplexor and QMUX also comes from the fact that the select qubits $\bar{p}$ can be in a superposition of basis states $|x\rangle$:

$$\left(\bigoplus_x C_x\right)\left(\sum_{x=0}^{2^m-1}\alpha_x|x\rangle|\psi_x\rangle\right) = \sum_{x=0}^{2^m-1}\alpha_x|x\rangle U_x|\psi_x\rangle$$

for any states $|\psi_x\rangle \in \mathcal{H}_{\bar{q}}$ ($0 \le x < 2^m$) and any complex numbers α_x with $\sum_x |\alpha_x|^2 = 1$. Obviously, the controlled gate introduced in Definition 2.2.5 is a special QMUX:

$$C^{(\bar{p})}(U) = I \oplus \ldots \oplus I \oplus U,$$

where the first $2^m - 1$ summands are the unit matrix of the same dimension as U.

Exercise 2.2.6. *Prove the multiplexor extension property:*

$$\left(\bigoplus_x C_x\right)\left(\bigoplus_x D_x\right) = \bigoplus_x (C_x D_x).$$

In the next section, we will see a simple application of QMUX in quantum walks. A close connection between QMUX and a quantum program construct – quantum case statement – will be revealed in Chapter 6. QMUXs have been successfully used for synthesis of quantum circuits (see [201]) and thus will be useful for compilation of quantum programs.

2.2.5 UNIVERSALITY OF GATES

We have already introduced several important classes of quantum gates in the last three subsections. A question naturally arises: are they sufficient for quantum computation? This section is devoted to answering this question.

To better understand this question, let us first consider the corresponding question in classical computation. For each $n \ge 0$, there are 2^{2^n} n-ary Boolean functions. Totally, we have infinitely many Boolean functions. However, there are some small sets of logic gates that are universal: they can generate all Boolean functions; for example, {NOT, AND}, {NOT, OR}. The notion of universality can be easily generalized to the quantum case:

Definition 2.2.7. *A set Ω of unitary matrices is universal if all unitary matrices can be generated by it; that is, for any positive integer n, and for any $2^n \times 2^n$ unitary matrix U, there exists a circuit C with $qvar(C) = \{q_1, \ldots, q_n\}$ constructed from the gates defined by unitary matrices in Ω such that*

$$U[q_1, \ldots, q_n] = C$$

(equivalence of circuits introduced in Definition 2.2.3).

One of the simplest universal sets of quantum gates is presented in the following:

Theorem 2.2.1. *The CNOT gate together with all one-qubit gates is universal.*

The universal sets of classical gates mentioned previously are all finite. However, the universal set of quantum gates given in Theorem 2.2.1 is infinite. Indeed, the set of unitary operators form a continuum, which is uncountably infinite. So, it is impossible to exactly implement an arbitrary unitary operator by a finite set of quantum gates. This forces us to consider approximate universality rather than the exact universality introduced in Definition 2.2.7.

Definition 2.2.8. *A set Ω of unitary matrices is approximately universal if for any unitary operator U and for any $\epsilon > 0$, there is a circuit C with $qvar(C) = \{q_1, \ldots, q_n\}$ constructed from the gates defined by unitary matrices in Ω such that*

$$d(U[q_1, \ldots, q_n], C) < \epsilon,$$

where the distance d is defined by equation (2.2).

Two well-known approximately universal sets of gates are given in the following:

Theorem 2.2.2. *The following two sets of gates are approximately universal:*

 (i) *Hadamard gate H, $\pi/8$ gate T and CNOT gate C;*
(ii) *Hadamard gate H, phase gate S, CNOT gate C and the Toffoli gate (see Example 2.2.5).*

The proofs of Theorems 2.2.1 and 2.2.2 are omitted here, but the reader can find them in book [174], Section 4.5.

2.2.6 MEASUREMENT IN CIRCUITS

The universality theorems presented in the last subsection indicate that any quantum computation can be carried out by a quantum circuit constructed from the basic quantum gates described in Subsections 2.2.2 and 2.2.3. But the output of a quantum circuit is usually a quantum state, which cannot be observed directly from the outside. In order to read out the outcome of computation, we have to perform a measurement at the end of the circuit. So, sometimes we need to consider a generalized notion of quantum circuit, namely circuit with quantum measurements.

As shown in Subsection 2.1.4, we only need to use projective measurements if it is allowed to introduce ancilla qubits. Furthermore, if the circuit contains n qubit variables, the measurement in the computational basis $\{|x\rangle : x \in \{0,1\}^n\}$ is sufficient because any orthonormal basis of these qubits can be obtained from the computational basis by a unitary transformation.

Actually, quantum measurements are not only used at the end of a computation. They are also often performed as an intermediate step of a computation and the measurement outcomes are used to conditionally control subsequent steps of the computation. But Nielsen and Chuang [174] explicitly pointed out:

- **Principle of deferred measurement:** Measurements can always be moved from an intermediate stage of a quantum circuit to the end of the circuit; if the measurement results are used at any stage of the circuit then the classically controlled operations can be replaced by conditional quantum operations.

Exercise 2.2.7. *Elaborate the principle of deferred measurement and prove it. This can be done in the following steps:*

(i) *We can formally define the notion of quantum circuit with measurements (mQC for short) by induction:*
  (a) *Each quantum gate is an mQC;*
  (b) *If $\bar{q}$ is a quantum register, $M = \{M_m\} = \{M_{m_1}, M_{m_2}, \ldots, M_{m_n}\}$ is a quantum measurement in $\mathcal{H}_{\bar{q}}$, and for each m, C_m is an mQC with $\bar{q} \cap qvar(C_m) = \emptyset$, then*

$$\text{if } (\square m \cdot M[\bar{q}] = m \rightarrow C_m) \text{ if} \equiv \text{fi } M[\bar{q}] = m_1 \rightarrow C_{m_1}$$
$$\square \qquad m_2 \rightarrow C_{m_2}$$
$$\cdots \cdots \qquad (2.13)$$
$$\square \qquad m_n \rightarrow C_{m_n}$$
$$\text{fi}$$

  is a mQC too;
  (c) *If C_1 and C_2 are mQCs, so is $C_1 C_2$.*
  Intuitively, equation (2.13) means that we perform measurement M on $\bar{q}$, and then the subsequent computation is selected based on the measurement outcome: if the outcome is m, then the corresponding circuit C_m follows.
(ii) *Generalize the notion of equivalence between quantum circuits (Definition 2.2.3) to the case of mQCs.*
(iii) *Show that for any mQC C, there is a quantum circuit C' (without measurements) and a quantum measurement $M[\bar{q}]$ such that $C = C'M[\bar{q}]$ (equivalence).*

If we remove the condition $\bar{q} \cap qvar(C_m) = \emptyset$ from clause (ii), then the post-measurement states of measured qubits can be used in the subsequent computation. Is the principle of deferred measurement still true for this case?

2.3 QUANTUM ALGORITHMS

Quantum circuits together with measurements described in the last section give us a complete (but low-level) model of quantum computation. Since the early 1990s, various quantum algorithms that can offer speed-up over their classical counterparts have been discovered. Partially due to historical reasons and partially due to lack of convenient quantum programming languages at that time, all of them were described in the model of quantum circuits.

In this section, we present several interesting quantum algorithms. Our aim is to provide examples of the quantum program constructs introduced in the subsequent chapters but not to provide a thorough discussion of quantum algorithms. If the reader would like to enter the core of this book as quickly as possible, she/he can skip this section for the first reading, and directly move to Chapter 3. Of course, she/he will need to come back to this point if she/he wishes to understand the examples in the subsequent chapters where the quantum algorithms presented in this section are programmed.

2.3.1 QUANTUM PARALLELISM AND INTERFERENCE

Let us start from two basic techniques for designing quantum algorithms – quantum parallelism and interference. They are two key ingredients that enable a quantum computer to outperform its classical counterpart.

Quantum Parallelism:

Quantum parallelism can be clearly illustrated through a simple example. Consider an n-ary Boolean function:

$$f : \{0,1\}^n \to \{0,1\}.$$

The task is to evaluate $f(x)$ for different values $x \in \{0,1\}^n$ simultaneously. Classical parallelism for this task can be roughly imagined as follows: *multiple* circuits each for computing the same function f are built, and they are executed simultaneously for different inputs x. In contrast, we only need to build a *single* quantum circuit that implements the unitary transformation:

$$U_f : |x,y\rangle \to |x, y \oplus f(x)\rangle \tag{2.14}$$

for any $x \in \{0,1\}^n$ and $y \in \{0,1\}$. Obviously, unitary operator U_f is generated from the Boolean function f. This circuit consists of $n+1$ qubits, the first n qubits form the "data" register, and the last is the " target" register. It can be proved that given a classical circuit for computing f we can construct a quantum circuit with comparable complexity that implements U_f.

Exercise 2.3.1. *Show that U_f is a multiplexor (see Definition 2.2.6):*

$$U_f = \bigoplus_x U_{f,x},$$

where the first n qubits are used as the select qubits, and for each $x \in \{0, 1\}^n$, $U_{f,x}$ is a unitary operator on the last qubit defined by

$$U_{f,x}|y\rangle = |y \oplus f(x)\rangle$$

for $y \in \{0, 1\}$; that is, $U_{f,x}$ is I (the identity operator) if $f(x) = 0$ and it is X (the NOT gate) if $f(x) = 1$.

The following procedure shows how quantum parallelism can accomplish the task of evaluating $f(x)$ simultaneously for all inputs $x \in \{0, 1\}^n$:

- An equal superposition of 2^n basis states of the data register is produced very efficiently by only n Hadamard gates:

$$|0\rangle^{\otimes n} \xrightarrow{H^{\otimes n}} |\psi\rangle \triangleq \frac{1}{\sqrt{2^n}} \sum_{x \in \{0,1\}^n} |x\rangle,$$

where $|0\rangle^{\otimes n} = |0\rangle \otimes \ldots \otimes |0\rangle$ (the tensor product of n $|0\rangle$'s), and $H^{\otimes n} = H \otimes \ldots \otimes H$ (the tensor product of n H's).
- Applying unitary transformation U_f to the data register in state $|\psi\rangle$ and the target register in state $|0\rangle$ yields:

$$|\psi\rangle|0\rangle = \frac{1}{\sqrt{2^n}} \sum_{x \in \{0,1\}^n} |x, 0\rangle \xrightarrow{U_f} \frac{1}{\sqrt{2^n}} \sum_{x \in \{0,1\}^n} |x, f(x)\rangle. \qquad (2.15)$$

It should be noticed that the unitary transformation U_f was executed *only once* in this equation, but the different terms in the right-hand side of the equation contain information about $f(x)$ for all $x \in \{0, 1\}^n$. In a sense, $f(x)$ was evaluated for 2^n different values of x *simultaneously*.

However, quantum parallelism is not enough for a quantum computer to outperform its classical counterpart. Indeed, to extract information from the state in the right-hand side of equation (2.15), a measurement must be performed on it; for example, if we perform the measurement in the computational basis $\{|x\rangle : x \in \{0, 1\}^n\}$ on the data register, then it would give $f(x)$ at the target register only for a single value of x (with probability $1/2^n$), and we cannot obtain $f(x)$ for all $x \in \{0, 1\}^n$ at the same time. Thus, a quantum computer has no advantage over a classical computer at all if such a naïve way of extracting information is used.

Quantum Interference:

In order to be really useful, quantum parallelism has to be combined with another feature of quantum systems – quantum interference. For example, let us consider a superposition

$$\sum_x \alpha_x |x, f(x)\rangle$$

of which the right-hand side of equation (2.15) is a special case. As said before, if we directly measure the data register in the computational basis, we can only get *local* information about $f(x)$ for a single value of x. But if we first perform a unitary operator U on the data register, then the original superposition is transformed to

$$U\left(\sum_x \alpha_x |x, f(x)\rangle\right) = \sum_x \alpha_x \left(\sum_{x'} U_{x'x} |x', f(x)\rangle\right)$$

$$= \sum_{x'}\left[|x'\rangle \otimes \left(\sum_x \alpha_x U_{x'x} |f(x)\rangle\right)\right],$$

where $U_{x'x} = \langle x'|U|x\rangle$, and now the measurement in the computational basis will give certain *global* information about $f(x)$ for all $x \in \{0,1\}^n$. This global information resides in

$$\sum_x \alpha_x U_{x'x} |f(x)\rangle$$

for some single value x'. In a sense, the unitary transformation U was able to merge information about $f(x)$ for different values of x. It is worth noting that the measurement in a basis after a unitary transformation is essentially the measurement in a different basis. So, an appropriate choice of a basis in which a measurement is performed is crucial in order to extract the desired global information.

2.3.2 DEUTSCH-JOZSA ALGORITHM

It is still not convincing from the general discussion in the previous subsection that quantum parallelism and interference can actually help us to solve some interesting computational problems. However, the power of combining quantum parallelism and interference can be clearly seen in the Deutsch-Jozsa algorithm that solves the following:

- *Deutsch Problem:* Given a Boolean function $f : \{0,1\}^n \to \{0,1\}$, known to be either constant, or balanced – $f(x)$ equals 0 for exactly half of all the possible x, and 1 for the other half. Determine whether it is constant or balanced.

The algorithm is described in Figure 2.1. It should be emphasized that in this algorithm, the unitary operator U_f determined by function f according to equation (2.14) is supplied as an oracle.

To understand this quantum algorithm, we need to carefully look at several key ideas in its design:

- In step 2, the target register (the last qubit) is cleverly initialized in state $|-\rangle = H|1\rangle$ rather than in state $|0\rangle$ as in equation (2.15). This special initialization is often referred to as the *phase kickback trick* since

$$U_f|x, -\rangle = |x\rangle \otimes (-1)^{f(x)}|-\rangle$$

$$= (-1)^{f(x)}|x, -\rangle.$$

- **Inputs:** A quantum oracle that implements the unitary operator U_f defined by equation (2.14).
- **Outputs:** 0 if and only if f is constant.
- **Runtime:** One application of U_f. Always succeeds.
- **Procedure:**

1. $|0\rangle^{\otimes n}|1\rangle$

2. $\overset{H^{\otimes(n+1)}}{\to} \dfrac{1}{\sqrt{2^n}} \sum\limits_{x\in\{0,1\}^n} |x\rangle|-\rangle$

3. $\overset{U_f}{\to} \dfrac{1}{\sqrt{2^n}} \sum\limits_{x}(-1)^{f(x)}|x\rangle|-\rangle$

4. $\overset{H^{\otimes n} \text{ on the first } n \text{ qubits}}{\to} \sum\limits_{z} \dfrac{\sum_x(-1)^{x\cdot z+f(x)}}{2^n}|z\rangle|-\rangle$

5. $\overset{\text{measure on the first } n \text{ qubits in the computational basis}}{\to} z$

FIGURE 2.1

Deutsch-Jozsa algorithm.

Here, only the phase of the target register is changed from 1 to $(-1)^{f(x)}$, which can be moved to the front of the data register.
- Quantum parallelism happens in step 3 when applying the oracle U_f.
- Quantum interference is used in step 4: n Hadamard gates acting on the data register (the first n qubits) yields

$$
\begin{aligned}
H^{\otimes n}&\left(\frac{1}{\sqrt{2^n}}\sum_x |x\rangle \otimes (-1)^{f(x)}|-\rangle\right)\\
&= \frac{1}{\sqrt{2^n}}\sum_x \left(H^{\otimes n}|x\rangle \otimes (-1)^{f(x)}|-\rangle\right)\\
&= \frac{1}{2^n}\sum_x \left(\sum_z (-1)^{x\cdot z}|z\rangle \otimes (-1)^{f(x)}|-\rangle\right)\\
&= \frac{1}{2^n}\sum_z \left[\left(\sum_x (-1)^{x\cdot z+f(x)}\right)|z\rangle \otimes |-\rangle\right].
\end{aligned}
\tag{2.16}
$$

- In step 5, we measure the data register in the computational basis $\{|z\rangle : z \in \{0,1\}^n\}$. The probability that we get outcome $z = 0$ (i.e., $|z\rangle = |0\rangle^{\otimes n}$) is

$$
\frac{1}{2^n}\left|\sum_x (-1)^{f(x)}\right|^2 = \begin{cases} 1 & \text{if } f \text{ is constant,}\\ 0 & \text{if } f \text{ is balanced.} \end{cases}
$$

It is interesting to note that the positive and negative contributions to the amplitude for $|0\rangle^{\otimes n}$ cancel when f is balanced.

Exercise 2.3.2. *Prove the equality used in equation (2.16):*

$$H^{\otimes n}|x\rangle = \frac{1}{\sqrt{2^n}} \sum_{z\in\{0,1\}^n} (-1)^{x\cdot z}|z\rangle$$

for any $x \in \{0,1\}^n$, where

$$x \cdot z = \sum_{i=1}^{n} x_i z_i$$

if $x = x_1,\ldots,x_n$ and $z = z_1,\ldots,z_n$.

Finally, let us briefly compare the query complexities of the Deutsch problem in classical computing and the Deutsch-Jozsa algorithm. A deterministic classical algorithm should repeatedly select a value $x \in \{0,1\}^n$ and calculate $f(x)$ until it can determine with certainty whether f is constant or balanced. So, a classical algorithm requires $2^{n-1} + 1$ evaluations of f. In contrast, U_f is executed only once in step 3 of the Deutsch-Jozsa algorithm.

2.3.3 GROVER SEARCH ALGORITHM

The Deutsch-Jozsa algorithm properly illustrates several key ideas for designing quantum algorithms, but the problem solved by it is somehow artificial. In this subsection, we introduce a quantum algorithm that is very useful for a wide range of practical applications, namely the Grover algorithm that solves the following:

- *Search Problem*: The task is to search through a database consisting of N elements, indexed by numbers $0, 1, \ldots, N-1$. For convenience, we assume that $N = 2^n$ so that the index can be stored in n bits. We also assume that the problem has exactly M solutions with $1 \le M \le N/2$.

As in the Deutsch-Jozsa algorithm, we are supplied with a quantum oracle – a black box with the ability to recognize a solution of the search problem. Formally, let function $f : \{0, 1, \ldots, N-1\} \to \{0, 1\}$ be defined as follows:

$$f(x) = \begin{cases} 1 & \text{if } x \text{ is a solution,} \\ 0 & \text{otherwise.} \end{cases}$$

We write

$$\mathcal{H}_N = \mathcal{H}_2^{\otimes n} = span\{|0\rangle, |1\rangle, \ldots, |N-1\rangle\}$$

with $\mathcal{H}_2$ being the state Hilbert space of a qubit. Then the oracle can be thought of as the unitary operator $O = U_f$ in $\mathcal{H}_N \otimes \mathcal{H}_2$ defined by

$$O|x, q\rangle = U_f|x, q\rangle = |x\rangle|q \oplus f(x)\rangle \tag{2.17}$$

for $x \in \{0, 1, \ldots, N-1\}$ and $q \in \{0, 1\}$, where $|x\rangle$ is the index register, and $|q\rangle$ is the oracle qubit which is flipped if x is a solution, and is unchanged otherwise. In particular, the oracle has the phase kickback property:

$$|x, -\rangle \xrightarrow{O} (-1)^{f(x)}|x, -\rangle.$$

Thus, if the oracle qubit is initially in state $|-\rangle$, then it remains $|-\rangle$ throughout the search algorithm and can be omitted. So, we can simply write:

$$|x\rangle \xrightarrow{O} (-1)^{f(x)}|x\rangle. \tag{2.18}$$

Grover Rotation:
One key subroutine of the Grover algorithm is called the Grover rotation. It consists of four steps, as described in Figure 2.2.

- **Procedure:**

  1. Apply the oracle O;
  2. Apply the Hadamard transform $H^{\otimes n}$;
  3. Perform a conditional phase shift :
     $$|0\rangle \to |0\rangle,$$
     $$|x\rangle \to -|x\rangle \text{ for all } x \neq 0;$$
  4. Apply the Hadamard transform $H^{\otimes n}$.

FIGURE 2.2

Grover rotation.

Let us see what the Grover rotation actually does. We write G for the unitary transformation defined by the procedure in Figure 2.2; i.e., the composition of the operators in steps 1-4. It should be pointed out that the oracle O used in step 1 is thought of as a unitary operator in the space $\mathcal{H}_N$ (rather than $\mathcal{H}_N \otimes \mathcal{H}_2$) defined by equation (2.18). The conditional phase shift in step 3 is defined in the basis $\{|0\rangle, |1\rangle, \ldots, |N-1\rangle\}$ of the space $\mathcal{H}_N$. The following lemma presents the unitary operator of the quantum circuit that implements the Grover rotation.

Lemma 2.3.1. $G = (2|\psi\rangle\langle\psi| - I)O$, where

$$|\psi\rangle = \frac{1}{\sqrt{N}} \sum_{x=0}^{N-1} |x\rangle$$

is the equal superposition in $\mathcal{H}_N$.

Exercise 2.3.3. *Prove Lemma 2.3.1.*

It is not easy to imagine from just the previous description that the operator G represents a rotation. A geometric visualization can help us to understand the Grover rotation better. Let us introduce two vectors in the space $\mathcal{H}_N$:

$$|\alpha\rangle = \frac{1}{\sqrt{N-M}} \sum_{x \text{ not solution}} |x\rangle,$$

$$|\beta\rangle = \frac{1}{\sqrt{M}} \sum_{x \text{ solution}} |x\rangle.$$

It is clear that the vectors $|\alpha\rangle$ and $|\beta\rangle$ are orthogonal. If we define angle θ by

$$\cos\frac{\theta}{2} = \sqrt{\frac{N-M}{N}} \ (0 \le \frac{\theta}{2} \le \frac{\pi}{2}),$$

then the equal superposition in Lemma 2.3.1 can be expressed as follows:

$$|\psi\rangle = \cos\frac{\theta}{2}|\alpha\rangle + \sin\frac{\theta}{2}|\beta\rangle.$$

Furthermore, we have:

Lemma 2.3.2. $G(\cos\delta|\alpha\rangle + \sin\delta|\beta\rangle) = \cos(\theta+\delta)|\alpha\rangle + \sin(\theta+\delta)|\beta\rangle.$

Intuitively, the Grover operator G is a rotation for angle θ in the two-dimensional space spanned by $|\alpha\rangle$ and $|\beta\rangle$. For any real number δ, the vector $\cos\delta|\alpha\rangle + \sin\delta|\beta\rangle$ can be represented by a point $(\cos\delta, \sin\delta)$. Thus, Lemma 2.3.2 indicates that the action of G is depicted by the mapping:

$$(\cos\delta, \sin\delta) \xrightarrow{G} (\cos(\theta+\delta), \sin(\theta+\delta)).$$

Exercise 2.3.4. *Prove Lemma 2.3.2.*

Grover Algorithm:

Using the Grover rotation as a subroutine, the quantum search algorithm can be described as shown in Figure 2.3.

It should be noted that k in Figure 2.3 is a constant integer; the value of k will be suitably fixed in the next paragraph.

Performance Analysis:

It can be shown that the search problem requires approximately N/M operations by a classical computer. Let us see how many iterations of G are needed in step 3 of the Grover algorithm. Note that in step 2 the index register (i.e., the first n qubits) is prepared in the state

$$|\psi\rangle = \sqrt{\frac{N-M}{N}}|\alpha\rangle + \sqrt{\frac{M}{N}}|\beta\rangle.$$

- **Inputs:** A quantum oracle O defined by equation (2.17).
- **Outputs:** A solution x.
- **Runtime:** $O(\sqrt{N})$ operations. Succeeds with probability $\Theta(1)$.
- **Procedure:**

1. $|0\rangle^{\otimes n}|1\rangle$

2. $\xrightarrow{H^{\otimes(n+1)}} \dfrac{1}{\sqrt{2^n}} \displaystyle\sum_{x=0}^{2^n-1} |x\rangle|-\rangle = \left(\cos\dfrac{\theta}{2}|\alpha\rangle + \sin\dfrac{\theta}{2}|\beta\rangle \right)|-\rangle$

3. $\xrightarrow{G^k \text{ on the first } n \text{ qubits}} \left[\cos\left(\dfrac{2k+1}{2}\theta\right)|\alpha\rangle + \sin\left(\dfrac{2k+1}{2}\theta\right)|\beta\rangle \right]|-\rangle$

4. $\xrightarrow{\text{measure the first } n \text{ qubits in the computational basis}} |x\rangle$

FIGURE 2.3

Grover search algorithm.

So, rotating through $\arccos\sqrt{\dfrac{M}{N}}$ radians takes the index register from $|\psi\rangle$ to $|\beta\rangle$. It is asserted by Lemma 2.3.2 that the Grover operator G is a rotation for angle θ. Let k be the integer closest to the real number

$$\frac{\arccos\sqrt{\dfrac{M}{N}}}{\theta}.$$

Then we have:

$$k \leq \left\lceil \frac{\arccos\sqrt{\dfrac{M}{N}}}{\theta} \right\rceil \leq \left\lceil \frac{\pi}{2\theta} \right\rceil$$

because $\arccos\sqrt{\dfrac{M}{N}} \leq \dfrac{\pi}{2}$. Consequently, k is a positive integer in the interval $\left[\dfrac{\pi}{2\theta} - 1, \dfrac{\pi}{2\theta} \right]$. By the assumption $M \leq \dfrac{N}{2}$, we have

$$\frac{\theta}{2} \geq \sin\frac{\theta}{2} = \sqrt{\frac{M}{N}}$$

and $k \leq \left\lceil \dfrac{\pi}{4}\sqrt{\dfrac{N}{M}} \right\rceil$, i.e., $k = O(\sqrt{N})$. On the other hand, by the definition of k we obtain:

$$\left| k - \frac{\arccos\sqrt{\dfrac{M}{N}}}{\theta} \right| \leq \frac{1}{2}.$$

It follows that

$$\arccos\sqrt{\frac{M}{N}} \le \frac{2k+1}{2}\theta \le \theta + \arccos\sqrt{\frac{M}{N}}.$$

Since $\cos\frac{\theta}{2} = \sqrt{\frac{N-M}{N}}$, we have $\arccos\sqrt{\frac{M}{N}} = \frac{\pi}{2} - \frac{\theta}{2}$ and

$$\frac{\pi}{2} - \frac{\theta}{2} \le \frac{2k+1}{2}\theta \le \frac{\pi}{2} + \frac{\theta}{2}.$$

Thus, since $M \le \frac{N}{2}$, it holds that the success probability

$$\Pr(\text{success}) = \sin^2\left(\frac{2k+1}{2}\theta\right) \ge \cos^2\frac{\theta}{2} = \frac{N-M}{N} \ge \frac{1}{2},$$

i.e., $\Pr(\text{success}) = \Theta(1)$. In particular, if $M \ll N$, then the success probability is very high.

The previous derivation can be summarized as follows: The Grover algorithm can find a solution x with success probability $O(1)$ within $k = O(\sqrt{N})$ steps.

2.3.4 QUANTUM WALKS

In the previous subsections, we saw how the power of quantum parallelism and interference can be exploited to design the Deutsch-Jozsa algorithm and the Grover search algorithm. We now turn to consider a class of quantum algorithms for which the design idea looks very different from that used in the Deutsch-Jozsa algorithm and the Grover algorithm. This class of algorithms was developed based on the notion of quantum walk, which is the quantum counterpart of random walk.

One-Dimensional Quantum Walk:

The simplest random walk is the one-dimensional walk where a particle moves on a discrete line whose nodes are denoted by integers $\mathbb{Z} = \{\ldots, -2, -1, 0, 1, 2, \ldots\}$. At each step, the particle moves one position left or right, depending on the flip of a "coin." A quantum variant of the one-dimensional random walk is the Hadamard walk defined in the following:

Example 2.3.1. *The state Hilbert space of the Hadamard walk is $\mathcal{H}_d \otimes \mathcal{H}_p$, where:*

- *$\mathcal{H}_d = span\{|L\rangle, |R\rangle\}$ is a two-dimensional Hilbert space, called the direction space, and $|L\rangle, |R\rangle$ are used to indicate the directions Left and Right, respectively;*
- *$\mathcal{H}_p = span\{|n\rangle : n \in \mathbb{Z}\}$ is an infinite-dimensional Hilbert space, and $|n\rangle$ indicates the position marked by integer n,*

and spanX for a nonempty set X is defined according to equation (2.1). One step of the Hadamard walk is represented by the unitary operator

$$W = T(H \otimes I_{\mathcal{H}_p}),$$

where the translation T is a unitary operator in $\mathcal{H}_d \otimes \mathcal{H}_p$ defined by

$$T|L,n\rangle = |L,n-1\rangle, \quad T|R,n\rangle = |R,n+1\rangle$$

for every $n \in \mathbb{Z}$, H is the Hadamard transformation in the direction space $\mathcal{H}_d$, and $I_{\mathcal{H}_p}$ is the identity operator in the position space $\mathcal{H}_p$. The Hadamard walk is then described by repeated applications of operator W.

Exercise 2.3.5. *We define the left and right translation operators T_L and T_R in the position space $\mathcal{H}_p$ by*

$$T_L|n\rangle = |n-1\rangle, \quad T_R|n\rangle = |n+1\rangle$$

for each $n \in \mathbb{Z}$. Then the translation operator T is the quantum conditional $T_L \oplus T_R$ with the direction variable d as the select qubit (see Example 2.2.6).

Although the Hadamard walk was defined by mimicking the one-dimensional random walk, some of their behaviors are very different:

- The translation operator T can be explained as follows: if the direction system is in state $|L\rangle$, then the walker moves from position n to $n-1$, and if the direction is in $|R\rangle$, then the walker moves from position n to $n+1$. This looks very similar to a random walk, but in a quantum walk, the direction can be in a superposition of $|L\rangle$ and $|R\rangle$, and intuitively the walker can move to the left and to the right simultaneously.

- In a random walk, we only need to specify the statistical behavior of the "coin"; for example, flipping a fair "coin" gives heads and tails with equal probability $\frac{1}{2}$. In a quantum walk, however, we have to explicitly define the dynamics of the " coin" underlying its statistical behavior; for example, the Hadamard transformation H can be seen as a quantum realization of the fair "coin"; but so does the following 2×2 unitary matrix (and many others):

$$C = \frac{1}{\sqrt{2}} \begin{pmatrix} 1 & i \\ i & 1 \end{pmatrix}.$$

- Quantum interference may happen in a quantum walk; for example, let the Hadamard walk start in state $|L\rangle|0\rangle$. Then we have:

$$
\begin{aligned}
|L\rangle|0\rangle &\xrightarrow{H} \frac{1}{\sqrt{2}}\big(|L\rangle + |R\rangle\big)|0\rangle \\
&\xrightarrow{T} \frac{1}{\sqrt{2}}\big(|L\rangle|-1\rangle + |R\rangle|1\rangle\big) \\
&\xrightarrow{H} \frac{1}{2}\big[\big(|L\rangle + |R\rangle\big)|-1\rangle + \big(|L\rangle - |R\rangle\big)|1\rangle\big] \\
&\xrightarrow{T} \frac{1}{2}\big(|L\rangle|-2\rangle + |R\rangle|0\rangle + |L\rangle|0\rangle - |R\rangle|2\rangle\big) \\
&\xrightarrow{H} \frac{1}{2\sqrt{2}}\big[\big(|L\rangle + |R\rangle\big)|-2\rangle + \big(|L\rangle - |R\rangle\big)|0\rangle \\
&\qquad\qquad + \big(|L\rangle + |R\rangle\big)|0\rangle - \big(|L\rangle - |R\rangle\big)|2\rangle\big]
\end{aligned}
$$

(2.19)

Here, $-|R\rangle|0\rangle$ and $|R\rangle|0\rangle$ are out of phase and thus cancel one another.

Quantum Walk on a Graph:

Random walks on graphs are a class of random walks widely used in the design and analysis of algorithms. Let $G = (V, E)$ be an n-regular directed graph; that is, a graph where each vertex has n neighbors. Then we can label each edge with a number between 1 and n such that for each $1 \leq i \leq n$, the directed edges labeled i form a permutation. In this way, for each vertex v, the ith neighbor v_i of v is defined to be the vertex linked from v by an edge labeled i. A random walk on G is defined as follows: the vertices v's of G are used to represent the states of the walk, and for each state v the walk goes from v to its every neighbor with a certain probability. Such a random walk also has a quantum counterpart, which is carefully described in the following:

Example 2.3.2. *The state Hilbert space of a quantum walk on an n-regular graph $G = (V, E)$ is $\mathcal{H}_d \otimes \mathcal{H}_p$, where:*

- *$\mathcal{H}_d = span\{|i\rangle\}_{i=1}^n$ is an n-dimensional Hilbert space. We introduce an auxiliary quantum system, called the direction "coin," with the state space $\mathcal{H}_d$. For each $1 \leq i \leq n$, the state $|i\rangle$ is used to denote the ith direction. The space $\mathcal{H}_d$ is referred to as the "coin space";*
- *$\mathcal{H}_p = span\{|v\rangle\}_{v \in V}$ is the position Hilbert space. For each vertex v of the graph, there is a basis state $|v\rangle$ in $\mathcal{H}_p$.*

The shift S is an operator in $\mathcal{H}_d \otimes \mathcal{H}_p$ defined as follows:

$$S|i, v\rangle = |i\rangle|v_i\rangle$$

for any $1 \leq i \leq n$ and $v \in V$, where v_i is the ith neighbor of v. Intuitively, for each i, if the "coin" is in state $|i\rangle$, then the walker moves in the ith direction. Of course, the "coin" can be in a superposition of states $|i\rangle$ $(1 \leq i \leq n)$ and the walker moves to all the directions simultaneously.

If we further choose a unitary operator C in the "coin" space $\mathcal{H}_d$, called the "coin-tossing operator," then a single step of a coined quantum walk on graph G can be modelled by the unitary operator:

$$W = S(C \otimes I_{\mathcal{H}_p}) \tag{2.20}$$

where $I_{\mathcal{H}_p}$ is the identity operator in the position space $\mathcal{H}_p$. For example, a fair "coin" can be implemented by choosing the discrete Fourier transform:

$$FT = \frac{1}{\sqrt{d}} \begin{pmatrix} 1 & 1 & 1 & \cdots & 1 \\ 1 & \omega & \omega^2 & \cdots & \omega^{d-1} \\ 1 & \omega^2 & \omega^4 & \cdots & \omega^{2(d-1)} \\ \cdots & \cdots & \cdots & & \\ 1 & \omega^{d-1} & \omega^{(d-1)2} & \cdots & \omega^{(d-1)(d-1)} \end{pmatrix} \tag{2.21}$$

as the "coin-tossing operator," where $\omega = \exp(2\pi i/d)$. The operator FT maps each direction into a superposition of directions such that after measurement each of them *is obtained with the equal probability $\frac{1}{d}$. The quantum walk is then an iteration of the single-step walk operator W.*

Exercise 2.3.6. *For each $1 \leq i \leq n$, we can define a shift operator S_i in the position space $\mathcal{H}_V$:*

$$S_i|v\rangle = |v_i\rangle$$

for any $v \in V$, where v_i stands for the ith neighbor of v. If we slightly generalize the notion of quantum multiplexor (QMUX) by allowing the select variable being any quantum variable but not only qubits, then the shift operator S in Example 2.3.2 is the QMUX $\bigoplus_i S_i$ with the direction d as the select variable.

It has been observed that sometimes quantum effect (e.g., interference) in a quantum walk can offer a significant speed-up; for example, it helps a quantum walk to hit a vertex from another much faster than a random walk.

2.3.5 QUANTUM-WALK SEARCH ALGORITHM

Is it possible to harness the quantum speed-up pointed out at the end of the last subsection to design quantum algorithms that outperform their classical counterparts? In this subsection, we present such an algorithm for solving the search problem considered in Subsection 2.3.3.

Assume that the database consists of $N = 2^n$ items, each of which is encoded as an n-bit string $x = x_1 \ldots x_n \in \{0, 1\}^n$. It was assumed in Subsection 2.3.3 that there are M solutions. Here, we only consider the special case of $M = 1$. So, the task is to find the single target item (solution) x^*. The search algorithm in this subsection is based upon a quantum walk over the n-cube – the hypercube of dimension n. The n-cube is a graph with $N = 2^n$ nodes, each of which corresponds to an item x. Two nodes x and y are connected by an edge if they have only a one-bit difference:

$$x_d \neq y_d \text{ for some } d, \text{ and } x_i = y_i \text{ for all } i \neq d;$$

that is, x and y differ by only a single-bit flip. Thus, each of the 2^n nodes of the n-cube has degree n – it is connected to n other nodes.

As a special case of Example 2.3.2, the quantum walk over the n-cube is described as follows:

- The state Hilbert space is $\mathcal{H}_d \otimes \mathcal{H}_p$, where $\mathcal{H}_d = span\{|1\rangle, \ldots, |n\rangle\}$,

$$\mathcal{H}_p = \mathcal{H}_2^{\otimes n} = span\{|x\rangle : x \in \{0, 1\}^n\},$$

and $\mathcal{H}_2$ is the state space of a qubit.
- The shift operator S maps $|d, x\rangle$ to $|d, x \oplus e_d\rangle$ (the dth bit of x is flipped), where $e_d = 0 \ldots 010 \ldots 0$ (the dth bit is 1 and all others are 0) is the dth basis vector of the n-cube. Formally,

$$S = \sum_{d=1}^{n} \sum_{x \in \{0,1\}^n} |d, x \oplus e_d\rangle \langle d, x|$$

where $\oplus$ is component-wise addition modulo 2.

- The "coin tossing" operator C is chosen to be the Grover rotation without the oracle (see Lemma 2.3.1):

$$C = 2|\psi_d\rangle\langle\psi_d| - I$$

where I is the identity operator in $\mathcal{H}_d$ and $|\psi_d\rangle$ is the equal superposition over all n directions:

$$|\psi_d\rangle = \frac{1}{\sqrt{n}} \sum_{d=1}^{n} |d\rangle.$$

As in the Grover algorithm, we are supplied with an oracle that can mark the target item x^*. Suppose that this oracle is implemented via a perturbation of C:

$$D = C \otimes \sum_{x \neq x^*} |x\rangle\langle x| + C' \otimes |x^*\rangle\langle x^*| \tag{2.22}$$

where C' is a unitary operator in $\mathcal{H}_d$. Intuitively, the oracle applies the original "coin tossing" operator C to the direction system whenever the position corresponds to a nontarget item, but marks the target item x^* by applying a special "coin" action C'.

Now the search algorithm works as follows:

- Initialize the quantum computer to the equal superposition over both all directions and all positions: $|\psi_0\rangle = |\psi_d\rangle \otimes |\psi_p\rangle$, where

$$|\psi_p\rangle = \frac{1}{\sqrt{N}} \sum_{x \in \{0,1\}^n} |x\rangle.$$

- Apply the perturbed single-step walk operator

$$W' = SD = W - S\big[(C - C') \otimes |x^*\rangle\langle x^*|\big]$$

$t = \left\lceil \frac{\pi}{2}\sqrt{N} \right\rceil$ times, where W is the single-step walk operator defined by equation (2.20).

- Measure the state of the quantum computer in the $|d, x\rangle$ basis.

There is a remarkable difference between the "coin tossing" operator D used in this algorithm and the original "coin tossing" operator C (more precisely, $C \otimes I$) in Example 2.3.2: the operator C acts only in the direction space and thus is position-independent. However, D is obtained by modifying $C \otimes I$ with C' marking the target item x^*, and it is obvious from equation (2.22) that D is position-dependent.

For the case of $C' = -I$, it was proved that the algorithm finds the target item with probability $\frac{1}{2} - O(\frac{1}{n})$, and thus the target item can be found with an arbitrarily small probability of error by repeating the algorithm a constant number of times. The performance analysis of this algorithm is involved and not included here, but the reader can find it in the original paper [203].

The reader is invited to carefully compare this search algorithm based on quantum walk with the Grover search algorithms introduced in Subsection 2.3.3.

2.3.6 QUANTUM FOURIER TRANSFORM

Another important class of quantum algorithms is based on the quantum Fourier transform. Recall that the discrete Fourier transform takes as input a vector of complex numbers $x_0, \ldots, x_{N-1}$, and it outputs a vector of complex numbers $y_0, \ldots, y_{N-1}$:

$$y_k = \frac{1}{\sqrt{N}} \sum_{j=0}^{N-1} e^{2\pi ijk/N} x_j \tag{2.23}$$

for each $0 \le j < N$. The quantum Fourier transform is a quantum counterpart of the discrete Fourier transform.

Definition 2.3.1. *The quantum Fourier transform on an orthonormal basis* $|0\rangle, \ldots, |N-1\rangle$ *is defined by*

$$FT : |j\rangle \to \frac{1}{\sqrt{N}} \sum_{k=0}^{N-1} e^{2\pi ijk/N} |k\rangle.$$

More generally, the quantum Fourier transform on a general state in the N-dimensional Hilbert space is given as follows:

$$FT : \sum_{j=0}^{N-1} x_j |j\rangle \to \sum_{k=0}^{N-1} y_k |k\rangle,$$

where the amplitudes $y_0, \ldots, y_{N-1}$ are obtained by the discrete Fourier (2.23) transform on amplitudes $x_0, \ldots, x_{N-1}$. The matrix representation of the quantum Fourier transform was given in equation (2.21).

Proposition 2.3.1. *The quantum Fourier transform FT is unitary.*

Exercise 2.3.7. *Prove Proposition 2.3.1.*

The Circuit of Quantum Fourier Transform:

An implementation of the quantum Fourier transform FT by one-qubit and two-qubit gates is presented in the following proposition and its proof.

Proposition 2.3.2. *Let* $N = 2^n$. *Then the quantum Fourier transform can be implemented by a quantum circuit consisting of n Hadamard gates and*

$$\frac{n(n-1)}{2} + 3\lfloor \frac{n}{2} \rfloor$$

controlled gates.

Proof. We prove this proposition by explicitly constructing a quantum circuit that fulfils the stated conditions. We use the binary representation:

- $j_1j_2\ldots j_n$ denotes

$$j = j_1 2^{n-1} + j_2 2^{n-2} + \ldots + j_n 2^0;$$

- $0.j_kj_{k+1}\ldots j_n$ denotes

$$j_k/2 + j_{k+1}/2^2 + \ldots + j_n/2^{n-k+1}$$

for any $k \geq 1$.

Then the proposition can be proved in three steps:

(i) Using the notation introduced in Section 2.2, we design the circuit:

$$\begin{aligned} D \equiv\ & H[q_1]C(R_2)[q_2,q_1]\ldots C(R_n)[q_n,q_1]H[q_2]C(R_2)[q_3,q_2] \\ & \ldots C(R_{n-1})[q_n,q_2]\ldots H[q_{n-1}]C(R_2)[q_n,q_{n-1}]H[q_n] \end{aligned} \tag{2.24}$$

where R_k is the phase shift (see Example 2.2.1):

$$R_k = P\left(2\pi/2^k\right) = \begin{pmatrix} 1 & 0 \\ 0 & e^{2\pi i/2^k} \end{pmatrix}$$

for $k = 2,\ldots,n$. If we input $|j\rangle = |j_1\ldots j_n\rangle$ into the circuit (2.24), then the output is :

$$\frac{1}{\sqrt{2^n}}(|0\rangle + e^{2\pi i 0.j_1\ldots j_n}|1\rangle)\ldots(|0\rangle + e^{2\pi i 0.j_n}|1\rangle) \tag{2.25}$$

by a routine calculation.

(ii) We observe that whenever $N = 2^n$, the quantum Fourier transform can be rewritten as follows:

$$\begin{aligned} |j\rangle \rightarrow\ & \frac{1}{\sqrt{2^n}} \sum_{k=0}^{2^n-1} e^{2\pi i jk/2^n}|k\rangle \\ =\ & \frac{1}{\sqrt{2^n}} \sum_{k_1=0}^{1} \ldots \sum_{k_n=0}^{1} e^{2\pi i j(k_1\cdot 2^{n-1}+\ldots+k_n\cdot 2^0)/2^n}|k_1\ldots k_n\rangle \\ =\ & \frac{1}{\sqrt{2^n}} \left(\sum_{k_1=0}^{1} e^{2\pi i jk_1/2^1}|k_1\rangle\right)\ldots\left(\sum_{k_n=0}^{1} e^{2\pi i jk_n/2^n}|k_n\rangle\right) \\ =\ & \frac{1}{\sqrt{2^n}} \left(|0\rangle + e^{2\pi i 0.j_n}|1\rangle\right)\ldots\left(|0\rangle + e^{2\pi i 0.j_1\ldots j_n}|1\rangle\right). \end{aligned} \tag{2.26}$$

(iii) Finally, by comparing equations (2.26) and (2.25), we see that adding $\lfloor \frac{n}{2} \rfloor$ swap gates at the end of the circuit (2.24) will reverse the order of the qubits, and thus yield the quantum Fourier transform. It is known that each swap gate can be accomplished by using 3 CNOT gates (see Exercise 2.2.3). □

2.3.7 PHASE ESTIMATION

Now we show how the quantum Fourier transform defined in the last subsection can be used in an algorithm for phase estimation. This quantum algorithm solves the following problem:

- *Phase Estimation*: A unitary operator U has an eigenvector $|u\rangle$ with eigenvalue $e^{2\pi i\varphi}$, where the value of φ is unknown. The goal is to estimate the phase φ.

The phase estimation algorithm is described in Figure 2.4. It uses two registers:

- The first consists of t qubits $q_1, \ldots, q_t$, all of which are initialized in state $|0\rangle$;
- The second is the system p which U applies to, initialized in state $|u\rangle$.

Using the notation introduced in Section 2.2, the circuit for this algorithm can be written as follows:

$$D \equiv E \cdot FT^\dagger[q_1, \ldots, q_t] \tag{2.27}$$

where:

$$E \equiv H[q_1]\ldots H[q_{t-2}]H[q_{t-1}]H[q_t]$$
$$C(U^{2^0})[q_t,p]C(U^{2^1})[q_{t-1},p]C(U^{2^2})[q_{t-2},p]\ldots C(U^{2^{t-1}})[q_1,p]$$

$C(\cdot)$ is the controlled gate (see Definition 2.2.5), and $FT^\dagger$ is the inverse quantum Fourier transform FT and can be obtained by reversing the circuit of FT given in the proof of Proposition 2.3.2.

Obviously, circuit (2.27) consists of $O(t^2)$ Hadamard and controlled gates together with one call to oracle U^{2^j} for $j = 0, 1, \ldots, t-1$. We further observe that

$$E|0\rangle_{q_1}\ldots|0\rangle_{q_{t-2}}|0\rangle_{q_{t-1}}|0\rangle_{q_t}|u\rangle_p = \frac{1}{\sqrt{2^t}}\left(|0\rangle + e^{2\pi i\varphi\cdot 2^{t-1}}|1\rangle\right)$$
$$\ldots\left(|0\rangle + e^{2\pi i\varphi\cdot 2^2}|1\rangle\right)\left(|0\rangle + e^{2\pi i\varphi\cdot 2^1}|1\rangle\right)\left(|0\rangle + e^{2\pi i\varphi\cdot 2^0}|1\rangle\right)|u\rangle$$
$$= \frac{1}{\sqrt{2^t}}\left(\sum_{k=0}^{2^t-1} e^{2\pi i\varphi k}|k\rangle\right)|u\rangle. \tag{2.28}$$

A Special Case:

To understand why the algorithm works, let us first consider a special case where φ can be exactly expressed in t bits:

$$\varphi = 0.\varphi_1\varphi_2\varphi_3\ldots\varphi_t.$$

- **Inputs:**

  (i) An oracle which performs controlled-U^{2^j} operators for $j = 0, 1, \ldots, t-1$;
  (ii) t qubits initialized to $|0\rangle$;
  (iii) An eigenvector $|u\rangle$ of U with eigenvalue $e^{2\pi i \varphi}$,

  where

  $$t = n + \left\lceil \log(2 + \frac{1}{2\epsilon}) \right\rceil .$$

- **Outputs:** An n-bit approximation $\tilde{\varphi} = m$ to φ.
- **Runtime:** $O(t^2)$ operations and one call to each oracle. Success with probability at least $1 - \epsilon$.
- **Procedure:**

  1. $|0\rangle^{\otimes t}|u\rangle \quad \xrightarrow{H^{\otimes t} \text{ on the first } t \text{ qubits}} \quad \frac{1}{\sqrt{2^t}} \sum_{j=0}^{2^t-1} |j\rangle |u\rangle$

  2. $\xrightarrow{\text{oracles}} \quad \frac{1}{\sqrt{2^t}} \sum_{j=0}^{2^t-1} |j\rangle U^j |u\rangle = \frac{1}{\sqrt{2^t}} \sum_{j=0}^{2^t-1} e^{2\pi i j \varphi} |j\rangle |u\rangle$

  3. $\xrightarrow{FT^\dagger} \quad \frac{1}{\sqrt{2^t}} \sum_{j=0}^{2^t-1} e^{2\pi i j \varphi} \left(\frac{1}{\sqrt{2^t}} \sum_{k=0}^{2^t-1} e^{-2\pi i j k / 2^t} |k\rangle \right) |u\rangle$

  $$= \sum_{k=0}^{2^t-1} \alpha_k |k\rangle |u\rangle$$

  4. $\xrightarrow{\text{measure the first } t \text{ qubits}} \quad |m\rangle |u\rangle,$

  where

  $$\alpha_k = \frac{1}{2^t} \sum_{j=0}^{2^t-1} e^{2\pi i j (\varphi - k/2^t)} = \frac{1}{2^t} \left[\frac{1 - e^{2\pi i (2^t \varphi - k)}}{1 - e^{2\pi i (\varphi - k/2^t)}} \right] .$$

FIGURE 2.4

Phase estimation.

Then equation (2.28) can be rewritten as:

$$E|0\rangle \ldots |0\rangle|0\rangle|0\rangle|u\rangle = \frac{1}{\sqrt{2^t}} \left(|0\rangle + e^{2\pi i 0.\varphi_t}|1\rangle \right) \ldots \left(|0\rangle + e^{2\pi i 0.\varphi_3 \ldots \varphi_t}|1\rangle \right)$$
$$\left(|0\rangle + e^{2\pi i 0.\varphi_2 \varphi_3 \ldots \varphi_t}|1\rangle \right) \left(|0\rangle + e^{2\pi i \varphi_1 \varphi_2 \varphi_3 \ldots \varphi_t}|1\rangle \right) |u\rangle. \qquad (2.29)$$

Furthermore, by equations (2.27) and (2.26) we obtain:

$$C|0\rangle\dots|0\rangle|0\rangle|0\rangle|u\rangle = FT^\dagger\,(E|0\rangle\dots|0\rangle|0\rangle|0\rangle)\,|u\rangle$$
$$= |\varphi_1\varphi_2\varphi_3\dots\varphi_t\rangle|u\rangle.$$

Performance Analysis:

The previous discussion about a special case should give the reader a hint why the algorithm is correct. Now we are ready to consider the general case. Let $0 \leq b < 2^t$ be such that $b/2^t = 0.b_1\dots b_t$ is the best t bit approximation to φ which is less than φ; i.e.,

$$b/2^t \leq \varphi < b/2^t + 1/2^t.$$

We write $\delta = \varphi - b/2^t$ for the difference. It is clear that $0 \leq \delta < 1/2^t$. Note that

$$|\alpha_k| \leq \frac{1}{2^{t-1}|1 - e^{2\pi i(\varphi-k)/2^t}|}$$

because $|1 - e^{i\theta}| \leq 2$ for all θ. Put $\beta_l = \alpha_{(b+l \mod 2^t)}$ for any $-2^{t-1} < l \leq 2^{t-1}$. Then

$$|\beta_l| \leq \frac{1}{2^{t-1}|1 - e^{2\pi i(\delta-l/2^t)}|} \leq \frac{1}{2|l - 2^t\delta|}$$

because

(i) $|1 - e^{i\theta}| \geq \frac{2|\theta|}{\pi}$ if $-\pi \leq \theta \leq \pi$; and
(ii) $-\frac{1}{2} \leq \delta - l/2^t \leq \frac{1}{2}$.

Suppose the outcome of the final measurement is m. Then for a positive integer d, we have:

$$P(|m - b| > d) = \sum_{m:|m-b|>d} |\alpha_m|^2$$

$$= \sum_{-2^{t-1}<l\leq-(d+1)} |\beta_l|^2 + \sum_{d+1\leq l\leq 2^{t-1}} |\beta_l|^2$$

$$\leq \frac{1}{4}\left[\sum_{l=-2^{t-1}+1}^{-(d+1)} \frac{1}{(l - 2^t\delta)^2} + \sum_{l=d+1}^{2^{t-1}} \frac{1}{(l - 2^t\delta)^2}\right]$$

$$\leq \frac{1}{4}\left[\sum_{l=-2^{t-1}+1}^{-(d+1)} \frac{1}{l^2} + \sum_{l=d+1}^{2^{t-1}} \frac{1}{(l-1)^2}\right] \quad (\text{note that } 0 \leq 2^t\delta < 1)$$

$$\leq \frac{1}{2}\sum_{l=d}^{2^{t-1}} \frac{1}{l^2}$$

$$\leq \frac{1}{2}\int_{d-1}^{2^{t-1}} \frac{dl}{l^2} \leq \frac{1}{2(d-1)}.$$

If we wish to approximate φ to a 2^{-n} accuracy and the success probability is at least $1 - \epsilon$, then we only need to choose $d = 2^{t-n} - 1$ and require $\frac{1}{2(d-1)} \leq \epsilon$. This leads to

$$t \geq T \triangleq n + \left\lceil \log(\frac{1}{2\epsilon} + 2) \right\rceil$$

and we can make use of $t = T$ qubits in the phase estimation algorithm.

Combining the preceding derivation with equation (2.27) and Proposition 2.3.2 gives us the conclusion: the algorithm presented in Figure 2.4 can compute the n-bit approximation of phase φ with at least success probability $1 - \epsilon$ within $O(t^2)$ steps, using

$$n + \left\lceil \log(\frac{1}{2\epsilon} + 2) \right\rceil$$

qubits.

The phase estimation algorithm is a key procedure in a class of important quantum algorithms, including the famous Shor algorithm for factoring [204] and the Harrow-Hassidim-Lloyd algorithm for systems of linear equations [112]. A detailed presentation of these two algorithms is out of the scope of this book.

2.4 BIBLIOGRAPHIC REMARKS

- *Quantum Mechanics*: The material on quantum mechanics presented in Section 2.1 is standard and can be found in any (advanced) textbook of quantum mechanics.
- *Quantum Circuits*: Part of Section 2.2 is based on [34] and Chapter 4 of book [174]. The quantum multiplexor in Subsection 2.2.4 was introduced by Shende et al. [201]. The notations for quantum gates and circuits as well as the notion of a quantum circuit with measurements in Exercise 2.2.7 come from [226]. Section 2.2 is merely an introduction to the basics of quantum circuits. Quantum circuits have been developed into a large research area since [34]. In particular, in recent years, research on quantum circuits, including synthesis (decomposition of large unitary matrices) and optimization of quantum circuits, became very active with applications to compilation of quantum programming languages; see Section 8.2 for further discussion. It is worth mentioning that synthesis and optimization of quantum circuits are much harder than the corresponding problems for classical circuits.
- *Quantum Algorithms*: The presentation of Subsections 2.3.1 to 2.3.3, 2.3.6 and 2.3.7 largely follows Sections 1.4, 5.1, 5.2 and 6.1 of [174]. The one-dimensional quantum walk and the quantum walk on a graph in Subsection 2.3.4 were defined in [9] and [19], respectively. The algorithm given in Subsection 2.3.5 was proposed by Shenvi et al. [203].

Quantum algorithms have been one of the most active research areas in quantum computing since Shor's factoring algorithm and Grover search were discovered. For the three major quantum algorithms in earlier times, namely the Shor algorithm, Grover algorithm and quantum simulation [154], and their variants, [174] is still one of the best expositions. Shor [205] proposed two explanations for why so few classes of quantum algorithms have been found and pointed out several lines of research that might lead to the discovery of new quantum algorithms. A large number of papers on quantum walks and algorithms based on them have been published in the last decade; see [18,192,214] for a thorough survey. A recent breakthrough in quantum algorithms is the Harrow-Hassidim-Lloyd algorithm for systems of linear equations [112]. It further led to active research on quantum machine learning algorithms [156,157,184] in the last few years; see [2] for some interesting discussions about this line of research.

Quantum programs with classical control

Syntax and semantics of quantum programs

3

In Section 2.3, several quantum algorithms were presented at the very low-level model of quantum computing – quantum circuits. How can we design and implement higher-level programming languages for quantum computers? From this chapter on, we systematically develop the foundations of quantum programming.

As the first step, let us see how a classical programming language can be directly extended for programming a quantum computer. As pointed out in Sections 1.1 and 1.2, this issue had been the main concern of early research on quantum programming. This chapter studies a class of simple quantum generalizations of classical programs – quantum programs with classical control: i.e., programs in the superposition-of-data paradigm. The design idea of this class of quantum programs was briefly introduced in Subsection 1.2.1. The control flow of these programs will be further discussed shortly.

The chapter is divided into three parts:

- The **while**-language constitutes the "kernel" of many classical programming languages. The first part of this chapter introduces a quantum extension of the **while**-language. This part consists of Sections 3.1 to 3.3: Section 3.1 defines the syntax of the quantum **while**-language. Sections 3.2 and 3.3 present its operational and denotational semantics, respectively.

  Along the way, we briefly prepare a theory of quantum domains needed for a characterization of the denotational semantics of the loop in the quantum **while**-language. For readability, the lengthy proofs of some lemmas about quantum domains are postponed to a separate section – Section 3.6 – at the end of the chapter.
- The second part – Section 3.4 – extends the quantum **while**-language by adding recursive quantum programs (with classical control). The operational and denotational semantics of recursive quantum programs are defined. Here, the theory of quantum domains is also needed to deal with the denotational semantics.
- The third part – Section 3.5 – presents an illustrative example showing how the Grover quantum search can be programmed in the language defined in this chapter.

3.1 SYNTAX

In this section, we define the syntax of a quantum extension of classical **while**-language. Recall that a classical **while**-program is generated by the grammar:

$$S ::= \textbf{skip} \mid u := t \mid S_1; S_2$$
$$\mid \textbf{if } b \textbf{ then } S_1 \textbf{ else } S_2 \textbf{ fi}$$
$$\mid \textbf{while } b \textbf{ do } S \textbf{ od}.$$

Here, S, S_1, S_2 are programs, u is a variable, t is an expression, and b is a Boolean expression. Intuitively, **while**-programs are executed as follows:

- The statement "**skip**" does nothing but terminates.
- The assignment "$u := t$" assigns the value of expression t to variable u.
- The sequential composition "$S_1; S_2$" first executes S_1, and when S_1 terminates, it executes S_2.
- The conditional statement "**if** b **then** S_1 **else** S_2 **fi**" starts from evaluating the Boolean expression b: if b is true, S_1 is executed; otherwise, S_2 is executed. The conditional statement can be generalized to the case statement:

$$
\begin{aligned}
&\textbf{if } G_1 \rightarrow S_1 \\
&\square \ G_2 \rightarrow S_2 \\
&\qquad \cdots\cdots \\
&\square \ G_n \rightarrow S_n \\
&\textbf{fi}
\end{aligned}
\tag{3.1}
$$

or more compactly

$$\textbf{if } (\square i \cdot G_i \rightarrow S_i) \textbf{ fi}$$

where $G_1, G_2, \ldots, G_n$ are Boolean expressions, called guards, and $S_1, S_2, \ldots, S_n$ are programs. The case statement starts from evaluating guards: if G_i is true, then the corresponding subprogram S_i is executed.

- The **while**-loop "**while** b **do** S **od**" starts from evaluating the loop guard b: if b is false, the loop terminates immediately; otherwise, the loop body S is executed, and when S terminates, the process is repeated.

Now we expand the **while**-language so that it can be used for quantum programming. We first fix the alphabet of the quantum **while**-language:

- A countably infinite set $qVar$ of quantum variables. The symbols $q, q', q_0, q_1, q_2, \ldots$ will be used as meta-variables ranging over quantum variables.

- Each quantum variable $q \in qVar$ has a type $\mathcal{H}_q$, which is a Hilbert space – the state space of the quantum system denoted by q. For simplicity, we only consider two basic types:

$$\textbf{Boolean} = \mathcal{H}_2, \qquad \textbf{integer} = \mathcal{H}_\infty.$$

Note that the sets denoted by types **Boolean** and **integer** in classical computation are exactly the computational bases of $\mathcal{H}_2$ and $\mathcal{H}_\infty$, respectively (see Examples 2.1.1 and 2.1.2). The main results presented in this chapter can be easily generalized to the case with more data types.

A quantum register is a finite sequence of distinct quantum variables. (The notion of quantum register in Section 2.2 is slightly generalized here by allowing it to contain other quantum variables than qubit variables.) The state Hilbert space of a quantum register $\bar{q} = q_1, \ldots, q_n$ is the tensor product of the state spaces of the quantum variables occurring in $\bar{q}$:

$$\mathcal{H}_{\bar{q}} = \bigotimes_{i=1}^{n} \mathcal{H}_{q_i}.$$

When necessary, we write $|\psi\rangle_{q_i}$ to indicate that $|\psi\rangle$ is a state of quantum variable q_i; that is, $|\psi\rangle$ is in $\mathcal{H}_{q_i}$. Thus, $|\psi\rangle_{q_i} \langle \varphi_i|$ denotes the outer product of states $|\psi\rangle$ and $|\varphi\rangle$ of q_i, and $|\psi_1\rangle_{q_1} \ldots |\psi_n\rangle_{q_n}$ is a state in $\mathcal{H}_{\bar{q}}$ in which q_i is in state $|\psi_i\rangle$ for every $1 \leq i \leq n$.

With these ingredients, we can define programs in the quantum **while**-language.

Definition 3.1.1. *Quantum programs are generated by the syntax:*

$$\begin{aligned} S ::= \ & \textbf{skip} \mid q := |0\rangle \mid \bar{q} := U[\bar{q}] \mid S_1; S_2 \\ & \mid \textbf{if} \ (\square m \cdot M[\bar{q}] = m \rightarrow S_m) \ \textbf{fi} \\ & \mid \textbf{while} \ M[\bar{q}] = 1 \ \textbf{do} \ S \ \textbf{od}. \end{aligned} \qquad (3.2)$$

This definition deserves a careful explanation:

- As in the classical **while**-language, statement "**skip**" does nothing and terminates immediately.
- The initialization statement "$q := |0\rangle$" sets quantum variable q to the basis state $|0\rangle$. For any pure state $|\psi\rangle \in \mathcal{H}_q$, there is obviously a unitary operator U in $\mathcal{H}_q$ such that $|\psi\rangle = U|0\rangle$. So, the system q can be prepared in state $|\psi\rangle$ by this initialization and the unitary transformation $q := U[q]$.
- The statement "$\bar{q} := U[\bar{q}]$" means that unitary transformation U is performed on quantum register $\bar{q}$, leaving the states of the quantum variables not in $\bar{q}$ unchanged.
- Sequential composition is similar to its counterpart in a classical programming language.

- The program construct

$$\textbf{if } (\square m \cdot M[\bar{q}] = m \rightarrow S_m) \textbf{ fi} \equiv \textbf{if } M[\bar{q}] = m_1 \rightarrow S_{m_1}$$
$$\square \qquad m_2 \rightarrow S_{m_2}$$
$$\ldots\ldots \qquad (3.3)$$
$$\square \qquad m_n \rightarrow S_{m_n}$$
$$\textbf{fi}$$

is a quantum generalization of the classical case statement (3.1). Recall that the first step of execution of statement (3.1) is to see which guard G_i is satisfied. However, according to the Postulate of quantum mechanics 3 (see Subsection 2.1.4), the way to acquire information about a quantum system is to perform a measurement on it. So, in executing the statement (3.3), quantum measurement

$$M = \{M_m\} = \{M_{m_1}, M_{m_2}, \ldots, M_{m_n}\}$$

will be performed on quantum register $\bar{q}$, and then a subprogram S_m will be selected to be executed next according to the outcome of the measurement. An essential difference between the measurement-based case statement (3.3) and a classical case statement is that the state of program variables is changed after performing the measurement in the former, whereas it is not changed after checking the guards in the latter.

- The statement

$$\textbf{while } M[\bar{q}] = 1 \textbf{ do } S \textbf{ od} \qquad (3.4)$$

is a quantum generalization of the classical loop "**while** b **do** S **od**". To acquire information about quantum register $\bar{q}$, a measurement M is performed on it. The measurement $M = \{M_0, M_1\}$ is a yes-no measurement with only two possible outcomes: 0 ("no"), 1 ("yes"). If the outcome 0 is observed, then the program terminates, and if the outcome 1 occurs, then the program executes the subprogram S and continues. The only difference between the quantum loop (3.4) and a classical loop is that checking the loop guard b in the classical loop does not change the state of program variables, but this is not the case in the quantum loop.

Classical Control Flow:

Now it is the right time to explain that the control flow of a program in the quantum **while**-language is *classical*, as indicated at the beginning of this chapter. Recall that the control flow of a program is the order of its execution. In the quantum **while**-language, there are only two statements – the case statement (3.3) and the loop (3.4) – whose execution is determined by a choice as to which of two or more paths should be followed. The case statement (3.3) selects a command to execute according to the outcome of measurement M: if the outcome is m_i, then the corresponding command S_{m_i} will be executed. Since the outcome of a quantum measurement is classical information, the control flow in statement (3.3) is classical. The same argument illustrates that the control flow in the loop (3.4) is classical too.

As pointed out in Subsection 1.2.2, it is also possible to define programs with quantum control flow. Quantum control flow of programs is much harder to understand, which will be the theme of Chapters 6 and 7.

Program Variables:

Before concluding this section, we present the following technical definition, which will be needed in the sequel.

Definition 3.1.2. *The set $qvar(S)$ of quantum variables in quantum program S is recursively defined as follows:*

(i) *If $S \equiv$ **skip**, then $qvar(S) = \emptyset$;*
(ii) *If $S \equiv q := |0\rangle$, then $qvar(S) = \{q\}$;*
(iii) *If $S \equiv \overline{q} := U[\overline{q}]$, then $qvar(S) = \overline{q}$;*
(iv) *If $S \equiv S_1; S_2$, then $qvar(S) = qvar(S_1) \cup qvar(S_2)$;*
(v) *If $S \equiv$ **if** $(\square m \cdot M[\overline{q}] = m \rightarrow S_m)$ **fi**, then*

$$qvar(S) = \overline{q} \cup \bigcup_m qvar(S_m);$$

(vi) *If $S \equiv$ **while** $M[\overline{q}] = 1$ **do** S **od**, then $qvar(S) = \overline{q} \cup qvar(S)$.*

3.2 OPERATIONAL SEMANTICS

The syntax of quantum **while**-programs was defined in the last section. This section defines the operational semantics of the quantum **while**-language. We first introduce several notations:

- A positive operator ρ in a Hilbert space $\mathcal{H}$ is called a *partial density operator* if $tr(\rho) \leq 1$. So, a density operator ρ (see Definition 2.1.21) is a partial density operator with $tr(\rho) = 1$. We write $\mathcal{D}(\mathcal{H})$ for the set of partial density operators in $\mathcal{H}$. In quantum programming theory, a partial density operator is a very useful notion, because a program with loops (or more generally, recursions) may not terminate with a certain probability, and its output is a partial density operator but not necessarily a density operator.
- We write $\mathcal{H}_{all}$ for the tensor product of the state Hilbert spaces of all quantum variables:

$$\mathcal{H}_{all} = \bigotimes_{q \in qVar} \mathcal{H}_q.$$

- Let $\overline{q} = q_1, \ldots, q_n$ be a quantum register. An operator A in the state Hilbert space $\mathcal{H}_{\overline{q}}$ of $\overline{q}$ has a cylindrical extension $A \otimes I$ in $\mathcal{H}_{all}$, where I is the identity operator in the state Hilbert space

$$\bigotimes_{q \in qVar \setminus \overline{q}} \mathcal{H}_q$$

of the quantum variables that are not in $\overline{q}$. In the sequel, we will simply write A for its cylindrical extension, and it can be easily recognized from the context, without any risk of confusion.
- We will use E to denote the empty program: i.e., termination.

As in the theory of classical programming, the execution of a quantum program can be properly described in terms of transition between configurations.

Definition 3.2.1. *A quantum configuration is a pair $\langle S, \rho \rangle$, where:*

(i) *S is a quantum program or the empty program E;*
(ii) *$\rho \in \mathcal{D}(\mathcal{H}_{all})$ is a partial density operator in $\mathcal{H}_{all}$, and it is used to indicate the (global) state of quantum variables.*

A transition between quantum configurations:

$$\langle S, \rho \rangle \rightarrow \langle S', \rho' \rangle$$

means that after executing quantum program S one step in state ρ, the state of quantum variables becomes ρ', and S' is the remainder of S still to be executed. In particular, if $S' = E$, then S terminates in state ρ'.

Definition 3.2.2. *The operational semantics of quantum programs is the transition relation $\rightarrow$ between quantum configurations defined by the transition rules in Figure 3.1.*

The operational semantics (i.e., the relation $\rightarrow$) defined previously should be understood as the smallest transition relation between quantum configurations that satisfies the rules in Figure 3.1. Obviously, the transition rules (IN), (UT), (IF), (L0) and (L1) are determined by the postulates of quantum mechanics. As you saw in Chapter 2, probabilities always arise from the measurements in a quantum computation. But it should be noticed that the operational semantics of quantum programs is an ordinary transition relation $\rightarrow$ rather than a probabilistic transition relation. Several remarks should help the reader to understand these transition rules:

- The symbol U in the target configuration of the rule (UT) stands indeed for the cylindrical extension of U in $\mathcal{H}_{all}$. A similar remark applies to the rules (IF), (L0) and (L1) for measurements and loops.
- In the rule (IF), the outcome m is observed with probability

$$p_m = tr(M_m \rho M_m^{\dagger}),$$

(SK)

$$\overline{\langle \mathbf{skip}, \rho \rangle \rightarrow \langle E, \rho \rangle}$$

(IN)

$$\overline{\langle q := |0\rangle, \rho \rangle \rightarrow \langle E, \rho_0^q \rangle}$$

where

$$\rho_0^q = \begin{cases} |0\rangle_q \langle 0|\rho|0\rangle_q \langle 0| + |0\rangle_q \langle 1|\rho|1\rangle_q \langle 0| & \text{if } type(q) = \textbf{Boolean}, \\ \sum_{n=-\infty}^{\infty} |0\rangle_q \langle n|\rho|n\rangle_q \langle 0| & \text{if } type(q) = \textbf{integer}. \end{cases}$$

(UT)

$$\overline{\langle \overline{q} := U[\overline{q}], \rho \rangle \rightarrow \langle E, U\rho U^\dagger \rangle}$$

(SC)

$$\frac{\langle S_1, \rho \rangle \rightarrow \langle S_1', \rho' \rangle}{\langle S_1; S_2, \rho \rangle \rightarrow \langle S_1'; S_2, \rho' \rangle}$$

where we make the convention that $E; S_2 = S_2$.

(IF)

$$\overline{\langle \mathbf{if}\ (\square m \cdot M[\overline{q}] = m \rightarrow S_m)\ \mathbf{fi}, \rho \rangle \rightarrow \langle S_m, M_m \rho M_m^\dagger \rangle}$$

for each possible outcome m of measurement $M = \{M_m\}$.

(L0)

$$\overline{\langle \mathbf{while}\ M[\overline{q}] = 1\ \mathbf{do}\ S\ \mathbf{od}, \rho \rangle \rightarrow \langle E, M_0 \rho M_0^\dagger \rangle}$$

(L1)

$$\overline{\langle \mathbf{while}\ M[\overline{q}] = 1\ \mathbf{do}\ S\ \mathbf{od}, \rho \rangle \rightarrow \langle S; \mathbf{while}\ M[\overline{q}] = 1\ \mathbf{do}\ S\ \mathbf{od}, M_1 \rho M_1^\dagger \rangle}$$

FIGURE 3.1

Transition rules for quantum **while**-programs.

and in this case, after the measurement the state becomes

$$\rho_m = M_m \rho M_m^\dagger / p_m.$$

So, a natural presentation of the rule (IF) is the probabilistic transition:

$$\overline{\langle \mathbf{if}\ (\square m \cdot M[\overline{q}] = m \rightarrow S_m)\ \mathbf{fi}, \rho \rangle \overset{p_m}{\rightarrow} \langle S_m, \rho_m \rangle}$$

However, if we encode both probability p_m and density operator ρ_m into a partial density operator

$$M_m \rho M_m^\dagger = p_m \rho_m,$$

then the rule can be presented as an ordinary (a nonprobabilistic) transition.

- Likewise, in the rules (L0) and (L1) the measurement outcomes 0 and 1 occur with probabilities:

$$p_0 = tr(M_0 \rho M_0^\dagger), \qquad p_1 = tr(M_1 \rho M_1^\dagger),$$

respectively, and the state becomes $M_0 \rho M_0^\dagger / p_0$ from ρ when the outcome is 0, and it becomes $M_1 \rho M_1^\dagger / p_1$ when the outcome is 1. These probabilities and postmeasurement states are encoded into partial density operators so that the rules (L0) and (L1) can be stated as ordinary transitions instead of probabilistic transitions.

From this discussion, we see that, exactly, the convention of combining probabilities with postmeasurement states enables us to define the operational semantics $\rightarrow$ as a nonprobabilistic transition relation.

Transition Rules for Pure States:

The transition rules in Figure 3.1 were stated in the language of density operators. As we will see in the next section, this general setting provides us with an elegant formulation of denotational semantics. However, pure states are usually more convenient in applications. So, we display the pure state variants of these transition rules in Figure 3.2. In the rules for pure states, a configuration is a pair

$$\langle S, |\psi\rangle \rangle$$

with S being a quantum program or the empty program E and $|\psi\rangle$ a pure state in $\mathcal{H}_{all}$. As indicated previously, transitions in Figure 3.1 are all nonprobabilistic. However, the transitions in rules (IF′), (L0′) and (L1′) are probabilistic in the form of

$$\langle S, |\psi\rangle \rangle \xrightarrow{p} \langle S', |\psi'\rangle \rangle.$$

Whenever the probability $p = 1$, then this transition is abbreviated to

$$\langle S, |\psi\rangle \rangle \rightarrow \langle S', |\psi'\rangle \rangle.$$

Of course, the rules in Figure 3.2 are special cases of the corresponding rules in Figure 3.1. Conversely, using the correspondence between density operators and ensembles of pure states, the rules in Figure 3.1 can be derived from their counterparts in Figure 3.2.

The reader might have noticed that Figure 3.2 does not include a pure state version of the initialization rule (IN). Actually, the rule (IN) has no pure state version because it is possible that an initialization will transfer a pure state into a mixed state: although

(SK')
$$\overline{\langle \mathbf{skip}, |\psi\rangle\rangle \to \langle E, |\psi\rangle\rangle}$$

(UT')
$$\overline{\langle \overline{q} := U[\overline{q}], |\psi\rangle\rangle \to \langle E, U|\psi\rangle\rangle}$$

(SC')
$$\frac{\langle S_1, |\psi\rangle\rangle \xrightarrow{p} \langle S_1', |\psi'\rangle\rangle}{\langle S_1; S_2, |\psi\rangle\rangle \xrightarrow{p} \langle S_1'; S_2, |\psi'\rangle\rangle}$$

where we make the convention that $E; S_2 = S_2$.

(IF')
$$\overline{\langle \mathbf{if}\ (\square m \cdot M[\overline{q}] = m \to S_m)\ \mathbf{fi}, |\psi\rangle\rangle \xrightarrow{||M_m|\psi\rangle||^2} \langle S_m, \frac{M_m|\psi\rangle}{||M_m|\psi\rangle||}\rangle}$$

for each outcome m of measurement $M = \{M_m\}$.

(L0')
$$\overline{\langle \mathbf{while}\ M[\overline{q}] = 1\ \mathbf{do}\ S\ \mathbf{od}, |\psi\rangle\rangle \xrightarrow{||M_0|\psi\rangle||^2} \langle E, \frac{M_0|\psi\rangle}{||M_0|\psi\rangle||}\rangle}$$

(L1')
$$\overline{\langle \mathbf{while}\ M[\overline{q}] = 1\ \mathbf{do}\ S\ \mathbf{od}, |\psi\rangle\rangle \xrightarrow{||M_1|\psi\rangle||^2} \langle S; \mathbf{while}\ M[\overline{q}] = 1\ \mathbf{do}\ S\ \mathbf{od}, \frac{M_1|\psi\rangle}{||M_1|\psi\rangle||}\rangle}$$

FIGURE 3.2

Transition rules for quantum **while**-programs in pure states.

the initialization $q := |0\rangle$ changes the state of local variable q into a pure state $|0\rangle$, its side effect on other variables may cause a transition of a global state $|\psi\rangle \in \mathcal{H}_{all}$ of all variables $qVar$ into a mixed state. To see the rule (IN) more clearly, let us look at the case of $type(q) = \mathbf{integer}$ as an example.

Example 3.2.1

(i) *We first consider the case where ρ is a pure state; that is, $\rho = |\psi\rangle\langle\psi|$ for some $|\psi\rangle \in \mathcal{H}_{all}$. We can write $|\psi\rangle$ in the form:*

$$|\psi\rangle = \sum_k \alpha_k |\psi_k\rangle,$$

where all $|\psi_k\rangle$ are product states, say

$$|\psi_k\rangle = \bigotimes_{p \in qVar} |\psi_{kp}\rangle.$$

Then

$$\rho = \sum_{k,l} \alpha_k \alpha_l^* |\psi_k\rangle \langle \psi_l|.$$

After the initialization $q := |0\rangle$ the state becomes:

$$
\begin{aligned}
\rho_0^q &= \sum_{n=-\infty}^{\infty} |0\rangle_q \langle n|\rho|n\rangle_q \langle 0| \\
&= \sum_{k,l} \alpha_k \alpha_l^* \left(\sum_{n=-\infty}^{\infty} |0\rangle_q \langle n|\psi_k\rangle \langle \psi_l|n\rangle_q \langle 0| \right) \\
&= \sum_{k,l} \alpha_k \alpha_l^* \left(\sum_{n=-\infty}^{\infty} \langle \psi_{lq}|n\rangle \langle n|\psi_{kq}\rangle \right) \left(|0\rangle_q \langle 0| \otimes \bigotimes_{p \neq q} |\psi_{kp}\rangle \langle \psi_{lp}| \right) \\
&= \sum_{k,l} \alpha_k \alpha_l^* \langle \psi_{lq}|\psi_{kq}\rangle \left(|0\rangle_q \langle 0| \otimes \bigotimes_{p \neq q} |\psi_{kp}\rangle \langle \psi_{lp}| \right) \\
&= |0\rangle_q \langle 0| \otimes \left(\sum_{k,l} \alpha_k \alpha_l^* \langle \psi_{lq}|\psi_{kq}\rangle \bigotimes_{p \neq q} |\psi_{kp}\rangle \langle \psi_{lp}| \right). \tag{3.5}
\end{aligned}
$$

It is obvious that ρ_0^q is not necessary to be a pure state although ρ is a pure state.

(ii) *In general, suppose that ρ is generated by an ensemble $\{(p_i, |\psi_i\rangle)\}$ of pure states; that is,*

$$\rho = \sum_i p_i |\psi_i\rangle \langle \psi_i|.$$

For each i, we write $\rho_i = |\psi_i\rangle \langle \psi_i|$ and assume that it becomes ρ_{i0}^q after the initialization. By the previous argument, we can write ρ_{i0}^q in the form:

$$\rho_{i0}^q = |0\rangle_q \langle 0| \otimes \left(\sum_k \alpha_{ik} |\varphi_{ik}\rangle \langle \varphi_{ik}| \right),$$

where $|\varphi_{ik}\rangle \in \mathcal{H}_{qVar\setminus\{q\}}$ *for all k. Then the initialization causes* ρ *to become*

$$\rho_0^q = \sum_{n=-\infty}^{\infty} |0\rangle_q \langle n|\rho|n\rangle_q \langle 0|$$

$$= \sum_i p_i \left(\sum_{n=-\infty}^{\infty} |0\rangle_q \langle n|\rho_i|n\rangle_q \langle 0| \right) \qquad (3.6)$$

$$= |0\rangle_q \langle 0| \otimes \left(\sum_{i,k} p_i \alpha_{ik} |\varphi_{ik}\rangle \langle \varphi_{ik}| \right).$$

From equations (3.5) and (3.6) we see that the state of quantum variable q is set to be $|0\rangle$ *and the states of the other quantum variables are unchanged.*

Exercise 3.2.1. *Find a necessary and sufficient condition under which* ρ_0^q *in equation (3.5) is a pure state. [Hint: A density operator* ρ *is a pure state if and only if* $tr(\rho^2) = 1$*; see [174], Exercise 2.71.]*

Computation of a Program:

Now the notion of computation of a quantum program can be naturally defined in terms of its transitions.

Definition 3.2.3. *Let S be a quantum program and* $\rho \in \mathcal{D}(\mathcal{H}_{all})$*.*

(i) *A transition sequence of S starting in* ρ *is a finite or infinite sequence of configurations in the following form:*

$$\langle S, \rho \rangle \rightarrow \langle S_1, \rho_1 \rangle \rightarrow \ldots \rightarrow \langle S_n, \rho_n \rangle \rightarrow \langle S_{n+1}, \rho_{n+1} \rangle \rightarrow \ldots$$

such that $\rho_n \neq 0$ *for all n (except the last n in the case of a finite sequence).*

(ii) *If this sequence cannot be extended, then it is called a computation of S starting in* ρ*.*

    (a) *If a computation is finite and its last configuration is* $\langle E, \rho' \rangle$*, then we say that it terminates in* ρ'*.*

    (b) *If it is infinite, then we say that it diverges. Moreover, we say that S can diverge from* ρ *whenever it has a diverging computation starting in* ρ*.*

To illustrate this definition, let us see a simple example.

Example 3.2.2. *Suppose that* $type(q_1) = $ **Boolean** *and* $type(q_2) = $ **integer***. Consider the program*

$$S \equiv q_1 := |0\rangle; \ q_2 := |0\rangle; \ q_1 := H[q_1]; \ q_2 := q_2 + 7;$$
$$\textbf{if } M[q_1] = 0 \rightarrow S_1$$
$$\square \qquad 1 \rightarrow S_2$$
$$\textbf{fi}$$

where:

- *H is the Hadamard transformation, $q_2 := q_2 + 7$ is a rewriting of*

$$q_2 := T_7[q_2]$$

  with T_7 being the translation operator defined in Example 2.1.4;
- *M is the measurement in the computational basis $|0\rangle, |1\rangle$ of $\mathcal{H}_2$; that is, $M = \{M_0, M_1\}$, $M_0 = |0\rangle\langle 0|$ and $M_1 = |1\rangle\langle 1|$;*
- *$S_1 \equiv$ **skip**;*
- *$S_2 \equiv$ **while** $N[q_2] = 1$ **do** $q_1 := X[q_1]$ **od**, where X is the Pauli matrix (i.e., the NOT gate), $N = \{N_0, N_1\}$, and*

$$N_0 = \sum_{n=-\infty}^{0} |n\rangle\langle n|, \qquad N_1 = \sum_{n=1}^{\infty} |n\rangle\langle n|.$$

Let $\rho = |1\rangle_{q_1}\langle 1| \otimes |-1\rangle_{q_2}\langle -1| \otimes \rho_0$ and

$$\rho_0 = \bigotimes_{q \neq q_1, q_2} |0\rangle_q\langle 0|.$$

Then the computations of S starting in ρ are:

$$
\begin{aligned}
\langle S, \rho\rangle &\to \langle q_2 := |0\rangle;\ q_1 := H[q_1];\ q_2 := q_2 + 7;\ \textbf{if} \ldots \textbf{fi}, \rho_1\rangle \\
&\to \langle q_1 := H[q_1];\ q_2 := q_2 + 7;\ \textbf{if} \ldots \textbf{fi}, \rho_2\rangle \\
&\to \langle q_2 := q_2 + 7;\ \textbf{if} \ldots \textbf{fi}, \rho_3\rangle \\
&\to \langle \textbf{if} \ldots \textbf{fi}, \rho_4\rangle \\
&\to \begin{cases} \langle S_1, \rho_5\rangle \to \langle E, \rho_5\rangle, \\ \langle S_2, \rho_6\rangle, \end{cases}
\end{aligned}
$$

$$
\begin{aligned}
\langle S_2, \rho_6\rangle &\to \langle q_1 := X[q_1];\ S_2, \rho_6\rangle \\
&\to \langle S_2, \rho_5\rangle \\
&\to \ldots \\
&\to \langle q_1 := X[q_1];\ S_2, \rho_6\rangle \quad \text{(after $2n-1$ transitions)} \\
&\to \langle S_2, \rho_5\rangle \\
&\to \ldots
\end{aligned}
$$

where:

$$
\begin{aligned}
\rho_1 &= |0\rangle_{q_1}\langle 0| \otimes |-1\rangle_{q_2}\langle -1| \otimes \rho_0, \\
\rho_2 &= |0\rangle_{q_1}\langle 0| \otimes |0\rangle_{q_2}\langle 0| \otimes \rho_0, \\
\rho_3 &= |+\rangle_{q_1}\langle +| \otimes |0\rangle_{q_2}\langle 0| \otimes \rho_0, \\
\rho_4 &= |+\rangle_{q_1}\langle +| \otimes |7\rangle_{q_2}\langle 7| \otimes \rho_0,
\end{aligned}
$$

$$\rho_5 = \frac{1}{2}|0\rangle_{q_1}\langle 0| \otimes |7\rangle_{q_2}\langle 7| \otimes \rho_0,$$

$$\rho_6 = \frac{1}{2}|1\rangle_{q_1}\langle 1| \otimes |7\rangle_{q_2}\langle 7| \otimes \rho_0.$$

So, S can diverge from ρ. Note that S_2 also has the transition

$$\langle S_2, \rho_6\rangle \to \langle E, 0_{\mathcal{H}_{all}}\rangle,$$

but we always discard the transitions in which the partial density operator of the target configuration is a zero operator.

Nondeterminism:

To conclude this section, let us observe an interesting difference between the operational semantics of classical and quantum **while**-programs. Classical **while**-programs are a typical class of deterministic programs that have exactly one computation starting in a given state. (Here, if not only the conditional statement "**if** ...**then** ...**else**" but also the case statement (3.1) is included, then it is assumed that the guards $G_1, G_2, \ldots, G_n$ do not overlap each other.) However, this example showed that quantum **while**-programs no longer possess such a determinism because probabilism is introduced by the measurements in the statements "**if** ($\square m \cdot M[\overline{q}] = m \to S_m$) **fi**" and "**while** $M[\overline{q}] = 1$ **do** S **od**". Essentially, the operational semantics $\to$ of quantum programs given in Definition 3.2.2 is a probabilistic transition relation. However, the after encoding probabilities into partial density operators, probabilism manifests as nondeterminism in the transition rules (IF), (L0) and (L2). Therefore, the semantics $\to$ should be understood as a nondeterministic transition relation.

3.3 DENOTATIONAL SEMANTICS

We defined the operational semantics of quantum programs in the previous section. Then the denotational semantics can be defined based on it, or more precisely on the notion of computation introduced in Definition 3.2.3. The denotational semantics of a quantum program is a semantic function that maps partial density operators to themselves. Intuitively, for any quantum program S, the semantic function of S sums up the computed results of all terminating computations of S.

If configuration $\langle S', \rho'\rangle$ can be reached from $\langle S, \rho\rangle$ in n steps through the transition relation $\to$, which means there are configurations $\langle S_1, \rho_1\rangle, \ldots, \langle S_{n-1}, \rho_{n-1}\rangle$ such that

$$\langle S, \rho\rangle \to \langle S_1, \rho_1\rangle \to \ldots \to \langle S_{n-1}, \rho_{n-1}\rangle \to \langle S', \rho'\rangle,$$

then we write:

$$\langle S, \rho\rangle \to^n \langle S', \rho'\rangle.$$

Furthermore, we write $\to^*$ for the reflexive and transitive closures of $\to$; that is,

$$\langle S, \rho\rangle \to^* \langle S', \rho'\rangle$$

if and only if $\langle S, \rho\rangle \to^n \langle S', \rho'\rangle$ for some $n \geq 0$.

Definition 3.3.1. *Let S be a quantum program. Then its semantic function*

$$\llbracket S \rrbracket : \mathcal{D}(\mathcal{H}_{all}) \rightarrow \mathcal{D}(\mathcal{H}_{all})$$

is defined by

$$\llbracket S \rrbracket(\rho) = \sum \left\{ | \rho' : \langle S, \rho \rangle \rightarrow^* \langle E, \rho' \rangle | \right\} \tag{3.7}$$

for all $\rho \in \mathcal{D}(\mathcal{H}_{all})$, where $\{| \cdot |\}$ stands for multi-set, which means a (generalized) set that allows multiple instances of an element.

The reason for using a multi-set rather than an ordinary set in equation (3.7) is that the same partial density operator may be obtained through different computational paths, as we can see from the rules (IF), (L0) and (L1) in the last section. The following simple example illustrates the case more explicitly.

Example 3.3.1. *Assume that type$(q) = $ **Boolean**. Consider the program:*

$$S \equiv q := |0\rangle);\ q := H[q];\ \textbf{if } M[q] = 0 \rightarrow S_0$$
$$\square \qquad\qquad 1 \rightarrow S_1$$
$$\textbf{fi}$$

where:

- *M is the measurement in the computational basis $|0\rangle, |1\rangle$ of the state space $\mathcal{H}_2$ of a qubit;*
- *$S_0 \equiv q := I[q]$ and $S_1 \equiv q := X[q]$ with I and X being the identity operator and the NOT gate, respectively.*

Let $\rho = |0\rangle_{all}\langle 0|$, where

$$|0\rangle_{all} = \bigotimes_{q \in qVar} |0\rangle_q.$$

Then the computations of S starting in ρ are:

$$\langle S, \rho \rangle \rightarrow \langle q := H[q]; \textbf{if} \ldots \textbf{fi}, \rho \rangle$$
$$\rightarrow \langle \textbf{if} \ldots \textbf{fi}, |+\rangle_q \langle +| \otimes \bigotimes_{p \neq q} |0\rangle_p \langle 0| \rangle$$
$$\rightarrow \begin{cases} \langle S_0, \frac{1}{2}|0\rangle_q \langle 0| \otimes \bigotimes_{p \neq q} |0\rangle_p \langle 0| \rangle \rightarrow \langle E, \frac{1}{2}\rho \rangle, \\ \langle S_1, \frac{1}{2}|1\rangle_q \langle 1| \otimes \bigotimes_{p \neq q} |0\rangle_p \langle 0| \rangle \rightarrow \langle E, \frac{1}{2}\rho \rangle. \end{cases}$$

So, we have:

$$\llbracket S \rrbracket(\rho) = \frac{1}{2}\rho + \frac{1}{2}\rho = \rho.$$

3.3.1 BASIC PROPERTIES OF SEMANTIC FUNCTIONS

As in classical programming theory, operational semantics is convenient for describing the execution of quantum programs. On the other hand, denotational semantics is suitable for studying mathematical properties of quantum programs. Now we establish several basic properties of semantic functions that are useful for reasoning about quantum programs.

First of all, we observe that the semantic function of any quantum program is linear.

Lemma 3.3.1 (Linearity). *Let $\rho_1, \rho_2 \in \mathcal{D}(\mathcal{H}_{all})$ and $\lambda_1, \lambda_2 \geq 0$. If $\lambda_1 \rho_1 + \lambda_2 \rho_2 \in \mathcal{D}(\mathcal{H}_{all})$, then for any quantum program S, we have:*

$$\llbracket S \rrbracket(\lambda_1 \rho_1 + \lambda_2 \rho_2) = \lambda_1 \llbracket S \rrbracket(\rho_1) + \lambda_2 \llbracket S \rrbracket(\rho_2).$$

Proof. We can prove the following fact by induction on the structure of S:

- Claim: If $\langle S, \rho_1 \rangle \rightarrow \langle S', \rho_1' \rangle$ and $\langle S, \rho_2 \rangle \rightarrow \langle S', \rho_2' \rangle$, then

$$\langle S, \lambda_1 \rho_1 + \lambda_2 \rho_2 \rangle \rightarrow \langle S', \lambda_1 \rho_1' + \lambda_2 \rho_2' \rangle.$$

Then the conclusion immediately follows. □

Exercise 3.3.1. *Prove the claim in the proof of Lemma 3.3.1.*

Secondly, we present a structural representation for the semantic functions of quantum programs except **while**-loops. The representation of the semantic function of a quantum loop requires some mathematical tools from lattice theory. So, it is postponed to Subsection 3.3.3 after we prepare the necessary tools in the next subsection.

Proposition 3.3.1 (Structural Representation).

(i) $\llbracket \mathbf{skip} \rrbracket(\rho) = \rho$.

(ii) **(a)** *If $type(q) = $ **Boolean**, then*

$$\llbracket q := |0\rangle \rrbracket(\rho) = |0\rangle_q \langle 0|\rho|0\rangle_q \langle 0| + |0\rangle_q \langle 1|\rho|1\rangle_q \langle 0|.$$

(b) *If $type(q) = $ **integer**, then*

$$\llbracket q := |0\rangle \rrbracket(\rho) = \sum_{n=-\infty}^{\infty} |0\rangle_q \langle n|\rho|n\rangle_q \langle 0|.$$

(iii) $\llbracket \overline{q} := U[\overline{q}] \rrbracket(\rho) = U\rho U^\dagger$.

(iv) $\llbracket S_1; S_2 \rrbracket(\rho) = \llbracket S_2 \rrbracket(\llbracket S_1 \rrbracket(\rho))$.

(v) $\llbracket \mathbf{if}\ (\square m \cdot M[\overline{q}] = m \rightarrow S_m)\ \mathbf{fi} \rrbracket(\rho) = \sum_m \llbracket S_m \rrbracket(M_m \rho M_m^\dagger)$.

Proof. (i), (ii) and (iii) are obvious.

(iv) By Lemma 3.3.1 and the rule (SC) we obtain:

$$
\begin{aligned}
[\![S_2]\!]([\![S_1]\!](\rho)) &= [\![S_2]\!]\left(\sum\left\{|\rho_1 : \langle S_1, \rho\rangle \to^* \langle E, \rho_1\rangle|\right\}\right) \\
&= \sum\left\{|[\![S_2]\!](\rho_1) : \langle S_1, \rho\rangle \to^* \langle E, \rho_1\rangle|\right\} \\
&= \sum\left\{|\sum\left\{|\rho' : \langle S_2, \rho_1\rangle \to^* \langle E, \rho'\rangle|\right\} : \langle S_1, \rho\rangle \to^* \langle E, \rho_1\rangle|\right\} \\
&= \sum\left\{|\rho' : \langle S_1, \rho\rangle \to^* \langle E, \rho_1\rangle \text{ and } \langle S_2, \rho_1\rangle \to^* \langle E, \rho'\rangle|\right\} \\
&= \sum\left\{|\rho' : \langle S_1; S_2, \rho\rangle \to^* \langle E, \rho'\rangle|\right\} \\
&= [\![S_1; S_2]\!](\rho).
\end{aligned}
$$

(v) follows immediately from the rule (IF). $\qquad\square$

3.3.2 QUANTUM DOMAINS

Before presenting a representation of the semantic function of a quantum **while**-loop, we first have to pave the road leading toward it. In this subsection, we examine the domains of partial density operators and quantum operations. The notions and lemmas presented in this subsection will also be used in Section 3.4 and Chapter 7.

Basic Lattice Theory:

We first review the requisite concepts from lattice theory.

Definition 3.3.2. *A partial order is a pair $(L, \sqsubseteq)$ where L is a nonempty set and $\sqsubseteq$ is a binary relation on L satisfying the following conditions:*

(i) *Reflexivity: $x \sqsubseteq x$ for all $x \in L$;*

(ii) *Antisymmetry: $x \sqsubseteq y$ and $y \sqsubseteq x$ imply $x = y$ for all $x, y \in L$;*

(iii) *Transitivity: $x \sqsubseteq y$ and $y \sqsubseteq z$ imply $x \sqsubseteq z$ for all $x, y, z \in L$.*

Definition 3.3.3. *Let $(L, \sqsubseteq)$ be a partial order.*

(i) *An element $x \in L$ is called the least element of L when $x \sqsubseteq y$ for all $y \in L$. The least element is usually denoted by 0.*

(ii) *An element $x \in L$ is called an upper bound of a subset $X \subseteq L$ if $y \sqsubseteq x$ for all $x \in X$.*

(iii) *x is called the least upper bound of X, written $x = \bigsqcup X$, if*

    (a) *x is an upper bound of X;*

    (b) *for any upper bound y of X, it holds that $x \sqsubseteq y$.*

We often write $\bigsqcup_{n=0}^{\infty} x_n$ or $\bigsqcup_n x_n$ for $\bigsqcup X$ when X is a sequence $\{x_n\}_{n=0}^{\infty}$.

Definition 3.3.4. *A complete partial order (CPO for short) is a partial order $(L, \sqsubseteq)$ satisfying the following conditions:*

(i) *it has the least element* 0;
(ii) $\bigsqcup_{n=0}^{\infty} x_n$ *exists for any increasing sequence* $\{x_n\}$ *in L; i.e.*

$$x_0 \sqsubseteq \ldots \sqsubseteq x_n \sqsubseteq x_{n+1} \sqsubseteq \ldots.$$

Definition 3.3.5. *Let* $(L, \sqsubseteq)$ *be a CPO. Then a function f from L into itself is said to be continuous if*

$$f\left(\bigsqcup_n x_n\right) = \bigsqcup_n f(x_n)$$

for any increasing sequence $\{x_n\}$ *in L.*

The following theorem has been widely used in programming theory for the description of semantics of loops and recursive programs.

Theorem 3.3.1. *(Knaster-Tarski) Let* $(L, \sqsubseteq)$ *be a CPO and function* $f : L \to L$ *is continuous. Then f has the least fixed point*

$$\mu f = \bigsqcup_{n=0}^{\infty} f^{(n)}(0)$$

(i.e., $f(\mu f) = \mu f$*, and if* $f(x) = x$ *then* $\mu f \sqsubseteq x$*), where*

$$\begin{cases} f^{(0)}(0) &= 0, \\ f^{(n+1)}(0) &= f(f^{(n)}(0)) \text{ for } n \geq 0. \end{cases}$$

Exercise 3.3.2. *Prove Theorem 3.3.1.*

Domain of Partial Density Operators:

We now consider the lattice-theoretic structures of quantum objects required in the representation of quantum **while**-loops. Actually, we need to deal with two levels of quantum objects. At the lower level are partial density operators. Let $\mathcal{H}$ be an arbitrary Hilbert space. A partial order in the set $\mathcal{D}(\mathcal{H})$ of partial density operators was already introduced in Definition 2.1.13. Recall that the Löwner order is defined as follows: for any operators $A, B \in \mathcal{L}(\mathcal{H})$, $A \sqsubseteq B$ if $B - A$ is a positive operator. The lattice-theoretic property of $\mathcal{D}(\mathcal{H})$ equipped with the Löwner order $\sqsubseteq$ is revealed in the following:

Lemma 3.3.2. $(\mathcal{D}(\mathcal{H}), \sqsubseteq)$ *is a CPO with the zero operator* $0_{\mathcal{H}}$ *as its least element.*

Domain of Quantum Operations:

We further consider the lattice-theoretic structure of quantum operations (see Definition 2.1.25).

Lemma 3.3.3. *Each quantum operation in a Hilbert space* $\mathcal{H}$ *is a continuous function from* $(\mathcal{D}(\mathcal{H}), \sqsubseteq)$ *into itself.*

We write $\mathcal{QO}(\mathcal{H})$ for the set of quantum operations in Hilbert space $\mathcal{H}$. Quantum operations should be considered as a class of quantum objects at a higher lever than partial density operators because $\mathcal{D}(\mathcal{H}) \subseteq \mathcal{L}(\mathcal{H})$, whereas $\mathcal{QO}(\mathcal{H}) \subseteq \mathcal{L}(\mathcal{L}(\mathcal{H}))$.

The Löwner order between operators induces a partial order between quantum operations in a natural way: for any $\mathcal{E}, \mathcal{F} \in \mathcal{QO}(\mathcal{H})$,

- $\mathcal{E} \sqsubseteq \mathcal{F} \Leftrightarrow \mathcal{E}(\rho) \sqsubseteq \mathcal{F}(\rho)$ for all $\rho \in \mathcal{D}(\mathcal{H})$.

In a sense, the Löwner order is lifted from lower-level objects $\mathcal{D}(\mathcal{H})$ to higher-level objects $\mathcal{QO}(\mathcal{H})$.

Lemma 3.3.4. $(\mathcal{QO}(\mathcal{H}), \sqsubseteq)$ *is a CPO.*

The proofs of Lemmas 3.3.2, 3.3.3 and 3.3.4 are quite involved. For readability, they are all postponed to Section 3.6.

3.3.3 SEMANTIC FUNCTION OF LOOP

Now we are ready to show that the semantic function of a quantum **while**-loop can be represented as the limit of the semantic functions of its finite syntactic approximations. To do this, we need an auxiliary notation: **abort** denotes a quantum program such that

$$\llbracket \textbf{abort} \rrbracket (\rho) = 0_{\mathcal{H}_{\text{all}}}$$

for all $\rho \in \mathcal{D}(\mathcal{H})$. Intuitively, program **abort** is never guaranteed to terminate; for example, we can choose

$$\textbf{abort} \equiv \textbf{while } M_{\text{trivial}}[q] = 1 \textbf{ do skip od},$$

where q is a quantum variable, and $M_{\text{trivial}} = \{M_0 = 0_{\mathcal{H}_q}, M_1 = I_{\mathcal{H}_q}\}$ is a trivial measurement in the state space $\mathcal{H}_q$. The program **abort** will serve as the basis for inductively defining the syntactic approximations of a quantum loop.

Definition 3.3.6. *Consider a quantum loop*

$$\textbf{while} \equiv \textbf{while } M[\overline{q}] = 1 \textbf{ do } S \textbf{ od}. \tag{3.8}$$

For any integer $k \geq 0$, the kth syntactic approximation $\textbf{while}^{(k)}$ of $\textbf{while}$ is inductively defined by

$$\begin{cases} \textbf{while}^{(0)} & \equiv \textbf{abort}, \\ \textbf{while}^{(k+1)} & \equiv \textbf{if } M[\overline{q}] = 0 \rightarrow \textbf{skip} \\ & \qquad \square \qquad 1 \rightarrow S; \textbf{while}^{(k)} \\ & \textbf{fi} \end{cases}$$

A representation of the semantic function of a quantum **while**-loop is then presented in the following:

Proposition 3.3.2. *Let $\textbf{while}$ be the loop (3.8). Then*

$$\llbracket \textbf{while} \rrbracket = \bigsqcup_{k=0}^{\infty} \llbracket \textbf{while}^{(k)} \rrbracket,$$

*where **while**$^{(k)}$ is the kth syntactic approximation of **while** for every $k \geq 0$, and the symbol $\bigsqcup$ stands for the supremum of quantum operations: i.e., the least upper bound in CPO $(\mathcal{QO}(\mathcal{H}_{all}), \sqsubseteq)$.*

Proof. For $i = 0, 1$, we introduce auxiliary operators

$$\mathcal{E}_i : \mathcal{D}(\mathcal{H}_{all}) \to \mathcal{D}(\mathcal{H}_{all})$$

defined by $\mathcal{E}_i(\rho) = M_i \rho M_i^{\dagger}$ for all $\rho \in \mathcal{D}(\mathcal{H})$.

First, we prove:

$$\left[\!\left[\mathbf{while}^{(k)}\right]\!\right](\rho) = \sum_{n=0}^{k-1} \left[\mathcal{E}_0 \circ \left([\![S]\!] \circ \mathcal{E}_1\right)^n\right](\rho)$$

for all $k \geq 1$ by induction on k. The symbol $\circ$ in the preceding equality stands for composition of quantum operations; that is, the composition $\mathcal{F} \circ \mathcal{E}$ of quantum operations $\mathcal{E}$ and $\mathcal{F}$ is defined by $(\mathcal{F} \circ \mathcal{E})(\rho) = \mathcal{F}(\mathcal{E}(\rho))$ for every $\rho \in \mathcal{D}(\mathcal{H})$. The case of $k = 1$ is obvious. Then by Proposition 3.3.1 (i), (iv) and (v) and the induction hypothesis on $k - 1$ we obtain:

$$
\begin{aligned}
\left[\!\left[\mathbf{while}^{(k)}\right]\!\right](\rho) &= [\![\mathbf{skip}]\!](\mathcal{E}_0(\rho)) + \left[\!\left[S; \mathbf{while}^{(k-1)}\right]\!\right](\mathcal{E}_1(\rho)) \\
&= \mathcal{E}_0(\rho) + \left[\!\left[\mathbf{while}^{(k-1)}\right]\!\right](([\![S]\!] \circ \mathcal{E}_1)(\rho)) \\
&= \mathcal{E}_0(\rho) + \sum_{n=0}^{k-2} \left[\mathcal{E}_0 \circ ([\![S]\!] \circ \mathcal{E}_1)^n\right](([\![S]\!] \circ \mathcal{E}_1)(\rho)) \qquad (3.9)\\
&= \sum_{n=0}^{k-1} \left[\mathcal{E}_0 \circ ([\![S]\!] \circ \mathcal{E}_1)^n\right](\rho).
\end{aligned}
$$

Secondly, we have:

$$
\begin{aligned}
[\![\mathbf{while}]\!](\rho) &= \sum \left\{ |\rho' : \langle \mathbf{while}, \rho \rangle \to^* \langle E, \rho' \rangle| \right\} \\
&= \sum_{k=1}^{\infty} \sum \left\{ |\rho' : \langle \mathbf{while}, \rho \rangle \to^k \langle E, \rho' \rangle| \right\}.
\end{aligned}
$$

So, it suffices to show that

$$\sum \left\{ |\rho' : \langle \mathbf{while}, \rho \rangle \to^k \langle E, \rho' \rangle| \right\} = \left[\mathcal{E}_0 \circ ([\![S]\!] \circ \mathcal{E}_1)^{k-1}\right](\rho)$$

for all $k \geq 1$. By the previous points, it is not hard to prove this equality by induction on k. $\qquad \square$

A fixed point characterization of the semantic function of a quantum loop can be derived from the preceding proposition.

Corollary 3.3.1. *Let* **while** *be the loop* (3.8). *Then for any* $\rho \in \mathcal{D}(\mathcal{H}_{all})$, *it holds that*

$$\llbracket \textbf{while} \rrbracket(\rho) = M_0 \rho M_0^\dagger + \llbracket \textbf{while} \rrbracket \left(\llbracket S \rrbracket \left(M_1 \rho M_1^\dagger \right) \right).$$

Proof. Immediate from Proposition 3.3.2 and equation (3.9).   □

3.3.4 CHANGE AND ACCESS OF QUANTUM VARIABLES

One key issue in understanding the behavior of a program is to observe how it changes the states of program variables and how it accesses program variables during its execution. As the first application of the semantic function just studied, we now address this issue for quantum programs.

To simplify the presentation, we introduce an abbreviation. Let $X \subseteq qVar$ be a set of quantum variables. For any operator $A \in \mathcal{L}(\mathcal{H}_{all})$, we write:

$$tr_X(A) = tr_{\bigotimes_{q \in X} \mathcal{H}_q}(A)$$

where $tr_{\bigotimes_{q \in X} \mathcal{H}_q}$ is the partial trace over system $\bigotimes_{q \in X} \mathcal{H}_q$ (see Definition 2.1.22). Then we have:

Proposition 3.3.3

(i) $tr_{qvar(S)}(\llbracket S \rrbracket(\rho)) = tr_{qvar(S)}(\rho)$ *whenever* $tr(\llbracket S \rrbracket(\rho)) = tr(\rho)$.

(ii) *If it holds that*

$$tr_{qVar \setminus qvar(S)}(\rho_1) = tr_{qVar \setminus qvar(S)}(\rho_2),$$

then we have:

$$tr_{qVar \setminus qvar(S)}(\llbracket S \rrbracket(\rho_1)) = tr_{qVar \setminus qvar(S)}(\llbracket S \rrbracket(\rho_2)).$$

Recall from Definition 2.1.22 that $tr_X(\rho)$ describes the state of the quantum variables not in X when the global state of all quantum variables is ρ. So, the preceding proposition can be intuitively explained as follows:

- Proposition 3.3.3(i) indicates that the state of the quantum variables not in $qvar(S)$ after executing program S is the same as that before executing S. This means that program S can only change the state of quantum variables in $qvar(S)$.
- Proposition 3.3.3(ii) shows that if two input states ρ_1 and ρ_2 coincide on the quantum variables in $qvar(S)$, then the computed outcomes of S, starting in ρ_1 and ρ_2, respectively, will also coincide on these quantum variables. In other words, if the output of program S with input ρ_1 is different from that with input ρ_2, then ρ_1 and ρ_2 must be different when restricted to $qvar(S)$. This means that program S can access at most the quantum variables in $qvar(S)$.

Exercise 3.3.3. *Prove Proposition 3.3.3. [Hint: use the representation of semantic functions presented in Propositions 3.3.1 and 3.3.2.]*

3.3.5 **TERMINATION AND DIVERGENCE PROBABILITIES**

Another key issue with the behavior of a program is its termination. The first consideration about this problem for quantum programs is based on the following proposition showing that a semantic function does not increase the trace of partial density operator of quantum variables.

Proposition 3.3.4. *For any quantum program S and for all partial density operators* $\rho \in \mathcal{D}(\mathcal{H}_{all})$, *it holds that*

$$tr([\![S]\!](\rho)) \leq tr(\rho).$$

Proof. We proceed by induction on the structure of S.

- Case 1. $S \equiv \mathbf{skip}$. Obvious.
- Case 2. $S \equiv q := |0\rangle$. If $type(q) = \mathbf{integer}$, then using the equality $tr(AB) = tr(BA)$ we obtain:

$$
\begin{aligned}
tr([\![S]\!](\rho)) &= \sum_{n=-\infty}^{\infty} tr(|0\rangle_q \langle n|\rho|n\rangle_q \langle 0|) \\
&= \sum_{n=-\infty}^{\infty} tr(_q\langle 0|0\rangle_q \langle n|\rho|n\rangle_q) \\
&= tr\left[\left(\sum_{n=-\infty}^{\infty} |n\rangle_q\langle n|\right)\rho\right] = tr(\rho).
\end{aligned}
$$

It can be proved in a similar way when $type(q) = \mathbf{Boolean}$.
- Case 3. $S \equiv \overline{q} := U[\overline{q}]$. Then

$$tr([\![S]\!](\rho)) = tr\left(U\rho U^\dagger\right) = tr\left(U^\dagger U\rho\right) = tr(\rho).$$

- Case 4. $S \equiv S_1; S_2$. It follows from the induction hypothesis on S_1 and S_2 that

$$
\begin{aligned}
tr([\![S]\!](\rho)) &= tr([\![S_2]\!]([\![S_1]\!](\rho))) \\
&\leq tr([\![S_1]\!](\rho)) \\
&\leq tr(\rho).
\end{aligned}
$$

- Case 5. $S \equiv \mathbf{if}\ (\square m \cdot M[\overline{q}] = m \rightarrow S_m)\ \mathbf{fi}$. Then by the induction hypothesis we obtain:

$$
\begin{aligned}
tr([\![S]\!](\rho)) &= \sum_m tr\left([\![S_m]\!]\left(M_m\rho M_m^\dagger\right)\right) \\
&\leq \sum_m tr\left(M_m\rho M_m^\dagger\right) \\
&= tr\left[\left(\sum_m M_m^\dagger M_m\right)\rho\right] = tr(\rho).
\end{aligned}
$$

- Case 6. $S \equiv$ **while** $M[\bar{q}] = 1$ **do** S' **od**. We write $(\textbf{while}')^n$ for the statement obtained through replacing S by S' in $(\textbf{while})^n$ given in Definition 3.3.6. With Proposition 3.3.2, it suffices to show that

$$tr\left(\llbracket(\textbf{while}')^n\rrbracket\,(\rho)\right) \leq tr(\rho)$$

for all $n \geq 0$. This can be carried out by induction on n. The case of $n = 0$ is obvious. By the induction hypothesis on n and S', we have:

$$
\begin{aligned}
tr\left(\llbracket(\textbf{while}')^{n+1}\rrbracket\,(\rho)\right) &= tr\left(M_0\rho M_0^\dagger\right) + tr\left(\llbracket(\textbf{while}')^n\rrbracket\left(\llbracket S'\rrbracket\left(M_1\rho M_1^\dagger\right)\right)\right)\\
&\leq tr\left(M_0\rho M_0^\dagger\right) + tr\left(\llbracket S'\rrbracket\left(M_1\rho M_1^\dagger\right)\right)\\
&\leq tr\left(M_0\rho M_0^\dagger\right) + tr\left(M_1\rho M_1^\dagger\right)\\
&= tr\left[\left(M_0^\dagger M_0 + M_1^\dagger M_1\right)\rho\right]\\
&= tr(\rho).
\end{aligned}
$$

$\square$

Intuitively, $tr(\llbracket S\rrbracket(\rho))$ is the probability that program S terminates when starting in state ρ. From the proof of the preceding proposition, we can see that the only program constructs that can cause $tr(\llbracket S\rrbracket(\rho)) < tr(\rho)$ are the loops occurring in S. Thus,

$$tr(\rho) - tr(\llbracket S\rrbracket(\rho))$$

is the probability that program S diverges from input state ρ. This can be further illustrated by the following example.

Example 3.3.2. *Let* $type(q) = $ **integer***, and let*

$$M_0 = \sum_{n=1}^{\infty}\sqrt{\frac{n-1}{2n}}(|n\rangle\langle n| + |-n\rangle\langle -n|),$$

$$M_1 = |0\rangle\langle 0| + \sum_{n=1}^{\infty}\sqrt{\frac{n+1}{2n}}(|n\rangle\langle n| + |-n\rangle\langle -n|).$$

Then $M = \{M_0, M_1\}$ *is a yes-no measurement in the state Hilbert space* $\mathcal{H}_q$ *(note that* M *is not a projective measurement). Consider the program:*

$$\textbf{while} \equiv \textbf{while } M[q] = 1 \textbf{ do } q := q + 1 \textbf{ od}$$

Let $\rho = |0\rangle_q\langle 0| \otimes \rho_0$ *with*

$$\rho_0 = \bigotimes_{p \neq q}|0\rangle_p\langle 0|.$$

Then after some calculations we have:

$$[\![(\mathbf{while})^n]\!](\rho) = \begin{cases} 0_{\mathcal{H}_{all}} & \text{if } n = 0, 1, 2, \\ \frac{1}{2}\left(\sum_{k=2}^{n-1} \frac{k-1}{k!} |k\rangle_q \langle k|\right) \otimes \rho_0 & \text{if } n \geq 3, \end{cases}$$

$$[\![\mathbf{while}]\!](\rho) = \frac{1}{2}\left(\sum_{n=2}^{\infty} \frac{n-1}{n!} |n\rangle_q \langle n|\right) \otimes \rho_0$$

and

$$tr([\![\mathbf{while}]\!](\rho)) = \frac{1}{2}\sum_{n=2}^{\infty} \frac{n-1}{n!} = \frac{1}{2}.$$

This means that program **while** *terminates on input ρ with probability $\frac{1}{2}$, and it diverges from input ρ with probability $\frac{1}{2}$.*

A more systematic study of the termination of quantum programs will be presented in Chapter 5.

3.3.6 SEMANTIC FUNCTIONS AS QUANTUM OPERATIONS

To conclude this section, we establish a connection between quantum programs and quantum operations (see Subsection 2.1.7).

The semantic function of a quantum program is defined to be a mapping from partial density operators in $\mathcal{H}_{all}$ to themselves. Let V be a subset of $qVar$. Whenever a quantum operation $\mathcal{E}$ in $\mathcal{H}_{all}$ is the cylindric extension of a quantum operation $\mathcal{F}$ in $\mathcal{H}_V = \bigotimes_{q \in V} \mathcal{H}_q$, meaning that

$$\mathcal{E} = \mathcal{F} \otimes \mathcal{I}$$

where $\mathcal{I}$ is the identity quantum operation in $\mathcal{H}_{qVar \setminus V}$, we always identify $\mathcal{E}$ with $\mathcal{F}$, and $\mathcal{E}$ can be seen as a quantum operation in $\mathcal{H}_V$. With this convention, we have:

Proposition 3.3.5. *For any quantum program S, its semantic function $[\![S]\!]$ is a quantum operation in $\mathcal{H}_{qvar(S)}$.*

Proof. It can be proved by induction on the structure of S. For the case that S is not a loop, it follows from Theorem 2.1.1 (iii) and Proposition 3.3.1. For the case that S is a loop, it follows from Proposition 3.3.2 and Lemma 3.3.4. $\qquad\square$

Conversely, one may ask: can every quantum operation be modelled by a quantum program? To answer this question, let us first introduce the notion of local quantum variable.

Definition 3.3.7. *Let S be a quantum program and $\overline{q}$ a sequence of quantum variables. Then:*

(i) *The block command defined by S with local variables $\overline{q}$ is:*

$$\textbf{begin local } \overline{q} : S \textbf{ end}. \tag{3.10}$$

(ii) *The quantum variables of the block command are:*

$$qvar\,(\textbf{begin local } \overline{q} : S \textbf{ end}) = qvar(S) \setminus \overline{q}.$$

(iii) *The denotational semantics of the block command is the quantum operation from $\mathcal{H}_{qvar(S)}$ to $\mathcal{H}_{qvar(S)\setminus\overline{q}}$ defined by*

$$[\![\textbf{begin local } \overline{q} : S \textbf{ end}]\!]\,(\rho) = tr_{\mathcal{H}_{\overline{q}}}([\![S]\!](\rho)) \tag{3.11}$$

for any density operator $\rho \in \mathcal{D}(\mathcal{H}_{qvar(S)})$, where $tr_{\mathcal{H}_{\overline{q}}}$ stands for the partial trace over $\mathcal{H}_{\overline{q}}$ (see Definition 2.1.22).

The intuitive meaning of block command (3.10) is that program S is running in the environment where $\overline{q}$ are local variables that will be initialized in S. After executing S, the auxiliary system denoted by the local variables $\overline{q}$ is discarded. This is why the trace over $\mathcal{H}_{\overline{q}}$ is taken in the defining equation (3.11) of the semantics of the block command. Note that (3.11) is a partial density operator in $\mathcal{H}_{qvar(S)\setminus\overline{q}}$.

A block command will be seen as a quantum program in the sequel. Then we are able to provide a positive answer to the question raised earlier. The following proposition is essentially a restatement of Theorem 2.1.1 (ii) in terms of quantum programs.

Proposition 3.3.6. *For any finite subset V of qVar, and for any quantum operation $\mathcal{E}$ in $\mathcal{H}_V$, there exists a quantum program (more precisely, a block command) S such that $[\![S]\!] = \mathcal{E}$.*

Proof. By Theorem 2.1.1 (ii), there exist:

(i) quantum variables $\overline{p} \subseteq qVar \setminus \overline{q}$,
(ii) a unitary transformation U in $\mathcal{H}_{\overline{p}\cup\overline{q}}$,
(iii) a projection P onto a closed subspace of $\mathcal{H}_{\overline{p}\cup\overline{q}}$, and
(iv) a state $|e_0\rangle$ in $\mathcal{H}_{\overline{p}}$

such that

$$\mathcal{E}(\rho) = tr_{\mathcal{H}_{\overline{p}}}\left[PU(|e_0\rangle\langle e_0| \otimes \rho)U^{\dagger}P\right]$$

for all $\rho \in \mathcal{D}(\mathcal{H}_{\overline{q}})$. Obviously, we can find a unitary operator U_0 in $\mathcal{H}_{\overline{p}}$ such that

$$|e_0\rangle = U_0|0\rangle_{\overline{p}}$$

where $|0\rangle_{\overline{p}} = |0\rangle \ldots |0\rangle$ (all quantum variables in $\overline{p}$ are initialized in state $|0\rangle$). On the other hand,

$$M = \{M_0 = P, M_1 = I - P\}$$

is a yes-no measurement in $\mathcal{H}_{\overline{p} \cup \overline{q}}$, where I is the identity operator in $\mathcal{H}_{\overline{p} \cup \overline{q}}$. We set

$$S \equiv \textbf{begin local } \overline{p} : \overline{p} := |0\rangle_{\overline{p}}; \ \overline{p} := U_0[\overline{p}]; \ \overline{p} \cup \overline{q} := U[\overline{p} \cup \overline{q}];$$
$$\textbf{if } M[\overline{p} \cup \overline{q}] = 0 \to \textbf{skip}$$
$$\square \qquad\qquad 1 \to \textbf{abort}$$
$$\textbf{fi}$$
$$\textbf{end}$$

Then it is easy to check that $[\![S]\!] = \mathcal{E}$. $\square$

3.4 CLASSICAL RECURSION IN QUANTUM PROGRAMMING

The notion of recursion allows the programming of repetitive tasks without a large number of similar steps to be specified individually. In the previous sections, we have studied the quantum extension of the **while**-language, which provides a program construct, namely the quantum **while**-loop, to implement a special kind of recursion – iteration – in quantum computation. The general form of recursive procedure has been widely used in classical programming. It renders a more powerful technique than iteration, in which a function can be defined, directly or indirectly, in terms of itself. In this section, we add the general notion of recursion into the quantum **while**-language in order to specify procedures in quantum computation that can call themselves.

The notion of recursion considered in this section should be properly termed as *classical recursion in quantum programming* because the control flow within it is still classical, or more precisely, the control is determined by the outcomes of quantum measurements. The notion of recursion with quantum control flow will be introduced in Chapter 7. To avoid confusion, a quantum program containing recursion with classical control will be called a *recursive quantum program*, whereas a quantum program containing recursion with quantum control will be referred to as a *quantum recursive program*. With the mathematical tools prepared in Subsection 3.3.2, the theory of recursive quantum programs presented in this section is more or less a straightforward generalization of the theory of classical recursive programs. However, as you will see in Chapter 7, the treatment of quantum recursive programs is much more difficult, and it requires some ideas that are radically different from those used in this section.

3.4.1 SYNTAX

We first define the syntax of recursive quantum programs. The alphabet of recursive quantum programs is the alphabet of quantum **while**-programs expanded by adding a set of procedure identifiers, ranged over by $X, X_1, X_2, \ldots$.

Quantum program schemes are defined as generalized quantum **while**-programs that may contain procedure identifiers. Formally, we have:

Definition 3.4.1. *Quantum program schemes are generated by the syntax:*

$$S ::= X \mid \textbf{skip} \mid q := |0\rangle \mid \overline{q} := U[\overline{q}] \mid S_1; S_2$$
$$\mid \textbf{if } (\square m \cdot M[\overline{q}] = m \rightarrow S_m) \textbf{ fi} \tag{3.12}$$
$$\mid \textbf{while } M[\overline{q}] = 1 \textbf{ do } S \textbf{ od.}$$

The only difference between the syntax (3.2) and (3.12) is that a clause for procedure identifiers X is added in the latter. If a program scheme S contains at most the procedure identifiers $X_1, \ldots, X_n$, then we write

$$S \equiv S[X_1, \ldots, X_n].$$

As in classical programming, procedure identifiers in a quantum program scheme are used as subprograms, which are usually called *procedure calls*. They are specified by declarations defined in the following:

Definition 3.4.2. *Let $X_1, \ldots, X_n$ be different procedure identifiers. A declaration for $X_1, \ldots, X_n$ is a system of equations:*

$$D : \begin{cases} X_1 \Leftarrow S_1, \\ \quad \ldots \ldots \\ X_n \Leftarrow S_n, \end{cases} \tag{3.13}$$

where for every $1 \le i \le n$, $S_i \equiv S_i[X_1, \ldots, X_n]$ is a quantum program scheme.

Now we are ready to introduce the key notion of this section.

Definition 3.4.3. *A recursive quantum program consists of:*

 (i) *a quantum program scheme $S \equiv S[X_1, \ldots, X_n]$, called the main statement; and*
 (ii) *a declaration D for $X_1, \ldots, X_n$.*

3.4.2 OPERATIONAL SEMANTICS

A recursive quantum program is a quantum program scheme together with a declaration of procedure identifiers within it. So, we first define the operational semantics of quantum program schemes with respect to a given declaration. To this end, we need to generalize the notion of configuration defined in Section 3.2.

Definition 3.4.4. *A quantum configuration is a pair $\langle S, \rho \rangle$, where:*

 (i) *S is a quantum program scheme or the empty program E;*
 (ii) *$\rho \in \mathcal{D}(\mathcal{H}_{all})$ is a partial density operator in $\mathcal{H}_{all}$.*

This definition is the same as Definition 3.2.1 except that S is allowed to be not only a program but also a program scheme.

Now the operational semantics of quantum programs given in Definition 3.2.2 can be easily generalized to the case of quantum program schemes.

Definition 3.4.5. *Let D be a given declaration. The operational semantics of quantum program schemes with respect to D is the transition relation $\rightarrow_D$ between* *quantum configurations defined by the transition rules in Figure 3.1 together with the following rule for recursion:*

$$\text{(REC)} \qquad \frac{}{\langle X_i, \rho \rangle \to_D \langle S_i, \rho \rangle} \text{ if } X_i \Leftarrow S_i \text{ is in the declaration } D.$$

FIGURE 3.3

Transition rule for recursive quantum programs.

Of course, when used in this definition, the rules in Figure 3.1 are extended by allowing program schemes to appear in configurations, and the transition symbol $\to$ is replaced by $\to_D$. As in classical programming, the rule (REC) in Figure 3.3 can be referred to as the *copy rule*, meaning that at runtime a procedure call is treated like the procedure body inserted at the place of call.

3.4.3 DENOTATIONAL SEMANTICS

Based on the operational semantics described in the last subsection, the denotational semantics of quantum program schemes can be easily defined by straightforward extending of Definitions 3.2.3 and 3.3.1.

Definition 3.4.6. *Let D be a given declaration. For any quantum program scheme S, its semantic function with respect to D is the mapping:*

$$[\![S|D]\!] : \mathcal{D}(\mathcal{H}_{all}) \to \mathcal{D}(\mathcal{H}_{all})$$

defined by

$$[\![S|D]\!](\rho) = \sum \left\{ |\rho' : \langle S, \rho \rangle \to_D^* \langle E, \rho' \rangle | \right\}$$

for every $\rho \in \mathcal{D}(\mathcal{H}_{all})$, where $\to_D^*$ is the reflexive and transitive closure of $\to_D$.

Suppose that a recursive quantum program consists of the main statement S and declaration D. Then its denotational semantics is defined to be $[\![S|D]\!]$. Obviously, if S is a program (i.e., a program scheme that contains no procedure identifiers), then $[\![S|D]\!]$ does not depend on D and it coincides with Definition 3.3.1, and thus we can simply write $[\![S]\!]$ for $[\![S|D]\!]$.

Example 3.4.1. *Consider the declaration*

$$D : \begin{cases} X_1 \Leftarrow S_1, \\ X_2 \Leftarrow S_2 \end{cases}$$

where:

$$S_1 \equiv \textbf{if } M[q] = 0 \rightarrow q := H[q]; X_2$$
$$\square \qquad 1 \rightarrow \textbf{skip}$$
$$\textbf{fi}$$

$$S_2 \equiv \textbf{if } N[q] = 0 \rightarrow q := Z[q]; X_1$$
$$\square \qquad 1 \rightarrow \textbf{skip}$$
$$\textbf{fi}$$

q is a qubit variable, M is the measurement in the computational basis $|0\rangle, |1\rangle$ and N the measurement in the basis $|+\rangle, |-\rangle$; that is,

$$M = \{M_0 = |0\rangle\langle 0|, M_1 = |1\rangle\langle 1|\},$$

$$N = \{N_0 = |+\rangle\langle +|, N_1 = |-\rangle\langle -|\}.$$

Then the computations of recursive quantum program X_1 with declaration D starting in $\rho = |+\rangle\langle +|$ are:

$$\langle X_1, \rho \rangle \rightarrow_D \langle S_1, \rho \rangle$$
$$\rightarrow_D \begin{cases} \langle q := H[q]; X_2, \frac{1}{2}|0\rangle\langle 0| \rangle \rightarrow_D \langle X_2, \frac{1}{2}\rho \rangle, \\ \langle \textbf{skip}, \frac{1}{2}|1\rangle\langle 1| \rangle \rightarrow_D \langle E, \frac{1}{2}|1\rangle\langle 1| \rangle \end{cases}$$

where:

$$\langle X_2, \frac{1}{2}\rho \rangle \rightarrow_D \langle S_2, \frac{1}{2}\rho \rangle \rightarrow_D \langle q := Z[q]; X_1, \frac{1}{2}\rho \rangle \rightarrow_D \langle X_1, \frac{1}{2}|-\rangle\langle -| \rangle \rightarrow_D \cdots.$$

and we have:

$$[\![X_1|D]\!](\rho) = \sum_{n=1}^{\infty} \frac{1}{2^n}|1\rangle\langle 1| = |1\rangle\langle 1|.$$

Before moving on to study various properties of general recursive programs, let us see how a quantum **while**-loop discussed in the previous sections can be treated as a special recursive quantum program. We consider the loop:

$$\textbf{while} \equiv \textbf{while } M[\overline{q}] = 1 \textbf{ do } S \textbf{ od}.$$

Here S is a quantum program (containing no procedure identifiers). Let X be a procedure identifier with the declaration D:

$$X \equiv \textbf{if } M[\overline{q}] = 0 \rightarrow \textbf{skip}$$
$$\square \qquad 1 \rightarrow S; X$$
$$\textbf{fi}$$

Then the quantum loop **while** is actually equivalent to the recursive quantum program with X as its main statement.

Exercise 3.4.1. *Show that* $\llbracket \mathbf{while} \rrbracket = \llbracket X|D \rrbracket$.

Basic Properties of Semantic Functions of Recursive Quantum Programs:

We now establish some basic properties of semantic functions of recursive quantum programs. The next proposition is a generalization of Propositions 3.3.1 and 3.3.2 to quantum program schemes with respect to a declaration.

Proposition 3.4.1. *Let D be the declaration given by equation (3.13). Then for any $\rho \in \mathcal{D}(\mathcal{H}_{all})$, we have:*

(i) $\llbracket X|D \rrbracket(\rho) = \begin{cases} 0_{\mathcal{H}_{all}} & \text{if } X \notin \{X_1, \ldots, X_n\}, \\ \llbracket S_i|D \rrbracket(\rho) & \text{if } X = X_i \ (1 \le i \le n); \end{cases}$

(ii) *if S is **skip**, initialization or unitary transformation, then $\llbracket S|D \rrbracket(\rho) = \llbracket S \rrbracket(\rho)$;*

(iii) $\llbracket T_1; T_2|D \rrbracket(\rho) = \llbracket T_2|D \rrbracket(\llbracket T_1|D \rrbracket(\rho))$;

(iv) $\llbracket \mathbf{if} \ (\square m \cdot M[\overline{q}] = m \to T_m) \ \mathbf{fi}|D \rrbracket(\rho) = \sum_m \llbracket T_m|D \rrbracket \left(M_m \rho M_m^{\dagger} \right)$;

(v) $\llbracket \mathbf{while} \ M[\overline{q}] = 1 \ \mathbf{do} \ S \ \mathbf{od}|D \rrbracket(\rho) = \bigsqcup_{k=0}^{\infty} \llbracket \mathbf{while}^{(k)}|D \rrbracket(\rho)$, *where $\mathbf{while}^{(k)}$ is the kth syntactic approximation of the loop (see Definition 3.3.6) for every integer $k \ge 0$.*

Proof. Similar to the proofs of Propositions 3.3.1 and 3.3.2.   □

Proposition 3.4.1(v) can be further generalized so that the denotational semantics of a recursive quantum program can be expressed in terms of that of its syntactic approximations.

Definition 3.4.7. *Consider the recursive quantum program with the main statement $S \equiv S[X_1, \ldots, X_m]$ and the declaration D given by equation (3.13). For any integer $k \ge 0$, the kth syntactic approximation $S_D^{(k)}$ of S with respect to D is inductively defined as follows:*

$$\begin{cases} S_D^{(0)} & \equiv \mathbf{abort}, \\ S_D^{(k+1)} & \equiv S\left[S_{1D}^{(k)}/X_1, \ldots, S_{nD}^{(k)}/X_n \right], \end{cases} \tag{3.14}$$

*where **abort** is as in Subsection 3.3.3, and*

$$S[P_1/X_1, \ldots, P_n/X_n]$$

stands for the result of simultaneous substitution of $X_1, \ldots, X_n$ by $P_1, \ldots, P_n$, respectively, in S.

It should be noticed that the preceding definition is given by induction on k with S being an arbitrary program scheme. Thus, $S_{1D}^{(k)}, \ldots, S_{nD}^{(k)}$ in equation (3.14) are assumed to be already defined in the induction hypothesis for k. It is clear that for all $k \ge 0$, $S_D^{(k)}$ is a program (containing no procedure identifiers). The following lemma clarifies the relationship of a substitution and a declaration when used to define the semantics of a program.

Lemma 3.4.1. *Let D be a declaration given by equation (3.13). Then for any program scheme S, we have:*

(i) $[\![S|D]\!] = [\![S[S_1/X_1, \ldots, S_n/X_n]|D]\!]$.

(ii) $[\![S_D^{(k+1)}]\!] = [\![S|D^{(k)}]\!]$ *for every integer* $k \geq 0$, *where declaration*

$$D^{(k)} = \begin{cases} X_1 \Leftarrow S_{1D}^{(k)}, \\ \quad \cdots\cdots \\ X_n \Leftarrow S_{nD}^{(k)}. \end{cases}$$

Proof.

(i) can be proved by induction on the structure of S together with Proposition 3.4.1.

(ii) It follows from (i) that

$$\begin{aligned} [\![S|D^{(k)}]\!] &= [\![S\left[S_{1D}^{(k)}/X_1, \ldots, S_{nD}^{(k)}/X_n\right]|D^{(k)}]\!] \\ &= [\![S\left[S_{1D}^{(k)}/X_1, \ldots, S_{nD}^{(k)}/X_n\right]]\!] \\ &= [\![S_D^{(k+1)}]\!]. \end{aligned}$$

$\square$

Based on the previous lemma, we obtain a representation of the semantic function of a recursive program by its syntactic approximations.

Proposition 3.4.2. *For any recursive program S with declaration D, we have:*

$$[\![S|D]\!] = \bigsqcup_{k=0}^{\infty} [\![S_D^{(k)}]\!].$$

Proof. For any $\rho \in \mathcal{D}(\mathcal{H}_{all})$, we want to show that

$$[\![S|D]\!](\rho) = \bigsqcup_{k=0}^{\infty} [\![S_D^{(k)}]\!](\rho).$$

It suffices to prove that for any integers $r, k \geq 0$, the following claims hold:

Claim 1: $\langle S, \rho \rangle \rightarrow_D^r \langle E, \rho' \rangle \Rightarrow \exists l \geq 0$ s.t. $\langle S_D^{(l)}, \rho \rangle \rightarrow^* \langle E, \rho' \rangle$.

Claim 2: $\langle S_D^{(k)}, \rho \rangle \rightarrow^r \langle E, \rho' \rangle \Rightarrow \langle S, \rho \rangle \rightarrow_D^* \langle E, \rho' \rangle$.

This can be done by induction on r, k and the depth of inference using the transition rules. $\square$

Exercise 3.4.2. *Complete the proof of Proposition 3.4.2.*

3.4.4 FIXED POINT CHARACTERIZATION

Proposition 3.4.2 can be seen as a generalization of Proposition 3.3.2 via Proposition 3.4.1(v). A fixed point characterization of quantum **while**-loop was given in Subsection 3.3.3 as a corollary of Proposition 3.3.2. In this section, we give a fixed point characterization of recursive quantum programs and thus obtain a generalization of Corollary 3.3.1. In classical programming theory, recursive equations are solved in a certain domain of functions. Here, we are going to solve recursive quantum equations in the domain of quantum operations defined in Subsection 3.3.2. To this end, we first introduce the following:

Definition 3.4.8. *Let* $S \equiv S[X_1, \ldots, X_n]$ *be a quantum program scheme, and let* $QO(\mathcal{H}_{all})$ *be the set of quantum operations in* $\mathcal{H}_{all}$. *Then its semantic functional is the mapping:*

$$\llbracket S \rrbracket : QO(\mathcal{H}_{all})^n \to QO(\mathcal{H}_{all})$$

defined as follows: for any $\mathcal{E}_1, \ldots, \mathcal{E}_n \in QO(\mathcal{H}_{all})$,

$$\llbracket S \rrbracket(\mathcal{E}_1, \ldots, \mathcal{E}_n) = \llbracket S|E \rrbracket$$

where

$$E : \begin{cases} X_1 \Leftarrow T_1, \\ \ldots \ldots \\ X_n \Leftarrow T_n \end{cases}$$

is a declaration such that for each $1 \leq i \leq n$, T_i *is a program (containing no procedure identifiers) with* $\llbracket T_i \rrbracket = \mathcal{E}_i$.

We argue that the semantic functional $\llbracket S \rrbracket$ is well-defined. It follows from Proposition 3.3.6 that the programs T_i always exist. On the other hand, if

$$E' : \begin{cases} X_1 \Leftarrow T'_1, \\ \ldots \ldots \\ X_n \Leftarrow T'_n \end{cases}$$

is another declaration with each program T'_i satisfying $\llbracket T'_i \rrbracket = \mathcal{E}_i$, then we can show that

$$\llbracket S|E \rrbracket = \llbracket S|E' \rrbracket.$$

Now we define the domain in which we are going to find a fixed point of the semantic functional defined by a declaration for procedure identifiers $X_1, \ldots, X_n$. Let us consider the Cartesian power $QO(\mathcal{H}_{all})^n$. An order $\sqsubseteq$ in $QO(\mathcal{H}_{all})^n$ is naturally induced by the order $\sqsubseteq$ in $QO(\mathcal{H}_{all})$: for any $\mathcal{E}_1, \ldots, \mathcal{E}_n, \mathcal{F}_1, \ldots, \mathcal{F}_n \in QO(\mathcal{H}_{all})$,

- $(\mathcal{E}_1, \ldots, \mathcal{E}_n) \sqsubseteq (\mathcal{F}_1, \ldots, \mathcal{F}_n) \Leftrightarrow$ for every $1 \leq i \leq n$, $\mathcal{E}_i \sqsubseteq \mathcal{F}_i$.

It follows from Lemma 3.3.4 that $(QO(\mathcal{H}_{all})^n, \sqsubseteq)$ is a CPO. Furthermore, we have:

Proposition 3.4.3. *For any quantum program scheme* $S \equiv S[X_1, \ldots, X_n]$, *its semantic functional*

$$[\![S]\!] : \left(\mathcal{QO}(\mathcal{H}_{all})^n, \sqsubseteq\right) \to \left(\mathcal{QO}(\mathcal{H}_{all}), \sqsubseteq\right)$$

is continuous.

Proof. For each $1 \leq i \leq n$, let $\{\mathcal{E}_{ij}\}_j$ be an increasing sequence in $(\mathcal{QO}(\mathcal{H}_{all}), \sqsubseteq)$. What we need to prove is:

$$[\![S]\!]\left(\bigsqcup_j \mathcal{E}_{1j}, \ldots, \bigsqcup_j \mathcal{E}_{nj}\right) = \bigsqcup_j [\![S]\!]\left(\mathcal{E}_{1j}, \ldots, \mathcal{E}_{nj}\right).$$

Suppose that

$$D : \begin{cases} X_1 \Leftarrow P_1, \\ \ldots\ldots \\ X_n \Leftarrow P_n, \end{cases} \qquad D_j : \begin{cases} X_1 \Leftarrow P_{1j}, \\ \ldots\ldots \\ X_n \Leftarrow P_{nj} \end{cases}$$

be declarations such that

$$[\![P_i]\!] = \bigsqcup_j \mathcal{E}_{ij} \text{ and } [\![P_{ij}]\!] = \mathcal{E}_{ij}$$

for any $1 \leq i \leq n$ and for any j. Then it suffices to show that

$$[\![S|D]\!] = \bigsqcup_j [\![S|D_j]\!] . \tag{3.15}$$

Using Proposition 3.4.1, this can be done by induction on the structure of S. $\qquad\square$

Exercise 3.4.3. *Prove equation (3.15).*

Let D be the declaration given by equation (3.13). Then D naturally induces a semantic functional:

$$[\![D]\!] : \mathcal{QO}(\mathcal{H}_{all})^n \to \mathcal{QO}(\mathcal{H}_{all})^n,$$

$$[\![D]\!](\mathcal{E}_1, \ldots, \mathcal{E}_n) = ([\![S_1]\!](\mathcal{E}_1, \ldots, \mathcal{E}_n), \ldots, [\![S_n]\!](\mathcal{E}_1, \ldots, \mathcal{E}_n))$$

for any $\mathcal{E}_1, \ldots, \mathcal{E}_n \in \mathcal{QO}(\mathcal{H}_{all})$. It follows from Proposition 3.4.3 that

$$[\![D]\!] : \left(\mathcal{QO}(\mathcal{H}_{all})^n, \sqsubseteq\right) \to \left(\mathcal{QO}(\mathcal{H}_{all})^n, \sqsubseteq\right)$$

is continuous. Then by the Knaster-Tarski Theorem (Theorem 3.3.1) we assert that $[\![D]\!]$ has a fixed point:

$$\mu[\![D]\!] = \left(\mathcal{E}_1^*, \ldots, \mathcal{E}_n^*\right) \in \mathcal{QO}(\mathcal{H}_{all})^n.$$

We now are able to present the fixed-point characterization of recursive quantum programs:

Theorem 3.4.1. *For the recursive quantum program with the main statement S and the declaration D, we have:*

$$[\![S|D]\!] = [\![S]\!](\mu[\![D]\!]) = [\![S]\!](\mathcal{E}_1^*, \ldots, \mathcal{E}_n^*).$$

Proof. First of all, we claim that for any program scheme $T \equiv T[X_1, \ldots, X_n]$ and for any programs $T_1, \ldots, T_n$,

$$[\![T[T_1/X_1, \ldots, T_n/X_n]]\!] = [\![T]\!]([\![T_1]\!], \ldots, [\![T_n]\!]). \tag{3.16}$$

In fact, let us consider declaration

$$E : \begin{cases} X_1 \Leftarrow T_1, \\ \ldots\ldots \\ X_n \Leftarrow T_n. \end{cases}$$

Then byDefinition 3.4.8 and Lemma 3.4.1 (i) we obtain:

$$\begin{aligned}
[\![T]\!]([\![T_1]\!], \ldots, [\![T_n]\!]) = [\![T|E]\!] &= [\![T[T_1/X_1, \ldots, T_n/X_n]|E]\!] \\
&= [\![T[T_1/X_1, \ldots, T_n/X_n]]\!]
\end{aligned}$$

because $T_1, \ldots, T_n$ are all programs (without procedure identifiers).

Secondly, we define the iteration of $[\![D]\!]$, starting from the least element $\overline{\mathbf{0}} = (\mathbf{0}, \ldots, \mathbf{0})$ in $\mathcal{QO}(\mathcal{H}_{all})^n$, as follows:

$$\begin{cases} [\![D]\!]^{(0)}(\overline{\mathbf{0}}) = (\mathbf{0}, \ldots, \mathbf{0}), \\ [\![D]\!]^{(k+1)}(\overline{\mathbf{0}}) = [\![D]\!]\left([\![D]\!]^{(k)}(\overline{\mathbf{0}})\right) \end{cases}$$

where $\mathbf{0}$ is the zero quantum operation in $\mathcal{H}_{all}$. Then it holds that

$$[\![D]\!]^{(k)}\left(\overline{\mathbf{0}}\right) = \left([\![S_{1D}^{(k)}]\!], \ldots, [\![S_{nD}^{(k)}]\!]\right) \tag{3.17}$$

for every integer $k \geq 0$. Equation (3.17) can by proved by induction on k. Indeed, the case of $k = 0$ is obvious. The induction hypothesis for k together with equation (3.16) yields:

$$\begin{aligned}
[\![D]\!]^{(k+1)}\left(\overline{\mathbf{0}}\right) &= [\![D]\!]\left([\![S_{1D}^{(k)}]\!], \ldots, [\![S_{nD}^{(k)}]\!]\right) \\
&= \left([\![S_1]\!]\left([\![S_{1D}^{(k)}]\!], \ldots, [\![S_{nD}^{(k)}]\!]\right), \ldots, [\![S_n]\!]\left([\![S_{1D}^{(k)}]\!], \ldots, [\![S_{nD}^{(k)}]\!]\right)\right) \\
&= \left([\![S_1[S_{1D}^{(k)}/X_1, \ldots, S_{nD}^{(k)}/X_n]]\!], \ldots, [\![S_n[S_{1D}^{(k)}/X_1, \ldots, S_{nD}^{(k)}/X_n]]\!]\right) \\
&= \left([\![S_{1D}^{(k+1)}]\!], \ldots, [\![S_{nD}^{(k+1)}]\!]\right).
\end{aligned}$$

Finally, using equation (3.16), Proposition 3.4.3, the Knaster-Tarski Theorem and Proposition 3.4.1 (iii), we obtain:

$$
\begin{aligned}
[\![S]\!] \left(\mu \, [\![D]\!] \right) &= [\![S]\!] \left(\bigsqcup_{k=0}^{\infty} [\![D]\!]^{(k)} \left(\bar{\mathbf{0}} \right) \right) \\
&= [\![S]\!] \left(\bigsqcup_{k=0}^{\infty} \left(\left[\!\left[S_{1D}^{(k)} \right]\!\right] , \ldots, \left[\!\left[S_{nD}^{(k)} \right]\!\right] \right) \right) \\
&= \bigsqcup_{k=0}^{\infty} [\![S]\!] \left(\left[\!\left[S_{1D}^{(k)} \right]\!\right] , \ldots, \left[\!\left[S_{nD}^{(k)} \right]\!\right] \right) \\
&= \bigsqcup_{k=0}^{\infty} \left[\!\left[S \left[S_{1D}^{(k)}, \ldots, S_{nD}^{(k)} \right] \right]\!\right] \\
&= \bigsqcup_{k=0}^{\infty} \left[\!\left[S_{D}^{(k+1)} \right]\!\right] \\
&= [\![S|D]\!].
\end{aligned}
$$

$\square$

To conclude this section, we leave the following two problems for the reader. As pointed out at the beginning of this section, the materials presented in this section are similar to the theory of classical recursive programs, but I believe that research on these two problems will reveal some interesting and subtle differences between recursive quantum programs and classical recursive programs.

Problem 3.4.1

(i) *Can a general measurement in a quantum program be implemented by a projective measurement together with a unitary transformation? If the program contains no recursions (and no loops), then this question was already answered by Proposition 2.1.1.*

(ii) *How can a measurement in a quantum program be deferred? For the case that the program contains no recursions (and no loops), this question was answered by the principle of deferred measurement in Subsection 2.2.6. The interesting case is a program with recursions or loops.*

Problem 3.4.2. *Only recursive quantum programs without parameters are considered in this section. How do we define recursive quantum programs with parameters? We will have to deal with two different kinds of parameters:*

(i) *classical parameters;*
(ii) *quantum parameters.*

Bernstein-Varzirani recursive Fourier sampling [1,37,38] and Grover fixed point quantum search [109] are two examples of recursive quantum programs with parameters.

3.5 ILLUSTRATIVE EXAMPLE: GROVER QUANTUM SEARCH

The quantum **while**-language and its extension with recursive quantum programs have been studied in the previous sections. We now use the quantum **while**-language to program the Grover search algorithm in order to illustrate its utility. For the convenience of the reader, let us first briefly recall the algorithm from Subsection 2.3.3. The database searched by the algorithm consists of $N = 2^n$ elements, indexed by numbers $0, 1, \ldots, N - 1$. It is assumed that the search problem has exactly L solutions with $1 \leq L \leq \frac{N}{2}$, and we are supplied with an oracle – a black box with the ability to recognize solutions to the search problem. We identify an integer $x \in \{0, 1, \ldots, N - 1\}$ with its binary representation $x \in \{0, 1\}^n$. The oracle is represented by the unitary operator O on $n + 1$ qubits:

$$|x\rangle|q\rangle \xrightarrow{O} |x\rangle|q \oplus f(x)\rangle$$

for all $x \in \{0, 1\}^n$ and $q \in \{0, 1\}$, where $f : \{0, 1\}^n \to \{0, 1\}$ defined by

$$f(x) = \begin{cases} 1 & \text{if } x \text{ is a solution,} \\ 0 & \text{otherwise} \end{cases}$$

is the characteristic function of solutions. The Grover operator G consists of the following steps:

(i) Apply the oracle O;
(ii) Apply the Hadamard transform $H^{\otimes n}$;
(iii) Perform a conditional phase shift Ph:

$$|0\rangle \to |0\rangle, \quad |x\rangle \to -|x\rangle \text{ for all } x \neq 0;$$

     that is, $Ph = 2|0\rangle\langle 0| - I$.
(iv) Apply the Hadamard transform $H^{\otimes n}$ again.

A geometric intuition of operator G as a rotation was carefully described in Subsection 2.3.3. Employing the Grover operator, the search algorithm is described in Figure 3.4, where the number k of iterations of the Grover operator is taken to be the positive integer in the interval $[\frac{\pi}{2\theta} - 1, \frac{\pi}{2\theta}]$, and θ is the angle rotated by the Grover operator and defined by the equation:

$$\cos\frac{\theta}{2} = \sqrt{\frac{N - L}{2}} \ (0 \leq \frac{\theta}{2} \leq \frac{\pi}{2}).$$

Now we program the Grover algorithm in the quantum **while**-language. We use $n + 2$ quantum variables: $q_0, q_1, \ldots, q_{n-1}, q, r$.

- Their types are as follows:

$$type(q_i) = type(q) = \textbf{Boolean} \ (0 \leq i < n),$$
$$type(r) = \textbf{integer}$$

- **Procedure:**

1. $|0\rangle^{\otimes n}|1\rangle$

2. $\overset{H^{\otimes(n+1)}}{\to} \dfrac{1}{\sqrt{2^n}} \sum_{x=0}^{2^n-1} |x\rangle|-\rangle = \left(\cos\dfrac{\theta}{2}|\alpha\rangle + \sin\dfrac{\theta}{2}|\beta\rangle\right)|-\rangle,$

3. $\overset{G^k}{\to} \left[\cos\left(\dfrac{2k+1}{2}\theta\right)|\alpha\rangle + \sin\left(\dfrac{2k+1}{2}\theta\right)|\beta\rangle\right]|-\rangle$

4. $\overset{\text{measure the first } n \text{ qubits in the computational basis}}{\to} |x\rangle|-\rangle$

FIGURE 3.4

Grover search algorithm.

- The variable r is introduced to count the number of iterations of the Grover operator. We use quantum variable r instead of a classical variable for this purpose since, for the reason of simplicity, classical variables are not included in the quantum **while**-language.

Then the Grover algorithm can be written as the program *Grover* in Figure 3.5. Note that the size of the searched database is $N = 2^n$, so n in the program *Grover* should be understood as a metavariable. Several ingredients in *Grover* are specified as follows:

- The measurement $M = \{M_0, M_1\}$ in the loop guard (line 7) is given as follows:

$$M_0 = \sum_{l\geq k} |l\rangle_r\langle l|, \quad M_1 = \sum_{l<k} |l\rangle_r\langle l|$$

with k being a positive integer in the interval $\left[\frac{\pi}{2\theta} - 1, \frac{\pi}{2\theta}\right]$;

- **Program:**

1. $q_0 := |0\rangle; \; q_1 := |0\rangle; \; \ldots\ldots; \; q_{n-1} := |0\rangle;$
2. $q := |0\rangle;$
3. $r := |0\rangle;$
4. $q := X[q];$
5. $q_0 := H[q_0]; \; q_1 := H[q_1]; \; \ldots\ldots; \; q_{n-1} := H[q_{n-1}];$
6. $q := H[q];$
7. **while** $M[r] = 1$ **do** D **od**;
8. **if** $(\Box x \cdot M'[q_0, q_1, \ldots, q_{n-1}] = x \to$ **skip**$)$ **fi**

FIGURE 3.5

Quantum search program *Grover*.

- The loop body D (line 7) is given in Figure 3.6;
- In the **if** . . . **fi** statement (line 8), N is the measurement in the computational basis of n qubits; that is,

$$M' = \{M'_x : x \in \{0,1\}^n\}$$

with $M'_x = |x\rangle\langle x|$ for every x.

- **Loop Body:**

  1. $q_0, q_1, \ldots, q_{n-1}, q := O[q_0, q_1, \ldots, q_{n-1}, q];$
  2. $q_0 := H[q_0];\ q_1 := H[q_1];\ \ldots\ldots;\ q_{n-1} := H[q_{n-1}];$
  3. $q_0, q_1, \ldots, q_{n-1} := Ph[q_0, q_1, \ldots, q_{n-1}];$
  4. $q_0 := H[q_0];\ q_1 := H[q_1];\ \ldots\ldots;\ q_{n-1} := H[q_{n-1}];$
  5. $r := r + 1$

FIGURE 3.6

Loop body D.

The correctness of this program will be proved in the next chapter using the program logic developed there.

3.6 PROOFS OF LEMMAS

Several lemmas about the domains of partial density operators and quantum operations were presented without proofs in Subsection 3.3.2. For completeness, we give their proofs in this section.

The proof of Lemma 3.3.2 requires the notion of square root of a positive operator, which in turn requires the spectral decomposition theorem for Hermitian operators in an infinite-dimensional Hilbert space $\mathcal{H}$. Recall from Definition 2.1.16 that an operator $M \in \mathcal{L}(\mathcal{H})$ is Hermitian if $M^\dagger = M$. As defined in Subsection 2.1.2, a projector P_X is associated with each closed subspace X of $\mathcal{H}$. A spectral family in $\mathcal{H}$ is a family

$$\{E_\lambda\}_{-\infty < \lambda < +\infty}$$

of projectors indexed by real numbers λ satisfying the following conditions:

  (i) $E_{\lambda_1} \sqsubseteq E_{\lambda_2}$ whenever $\lambda_1 \le \lambda_2$;
  (ii) $E_\lambda = \lim_{\mu \to \lambda+} E_\mu$ for each λ; and
  (iii) $\lim_{\lambda \to -\infty} E_\lambda = 0_{\mathcal{H}}$ and $\lim_{\lambda \to +\infty} E_\lambda = I_{\mathcal{H}}$.

Theorem 3.6.1 ([182], Theorem III.6.3). *(Spectral decomposition) If M is a Hermitian operator with $spec(M) \subseteq [a,b]$, then there is a spectral family $\{E_\lambda\}$ such that*

$$M = \int_a^b \lambda dE_\lambda,$$

where the integral in the right-hand side is defined to be an operator satisfying the following condition: for any $\epsilon > 0$, there exists $\delta > 0$ such that for any $n \geq 1$ and $x_0, x_1, \ldots, x_{n-1}, x_n, y_1, \ldots, y_{n-1}, y_n$ with

$$a = x_0 \leq y_1 \leq x_1 \leq \ldots \leq y_{n-1} \leq x_{n-1} \leq y_n \leq x_n = b,$$

it holds that

$$d\left(\int_a^b \lambda dE_\lambda, \sum_{i=1}^n y_i(E_{x_i} - E_{x_{i-1}})\right) < \epsilon$$

whenever $\max_{i=1}^n (x_i - x_{i-1}) < \delta$. Here, $d(\cdot, \cdot)$ stands for the distance between operators (see Definition 2.1.14).

Now we are able to define the square root of a positive operator A. Since A is a Hermitian operator, it enjoys a spectral decomposition:

$$A = \int \lambda dE_\lambda.$$

Then its square root is defined to be

$$\sqrt{A} = \int \sqrt{\lambda} dE_\lambda.$$

With these preliminaries, we can give:

Proof of lemma 3.3.2. First, for any positive operator A, we get:

$$|\langle\varphi|A|\psi\rangle|^2 = \left|\left(\sqrt{A}|\varphi\rangle, \sqrt{A}|\psi\rangle\right)\right|^2 \leq \langle\varphi|A|\varphi\rangle\langle\psi|A|\psi\rangle \quad (3.18)$$

by the Cauchy-Schwarz inequality (see [174], page 68).

Now let $\{\rho_n\}$ be an increasing sequence in $(\mathcal{D}(\mathcal{H}), \sqsubseteq)$. For any $|\psi\rangle \in \mathcal{H}$, put $A = \rho_n - \rho_m$ and $|\varphi\rangle = A|\psi\rangle$. Then

$$\langle\psi|A|\psi\rangle \leq \langle\psi|\rho_n|\psi\rangle \leq \|\psi\|^2 \cdot tr(\rho_n) \leq \|\psi\|^2,$$

and similarly we have $\langle\varphi|A|\varphi\rangle \leq \|\varphi\|^2$. Thus, it follows from equation (3.18) that

$$|\langle\varphi|A|\psi\rangle|^2 \leq \|\psi\|^2 \cdot \|\varphi\|^2.$$

Furthermore, we obtain:

$$\begin{aligned}
\|A\|^4 &= \sup_{|\psi\rangle \neq 0} \frac{\|A|\psi\rangle\|^4}{\|\psi\|^4} \\
&= \sup_{|\psi\rangle \neq 0} \frac{\langle\varphi|A|\psi\rangle^2}{\|\psi\|^4} \\
&\leq \sup_{|\psi\rangle \neq 0} \frac{\|\varphi\|^2}{\|\psi\|^2} \\
&= \sup_{|\psi\rangle \neq 0} \frac{\|A|\psi\rangle\|^2}{\|\psi\|^2} = \|A\|^2
\end{aligned}$$

and $\|A\| \leq 1$. This leads to

$$\begin{aligned}
\langle\varphi|A|\varphi\rangle &= \left(A\sqrt{A}|\psi\rangle, A\sqrt{A}|\psi\rangle \right) \\
&= \left\| A\sqrt{A}|\psi\rangle \right\|^2 \\
&\leq \|A\|^2 \cdot \left\| \sqrt{A}|\psi\rangle \right\|^2 \\
&= \left(\sqrt{A}|\psi\rangle, \sqrt{A}|\psi\rangle \right) \\
&= \langle\psi|A|\psi\rangle.
\end{aligned}$$

Using equation (3.18) once again we get:

$$\begin{aligned}
\|\rho_n|\psi\rangle - \rho_m|\psi\rangle\|^4 &= |\langle\varphi|A|\psi\rangle|^2 \\
&\leq \langle\psi|A|\psi\rangle^2 = |\langle\psi|\rho_n|\psi\rangle - \langle\psi|\rho_m|\psi\rangle|^2.
\end{aligned} \tag{3.19}$$

Note that $\{\langle\psi|\rho_n|\psi\rangle\}$ is an increasing sequence of real numbers bounded by $\|\psi\|^2$, and thus it is a Cauchy sequence. This together with equation (3.19) implies that $\{\rho_n|\psi\rangle\}$ is a Cauchy sequence in $\mathcal{H}$. So, we can define:

$$\left(\lim_{n\to\infty} \rho_n \right) |\psi\rangle = \lim_{n\to\infty} \rho_n|\psi\rangle.$$

Furthermore, for any complex numbers $\lambda_1, \lambda_2 \in \mathbb{C}$ and $|\psi_1\rangle, |\psi_2\rangle \in \mathcal{H}$, it holds that

$$\begin{aligned}
\left(\lim_{n\to\infty} \rho_n \right) (\lambda_1|\psi_1\rangle + \lambda_2|\psi_2\rangle) &= \lim_{n\to\infty} \rho_n (\lambda_1|\psi_1\rangle + \lambda_2|\psi_2\rangle) \\
&= \lim_{n\to\infty} (\lambda_1\rho_n|\psi_1\rangle + \lambda_2\rho_n|\psi_2\rangle) \\
&= \lambda_1 \lim_{n\to\infty} \rho_n|\psi_1\rangle + \lambda_2 \lim_{n\to\infty} \rho_n|\psi_2\rangle \\
&= \lambda_1 \left(\lim_{n\to\infty} \rho_n \right) |\psi_1\rangle + \lambda_2 \left(\lim_{n\to\infty} \rho_n \right) |\psi_2\rangle,
\end{aligned}$$

and $\lim_{n\to\infty} \rho_n$ is a linear operator. For any $|\psi\rangle \in \mathcal{H}$, we have:

$$\langle\psi|\lim_{n\to\infty}\rho_n|\psi\rangle = \left(|\psi\rangle, \lim_{n\to\infty}\rho_n|\psi\rangle\right) = \lim_{n\to\infty}\langle\psi|\rho_n|\psi\rangle \geq 0.$$

Thus, $\lim_{n\to\infty} \rho_n$ is positive. Let $\{|\psi_i\rangle\}$ be an orthonormal basis of $\mathcal{H}$. Then

$$\begin{aligned}
tr\left(\lim_{n\to\infty}\rho_n\right) &= \sum_i \langle\psi_i|\lim_{n\to\infty}\rho_n|\psi_i\rangle \\
&= \sum_i \left(|\psi_i\rangle, \lim_{n\to\infty}\rho_n|\psi_i\rangle\right) \\
&= \lim_{n\to\infty}\sum_i \langle\psi_i|\rho_n|\psi_i\rangle \\
&= \lim_{n\to\infty} tr(\rho_n) \leq 1,
\end{aligned}$$

and $\lim_{n\to\infty} \rho_n \in \mathcal{D}(\mathcal{H})$. So, it suffices to show that

$$\lim_{n\to\infty}\rho_n = \bigsqcup_{n=0}^{\infty} \rho_n;$$

that is,

(i) $\rho_m \sqsubseteq \lim_{n\to\infty} \rho_n$ for all $m \geq 0$; and
(ii) if $\rho_m \sqsubseteq \rho$ for all $m \geq 0$, then $\lim_{n\to\infty} \rho_n \sqsubseteq \rho$.

Note that for any positive operators B and C, $B \sqsubseteq C$ if and only if $\langle\psi|B|\psi\rangle \leq \langle\psi|C|\psi\rangle$ for all $|\psi\rangle \in \mathcal{H}$. Then both (i) and (ii) follow immediately from

$$\langle\psi|\lim_{n\to\infty}\rho_n|\psi\rangle = \lim_{n\to\infty}\langle\psi|\rho_n|\psi\rangle.$$

This completes the proof of Lemma 3.3.2.

The proof of Lemma 3.3.3 can be easily done based on Lemma 3.3.2.

Proof of Lemma 3.3.3. Suppose that $\mathcal{E}$ is a quantum operation with Kraus representation $\mathcal{E} = \sum_i E_i \circ E_i^\dagger$ (see Theorem 2.1.1), and $\{\rho_n\}$ is an increasing sequence in $\mathcal{D}(\mathcal{H})$. Then by Lemma 3.3.2 we obtain:

$$\begin{aligned}
\mathcal{E}\left(\bigsqcup_n \rho_n\right) &= \mathcal{E}\left(\lim_{n\to\infty}\rho_n\right) \\
&= \sum_i E_i\left(\lim_{n\to\infty}\rho_n\right)E_i^\dagger \\
&= \lim_{n\to\infty}\sum_i E_i\rho_n E_i^\dagger \\
&= \lim_{n\to\infty}\mathcal{E}(\rho_n) \\
&= \bigsqcup_n \mathcal{E}(\rho_n).
\end{aligned}$$

Finally, we can prove Lemma 3.3.4.

Proof of Lemma 3.3.4. Let $\{\mathcal{E}_n\}$ be an increasing sequence in $(\mathcal{QO}(\mathcal{H}), \sqsubseteq)$. Then for any $\rho \in \mathcal{D}(\mathcal{H})$, $\{\mathcal{E}_n(\rho)\}$ is an increasing sequence in $(\mathcal{D}(\mathcal{H}), \sqsubseteq)$. With Lemma 3.3.2 we can define:

$$\left(\bigsqcup_n \mathcal{E}_n\right)(\rho) = \bigsqcup_n \mathcal{E}_n(\rho) = \lim_{n\to\infty} \mathcal{E}_n(\rho),$$

and it holds that

$$tr\left(\left(\bigsqcup_n \mathcal{E}_n\right)(\rho)\right) = tr\left(\lim_{n\to\infty} \mathcal{E}_n(\rho)\right) = \lim_{n\to\infty} tr(\mathcal{E}_n(\rho)) \leq 1$$

because $tr(\cdot)$ is continuous. Furthermore, $\bigsqcup_n \mathcal{E}_n$ can be defined on the whole of $\mathcal{L}(\mathcal{H})$ by linearity. The defining equation of $\bigsqcup_n \mathcal{E}_n$ implies:

(i) $\mathcal{E}_m \sqsubseteq \bigsqcup_n \mathcal{E}_n$ for all $m \geq 0$;
(ii) if $\mathcal{E}_m \sqsubseteq \mathcal{F}$ for all $m \geq 0$ then $\bigsqcup_n \mathcal{E}_n \sqsubseteq \mathcal{F}$.

So, it suffices to show that $\bigsqcup_n \mathcal{E}_n$ is completely positive. Suppose that $\mathcal{H}_R$ is an extra Hilbert space. For any $C \in \mathcal{L}(\mathcal{H}_R)$ and $D \in \mathcal{L}(\mathcal{H})$, we have:

$$\left(\mathcal{I}_R \otimes \bigsqcup_n \mathcal{E}_n\right)(C \otimes D) = C \otimes \left(\bigsqcup_n \mathcal{E}_n\right)(D)$$

$$= C \otimes \lim_{n\to\infty} \mathcal{E}_n(D)$$

$$= \lim_{n\to\infty} (C \otimes \mathcal{E}_n(D))$$

$$= \lim_{n\to\infty} (\mathcal{I}_R \otimes \mathcal{E}_n)(C \otimes D).$$

Then for any $A \in \mathcal{L}(\mathcal{H}_R \otimes \mathcal{H})$ we get:

$$\left(\mathcal{I}_R \otimes \bigsqcup_n \mathcal{E}_n\right)(A) = \lim_{n\to\infty} (\mathcal{I}_R \otimes \mathcal{E}_n)(A)$$

by linearity. Thus, if A is positive, then $(\mathcal{I}_R \otimes \mathcal{E}_n)(A)$ is positive for all n, and $\left(\mathcal{I}_R \otimes \bigsqcup_n \mathcal{E}_n\right)(A)$ is positive.

3.7 BIBLIOGRAPHIC REMARKS

The quantum **while**-language presented in Section 3.1 was defined in [221], but various quantum program constructs in it were introduced in the previous works by Sanders and Zuliani [191,241] and Selinger [194], among others. A general form of quantum **while**-loops was introduced and their properties were thoroughly investigated in [227]. A discussion about the existing quantum programming languages was already given in Subsection 1.1.1; it is worth comparing the quantum programming language described in this chapter with the languages mentioned there.

The presentation of operational and denotational semantics in Sections 3.2 and 3.3 is mainly based on [221]. The denotational semantics was actually first given by Feng et al. in [82], but the treatments of denotational semantics in [82] and [221] are different: in [82], the denotational semantics is directly defined, whereas in [221], the operational semantics comes first and then the denotational semantics is derived from the operational semantics. The idea of encoding a probability and a density operator into a partial density operator in the transition rules was suggested by Selinger [194]. A domain theory for quantum computation was first considered by Kashefi [133]. Lemmas 3.3.2 and 3.3.4 were obtained by Selinger [194] in the case of finite-dimensional Hilbert spaces. The proof of Lemma 3.3.2 for the general case was given in [225], and it is essentially a modification of the proof of Theorem III.6.2 in [182]. A form of Proposition 3.3.6 was first presented by Selinger in [194]. The current statement of Proposition 3.3.6 is given based on the notion of local quantum variable, which was introduced in [233].

Recursion in quantum programming was first considered by Selinger in [194]. But the materials presented in Section 3.4 are slightly different from those in [194] and unpublished elsewhere.

Finally, it should be pointed out that this chapter is essentially the quantum generalization of the semantics of the classical **while**-programs and recursive programs as presented by Apt, de Boer and Olderog in [21].

Logic for quantum programs 4

A simple quantum programming language was defined in Chapter 3 to write quantum programs with classical control. It was shown by several examples to be convenient to program some quantum algorithms.

As is well-known, programming is error-prone. It is even worse when programming a quantum computer, because human intuition is much better adapted to the classical world than to the quantum world. Thus, it is critical to develop methodologies and techniques for verification of quantum programs.

In this chapter, we build logical foundations for reasoning about correctness of quantum programs. This chapter consists of the following parts:

- The first step in developing a logic for quantum programs is to define the notion of quantum predicate, which can properly describe properties of quantum systems. We introduce the notion of quantum predicate as a physical observable in Section 4.1. Moreover, the notion of weakest precondition is generalized to the case of quantum programs.
- Floyd-Hoare logic is an effective proof system for correctness of classical programs. Based on Section 4.1, we develop a logic of the Floyd-Hoare style for quantum programs in Section 4.2, where soundness and (relative) completeness of such a logic are proved, and an example is given to show how this logic can be used in verification of quantum programs.
- A logic for quantum programs is not a straightforward extension of the corresponding logic for classical programs. We have to carefully consider how various quantum features can be incorporated into a logical system. It is well-known that a distinctive feature between classical and quantum systems is non-commutativity of observables about quantum systems. Section 4.3 is devoted to examining (non-)commutativity of the quantum weakest preconditions.

4.1 QUANTUM PREDICATES

In classical logic, predicates are used to describe properties of individuals or systems. Then what is a quantum predicate? A natural idea is that a quantum predicate should be a physical observable. Recall from Section 2.1.4 that an observable of a quantum system is expressed by a Hermitian operator M in its state Hilbert space $\mathcal{H}$. At this moment, for simplicity, we assume that $\mathcal{H}$ is finite-dimensional. If $\lambda \in \mathbb{C}$ and a nonzero vector $|\psi\rangle \in \mathcal{H}$ satisfy

$$M|\psi\rangle = \lambda|\psi\rangle,$$

then λ is called an eigenvalue of M and $|\psi\rangle$ the eigenvector of M corresponding to λ. It turns out that all eigenvalues of M are real numbers. We write $spec(M)$ for the set of eigenvalues of M – the (point) spectrum of M. For each eigenvalue $\lambda \in spec(M)$, the eigenspace of M corresponding to λ is the (closed) subspace

$$X_\lambda = \{|\psi\rangle \in \mathcal{H} : A|\psi\rangle = \lambda|\psi\rangle\}.$$

In order to see what a quantum predicate should be, let us first consider a special class of quantum observables (Hermitian operators), namely projections. Historically, Birkhoff-von Neumann quantum logic is the first logic for reasoning about the properties of quantum systems. One of its basic ideas is that a proposition about a quantum system can be modelled by a (closed) subspace X of the system's state Hilbert space $\mathcal{H}$. The subspace X can be seen as the eigenspace of the projection P_X (see Definition 2.1.10) corresponding to eigenvalue 1, and eigenvalue 1 can be understood as the truth value of the proposition modelled by X.

Extending this idea, whenever an observable (a Hermitian operator) M is considered as a quantum predicate, its eigenvalue λ should be understood as the truth value of the proposition described by the eigenspace X_λ. Note that the truth value of a classical proposition is either 0 (false) or 1 (true), and the truth value of a probabilistic proposition is given as a real number between 0 and 1. This observation leads to the following:

Definition 4.1.1. *A quantum predicate in a Hilbert space $\mathcal{H}$ is a Hermitian operator M in $\mathcal{H}$ with all its eigenvalues lying within the unit interval* $[0, 1]$.

The set of predicates in $\mathcal{H}$ is denoted $\mathcal{P}(\mathcal{H})$. The state space $\mathcal{H}$ in the preceding definition and the following development can be infinite-dimensional unless it is explicitly stated to be finite-dimensional, although for simplicity, we assumed it is finite-dimensional in the discussion at the beginning of this section.

Satisfaction of Quantum Predicates:

Now we consider how a quantum state can satisfy a quantum predicate. Recall from Exercise 2.1.8 that $tr(M\rho)$ is the expectation value of measurement outcomes when a quantum system is in the mixed state ρ and we perform the projective measurement determined by observable M on it. Now if M is seen as a quantum predicate, then $tr(M\rho)$ may be interpreted as the degree to which quantum state ρ satisfies quantum predicate M, or more precisely the average truth value of the proposition represented by M in a quantum system of the state ρ. The reasonableness of the previous definition is further indicated by the following fact:

Lemma 4.1.1. *Let M be a Hermitian operator in $\mathcal{H}$. Then the following statements are equivalent:*

(i) $M \in \mathcal{P}(\mathcal{H})$ *is a quantum predicate.*
(ii) $0_{\mathcal{H}} \sqsubseteq M \sqsubseteq I_{\mathcal{H}}$, *where* $0_{\mathcal{H}}, I_{\mathcal{H}}$ *are the zero and identity operators in $\mathcal{H}$, respectively.*
(iii) $0 \leq tr(M\rho) \leq 1$ *for all density operators ρ in $\mathcal{H}$.*

An operator M satisfying $0_{\mathcal{H}} \sqsubseteq M \sqsubseteq I_{\mathcal{H}}$ is commonly called an effect in the literature of quantum logic and quantum foundations. Intuitively, clause (iii) in the previous lemma means that the satisfaction degree of a quantum predicate M by a quantum state ρ is always in the unit interval.

Exercise 4.1.1. *Prove Lemma 4.1.1.*

The following two lemmas show some basic properties of quantum predicates that will be frequently used in this chapter. The first one gives a characterization of the Löwner order between quantum predicates in terms of satisfaction degrees.

Lemma 4.1.2. *For any observables M, N, the following two statements are equivalent:*

(i) $M \sqsubseteq N$;
(ii) *for all density operators ρ, $tr(M\rho) \leq tr(N\rho)$.*

Exercise 4.1.2. *Prove Lemma 4.1.2.*

Furthermore, the next lemma examines the lattice-theoretic structure of quantum predicates with respect to the Löwner partial order.

Lemma 4.1.3. *The set $(\mathcal{P}(\mathcal{H}), \sqsubseteq)$ of quantum predicates with the Löwner partial order is a complete partial order (CPO) (see Definition 3.3.4).*

Proof. Similar to the proof of Proposition 3.3.2. □

It is worthwhile to point out that $(\mathcal{P}(\mathcal{H}), \sqsubseteq)$ is not a lattice except in the trivial case of one-dimensional state space $\mathcal{H}$; that is, the greatest lower bound and least upper bound of elements in $(\mathcal{P}(\mathcal{H}), \sqsubseteq)$ are not always defined.

4.1.1 QUANTUM WEAKEST PRECONDITIONS

Quantum predicates as defined previously can be used to describe the properties of quantum states. The next question that we need to answer in developing a logic for reasoning about quantum programs is: How do we describe the properties of quantum programs that transform a quantum state into another quantum state?

In classical programming theory, the notion of weakest precondition was extensively used for specifying the properties of programs. The weakest precondition describes a program in a backward way; that is, it determines the weakest property that the input must satisfy in order to achieve a given property of the output. This notion can be generalized to the quantum case. Actually, the quantum generalization of weakest precondition will play a key role in logics for quantum programs. In this subsection, we introduce a purely semantic (syntax-independent) notion of quantum weakest precondition. We saw that the denotational semantics of a quantum program is usually represented by a quantum operation in the last chapter. So, in this subsection, a quantum program is simply abstracted as a quantum operation.

Definition 4.1.2. *Let* $M, N \in \mathcal{P}(\mathcal{H})$ *be quantum predicates, and let* $\mathcal{E} \in \mathcal{QO}(\mathcal{H})$ *be a quantum operation (see Definition 2.1.25). Then* M *is called a precondition of* N *with respect to* $\mathcal{E}$, *written* $\{M\}\mathcal{E}\{N\}$, *if*

$$tr(M\rho) \leq tr(N\mathcal{E}(\rho)) \tag{4.1}$$

for all density operators ρ *in* $\mathcal{H}$.

The intuitive meaning of condition (4.1) comes immediately from the interpretation of satisfaction relation between quantum states and quantum predicates: $tr(M\rho)$ is the expectation of truth value of predicate M in state ρ. More explicitly, inequality (4.1) can be seen as a probabilistic version of the statement: if state ρ satisfies predicate M, then the state after transformation $\mathcal{E}$ from ρ satisfies predicate N.

Definition 4.1.3. *Let* $M \in \mathcal{P}(\mathcal{H})$ *be a quantum predicate and* $\mathcal{E} \in \mathcal{QO}(\mathcal{H})$ *a quantum operation. Then the weakest precondition of* M *with respect to* $\mathcal{E}$ *is a quantum predicate* $wp(\mathcal{E})(M)$ *satisfying the following conditions:*

(i) $\{wp(\mathcal{E})(M)\}\mathcal{E}\{M\}$;
(ii) *for all quantum predicates* N, $\{N\}\mathcal{E}\{M\}$ *implies* $N \sqsubseteq wp(\mathcal{E})(M)$,
  where $\sqsubseteq$ *stands for the Löwner order.*

Intuitively, condition (i) indicates that $wp(\mathcal{E})(M)$ is a precondition of M with respect to $\mathcal{E}$, and condition (ii) means that whenever N is also a precondition of M, then $wp(\mathcal{E})(M)$ is weaker than N.

The preceding abstract definition of quantum weakest precondition is often not easy to use in applications. So, it is desirable to find an explicit representation of quantum weakest precondition. We learned from Theorem 2.1.1 that there are two convenient representations of a quantum operation, namely the Kraus operator-sum representation and the system-environment model. If (the denotational) semantics of a quantum program is represented in one of these two forms, its weakest precondition also enjoys an elegant representation. Let us first consider the Kraus operator-sum representation.

Proposition 4.1.1. *Suppose that quantum operation* $\mathcal{E} \in \mathcal{QO}(\mathcal{H})$ *is represented by the set* $\{E_i\}$ *of operators; that is,*

$$\mathcal{E}(\rho) = \sum_i E_i \rho E_i^\dagger$$

for every density operator ρ. *Then for each predicate* $M \in \mathcal{P}(\mathcal{H})$, *we have:*

$$wp(\mathcal{E})(M) = \sum_i E_i^\dagger M E_i. \tag{4.2}$$

Proof. We see from condition (ii) in Definition 4.1.3 that weakest precondition $wp(\mathcal{E})(M)$ is unique when it exists. Then we only need to check that $wp(\mathcal{E})(M)$ given by equation (4.2) satisfies the two conditions in Definition 4.1.3.

(i) Since $tr(AB) = tr(BA)$ for any operators A, B in $\mathcal{H}$, we have:

$$
\begin{aligned}
tr(wp(\mathcal{E})(M)\rho) &= tr\left(\left(\sum_i E_i^\dagger M E_i\right)\rho\right) \\
&= \sum_i tr\left(E_i^\dagger M E_i \rho\right) \\
&= \sum_i tr\left(M E_i \rho E_i^\dagger\right) \\
&= tr\left(M\left(\sum_i E_i \rho E_i^\dagger\right)\right) \\
&= tr(M\mathcal{E}(\rho))
\end{aligned}
\tag{4.3}
$$

for each density operator ρ in $\mathcal{H}$. Thus, $\{wp(\mathcal{E})(M)\}\mathcal{E}\{M\}$.

(ii) It is known that $M \sqsubseteq N$ if and only if $tr(M\rho) \leq tr(N\rho)$ for all ρ. Thus, if $\{N\}\mathcal{E}\{M\}$, then for any density operator ρ we have:

$$
tr(N\rho) \leq tr(M\mathcal{E}(\rho)) = tr(wp(\mathcal{E})(M)\rho).
$$

Therefore, it follows immediately that $N \sqsubseteq wp(\mathcal{E})(M)$. $\qquad\square$

We can also give an intrinsic characterization of $wp(\mathcal{E})$ in the case that the denotational semantics $\mathcal{E}$ of a quantum program is given in a system-environment model:

$$
\mathcal{E}(\rho) = tr_E\left[PU(|e_0\rangle\langle e_0| \otimes \rho)U^\dagger P\right]
\tag{4.4}
$$

for all density operator ρ in $\mathcal{H}$, where E is an environment system with state Hilbert space $\mathcal{H}_E$, U is a unitary transformation in $\mathcal{H}_E \otimes \mathcal{H}$, P is a projector onto some closed subspace of $\mathcal{H}_E \otimes \mathcal{H}$, and $|e_0\rangle$ is a fixed state in $\mathcal{H}_E$.

Proposition 4.1.2. *If quantum operation $\mathcal{E}$ is given by equation (4.4), then we have:*

$$
wp(\mathcal{E})(M) = \langle e_0|U^\dagger P(M \otimes I_E)PU|e_0\rangle
$$

for each $M \in \mathcal{P}(\mathcal{H})$, where I_E is the identity operator in the environment system's state space $\mathcal{H}_E$.

Proof. Let $\{|e_k\rangle\}$ be an orthonormal basis of $\mathcal{H}_E$. Then

$$
\mathcal{E}(\rho) = \sum_k \langle e_k|PU|e_0\rangle \,\rho\langle e_0|U^\dagger P|e_k\rangle,
$$

and using Proposition 4.1.1 we obtain:

$$wp(\mathcal{E})(M) = \sum_k \langle e_0|U^\dagger P|e_k\rangle M\langle e_k|PU|e_0\rangle$$

$$= \langle e_0|U^\dagger P \left(\sum_k |e_k\rangle M\langle e_k| \right) PU|e_0\rangle.$$

Note that

$$\sum_k |e_k\rangle M\langle e_k| = M \otimes \left(\sum_k |e_k\rangle\langle e_k| \right) = M \otimes I_E$$

because $\{|e_k\rangle\}$ is an orthonormal basis of $\mathcal{H}_E$, and M is an operator in $\mathcal{H}$. This completes the proof. $\square$

Schrödinger-Heisenberg Duality:

As in classical programming theory, the denotational semantics $\mathcal{E}$ of a quantum program is a forward state transformer:

$$\mathcal{E} : \mathcal{D}(\mathcal{H}) \to \mathcal{D}(\mathcal{H}),$$
$$\rho \mapsto \mathcal{E}(\rho) \text{ for each } \rho \in \mathcal{D}(\mathcal{H})$$

where $\mathcal{D}(\mathcal{H})$ stands for the set of partial density operators in $\mathcal{H}$: i.e., positive operators with traces ≤ 1. On the other hand, the notion of weakest precondition defines a backward quantum predicate transformer:

$$wp(\mathcal{E}) : \mathcal{P}(\mathcal{H}) \to \mathcal{P}(\mathcal{H}),$$
$$M \mapsto wp(\mathcal{E})(M) \text{ for each } M \in \mathcal{P}(\mathcal{M}).$$

They provide us with two complementary ways to look at a quantum program.

The duality between forward and backward semantics has been extensively exploited to cope with classical programs. It will be equally useful for the studies of quantum programs. Moreover, the relationship between a quantum program and its weakest precondition can even be considered from a physics point of view – the Schrödinger-Heisenberg duality (Figure 4.1) between quantum states (described as density operators) and quantum observables (described as Hermitian operators).

Definition 4.1.4. *Let $\mathcal{E}$ be a quantum operation mapping (partial) density operators to (partial) density operators, and let $\mathcal{E}^*$ be an operator mapping Hermitian operators to Hermitian operators. If we have*

(Duality) $$tr[M\mathcal{E}(\rho)] = tr[\mathcal{E}^*(M)\rho]$$ (4.5)

for any (partial) density operator ρ, and for any Hermitian operator M, then we say that $\mathcal{E}$ and $\mathcal{E}^*$ are (Schrödinger-Heisenberg) dual.

It follows from the definition that the dual $\mathcal{E}^*$ of a quantum operation $\mathcal{E}$ is unique whenever it exists.

$$\rho \quad \models \quad \mathcal{E}^*(M)$$

$$\mathcal{E} \downarrow \qquad \uparrow \mathcal{E}^*$$

$$\mathcal{E}(\rho) \quad \models \quad M$$

The mapping $\rho \mapsto \mathcal{E}(\rho)$ is the Schrödinger picture, and the mapping $M \mapsto \mathcal{E}^*(M)$ is the Heisenberg picture. The symbol $\models$ stands for satisfaction relation; that is, $tr(M\rho) = \Pr\{\rho \models M\}$ (the probability that ρ satisfies M).

FIGURE 4.1

Schrödinger-Heisenberg duality.

The following proposition indicates that the notion of weakest precondition in programming theory coincides with the notion of Schrödinger-Heisenberg duality in physics.

Proposition 4.1.3. *Any quantum operation $\mathcal{E} \in \mathcal{QO}(\mathcal{H})$ and its weakest precondition $wp(\mathcal{E})$ are dual to each other.*

Proof. Immediate from equation (4.3). $\qquad\qquad\qquad\qquad\qquad \square$

To conclude this section, we collect several basic algebraic properties of quantum weakest preconditions in the following proposition.

Proposition 4.1.4. *Let $\lambda \geq 0$ and $\mathcal{E}, \mathcal{F} \in \mathcal{QO}(\mathcal{H})$, and let $\{\mathcal{E}_n\}$ be an increasing sequence in $\mathcal{QO}(\mathcal{H})$. Then*

(i) $wp(\lambda\mathcal{E}) = \lambda wp(\mathcal{E})$ *provided* $\lambda\mathcal{E} \in \mathcal{QO}(\mathcal{H})$;

(ii) $wp(\mathcal{E} + \mathcal{F}) = wp(\mathcal{E}) + wp(\mathcal{F})$ *provided* $\mathcal{E} + \mathcal{F} \in \mathcal{QO}(\mathcal{H})$;

(iii) $wp(\mathcal{E} \circ \mathcal{F}) = wp(\mathcal{F}) \circ wp(\mathcal{E})$;

(iv) $wp\left(\bigsqcup_{n=0}^{\infty} \mathcal{E}_n\right) = \bigsqcup_{n=0}^{\infty} wp(\mathcal{E}_n)$, *where* $\bigsqcup_{n=0}^{\infty} wp(\mathcal{E}_n)$ *is defined by*

$$\left(\bigsqcup_{n=0}^{\infty} wp(\mathcal{E}_n)\right)(M) \overset{\triangle}{=} \bigsqcup_{n=0}^{\infty} wp(\mathcal{E}_n)(M)$$

for any $M \in \mathcal{P}(\mathcal{H})$.

Proof. **(i)** and **(ii)** are immediately from Proposition 4.1.1.

(iii) It is easy to see that $\{L\}\mathcal{E}\{M\}$ and $\{M\}\mathcal{F}\{N\}$ implies $\{L\}\mathcal{E} \circ \mathcal{F}\{N\}$. Thus, we have:

$$\{wp(\mathcal{E})(wp(\mathcal{F})(M))\}\mathcal{E} \circ \mathcal{F}\{M\}.$$

On the other hand, we need to show that $N \sqsubseteq wp(\mathcal{E})(wp(\mathcal{F})(M))$ whenever $\{N\}\mathcal{E} \circ \mathcal{F}\{M\}$. In fact, for any density operator ρ, it follows from equation (4.3) that

$$tr(N\rho) \le tr(M(\mathcal{E} \circ \mathcal{F})(\rho))$$
$$= tr(M\mathcal{F}(\mathcal{E}(\rho)))$$
$$= tr(wp(\mathcal{F})(M)\mathcal{E}(\rho))$$
$$= tr(wp(\mathcal{E})(wp(\mathcal{F})(M))\rho).$$

Therefore, we obtain

$$wp(\mathcal{E} \circ \mathcal{F})(M) = wp(\mathcal{E})(wp(\mathcal{F})(M)) = (wp(\mathcal{F}) \circ wp(\mathcal{E}))(M).$$

(iv) First, we note that the following two equalities follow immediately from the definition of $\bigsqcup$ in CPO $(\mathcal{P}(\mathcal{H}), \sqsubseteq)$:

$$M\left(\bigsqcup_{n=0}^{\infty} M_n\right) = \lim_{n\to\infty} MM_n,$$

$$tr\left(\bigsqcup_{n=0}^{\infty} M_n\right) = \bigsqcup_{n=0}^{\infty} tr(M_n).$$

Then we can prove that

$$\left\{\bigsqcup_{n=0}^{\infty} wp(\mathcal{E}_n)(M)\right\} \bigsqcup_{n=0}^{\infty} \mathcal{E}_n\{M\}.$$

Indeed, for any $\rho \in \mathcal{D}(\mathcal{H})$, we have:

$$tr\left(\bigsqcup_{n=0}^{\infty} wp(\mathcal{E}_n)(M)\rho\right) = \bigsqcup_{n=0}^{\infty} tr(wp(\mathcal{E}_n)(M)\rho)$$

$$\le \bigsqcup_{n=0}^{\infty} tr(M\mathcal{E}_n(\rho))$$

$$= tr\left(\lim_{n\to\infty} M\mathcal{E}_n(\rho)\right)$$

$$= tr\left(M\left(\bigsqcup_{n=0}^{\infty} \mathcal{E}_n\right)(\rho)\right).$$

Second, we show that $\{N\} \bigsqcup_{n=0}^{\infty} \mathcal{E}_n\{M\}$ implies $N \sqsubseteq \bigsqcup_{n=0}^{\infty} wp(\mathcal{E}_n)(M)$. It suffices to note that

$$tr(N\rho) \le tr\left(M\left(\bigsqcup_{n=0}^{\infty} \mathcal{E}_n\right)(\rho)\right)$$

$$= tr\left(\lim_{n\to\infty} M\mathcal{E}_n(\rho)\right)$$

$$= \bigsqcup_{n=0}^{\infty} tr(M\mathcal{E}_n(\rho))$$

$$= \bigsqcup_{n=0}^{\infty} tr(wp(\mathcal{E}_n)(M)\rho)$$

$$= tr\left(\left(\bigsqcup_{n=0}^{\infty} wp(\mathcal{E}_n)\right)(M)\rho\right)$$

for all density operators ρ. Thus, it holds that

$$wp\left(\bigsqcup_{n=0}^{\infty} \mathcal{E}_n\right)(M) = \bigsqcup_{n=0}^{\infty} wp(\mathcal{E}_n)(M).$$
□

4.2 FLOYD-HOARE LOGIC FOR QUANTUM PROGRAMS

Floyd-Hoare logic is a logical system widely used in classical programming methodology for reasoning about correctness of programs. It consists of a set of inference rules defined in terms of preconditions and postconditions.

The notions of quantum predicate and weakest precondition were introduced in the last section for abstract quantum programs modelled by quantum operations. Based on them, in this section, we present a logic of the Floyd-Hoare style for reasoning about correctness of quantum programs in the **while**-language introduced in Section 3.1.

4.2.1 CORRECTNESS FORMULAS

In the classical Floyd-Hoare logic, correctness of a program is expressed by a Hoare triple which consists of a predicate describing the input state and a predicate describing the output states of the program. The notion of Hoare triple can be directly generalized into the quantum setting.

Let $qVar$ be the set of quantum variables in the **while**-language defined in Section 3.1. For any set $X \subseteq qVar$, we write

$$\mathcal{H}_X = \bigotimes_{q \in X} \mathcal{H}_q$$

for the state Hilbert space of the system consisting of quantum variables in X, where $\mathcal{H}_q$ is the state space of quantum variable q. In particular, we set

$$\mathcal{H}_{all} = \bigotimes_{q \in qVar} \mathcal{H}_q.$$

Recall from the last section, a quantum predicate in $\mathcal{H}_X$ is a Hermitian operator P in $\mathcal{H}_X$ such that $0_{\mathcal{H}_X} \sqsubseteq P \sqsubseteq I_{\mathcal{H}_X}$. We write $\mathcal{P}(\mathcal{H}_X)$ for the set of quantum predicates in $\mathcal{H}_X$.

Definition 4.2.1. *A correctness formula is a statement of the form:*

$$\{P\}S\{Q\}$$

where S is a quantum program, and both $P, Q \in \mathcal{P}(\mathcal{H}_{all})$ *are quantum predicates in* $\mathcal{H}_{all}$. *The quantum predicate P is called the precondition of the correctness formula and Q the postcondition.*

In the Floyd-Hoare logic for classical programs, P and Q in a Hoare triple $\{P\}S\{Q\}$ are two first-order logical formulas. The Hoare logical formula $\{P\}S\{Q\}$ can be used to describe two different kinds of correctness of programs:

- *Partial correctness*: If an input to program S satisfies the precondition P, then either S does not terminate, or it terminates in a state satisfying the postcondition Q.
- *Total correctness*: If an input to program S satisfies the precondition P, then S must terminate and it terminates in a state satisfying the postcondition Q.

Although the appearance of a Hoare triple $\{P\}S\{Q\}$ in the quantum case is the same as that in the classical case, precondition P and postcondition Q in the former are two quantum predicates, i.e. observables represented by Hermitian operators. We write $\mathcal{D}(\mathcal{H}_X)$ for the set of partial density operators, i.e. positive operators with traces ≤ 1, in $\mathcal{H}_X$. Intuitively, for any quantum predicate $P \in \mathcal{P}(\mathcal{H}_X)$ and state $\rho \in \mathcal{D}(\mathcal{H}_X)$, $tr(P\rho)$ stands for the probability that predicate P is satisfied in state ρ. As in the classical programming theory, a correctness formula can also be interpreted in two different ways:

Definition 4.2.2

(i) *The correctness formula* $\{P\}S\{Q\}$ *is true in the sense of total correctness, written*

$$\models_{tot} \{P\}S\{Q\},$$

if we have:

$$tr(P\rho) \leq tr(Q[\![S]\!](\rho)) \tag{4.6}$$

for all $\rho \in \mathcal{D}(\mathcal{H}_{all})$, *where* $[\![S]\!]$ *is the semantic function of S (see Definition 3.3.1).*

(ii) *The correctness formula* $\{P\}S\{Q\}$ *is true in the sense of partial correctness, written*

$$\models_{par} \{P\}S\{Q\},$$

if we have:

$$tr(P\rho) \leq tr(Q[\![S]\!](\rho)) + [tr(\rho) - tr([\![S]\!](\rho))] \tag{4.7}$$

for all $\rho \in \mathcal{D}(\mathcal{H}_{all})$.

The intuitive meaning of the defining inequality (4.6) of total correctness is:

- The probability that input ρ satisfies quantum predicate P is not greater than the probability that quantum program S terminates on ρ and its output $[\![S]\!](\rho)$ satisfies quantum predicate Q.

It is obvious from Definition 4.1.2 that $\models_{tot} \{P\}S\{Q\}$ is a restatement of the fact that P is a precondition of Q with respect to quantum operation $[\![S]\!]$, i.e.,

$$\{P\}[\![S]\!]\{Q\}.$$

Recall that $tr(\rho) - tr([\![S]\!](\rho))$ is the probability that quantum program S diverges from input ρ. Thus, the defining inequality (4.7) of partial correctness intuitively means:

- If input ρ satisfies predicate P, then either program S terminates on it and its output $[\![S]\!](\rho)$ satisfies Q, or S diverges from it.

To better understand this definition, let us see a simple example. This example clearly illustrates the difference between total correctness and partial correctness.

Example 4.2.1. *Assume that* $type(q) = $ **Boolean**. *Consider the program:*

$$S \equiv \textbf{while } M[q] = 1 \textbf{ do } q := \sigma_z[q] \textbf{ od}$$

where $M_0 = |0\rangle\langle 0|$, $M_1 = |1\rangle\langle 1|$, *and* σ_z *is the Pauli matrix. Let*

$$P = |\psi\rangle_q\langle\psi| \otimes P'$$

where $|\psi\rangle = \alpha|0\rangle + \beta|1\rangle \in \mathcal{H}_2$, *and* $P' \in \mathcal{P}\left(\mathcal{H}_{qVar\setminus\{q\}}\right)$. *Then*

(i) *We see that the total correctness*

$$\models_{tot} \{P\}S\{|0\rangle_q\langle 0| \otimes P'\}$$

does not hold if $\beta \neq 0$ *and* $P' \neq 0_{\mathcal{H}_{qVar\setminus\{q\}}}$. *In fact, put*

$$\rho = |\psi\rangle_q\langle\psi| \otimes I_{\mathcal{H}_{qVar\setminus\{q\}}}.$$

Note that ρ *is not normalized for simplicity of presentation. Then*

$$[\![S]\!](\rho) = |\alpha|^2 |0\rangle_q\langle 0| \otimes I_{\mathcal{H}_{qVar\setminus\{q\}}}$$

and

$$tr(P\rho) = tr(P') > |\alpha|^2 tr(P') = tr((|0\rangle_q\langle 0| \otimes P')[\![S]\!](\rho)).$$

(ii) *We have the partial correctness:*

$$\models_{par} \{P\}S\{|0\rangle_q\langle 0| \otimes P'\};$$

that is,

$$tr(P\rho) \leq tr((|0\rangle_q\langle 0| \otimes P')[\![S]\!](\rho)) + [tr(\rho) - tr([\![S]\!](\rho))]. \tag{4.8}$$

Here, we only consider a special class of partial density operators in $\mathcal{H}_{Var\setminus\{q\}}$:

$$\rho = |\varphi\rangle_q\langle\varphi| \otimes \rho'$$

where $|\varphi\rangle = a|0\rangle + b|1\rangle \in \mathcal{H}_2$, and $\rho' \in \mathcal{D}\left(\mathcal{H}_{qVar\setminus\{q\}}\right)$. A routine calculation yields:

$$[\![S]\!](\rho) = |a|^2|0\rangle_q\langle0| \otimes \rho'$$

and

$$\begin{aligned}
tr(P\rho) &= |\langle\varphi|\varphi\rangle|^2 tr(P'\rho')\\
&\leq |a|^2 tr(P'\rho') + [tr(\rho') - |a|^2 tr(\rho')]\\
&= tr((|0\rangle_q\langle0| \otimes P')[\![S]\!](\rho)) + [tr(\rho) - tr([\![S]\!](\rho))].
\end{aligned}$$

Exercise 4.2.1. *Prove inequality (4.8) for all $\rho \in \mathcal{D}(\mathcal{H}_{all})$.*

The following proposition presents several basic properties of total and partial correctness formulas.

Proposition 4.2.1

(i) *If $\models_{tot} \{P\}S\{Q\}$, then $\models_{par} \{P\}S\{Q\}$.*
(ii) *For any quantum program S, and for any $P, Q \in \mathcal{P}(\mathcal{H}_{all})$, we have:*

$$\models_{tot} \{0_{\mathcal{H}_{all}}\}S\{Q\}, \quad \models_{par} \{P\}S\{I_{\mathcal{H}_{all}}\}.$$

(iii) *(Linearity) For any $P_1, P_2, Q_1, Q_2 \in \mathcal{P}(\mathcal{H}_{all})$ and $\lambda_1, \lambda_2 \geq 0$ with $\lambda_1 P_1 + \lambda_2 P_2, \lambda_1 Q_1 + \lambda_2 Q_2 \in \mathcal{P}(\mathcal{H}_{all})$, if*

$$\models_{tot} \{P_i\}S\{Q_i\} \ (i = 1, 2),$$

then

$$\models_{tot} \{\lambda_1 P_1 + \lambda_2 P_2\}S\{\lambda_1 Q_1 + \lambda_2 Q_2\}.$$

The same conclusion holds for partial correctness if $\lambda_1 + \lambda_2 = 1$.

Proof. Immediate from definition. $\qquad\square$

4.2.2 WEAKEST PRECONDITIONS OF QUANTUM PROGRAMS

In Subsection 4.1.1, we already defined the notion of weakest precondition for a general quantum operation (thought of as the denotational semantics of a quantum program). In this subsection, we consider its syntactic counterpart, namely weakest precondition for a quantum program written in the **while**-language defined in Section 3.1. As in the case of classical Floyd-Hoare logic, weakest preconditions and weakest liberal preconditions can be defined for quantum programs corresponding to total correctness and partial correctness, respectively. They will play a key role in establishing the (relative) completeness of Floyd-Hoare logic for quantum programs.

Definition 4.2.3. *Let S be a quantum **while**-program and $P \in \mathcal{P}(\mathcal{H}_{all})$ be a quantum predicate in $\mathcal{H}_{all}$.*

(i) *The weakest precondition of S with respect to P is defined to be the quantum predicate $wp.S.P \in \mathcal{P}(\mathcal{H}_{all})$ satisfying the following conditions:*
  (a) $\models_{tot} \{wp.S.P\}S\{P\}$;
  (b) *if quantum predicate $Q \in \mathcal{P}(\mathcal{H}_{all})$ satisfies $\models_{tot} \{Q\}S\{P\}$ then $Q \sqsubseteq wp.S.P$.*
(ii) *The weakest liberal precondition of S with respect to P is defined to be the quantum predicate $wlp.S.P \in \mathcal{P}(\mathcal{H}_{all})$ satisfying the following conditions:*
  (a) $\models_{par} \{wlp.S.P\}S\{P\}$;
  (b) *if quantum predicate $Q \in \mathcal{P}(\mathcal{H}_{all})$ satisfies $\models_{par} \{Q\}S\{P\}$ then $Q \sqsubseteq wlp.S.P$.*

By comparing the previous definition and Definition 4.1.3, we can see that they are compatible; that is,

$$wp.S.P = wp(\llbracket S \rrbracket)(P). \tag{4.9}$$

Note that the left-hand side of this equality is given directly in terms of program S, whereas the right-hand side is given in terms of the semantics of S.

The next two propositions give explicit representations of weakest preconditions and weakest liberal preconditions, respectively, for programs written in the quantum **while**-language. They will be essentially used in the proof of completeness of quantum Floyd-Hoare logic for total and partial correctness. Let us first consider weakest preconditions of quantum programs.

Proposition 4.2.2

(i) $wp.\mathbf{skip}.P = P$.
(ii) (a) *If $type(q) = $ **Boolean**, then*

$$wp.q := |0\rangle.P = |0\rangle_q \langle 0|P|0\rangle_q \langle 0| + |1\rangle_q \langle 0|P|0\rangle_q \langle 1|.$$

(b) *If $type(q) = $ **integer**, then*

$$wp.q := |0\rangle.P = \sum_{n=-\infty}^{\infty} |n\rangle_q \langle 0|P|0\rangle_q \langle n|.$$

(iii) $wp.\overline{q} := U[\overline{q}].P = U^{\dagger}PU$.
(iv) $wp.S_1; S_2.P = wp.S_1.(wp.S_2.P)$.
(v) $wp.\mathbf{if}\ (\square m \cdot M[\overline{q}] = m \rightarrow S_m)\ \mathbf{fi}.P = \sum_m M_m^{\dagger}(wp.S_m.P)M_m$.
(vi) $wp.\mathbf{while}\ M[\overline{q}] = 1\ \mathbf{do}\ S\ \mathbf{od}.P = \bigsqcup_{n=0}^{\infty} P_n$, *where*

$$\begin{cases} P_0 = 0_{\mathcal{H}_{all}}; \\ P_{n+1} = M_0^{\dagger}PM_0 + M_1^{\dagger}(wp.S.P_n)M_1 \ \text{for all } n \geq 0. \end{cases}$$

Proof. The trick is to simultaneously prove this proposition and Corollary 4.2.1 following by induction on the structure of quantum program S.

- Case 1. $S \equiv$ **skip**. Obvious.
- Case 2. $S \equiv q := |0\rangle$. We only consider the case of $type(q) =$ **integer**, and the case of $type(q) =$ **Boolean** is similar. First, it holds that

$$tr\left(\left(\sum_{n=-\infty}^{\infty} |n\rangle_q \langle 0|P|0\rangle_q \langle n|\right)\rho\right) = tr\left(P\sum_{n=-\infty}^{\infty}|0\rangle_q\langle n|\rho|n\rangle_q\langle 0|\right)$$
$$= tr(P[\![q := |0\rangle]\!](\rho)).$$

On the other hand, for any quantum predicate $Q \in \mathcal{P}(\mathcal{H}_{all})$, if

$$\models_{tot} \{Q\}q := |0\rangle\{P\},$$

i.e.,

$$tr(Q\rho) \leq tr(P[\![q := |0\rangle]\!](\rho))$$
$$= tr\left(\left(\sum_{n=-\infty}^{\infty} |n\rangle_q \langle 0|P|0\rangle_q \langle n|\right)\rho\right)$$

for all $\rho \in \mathcal{D}(\mathcal{H}_{all})$, then it follows from Lemma 4.1.2 that

$$Q \sqsubseteq \sum_{n=-\infty}^{\infty} |n\rangle_q \langle 0|P|0\rangle_q \langle n|.$$

- Case 3. $S \equiv \bar{q} := U[\bar{q}]$. Similar to Case 2.
- Case 4. $S \equiv S_1; S_2$. It follows from the induction hypothesis on S_1 and S_2 that

$$tr((wp.S_1.(wp.S_2.P))\rho) = tr((wp.S_2.P)[\![S_1]\!](\rho))$$
$$= tr(P[\![S_2]\!]([\![S_1]\!](\rho)))$$
$$= tr(P[\![S_1; S_2]\!](\rho)).$$

If $\models_{tot} \{Q\}S_1; S_2\{P\}$, then for all $\rho \in \mathcal{D}(\mathcal{H}_{all})$, we have:

$$tr(QP) \leq tr(P[\![S_1; S_2]\!](\rho)) = tr((wp.S_1.(wp.S_2.P))\rho).$$

Therefore, it follows from Lemma 4.1.2 that $Q \sqsubseteq wp.S_1.(wp.S_2.P)$.

- Case 5. $S \equiv \mathbf{if} \ (\square m \cdot M[\overline{q}] = m \rightarrow S_m) \ \mathbf{fi}$. Applying the induction hypothesis on S_m, we obtain:

$$
\begin{aligned}
tr\left(\left(\sum_m M_m^\dagger (wp.S_m.P)M_m\right)\rho\right) &= \sum_m tr((wp.S_m.P)M_m\rho M_m^\dagger) \\
&= \sum_m tr(P[\![S_m]\!](M_m\rho M_m^\dagger)) \\
&= tr\left(P\sum_m [\![S_m]\!]\left(M_m\rho M_m^\dagger\right)\right) \\
&= tr(P[\![\mathbf{if} \ (\square m \cdot M[\overline{q}] = m \rightarrow S_m)\ \mathbf{fi}]\!](\rho)).
\end{aligned}
$$

If

$$
\models_{tot} \{Q\}\mathbf{if}\ (\square m \cdot M[\overline{q}] = m \rightarrow S_m)\ \mathbf{fi}\{P\},
$$

then

$$
tr(Q\rho) \leq tr\left(\left(\sum_m M_m^\dagger (wp.S_m.P)M_m\right)\rho\right)
$$

for all ρ, and it follows from Lemma 4.1.2 that

$$
Q \sqsubseteq \sum_m M_m^\dagger (wlp.S_m.P)M_m.
$$

- Case 6. $S \equiv \mathbf{while}\ M[\overline{q}] = 1\ \mathbf{do}\ S'\ \mathbf{od}$. For simplicity, we write $(\mathbf{while})^n$ for the nth syntactic approximation "$(\mathbf{while}\ M[\overline{q}] = 1\ \mathbf{do}\ S'\ \mathbf{od})^n$" of loop S (see Definition 3.3.6). First, we have:

$$
tr(P_n\rho) = tr(P[\![(\mathbf{while})^n]\!](\rho)).
$$

This claim can be proved by induction on n. The basis case of $n = 0$ is obvious. By the induction hypotheses on n and S', we obtain:

$$
\begin{aligned}
tr(P_{n+1}\rho) &= tr(M_0^\dagger P M_0 \rho) + tr(M_1^\dagger (wp.S'.P_n)M_1\rho) \\
&= tr(PM_0\rho M_0^\dagger) + tr((wp.S'.P_n)M_1\rho M_1^\dagger) \\
&= tr(PM_0\rho M_0^\dagger) + tr(P_n[\![S']\!](M_1\rho M_1^\dagger)) \\
&= tr(PM_0\rho M_0^\dagger) + tr(P[\![(\mathbf{while})^n]\!]([\![S']\!](M_1\rho M_1^\dagger))) \\
&= tr[P(M_0\rho M_0^\dagger + [\![S';(\mathbf{while})^n]\!](M_1\rho M_1^\dagger))] \\
&= tr(P[\![(\mathbf{while})^{n+1}]\!](\rho)).
\end{aligned}
$$

Now continuity of trace operator yields:

$$tr\left(\left(\bigsqcup_{n=0}^{\infty} P_n\right)\rho\right) = \bigsqcup_{n=0}^{\infty} tr(P_n\rho)$$

$$= \bigsqcup_{n=0}^{\infty} tr(P[\![(\textbf{while})^n]\!](\rho))$$

$$= tr\left(P\bigsqcup_{n=0}^{\infty} [\![(\textbf{while})^n]\!](\rho)\right)$$

$$= tr(P[\![\textbf{while } M[\bar{q}] = 1 \textbf{ do } S' \textbf{ od}]\!](\rho)).$$

So, if

$$\models_{tot} \{Q\}\textbf{while } M[\bar{q}] = 1 \textbf{ do } S' \textbf{ od}\{P\},$$

then

$$tr(Q\rho) \leq tr\left(\left(\bigsqcup_{n=0}^{\infty} P_n\right)\rho\right)$$

for all ρ, and by Lemma 4.1.2 we obtain $Q \sqsubseteq \bigsqcup_{n=0}^{\infty} P_n$.

□

The following corollary shows that the probability that an initial state ρ satisfies the weakest precondition $wp.S.P$ is equal to the probability that the terminal state $[\![S]\!](\rho)$ satisfies P. It follows from the proof of the previous proposition. But it can also be derived from equations (4.3) and (4.9).

Corollary 4.2.1. *For any quantum* **while**-*program S, for any quantum predicate* $P \in \mathcal{P}(\mathcal{H}_{all})$, *and for any partial density operator* $\rho \in \mathcal{D}(\mathcal{H}_{all})$, *we have:*

$$tr((wp.S.P)\rho) = tr(P[\![S]\!](\rho)).$$

We can also give explicit representations of weakest liberal preconditions of quantum programs.

Proposition 4.2.3

(i) $wlp.\textbf{skip}.P = P$.

(ii) (a) *If* $type(q) = $ **Boolean**, *then*

$$wlp.q := |0\rangle.P = |0\rangle_q \langle 0|P|0\rangle_q \langle 0| + |1\rangle_q \langle 0|P|0\rangle_q \langle 1|.$$

(b) If $type(q) = $ **integer**, then

$$wlp.q := |0\rangle.P = \sum_{n=-\infty}^{\infty} |n\rangle_q \langle 0|P|0\rangle_q \langle n|.$$

(iii) $wlp.\overline{q} := U[\overline{q}].P = U^\dagger PU.$
(iv) $wlp.S_1; S_2.P = wlp.S_1.(wlp.S_2.P).$
(v) $wlp.\textbf{if } (\square m \cdot M[\overline{q}] := m \rightarrow S_m) \textbf{ fi}.P = \sum_m M_m^\dagger(wlp.S_m.P)M_m.$
(vi) $wlp.\textbf{while } M[\overline{q}] = 1 \textbf{ do } S \textbf{ od}.P = \prod_{n=0}^{\infty} P_n,$ where

$$\begin{cases} P_0 = I_{\mathcal{H}_{all}}, \\ P_{n+1} = M_0^\dagger PM_0 + M_1^\dagger(wlp.S.P_n)M_1 \text{ for all } n \geq 0. \end{cases}$$

Proof. Similar to the case of weakest precondition, we prove this proposition and its corollary following simultaneously by induction on the structure of quantum program S.

- Case 1. $S \equiv \textbf{skip}$, or $q := |0\rangle$, or $\overline{q} := U[\overline{q}]$. Similar to Cases 1, 2 and 3 in the proof of Proposition 4.2.2.
- Case 2. $S \equiv S_1; S_2$. First, with the induction hypothesis on S_1 and S_2, we have:

$$\begin{aligned} tr(wlp.S_1.(wlp.S_2.P)\rho) &= tr(wlp.S_2.P[\![S_1]\!](\rho)) + [tr(\rho) - tr([\![S_1]\!](\rho))] \\ &= tr(P[\![S_2]\!]([\![S_1]\!](\rho)) + [tr([\![S_1]\!](\rho)) - tr([\![S_2]\!]([\![S_1]\!](\rho)))] \\ &\qquad + [tr(\rho) - tr([\![S_1]\!](\rho))] \\ &= tr(P[\![S_2]\!]([\![S_1]\!](\rho)) + [tr(\rho) - tr([\![S_2]\!]([\![S_1]\!](\rho)))] \\ &= tr(P[\![S]\!](\rho)) + [tr(\rho) - tr([\![S]\!](\rho))]. \end{aligned}$$

If $\models_{par} \{Q\}S\{P\}$, then it holds that

$$\begin{aligned} tr(Q\rho) &\leq tr(P[\![S]\!](\rho)) + [tr(\rho) - tr([\![S]\!](\rho))] \\ &= tr(wlp.S_1.(wlp.S_2.P)\rho) \end{aligned}$$

for all $\rho \in \mathcal{D}(\mathcal{H}_{all})$, and by Lemma 4.1.2 we obtain:

$$Q \sqsubseteq wlp.S_1.(wlp.S_2.P).$$

- Case 3. $S \equiv \textbf{if } (\square m \cdot M[\overline{q}] = m \rightarrow S_m) \textbf{ fi}$. It can be derived by the induction hypothesis on all S_m that

$$tr\left(\sum_m M_m^\dagger(wlp.S_m.P)M_m\rho\right) = \sum_m tr(M_m^\dagger(wlp.S_m.P)M_m\rho)$$

$$= \sum_m tr((wlp.S_m.P)M_m\rho M_m^\dagger)$$

$$= \sum_m \left\{tr(P[\![S_m]\!](M_m\rho M_m^\dagger)) + [tr(M_m\rho M_m^\dagger) - tr([\![S_m]\!](M_m\rho M_m^\dagger))]\right\}$$

$$= \sum_m tr\left(P[\![S_m]\!](M_m\rho M_m^\dagger)\right) + \left[\sum_m tr(M_m\rho M_m^\dagger) - \sum_m tr([\![S_m]\!](M_m\rho M_m^\dagger))\right]$$

$$= tr\left(P\sum_m [\![S_m]\!](M_m\rho M_m^\dagger)\right)$$

$$+ \left[tr\left(\rho\sum_m M_m^\dagger M_m\right) - tr\left(\sum_m [\![S_m]\!](M_m\rho M_m^\dagger)\right)\right]$$

$$= tr(P[\![S]\!](\rho)) + [tr(\rho) - tr([\![S]\!](\rho))]$$

because

$$\sum_m M_m^\dagger M_m = I_{\mathcal{H}_{\bar{q}}}.$$

If $\models_{par} \{Q\}S\{P\}$, then for all $\rho \in \mathcal{D}(\mathcal{H}_{all})$, it holds that

$$tr(Q\rho) \leq tr(P[\![S]\!](\rho)) + [tr(\rho) - tr([\![S]\!](\rho))]$$

$$= tr\left(\sum_m M_m^\dagger(wlp.S_m.P)M_m\rho\right).$$

This together with Lemma 4.1.2 implies

$$Q \sqsubseteq \sum_m M_m^\dagger(wlp.S_m.P)M_m.$$

- Case 4. $S \equiv$ **while** $M[\bar{q}] = 1$ **do** S' **od**. We first prove that

$$tr(P_n\rho) = tr(P[\![(\mathbf{while})^n]\!](\rho)) + [tr(\rho) - tr([\![(\mathbf{while})^n]\!](\rho))] \tag{4.10}$$

by induction on n, where $(\mathbf{while})^n$ is an abbreviation of the syntactic approximation $(\mathbf{while}\ M[\bar{q}] = 1\ \mathbf{do}\ S'\ \mathbf{od})^n$. The case of $n = 0$ is obvious.

By induction on S' and the induction hypothesis on n, we observe:

$$
\begin{aligned}
tr(P_{n+1}\rho) &= tr[(M_0^\dagger P M_0) + M_1^\dagger (wlp.S'.P_n)M_1\rho] \\
&= tr(M_0^\dagger P M_0 \rho) + tr(M_1^\dagger (wlp.S'.P_n)M_1\rho) \\
&= tr(P M_0 \rho M_0^\dagger) + tr((wlp.S'.P_n)M_1\rho M_1^\dagger) \\
&= tr(P M_0 \rho M_0^\dagger) + tr(P_n[\![S']\!](M_1\rho M_1^\dagger)) + [tr(M_1\rho M_1^\dagger) - tr([\![S']\!](M_1\rho M_1^\dagger))] \\
&= tr(P M_0 \rho M_0^\dagger) + tr(P[\![(\textbf{while})^n]\!]([\![S]\!](M_1\rho M_1^\dagger))) + [tr([\![S]\!](M_1\rho M_1^\dagger)) \\
&\quad - tr([\![(\textbf{while})^n]\!]([\![S]\!](M_1\rho M_1^\dagger)))] + [tr(M_1\rho M_1^\dagger) - tr([\![S']\!](M_1\rho M_1^\dagger))] \\
&= tr(P[M_0\rho M_0^\dagger + [\![(\textbf{while})^n]\!]([\![S]\!](M_1\rho M_1^\dagger))] \\
&\quad + [tr(\rho) - tr(M_0\rho M_0^\dagger + [\![(\textbf{while})^n]\!]([\![S]\!](M_1\rho M_1^\dagger)))] \\
&= tr(P[\![(\textbf{while})^{n+1}]\!](\rho)) + [tr(\rho) - tr([\![(\textbf{while})^{n+1}]\!](\rho)].
\end{aligned}
$$

This completes the proof of equation (4.10). Note that quantum predicate $P \sqsubseteq I$. Then $I - P$ is positive, and by continuity of trace operator we obtain:

$$
\begin{aligned}
tr\left(\left(\bigsqcap_{n=0}^{\infty} P_n\right)\rho\right) &= \bigsqcap_{n=0}^{\infty} tr(P_n\rho) \\
&= \bigsqcap_{n=0}^{\infty} \left\{ tr\left(P[\![(\textbf{while})^n]\!](\rho)\right) + [tr(\rho) - tr([\![(\textbf{while})^n]\!](\rho))] \right\} \\
&= tr(\rho) + \bigsqcap_{n=0}^{\infty} tr\left[(P - I)[\![(\textbf{while})^n]\!](\rho)\right] \\
&= tr(\rho) + tr\left[(P - I)\bigsqcup_{n=0}^{\infty}[\![(\textbf{while})^n]\!](\rho)\right] \\
&= tr(\rho) + tr[(P - I)[\![S]\!](\rho)] \\
&= tr(P[\![S]\!](\rho)) + [tr(\rho) - tr([\![S]\!](\rho))].
\end{aligned}
$$

For any $Q \in \mathcal{P}(\mathcal{H}_{all})$, $\models_{par} \{Q\}S\{P\}$ implies:

$$
\begin{aligned}
tr(Q\rho) &\le tr(P[\![S]\!](\rho)) + [tr(\rho) - tr([\![S]\!](\rho)) \\
&= tr\left(\left(\bigsqcap_{n=0}^{\infty} P_n\right)\rho\right)
\end{aligned}
$$

for all $\rho \in \mathcal{D}(\mathcal{H}_{all})$. This together with Lemma 4.1.2 leads to $Q \sqsubseteq \bigsqcap_{n=0}^{\infty} P_n$. $\square$

Corollary 4.2.2. *For any quantum **while**-program S, for any quantum predicate $P \in \mathcal{P}(\mathcal{H}_{all})$, and for any partial density operator $\rho \in \mathcal{D}(\mathcal{H}_{all})$, we have:*

$$
tr((wlp.S.P)\rho) = tr(P[\![S]\!](\rho)) + [tr(\rho) - tr([\![S]\!](\rho)].
$$

The previous lemma means that the probability that an initial state ρ satisfies the weakest liberal precondition $wlp.S.P$ is equal to the sum of the probability that the terminal state $[\![S]\!](\rho)$ satisfies P and the probability that S does not terminate when starting from ρ.

To conclude this subsection, we present a recursive characterization of weakest precondition and weakest liberal precondition of the quantum **while**-loop. This characterization provides a key step in the proof of completeness of quantum Floyd-Hoare logic.

Proposition 4.2.4. *We write* **while** *for quantum loop* "**while** $M[\bar{q}] = 1$ **do** S **od**". *Then for any* $P \in \mathcal{P}(\mathcal{H}_{all})$, *we have:*

(i) $wp.\mathbf{while}.P = M_0^\dagger P M_0 + M_1^\dagger (wp.S.(wp.\mathbf{while}.P))M_1.$

(ii) $wlp.\mathbf{while}.P = M_0^\dagger P M_0 + M_1^\dagger (wlp.S.(wlp.\mathbf{while}.P))M_1.$

Proof. We only prove (ii), and the proof of (i) is similar and easier. For every $\rho \in \mathcal{D}(\mathcal{H}_{all})$, by Proposition 4.2.3 (iv) we observe:

$$tr[(M_0^\dagger P M_0 + M_1^\dagger (wlp.S.(wlp.\mathbf{while}.P))M_1)\rho]$$
$$= tr(P M_0 \rho M_0^\dagger) + tr[(wlp.S.(wlp.\mathbf{while}.P))M_1 \rho M_1^\dagger]$$
$$= tr(P M_0 \rho M_0^\dagger) + tr[(wlp.\mathbf{while}.P)[\![S]\!](M_1 \rho M_1^\dagger)]$$
$$+ [tr(M_1 \rho M_1^\dagger) - tr([\![S]\!](M_1 \rho M_1^\dagger))]$$
$$= tr(P M_0 \rho M_0^\dagger) + tr[P[\![\mathbf{while}]\!]([\![S]\!](M_1 \rho M_1^\dagger))] + [tr([\![S]\!](M_1 \rho M_1^\dagger))$$
$$- tr([\![\mathbf{while}]\!]([\![S]\!](M_1 \rho M_1^\dagger))] + [tr(M_1 \rho M_1^\dagger) - tr([\![S]\!](M_1 \rho M_1^\dagger))]$$
$$= tr[P(M_0 \rho M_0^\dagger + [\![\mathbf{while}]\!]([\![S]\!](M_1 \rho M_1^\dagger)))]$$
$$+ [tr(M_1 \rho M_1^\dagger) - tr([\![\mathbf{while}]\!]([\![S]\!](M_1 \rho M_1^\dagger)))]$$
$$= tr(P[\![\mathbf{while}]\!](\rho)) + [tr(\rho M_1^\dagger M_1) - tr([\![\mathbf{while}]\!]([\![S]\!](M_1 \rho M_1^\dagger)))]$$
$$= tr(P[\![\mathbf{while}]\!](\rho)) + [tr(\rho (I - M_0^\dagger M_0)) - tr([\![\mathbf{while}]\!]([\![S]\!](M_1 \rho M_1^\dagger)))]$$
$$= tr(P[\![\mathbf{while}]\!](\rho)) + [tr(\rho) - tr(M_0 \rho M_0^\dagger + [\![\mathbf{while}]\!]([\![S]\!](M_1 \rho M_1^\dagger)))]$$
$$= tr(P[\![\mathbf{while}]\!](\rho)) + [tr(\rho) - tr([\![\mathbf{while}]\!](\rho))].$$

This means that

$$\left\{M_0^\dagger P M_0 + M_1^\dagger (wlp.S.(wlp.\mathbf{while}.P))M_1\right\} \mathbf{while}\{P\},$$

and

$$Q \sqsubseteq M_0^\dagger P M_0 + M_1^\dagger (wlp.S.(wlp.\mathbf{while}.P))M_1$$

provided $\models_{par} \{Q\}\mathbf{while}\{P\}$. $\qquad\square$

From Propositions 4.2.2 (vi) and 4.2.3 (vi) we see that the previous proposition can be actually strengthened as follows:

- $wp.\textbf{while}.P$ and $wlp.\textbf{while}.P$ are the least fixed point and the greatest fixed point of function:

$$X \mapsto M_0^\dagger P M_0 + M_1^\dagger (wp.S.X) M_1,$$

respectively.

4.2.3 PROOF SYSTEM FOR PARTIAL CORRECTNESS

Now we are ready to present an axiomatic system of Floyd-Hoare logic for quantum **while**-programs. The axiomatic system is given in terms of correctness formulas defined in Subsection 4.2.1. The quantum Floyd-Hoare logic can be divided into two proof systems, one for partial correctness and one for total correctness. In this subsection, we introduce the proof system qPD for partial correctness of quantum programs. It consists of the axioms and inference rules in Figure 4.2.

An application of the proof system qPD and the proof system qTD for total correctness presented in the next subsection will be given in Subsection 4.2.5 below where the correctness of the Grover algorithm is proved using qPD and qTD. The reader who is mainly interested in the applications of quantum Floyd-Hoare logic may first leave here to learn the rule (R-LT) of the system qTD in the next subsection and then directly move to Subsection 4.2.5. If she/he likes, the reader can return to this point after finishing Subsection 4.2.5.

As we know, the most important issue for any logical system is its soundness and completeness. In the remainder of this subsection, we study ·soundness and completeness of the proof system qPD. We say that a correctness formula $\{P\}S\{Q\}$ is provable in qTD, written

$$\vdash_{qPD} \{P\}S\{Q\}$$

if it can be derived by a finite number of applications of the axioms and inference rules given in Figure 4.2.

We first prove the soundness of qPD with respect to the semantics of partial correctness:

- provability of a correctness formula in the proof system qPD implies its truth in the sense of partial correctness.

Before doing this, let us introduce an auxiliary notation: for $i = 0, 1$, the quantum operation $\mathcal{E}_i$ is defined by

$$\mathcal{E}_i(\rho) = M_i \rho M_i^\dagger$$

for all $\rho \in \mathcal{D}(\mathcal{H}_{all})$. This notation was already used in the proof of Proposition 3.3.2. It will be frequently used in this subsection and the next as well as in Chapter 5.

(Ax-Sk) $\qquad\qquad$ $\{P\}\textbf{Skip}\{P\}$

(Ax-In) If $type(q) = \textbf{Boolean},$ then

$$\{|0\rangle_q\langle 0|P|0\rangle_q\langle 0| + |1\rangle_q\langle 0|P|0\rangle_q\langle 1|\}q := |0\rangle\{P\}$$

If $type(q) = \textbf{integer},$ then

$$\left\{\sum_{n=-\infty}^{\infty} |n\rangle_q\langle 0|P|0\rangle_q\langle n|\right\} q := |0\rangle\{P\}$$

(Ax-UT) $\qquad$ $\{U^\dagger PU\}\bar{q} := U[\bar{q}]\{P\}$

(R-SC) $\qquad$ $\dfrac{\{P\}S_1\{Q\} \qquad \{Q\}S_2\{R\}}{\{P\}S_1;S_2\{R\}}$

(R-IF) $\qquad$ $\dfrac{\{P_m\}S_m\{Q\} \text{ for all } m}{\left\{\sum_m M_m^\dagger P_m M_m\right\}\textbf{if } (\square m \cdot M[\bar{q}] = m \to S_m)\ \textbf{fi}\{Q\}}$

(R-LP) $\qquad$ $\dfrac{\{Q\}S\left\{M_0^\dagger PM_0 + M_1^\dagger QM_1\right\}}{\{M_0^\dagger PM_0 + M_1^\dagger QM_1\}\textbf{while } M[\bar{q}] = 1 \textbf{ do } S \textbf{ od}\{P\}}$

(R-Or) $\qquad$ $\dfrac{P \sqsubseteq P' \quad \{P'\}S\{Q'\} \quad Q' \sqsubseteq Q}{\{P\}S\{Q\}}$

FIGURE 4.2

Proof system *qPD* of partial correctness.

Theorem 4.2.1 (Soundness). *The proof system qPD is sound for partial correctness of quantum **while**-programs; that is, for any quantum **while**-program S and quantum predicates $P, Q \in \mathcal{P}(\mathcal{H}_{all})$, we have:*

$$\vdash_{qPD} \{P\}S\{Q\} \text{ implies } \models_{par} \{P\}S\{Q\}.$$

Proof. We only need to show that the axioms of *qPD* are valid in the sense of partial correctness and inference rules of *qPD* preserve partial correctness.

- (Ax-Sk) It is obvious that $\models_{par} \{P\}\mathbf{skip}\{P\}$.
- (Ax-In) We only prove the case of $type(q) = \mathbf{integer}$, and the case of $type(q) = \mathbf{Boolean}$ is similar. For any $\rho \in \mathcal{D}(\mathcal{H}_{all})$, it follows from Proposition 3.3.1 (ii) that

$$
\begin{aligned}
tr\left[\left(\sum_{n=-\infty}^{\infty} |n\rangle_q \langle 0|P|0\rangle_q \langle n|\right)\rho\right] &= \sum_{n=-\infty}^{\infty} tr(|n\rangle_q \langle 0|P|0\rangle_q \langle n|\rho) \\
&= \sum_{n=-\infty}^{\infty} tr(P|0\rangle_q \langle n|\rho|n\rangle_q \langle 0|) \\
&= tr\left(P \sum_{n=-\infty}^{\infty} |0\rangle_q \langle n|\rho|n\rangle_q \langle 0|\right) \\
&= tr(P[\![q := |0\rangle]\!](\rho)).
\end{aligned}
$$

Therefore, we have:

$$
\models_{par} \left\{\sum_{n=-\infty}^{\infty} |n\rangle_q \langle 0|P|0\rangle_q \langle n|\right\} q := |0\rangle \{P\}.
$$

- (Ax-UT) It is easy to see that

$$
\models_{par} \{U^{\dagger}PU\}\overline{q} := U[\overline{q}]\{P\}.
$$

- (R-SC) If $\models_{par} \{P\}S_1\{Q\}$ and $\models_{par} \{Q\}S_2\{R\}$, then for any $\rho \in \mathcal{D}(\mathcal{H}_{all})$ we have:

$$
\begin{aligned}
tr(P\rho) &\leq tr(Q[\![S_1]\!](\rho)) + [tr(\rho) - tr([\![S_1]\!](\rho))] \\
&\leq tr(R[\![S_2]\!]([\![S_1]\!](\rho))) + [tr([\![S_1]\!](\rho)) - tr([\![S_2]\!]([\![S_1]\!](\rho)))] \\
&\qquad\qquad + [tr(\rho) - tr([\![S_1]\!](\rho))] \\
&= tr(R[\![S_1; S_2]\!](\rho)) + [tr(\rho) - tr([\![S_1; S_2]\!](\rho))].
\end{aligned}
$$

Therefore, $\models_{par} \{P\}S_1; S_2\{R\}$ holds as desired.
- (R-IF) Assume that $\models_{par} \{P_m\}S_m\{Q\}$ for all possible measurement outcomes m. Then for all $\rho \in \mathcal{D}(\mathcal{H}_{all})$, since

$$
\sum_m M_m^{\dagger}M_m = I_{\mathcal{H}_{\overline{q}}},
$$

it holds that

$$tr\left(\sum_m M_m^\dagger P_m M_m \rho\right) = \sum_m tr(M_m^\dagger P_m M_m \rho)$$

$$= \sum_m tr(P_m M_m \rho M_m^\dagger)$$

$$\leq \sum_m \left\{ tr(Q[\![S_m]\!](M_m \rho M_m^\dagger)) + [tr(M_m \rho M_m^\dagger) - tr([\![S_m]\!](M_m \rho M_m^\dagger))] \right\}$$

$$\leq \sum_m tr\left(Q[\![S_m]\!](M_m \rho M_m^\dagger)\right) + \left[\sum_m tr(M_m \rho M_m^\dagger) - \sum_m tr([\![S_m]\!](M_m \rho M_m^\dagger))\right]$$

$$= tr\left(Q\sum_m [\![S_m]\!](M_m \rho M_m^\dagger)\right) + \left[tr\left(\sum_m \rho M_m^\dagger M_m\right) - tr\left(\sum_m [\![S_m]\!](M_m \rho M_m^\dagger)\right)\right]$$

$$= tr(Q[\![\mathbf{if}\ldots\mathbf{fi}]\!](\rho)) + [tr(\rho) - tr([\![\mathbf{if}\ldots\mathbf{fi}]\!](\rho))],$$

and

$$\models_{par} \left\{\sum_m M_m^\dagger P_m M_m\right\} \mathbf{if}\ldots\mathbf{fi}\{Q\},$$

where **if...fi** is an abbreviation of statement "**if** $(\Box m \cdot M[\bar{q}] = m \to S_m)$ **fi**".
- (R-LP) Suppose that

$$\models_{par} \{Q\}S\left\{M_0^\dagger P M_0 + M_1^\dagger Q M_1\right\}.$$

Then for all $\rho \in \mathcal{D}(\mathcal{H}_{all})$, it holds that

$$tr(Q\rho) \leq tr((M_0^\dagger P M_0 + M_1^\dagger Q M_1)[\![S]\!](\rho)) + [tr(\rho) - tr([\![S]\!](\rho))]. \quad (4.11)$$

Furthermore, we have:

$$tr\left[\left(M_0^\dagger P M_0 + M_1^\dagger Q M_1\right)\rho\right] \leq \sum_{k=0}^n tr\left(P\left(\mathcal{E}_0 \circ ([\![S]\!] \circ \mathcal{E}_1)^k\right)(\rho)\right)$$
$$+ tr\left(Q\left(\mathcal{E}_1 \circ ([\![S]\!] \circ \mathcal{E}_1)^n\right)(\rho)\right) \quad (4.12)$$
$$+ \sum_{k=0}^{n-1}\left[tr(\mathcal{E}_1 \circ ([\![S]\!] \circ \mathcal{E}_1)^k(\rho)) - tr\left(([\![S]\!] \circ \mathcal{E}_1)^{k+1}(\rho)\right)\right]$$

for all $n \geq 1$. In fact, equation (4.12) may be proved by induction on n. The case of $n = 1$ is obvious. Using equation (4.11), we obtain:

$$tr\left(Q\left(\mathcal{E}_1 \circ ([\![S]\!] \circ \mathcal{E}_1)^n\right)(\rho)\right) \leq tr\left(\left(M_0^\dagger P M_0 + M_1^\dagger Q M_1\right)([\![S]\!] \circ \mathcal{E}_1)^{n+1}(\rho)\right)$$
$$+ \left[tr\left((\mathcal{E}_1 \circ ([\![S]\!] \circ \mathcal{E}_1)^n)(\rho)\right) - tr\left(([\![S]\!] \circ \mathcal{E}_1)^{n+1}(\rho)\right)\right]$$
$$= tr\left(P\left(\mathcal{E}_0 \circ ([\![S]\!] \circ \mathcal{E}_1)^{n+1}\right)(\rho)\right) + tr\left(Q\left(\mathcal{E}_1 \circ ([\![S]\!] \circ \mathcal{E}_1)^{n+1}\right)(\rho)\right)$$
$$+ \left[tr\left((\mathcal{E}_1 \circ ([\![S]\!] \circ \mathcal{E}_1)^n)(\rho)\right) - tr\left(([\![S]\!] \circ \mathcal{E}_1)^{n+1}(\rho)\right)\right]. \tag{4.13}$$

Combining equations (4.12) and (4.13), we assert that

$$tr\left[\left(M_0^\dagger P M_0 + M_1^\dagger Q M_1\right)\rho\right] \leq \sum_{k=0}^{n+1} tr\left(P\left(\mathcal{E}_0 \circ ([\![S]\!] \circ \mathcal{E}_1)^k\right)(\rho)\right)$$
$$+ tr\left(Q\left(\mathcal{E}_1 \circ ([\![S]\!] \circ \mathcal{E}_1)^{n+1}\right)(\rho)\right)$$
$$+ \sum_{k=0}^{n} \left[tr\left(\mathcal{E}_1 \circ ([\![S]\!] \circ \mathcal{E}_1)^k(\rho)\right) - tr\left(([\![S]\!] \circ \mathcal{E}_1)^{k+1}(\rho)\right)\right].$$

Therefore, equation (4.12) holds in the case of $n+1$ provided it is true in the case of n, and we complete the proof of equation (4.12).
Now we note that

$$tr\left(\mathcal{E}_1 \circ ([\![S]\!] \circ \mathcal{E}_1)^k(\rho)\right) = tr\left(M_1([\![S]\!] \circ \mathcal{E}_1)^k(\rho)M_1^\dagger\right)$$
$$= tr\left(([\![S]\!] \circ \mathcal{E}_1)^k(\rho)M_1^\dagger M_1\right)$$
$$= tr\left(([\![S]\!] \circ \mathcal{E}_1)^k(\rho)\left(I - M_0^\dagger M_0\right)\right)$$
$$= tr\left(([\![S]\!] \circ \mathcal{E}_1)^k(\rho)\right) - tr\left((\mathcal{E}_0 \circ ([\![S]\!] \circ \mathcal{E}_1)^k)(\rho)\right).$$

Then it follows that

$$\sum_{k=0}^{n-1} \left[tr\left(\mathcal{E}_1 \circ ([\![S]\!] \circ \mathcal{E}_1)^k(\rho)\right) - tr\left(([\![S]\!] \circ \mathcal{E}_1)^{k+1}(\rho)\right)\right] = \sum_{k=0}^{n-1} tr\left(([\![S]\!] \circ \mathcal{E}_1)^k(\rho)\right)$$
$$- \sum_{k=0}^{n-1}\left[tr\left(\mathcal{E}_0 \circ ([\![S]\!] \circ \mathcal{E}_1)^k(\rho)\right) - \sum_{k=0}^{n-1} tr\left(([\![S]\!] \circ \mathcal{E}_1)^{k+1}(\rho)\right)\right]$$
$$= tr(\rho) - tr\left(([\![S]\!] \circ \mathcal{E}_1)^n(\rho)\right) - \sum_{k=0}^{n-1} tr\left(\mathcal{E}_0 \circ ([\![S]\!] \circ \mathcal{E}_1)^k(\rho)\right).$$

$$\tag{4.14}$$

On the other hand, we have:

$$tr(Q(\mathcal{E}_1 \circ ([\![S]\!] \circ \mathcal{E}_1)^n)(\rho)) = tr(Q M_1([\![S]\!] \circ \mathcal{E}_1)^n)(\rho)M_1^\dagger)$$
$$\leq tr(M_1([\![S]\!] \circ \mathcal{E}_1)^n)(\rho)M_1^\dagger)$$
$$= tr(([\![S]\!] \circ \mathcal{E}_1)^n)(\rho)M_1^\dagger M_1) \tag{4.15}$$
$$= tr(([\![S]\!] \circ \mathcal{E}_1)^n)(\rho)(I - M_0^\dagger M_0))$$
$$= tr(([\![S]\!] \circ \mathcal{E}_1)^n)(\rho)) - tr((\mathcal{E}_0 \circ ([\![S]\!] \circ \mathcal{E}_1)^n)(\rho)).$$

Putting equations (4.14) and (4.15) into equation (4.12), we obtain:

$$tr\left[(M_0^\dagger P M_0 + M_1^\dagger Q M_1)\rho\right] \le \sum_{k=0}^{n} tr\left(P(\mathcal{E}_0 \circ (\llbracket S \rrbracket \circ \mathcal{E}_1)^k)(\rho)\right)$$

$$+ \left[tr(\rho) - \sum_{k=0}^{n} tr((\mathcal{E}_0 \circ (\llbracket S \rrbracket \circ \mathcal{E}_1)^k)(\rho))\right]$$

$$= tr\left(P \sum_{k=0}^{n}(\mathcal{E}_0 \circ (\llbracket S \rrbracket \circ \mathcal{E}_1)^k)(\rho)\right)$$

$$+ \left[tr(\rho) - tr\left(\sum_{k=0}^{n}(\mathcal{E}_0 \circ (\llbracket S \rrbracket \circ \mathcal{E}_1)^k)(\rho)\right)\right].$$

Let $n \to \infty$. Then it follows that

$$tr\left[(M_0^\dagger P M_0 + M_1^\dagger Q M_1)\rho\right] \le tr(P\llbracket \mathbf{while} \rrbracket(\rho) + [tr(\rho) - tr(\llbracket \mathbf{while} \rrbracket(\rho))]$$

and

$$\models_{par} \{M_0^\dagger P M_0 + M_1^\dagger Q M_1\}\mathbf{while}\{P\},$$

where **while** is an abbreviation of quantum loop "**while** $M[\overline{q}] = 1$ **do** S".
- (R-Or) The validity of this rule follows immediately from Lemma 4.1.2 and Definition 4.2.2. □

Now we are going to establish completeness for the proof system qPD with respect to the semantics of partial correctness:

- truth of a quantum program in the sense of partial correctness implies its provability in the proof system qPD.

Note that the Löwner ordering assertions between quantum predicates in the rule (R-Or) are statements about complex numbers. So, only a completeness of qPD relative to the theory of the field of complex numbers may be anticipated; more precisely, we can add all statements that are true in the field of complex numbers into qPD in order to make it complete. The following theorem should be understood exactly in the sense of such a relative completeness.

Theorem 4.2.2 (Completeness). *The proof system qPD is complete for partial correctness of quantum **while**-programs; that is, for any quantum **while**-program S and quantum predicates $P, Q \in \mathcal{P}(\mathcal{H}_{all})$, we have:*

$$\models_{par} \{P\}S\{Q\} \text{ implies } \vdash_{qPD} \{P\}S\{Q\}.$$

Proof. If $\models_{par} \{P\}S\{Q\}$, then by Definition 4.2.3 (ii) we have $P \sqsubseteq wlp.S.Q$. Therefore, by the rule (R-Or) it suffices to prove the following:

- Claim:

$$\vdash_{qPD} \{wlp.S.Q\}S\{Q\}.$$

We proceed by induction on the structure of S to prove this claim.

- Case 1. $S \equiv$ **skip**. Immediate from the axiom (Ax-Sk).
- Case 2. $S \equiv q := 0$. Immediate from the axiom (Ax-In).
- Case 3. $S \equiv \overline{q} := U[\overline{q}]$. Immediate from the axiom (Ax-UT).
- Case 4. $S \equiv S_1; S_2$. It follows from the induction hypothesis on S_1 and S_2 that

$$\vdash_{qPD} \{wlp.S_1.(wlp.S_2.Q)\}S_1\{wlp.S_2.Q\}$$

and

$$\vdash_{qPD} \{wlp.S_2.Q\}S_2\{Q\}.$$

We obtain:

$$\vdash_{qPD} \{wlp.S_1.(wlp.S_2.Q)\}S_1; S_2\{Q\}$$

by the rule (R-SC). Then with Proposition 4.2.3 (iv) we see that

$$\vdash_{qPD} \{wlp.S_1; S_2.Q\}S_1; S_2\{Q\}.$$

- Case 5. $S \equiv$ **if** $(\square m \cdot M[\overline{q}] = m \rightarrow S_m)$ **fi**. For all m, by the induction hypothesis on S_m we obtain:

$$\vdash_{qPD} \{wlp.S_m.Q\}S_m\{Q\}.$$

Then applying the rule (R-IF) yields:

$$\vdash_{qPD} \left\{\sum_m M_m^\dagger(wlp.S_m.Q)M_m\right\} \textbf{if } (\square m \cdot M[\overline{q}] = m \rightarrow S_m) \textbf{ fi}\{Q\},$$

and using Proposition 4.2.3 (v) we have:

$$\vdash_{qPD} \{wlp.\textbf{if } (\square m \cdot M[\overline{q}] = m \rightarrow S_m) \textbf{ fi}.Q\}\textbf{if } (\square m \cdot M[\overline{q}] = m \rightarrow S_m) \textbf{ fi}\{Q\}.$$

- Case 6. $S \equiv$ **while** $M[\overline{q}] = 1$ **do** S' **od**. For simplicity, we write **while** for quantum loop "**while** $M[\overline{q}] = 1$ **do** S' **od**". The induction hypothesis on S asserts that

$$\vdash_{qPD} \{wlp.S.(wlp.\textbf{while}.P)\}S\{wlp.\textbf{while}.P\}.$$

By Proposition 4.2.4 (ii) we have:

$$wlp.\textbf{while}.P = M_0^\dagger PM_0 + M_1^\dagger(wlp.S.(wlp.\textbf{while}.P))M_1.$$

Then by the rule (R-LP) we obtain:

$$\vdash_{qPD} \{wlp.\textbf{while}.P\}\textbf{while}\{P\}$$

as desired. □

4.2.4 PROOF SYSTEM FOR TOTAL CORRECTNESS

We studied the proof system qPD for partial correctness of quantum **while**-programs in the last subsection. In this subsection, we further study a proof system qTD for total correctness of quantum **while**-programs. The only difference between qTD and qPD is the inference rule for quantum **while**-loops. In the system qPD, we do not need to consider termination of quantum loops. However, it is crucial in the system qTD to have a rule that can infer termination of quantum loops. To give the rule for total correctness of quantum loops, we need a notion of bound function which expresses the number of iterations of a quantum loop in its computation.

Definition 4.2.4. *Let $P \in \mathcal{P}(\mathcal{H}_{all})$ be a quantum predicate and a real number $\epsilon > 0$. A function*

$$t : \mathcal{D}(\mathcal{H}_{all}) \rightarrow \mathbb{N} \ (\textit{nonnegative integers})$$

is called a (P, ϵ)-bound function of quantum loop "$\textbf{while } M[\bar{q}] = 1 \textbf{ do } S \textbf{ od}$" if it satisfies the following two conditions:

(i) $t\left(\llbracket S \rrbracket \left(M_1 \rho M_1^\dagger\right)\right) \leq t(\rho);$ *and*

(ii) $tr(P\rho) \geq \epsilon$ *implies*

$$t\left(\llbracket S \rrbracket \left(M_1 \rho M_1^\dagger\right)\right) < t(\rho)$$

for all $\rho \in \mathcal{D}(\mathcal{H}_{all})$.

A bound function is also often called a ranking function in the programming theory literature. The purpose of a bound function of a loop is to warrant termination of the loop. The basic idea is that the value of the bound function is always nonnegative and it is decreased with each iteration of the loop, and thus the loop should terminate after a finite number of iterations. A bound function t of a classical loop "$\textbf{while } B \textbf{ do } S \textbf{ od}$" is required to satisfy the inequality

$$t(\llbracket S \rrbracket(s)) < t(s)$$

for any input state s. It is interesting to compare this inequality with conditions (i) and (ii) of the previous definition. We see that the conditions (i) and (ii) are two inequalities between

$$t\left(\llbracket S \rrbracket \left(M_1 \rho M_1^\dagger\right)\right)$$

and $t(\rho)$, but not between $t([\![S]\!](\rho))$ and $t(\rho)$. This is because in the implementation of the quantum loop "**while** $M[\bar{q}] = 1$ **do** S **od**", we need to perform the yes-no measurement M on ρ when checking the loop guard "$M[\bar{q}] = 1$", and the states of quantum variables will become $M_1 \rho M_1^\dagger$ from ρ whence the measurement outcome "yes" is observed.

The following lemma gives a characterization of the existence of a bound function of a quantum loop in terms of the limit of the state of quantum variables when the number of iterations of the loop goes to infinity. It provides a key step for the proof of soundness and completeness of the proof system qTD.

Lemma 4.2.1. *Let $P \in \mathcal{P}(\mathcal{H}_{all})$ be a quantum predicate. Then the following two statements are equivalent:*

(i) *for any $\epsilon > 0$, there exists a (P, ϵ)-bound function t_ϵ of the **while**-loop "**while** $M[\bar{q}] = 1$ **do** S **od**";*

(ii) $\lim_{n\to\infty} tr\left(P([\![S]\!] \circ \mathcal{E}_1)^n(\rho)\right) = 0$ *for all $\rho \in \mathcal{D}(\mathcal{H}_{all})$.*

Proof. (i) $\Rightarrow$ (ii) We prove this implication by refutation. If

$$\lim_{n\to\infty} tr\left(P([\![S]\!] \circ \mathcal{E}_1)^n(\rho)\right) \neq 0,$$

then there exist $\epsilon_0 > 0$ and a strictly increasing sequence $\{n_k\}$ of nonnegative integers such that

$$tr\left(P([\![S]\!] \circ \mathcal{E}_1)^{n_k}(\rho)\right) \geq \epsilon_0$$

for all $k \geq 0$. Thus, we have a (P, ϵ_0)-bound function of loop "**while** $M[\bar{q}] = 1$ **do** S **od**". For each $k \geq 0$, we set

$$\rho_k = ([\![S]\!] \circ \mathcal{E}_1)^{n_k}(\rho).$$

Then it holds that $tr(P\rho_k) \geq \epsilon_0$, and by conditions (i) and (ii) in Definition 4.2.4 we obtain:

$$\begin{aligned}
t_{\epsilon_0}(\rho_k) &> t_{\epsilon_0}\left([\![S]\!](M_1\rho_k M_1^\dagger)\right) \\
&= t_{\epsilon_0}\left(([\![S]\!] \circ \mathcal{E}_1)(\rho_k)\right) \\
&\geq t_{\epsilon_0}\left(([\![S]\!] \circ \mathcal{E}_1)^{n_{k+1}-n_k}(\rho_k)\right) \\
&= t_{\epsilon_0}(\rho_{k+1}).
\end{aligned}$$

Consequently, we have an infinitely descending chain $\{t_{\epsilon_0}(\rho_k)\}$ in $\mathbb{N}$. This is a contradiction because $\mathbb{N}$ is a well-founded set.

(ii) $\Rightarrow$ (i) For each $\rho \in \mathcal{D}(\mathcal{H}_{all})$, if

$$\lim_{n\to\infty} tr\left(P([\![S]\!] \circ \mathcal{E}_1)^n(\rho)\right) = 0,$$

then for any $\epsilon > 0$, there exists $N \in \mathbb{N}$ such that

$$tr\left(P(\llbracket S \rrbracket \circ \mathcal{E}_1)^n(\rho)\right) < \epsilon$$

for all $n \geq N$. We define:

$$t_\epsilon(\rho) = \min\left\{N \in \mathbb{N} : tr\left(P(\llbracket S \rrbracket \circ \mathcal{E}_1)^n(\rho)\right) < \epsilon \ \text{ for all } n \geq N\right\}.$$

Now it suffices to show that t_ϵ is a (P, ϵ)-bound function of loop "**while** $M[\bar{q}] = 1$ **do** S **od**". To this end. we consider the following two cases:

- Case 1. $tr(P\rho) \geq \epsilon$. Suppose that $t_\epsilon(\rho) = N$. Then $tr(P\rho) \geq \epsilon$ implies $N \geq 1$. By the definition of t_ϵ, we assert that

$$tr\left(P(\llbracket S \rrbracket \circ \mathcal{E}_1)^n(\rho)\right) < \epsilon$$

for all $n \geq N$. Thus, for all $n \geq N - 1 \geq 0$,

$$tr\left(P(\llbracket S \rrbracket \circ \mathcal{E}_1)^n\left(\llbracket S \rrbracket\left(M_1^\dagger \rho M_1\right)\right)\right) = tr\left(P(\llbracket S \rrbracket \circ \mathcal{E}_1)^{n+1}(\rho)\right) < \epsilon.$$

Therefore, we have:

$$t_\epsilon\left(\llbracket S \rrbracket\left(M_1^\dagger \rho M_1\right)\right) \leq N - 1 < N = t_\epsilon(\rho).$$

- Case 2. $tr(P\rho) < \epsilon$. Again, suppose that $t_\epsilon(\rho) = N$. Now we have the following two sub-cases:
  - ▶ Subcase 2.1. $N = 0$. Then for all $n \geq 0$, it holds that

$$tr\left(P(\llbracket S \rrbracket \circ \mathcal{E}_1)^n(\rho)\right) < \epsilon.$$

Furthermore, it is easy to see that

$$t_\epsilon\left(\llbracket S \rrbracket\left(M_1 \rho M_1^\dagger\right)\right) = 0 = t_\epsilon(\rho).$$

  - ▶ Subcase 2.2. $N \geq 1$. We can derive that

$$t_\epsilon(\rho) > t_\epsilon\left(\llbracket S \rrbracket\left(M_1 \rho M_1^\dagger\right)\right)$$

in the way of Case 1. □

Now we are ready to present the proof system qTD for total correctness of quantum **while**-programs. As mentioned before, the system qTD differs from the proof system qPD for partial correctness of quantum programs only in the inference rule for loops. More precisely, the proof system qTD consists of the axioms (Ax-Sk), (Ax-In) and (Ax-UT) and inference rules (R-SC), (R-IF) and (R-Or) in Figure 4.2 as well as inference rule (R-LT) in Figure 4.3.

- $\{Q\}S\{M_0^\dagger PM_0 + M_1^\dagger QM_1\}$
- for each $\epsilon > 0$, t_ϵ is a $(M_1^\dagger QM_1, \epsilon)$-bound function

(R-LT) $$\dfrac{\text{of loop } \textbf{while } M[\overline{q}] = 1 \textbf{ do } S \textbf{ od}}{\{M_0^\dagger PM_0 + M_1^\dagger QM_1\}\textbf{while } M[\overline{q}] = 1 \textbf{ do } S \textbf{ od}\{P\}}$$

FIGURE 4.3

Proof system *qTD* of total correctness.

An application of the rule (R-LT) to prove total correctness of the Grover search algorithm will be presented in Subsection 4.2.5 following.

The remainder of this subsection is devoted to establishing soundness and completeness of *qTD*:

- provability of a correctness formula in the proof system *qTD* is equivalent to its truth in the sense of total correctness.

We write:

$$\vdash_{qTD} \{P\}S\{Q\}$$

whenever the correctness formula $\{P\}S\{Q\}$ can be derived by a finite number of applications of the axioms and inference rules in *qTD*.

Theorem 4.2.3 (Soundness). *The proof system qTD is sound for total correctness of quantum **while**-programs; that is, for any quantum program S and quantum predicates $P, Q \in \mathcal{P}(\mathcal{H}_{all})$, we have:*

$$\vdash_{qTD} \{P\}S\{Q\} \text{ implies } \models_{tot} \{P\}S\{Q\}.$$

Proof. It suffices to show that the axioms of *qTD* are valid in the sense of total correctness, and inference rules of *qTD* preserve total correctness.

The proof for soundness of (Ax-Sk), (Ax-In) and (Ax-UT) is similar to the case of partial correctness. The proof of the remaining inference rules are given as follows:

- (R-SC) Suppose that $\models_{tot} \{P\}S_1\{Q\}$ and $\models_{tot} \{Q\}S_2\{R\}$. Then for any $\rho \in \mathcal{D}(\mathcal{H}_{all})$, with Proposition 3.3.1 (iv) we obtain:

$$tr(P\rho) \leq tr(Q\llbracket S_1 \rrbracket(\rho))$$
$$\leq tr(R\llbracket S_2 \rrbracket(\llbracket S_1 \rrbracket(\rho)))$$
$$= tr(P\llbracket S_1; S_2 \rrbracket(\rho)).$$

Therefore, $\models_{tot} \{P\}S_1; S_2\{R\}$.
- (R-IF) Suppose that $\models_{tot} \{P_m\}S_m\{Q\}$ for all possible measurement outcomes m. Then for any $\rho \in \mathcal{D}(\mathcal{H}_{all})$, it holds that

$$tr\left(P_m M_m \rho M_m^\dagger\right) \leq tr\left(Q[\![S_m]\!]\left(M_m \rho M_m^\dagger\right)\right).$$

Therefore, we have:

$$tr\left(\sum_m M_m^\dagger P_m M_m \rho\right) = \sum_m tr\left(P_m M_m \rho M_m^\dagger\right)$$

$$\leq \sum_m tr\left(Q[\![S_m]\!]\left(M_m \rho M_m^\dagger\right)\right)$$

$$= tr\left(Q \sum_m [\![S_m]\!]\left(M_m \rho M_m^\dagger\right)\right)$$

$$= tr(Q[\![\mathbf{if}\ (\Box m \cdot M[\overline{q}] = m \to S_m)\ \mathbf{fi}]\!](\rho)),$$

and it follows that

$$\models_{tot} \left\{\sum_m M_m^\dagger P M_m\right\} \mathbf{if}\ (\Box m \cdot M[\overline{q}] = m \to S_m)\ \mathbf{fi}\{Q\}.$$

- (R-LT) We assume that

$$\models_{tot} \{Q\}S\left\{M_0^\dagger P M_0 + M_1^\dagger Q M_1\right\}.$$

Then for any $\rho \in \mathcal{D}(\mathcal{H}_{all})$, we have:

$$tr(Q\rho) \leq tr\left((M_0^\dagger P M_0 + M_1^\dagger Q M_1)[\![S]\!](\rho)\right). \tag{4.16}$$

We first prove the following inequality:

$$tr\left[\left(M_0^\dagger P M_0 + M_1^\dagger Q M_1\right)\rho\right]$$
$$\leq \sum_{k=0}^n tr\left(P[\mathcal{E}_0 \circ ([\![S]\!] \circ \mathcal{E}_1)]^k(\rho)\right) + tr\left(Q\left[\mathcal{E}_1 \circ ([\![S]\!] \circ \mathcal{E}_1)^n\right](\rho)\right) \tag{4.17}$$

by induction on n. Indeed, it holds that

$$tr\left[\left(M_0^\dagger P M_0 + M_1^\dagger Q M_1\right)\rho\right] = tr\left(P M_0 \rho M_0^\dagger\right) + tr\left(Q M_1 \rho M_1^\dagger\right)$$
$$= tr(P\mathcal{E}_0(\rho)) + tr(Q\mathcal{E}_1(\rho)).$$

So, equation (4.17) is correct for the base case of $n = 0$. Assume that equation (4.17) is correct for the case of $n = m$. Then applying equation (4.16), we obtain:

$$tr\left[\left(M_0^\dagger P M_0 + M_1^\dagger Q M_1\right)\rho\right] = tr(P\mathcal{E}_0(\rho)) + tr\left(QM_1\rho M_1^\dagger\right)$$

$$\leq \sum_{k=0}^{m} tr\left(P[\mathcal{E}_0 \circ ([\![S]\!] \circ \mathcal{E}_1)]^k(\rho)\right) + tr\left(Q\left[\mathcal{E}_1 \circ ([\![S]\!] \circ \mathcal{E}_1)^m\right](\rho)\right)$$

$$\leq \sum_{k=0}^{m} tr\left(P[\mathcal{E}_0 \circ ([\![S]\!] \circ \mathcal{E}_1)]^k(\rho)\right)$$

$$+ tr\left(\left(M_0^\dagger P M_0 + M_1^\dagger Q M_1\right)[\![S]\!]\left([\mathcal{E}_1 \circ ([\![S]\!] \circ \mathcal{E}_1)^m](\rho)\right)\right)$$

$$= \sum_{k=0}^{m} tr\left(P[\mathcal{E}_0 \circ ([\![S]\!] \circ \mathcal{E}_1)]^k(\rho)\right) + tr\left(PM_0[\![S]\!]\left([\mathcal{E}_1 \circ ([\![S]\!] \circ \mathcal{E}_1)^m](\rho)\right)M_0^\dagger\right)$$

$$+ tr\left(QM_1[\![S]\!]\left([\mathcal{E}_1 \circ ([\![S]\!] \circ \mathcal{E}_1)^m](\rho)\right)M_1^\dagger\right)$$

$$= \sum_{k=0}^{m+1} tr\left(P[\mathcal{E}_0 \circ ([\![S]\!] \circ \mathcal{E}_1)]^k(\rho)\right) + tr\left(Q\left[\mathcal{E}_1 \circ ([\![S]\!] \circ \mathcal{E}_1)^{m+1}\right](\rho)\right).$$

Therefore, equation (4.17) also holds for the case of $n = m + 1$. This completes the proof of equation (4.17).

Now, since for any $\epsilon > 0$, there exists $(M_1^\dagger Q M_1, \epsilon)$-bound function t_ϵ of quantum loop "**while** $M[\bar{q}] = 1$ **do** S **od**", by Lemma 4.2.1 we obtain:

$$\lim_{n \to \infty} tr(Q[\mathcal{E}_1 \circ ([\![S]\!] \circ \mathcal{E}_1)^n(\rho)) = \lim_{n \to \infty} tr(QM_1([\![S]\!] \circ \mathcal{E}_1)^n(\rho)M_1^\dagger)$$

$$= \lim_{n \to \infty} tr(M_1^\dagger Q M_1([\![S]\!] \circ \mathcal{E}_1)^n(\rho))$$

$$= 0.$$

Consequently, it holds that

$$tr[(M_0^\dagger P M_0 + M_1^\dagger Q M_1)\rho] \leq \lim_{n \to \infty} \sum_{k=0}^{n} tr(P[\mathcal{E}_0 \circ ([\![S]\!] \circ \mathcal{E}_1)]^k(\rho))$$

$$+ \lim_{n \to \infty} tr(Q[\mathcal{E}_1 \circ ([\![S]\!] \circ \mathcal{E}_1)^n](\rho))$$

$$= \sum_{n=0}^{\infty} tr(P[\mathcal{E}_0 \circ ([\![S]\!] \circ \mathcal{E}_1)]^n(\rho))$$

$$= tr\left(P \sum_{n=0}^{\infty} [\mathcal{E}_0 \circ ([\![S]\!] \circ \mathcal{E}_1)^n](\rho)\right)$$

$$= tr\left(P[\![\textbf{while } M[\bar{q}] = 1 \textbf{ do } S \textbf{ od}]\!](\rho)\right).$$

□

Theorem 4.2.4 (Completeness). *The proof system qTD is complete for total correctness of quantum **while**-programs; that is, for any quantum program S and quantum predicates $P, Q \in \mathcal{P}(\mathcal{H}_{all})$, we have:*

$$\models_{tot} \{P\}S\{Q\} \text{ implies } \vdash_{qTD} \{P\}S\{Q\}.$$

Proof. Similar to the case of partial correctness, it suffices to prove the following:

- Claim:

$$\vdash_{qTD} \{wp.S.Q\}S\{Q\}$$

for any quantum program S and quantum predicate $P \in \mathcal{P}(\mathcal{H}_{all})$, because by Definition 4.2.3 (i) we have $P \sqsubseteq wp.S.Q$ when $\models_{tot} \{P\}S\{Q\}$. This claim can be proved by induction on the structure of S. We only consider the case of $S \equiv$ **while** $M[\bar{q}] = 1$ **do** S' **od**. The other cases are similar to the proof of Theorem 4.2.2.

We write **while** for quantum loop "**while** $M[\bar{q}] = 1$ **do** S' **od**". It follows from Proposition 4.2.4(i) that

$$wp.\textbf{while}.Q = M_0^\dagger Q M_0 + M_1^\dagger (wp.S'.(wp.\textbf{while}.Q))M_1.$$

So, our aim is to derive that

$$\vdash_{qTD} \left\{ M_0^\dagger Q M_0 + M_1^\dagger (wp.S'.(wp.\textbf{while}.Q))M_1 \right\} \textbf{while}\{Q\}.$$

By the induction hypothesis on S' we get:

$$\vdash_{qTD} \left\{ wp.S'.(wp.\textbf{while}.Q) \right\} S'\{wp.\textbf{while}.Q\}.$$

Then by the rule (R-LT) it suffices to show that for any $\epsilon > 0$, there exists a $(M_1^\dagger (wp.S'.(wp.\textbf{while}.Q))M_1, \epsilon)$-bound function of the quantum loop **while**. Applying Lemma 4.2.1, we only need to prove:

$$\lim_{n \to \infty} tr\left(M_1^\dagger (wp.S'.(wp.\textbf{while}.Q))M_1(\llbracket S' \rrbracket \circ \mathcal{E}_1)^n(\rho) \right) = 0. \tag{4.18}$$

The proof of equation (4.18) is carried out in two steps. First, by Propositions 4.2.2 (iv) and 3.3.1 (iv) we observe:

$$
\begin{aligned}
&tr\left(M_1^\dagger(wp.S'.(wp.\textbf{while}.Q))M_1([\![S']\!] \circ \mathcal{E}_1)^n(\rho))\right) \\
&= tr\left(wp.S'.(wp.\textbf{while}.Q)M_1([\![S']\!] \circ \mathcal{E}_1)^n(\rho)M_1^\dagger)\right) \\
&= tr\left(wp.\textbf{while}.Q[\![S']\!]\left(M_1([\![S']\!] \circ \mathcal{E}_1)^n(\rho)M_1^\dagger)\right)\right) \\
&= tr\left(wp.\textbf{while}.Q([\![S']\!] \circ \mathcal{E}_1)^{n+1}(\rho))\right) \\
&= tr\left(Q[\![\textbf{while}]\!]([\![S']\!] \circ \mathcal{E}_1)^{n+1}(\rho))\right) \\
&= \sum_{k=n+1}^{\infty} tr\left(Q\left[\mathcal{E}_0 \circ ([\![S']\!] \circ \mathcal{E}_1)^k\right](\rho))\right).
\end{aligned}
$$

(4.19)

Secondly, we consider the following infinite series of nonnegative real numbers:

$$
\sum_{n=0}^{\infty} tr\left(Q\left[\mathcal{E}_0 \circ ([\![S']\!] \circ \mathcal{E}_1)^k\right](\rho)\right) = tr\left(Q\sum_{n=0}^{\infty}\left[\mathcal{E}_0 \circ ([\![S']\!] \circ \mathcal{E}_1)^k\right](\rho)\right).
$$

(4.20)

Since $Q \sqsubseteq I_{\mathcal{H}_{all}}$, it follows from Propositions 3.3.1 (iv) and 3.3.4 that

$$
\begin{aligned}
tr\left(Q\sum_{n=0}^{\infty}\left[\mathcal{E}_0 \circ ([\![S']\!] \circ \mathcal{E}_1)^k\right](\rho)\right) &= tr(Q[\![\textbf{while}]\!](\rho)) \\
&\leq tr([\![\textbf{while}]\!](\rho)) \\
&\leq tr(\rho) \leq 1.
\end{aligned}
$$

Therefore, the infinite series in equation (4.20) converges. Note that equation (4.19) is the sum of the remaining terms of the infinite series in equation (4.20) after the nth term. Then convergence of the infinite series in equation (4.20) implies equation (4.18), and we complete the proof. □

It should be pointed out that, as remarked for Theorem 4.2.2, the preceding theorem is also merely a relative completeness of the proof system qTD with respect to the theory of the fields of complex numbers because, except that the rule (R-Or) is employed in qTD, the existence of bound functions in the rule (R-LT) is a statement about complex numbers too.

4.2.5 AN ILLUSTRATIVE EXAMPLE: REASONING ABOUT THE GROVER ALGORITHM

In the last two subsections, we developed the proof system qPD for partial correctness and qTD for total correctness of quantum **while**-programs, and established their soundness and (relative) completeness. The purpose of this subsection is to show how the proof systems qPD and qTD can actually be used to verify correctness of quantum programs. We consider the Grover quantum search algorithm as an example.

Recall from Subsection 2.3.3 and Section 3.5 the search problem can be stated as follows. The search space consists of $N = 2^n$ elements, indexed by numbers $0, 1, \ldots, N - 1$. It is assumed that the search problem has exactly L solutions with $1 \leq L \leq \frac{N}{2}$, and we are supplied with an oracle – a black box with the ability to recognize solutions to the search problem. Each element $x \in \{0, 1, \ldots, N - 1\}$ is identified with its binary representation $x \in \{0, 1\}^n$. In the quantum **while**-language, the Grover algorithm solving this problem can be written as the program *Grover* in Figure 4.4, where:

- **Program:**

  1. $q_0 := |0\rangle;\ q_1 := |0\rangle;\ \ldots\ldots;\ q_{n-1} := |0\rangle;$
  2. $q := |0\rangle;$
  3. $r := |0\rangle;$
  4. $q := X[q];$
  5. $q_0 := H[q_0];\ q_1 := H[q_1];\ \ldots\ldots;\ q_{n-1} := H[q_{n-1}];$
  6. $q := H[q];$
  7. **while** $M[r] = 1$ **do** D **od**;
  8. **if** $(\Box x \cdot M'[q_0, q_1, \ldots, q_{n-1}] = x \rightarrow$ **skip**$)$ **fi**

FIGURE 4.4

Quantum search program *grover*.

- $q_0, q_1, \ldots, q_{n-1}, q$ are quantum variables with type **Boolean** and r with type **integer**;
- X is the NOT gate and H the Hadamard gate;
- $M = \{M_0, M_1\}$ is a measurement with

$$M_0 = \sum_{l \geq k} |l\rangle_r \langle l|, \quad M_1 = \sum_{l < k} |l\rangle_r \langle l|,$$

and k being a positive integer in the interval $\left[\frac{\pi}{2\theta} - 1, \frac{\pi}{2\theta}\right]$ with θ being determined by the equation

$$\cos \frac{\theta}{2} = \sqrt{\frac{N - L}{2}} \quad (0 \leq \theta \leq \frac{\pi}{2});$$

- M' is the measurement in the computational basis of n qubits; that is,

$$M' = \{M'_x : x \in \{0, 1\}^n\}$$

with $M'_x = |x\rangle\langle x|$ for every x;

- D is the subprogram given in Figure 4.5.

- **Loop Body:**

    1. $q_0, q_1, \ldots, q_{n-1}, q := O[q_0, q_1, \ldots, q_{n-1}, q]$;
    2. $q_0 := H[q_0]$; $q_1 := H[q_1]$; $\ldots \ldots$; $q_{n-1} := H[q_{n-1}]$;
    3. $q_0, q_1, \ldots, q_{n-1} := Ph[q_0, q_1, \ldots, q_{n-1}]$;
    4. $q_0 := H[q_0]$; $q_1 := H[q_1]$; $\ldots \ldots$; $q_{n-1} := H[q_{n-1}]$;
    5. $r := r + 1$

FIGURE 4.5

Loop body D.

In Figure 4.5, O is the oracle represented by the unitary operator on $n + 1$ qubits:

$$|x\rangle|q\rangle \xrightarrow{O} |x\rangle|q \oplus f(x)\rangle$$

for all $x \in \{0, 1\}^n$ and $q \in \{0, 1\}$, where $f : \{0, 1\}^n \to \{0, 1\}$ defined by

$$f(x) = \begin{cases} 1 & \text{if } x \text{ is a solution,} \\ 0 & \text{otherwise} \end{cases}$$

is the characteristic function of solutions. The gate Ph is a conditional phase shift:

$$|0\rangle \to |0\rangle, \quad |x\rangle \to -|x\rangle \quad \text{for all } x \neq 0;$$

that is, $Ph = 2|0\rangle\langle 0| - I$.

Correctness Formula for Grover Search:

It was shown in Subsection 2.3.3 that the Grover algorithm can achieve success probability

$$\Pr(\text{success}) = \sin^2\left(\frac{2k + 1}{2}\theta\right) \geq \frac{N - L}{N}$$

where k is the integer closest to the real number

$$\frac{\arccos\sqrt{\frac{L}{N}}}{\theta};$$

that is, k is an integer in the interval $\left[\frac{\pi}{2\theta} - 1, \frac{\pi}{2\theta}\right]$. The success probability is at least one-half because $L \leq \frac{N}{2}$. In particular, if $L \ll N$, then it is very high. Using the ideas introduced in the previous subsections, this fact can be expressed by the total correctness of the program $Grover$:

$$\models_{tot} \{p_{succ}I\}Grover\{P\},$$

where the precondition is the product of the success probability $p_{succ} \overset{\triangle}{=} \Pr(\text{success})$ and the identity operator:

$$I = \bigotimes_{i=0}^{n-1} I_{q_i} \otimes I_q \otimes I_r,$$

and the postcondition is defined by

$$P = \left(\sum_{t \text{ solution}} |t\rangle_{\overline{q}} \langle t| \right) \otimes I_q \otimes I_r,$$

I_{q_i} ($i = 0, 1, \ldots, n-1$) and I_q are the identity operator in $\mathcal{H}_2$ (type **Boolean**), I_r is the identity operator in $\mathcal{H}_\infty$ (type **integer**) and $\overline{q} = q_0, q_1, \ldots, q_{n-1}$.

To avoid an overly complicated calculation, we choose to consider a very special case: $L = 1$ and $k = \frac{\pi}{2\theta} - \frac{1}{2}$ is the midpoint of the interval $\left[\frac{\pi}{2\theta} - 1, \frac{\pi}{2\theta} \right]$. In this case, there is a unique solution, say s, and the postcondition

$$P = |s\rangle_{\overline{q}} \langle s| \otimes I_q \otimes I_r.$$

Also, we have $p_{succ} = 1$. So, what we need to prove is then simply

$$\models_{tot} \{I\} Grover \{P\}.$$

By the soundness of qTD (Theorem 4.2.3), it suffices to show that

$$\vdash_{qTD} \{I\} Grover \{P\}. \tag{4.21}$$

We can prove it by using the proof rules presented in Figures 4.2 and 4.3.

Verification of Loop Body D:

For better understanding, we divide the proof of equation (4.21) into several steps. First, we verify the loop body D given in Figure 4.5. For this purpose, the following simple lemma is useful.

Lemma 4.2.2. *For each $i = 1, 2, \ldots, n$, suppose that $\overline{q}_i$ is a quantum register and U_i is a unitary operator in $\mathcal{H}_{\overline{q}_i}$. Let $U = U_n \ldots U_2 U_1$, where U_i actually stands for its cylinder extension in $\bigotimes_{i=1}^n \mathcal{H}_{\overline{q}_i}$ for every $i \leq n$. Then for any quantum predicate P, we have:*

$$\vdash_{qPD} \{U^\dagger P U\} \overline{q}_1 := U_1[\overline{q}_1]; \overline{q}_2 := U_2[\overline{q}_2]; \ldots; \overline{q}_n := U_n[\overline{q}_n] \{P\}.$$

Proof. By repeatedly using the axiom (Ax-UT). $\qquad\qquad\square$

With the previous lemma, we can prove the correctness of loop body D. First, it is easy to see that

$$\sum_{t \in \{0, q\}^n} M_t'^\dagger P M_t' = P.$$

By the axiom (Ax-Sk) and the rule (R-IF) we obtain:

$$\vdash_{qTD} \{P\}\text{if } (\Box x \cdot M'[q_0, q_1, \ldots, q_{n-1}] = x \to \textbf{skip}) \textbf{ fi}\{P\} \tag{4.22}$$

We put:

$$P' = |s\rangle_{\overline{q}}\langle s| \otimes |-\rangle_q \langle -| \otimes |k\rangle_r \langle k|,$$

$$|\psi_l\rangle = \cos\left[\frac{\pi}{2} + (l-k)\theta\right]|\alpha\rangle + \sin\left[\frac{\pi}{2} + (l-k)\theta\right]|s\rangle$$

for every integer l, and

$$Q = \sum_{l<k}(|\psi_l\rangle_{\overline{q}}\langle\psi_l| \otimes |-\rangle_q\langle-| \otimes |l\rangle_r\langle l|).$$

Then we have:

$$M_0^\dagger P' M_0 + M_1^\dagger Q M_1 = \sum_{l\leq k}(|\psi_l\rangle_{\overline{q}}\langle\psi_l| \otimes |-\rangle_q\langle-| \otimes |l\rangle_r\langle l|),$$

$$(G^\dagger \otimes I_q \otimes U_{+1}^\dagger)(M_0^\dagger P' M_0 + M_1^\dagger Q M_1)(G \otimes I_q \otimes U_{+1})$$
$$= \sum_{l\leq k}(|\psi_{l-1}\rangle_{\overline{q}}\langle\psi_{l-1}| \otimes |-\rangle_q\langle-| \otimes |l-1\rangle_r\langle l-1|)$$
$$= Q$$

where G is the Grover rotation defined in Figure 2.2 (see Subsection 2.3.3). Thus, it follows from Lemma 4.2.2 that

$$\vdash_{qTD} \{Q\}D\{M_0^\dagger P' M_0 + M_1^\dagger Q M_1\}.$$

Termination of Loop "**while** $M[r] = 1$ **do** D **od**":
A key step in proving the correctness of the Grover algorithm is to show termination of the loop in line 8 of Figure 4.4. We define a bound function

$$t : \mathcal{D}(\mathcal{H}_{\overline{q}} \otimes \mathcal{H}_q \otimes \mathcal{H}_r) \to \mathbb{N}$$

as follows:

- if $\rho \in \mathcal{D}(\mathcal{H}_{\overline{q}} \otimes \mathcal{H}_q \otimes \mathcal{H}_r)$ can be written as

$$\rho = \sum_{l,t=-\infty}^{\infty} \rho_{lt} \otimes |l\rangle\langle t|$$

with ρ_{lt} being an operator (but not necessarily a partial density operator) in $\mathcal{H}_{\overline{q}} \otimes \mathcal{H}_q$ for all $-\infty \leq l, t \leq \infty$, then

$$t(\rho) = k - \max\{\max(l,t)|\rho_{lt} \neq 0 \text{ and } l, t \leq k\}.$$

Then we have:

$$[\![D]\!](M_1 \rho M_1^\dagger) = [\![D]\!]\left(\sum_{l,t<k} \rho_{l,t} \otimes |l\rangle_r\langle t|\right)$$

$$= \sum_{l,t<k}\left[(G \otimes I_q)\,\rho_{lt}\left(G^\dagger \otimes I_q\right) \otimes |l+1\rangle_r\langle t+1|\right],$$

and it follows that

$$t([\![D]\!](M_1 \rho M_1^\dagger)) < t(\rho),$$

where G is the Grover rotation. So, t is a $(M_1^\dagger Q M_1, \epsilon)$-bound function for any ϵ. By the rule (R-LT) we assert that

$$\vdash_{qTD} \{M_0^\dagger P'M_0 + M_1^\dagger QM_1\}\textbf{while } M[r]=1 \textbf{ do } D \textbf{ od}\{P'\}. \tag{4.23}$$

Correctness of the Grover Algorithm:

Finally, we can assemble all the ingredients prepared before to prove the correctness of the Grover algorithm. Using the axiom (Ax-In) we obtain:

$$\left\{\bigotimes_{i=0}^{m-1}|0\rangle_{q_i}\langle 0| \otimes \bigotimes_{i=m}^{n-1} I_{q_i} \otimes I_q \otimes I_r\right\} q_m := |0\rangle \left\{\bigotimes_{i=0}^{m}|0\rangle_{q_i}\langle 0| \otimes \bigotimes_{i=m+1}^{n-1} I_{q_i} \otimes I_q \otimes I_r\right\}$$

for $m=0,1,\ldots n-1$, and they can be combined by the rule (R-SC) to yield:

$$\{I\}q_0 := |0\rangle; q_1 := |0\rangle; \ldots; q_{n-1} := |0\rangle \left\{\bigotimes_{i=0}^{n-1}|0\rangle_{q_i}\langle 0| \otimes I_q \otimes I_r\right\}$$

$$q := |0\rangle \left\{\bigotimes_{i=0}^{n-1}|0\rangle_{q_i}\langle 0| \otimes |0\rangle_q\langle 0| \otimes I_r\right\}$$

$$r := |0\rangle \left\{\bigotimes_{i=0}^{n-1}|0\rangle_{q_i}\langle 0| \otimes |0\rangle_q\langle 0| \otimes |0\rangle_r\langle 0|\right\}$$

$$q := X[q]; q_0 := H[q_0]; q_1 := H[q_1]; \ldots;$$
$$q_{n-1} := H[q_{n-1}]; q := H[q]\left\{|\psi\rangle_{\overline{q}}\langle\psi| \otimes |-\rangle_q\langle -| \otimes |0\rangle_r\langle -|\right\}, \tag{4.24}$$

where

$$|\psi\rangle = \frac{1}{\sqrt{2^n}}\sum_{x\in\{0,1\}^n}|x\rangle$$

is the equal superposition. Note that the last part of equation (4.24) is derived by Lemma 4.2.2 and the following equality:

$$\left[\left(H^{\dagger}\right)^{\otimes n} \otimes X^{\dagger}H^{\dagger} \otimes I_r\right]\left(|\psi\rangle_{\overline{q}}\langle\psi| \otimes |-\rangle_q\langle-| \otimes |0\rangle_r\langle0|\right)\left(H^{\otimes n} \otimes HX \otimes I_r\right)$$

$$= \bigotimes_{i=0}^{n-1} |0\rangle_{q_i}\langle0| \otimes |0\rangle_q\langle0| \otimes |0\rangle_r\langle0|.$$

It is obvious that $P' \sqsubseteq P$. On the other hand, it follows from the assumption $k = \frac{\pi}{2\theta} - \frac{1}{2}$ that $|\psi\rangle = |\psi_0\rangle$. Then we obtain:

$$|\psi\rangle_{\overline{q}}\langle\psi| \otimes |-\rangle_q\langle-| \otimes |0\rangle_r\langle0| = |\psi_0\rangle_{\overline{q}}\langle\psi_0| \otimes |-\rangle_q\langle-| \otimes |0\rangle_r\langle0|$$

$$\sqsubseteq M_0^{\dagger}P'M_0 + M_1^{\dagger}QM_1.$$

We complete the proof by using the rules (R-Or) and (R-SC) to combine equations (4.22), (4.23) and (4.24).

4.3 COMMUTATIVITY OF QUANTUM WEAKEST PRECONDITIONS

In the previous sections of this chapter, we have built a logical foundation for reasoning about correctness of quantum programs, including the quantum weakest precondition semantics and the Floyd-Hoare logic for quantum **while**-programs. This logical foundation is, of course, a generalization of the corresponding theories for classical and probabilistic programs, but it is certainly not a simple generalization. Indeed, it has to answer some problems that would not arise in the realm of classical and probabilistic programming. This section deals with one of these problems, namely (non-)commutativity of quantum predicates. The influence of other fundamental differences between quantum systems and classical systems on quantum programming will be revealed in Chapters 6 and 7 and discussed in Sections 8.5 and 8.6.

The significance of the (non-)commutativity problem of quantum predicates comes from the following observation that more than one predicate may be involved in specifying and reasoning about a complicated property of a quantum program, but:

- quantum predicates are observables, and their physical simultaneous verifiability depends on commutativity between them, according to the Heisenberg uncertainty principle (see [174], page 89).
- mathematically, a logical combination like conjunction and disjunction of two quantum predicates is well-defined only when they commute.

We consider the (non-)commutativity problem of quantum weakest preconditions defined in Section 4.1.1. For any two operators A and B in a Hilbert space $\mathcal{H}$, it is said that A and B commute if

$$AB = BA.$$

So, what concerns us is the question:

- Given a quantum operation $\mathcal{E} \in \mathcal{QO}(\mathcal{H})$ (as the denotational semantics of a quantum program). For two quantum predicates $M, N \in \mathcal{P}(\mathcal{H})$, when do $wp(\mathcal{E})(M)$ and $wp(\mathcal{E})(N)$ commute?

This question is interesting because one might need to deal with logical combinations of quantum predicates when reasoning about complicated quantum programs. For example, one might like to know whether the conjunction "M and N" is satisfied after a quantum program $\mathcal{E}$ is executed. Then she/he would consider whether the conjunction "$wp(\mathcal{E})(M)$ and $wp(\mathcal{E})(N)$" of weakest preconditions is satisfied before the program is executed. However, as pointed out previously, these conjunctions are well-defined only if the involved quantum predicates commute. (A further discussion about related issues is left as Problem 4.3.2 at the end of this section.)

Now we start to address this question. To warm up, we first see a simple example.

Example 4.3.1 (Bit flip and phase flip channels). *Bit flip and phase flip are quantum operations on a single qubit, and they are widely used in the theory of quantum error-correction. Let X, Y, Z stand for the Pauli matrices (see Example 2.2.2).*

- *The bit flip is defined by*

$$\mathcal{E}(\rho) = E_0 \rho E_0^{\dagger} + E_1 \rho E_1^{\dagger}, \tag{4.25}$$

where $E_0 = \sqrt{p}I$ and $E_1 = \sqrt{1-p}X$. It is easy to see that $wp(\mathcal{E})(M)$ and $wp(\mathcal{E})(N)$ commute when $MN = NM$ and $MXN = NXM$.
- *If E_1 in equation (4.25) is replaced by $\sqrt{1-p}Z$ (respectively $\sqrt{1-p}Y$), then $\mathcal{E}$ is the phase flip (respectively bit-phase flip), and $wp(\mathcal{E})(M)$ and $wp(\mathcal{E})(N)$ commute when $MN = NM$ and $MZN = NZM$ (respectively $MYN = NYM$).*

Secondly, we consider two simplest classes of quantum operations: unitary transformations and projective measurements.

Proposition 4.3.1

(i) *Let $\mathcal{E} \in \mathcal{QO}(\mathcal{H})$ be a unitary transformation; that is,*

$$\mathcal{E}(\rho) = U\rho U^{\dagger}$$

for any $\rho \in \mathcal{D}(\mathcal{H})$, where U is a unitary operator in $\mathcal{H}$. Then $wp(\mathcal{E})(M)$ and $wp(\mathcal{E})(N)$ commute if and only if M and N commute.

(ii) *Let $\{P_k\}$ be a projective measurement in $\mathcal{H}$; that is, $P_{k_1}P_{k_2} = \delta_{k_1 k_2}P_{k_1}$ and $\sum_k P_k = I_{\mathcal{H}}$, where*

$$\delta_{k_1 k_2} = \begin{cases} 1, & \text{if } k_1 = k_2, \\ 0, & \text{otherwise.} \end{cases}$$

If $\mathcal{E}$ is given by this measurement, with the result of the measurement unknown:

$$\mathcal{E}(\rho) = \sum_k P_k \rho P_k$$

for each $\rho \in \mathcal{D}(\mathcal{H})$, then $wp(\mathcal{E})(M)$ and $wp(\mathcal{E})(N)$ commute if and only if $P_k M P_k$ and $P_k N P_k$ commute for all indices k.
In particular, let $\{|i\rangle\}$ be an orthonormal basis of $\mathcal{H}$. If $\mathcal{E}$ is given by the measurement in the basis $\{|i\rangle\}$:

$$\mathcal{E}(\rho) = \sum_i P_i \rho P_i,$$

where $P_i = |i\rangle\langle i|$ for each basis state $|i\rangle$, then $wp(\mathcal{E})(M)$ and $wp(\mathcal{E})(N)$ commute for any $M, N \in \mathcal{P}(\mathcal{H})$.

Exercise 4.3.1. *Prove Proposition 4.3.1.*

After dealing with the previous example and special case, we now consider the weakest preconditions with respect to a general quantum operation $\mathcal{E}$. Unfortunately, we are only able to give some useful sufficient (but not necessary) conditions for commutativity of $wp(\mathcal{E})(M)$ and $wp(\mathcal{E})(N)$.

As usual, we consider two representations of $\mathcal{E}$, namely the Kraus operator-sum representation and the system-environment model. Let us first work in the case where quantum operation $\mathcal{E}$ is given in the Kraus operator-sum form. The following proposition presents a sufficient condition for commutativity of $wp(\mathcal{E})(M)$ and $wp(\mathcal{E})(N)$ in the case where M and N already commute.

Proposition 4.3.2. *Suppose that $\mathcal{H}$ is finite-dimensional. Let $M, N \in \mathcal{P}(\mathcal{H})$ and they commute, i.e., there exists an orthonormal basis $\{|\psi_i\rangle\}$ of $\mathcal{H}$ such that*

$$M = \sum_i \lambda_i |\psi_i\rangle\langle\psi_i|, \quad N = \sum_i \mu_i |\psi_i\rangle\langle\psi_i|$$

where λ_i, μ_i are reals for each i ([174], Theorem 2.2), and let quantum operation $\mathcal{E} \in \mathcal{SO}(\mathcal{H})$ be represented by the set $\{E_i\}$ of operators, i.e. $\mathcal{E} = \sum_i E_i \circ E_i^\dagger$. If for any i, j, k, l, we have either $\lambda_k \mu_l = \lambda_l \mu_k$ or

$$\sum_m \langle\psi_k|E_i|\psi_m\rangle\langle\psi_l|E_j|\psi_m\rangle = 0,$$

then $wp(\mathcal{E})(M)$ and $wp(\mathcal{E})(N)$ commute.

Exercise 4.3.2. *Prove Proposition 4.3.2.*

To present another sufficient condition for commutativity of quantum weakest preconditions, we need to introduce commutativity between a quantum operation and a quantum predicate.

Definition 4.3.1. *Let quantum operation $\mathcal{E} \in \mathcal{QO}(\mathcal{H})$ be represented by the set $\{E_i\}$ of operators, i.e., $\mathcal{E} = \sum_i E_i \circ E_i^\dagger$, and let quantum predicate $M \in \mathcal{P}(\mathcal{H})$. Then we say that M and $\mathcal{E}$ commute if M and E_i commute for each i.*

It seems that in this definition commutativity between quantum predicate M and quantum program $\mathcal{E}$ depends on the choice of operators E_i in the Kraus representation of $\mathcal{E}$. Thus, one may wonder if this definition is intrinsic because the Kraus operators E_i are not unique. To address this problem, we need the following:

Lemma 4.3.1 ([174], Theorem 8.2). *(Unitary freedom in the operator-sum representation) Suppose that $\{E_i\}$ and $\{F_j\}$ are operator elements giving rise to quantum operations $\mathcal{E}$ and $\mathcal{F}$, respectively; that is,*

$$\mathcal{E} = \sum_i E_i \circ E_i^\dagger, \quad \mathcal{F} = \sum_j F_j \circ F_j^\dagger.$$

By appending zero operators to the shortest list of operation elements we may ensure that the numbers of E_i and F_j are the same. Then $\mathcal{E} = \mathcal{F}$ if and only if there exist complex numbers u_{ij} such that

$$E_i = \sum_j u_{ij} F_j$$

for all i, and $U = (u_{ij})$ is (the matrix representation of) a unitary operator.

As a simple corollary, we can see that the definition of commutativity between a quantum predicate M and a quantum operation $\mathcal{E}$ does not depend on the choice of the Kraus representation operators of $\mathcal{E}$.

Lemma 4.3.2. *The notion of commutativity between observables and quantum operations is well-defined. More precisely, suppose that $\mathcal{E}$ is represented by both $\{E_i\}$ and $\{F_j\}$:*

$$\mathcal{E} = \sum_i E_i \circ E_i^\dagger = \sum_j F_j \circ F_j^\dagger.$$

Then M and E_i commute for all i if and only if M and F_j commute for all j.

Furthermore, commutativity between observables and quantum operations is preserved by composition of quantum operations.

Proposition 4.3.3. *Let $M \in \mathcal{P}(\mathcal{H})$ be a quantum predicate, and let $\mathcal{E}_1, \mathcal{E}_2 \in \mathcal{QO}(\mathcal{H})$ be two quantum operations. If M and $\mathcal{E}_i$ commute for $i = 1, 2$, then M commutes with the composition $\mathcal{E}_1 \circ \mathcal{E}_2$ of $\mathcal{E}_1$ and $\mathcal{E}_2$.*

Exercise 4.3.3. *Prove Proposition 4.3.3.*

The following proposition gives another sufficient condition for commutativity of $wp(\mathcal{E})(M)$ and $wp(\mathcal{E})(N)$ also in the case where M and N commute. This condition is presented in terms of commutativity of quantum operations and quantum predicates.

Proposition 4.3.4. *Let $M, N \in \mathcal{P}(\mathcal{H})$ be two quantum predicates, and let $\mathcal{E} \in \mathcal{QO}(\mathcal{H})$ be a quantum operation. If M and N commute, M and $\mathcal{E}$ commute, and N and $\mathcal{E}$ commute, then $wp(\mathcal{E})(M)$ and $wp(\mathcal{E})(N)$ commute.*

Exercise 4.3.4. *Prove Proposition 4.3.4.*

Now we turn to consider the system-environment model of quantum operation:

$$\mathcal{E}(\rho) = tr_E \left[PU \left(|e_0\rangle\langle e_0| \otimes \rho\right) U^\dagger P \right] \tag{4.26}$$

for all density operators ρ in $\mathcal{H}$, where E is an environment system of which the state Hilbert space is $\mathcal{H}_E$, U is a unitary operator in $\mathcal{H}_E \otimes \mathcal{H}$, P is a projector onto a closed subspace of $\mathcal{H}_E \otimes \mathcal{H}$, and $|e_0\rangle$ is a given state in $\mathcal{H}_E$. To this end, we need two generalized notions of commutativity between linear operators.

Definition 4.3.2. *Let $M, N, A, B, C \in \mathcal{L}(\mathcal{H})$ be operators in $\mathcal{H}$. Then:*

(i) *We say that M and N (A, B, C)-commute if*

$$AMBNC = ANBMC.$$

In particular, it is simply said that M and N A-commute when M and N (A, A, A)-commute;

(ii) *We say that A and B conjugate-commute if*

$$AB^\dagger = BA^\dagger.$$

Obviously, commutativity is exactly $I_{\mathcal{H}}$-commutativity.

The next two propositions present several sufficient conditions for commutativity of quantum weakest preconditions when quantum operation $\mathcal{E}$ is given in the system-environment model.

Proposition 4.3.5. *Let quantum operation $\mathcal{E}$ be given by equation (4.26), and we write $A = PU|e_0\rangle$. Then:*

(i) *$wp(\mathcal{E})(M)$ and $wp(\mathcal{E})(N)$ commute if and only if $M \otimes I_E$ and $N \otimes I_E$ $(A^\dagger, AA^\dagger, A)$-commute;*

(ii) *$wp(\mathcal{E})(M)$ and $wp(\mathcal{E})(N)$ commute whenever $(M \otimes I_E)A$ and $(N \otimes I_E)A$ conjugate-commute,*

where $I_E = I_{\mathcal{H}_E}$ is the identity operator in $\mathcal{H}_E$.

Proposition 4.3.6. *Suppose that $\mathcal{H}$ is finite-dimensional. Let $\mathcal{E}$ be given by equation (4.26), and let $M, N \in \mathcal{P}(\mathcal{H})$ be quantum predicates and they commute, i.e., there exists an orthonormal basis $\{|\psi_i\rangle\}$ of $\mathcal{H}$ such that*

$$M = \sum_i \lambda_i |\psi_i\rangle\langle\psi_i|, \quad N = \sum_i \mu_i |\psi_i\rangle\langle\psi_i|$$

where λ_i, μ_i are reals for each i. If for any i, j, k, l, we have $\lambda_i \mu_j = \lambda_j \mu_i$ or

$$\langle e_0 | U^\dagger P | \psi_i e_k \rangle \perp \langle e_0 | U^\dagger P | \psi_j e_l \rangle,$$

then $wp(\mathcal{E})(M)$ and $wp(\mathcal{E})(N)$ commute.

Exercise 4.3.5. *Prove Propositions 4.3.5 and 4.3.6.*

Obviously, (non-)commutativity of quantum weakest preconditions is still not fully understood. To conclude this section, we propose two problems for further studies.

Problem 4.3.1. *The main results obtained in this section for commutativity of the weakest preconditions wp($\mathcal{E}$)(M) and wp($\mathcal{E}$)(N) (Propositions 4.3.2, 4.3.4 and 4.3.6) deal with the special case where M and N commute. So, an interesting problem is to find a sufficient and necessary condition for commutativity of wp($\mathcal{E}$)(M) and wp($\mathcal{E}$)(N) of a general quantum operation $\mathcal{E}$ in the case where M and N may not commute.*

An even more general problem would be: How to characterize [wp($\mathcal{E}$)(M), wp($\mathcal{E}$)(N)] in terms of [M, N], where for any operators X and Y, [X, Y] stands for their commutator, i.e., [X, Y] = XY − YX?

Problem 4.3.2. *Various healthiness conditions for predicate transformer semantics of classical programs were introduced by Dijkstra [75], e.g., conjunctivity and disjunctivity. These conditions were also carefully examined for probabilistic predicate transformers [166]. An interesting problem is to study healthiness conditions for quantum predicate transformers in the light of noncommutativity of quantum predicates. Note that this problem was considered in [225] for a special class of quantum predicates, namely projection operators.*

4.4 BIBLIOGRAPHIC REMARKS

Birkhoff-von Neumann quantum logic mentioned in Section 4.1 was first introduced in [42]. After development over 80 years, it has become a rich subject at the intersection of logic and quantum foundations; for a systematic exposition, see book [62].

The notion of quantum predicate as a Hermitian operator was conceived by D'Hondt and Panangaden, and the notion of quantum weakest precondition was first introduced by them in the seminal paper [70].

The exposition of Floyd-Hoare logic for quantum programs in Section 4.2 is based on [221]. Several other approaches to quantum Floyd-Hoare logic were briefly discussed in Subsection 1.1.3. In addition, Kakutani [132] proposed an extension of Hartog's probabilistic Hoare logic [114] for reasoning about quantum programs written in Selinger's language QPL [194]. Adams [8] defined a logic QPEL (Quantum Program and Effect Language) and its categorical semantics in terms of state-and-effect triangles.

The discussion about (non-)commutativity of quantum weakest preconditions given in Section 4.3 is based on [224]. A basis for solving Problem 4.3.2 is lattice-theoretic operations of quantum predicates (i.e., quantum effects), which have been widely studied in the mathematical literature since the 1950s; see for example [110,131].

Analysis of quantum programs

5

Chapter 4 developed logical tools for reasoning about correctness of quantum programs. This chapter turns to algorithmic analysis of the behavior of quantum programs, with a focus on termination analysis. The theoretical results and algorithms presented in this chapter will be useful for the design of compilers for quantum programming languages and optimization of quantum programs.

The chapter is organized as follows:

- In Section 5.1, we examine the behavior of quantum extension of the **while**-loop defined in Section 3.1, including termination and average running time. This section is divided into three subsections: Subsection 5.1.1 considers a class of simple quantum loops with a unitary operator as their body, Subsection 5.1.2 further deals with quantum loops with a general quantum operation as their body, and Subsection 5.1.3 presents an example that computes the average running time of a quantum walk on an n-circle.

- Motivated by quantum **while**-loops, we identify quantum Markov chains as the semantic model of quantum programs. Furthermore, we argue that termination analysis of quantum programs can be reduced to the reachability problem of quantum Markov chains. Reachability analysis techniques for classical Markov chains heavily depend on algorithms for graph-reachability problems. Likewise, a kind of graphical structure in Hilbert spaces, called quantum graphs, play a crucial role in the reachability analysis of quantum Markov chains. So, Section 5.2 gives an introduction to quantum graph theory, which provides a mathematical basis of Section 5.3.

- In Section 5.3, we study the reachability problems for quantum Markov chains. In particular, we present several (classical) algorithms for computing the reachability, repeated reachability and persistence probabilities of quantum Markov chains.

- For readability, the proofs of several technical lemmas in Sections 5.1 to 5.3 are postponed to the last section of this chapter, Section 5.4.

Since our main aim is to develop algorithms for analyzing quantum programs, the state Hilbert spaces considered in this chapter are always assumed to be finite-dimensional. Although a few results in this chapter may also be used in an infinite-dimensional state Hilbert space, the majority cannot be. Analysis of quantum programs in infinite-dimensional state spaces is a challenging problem and requires radically new ideas, and it should be a very important topic for future research.

5.1 TERMINATION ANALYSIS OF QUANTUM WHILE-LOOPS

As in classical programming, difficulty in the analysis of quantum programs essentially comes from loops and recursions. This section focuses on the quantum extension of the **while**-loop introduced in Section 3.1. We mainly consider termination of a quantum loop, but its average running time is also briefly discussed.

5.1.1 QUANTUM WHILE-LOOPS WITH UNITARY BODIES

To ease understanding, let us start from a special form of quantum **while**-loop:

$$S \equiv \textbf{while } M[\overline{q}] = 1 \textbf{ do } \overline{q} := U[\overline{q}] \textbf{ od} \tag{5.1}$$

where:

- $\overline{q}$ denotes quantum register $q_1, \ldots, q_n$, and its state Hilbert space is $\mathcal{H} = \bigotimes_{i=1}^{n} \mathcal{H}_{q_i}$;
- the loop body is the unitary transformation $\overline{q} := U[\overline{q}]$ with U being a unitary operator in $\mathcal{H}$;
- the yes-no measurement $M = \{M_0, M_1\}$ in the loop guard is projective; that is, $M_0 = P_{X^\perp}$ and $M_1 = P_X$ with X being a subspace of $\mathcal{H}$ and $X^\perp$ being the orthocomplement of X (see Definition 2.1.7(ii)).

The execution of the quantum loop S in equation (5.1) is clearly described by its operational and denotational semantics presented in Sections 3.2 and 3.3. To help the reader further understand the behavior of loop S, here we examine its computational process in a slightly different manner. For any input state $\rho \in \mathcal{D}(\mathcal{H})$, the behavior of the loop S can be described in the following unwound way:

(i) *Initial step*: The loop performs the projective measurement

$$M = \{M_0 = P_{X^\perp}, M_1 = P_X\}$$

on the input state ρ. If the outcome is 1, then the program performs the unitary operation U on the post-measurement state. Otherwise, the program terminates. More precisely, we have:

- The loop terminates with probability

$$p_T^{(1)}(\rho) = tr(P_{X^\perp}\rho).$$

In this case, the output at this step is

$$\rho_{out}^{(1)} = \frac{P_{X^\perp} \rho P_{X^\perp}}{p_T^{(1)}(\rho)}.$$

- The loop continues with probability

$$p_{NT}^{(1)}(\rho) = 1 - p_T^{(1)}(\rho) = tr(P_X \rho).$$

In this case, the program state after the measurement is

$$\rho_{mid}^{(1)} = \frac{P_X \rho P_X}{p_{NT}^{(1)}(\rho)}.$$

Furthermore, $\rho_{mid}^{(1)}$ is fed to the unitary operation U and then the state

$$\rho_{in}^{(2)} = U \rho_{mid}^{(1)} U^\dagger$$

is returned. Note that $\rho_{in}^{(2)}$ will be used as the input state in the next step.

(ii) *Induction step*: Suppose that the loop has run n steps, and it did not terminate at the nth step; that is, $p_{NT}^{(n)} > 0$. If $\rho_{in}^{(n+1)}$ is the program state at the end of the nth step, then in the $(n+1)$th step, $\rho_{in}^{(n+1)}$ is the input, and we have:

- The termination probability is

$$p_T^{(n+1)}(\rho) = tr(P_{X^\perp} \rho_{in}^{(n+1)})$$

and the output at this step is

$$\rho_{out}^{(n+1)} = \frac{P_{X^\perp} \rho_{in}^{(n+1)} P_{X^\perp}}{p_T^{(n+1)}(\rho)}.$$

- The loop continues to perform the unitary operation U on the post-measurement state

$$\rho_{mid}^{(n+1)} = \frac{P_X \rho_{in}^{(n+1)} P_X}{p_{NT}^{(n+1)}(\rho)}$$

with probability

$$p_{NT}^{(n+1)}(\rho) = 1 - p_T^{(n+1)}(\rho) = tr(P_X \rho_{in}^{(n+1)}),$$

and the state

$$\rho_{in}^{(n+2)} = U \rho_{mid}^{(n+1)} U^\dagger$$

will be returned. Then state $\rho_{in}^{(n+2)}$ will be the input of the $(n+2)$th step.

The reader may like to compare this description of the execution of quantum loop S with its semantics given in Section 3.2. Based on this description, we can introduce the notion of termination.

Definition 5.1.1

(i) *If probability* $p_{NT}^{(n)}(\rho) = 0$ *for some positive integer n, then we say that the loop* (5.1) *terminates from input* ρ.

(ii) *The nontermination probability of the loop* (5.1) *from input* ρ *is*

$$p_{NT}(\rho) = \lim_{n \to \infty} p_{NT}^{(\leq n)}(\rho)$$

where

$$p_{NT}^{(\leq n)}(\rho) = \prod_{i=1}^{n} p_{NT}^{(i)}(\rho)$$

denotes the probability that the loop does not terminate after n steps.

(iii) *We say that the loop* (5.1) *almost surely terminates from input* ρ *whenever nontermination probability* $p_{NT}(\rho) = 0$.

Intuitively, a quantum loop almost surely terminates if for any $\epsilon > 0$, there exists a large enough positive integer $n(\epsilon)$ such that the probability that the loop terminates within $n(\epsilon)$ steps is greater than $1 - \epsilon$.

In this definition, termination was considered for a single input. We can also define termination for all possible inputs.

Definition 5.1.2. *A quantum loop is terminating (respectively, almost surely terminating) if it terminates (respectively, almost surely terminates) from all input* $\rho \in \mathcal{D}(\mathcal{H})$.

In the computational process of a quantum loop, a density operator is taken as input, and a density operator is given as output with a certain probability at each step. Thus, we can obtain the overall output by synthesizing these density operators returned at all steps into a single one according to the respective probabilities. Note that sometimes the loop does not terminate with a nonzero probability. So, the synthesized output may not be a density operator but only a partial density operator, and thus a quantum loop defines a function from density operators to partial density operators in $\mathcal{H}$.

Definition 5.1.3. *The function* $\mathcal{F} : \mathcal{D}(\mathcal{H}) \to \mathcal{D}(\mathcal{H})$ *computed by the quantum loop* (5.1) *is defined by*

$$\mathcal{F}(\rho) = \sum_{n=1}^{\infty} p_{NT}^{(\leq n-1)}(\rho) \cdot p_T^{(n)}(\rho) \cdot \rho_{out}^{(n)}$$

for each $\rho \in \mathcal{D}(\mathcal{H})$.

It should be noted that in the defining equation of $\mathcal{F}(\rho)$ the quantity

$$p_{NT}^{(\leq n-1)}(\rho) \cdot p_T^{(n)}(\rho)$$

is the probability that the loop does not terminate at steps from 1 to $n-1$ but it terminates at the nth step.

For any operator A in the Hilbert space $\mathcal{H}$ and any subspace X of $\mathcal{H}$, we write:

$$A_X = P_X A P_X$$

where P_X is the projection onto X; that is, A_X is the restriction of A in X. Then the computational process of quantum loop (5.1) can be summarized as:

Lemma 5.1.1. *Let ρ be an input state to the loop (5.1). Then we have:*

(i)

$$p_{NT}^{(\leq n)}(\rho) = tr(U_X^{n-1} \rho_X U_X^{\dagger n-1})$$

for any positive integer n;

(ii)

$$\mathcal{F}(\rho) = P_{X^\perp} \rho P_{X^\perp} + P_{X^\perp} U \left(\sum_{n=0}^{\infty} U_X^n \rho_X U_X^{\dagger n} \right) U^\dagger P_{X^\perp},$$

where X is the subspace defining the projective measurement in the loop guard, and U is the unitary transformation in the loop body.

Exercise 5.1.1. *Prove Lemma 5.1.1.*

The following exercise further shows that the function computed by quantum loop S in equation (5.1) coincides with the denotational semantics of S according to Definition 3.3.1.

Exercise 5.1.2. *Prove that $\mathcal{F}(\rho) = [\![S]\!](\rho)$ for any $\rho \in \mathcal{D}(\mathcal{H})$.*

As shown in the following exercise, almost sure termination of a quantum loop can also be characterized in terms of the function computed by it.

Exercise 5.1.3. *Show that for each $\rho \in \mathcal{D}(\mathcal{H})$, we have:*

(i) $\langle \varphi | \mathcal{F}(\rho) | \psi \rangle = 0$ *if $|\varphi\rangle$ or $|\psi\rangle \in X$;*

(ii) $tr(\mathcal{F}(\rho)) = tr(\rho) - p_{NT}(\rho)$. *Thus, $tr(\mathcal{F}(\rho)) = tr(\rho)$ if and only if the loop (5.1) almost surely terminates from input state ρ.*

Termination:

Obviously, it is hard to decide directly by Definition 5.1.1 when the quantum loop (5.1) terminates. Now we try to find a necessary and sufficient condition for its termination. This can be done through several reduction steps.

First of all, the next lemma allows us to decompose an input density matrix into a sequence of simpler input density matrices when examining termination of a quantum loop.

Lemma 5.1.2. *Let* $\rho = \sum_i p_i \rho_i$ *with* $p_i > 0$ *for all* i. *Then the loop* (5.1) *terminates from input* ρ *if and only if it terminates from input* ρ_i *for all* i.

Exercise 5.1.4. *Prove Lemma 5.1.2.*

If $\{(p_i, |\psi_i\rangle)\}$ is an ensemble with $p_i > 0$ for all i, and density operator

$$\rho = \sum_i p_i |\psi_i\rangle\langle\psi_i|,$$

then the previous lemma asserts that the loop (5.1) terminates from input mixed state ρ if and only if it terminates from input pure state $|\psi_i\rangle$ for all i. In particular, we have:

Corollary 5.1.1. *A quantum loop is terminating if and only if it terminates from all pure input states.*

Secondly, the termination problem of a quantum loop may be reduced to a corresponding problem of a classical loop in the field of complex numbers. We decompose the subspace X and its ortho-complement $X^\perp$ defining the projective measurement in the guard of quantum loop (5.1). Let $\{|m_1\rangle, \ldots, |m_l\rangle\}$ be an orthonormal basis of $\mathcal{H}$ such that

$$\sum_{i=1}^{k} |m_i\rangle\langle m_i| = P_X \text{ and } \sum_{i=k+1}^{l} |m_i\rangle\langle m_i| = P_{X^\perp},$$

where $1 \leq k \leq l$. In other words, the basis $\{|m_1\rangle, \ldots, |m_l\rangle\}$ of $\mathcal{H}$ is divided into two parts $\{|m_1\rangle, \ldots, |m_k\rangle\}$ and $\{|m_{k+1}\rangle, \ldots, |m_l\rangle\}$ with the former being a basis of X and the latter a basis of $X^\perp$. Without any loss of generality, we assume in the sequel that the matrix representations of operators U (the unitary transformation in the loop body), U_X (the restriction of U in X), ρ_X (the restriction of input ρ in X), denoted also by U, U_X, ρ_X respectively for simplicity, are taken according to this basis. Also, for each pure state $|\psi\rangle$ we write $|\psi\rangle_X$ for the vector representation of projection $P_X|\psi\rangle$ in this basis.

Lemma 5.1.3. *The following two statements are equivalent:*

(i) *The quantum loop* (5.1) *terminates from input* $\rho \in \mathcal{D}(\mathcal{H})$;

(ii) $U_X^n \rho_X U_X^{\dagger n} = \mathbf{0}_{k \times k}$ *for some nonnegative integer n, where* $\mathbf{0}_{k \times k}$ *is the* $(k \times k)$-*zero matrix.*

In particular, it terminates from pure input state $|\psi\rangle$ *if and only if* $U_X^n |\psi\rangle_X = \mathbf{0}$ *for some nonnegative integer n, where* $\mathbf{0}$ *is the k-dimensional zero vector.*

Proof. This result follows from Lemma 5.1.1 (i) and the fact that $tr(A) = 0$ if and only if $A = \mathbf{0}$ when A is positive. $\qquad\square$

It should be noticed that the condition $U_X^n |\psi\rangle_X = \mathbf{0}$ in Lemma 5.1.3 is actually a termination condition for the following loop:

$$\textbf{while } \mathbf{v} \neq \mathbf{0} \textbf{ do } \mathbf{v} := U_X \mathbf{v} \textbf{ od} \tag{5.2}$$

This loop must be understood as a classical computation in the field of complex numbers.

Thirdly, we can show certain invariance of termination of a classical loop under a nonsingular transformation.

Lemma 5.1.4. *Let S be a nonsingular $(k \times k)$-complex matrix. Then the following two statements are equivalent:*

(i) *The classical loop (5.2) (with $\mathbf{v} \in \mathbf{C}^k$) terminates from input $\mathbf{v}_0 \in \mathbf{C}^k$.*
(ii) *The classical loop:*

$$\textbf{while } \mathbf{v} \neq \mathbf{0} \textbf{ do } \mathbf{v} := (SU_XS^{-1})\mathbf{v} \textbf{ od}$$

(with $\mathbf{v} \in \mathbf{C}^k$) terminates from input $S\mathbf{v}_0$.

Proof. Note that $S\mathbf{v} \neq \mathbf{0}$ if and only if $\mathbf{v} \neq \mathbf{0}$ because S is nonsingular. Then the conclusion follows from a simple calculation. □

Furthermore, we shall need the Jordan normal form theorem in the proof of the main results in this section. The proof of this normal form theorem can be found in any standard textbook on matrix theory; e.g., [40].

Lemma 5.1.5. *[Jordan normal form theorem] For any $(k \times k)$-complex matrix A, there is a nonsingular $(k \times k)$-complex matrix S such that*

$$A = SJ(A)S^{-1}$$

where

$$
\begin{aligned}
J(A) &= \bigoplus_{i=1}^{l} J_{k_i}(\lambda_i) \\
&= diag(J_{k_1}(\lambda_1), J_{k_2}(\lambda_2), \dots, J_{k_l}(\lambda_l)) \\
&= \begin{pmatrix} J_{k_1}(\lambda_1) & & & & \\ & J_{k_2}(\lambda_2) & & & \\ & & \ddots & & \\ & & & \ddots & \\ & & & & J_{k_l}(\lambda_l) \end{pmatrix}
\end{aligned}
$$

is the Jordan normal form of A, $\sum_{i=1}^{l} k_i = k$, and

$$
J_{k_i}(\lambda_i) = \begin{pmatrix} \lambda_i & 1 & & & \\ & \lambda_i & 1 & & \\ & & \ddots & \ddots & \\ & & & \ddots & 1 \\ & & & & \lambda_i \end{pmatrix}. \tag{5.3}
$$

is a $(k_i \times k_i)$-Jordan block for each $1 \leq i \leq l$. Furthermore, if the Jordan blocks corresponding to each distinct eigenvalue are presented in decreasing order of the *block size, then the Jordan normal form is uniquely determined once the ordering of the eigenvalues is given.*

The following technical lemma about the powers of Jordan blocks is also needed in the discussions following.

Lemma 5.1.6. *Let $J_r(\lambda)$ be a $(r \times r)$-Jordan block and $\mathbf{v}$ an r-dimensional complex vector. Then*

$$J_r(\lambda)^n \mathbf{v} = \mathbf{0}$$

for some nonnegative integer n if and only if $\lambda = 0$ or $\mathbf{v} = \mathbf{0}$, where $\mathbf{0}$ is the r-dimensional zero vector.

Proof. The "if" part is clear. We now prove the "only if" part. By a routine calculation we obtain:

$$J_r(\lambda)^n = \begin{pmatrix} \lambda^n & \binom{n}{1}\lambda^{n-1} & \binom{n}{2}\lambda^{n-2} & \cdots & \binom{n}{r-2}\lambda^{n-r+2} & \binom{n}{r-1}\lambda^{n-r+1} \\ 0 & \lambda^n & \binom{n}{1}\lambda^{n-1} & \cdots & \binom{n}{r-3}\lambda^{n-r+3} & \binom{n}{r-2}\lambda^{n-r+2} \\ 0 & 0 & \lambda^n & \cdots & \binom{n}{r-4}\lambda^{n-r+4} & \binom{n}{r-3}\lambda^{n-r+3} \\ & & & \cdots & & \\ 0 & 0 & 0 & \cdots & \lambda^n & \binom{n}{1}\lambda^{n-1} \\ 0 & 0 & 0 & \cdots & 0 & \lambda^n \end{pmatrix}.$$

Notice that $J_r(\lambda)^n$ is an upper triangular matrix with the diagonal entries being λ^n. So if $\lambda \neq 0$ then $J_r(\lambda)^n$ is nonsingular, and $J_r(\lambda)^n \mathbf{v} = \mathbf{0}$ implies $\mathbf{v} = \mathbf{0}$. $\square$

Now we are able to present one of the main results of this section, which gives a necessary and sufficient condition for termination of a quantum loop from a pure input state.

Theorem 5.1.1. *Suppose the Jordan decomposition of U_X is*

$$U_X = SJ(U_X)S^{-1}$$

where

$$J(U_X) = \bigoplus_{i=1}^{l} J_{k_i}(\lambda_i) = diag(J_{k_1}(\lambda_1), J_{k_2}(\lambda_2), \ldots, J_{k_l}(\lambda_l)).$$

Let $S^{-1}|\psi\rangle_X$ be divided into l sub-vectors $\mathbf{v}_1, \mathbf{v}_2, \ldots, \mathbf{v}_l$ such that the length of $\mathbf{v}_i$ is k_i. Then the quantum loop (5.1) terminates from input $|\psi\rangle$ if and only if for each $1 \leq i \leq l$, $\lambda_i = 0$ or $\mathbf{v}_i = \mathbf{0}$, where $\mathbf{0}$ is the k_i-dimensional zero vector.

Proof. Using Lemmas 5.1.3 and 5.1.4 we know that the quantum loop (5.1) terminates from input $|\psi\rangle$ if and only if

$$J(U_X)^n S^{-1}|\psi\rangle_X = \mathbf{0} \tag{5.4}$$

for some nonnegative integer n. A simple calculation yields

$$J(U_X)^n S^{-1} |\psi\rangle_X = ((J_{k_1}(\lambda_1)^n \mathbf{v}_1)^T, (J_{k_2}(\lambda_2)^n \mathbf{v}_2)^T, \ldots, (J_{k_l}(\lambda_l)^n \mathbf{v}_l)^T)^T$$

where $\mathbf{v}^T$ stands for the transpose of vector $\mathbf{v}$; that is, if $\mathbf{v}$ is a column vector then $\mathbf{v}^T$ is a row vector, and vice versa. Therefore, equation (5.4) holds for some nonnegative integer n if and only if for each $1 \le i \le l$, there exists a nonnegative integer n_i such that

$$J_{k_i}(\lambda_i)^{n_i} \mathbf{v}_i = \mathbf{0}.$$

Then we complete the proof by using Lemma 5.1.6. $\square$

Obviously, we can decide whether the quantum loop (5.1) terminates from any given mixed state by combining Lemma 5.1.2 and Theorem 5.1.1.

Corollary 5.1.2. *The quantum loop* (5.1) *is terminating if and only if U_X has only zero eigenvalues.*

Almost sure termination:

We now turn to consider almost sure termination. A necessary and sufficient condition for almost sure termination of the quantum loop (5.1) can also be derived by several steps of reduction. We first give a lemma similar to Lemma 5.1.2 so that a mixed input state can be reduced to a family of pure input states.

Lemma 5.1.7. *Let $\rho = \sum_i p_i \rho_i$ with $p_i > 0$ for all i. Then the quantum loop* (5.1) *almost surely terminates from input ρ if and only if it almost surely terminates from input ρ_i for all i.*

Exercise 5.1.5. *Prove Lemma 5.1.7.*

Corollary 5.1.3. *A quantum loop is almost surely terminating if and only if it almost surely terminates from all pure input states.*

We then present a technical lemma, which forms a key step in the proof of Theorem 5.1.2 following.

Lemma 5.1.8. *The quantum loop* (5.1) *almost surely terminates from pure input state $|\psi\rangle$ if and only if*

$$\lim_{n\to\infty} ||U_X^n |\psi\rangle|| = 0.$$

Proof. From Lemma 5.1.1, we have:

$$p_{NT}^{(\le n)}(|\psi\rangle) = ||U_X^{n-1} |\psi\rangle||^2.$$

Note that in the left-hand side of the preceding equation $|\psi\rangle$ actually stands for its corresponding density operator $|\psi\rangle\langle\psi|$. So $p_{NT}(|\psi\rangle) = 0$ if and only if $\lim_{n\to\infty} ||U_X^n |\psi\rangle|| = 0$. $\square$

The following theorem gives a necessary and sufficient condition for almost sure termination of a quantum loop from a pure input state.

Theorem 5.1.2. *Suppose that U_X, S, $J(U_X)$, $J_{k_i}(\lambda_i)$ and $\mathbf{v}_i$ ($1 \le i \le l$) are given as in Theorem 5.1.1. Then the quantum loop* (5.1) *almost surely terminates from input*

$|\psi\rangle$ *if and only if for each* $1 \leq i \leq l$, $|\lambda_i| < 1$ *or* $\mathbf{v}_i = \mathbf{0}$, *where* $\mathbf{0}$ *is the* k_i-*dimensional zero vector.*

Proof. First, for any nonnegative integer n, we have:

$$U_X^n|\psi\rangle = SJ(U_X)^n S^{-1}|\psi\rangle.$$

Then $\lim_{n\to\infty} ||U_X^n|\psi\rangle|| = 0$ if and only if

$$\lim_{n\to\infty} ||J(U_X)^n S^{-1}|\psi\rangle|| = 0 \tag{5.5}$$

since S is nonsingular. Using Lemma 5.1.8 we know that the loop (5.1) almost surely terminates from input $|\psi\rangle$ if and only if equation (5.5) holds. Note that

$$J(U_X)^n S^{-1}|\psi\rangle = ((J_{k_1}(\lambda_1)^n \mathbf{v}_1)^T, (J_{k_2}(\lambda_2)^n \mathbf{v}_2)^T, \ldots, (J_{k_l}(\lambda_l)^n \mathbf{v}_l)^T)^T$$

where $\mathbf{v}^T$ stands for the transpose of vector $\mathbf{v}$. Then equation (5.5) holds if and only if

$$\lim_{n\to\infty} ||J_{k_i}(\lambda_i)^n \mathbf{v}_i|| = 0 \tag{5.6}$$

for all $1 \leq i \leq l$. Furthermore, we have:

$$J_r(\lambda)^n\mathbf{v} = \left(\sum_{i=0}^{r-1}\binom{n}{i}\lambda^{n-i}v_{i+1}, \sum_{i=0}^{r-2}\binom{n}{i}\lambda^{n-i}v_{i+2}, \cdots, \lambda^n v_{r-1} + \binom{n}{1}\lambda^{n-1}v_r, \lambda^n v_r\right)^T.$$

So, equation (5.6) holds if and only if the following system of k_i equations are valid:

$$\begin{cases} \lim_{n\to\infty}\sum_{j=0}^{k_i-1}\binom{n}{j}\lambda_i^{n-j}v_{i(j+1)} = 0, \\ \lim_{n\to\infty}\sum_{j=0}^{k_i-2}\binom{n}{j}\lambda_i^{n-j}v_{i(j+2)} = 0, \\ \ldots\ldots\ldots\ldots \\ \lim_{n\to\infty}[\lambda_i^n v_{i(k_i-1)} + \binom{n}{1}\lambda_i^{n-1}v_{ik_i}] = 0, \\ \lim_{n\to\infty}\lambda_i^n v_{ik_i} = 0, \end{cases} \tag{5.7}$$

where it is assumed that $\mathbf{v}_i = (v_{i1}, v_{i2}, \ldots, v_{ik_i})$.

We now consider two cases. If $|\lambda_i| < 1$, then

$$\lim_{n\to\infty}\binom{n}{j}\lambda_i^{n-j} = 0$$

for any $0 \leq j \leq k_i - 1$, and all of the equations in (5.7) follow. On the other hand, if $|\lambda_i| \geq 1$, then from the last equation in (5.7) we know that $v_{ik} = 0$. Putting $v_{ik} = 0$ into the second equation from the bottom in (5.7) we obtain $v_{i(k-1)} = 0$. We can further move from bottom to top in the system (5.7) of equations in this way, and finally we get:

$$v_{i1} = v_{i2} = \cdots = v_{i(k_i-1)} = v_{ik_i} = 0.$$

This completes the proof.   □

Corollary 5.1.4. *Quantum loop* (5.1) *is almost surely terminating if and only if all the eigenvalues of* U_X *have norms less than 1.*

This subsection only considered a special class of quantum loops with a unitary transformation as their body. It can be seen as a warming up for the next subsection. But the termination conditions presented in this subsection are of independent significance because they are much easier to check than the corresponding conditions in the next subsection given for more general quantum loops.

5.1.2 GENERAL QUANTUM WHILE-LOOPS

Termination of a special class of quantum **while**-loops with unitary bodies was carefully studied in the last subsection. However, the expressive power of this kind of quantum loop is very limited; for example, they cannot model the case where a measurement occurs in the loop body or a quantum loop is nested in another. Now we consider a general quantum **while**-loop as defined in Section 3.1:

$$\textbf{while } M[\overline{q}] = 1 \textbf{ do } S \textbf{ od} \tag{5.8}$$

where $M = \{M_0, M_1\}$ is a yes-no measurement, $\overline{q}$ is a quantum register, and the loop body S is a general quantum program. As we saw in Section 3.3, the denotational semantics of S is a quantum operation $[\![S]\!] = \mathcal{E}$ in the state Hilbert space of $\overline{q}$ (if the quantum variables $qvar(S) \subseteq \overline{p}$). So, the loop (5.8) can be equivalently rewritten as:

$$\textbf{while } M[\overline{q}] = 1 \textbf{ do } \overline{q} := \mathcal{E}[\overline{q}] \textbf{ od}. \tag{5.9}$$

This subsection focuses on quantum loop (5.9). Let us see how the loop (5.9) is executed. Roughly speaking, the loop consists of two parts. The loop body "$\overline{q} := \mathcal{E}[\overline{q}]$" transforms a density operator σ to density operator $\mathcal{E}(\sigma)$. The loop guard "$M[\overline{q}] = 1$" is checked at each execution step. For $i = 0, 1$, we define quantum operation $\mathcal{E}_i$ from the measurement $M = \{M_0, M_1\}$ in the loop guard as follows:

$$\mathcal{E}_i(\sigma) = M_i \sigma M_i^\dagger \tag{5.10}$$

for any density operator σ. Moreover, for any two quantum operations $\mathcal{F}_1, \mathcal{F}_2$, we write $\mathcal{F}_2 \circ \mathcal{F}_1$ for their composition; that is,

$$(\mathcal{F}_2 \circ \mathcal{F}_1)(\rho) = \mathcal{F}_2(\mathcal{F}_1(\rho))$$

for all $\rho \in \mathcal{D}(\mathcal{H})$. For a quantum operation $\mathcal{F}$, $\mathcal{F}^n$ denotes the nth power of $\mathcal{F}$, i.e., the composition of n copies of $\mathcal{F}$. Then the execution of the loop with input state ρ can be more precisely described as follows:

(i) *Initial step*: We first perform the termination measurement $\{M_0, M_1\}$ on the input state ρ.

- The probability that the program terminates, that is, the measurement outcome is 0, is

$$p_T^{(1)}(\rho) = tr[\mathcal{E}_0(\rho)],$$

and the program state after termination is

$$\rho_{out}^{(1)} = \mathcal{E}_0(\rho)/p_T^{(1)}(\rho).$$

We encode probability $p_T^{(1)}(\rho)$ and density operator $\rho_{out}^{(1)}$ into a partial density operator

$$p_T^{(1)}(\rho)\rho_{out}^{(1)} = \mathcal{E}_0(\rho).$$

So, $\mathcal{E}_0(\rho)$ is the partial output state at the first step.

- The probability that the program does not terminate, that is, the measurement outcome is 1, is

$$p_{NT}^{(1)}(\rho) = tr[\mathcal{E}_1(\rho)], \tag{5.11}$$

and the program state after the outcome 1 is obtained is

$$\rho_{mid}^{(1)} = \mathcal{E}_1(\rho)/p_{NT}^{(1)}(\rho).$$

Then it is transformed by the loop body $\mathcal{E}$ to

$$\rho_{in}^{(2)} = (\mathcal{E} \circ \mathcal{E}_1)(\rho)/p_{NT}^{(1)}(\rho),$$

upon which the second step will be executed. We can combine $p_{NT}^{(1)}$ and $\rho_{in}^{(2)}$ into a partial density operator

$$p_{NT}^{(1)}(\rho)\rho_{in}^{(2)} = (\mathcal{E} \circ \mathcal{E}_1)(\rho).$$

(ii) *Induction step*: We write

$$p_{NT}^{(\leq n)} = \prod_{i=1}^{n} p_{NT}^{(i)}$$

for the probability that the program does not terminate within n steps, where $p_{NT}^{(i)}$ is the probability that the program does not terminate at the ith step for every $1 \leq i \leq n$. The program state after the nth measurement with outcome 1 is

$$\rho_{mid}^{(n)} = \frac{\left[\mathcal{E}_1 \circ (\mathcal{E} \circ \mathcal{E}_1)^{n-1}\right](\rho)}{p_{NT}^{(\leq n)}},$$

which is then transformed by the loop body $\mathcal{E}$ into

$$\rho_{in}^{(n+1)} = \frac{(\mathcal{E} \circ \mathcal{E}_1)^n(\rho)}{p_{NT}^{(\leq n)}}.$$

We combine $p_{NT}^{(\leq n)}$ and $\rho_{in}^{(n+1)}$ into a partial density operator

$$p_{NT}^{(\leq n)}(\rho)\rho_{in}^{(n+1)} = (\mathcal{E} \circ \mathcal{E}_1)^n(\rho).$$

Now the $(n+1)$st step is executed upon $\rho_{in}^{(n+1)}$.

- The probability that the program terminates at the $(n+1)$st step is then

$$p_T^{(n+1)}(\rho) = tr\left[\mathcal{E}_0\left(\rho_{in}^{(n+1)}\right)\right],$$

and the probability that the program does not terminate within n steps but it terminates at the $(n+1)$st step is

$$q_T^{(n+1)}(\rho) = tr\left(\left[\mathcal{E}_0 \circ (\mathcal{E} \circ \mathcal{E}_1)^n\right](\rho)\right).$$

The program state after the termination is

$$\rho_{out}^{(n+1)} = [\mathcal{E}_0 \circ (\mathcal{E} \circ \mathcal{E}_1)^n](\rho)/q_T^{(n+1)}(\rho).$$

Combining $q_T^{(n+1)}(\rho)$ and $\rho_{out}^{(n+1)}$ yields the partial output state of the program at the $(n+1)$st step:

$$q_T^{(n+1)}(\rho)\rho_{out}^{(n+1)} = [\mathcal{E}_0 \circ (\mathcal{E} \circ \mathcal{E}_1)^n](\rho).$$

- The probability that the program does not terminate within $(n+1)$ steps is then

$$p_{NT}^{(\leq n+1)}(\rho) = tr([\mathcal{E}_1 \circ (\mathcal{E} \circ \mathcal{E}_1)^n](\rho)). \tag{5.12}$$

As pointed out in Section 3.1, the major difference between a classical loop and a quantum loop comes from the checking of the loop guard. During checking the guard of a classical loop, the program state is not changed. However, the quantum measurement in the guard of a quantum loop disturbs the state of the system. Thus, the quantum program state after checking the loop guard may be different from that before checking. The change of program state caused by measurement M is depicted by quantum operations $\mathcal{E}_0$ and $\mathcal{E}_1$.

The preceding description of the computational process of quantum loop (5.9) is a generalization of the execution of loop (5.1) described in Subsection 5.1.1. Now Definitions 5.1.1, 5.1.2 and 5.1.3 for the special quantum loop (5.1) can be easily extended to the general quantum loop (5.9).

Definition 5.1.4

(i) *We say that quantum loop (5.9) terminates from input state ρ if probability $p_{NT}^{(n)}(\rho) = 0$ for some positive integer n.*

(ii) *We say that loop (5.9) almost surely terminates from input state ρ if the nontermination probability*

$$p_{NT}(\rho) = \lim_{n \to \infty} p_{NT}^{(\leq n)}(\rho) = 0$$

where $p_{NT}^{(\leq n)}$ is the probability that the program does not terminate within n steps.

Definition 5.1.5. *The quantum loop (5.9) is terminating (respectively, almost surely terminating) if it terminates (respectively, almost surely terminates) from any input ρ.*

The (total) output state of a quantum loop is obtained by summing up its partial computing results obtained at all steps. Formally, we have:

Definition 5.1.6. *The function $\mathcal{F} : \mathcal{D}(H) \to \mathcal{D}(H)$ computed by the quantum loop (5.9) is defined by*

$$\mathcal{F}(\rho) = \sum_{n=1}^{\infty} q_T^{(n)}(\rho)\rho_{out}^{(n)} = \sum_{n=0}^{\infty} \left[\mathcal{E}_0 \circ (\mathcal{E} \circ \mathcal{E}_1)^n\right](\rho)$$

for each $\rho \in \mathcal{D}(\mathcal{H})$, where

$$q_T^{(n)} = p_{NT}^{(\leq n-1)} p_T^{(n)}$$

is the probability that the program does not terminate within $n - 1$ steps but it terminates at the nth step.

Obviously, the previous three definitions degenerate to the corresponding definitions in the last subsection whence the loop body is a unitary operator.

The following proposition gives a recursive characterization of the function $\mathcal{F}$ computed by quantum loop (5.9). It is essentially a restatement of Corollary 3.3.1, and can be easily proved by definition.

Proposition 5.1.1. *The quantum operation $\mathcal{F}$ computed by loop (5.9) satisfies the following recursive equation:*

$$\mathcal{F}(\rho) = \mathcal{E}_0(\rho) + \mathcal{F}[(\mathcal{E} \circ \mathcal{E}_1)(\rho)]$$

for all density operators ρ.

Matrix Representation of Quantum Operations:

The remaindering part of this subsection is devoted to termination and running time analysis of quantum loop (5.9). Since iterations of quantum operations $\mathcal{E}, \mathcal{E}_0, \mathcal{E}_1$ are involved in the definitions of termination and the computed function $\mathcal{F}$ of loop (5.9), dealing with these iterations in its analysis is unavoidable. However, it is usually very difficult to compute the iterations of quantum operations. To overcome this difficulty, we introduce a useful mathematical tool, namely the matrix representation of a quantum operation, which is usually easier to manipulate than the quantum operation itself.

Definition 5.1.7. *Suppose quantum operation $\mathcal{E}$ in a d-dimensional Hilbert space $\mathcal{H}$ has the Kraus operator-sum representation:*

$$\mathcal{E}(\rho) = \sum_i E_i \rho E_i^\dagger$$

for all density operators ρ. Then the matrix representation of $\mathcal{E}$ is the $d^2 \times d^2$ matrix:

$$M = \sum_i E_i \otimes E_i^*,$$

where A^* stands for the conjugate of matrix A, i.e., $A^* = (a_{ij}^*)$ with a_{ij}^* being the conjugate of complex number a_{ij}, whenever $A = (a_{ij})$.

The effect of matrix representation of quantum operations in analysis of quantum programs is mainly based on the next lemma, which establishes a connection between the image of a matrix A under a quantum operation $\mathcal{E}$ and the multiplication of the matrix representation of $\mathcal{E}$ and the cylindrical extension of A. Actually, this lemma will play a key role in the proofs of all the main results in this subsection.

Lemma 5.1.9. *Suppose that* $\dim \mathcal{H} = d$. *We write*

$$|\Phi\rangle = \sum_j |jj\rangle$$

for the (unnormalized) maximally entangled state in $\mathcal{H} \otimes \mathcal{H}$, where $\{|j\rangle\}$ is an orthonormal basis of $\mathcal{H}$. Let M be the matrix representation of quantum operation $\mathcal{E}$. Then for any $d \times d$ matrix A, we have:

$$(\mathcal{E}(A) \otimes I)|\Phi\rangle = M(A \otimes I)|\Phi\rangle \tag{5.13}$$

where I stands for the $d \times d$-unit matrix.

Proof. We first observe the matrix equality: for any matrices A, B and C,

$$(A \otimes B)(C \otimes I)|\Phi\rangle = (ACB^T \otimes I)|\Phi\rangle,$$

where B^T stands for the transpose of matrix B. This equality can be easily proved by a routine matrix calculation. Now it follows that

$$M(A \otimes I)|\Phi\rangle = \sum_i \left(E_i \otimes E_i^*\right)(A \otimes I)|\Phi\rangle$$

$$= \sum_i \left(E_i A E_i^\dagger \otimes I\right)|\Phi\rangle$$

$$= (\mathcal{E}(A) \otimes I)|\Phi\rangle.$$

$\square$

It is interesting to observe that the maximally entangled state $|\Phi\rangle$ enables us to represent a $d \times d$-matrix $A = (a_{ij})$ to a d^2-dimensional vector in the following way:

$$(A \otimes I)|\Phi\rangle = (a_{11}, \ldots, a_{1d}, a_{21}, \ldots, a_{2d}, \ldots, a_{d1}, \ldots, a_{dd})^T.$$

Furthermore, it helps to translate a quantum operation $\mathcal{E}$ in a d-dimensional Hilbert space to a $d^2 \times d^2$-matrix M through equation (35).

The preceding lemma has an immediate application showing that the matrix representation of a quantum operation is well-defined: if

$$\mathcal{E}(\rho) = \sum_i E_i \rho E_i^\dagger = \sum_j F_j \rho F_j^\dagger$$

for all density operators ρ, then

$$\sum_i E_i \otimes E_i^* = \sum_j F_j \otimes F_j^*.$$

This conclusion can be easily seen from the arbitrariness of matrix A in equation (5.13).

After preparing the mathematical tool of the matrix representation of a quantum operation, we now come back to consider the quantum loop (5.9). Assume that the quantum operation $\mathcal{E}$ in the loop body has the operator-sum representation:

$$\mathcal{E}(\rho) = \sum_i E_i \rho E_i^\dagger$$

for all density operators ρ. Let $\mathcal{E}_i$ ($i = 0, 1$) be the quantum operations defined by the measurement operations M_0, M_1 in the loop guard according to equation (5.10). We write $\mathcal{G}$ for the composition of $\mathcal{E}$ and $\mathcal{E}_1$:

$$\mathcal{G} = \mathcal{E} \circ \mathcal{E}_1.$$

Then $\mathcal{G}$ has the operator-sum representation:

$$\mathcal{G}(\rho) = \sum_i (E_i M_1) \rho (M_1^\dagger E_i^\dagger)$$

for all density operators ρ. Furthermore, the matrix representations of $\mathcal{E}_0$ and $\mathcal{G}$ are

$$N_0 = M_0 \otimes M_0^*,$$
$$R = \sum_i (E_i M_1) \otimes (E_i M_1)^*, \qquad (5.14)$$

respectively. Suppose that the Jordan decomposition of R is

$$R = SJ(R)S^{-1}$$

where S is a nonsingular matrix, and $J(R)$ is the Jordan normal form of R:

$$J(R) = \bigoplus_{i=1}^{l} J_{k_i}(\lambda_i) = diag(J_{k_1}(\lambda_1), J_{k_2}(\lambda_2), \cdots, J_{k_l}(\lambda_l))$$

with $J_{k_s}(\lambda_s)$ being a $k_s \times k_s$-Jordan block of eigenvalue λ_s ($1 \leq s \leq l$) (see Lemma 5.1.5).

The following is a key technical lemma that describes the structure of the matrix representation R of quantum operation $\mathcal{G}$.

Lemma 5.1.10

(i) $|\lambda_s| \leq 1$ *for all* $1 \leq s \leq l$.

(ii) *If* $|\lambda_s| = 1$ *then the sth Jordan block is* 1-*dimensional; that is,* $k_s = 1$.

For readability, we postpone the lengthy proof of this lemma to Section 5.4.

Termination and Almost Sure Termination:

Now we are ready to study termination of the quantum loop (5.9). First of all, the following lemma gives a simple termination condition in terms of the matrix representation of quantum operations.

Lemma 5.1.11. *Let R be defined by equation (5.14), and let*

$$|\Phi\rangle = \sum_j |jj\rangle$$

be the (unnormalized) maximally entangled state in $\mathcal{H} \otimes \mathcal{H}$. Then we have:

(i) *Quantum loop (5.9) terminates from input ρ if and only if*

$$R^n(\rho \otimes I)|\Phi\rangle = \mathbf{0}$$

for some integer $n \geq 0$;

(ii) *Quantum loop (5.9) almost surely terminates from input ρ if and only if*

$$\lim_{n \to \infty} R^n(\rho \otimes I)|\Phi\rangle = \mathbf{0},$$

Proof. We only prove part (i), as the proof of part (ii) is similar. First, it follows from Lemma 5.1.9 that

$$[\mathcal{G}(\rho) \otimes I]|\Phi\rangle = R(\rho \otimes I)|\Phi\rangle.$$

Repeated applications of this equality yield:

$$[\mathcal{G}^n(\rho) \otimes I]|\Phi\rangle = R^n(\rho \otimes I)|\Phi\rangle.$$

On the other hand, it holds that

$$tr(A) = \langle\Phi|A \otimes I|\Phi\rangle$$

for any matrix A. Therefore, since $\mathcal{E}$ is trace-preserving, we obtain:

$$
\begin{aligned}
tr\left(\left[\mathcal{E}_1 \circ (\mathcal{E} \circ \mathcal{E}_1)^{n-1}\right](\rho)\right) &= tr\left((\mathcal{E} \circ \mathcal{E}_1)^n(\rho)\right) \\
&= tr(\mathcal{G}^n(\rho)) \\
&= \langle\Phi|R^n(\rho \otimes I)|\Phi\rangle.
\end{aligned}
$$

Moreover, it is clear that $\langle\Phi|R^n(\rho \otimes I)|\Phi\rangle = 0$ if and only if $R^n(\rho \otimes I)|\Phi\rangle = \mathbf{0}$. □

As a direct application of the preceding lemma, we have:

Lemma 5.1.12. *Let R and $|\Phi\rangle$ be as in Lemma 5.1.11.*

(i) *Quantum loop (5.9) is terminating if and only if $R^n|\Phi\rangle = \mathbf{0}$ for some integer $n \geq 0$;*

(ii) *Quantum loop (5.9) is almost surely terminating if and only if $\lim_{n\to\infty} R^n|\Phi\rangle = \mathbf{0}$.*

Proof. Notice that a quantum loop is terminating if and only if it terminates from a special input (mixed) state:

$$\rho_0 = \frac{1}{d} \cdot I,$$

where $d = \dim \mathcal{H}$ and I is the identity operator in $\mathcal{H}$. Then this lemma follows immediately from Lemma 5.1.11. □

We can now present one of the main results of this subsection, which gives a necessary and sufficient terminating condition for a quantum loop in terms of the eigenvalues of the matrix representations of the quantum operations involved in the loop.

Theorem 5.1.3. *Let R and $|\Phi\rangle$ be as in Lemma 5.1.11. Then we have:*

(i) *If $R^k|\Phi\rangle = \mathbf{0}$ for some integer $k \geq 0$, then quantum loop (5.9) is terminating. Conversely, if loop (5.9) is terminating, then $R^k|\Phi\rangle = \mathbf{0}$ for all integer $k \geq k_0$, where k_0 is the maximal size of Jordan blocks of R corresponding to eigenvalue 0.*

(ii) *Quantum loop (5.9) is almost surely terminating if and only if $|\Phi\rangle$ is orthogonal to all eigenvectors of $R^\dagger$ corresponding to eigenvalues λ with $|\lambda| = 1$, where $R^\dagger$ is the transpose conjugate of R.*

Proof. We first prove part (i). If $R^k|\Phi\rangle = 0$ for some $k \geq 0$, then by Lemma 5.1.12 we conclude that loop (5.9) is terminating. Conversely, suppose that loop (5.9) is terminating. Again by Lemma 5.1.12, there exists some integer $n \geq 0$ such that $R^n|\Phi\rangle = 0$. For any integer $k \geq$ the maximal size of Jordan blocks of R corresponding to eigenvalue 0, we want to show that $R^k|\Phi\rangle = 0$. Without any loss of generality, we assume the Jordan decomposition of R:

$$R = SJ(R)S^{-1}$$

where

$$J(R) = \bigoplus_{i=1}^{l} J_{k_i}(\lambda_i) = diag(J_{k_1}(\lambda_1), J_{k_2}(\lambda_2), \cdots, J_{k_l}(\lambda_l))$$

with $|\lambda_1| \geq \cdots \geq |\lambda_s| > 0$ and $\lambda_{s+1} = \cdots = \lambda_l = 0$. Observe that

$$R^n = SJ(R)^n S^{-1}.$$

Since S is nonsingular, it follows immediately from $R^n|\Phi\rangle = 0$ that

$$J(R)^n S^{-1}|\Phi\rangle = \mathbf{0}.$$

We can divide both matrix $J(R)$ and vector $S^{-1}|\Phi\rangle$ into two parts:

$$J(R) = \begin{pmatrix} A & 0 \\ 0 & B \end{pmatrix}, \quad S^{-1}|\Phi\rangle = \begin{pmatrix} |x\rangle \\ |y\rangle \end{pmatrix},$$

where

$$A = \bigoplus_{i=1}^{s} J_{k_i}(\lambda_i) = diag(J_{k_1}(\lambda_1), \ldots, J_{k_s}(\lambda_s)),$$

$$B = \bigoplus_{i=s+1}^{l} J_{k_i}(\lambda_i) = diag(J_{k_{s+1}}(0), \ldots, J_{k_l}(0)),$$

$|x\rangle$ is a t-dimensional vector, $|y\rangle$ is a $(d^2 - t)$-dimensional vector, and $t = \sum_{j=1}^{s} k_j$. Then it holds that

$$J(R)^n S^{-1}|\Phi\rangle = \begin{pmatrix} A^n|x\rangle \\ B^n|y\rangle \end{pmatrix}.$$

Note that $\lambda_1, \ldots, \lambda_s \neq 0$. So, $J_{k_1}(\lambda_1), \ldots, J_{k_s}(\lambda_s)$ are nonsingular, and A is nonsingular too. Thus, $J(R)^n S^{-1} |\Phi\rangle = \mathbf{0}$ implies $A^n |x\rangle = \mathbf{0}$ and furthermore $|x\rangle = \mathbf{0}$. On the other hand, for each j with $s+1 \leq j \leq l$, since $k \geq k_j$, it holds that $J_{k_j}(0)^k = \mathbf{0}$. Consequently, $B^k = \mathbf{0}$. This together with $|x\rangle = \mathbf{0}$ implies

$$J(R)^k S^{-1} |\Phi\rangle = \mathbf{0}$$

and

$$R^k |\Phi\rangle = SJ(R)^k S^{-1} |\Phi\rangle = \mathbf{0}.$$

Now we prove part (ii). First, we know by Lemma 5.1.12 that program (5.9) is almost terminating if and only if

$$\lim_{n \to \infty} J(R)^n S^{-1} |\Phi\rangle = \mathbf{0}.$$

We assume that

$$1 = |\lambda_1| = \cdots = |\lambda_r| > |\lambda_{r+1}| \geq \cdots \geq |\lambda_l|$$

in the Jordan decomposition of R, and we write:

$$J(R) = \begin{pmatrix} C & 0 \\ 0 & D \end{pmatrix}, \quad S^{-1} |\Phi\rangle = \begin{pmatrix} |u\rangle \\ |v\rangle \end{pmatrix}$$

where

$$C = diag(\lambda_1, \ldots, \lambda_r),$$
$$D = diag(J_{k_{r+1}}(\lambda_{r+1}), \ldots, J_{k_l}(\lambda_l)),$$

$|u\rangle$ is an r-dimensional vector, and $|v\rangle$ is a $(d^2 - r)$-dimensional vector. (Note that $J_{k_1}(\lambda_1), \ldots, J_{k_r}(\lambda_r)$ are all 1×1 matrices because $|\lambda_1| = \ldots = |\lambda_r| = 1$; see Lemma 5.1.10.)

If $|\Phi\rangle$ is orthogonal to all the eigenvectors of $R^\dagger$ corresponding to the eigenvalue with module 1, then by definition we have $|u\rangle = \mathbf{0}$. On the other hand, for each j with $r + 1 \leq j \leq l$, since $|\lambda_j| < 1$, we have

$$\lim_{n \to \infty} J_{k_j}(\lambda_j)^n = \mathbf{0}.$$

Thus, $\lim_{n \to \infty} D^n = \mathbf{0}$. So, it follows that

$$\lim_{n \to \infty} J(R)^n S^{-1} |\Phi\rangle = \lim_{n \to \infty} \begin{pmatrix} C^n |u\rangle \\ D^n |v\rangle \end{pmatrix} = \mathbf{0}.$$

Conversely, if

$$\lim_{n \to \infty} J(R)^n S^{-1} |\Phi\rangle = \mathbf{0},$$

then $\lim_{n \to \infty} C^n |u\rangle = \mathbf{0}$. This implies $|u\rangle = \mathbf{0}$ because C is a diagonal unitary. Consequently, $|\Phi\rangle$ is orthogonal to all the eigenvectors of $R^\dagger$ corresponding to the eigenvalue with module 1. $\qquad\square$

Expectation of Observables at the Outputs:

In addition to program termination, which we've already discussed, computing the expected value of a program variable is another important problem in classical program analysis. We now consider its quantum counterpart – computing the expectation of an observable at the output of a quantum program.

Recall from Exercise 2.1.8 that an observable is modelled by a Hermitian operator P, and the expectation (average value) of P in a state σ is $tr(P\sigma)$. In particular, whenever P is a quantum predicate, i.e., $0_{\mathcal{H}} \sqsubseteq P \sqsubseteq I_{\mathcal{H}}$, then the expectation $tr(P\sigma)$ can be understood as the probability that predicate P is satisfied in state σ. Actually, for a given input state ρ, many interesting properties of the quantum loop (5.9) can be expressed in terms of the expectation $tr(P\mathcal{F}(\rho))$ of observable P in the output state $\mathcal{F}(\rho)$. Thus, analysis of quantum programs can often be reduced to the problem of computing expectation $tr(P\mathcal{F}(\rho))$.

Now we develop a method for computing the expectation $tr(P\mathcal{F}(\rho))$. As will be seen in the proof of Theorem 5.1.4 following, our method depends on the convergence of power series

$$\sum_n R^n$$

where R is the matrix representation of $\mathcal{G} = \mathcal{E} \circ \mathcal{E}_1$ given by equation (5.14). But this series may not converge when some eigenvalues of R have module 1. A natural idea for overcoming this objection is to modify the Jordan normal form $J(R)$ of R by vanishing the Jordan blocks corresponding to those eigenvalues with module 1, which are all 1-dimensional according to Lemma 5.1.10. This yields the matrix:

$$N = SJ(N)S^{-1} \tag{5.15}$$

where $J(N)$ is obtained by modifying $J(R)$ as follows:

$$J(N) = diag(J'_1, J'_2, \cdots, J'_3), \tag{5.16}$$

$$J'_s = \begin{cases} 0 & \text{if } |\lambda_s| = 1, \\ J_{k_s}(\lambda_s) & \text{otherwise,} \end{cases}$$

for each $1 \leq s \leq l$.

Fortunately, as shown in the following lemma, such a modification of the matrix representation R of $\mathcal{G}$ does not change the behavior of its powers when combined with the measurement operator M_0 in the loop guard.

Lemma 5.1.13. *For any integer $n \geq 0$, we have:*

$$N_0 R^n = N_0 N^n,$$

where $N_0 = M_0 \otimes M_0^*$ is the matrix representation of $\mathcal{E}_0$.

The proof of this lemma is quite involved and thus also postponed to Section 5.4.

Now we are ready to present another main result of this subsection, which gives an explicit formula for computing the expected value of an observable at the output of a quantum loop.

Theorem 5.1.4. *The expectation of observable P in the output state $\mathcal{F}(\rho)$ of quantum loop (5.9) with input state ρ is*

$$tr(P\mathcal{F}(\rho)) = \langle\Phi|(P \otimes I)N_0(I \otimes I - N)^{-1}(\rho \otimes I)|\Phi\rangle,$$

where symbol I stands for the identity operator in $\mathcal{H}$, and

$$|\Phi\rangle = \sum_j |jj\rangle$$

is the (unnormalized) maximally entangled state in $\mathcal{H} \otimes \mathcal{H}$, with $\{|j\rangle\}$ being an orthonormal basis of $\mathcal{H}$.

Proof. With the previous preparations, this proof is more or less a straightforward calculation based on Definition 5.1.6. First, it follows from Lemma 5.1.9 together with the defining equations of quantum operations $\mathcal{E}_0$ and $\mathcal{G}$ that

$$[\mathcal{E}_0(\rho) \otimes I]|\Phi\rangle = N_0(\rho \otimes I)|\Phi\rangle, \tag{5.17}$$

$$[\mathcal{G}(\rho) \otimes I]|\Phi\rangle = R(\rho \otimes I)|\Phi\rangle. \tag{5.18}$$

By first applying equation (5.17) and then repeatedly applying equation (5.18), we obtain:

$$
\begin{aligned}
[\mathcal{F}(\rho) \otimes I]|\Phi\rangle &= \left[\sum_{n=0}^{\infty} \mathcal{E}_0\left(\mathcal{G}^n(\rho)\right) \otimes I\right]|\Phi\rangle \\
&= \sum_{n=0}^{\infty}\left[\mathcal{E}_0\left(\mathcal{G}^n(\rho)\right) \otimes I\right]|\Phi\rangle \\
&= \sum_{n=0}^{\infty} N_0\left(\mathcal{G}^n(\rho) \otimes I\right)|\Phi\rangle \\
&= \sum_{n=0}^{\infty} N_0 R^n(\rho \otimes I)|\Phi\rangle
\end{aligned}
$$

$$\overset{(a)}{=} \sum_{n=0}^{\infty} N_0 N^n \, (\rho \otimes I) \, |\Phi\rangle$$

$$= N_0 \left(\sum_{n=0}^{\infty} N^n \right) (\rho \otimes I) \, |\Phi\rangle$$

$$= N_0 (I \otimes I - N)^{-1} (\rho \otimes I) |\Phi\rangle.$$

The equality labeled by (a) follows from Lemma 5.1.13. Finally, a routine calculation yields $tr(\rho) = \langle \Phi | \rho \otimes I | \Phi \rangle$, and thus we have:

$$tr(P\mathcal{F}(\rho)) = \langle \Phi | P\mathcal{F}(\rho) \otimes I | \Phi \rangle$$

$$= \langle \Phi | (P \otimes I)(\mathcal{F}(\rho) \otimes I) | \Phi \rangle$$

$$= \langle \Phi | (P \otimes I) N_0 (I \otimes I - N)^{-1} (\rho \otimes I) | \Phi \rangle.$$

$\square$

Average Running Time:

We already studied two program analysis problems, namely termination and expected value, for quantum loop (5.9) using matrix representation of quantum operations. To further illustrate the power of the method just introduced, we compute the average running time of loop (5.9) with input state ρ:

$$\sum_{n=1}^{\infty} n p_T^{(n)}$$

where for each $n \geq 1$,

$$p_T^{(n)} = tr\left[\left(\mathcal{E}_0 \circ (\mathcal{E} \circ \mathcal{E}_1)^{n-1} \right)(\rho) \right] = tr\left[\left(\mathcal{E}_0 \circ \mathcal{G}^{n-1} \right)(\rho) \right]$$

is the probability that the loop (5.9) terminates at the nth step. It is clear that this cannot be done by a direct application of Theorem 5.1.4. But a procedure similar to the proof of Theorem 5.1.4 leads to:

Proposition 5.1.2. *The average running time of quantum loop* (5.9) *with input state ρ is*

$$\langle \Phi | N_0 (I \otimes I - N)^{-2} (\rho \otimes I) | \Phi \rangle.$$

Proof. This proof is also a straightforward calculation based on Definition 5.1.6. Using equations (5.17) and (5.18) and Lemma 5.1.13, we have:

$$\sum_{n=1}^{\infty} np_n = \sum_{n=1}^{\infty} n \cdot tr\left[\left(\mathcal{E}_0 \circ \mathcal{G}^{n-1}\right)(\rho)\right]$$

$$= \sum_{n=1}^{\infty} n\langle\Phi|\left(\mathcal{E}_0 \circ \mathcal{G}^{n-1}\right)(\rho) \otimes I|\Phi\rangle$$

$$= \sum_{n=1}^{\infty} n\langle\Phi|N_0 R^{n-1}(\rho \otimes I)|\Phi\rangle$$

$$= \sum_{n=1}^{\infty} n\langle\Phi|N_0 N^{n-1}(\rho \otimes I)|\Phi\rangle$$

$$= \langle\Phi|N_0 \left(\sum_{n=1}^{\infty} nN^{n-1}\right)(\rho \otimes I)|\Phi\rangle$$

$$= \langle\Phi|N_0 (I \otimes I - N)^{-2}(\rho \otimes I)|\Phi\rangle.$$

$\square$

5.1.3 **AN EXAMPLE**

We now give an example to show how Proposition 5.1.2 can be applied to quantum walks in order to compute their average running time. We consider a quantum walk on an n-circle. It can be seen as a variant of a one-dimensional quantum walk, and it is also a special case of quantum walk on a graph defined in Subsection 2.3.4.

Let $\mathcal{H}_d$ be the direction space, which is a 2-dimensional Hilbert space with orthonormal basis state $|L\rangle$ and $|R\rangle$, indicating directions Left and Right, respectively. Assume that the n different positions on the n-circle are labelled by numbers $0, 1, \ldots, n - 1$. Let $\mathcal{H}_p$ be an n-dimensional Hilbert space with orthonormal basis states $|0\rangle, |1\rangle, \ldots, |n - 1\rangle$, where for each $0 \leq i \leq n - 1$, the basis vector $|i\rangle$ corresponds to position i on the n-circle. Thus, the state space of the quantum walk is $\mathcal{H} = \mathcal{H}_d \otimes \mathcal{H}_p$. The initial state is assumed to be $|L\rangle|0\rangle$. Different from the quantum walks considered in Subsection 2.3.4, this walk has an absorbing boundary at position 1. So, each step of the walk consists of:

(i) Measure the position of the system to see whether the current position is 1. If the outcome is "yes", then the walk terminates; otherwise, it continues. This measurement is used to model the absorbing boundary. It can be described by

$$M = \{M_{yes} = I_d \otimes |1\rangle\langle 1|, M_{no} = I - M_{yes}\},$$

where I_d and I are the identity operators in $\mathcal{H}_d$ and $\mathcal{H}$, respectively;

(ii) A "coin-tossing" operator

$$H = \frac{1}{\sqrt{2}}\begin{pmatrix} 1 & 1 \\ 1 & -1 \end{pmatrix}$$

is applied in the direction space $\mathcal{H}_d$. Here, the Hadamard gate is chosen to model the "coin-tossing";

(iii) A shift operator

$$S = \sum_{i=0}^{n-1} |L\rangle\langle L| \otimes |i \ominus 1\rangle\langle i| + \sum_{i=0}^{n-1} |R\rangle\langle R| \otimes |i \oplus 1\rangle\langle i|$$

is performed in the space $\mathcal{H}$. The intuitive meaning of the operator S is that the system walks one step left or right according to the direction state. Here, $\oplus$ and $\ominus$ stand for addition and subtraction modulo n, respectively.

Using the quantum **while**-language defined in Section 3.1, this quantum walk can be written as quantum loop:

$$\textbf{while } M[d,p] = yes \textbf{ do } d,p := W[d,p] \textbf{ od}$$

where the quantum variables d, p are used to denote direction and position, respectively,

$$W = S(H \otimes I_p)$$

is the single-step walk operator, and I_p is the identity operator in $\mathcal{H}_p$.

We now compute the average running time of the quantum walk. A direct application of Proposition 5.1.2 tells us that the average running time of this walk is

$$\langle\Phi|N_0(I \otimes I - N)^{-2}(\rho \otimes I)|\Phi\rangle, \tag{5.19}$$

where

$$N_0 = M_{no} \otimes M_{no}, \quad N = (WM_{yes}) \otimes (WM_{yes})^*,$$

I is the identity matrix in $\mathcal{H} = \mathcal{H}_d \otimes \mathcal{H}_p$, and $\rho = |L\rangle\langle L| \otimes |0\rangle\langle 0|$. Note that here we do not need to use the modification procedure given by equations (5.15) and (5.16). A MATLAB program is developed to compute (5.19); see Algorithm 1. This algorithm was run on a laptop for $n < 30$, and the computational result showed that the average running time of the quantum walk on an n-circle is n.

Problem 5.1.1. *Prove or disprove that the average running time of the quantum walk on an n-circle is n for all $n \geq 30$.*

Algorithm 1 COMPUTE AVERAGE RUNNING TIME OF QUANTUM WALK ON n-CIRCLE

input : integer n
output: b (the average running time of quantum walk on a n-circle)
$n \times n$ **matrix** $I \leftarrow E(n)$; (*n-dimensional identity*)
integer $m \leftarrow 2n$;
$m \times m$ **matrix** $I_2 \leftarrow E(m)$; (*m-dimensional identity*)
m^2-**dimensional vector** $|\Phi\rangle \leftarrow \vec{I_2}$; (*maximally entangled state*)
$m \times m$ **matrix** $\rho \leftarrow |1\rangle\langle 1|$; (*initial state*)
2×2 **matrix** $H \leftarrow [1\ 1; 1\ -1]/\sqrt{2}$; (*Hadamard matrix*)
$m \times m$ **matrix** $M_0 \leftarrow |0\rangle\langle 0| \otimes E(2)$; (*termination test measurement*)
$m \times m$ **matrix** $M_1 \leftarrow I_2 - M_0$;
$n \times n$ **matrix** $X \leftarrow I * 0$; (*shift unitary*)
for $j = 1 : n - 1$ **do**
$\quad|\quad X(j, j+1) \leftarrow 1$;
end
$X(n, 1) \leftarrow 1$;
$C \leftarrow X^\dagger$;
$m \times m$ **matrix** $S \leftarrow X \otimes |0\rangle\langle 0| + C \otimes |1\rangle\langle 1|$; (*shift operator*)
$m \times m$ **matrix** $W \leftarrow S(I \otimes H)M_1$;
$m^2 \times m^2$ **matrix** $M_T \leftarrow M_0 \otimes M_0$;
$m^2 \times m^2$ **matrix** $N_T \leftarrow W_1 \otimes W_1$;
$m^2 \times m^2$ **matrix** $I_3 \leftarrow E(m^2)$; (*m^2-dimensional identity*)
real number $b \leftarrow \langle\Phi|M_T(I_3 - N_T)^{-2}(\rho \otimes I_2)|\Phi\rangle$; (*calculate the average running time*)
return b

5.2 QUANTUM GRAPH THEORY

We carefully studied termination and almost termination for quantum **while**-loops in the last section. As we will see later in the next section, the termination problem for quantum loops is a special case of reachability problem for quantum Markov chains. Indeed, classical Markov chains have been widely used in verification and analysis of randomized algorithms and probabilistic programs. So, this and the next sections are devoted to developing a theoretical framework and several algorithms for reachability analysis of quantum Markov chains. Hopefully, this will pave the way toward further research on algorithmic analysis of quantum programs.

Reachability analysis techniques for classical Markov chains heavily rely on algorithms for graph-reachability problems. Similarly, a kind of graph structures in Hilbert spaces, called quantum graphs, play a crucial role in the reachability analysis of quantum Markov chains. Therefore, in this section, we present a brief introduction to the theory of quantum graphs.

This section and the next one can be seen as the quantum generalization of reachability analysis of classical Markov chains; the reader should consult Chapter 10 of book [29] for their classical counterparts in case she/he finds some parts of these two sections hard to understand.

5.2.1 BASIC DEFINITIONS

A quantum graph structure naturally resides in a quantum Markov chain. So, let us start from the definition of quantum Markov chain. Recall that a classical Markov chain is a pair $\langle S, P \rangle$, where S is a finite set of states, and P is a matrix of transition probabilities, i.e., a mapping $P : S \times S \to [0, 1]$ such that

$$\sum_{t \in S} P(s, t) = 1$$

for every $s \in S$, where $P(s, t)$ is the probability of the system going from s to t. There is a directed graph underlying a Markov chain $\langle S, P \rangle$. The elements of S are vertices of the graph. The adjacency relation of this graph is defined as follows: for any $s, t \in S$, if $P(s, t) > 0$, then the graph has an edge from s to t. Understanding the structure of this graph is often very helpful for analysis of Markov chain $\langle S, P \rangle$ itself.

A quantum Markov chain is a quantum generalization of a Markov chain where the state space of a Markov chain is replaced by a Hilbert space and its transition matrix is replaced by a quantum operation which, as we saw in Subsection 2.1.7, is a mathematical formalism of the discrete-time evolution of (open) quantum systems.

Definition 5.2.1. *A quantum Markov chain is a pair* $\mathcal{C} = \langle \mathcal{H}, \mathcal{E} \rangle$, *where:*

(i) $\mathcal{H}$ *is a finite-dimensional Hilbert space;*
(ii) $\mathcal{E}$ *is a quantum operation (or super-operator) in* $\mathcal{H}$.

The behavior of a quantum Markov chain can be roughly described as follows: if currently the process is in a mixed state ρ, then it will be in state $\mathcal{E}(\rho)$ in the next step. So, a quantum Markov chain $\langle \mathcal{H}, \mathcal{E} \rangle$ is a discrete-time quantum system of which the state space is $\mathcal{H}$ and the dynamics is described by quantum operation $\mathcal{E}$. From the viewpoint of quantum programming, it can be used to model the body of quantum loop (5.9).

Now we examine the graph structure underlying a quantum Markov chain $\mathcal{C} = \langle \mathcal{H}, \mathcal{E} \rangle$. First of all, we introduce the adjacency relation between quantum states in $\mathcal{H}$ induced by the quantum operation $\mathcal{E}$. To this end, we need several auxiliary notions. Recall that $\mathcal{D}(\mathcal{H})$ denotes the set of partial density operators in $\mathcal{H}$, that is, positive operators ρ with trace $tr(\rho) \leq 1$. For any subset X of $\mathcal{H}$, we write $spanX$ for the subspace of $\mathcal{H}$ spanned by X, that is, it consists of all finite linear combinations of vectors in X.

Definition 5.2.2. *The support* $supp(\rho)$ *of a partial density operator* $\rho \in \mathcal{D}(\mathcal{H})$ *is the subspace of* $\mathcal{H}$ *spanned by the eigenvectors of* ρ *with nonzero eigenvalues.*

Definition 5.2.3. *Let* $\{X_k\}$ *be a family of subspaces of* $\mathcal{H}$. *Then the join of* $\{X_k\}$ *is defined by*

$$\bigvee_k X_k = span \left(\bigcup_k X_k \right).$$

In particular, we write $X \vee Y$ for the join of two subspaces X and Y. It is easy to see that $\bigvee_k X_k$ is the smallest subspace of $\mathcal{H}$ that contains all X_k.

Definition 5.2.4. *The image of a subspace X of $\mathcal{H}$ under a quantum operation $\mathcal{E}$ is*

$$\mathcal{E}(X) = \bigvee_{|\psi\rangle \in X} supp(\mathcal{E}(|\psi\rangle\langle\psi|)).$$

Intuitively, $\mathcal{E}(X)$ is the subspace of $\mathcal{H}$ spanned by the images under $\mathcal{E}$ of all states in X. Note that in the defining equation of $\mathcal{E}(X)$, $|\psi\rangle\langle\psi|$ is the density operator of pure state $|\psi\rangle$.

We collect several simple properties of the supports of density operators and images of quantum operations for later use.

Proposition 5.2.1

(i) *If $\rho = \sum_k \lambda_k |\psi_k\rangle\langle\psi_k|$ where all $\lambda_k > 0$ (but $|\psi_k\rangle$'s are not required to be pairwise orthogonal), then $supp(\rho) = span\{|\psi_k\rangle\}$;*

(ii) $supp(\rho + \sigma) = supp(\rho) \vee supp(\sigma)$;

(iii) *If $\mathcal{E}$ has the Kraus operator-sum representation $\mathcal{E} = \sum_{i \in I} E_i \circ E_i^\dagger$, then*

$$\mathcal{E}(X) = span\{E_i|\psi\rangle : i \in I \text{ and } |\psi\rangle \in X\};$$

(iv) $\mathcal{E}(X_1 \vee X_2) = \mathcal{E}(X_1) \vee \mathcal{E}(X_2)$. *Thus, $X \subseteq Y \Rightarrow \mathcal{E}(X) \subseteq \mathcal{E}(Y)$;*

(v) $\mathcal{E}(supp(\rho)) = supp(\mathcal{E}(\rho))$.

Exercise 5.2.1. *Prove Proposition 5.2.1.*

Based on Definitions 5.2.2 and 5.2.4, we can define the adjacency relation between (pure and mixed) states in a quantum Markov chain.

Definition 5.2.5. *Let $\mathcal{C} = \langle \mathcal{H}, \mathcal{E} \rangle$ be a quantum Markov chain, and let $|\varphi\rangle, |\psi\rangle \in \mathcal{H}$ be pure states and $\rho, \sigma \in \mathcal{D}(\mathcal{H})$ be mixed states in $\mathcal{H}$. Then*

(i) $|\varphi\rangle$ *is adjacent to* $|\psi\rangle$ *in $\mathcal{C}$, written $|\psi\rangle \to |\varphi\rangle$, if $|\varphi\rangle \in supp(\mathcal{E}(|\psi\rangle\langle\psi|))$.*

(ii) $|\varphi\rangle$ *is adjacent to ρ, written $\rho \to |\varphi\rangle$, if $|\varphi\rangle \in \mathcal{E}(supp(\rho))$.*

(iii) σ *is adjacent to ρ, written $\rho \to \sigma$, if $supp(\sigma) \subseteq \mathcal{E}(supp(\rho))$.*

Intuitively, $\langle \mathcal{H}, \to \rangle$ can be imagined as a "directed graph." However, there are two major differences between this graph and a classical graph:

- The set of vertices of a classical graph is usually finite, whereas the state Hilbert space $\mathcal{H}$ is a continuum;
- A classical graph has no mathematical structure other than the adjacency relation, but the space $\mathcal{H}$ possesses a linear algebraic structure that must be preserved by an algorithm searching through the graph $\langle \mathcal{H}, \to \rangle$.

As we will see in the following, these differences between a quantum graph and a classical graph make analysis of the former much harder than that of the latter.

We now can define the core notion of this section, namely reachability in a quantum graph, based on the adjacency relation in the same way as in the classical graph theory.

Definition 5.2.6

(i) *A path from ρ to σ in a quantum Markov chain $\mathcal{C}$ is a sequence*

$$\pi = \rho_0 \to \rho_1 \to \cdots \to \rho_n \ (n \geq 0)$$

of adjacent density operators in $\mathcal{C}$ such that $supp(\rho_0) \subseteq supp(\rho)$ and $\rho_n = \sigma$.

(ii) *For any density operators ρ and σ, if there is a path from ρ to σ then we say that σ is reachable from ρ in $\mathcal{C}$.*

Definition 5.2.7. *Let $\mathcal{C} = \langle \mathcal{H}, \mathcal{E} \rangle$ be a quantum Markov chain. For any $\rho \in \mathcal{D}(\mathcal{H})$, its reachable space in $\mathcal{C}$ is the subspace of $\mathcal{H}$ spanned by the states reachable from ρ:*

$$\mathcal{R}_{\mathcal{C}}(\rho) = span\{|\psi\rangle \in \mathcal{H} : |\psi\rangle \text{ is reachable from } \rho \text{ in } \mathcal{C}\}. \tag{5.20}$$

Note that in equation (5.20), $|\psi\rangle$ is identified with its density operator $|\psi\rangle\langle\psi|$.

Reachability in classical graph theory is transitive: that is, if a vertex v is reachable from u, and w is reachable from v, then w is also reachable from u. As expected, the following lemma shows that reachability in a quantum Markov chain is transitive too.

Lemma 5.2.1. *(Transitivity of reachability) For any $\rho, \sigma \in \mathcal{D}(\mathcal{H})$, if $supp(\rho) \subseteq \mathcal{R}_{\mathcal{C}}(\sigma)$, then $\mathcal{R}_{\mathcal{C}}(\rho) \subseteq \mathcal{R}_{\mathcal{C}}(\sigma)$.*

Exercise 5.2.2. *Prove Lemma 5.2.1.*

We now consider how to compute the reachable space of a state in a quantum Markov chain. To motivate our method, let us consider a classical directed graph $\langle V, E \rangle$, where V is the set of vertices and $E \subseteq V \times V$ is the adjacency relation. The transitive closure of E is defined as follows:

$$t(E) = \bigcup_{n=0}^{\infty} E^n = \{\langle v, v' \rangle : v' \text{ is reachable from } v \text{ in } \langle V, E \rangle\}.$$

It is well-known that the transitive closure can be computed as follows:

$$t(E) = \bigcup_{n=0}^{|V|-1} E^n$$

where $|V|$ is the number of vertices. As a quantum generalization of this fact, we have:

Theorem 5.2.1. *Let $\mathcal{C} = \langle \mathcal{H}, \mathcal{E} \rangle$ be a quantum Markov chain. If $d = \dim \mathcal{H}$, then for any $\rho \in \mathcal{D}(\mathcal{H})$, we have*

$$\mathcal{R}_{\mathcal{C}}(\rho) = \bigvee_{i=0}^{d-1} supp\left(\mathcal{E}^i(\rho)\right) \tag{5.21}$$

where $\mathcal{E}^i$ is the ith power of $\mathcal{E}$; that is, $\mathcal{E}^0 = \mathcal{I}$ (the identity operation in $\mathcal{H}$) and

$$\mathcal{E}^{i+1} = \mathcal{E} \circ \mathcal{E}^i$$

for $i \geq 0$.

Proof. We first show that $|\psi\rangle$ is reachable from ρ if and only if $|\psi\rangle \in supp\left(\mathcal{E}^i(\rho)\right)$ for some $i \geq 0$. In fact, if $|\psi\rangle$ is reachable from ρ, then there exist $\rho_1, \ldots, \rho_{i-1}$ such that

$$\rho \rightarrow \rho_1 \rightarrow \ldots \rightarrow \rho_{i-1} \rightarrow |\psi\rangle.$$

Using Proposition 5.2.1 (v), we obtain:

$$\begin{aligned}
|\psi\rangle \in supp(\mathcal{E}(\rho_{i-1})) &= \mathcal{E}(supp(\rho_{i-1})) \\
&\subseteq \mathcal{E}(supp(\mathcal{E}(\rho_{i-2})) \\
&= supp\left(\mathcal{E}^2(\rho_{i-2})\right) \subseteq \ldots \subseteq supp\left(\mathcal{E}^i(\rho)\right).
\end{aligned}$$

Conversely, if $|\psi\rangle \in supp(\mathcal{E}^i(\rho))$, then

$$\rho \rightarrow \mathcal{E}(\rho) \rightarrow \ldots \rightarrow \mathcal{E}^{i-1}(\rho) \rightarrow |\psi\rangle$$

and $|\psi\rangle$ is reachable from ρ. Therefore, it holds that

$$\begin{aligned}
\mathcal{R}_{\mathcal{C}}(\rho) &= span\{|\psi\rangle : |\psi\rangle \text{ is reachable from } \rho\} \\
&= span\left[\bigcup_{i=0}^{\infty} supp\left(\mathcal{E}^i(\rho)\right) \right] \\
&= \bigvee_{i=0}^{\infty} supp\left(\mathcal{E}^i(\rho)\right).
\end{aligned}$$

Now for each $n \geq 0$, we put

$$X_n = \bigvee_{i=0}^{n} supp\left(\mathcal{E}^i(\rho)\right).$$

Then we obtain an increasing sequence

$$X_0 \subseteq X_1 \subseteq \ldots \subseteq X_n \subseteq X_{n+1} \subseteq \ldots$$

of subspaces of $\mathcal{H}$. Let $d_n = \dim X_n$ for every $n \geq 0$. Then

$$d_0 \leq d_1 \leq \ldots \leq d_n \leq d_{n+1} \leq \ldots.$$

Note that $d_n \leq d$ for all n. Thus, there must be some n such that $d_n = d_{n+1}$. Assume that N is the smallest integer n such that $d_n = d_{n+1}$. Then we have

$$0 < \dim supp(\rho) = d_0 < d_1 < \ldots < d_{N-1} < d_N \leq d$$

and $N \leq d-1$. On the other hand, both X_N and X_{N+1} are subspaces of $\mathcal{H}$, $X_N \subseteq X_{N+1}$ and $\dim X_N = \dim X_{N+1}$. Thus, $X_N = X_{N+1}$. We can prove that

$$supp\left(\mathcal{E}^{N+k}(\rho)\right) \subseteq X_N$$

for all $k \geq 1$ by induction on k. So, $\mathcal{R}_{\mathcal{C}}(\rho) = X_N$. $\square$

5.2.2 BOTTOM STRONGLY CONNECTED COMPONENTS

We carefully defined the graph underlying a quantum Markov chain in the previous subsection. Now we move forward to examine its mathematical structure. In classical graph theory, the notion of bottom strongly connected component (BSCC) is an important tool in the studies of reachability problems. It has also been extensively applied in analysis of probabilistic programs modelled by Markov chains. In this subsection, we extend this notion to the quantum case. The quantum version of BSCC will be a basis of the reachability analysis algorithms for quantum Markov chains given in the next section.

We first introduce an auxiliary notation. Let X be a subspace of $\mathcal{H}$ and $\mathcal{E}$ a quantum operation in $\mathcal{H}$. Then the restriction of $\mathcal{E}$ on X is the quantum operation $\mathcal{E}_X$ in X defined by

$$\mathcal{E}_X(\rho) = P_X \mathcal{E}(\rho) P_X$$

for all $\rho \in \mathcal{D}(X)$, where P_X is the projection onto X. With this notation, we are able to define strong connectivity in a quantum Markov chain.

Definition 5.2.8. *Let $\mathcal{C} = \langle \mathcal{H}, \mathcal{E} \rangle$ be a quantum Markov chain. A subspace X of $\mathcal{H}$ is called strongly connected in $\mathcal{C}$ if for any $|\varphi\rangle, |\psi\rangle \in X$, we have:*

$$|\varphi\rangle \in \mathcal{R}_{\mathcal{C}_X}(\psi) \text{ and } |\psi\rangle \in \mathcal{R}_{\mathcal{C}_X}(\varphi) \tag{5.22}$$

where $\varphi = |\varphi\rangle\langle\varphi|$ and $\psi = |\psi\rangle\langle\psi|$ are the density operators corresponding to pure states $|\varphi\rangle$ and $\psi\rangle$, respectively, quantum Markov chain $\mathcal{C}_X = \langle X, \mathcal{E}_X \rangle$ is the restriction of $\mathcal{C}$ on X, and $\mathcal{R}_{\mathcal{C}_X}(\cdot)$ denotes a reachable subspace in $\mathcal{C}_X$.

Intuitively, condition (5.22) means that for any two states $|\varphi\rangle, |\psi\rangle$ in X, $|\varphi\rangle$ is reachable from $|\psi\rangle$ and $|\psi\rangle$ is reachable from $|\varphi\rangle$.

We write $SC(\mathcal{C})$ for the set of all strongly connected subspaces of $\mathcal{H}$ in $\mathcal{C}$. It is clear that $SC(\mathcal{C})$ with set inclusion $\subseteq$, i.e., $(SC(\mathcal{C}), \subseteq)$ is a partial order (see Definition 3.3.2). To further examine this partial order, we recall several concepts from lattice theory. Let $(L, \sqsubseteq)$ be a partial order. If any two elements $x, y \in L$ are comparable, that is, either $x \sqsubseteq y$ or $y \sqsubseteq x$, then we say that L is linearly ordered by $\sqsubseteq$. A partial order $(L, \sqsubseteq)$ is said to be inductive if for any subset K of L that is linearly ordered by $\sqsubseteq$, the least upper bound $\bigsqcup K$ exists in L.

Lemma 5.2.2. *The partial order $(SC(\mathcal{C}), \subseteq)$ is inductive.*

Exercise 5.2.3. *Prove Lemma 5.2.2.*

Now we further consider some special elements in the partial order $(SC(\mathcal{C}), \subseteq)$. Recall that an element x of a partial order $(L, \sqsubseteq)$ is called a maximal element of L if for any $y \in L$, $x \sqsubseteq y$ implies $x = y$. The Zorn lemma in set theory asserts that every inductive partial order has (at least one) maximal elements.

Definition 5.2.9. *A maximal element of $(SC(\mathcal{C}), \subseteq)$ is called a strongly connected component (SCC) of $\mathcal{C}$.*

To define the concept of BSCC (bottom strongly connected component) in a quantum Markov chain, we need one more auxiliary notion, namely invariant subspace.

Definition 5.2.10. *We say that a subspace X of $\mathcal{H}$ is invariant under a quantum operation $\mathcal{E}$ if $\mathcal{E}(X) \subseteq X$.*

The intuition behind the inclusion $\mathcal{E}(X) \subseteq X$ is that quantum operation $\mathcal{E}$ cannot transfer a state in X into a state outside X. Suppose that quantum operation $\mathcal{E}$ has the Kraus representation $\mathcal{E} = \sum_i E_i \circ E_i^\dagger$. Then it follows from Proposition 5.2.1 that X is invariant under $\mathcal{E}$ if and only if it is invariant under the Kraus operators E_i: $E_i X \subseteq X$ for all i.

The following theorem presents a useful property of invariant subspaces showing that a quantum operation does not decrease the probability of falling into an invariant subspace.

Theorem 5.2.2. *Let $\mathcal{C} = \langle \mathcal{H}, \mathcal{E} \rangle$ be a quantum Markov chain. If subspace X of $\mathcal{H}$ is invariant under $\mathcal{E}$, then we have:*

$$tr(P_X \mathcal{E}(\rho)) \geq tr(P_X \rho)$$

for all $\rho \in \mathcal{D}(\mathcal{H})$.

Proof. It suffices to show that

$$tr(P_X \mathcal{E}(|\psi\rangle \langle \psi|)) \geq tr(P_X |\psi\rangle \langle \psi|)$$

for each $|\psi\rangle \in \mathcal{H}$. Assume that $\mathcal{E} = \sum_i E_i \circ E_i^\dagger$, and $|\psi\rangle = |\psi_1\rangle + |\psi_2\rangle$ where $|\psi_1\rangle \in X$ and $|\psi_2\rangle \in X^\perp$. Since X is invariant under $\mathcal{E}$, we have $E_i|\psi_1\rangle \in X$ and $P_X E_i|\psi_1\rangle = E_i|\psi_1\rangle$. Then

$$a \stackrel{\triangle}{=} \sum_i tr\left(P_X E_i |\psi_2\rangle \langle \psi_1| E_i^\dagger\right) = \sum_i tr\left(E_i |\psi_2\rangle \langle \psi_1| E_i^\dagger P_X\right)$$

$$= \sum_i tr\left(E_i |\psi_2\rangle \langle \psi_1| E_i^\dagger\right) = \sum_i \langle \psi_1| E_i^\dagger E_i |\psi_2\rangle = \langle \psi_1 | \psi_2 \rangle = 0.$$

Similarly, it holds that

$$b \stackrel{\triangle}{=} \sum_i tr\left(P_X E_i |\psi_1\rangle \langle \psi_2| E_i^\dagger\right) = 0.$$

Moreover, we have:

$$c \overset{\triangle}{=} \sum_i tr\left(P_X E_i |\psi_2\rangle\langle\psi_2| E_i^\dagger\right) \geq 0.$$

Therefore,

$$tr(P_X \mathcal{E}(|\psi\rangle\langle\psi|)) = \sum_i tr\left(P_X E_i |\psi_1\rangle\langle\psi_1| E_i^\dagger\right) + a + b + c$$

$$\geq \sum_i tr\left(P_X E_i |\psi_1\rangle\langle\psi_1| E_i^\dagger\right) = \sum_i \langle\psi_1| E_i^\dagger E_i |\psi_1\rangle$$

$$= \langle\psi_1|\psi_1\rangle = tr(P_X|\psi\rangle\langle\psi|).$$

$\square$

Now we are ready to introduce the key notion of this subsection, namely bottom strongly connected component.

Definition 5.2.11. *Let* $\mathcal{C} = \langle\mathcal{H}, \mathcal{E}\rangle$ *be a quantum Markov chain. Then a subspace* X *of* $\mathcal{H}$ *is called a bottom strongly connected component (BSCC) of* $\mathcal{C}$ *if it is an SCC of* $\mathcal{C}$ *and it is invariant under* $\mathcal{E}$.

Example 5.2.1. *Consider quantum Markov chain* $\mathcal{C} = \langle\mathcal{H}, \mathcal{E}\rangle$ *with state Hilbert space* $\mathcal{H} = span\{|0\rangle, \cdots, |4\rangle\}$ *and quantum operation* $\mathcal{E} = \sum_{i=1}^5 E_i \circ E_i^\dagger$, *where the Kraus operators are given by*

$$E_1 = \frac{1}{\sqrt{2}}(|1\rangle\langle\theta_{01}^+| + |3\rangle\langle\theta_{23}^+|), \quad E_2 = \frac{1}{\sqrt{2}}(|1\rangle\langle\theta_{01}^-| + |3\rangle\langle\theta_{23}^-|),$$

$$E_3 = \frac{1}{\sqrt{2}}(|0\rangle\langle\theta_{01}^+| + |2\rangle\langle\theta_{23}^+|), \quad E_4 = \frac{1}{\sqrt{2}}(|0\rangle\langle\theta_{01}^-| + |2\rangle\langle\theta_{23}^-|),$$

$$E_5 = \frac{1}{10}(|0\rangle\langle 4| + |1\rangle\langle 4| + |2\rangle\langle 4| + 4|3\rangle\langle 4| + 9|4\rangle\langle 4|),$$

and

$$|\theta_{ij}^\pm\rangle = (|i\rangle \pm |j\rangle)/\sqrt{2}. \tag{5.23}$$

It is easy to verify that $B = span\{|0\rangle, |1\rangle\}$ *is a BSCC of quantum Markov chain* $\mathcal{C}$. *Indeed, for any* $|\psi\rangle = \alpha|0\rangle + \beta|1\rangle \in B$, *we have*

$$\mathcal{E}(|\psi\rangle\langle\psi|) = (|0\rangle\langle 0| + |1\rangle\langle 1|)/2.$$

Characterizations of BSCCs:

To help the reader have a better understanding of them, we give two characterizations of BSCCs. The first characterization is simple and it is presented in terms of reachable subspaces.

Lemma 5.2.3. *A subspace* X *is a BSCC of quantum Markov chain* $\mathcal{C}$ *if and only if* $\mathcal{R}_\mathcal{C}(|\varphi\rangle\langle\varphi|) = X$ *for any* $|\varphi\rangle \in X$.

Proof. We only prove the "only if" part because the "if" part is obvious. Suppose X is a BSCC. By the strong connectivity of X, we have $\mathcal{R}_\mathcal{C}(|\varphi\rangle\langle\varphi|) \supseteq X$ for all

$|\varphi\rangle \in X$. On the other hand, for any vector $|\varphi\rangle$ in X, using the invariance of X, i.e., $\mathcal{E}(X) \subseteq X$, it is easy to show that if $|\psi\rangle$ is reachable from $|\varphi\rangle$ then $|\psi\rangle \in X$. So, $\mathcal{R}_{\mathcal{C}}(|\varphi\rangle\langle\varphi|) \subseteq X$. $\qquad\square$

The second characterization of BSCCs is a little bit more complicated. To present it, we need the notion of fixed point of a quantum operation.

Definition 5.2.12

(i) *A density operator ρ in $\mathcal{H}$ is called a fixed point state of quantum operation $\mathcal{E}$ if $\mathcal{E}(\rho) = \rho$.*

(ii) *A fixed point state ρ of quantum operation $\mathcal{E}$ is called minimal if for any fixed point state σ of $\mathcal{E}$, it holds that $supp(\sigma) \subseteq supp(\rho)$ implies $\sigma = \rho$.*

The following lemma shows a close connection between the invariant subspaces under a quantum operation $\mathcal{E}$ and the fixed point states of $\mathcal{E}$. It provides a key step in the proof of Theorem 5.2.3 to follow.

Lemma 5.2.4. *If ρ is a fixed point state of $\mathcal{E}$, then $supp(\rho)$ is invariant under $\mathcal{E}$. Conversely, if X is invariant under $\mathcal{E}$, then there exists a fixed point state ρ_X of $\mathcal{E}$ such that $supp(\rho_X) \subseteq X$.*

Exercise 5.2.4. *Prove Lemma 5.2.4.*

Now we are able to give the second characterization, which establishes a connection between BSCCs and minimal fixed point states.

Theorem 5.2.3. *A subspace X is a BSCC of quantum Markov chain $\mathcal{C} = \langle \mathcal{H}, \mathcal{E} \rangle$ if and only if there exists a minimal fixed point state ρ of $\mathcal{E}$ such that $supp(\rho) = X$.*

Proof. We first prove the "if" part. Let ρ be a minimal fixed point state such that $supp(\rho) = X$. Then by Lemma 5.2.4, X is invariant under $\mathcal{E}$. To show that X is a BSCC, by Lemma 5.2.3 it suffices to prove that for any $|\varphi\rangle \in X$, $\mathcal{R}_{\mathcal{C}}(|\varphi\rangle\langle\varphi|) = X$. Suppose conversely that there exists $|\psi\rangle \in X$ such that $\mathcal{R}_{\mathcal{C}}(|\psi\rangle\langle\psi|) \subsetneq X$. Then by Lemma 5.2.1 we can show that $\mathcal{R}_{\mathcal{C}}(|\psi\rangle\langle\psi|)$ is invariant under $\mathcal{E}$. By Lemma 5.2.4, we can find a fixed point state ρ_ψ with

$$supp(\rho_\psi) \subseteq \mathcal{R}_{\mathcal{C}}(|\psi\rangle\langle\psi|) \subsetneq X.$$

This contradicts the assumption that ρ is minimal.

For the "only if" part, suppose that X is a BSCC. Then X is invariant under $\mathcal{E}$, and by Lemma 5.2.4, we can find a minimal fixed point state ρ_X of $\mathcal{E}$ with $supp(\rho_X) \subseteq X$. Take $|\varphi\rangle \in supp(\rho_X)$. By Lemma 5.2.5 we have $\mathcal{R}_{\mathcal{C}}(|\varphi\rangle\langle\varphi|) = X$. But using Lemma 5.2.4 again, we know that $supp(\rho_X)$ is invariant under $\mathcal{E}$, so $\mathcal{R}_{\mathcal{C}}(|\varphi\rangle\langle\varphi|) \subseteq supp(\rho_X)$. Therefore, $supp(\rho_X) = X$. $\qquad\square$

As mentioned previously, BSCCs will play a key role in analysis of quantum Markov chains. This application of BSCCs is based on not only our understanding of their structure described in Lemma 5.2.3 and Theorem 5.2.3 but also their relationship to each other. The following lemma clarifies the relationship between two different BSCCs.

Lemma 5.2.5

(i) *For any two different BSCCs X and Y of quantum Markov chain C, we have*
$X \cap Y = \{0\}$ *(0-dimensional Hilbert space).*

(ii) *If X and Y are two BSCCs of C with* $\dim X \neq \dim Y$, *then they are orthogonal,*
i.e., $X \perp Y$.

Proof.

(i) Suppose conversely that there exists a nonzero vector $|\varphi\rangle \in X \cap Y$. Then by
Lemma 5.2.3, we have $X = \mathcal{R}_{\mathcal{C}}(|\varphi\rangle\langle\varphi|) = Y$, contradicting the assumption that
$X \neq Y$. Therefore $X \cap Y = \{0\}$.

(ii) We postpone this part to Section 5.4 because it needs to use Theorem 5.2.5 in
the following section.   □

5.2.3 DECOMPOSITION OF THE STATE HILBERT SPACE

In the previous two subsections, a graph structure in a quantum Markov chain was
defined, and the notion of BSCC was generalized to the quantum case. In this
subsection, we further study such a graph structure in a quantum Markov chain
through a decomposition of the state Hilbert space.

Recall that a state in a classical Markov chain is transient if there is a nonzero
probability that the process will never return to it, and a state is recurrent if from it
the returning probability is 1. It is well-known that in a finite-state Markov chain a
state is recurrent if and only if it belongs to some BSCC, and thus the state space
of the Markov chain can be decomposed into the union of some BSCCs and a
transient subspace. The aim of this subsection is to prove a quantum generalization
of this result. Such a decomposition of the state Hilbert space forms a basis of our
algorithms for reachability analysis of quantum Markov chains, to be presented in
the next section.

Transient Subspaces:

Let us first define the notion of a transient subspace of a quantum Markov
chain. Transient states in a finite-state classical Markov chain can be equivalently
characterized as follows: a state is transient if and only if the probability that the
system stays at it will eventually become 0. This observation motivates the following:

Definition 5.2.13. *A subspace* $X \subseteq \mathcal{H}$ *is transient in a quantum Markov chain*
$\mathcal{C} = \langle \mathcal{H}, \mathcal{E} \rangle$ *if*

$$\lim_{k \to \infty} tr\left(P_X \mathcal{E}^k(\rho)\right) = 0 \tag{5.24}$$

for any $\rho \in \mathcal{D}(\mathcal{H})$, *where* P_X *is the projection onto X.*

Intuitively, $tr_X\left(P_X\mathcal{E}^k(\rho)\right)$ is the probability that the system's state falls into the
subspace X after executing quantum operation $\mathcal{E}$ for k times. So, equation (5.24)
means that the probability that the system stays in subspace X is eventually 0.

It is obvious from this definition that if subspaces $X \subseteq Y$ and Y is transient then X is transient too. So, it is sufficient to understand the structure of the largest transient subspace. Fortunately, we have an elegant characterization of the largest transient subspace. To give such a characterization, we need the following:

Definition 5.2.14. *Let $\mathcal{E}$ be a quantum operation in $\mathcal{H}$. Then its asymptotic average is*

$$\mathcal{E}_{\infty} = \lim_{N \to \infty} \frac{1}{N} \sum_{n=1}^{N} \mathcal{E}^n. \tag{5.25}$$

It follows from Lemma 3.3.4 that $\mathcal{E}_{\infty}$ is a quantum operation as well.

The following lemma points out a link between fixed point states of a quantum operation and its asymptotic average. This link will be used in the proof of Theorem 5.2.4 following.

Lemma 5.2.6

(i) *For any density operator ρ, $\mathcal{E}_{\infty}(\rho)$ is a fixed point state of $\mathcal{E}$;*
(ii) *For any fixed point state σ, it holds that $supp(\sigma) \subseteq \mathcal{E}_{\infty}(\mathcal{H})$.*

Exercise 5.2.5. *Prove Lemma 5.2.6.*

Now we can give a characterization of the largest transient subspace in terms of asymptotic average.

Theorem 5.2.4. *Let $C = \langle \mathcal{H}, \mathcal{E} \rangle$ be a quantum Markov chain. Then the orthocomplement of the image of $\mathcal{H}$ under the asymptotic average of $\mathcal{E}$:*

$$T_{\mathcal{E}} = \mathcal{E}_{\infty}(\mathcal{H})^{\perp}$$

is the largest transient subspace in C, where $\perp$ stands for orthocomplement (see Definition 2.1.7(ii)).

Proof. Let P be the projection onto the subspace $T_{\mathcal{E}}$. For any $\rho \in \mathcal{D}(\mathcal{H})$, we put $p_k = tr\left(P\mathcal{E}^k(\rho)\right)$ for every $k \geq 0$. Since $\mathcal{E}_{\infty}(\mathcal{H})$ is invariant under $\mathcal{E}$, by Theorem 5.2.2 we know that the sequence $\{p_k\}$ is non-increasing. Thus the limit $p_{\infty} = \lim_{k \to \infty} p_k$ does exist. Furthermore, noting that

$$supp(\mathcal{E}_{\infty}(\rho)) \subseteq \mathcal{E}_{\infty}(\mathcal{H})$$

we have

$$0 = tr(P\mathcal{E}_{\infty}(\rho)) = tr\left(P \lim_{N \to \infty} \frac{1}{N} \sum_{n=1}^{N} \mathcal{E}^n(\rho)\right)$$

$$= \lim_{N \to \infty} \frac{1}{N} \sum_{n=1}^{N} tr\left(P\mathcal{E}^n(\rho)\right)$$

$$= \lim_{N \to \infty} \frac{1}{N} \sum_{n=1}^{N} p_n$$

$$\geq \lim_{N \to \infty} \frac{1}{N} \sum_{n=1}^{N} p_\infty = p_\infty.$$

Thus $p_\infty = 0$, and $T_\mathcal{E}$ is transient by the arbitrariness of ρ.

To show that $T_\mathcal{E}$ is the largest transient subspace of $\mathcal{C}$, we first note that

$$supp\,(\mathcal{E}_\infty(I)) = \mathcal{E}_\infty(\mathcal{H}).$$

Let $\sigma = \mathcal{E}_\infty(I/d)$. Then by Lemma 5.2.6, σ is a fixed point state with $supp(\sigma) = T_\mathcal{E}^\perp$. Suppose Y is a transient subspace. We have

$$tr(P_Y \sigma) = \lim_{i \to \infty} tr\left(P_Y \mathcal{E}^i(\sigma)\right) = 0.$$

This implies $Y \perp supp(\sigma) = T_\mathcal{E}^\perp$. So, we have $Y \subseteq T_\mathcal{E}$.   □

BSCC Decomposition:

After introducing the notion of transient subspace, we now consider how to decompose the state Hilbert space of a quantum Markov chain $\mathcal{C} = \langle \mathcal{H}, \mathcal{E} \rangle$. First, it can be simply divided into two parts:

$$\mathcal{H} = \mathcal{E}_\infty(\mathcal{H}) \oplus \mathcal{E}_\infty(\mathcal{H})^\perp$$

where $\oplus$ stands for (orthogonal) sum (see Definition 2.1.8), and $\mathcal{E}_\infty(\mathcal{H})$ is the image of the whole state Hilbert space under the asymptotic average. We already know from Theorem 5.2.4 that $\mathcal{E}_\infty(\mathcal{H})^\perp$ is the largest transient subspace. So, what we need to do next is to examine the structure of $\mathcal{E}_\infty(\mathcal{H})$.

Our procedure for decomposition of $\mathcal{E}_\infty(\mathcal{H})$ is based on the following key lemma that shows how a fixed point state can be subtracted by another.

Lemma 5.2.7. *Let ρ and σ be two fixed point states of $\mathcal{E}$, and $supp(\sigma) \subsetneq supp(\rho)$. Then there exists another fixed point state η such that*

(i) *$supp(\eta) \perp supp(\sigma)$; and*
(ii) *$supp(\rho) = supp(\eta) \oplus supp(\sigma)$.*

Intuitively, state η in the preceding lemma can be understood as the subtraction of ρ by σ. For readability, the proof of this lemma is postponed to Section 5.4.

Now the BSCC decomposition of $\mathcal{E}_\infty(\mathcal{H})$ can be derived simply by repeated applications of the preceding lemma.

Theorem 5.2.5. *Let $\mathcal{C} = \langle \mathcal{H}, \mathcal{E} \rangle$ be a quantum Markov chain. Then $\mathcal{E}_\infty(\mathcal{H})$ can be decomposed into the direct sum of orthogonal BSCCs of $\mathcal{C}$.*

Proof. We notice that $\mathcal{E}_\infty\left(\frac{I}{d}\right)$ is a fixed point state of $\mathcal{E}$ and

$$supp\left(\mathcal{E}_\infty\left(\frac{I}{d}\right)\right) = \mathcal{E}_\infty(\mathcal{H})$$

where $d = \dim \mathcal{H}$. Then it suffices to prove the following:

- *Claim*: Let ρ be a fixed point state of $\mathcal{E}$. Then $supp(\rho)$ can be decomposed into the direct sum of some orthogonal BSCCs.

In fact, if ρ is minimal, then by Theorem 5.2.3, $supp(\rho)$ is itself a BSCC and we are done. Otherwise, we apply Lemma 5.2.7 to obtain two fixed point states of $\mathcal{E}$ with smaller orthogonal supports. Repeating this procedure, we can get a set of minimal fixed point states $\rho_1, \cdots, \rho_k$ with mutually orthogonal supports such that

$$supp(\rho) = \bigoplus_{i=1}^{k} supp(\rho_i).$$

Finally, from Lemma 5.2.4 and Theorem 5.2.3, we know that each $supp(\rho_i)$ is a BSCC. $\qquad\square$

Now we eventually achieve the decomposition promised at the beginning of this subsection. Combining Theorems 5.2.4 and 5.2.5, we see that the state Hilbert space of a quantum Markov chain $\mathcal{C} = \langle \mathcal{H}, \mathcal{E} \rangle$ can be decomposed into the direct sum of a transient subspace and a family of BSCCs:

$$\mathcal{H} = B_1 \oplus \cdots \oplus B_u \oplus T_{\mathcal{E}} \qquad (5.26)$$

where B_i's are orthogonal BSCCs of $\mathcal{C}$, and $T_{\mathcal{E}}$ is the largest transient subspace.

The preceding theorem shows the existence of BSCC decomposition for quantum Markov chains. Then a question immediately arises: is such a decomposition unique? It is well known that the BSCC decomposition of a classical Markov chain is unique. However, it is not the case for quantum Markov chains, as shown in the following:

Example 5.2.2. *Let quantum Markov chain* $\mathcal{C} = \langle \mathcal{H}, \mathcal{E} \rangle$ *be given as in Example 5.2.1. Then*

$$B_1 = span\{|0\rangle, |1\rangle\}, \quad B_2 = span\{|2\rangle, |3\rangle\},$$
$$D_1 = span\{|\theta_{02}^{+}\rangle, |\theta_{13}^{+}\rangle\}, \quad D_2 = span\{|\theta_{02}^{-}\rangle, |\theta_{13}^{-}\rangle\}$$

are all BSCCs, where the states $|\theta_{ij}^{\pm}\rangle$ *are defined by equation (5.23). It is easy to see that* $T_{\mathcal{E}} = span\{|4\rangle\}$ *is the largest transient subspace. Furthermore, we have two different decompositions:*

$$\mathcal{H} = B_1 \oplus B_2 \oplus T_{\mathcal{E}} = D_1 \oplus D_2 \oplus T_{\mathcal{E}}.$$

Although the BSCC decomposition of a quantum Markov chain is not unique, fortunately we have the following weak uniqueness in the sense that any two decompositions have the same number of BSCCs, and the corresponding BSCCs in them must have the same dimension.

Theorem 5.2.6. *Let* $\mathcal{C} = \langle \mathcal{H}, \mathcal{E} \rangle$ *be a quantum Markov chain, and let*

$$\mathcal{H} = B_1 \oplus \cdots \oplus B_u \oplus T_{\mathcal{E}} = D_1 \oplus \cdots \oplus D_v \oplus T_{\mathcal{E}}$$

be two decompositions in the form of equation (5.26), and B_is and D_is are arranged, respectively, according to the increasing order of the dimensions. Then

(i) *$u = v$; and*
(ii) *$\dim B_i = \dim D_i$ for each $1 \leq i \leq u$.*

Proof. For simplicity, we write $b_i = \dim B_i$ and $d_i = \dim D_i$. We prove by induction on i that $b_i = d_i$ for any $1 \leq i \leq \min\{u, v\}$, and thus $u = v$ as well.

First, we claim $b_1 = d_1$. Otherwise let, say, $b_1 < d_1$. Then $b_1 < d_j$ for all j. Thus by Lemma 5.2.5 (ii), we have:

$$B_1 \perp \bigoplus_{j=1}^{v} D_j.$$

But we also have $B_1 \perp T_{\mathcal{E}}$. This is a contradiction, as it holds that

$$\left(\bigoplus_{j=1}^{v} D_j \right) \oplus T_{\mathcal{E}} = \mathcal{H}.$$

Now suppose we already have $b_i = d_i$ for all $i < n$. We claim $b_n = d_n$. Otherwise let, say, $b_n < d_n$. Then from Lemma 5.2.5 (ii), we have

$$\bigoplus_{i=1}^{n} B_i \perp \bigoplus_{i=n}^{v} D_i,$$

and consequently

$$\bigoplus_{i=1}^{n} B_i \subseteq \bigoplus_{i=1}^{n-1} D_i.$$

On the other hand, we have

$$\dim \left(\bigoplus_{i=1}^{n} B_i \right) = \sum_{i=1}^{n} b_i > \sum_{i=1}^{n-1} d_i = \dim \left(\bigoplus_{i=1}^{n-1} D_i \right),$$

a contradiction.   □

Decomposition Algorithm:

We have proved the existence and weak uniqueness of BSCC decomposition for quantum Markov chains. With these theoretical preparations, we can now present an algorithm for finding a BSCC and transient subspace decomposition of a quantum Markov chain; see Algorithm 2 together with the procedure Decompose(X).

To conclude this section, we consider correctness and complexity of the BSCC decomposition algorithms. The following lemma is the key in settling the complexity of Algorithm 2.

Algorithm 2 **DECOMPOSE**($\mathcal{C}$)

input : A quantum Markov chain $\mathcal{C} = \langle \mathcal{H}, \mathcal{E} \rangle$
output: A set of orthogonal BSCCs $\{B_i\}$ and a transient subspace $T_{\mathcal{E}}$ such that $\mathcal{H} = (\bigoplus_i B_i) \oplus T_{\mathcal{E}}$
begin
    $\mathcal{B} \leftarrow \text{Decompose}(\mathcal{E}_\infty(\mathcal{H}))$;
    return $\mathcal{B}$, $\mathcal{E}_\infty(\mathcal{H})^\perp$;
end

Procedure Decompose(X)

input : A subspace X which is the support of a fixed point state of $\mathcal{E}$
output: A set of orthogonal BSCCs $\{B_i\}$ such that $X = \bigoplus B_i$
begin
    $\mathcal{E}' \leftarrow P_X \circ \mathcal{E}$;
    $\mathcal{B} \leftarrow$ a density operator basis of the set $\{$operators A in $\mathcal{H} : \mathcal{E}'(A) = A\}$;
    if $|\mathcal{B}| = 1$ **then**
        $\rho \leftarrow$ the unique element of $\mathcal{B}$;
        return $\{supp(\rho)\}$;
    else
        $\rho_1, \rho_2 \leftarrow$ two arbitrary elements of $\mathcal{B}$;
        $\rho \leftarrow$ positive part of $\rho_1 - \rho_2$;
        $Y \leftarrow supp(\rho)^\perp$;   (* the orthocomplement of $supp(\rho)$ in X*)
        return $\text{Decompose}(supp(\rho)) \cup \text{Decompose}(Y)$;
    end
end

Lemma 5.2.8. *Let $\langle \mathcal{H}, \mathcal{E} \rangle$ be a quantum Markov chain with $d = \dim \mathcal{H}$, and $\rho \in \mathcal{D}(\mathcal{H})$. Then*

(i) *The asymptotic average state $\mathcal{E}_\infty(\rho)$ can be computed in time $O(d^8)$.*
(ii) *A density operator basis of the set of fixed points of $\mathcal{E}$:*

$$\{operators\ A\ in\ \mathcal{H} : \mathcal{E}(A) = A\}$$

can be computed in time $O(d^6)$.

For readability, we postpone the proof of this lemma into Section 5.4.

Now the correctness and complexity of Algorithm 2 are shown in the following:

Theorem 5.2.7. *Given a quantum Markov chain $\langle \mathcal{H}, \mathcal{E} \rangle$, Algorithm 2 decomposes the Hilbert space $\mathcal{H}$ into the direct sum of a family of orthogonal BSCCs and a transient subspace of $\mathcal{C}$ in time $O(d^8)$, where $d = \dim \mathcal{H}$.*

Proof. The correctness of Algorithm 2 is easy to prove. Actually, it follows immediately from Theorem 5.2.4.

For the time complexity, we first notice that the nonrecursive part of the procedure Decompose(X) runs in time $O(d^6)$. Thus, total complexity of Decompose(X) is $O(d^7)$, as the procedure calls itself at most $O(d)$ times. Algorithm 2 first computes $\mathcal{E}_\infty(\mathcal{H})$, which, as indicated by Lemma 5.2.8 (i), costs time $O(d^8)$, and then feeds it into the procedure Decompose(X). Thus the total complexity of Algorithm 2 is $O(d^8)$. □

Problem 5.2.1. *Quantum graph theory has been developed in this section merely to provide necessary mathematical tools for reachability analysis of quantum Markov chains in the next section. It is desirable to build a richer theory of quantum graphs by generalizing more results in (di-)graphs theory [33] into the quantum setting and by understanding the essential differences between classical and quantum graphs.*

Problem 5.2.2. *The notion of a noncommutative graph was introduced in [76] in order to give a characterization of channel capacity in quantum Shannon information theory. It is interesting to find some connections between non-commutative graphs and quantum graphs defined in this section.*

5.3 REACHABILITY ANALYSIS OF QUANTUM MARKOV CHAINS

The graph structures of quantum Markov chains were carefully examined in the last section. This prepares necessary mathematical tools for reachability analysis of quantum Markov chains. In this section, we study reachability and its two variants – repeated reachability and persistence – of quantum Markov chains using the quantum graph theory developed in the last section.

As will be shown in Exercise 5.3.1 following, termination of a quantum **while**-loop can be reduced to a reachability problem of a quantum Markov chain. Indeed, as in classical and probabilistic programming theory, many other behaviors of quantum programs can be described in terms of the reachability and persistence discussed in this section when their semantics are modelled as quantum Markov chains. Furthermore, this section provides a basis for further research on analysis of more complicated quantum programs such as recursive quantum programs defined in Section 3.4, as well as nondeterministic and concurrent quantum programs, because various extensions of quantum Markov chains, e.g., recursive quantum Markov chains and quantum Markov decision processes, can serve as their semantic models.

5.3.1 REACHABILITY PROBABILITY

We first consider reachability probability in a quantum Markov chain, which is formally defined in the following:

Definition 5.3.1. *Let $\langle \mathcal{H}, \mathcal{E} \rangle$ be a quantum Markov chain, $\rho \in \mathcal{D}(\mathcal{H})$ an initial state, and $X \subseteq \mathcal{H}$ a subspace. Then the probability of reaching X, starting from ρ, is*

$$\Pr(\rho \vDash \Diamond X) = \lim_{i \to \infty} tr\left(P_X \widetilde{\mathcal{E}}^i(\rho)\right) \tag{5.27}$$

where $\widetilde{\mathcal{E}}^i$ is the composition of i copies of $\widetilde{\mathcal{E}}$, and $\widetilde{\mathcal{E}}$ is the quantum operation defined by

$$\widetilde{\mathcal{E}}(\sigma) = P_X \sigma P_X + \mathcal{E}\left(P_{X^\perp} \sigma P_{X^\perp}\right)$$

for all density operators σ.

Obviously, the limit in the preceding definition exists, as the probabilities $tr\left(P_X \widetilde{\mathcal{E}}^i(\rho)\right)$ are nondecreasing in number i. Intuitively, $\widetilde{\mathcal{E}}$ can be seen as a procedure that first performs the projective measurement $\{P_X, P_{X^\perp}\}$ and then applies the identity operator $\mathcal{I}$ or $\mathcal{E}$ depending on the measurement outcome.

Exercise 5.3.1

(i) *Consider the special form of quantum **while**-loop (5.9) where the measurement in the loop guard is projective:*

$$M = \{M_0 = P_X, M_1 = P_{X^\perp}\}.$$

Find a connection between the reachability probability $\Pr(\rho \vDash \Diamond X)$ in quantum Markov chain $\langle \mathcal{H}, \mathcal{E} \rangle$ and the termination probability

$$p_T(\rho) = 1 - \lim_{n \to \infty} p_{NT}^{(n)}(\rho)$$

where ρ is the initial state, $\mathcal{E}$ is the quantum operation in the loop body, and $p_{NT}^{(n)}(\rho)$ is defined by equations (5.11) and (5.12).

(ii) *Note that a general measurement can be implemented by a projective measurement together with a unitary transformation (see Subsection 2.1.5). Show how the termination problem of loop (5.9) in its full generality can be reduced to the reachability problem of a quantum Markov chain.*

Computation of Reachability Probability:

Now we see how the reachability probability (5.27) can be computed using the quantum BSCC decomposition given in the last section. We first note that the subspace X in equation (5.27) is invariant under $\widetilde{\mathcal{E}}$. Thus $\langle X, \widetilde{\mathcal{E}} \rangle$ is a quantum Markov chain. It is easy to verify that $\widetilde{\mathcal{E}}_\infty(X) = X$. Thus, we can decompose X into a set of orthogonal BSCCs according to $\widetilde{\mathcal{E}}$ by Theorem 5.2.5.

The following lemma shows a connection between the limit probability of hitting a BSCC and the probability that the asymptotic average of the initial state lies in the same BSCC.

Lemma 5.3.1. *Let $\{B_i\}$ be a BSCC decomposition of $\mathcal{E}_\infty(\mathcal{H})$, and P_{B_i} the projection onto B_i. Then for each i, we have*

$$\lim_{k\to\infty} tr\left(P_{B_i}\mathcal{E}^k(\rho)\right) = tr\left(P_{B_i}\mathcal{E}_\infty(\rho)\right) \tag{5.28}$$

for all $\rho \in \mathcal{D}(\mathcal{H})$.

Proof. We write P for the projection onto $T_{\mathcal{E}} = \mathcal{E}_\infty(\mathcal{H})^\perp$. Then similar to the proof of Theorem 5.2.4, we see that the limit

$$q_i \overset{\triangle}{=} \lim_{k\to\infty} tr\left(P_{B_i}\mathcal{E}^k(\rho)\right)$$

does exist, and $tr\left(P_{B_i}\mathcal{E}_\infty(\rho)\right) \le q_i$. Moreover, we have:

$$1 = tr((I-P)\mathcal{E}_\infty(\rho)) = \sum_i tr\left(P_{B_i}\mathcal{E}_\infty(\rho)\right)$$
$$\le \sum_i q_i$$
$$= \lim_{k\to\infty} tr\left((I-P)\mathcal{E}^k(\rho)\right) = 1.$$

This implies $q_i = tr\left(P_{B_i}\mathcal{E}_\infty(\rho)\right)$. $\square$

The preceding lemma together with Theorem 5.2.4 gives us an elegant way to compute the reachability probability of a subspace in a quantum Markov chain.

Theorem 5.3.1. *Let $\langle\mathcal{H},\mathcal{E}\rangle$ be a quantum Markov chain, $\rho \in \mathcal{D}(\mathcal{H})$, and $X \subseteq \mathcal{H}$ a subspace. Then*

$$\Pr(\rho \vDash \Diamond X) = tr\left(P_X\widetilde{\mathcal{E}}_\infty(\rho)\right),$$

and this probability can be computed in time $O(d^8)$ where $d = \dim(\mathcal{H})$.

Proof. The claim that

$$\Pr(\rho \vDash \Diamond X) = tr\left(P_X\widetilde{\mathcal{E}}_\infty(\rho)\right)$$

follows directly from Lemma 5.3.1 and Theorem 5.2.4. The time complexity of computing reachability probability follows from Lemma 5.2.8 (i). $\square$

It should be pointed out that the reachability probability $\Pr(\rho \vDash \Diamond X)$ can also be computed directly by the techniques used in the proofs of Theorem 5.1.4 and Proposition 5.1.2.

5.3.2 REPEATED REACHABILITY PROBABILITY

Reachability of quantum Markov chains was discussed in the last subsection. In this subsection, we further study repeated reachability of quantum Markov chains using the quantum BSCC decomposition. Intuitively, repeated reachability means that a system satisfies a desired condition infinitely often. Repeated reachability is particularly useful in specifying a fairness condition for a concurrent program consisting of a group of processes, which requires that each process participates in the computation infinitely often, provided it is enabled.

A Special Case:

To warm up, let us first consider a special case of this problem: if a quantum Markov chain $\langle \mathcal{H}, \mathcal{E} \rangle$ starts from a pure state $|\psi\rangle$, how can its evolution sequence

$$|\psi\rangle\langle\psi|, \mathcal{E}(|\psi\rangle\langle\psi|), \mathcal{E}^2(|\psi\rangle\langle\psi|), \dots$$

reach a subspace X of $\mathcal{H}$?

Since a quantum measurement can change the state of the measured system, we have two different scenarios. The first scenario is as follows: for each $i \geq 0$, in the i steps of evolution from $|\psi\rangle\langle\psi|$ to $\mathcal{E}^i(|\psi\rangle\langle\psi|)$, the projective measurement $\{P_X, P_{X\perp}\}$ is performed only at the end.

Lemma 5.3.2 (Measure-once). *Let B be a BSCC of quantum Markov chain $\mathcal{C} = \langle \mathcal{H}, \mathcal{E} \rangle$, and X a subspace which is not orthogonal to B. Then for any $|\psi\rangle \in B$, it holds that*

$$tr\left(P_X \mathcal{E}^i(|\psi\rangle\langle\psi|)\right) > 0$$

for infinitely many i.

Proof. As X is not orthogonal to B, we can always find a pure state $|\varphi\rangle \in B$ such that $P_X|\varphi\rangle \neq 0$. Now for any $|\psi\rangle \in B$, if there exists N such that

$$tr\left(P_X \mathcal{E}^k(|\psi\rangle\langle\psi|)\right) = 0$$

for any $k > N$, then

$$|\varphi\rangle \notin \mathcal{R}_{\mathcal{C}}\left(\mathcal{E}^{N+1}(|\psi\rangle\langle\psi|)\right)$$

which means that the reachable space $\mathcal{R}_{\mathcal{C}}\left(\mathcal{E}^{N+1}(|\psi\rangle\langle\psi|)\right)$ is a proper invariant subspace of B. This contradicts the assumption that B is a BSCC. Thus we have

$$tr\left(P_X \mathcal{E}^i(|\psi\rangle\langle\psi|)\right) > 0$$

for infinitely many i. $\qquad\square$

In the second scenario, the measurement $\{P_X, P_{X\perp}\}$ is performed at each of the i steps of evolution from $|\psi\rangle\langle\psi|$ to $\mathcal{E}^i(|\psi\rangle\langle\psi|)$: if the outcome corresponding to P_X is observed, the process terminates immediately; otherwise, it continues with another round of applying $\mathcal{E}$.

Lemma 5.3.3 (Measure-many). *Let B be a BSCC of a quantum Markov chain $\mathcal{C} = \langle \mathcal{H}, \mathcal{E} \rangle$, and $X \subseteq B$ a subspace of B. Then for any $|\psi\rangle \in B$, we have*

$$\lim_{i \to \infty} tr\left(\mathcal{G}^i(|\psi\rangle\langle\psi|)\right) = 0,$$

where the quantum operation $\mathcal{G}$ is the restriction of $\mathcal{E}$ in $X^\perp$; that is,

$$\mathcal{G}(\rho) = P_{X^\perp}\mathcal{E}(\rho)P_{X^\perp}$$

for all density operators ρ, and $X^\perp$ is the orthocomplement of X in $\mathcal{H}$.

Proof. By Lemma 3.3.4 we know that the limit

$$\mathcal{G}_\infty \triangleq \lim_{N\to\infty} \frac{1}{N} \sum_{n=1}^{N} \mathcal{G}^n$$

exists. For any $|\psi\rangle \in B$, we claim that

$$\rho_\psi \triangleq \mathcal{G}_\infty(|\psi\rangle\langle\psi|)$$

is a zero operator. Otherwise, it is easy to check that ρ_ψ is a fixed point of $\mathcal{G}$. Furthermore, from the fact that

$$\mathcal{E}(\rho_\psi) = \mathcal{G}(\rho_\psi) + P_X\mathcal{E}(\rho_\psi)P_X = \rho_\psi + P_X\mathcal{E}(\rho_\psi)P_X,$$

we have $tr(P_X\mathcal{E}(\rho_\psi)) = 0$ as $\mathcal{E}$ is trace-preserving. Thus $P_X\mathcal{E}(\rho_\psi) = 0$, and ρ_ψ is also a fixed point of $\mathcal{E}$. Note that

$$supp(\rho_\psi) \subseteq X^\perp \cap B.$$

By Theorem 5.2.3, we see that this contradicts the assumption that B is a BSCC.

Now with the preceding claim and the fact that $tr(\mathcal{G}^i(|\psi\rangle\langle\psi|))$ is nonincreasing in i, we immediately obtain:

$$\lim_{i\to\infty} tr\left(\mathcal{G}^i(|\psi\rangle\langle\psi|)\right) = 0.$$

$\square$

The preceding lemma actually shows that if we set X as an absorbing boundary, which is included in BSCC B, the reachability probability will be absorbed eventually.

Now we turn to consider the general case where the initial state is a mixed state expressed as a density operator ρ. First of all, the preceding lemma can be strengthened as the following:

Theorem 5.3.2. *Let $C = \langle \mathcal{H}, \mathcal{E} \rangle$ be a quantum Markov chain, and let X be a subspace of $\mathcal{H}$ and*

$$\mathcal{G}(\rho) = P_{X^\perp}\mathcal{E}(\rho)P_{X^\perp}$$

for all density operators ρ. Then the following two statements are equivalent:

(i) *The subspace $X^\perp$ contains no BSCC;*

(ii) *For any $\rho \in \mathcal{D}(\mathcal{H})$, we have*

$$\lim_{i \to \infty} tr(\mathcal{G}^i(\rho)) = 0.$$

Proof. Similar to the proof of Lemma 5.3.3.   □

The following example gives a simple application of Theorem 5.3.2.

Example 5.3.1. *Consider the quantum walk on an n-cycle described in Subsection 5.1.3. Let us set an absorbing boundary at position 0 (rather than at position 1 as in Subsection 5.1.3). Then from any initial state $|\psi\rangle$, we know from Theorem 5.3.2 that the probability of nontermination is asymptotically 0 because there is no BSCC which is orthogonal to the absorbing boundaries.*

The above discussions, in particular Lemma 5.3.3 and Theorem 5.3.2, provide us with a basis for defining a general form of repeated reachability in a quantum Markov chain $\langle \mathcal{H}, \mathcal{E} \rangle$. Note that $\mathcal{E}_\infty(\mathcal{H})^\perp$ is a transient subspace. So, we can focus our attention on $\mathcal{E}_\infty(\mathcal{H})$.

Let $\mathcal{C} = \langle \mathcal{H}, \mathcal{E} \rangle$ be a quantum Markov chain and X a subspace of $\mathcal{E}_\infty(\mathcal{H})$. Then we define:

$$\mathcal{X}(X) = \left\{ |\psi\rangle \in \mathcal{E}_\infty(\mathcal{H}) : \lim_{k \to \infty} tr\left(\mathcal{G}^k(|\psi\rangle\langle\psi|) \right) = 0 \right\}$$

where

$$\mathcal{G}(\rho) = P_{X^\perp} \mathcal{E}(\rho) P_{X^\perp}$$

for all $\rho \in \mathcal{D}(\mathcal{H})$. Intuitively, starting from a state $|\psi\rangle$ in $\mathcal{X}(X)$, we repeatedly run quantum operation $\mathcal{E}$, and at the end of each step we perform the measurement $\{X, X^\perp\}$. The defining equation of $\mathcal{X}(X)$ means that the probability that the system always eventually falls into $X^\perp$ is 0; in other words, the system infinitely often reaches X. It is easy to see that $\mathcal{X}(X)$ is a subspace of $\mathcal{H}$. Then the repeated reachability probability can be defined based on $\mathcal{X}(X)$.

Definition 5.3.2. *Let $\mathcal{C} = \langle \mathcal{H}, \mathcal{E} \rangle$ be a quantum Markov chain, X a subspace of $\mathcal{H}$ and ρ a density operator in $\mathcal{H}$. Then the probability that state ρ satisfies the repeated reachability $rep(X)$ is*

$$\Pr(\rho \vDash rep(X)) = \lim_{k \to \infty} tr\left(P_{\mathcal{X}(X)} \mathcal{E}^k(\rho) \right). \tag{5.29}$$

The well-definedness of $\Pr(\rho \vDash rep(X))$ comes from the fact that $\mathcal{X}(X)$ is invariant under $\mathcal{E}$. By Theorem 5.2.2 we know that the sequences

$$\left\{ tr\left(P_{\mathcal{X}(X)} \mathcal{E}^k(\rho) \right) \right\}$$

is nondecreasing, and thus its limit exists. The preceding definition is not easy to understand. To give the reader a better understanding of this definition, let us look at the defining equation (5.29) of repeated reachability probability in the following way: First, for any $0 \le \lambda < 1$, it follows from (5.29) that $\Pr(\rho \vDash rep(X)) \ge \lambda$ if and only if for any $\epsilon > 0$, there exists N such that for all $k \geq N$, $\mathcal{E}^k(\rho)$ falls into subspace $\mathcal{X}(X)$ with probability $\geq \lambda - \epsilon$. On the other hand, we already noticed previously that starting from any state in $\mathcal{X}(X)$, the system can infinitely often reach X. Combining these two observations gives us the intuition that starting from ρ, the system infinitely often reaches X.

The problem of computing repeated reachability probability will be discussed in the next subsection, together with the computation of persistence probability.

5.3.3 PERSISTENCE PROBABILITY

The aim of this subsection is to study another kind of reachability of quantum Markov chains, namely persistence. Intuitively, persistence means that a desired condition is always satisfied from a certain point of time. As pointed out in the last subsection, we can focus our attention on $\mathcal{E}_\infty(\mathcal{H})$ because $\mathcal{E}_\infty(\mathcal{H})^\perp$ is a transient subspace.

Definition 5.3.3. *Let $C = \langle \mathcal{H}, \mathcal{E} \rangle$ be a quantum Markov chain and X a subspace of $\mathcal{E}_\infty(\mathcal{H})$. Then the set of states in $\mathcal{E}_\infty(\mathcal{H})$ that are eventually always in X is*

$$\mathcal{Y}(X) = \left\{ |\psi\rangle \in \mathcal{E}_\infty(\mathcal{H}) : (\exists N \geq 0)(\forall k \geq N) \; supp\left(\mathcal{E}^k(|\psi\rangle\langle\psi|) \right) \subseteq X \right\}.$$

It is clear from its defining equation that $\mathcal{Y}(X)$ consists of the pure states from which the states reachable after some time point N are all in X. Here, we give a simple example to illustrate the notion $\mathcal{Y}(X)$ as well as $\mathcal{X}(X)$ defined in the last subsection.

Example 5.3.2. *Let us revisit Example 5.2.1 where*

$$\mathcal{E}_\infty(\mathcal{H}) = span\{|0\rangle, |1\rangle, |2\rangle, |3\rangle\}.$$

(i) *If $X = span\{|0\rangle, |1\rangle, |2\rangle\}$, then*

$$\mathcal{E}_\infty(X^\perp) = supp(\mathcal{E}_\infty(|3\rangle\langle3|)) = supp((|2\rangle\langle2| + |3\rangle\langle3|)/2)$$

and $\mathcal{E}_\infty(X) = \mathcal{E}_\infty(\mathcal{H})$. Thus $\mathcal{Y}(X) = B_1$ and $\mathcal{X}(X) = \mathcal{E}_\infty(\mathcal{H})$.

(ii) *If $X = span\{|3\rangle\}$, then*

$$\mathcal{E}_\infty(X^\perp) = B_1 \oplus B_2$$

and $\mathcal{E}_\infty(X) = B_2$. Thus $\mathcal{Y}(X) = \{0\}$ and $\mathcal{X}(X) = B_2$.

The following lemma gives a characterization of $\mathcal{X}(X)$ and $\mathcal{Y}(X)$ and also clarifies the relationship between them.

Lemma 5.3.4. *For any subspace X of $\mathcal{E}_\infty(\mathcal{H})$, both $\mathcal{X}(X)$ and $\mathcal{Y}(X)$ are invariant subspaces of $\mathcal{H}$ under $\mathcal{E}$. Furthermore, we have:*

(i) *$\mathcal{X}(X) = \mathcal{E}_\infty(X)$;*
(ii) *$\mathcal{Y}(X) = \bigvee_{B \subseteq X} B = \mathcal{X}(X^\perp)^\perp$, where B ranges over all BSCCs, and the orthogonal complements are taken in $\mathcal{E}_\infty(\mathcal{H})$.*

The proof of this lemma is postponed into Section 5.4.

Now we can define persistence probability of a quantum Markov chain.

Definition 5.3.4. *Let* $C = \langle \mathcal{H}, \mathcal{E} \rangle$ *be a quantum Markov chain,* $X \subseteq \mathcal{H}$ *a subspace and* ρ *a density operator in* $\mathcal{H}$. *Then the probability that state* ρ *satisfies the persistence property pers(X) is*

$$\Pr(\rho \vDash pers(X)) = \lim_{k \to \infty} tr\left(P_{\mathcal{Y}(X)}\mathcal{E}^k(\rho)\right).$$

Since $\mathcal{Y}(X)$ is invariant under $\mathcal{E}$, it follows from Theorem 5.2.2 that the sequence

$$\left\{tr\left(P_{\mathcal{Y}(X)}\mathcal{E}^k(\rho)\right)\right\}$$

is nondecreasing, and thus $\Pr(\rho \vDash pers(X))$ is well-defined. The preceding definition can be understood in a way similar to that given for Definition 5.3.2. For any $0 \leq \lambda < 1$, $\Pr(\rho \vDash pers(X)) \geq \lambda$ if and only if for any $\epsilon > 0$, there exists integer N such that for all $k \geq N$, $\mathcal{E}^k(\rho)$ falls into subspace $\mathcal{Y}(X)$ with probability $\geq \lambda - \epsilon$. Furthermore, starting from any state in $\mathcal{Y}(X)$, all the reachable states after some time point must be in X. Therefore, Definition 5.3.4 coincides with our intuition for persistence that a desired condition always holds after a certain point of time.

Combining Theorem 5.3.1 and Lemma 5.3.4, we obtain the main result of this subsection:

Theorem 5.3.3

(i) *The repeated reachability probability is*

$$\Pr(\rho \vDash rep(X)) = 1 - tr\left(P_{\mathcal{X}(X)^\perp}\mathcal{E}_\infty(\rho)\right)$$
$$= 1 - \Pr\left(\rho \vDash pers\left(X^\perp\right)\right).$$

(ii) *The persistence probability is*

$$\Pr(\rho \vDash pers(X)) = tr(P_{\mathcal{Y}(X)}\mathcal{E}_\infty(\rho)).$$

Computation of Repeated Reachability and Persistence Probabilities:

Now we consider how to compute the repeated reachability and persistence probabilities in a quantum Markov chain. Based on Theorem 5.3.3 (ii), we are able to give an algorithm for computing persistence probability; see Algorithm 3.

Theorem 5.3.4. *Give a quantum Markov chain* $\langle \mathcal{H}, \mathcal{E} \rangle$, *an initial state* $\rho \in \mathcal{D}(\mathcal{H})$, *and a subspace* $X \subseteq \mathcal{H}$, *Algorithm 3 computes persistence probability* $\Pr(\rho \vDash pers(X))$ *in time* $O(d^8)$, *where* $d = \dim \mathcal{H}$.

Proof. The correctness of Algorithm 3 follows immediately from Theorem 5.3.3 (ii). The time complexity is again dominated by the Jordan decomposition used in computing $\mathcal{E}_\infty(\rho)$ and $\mathcal{E}_\infty(X^\perp)$, thus it is $O(d^8)$. $\qquad\square$

Algorithm 3   PERSISTENCE(X, ρ)

input : A quantum Markov chain $\langle \mathcal{H}, \mathcal{E} \rangle$, a subspace $X \subseteq \mathcal{H}$, and an initial state $\rho \in \mathcal{D}(\mathcal{H})$
output: The probability $\Pr(\rho \vDash \text{pers}(X))$
begin
  $\rho_\infty \leftarrow \mathcal{E}_\infty(\rho)$;
  $Y \leftarrow \mathcal{E}_\infty(X^\perp)$;
  $P \leftarrow$ the projection onto $Y^\perp$;   (* $Y^\perp$ is the orthocomplement of Y in $\mathcal{E}_\infty(\mathcal{H})$ *)
  return $tr(P\rho_\infty)$;
end

With Theorem 5.3.3 (i), Algorithm 3 can also be used to compute repeated reachability probability $\Pr(\rho \vDash \text{rep}(X))$.

We conclude this section by raising a research problem:

Problem 5.3.1. *All algorithms for analysis of quantum programs presented in this chapter are classical; that is, they were developed for analysis of quantum programs using classical computers. It is desirable to develop quantum algorithms for the same purpose that can improve the complexities of the corresponding algorithms given in this chapter.*

5.4 PROOFS OF TECHNICAL LEMMAS

Several technical lemmas were used in the previous sections without proofs. For convenience of the reader, here we collect their proofs.

Proof of Lemma 5.1.10. We first give a series of lemmas that will serve as key steps in the proof of Lemma 5.1.10. Recall from Subsection 5.1.2 that $\mathcal{E}$ is a quantum operation and $M = \{M_0, M_1\}$ a quantum measurement. The quantum operations $\mathcal{E}_0, \mathcal{E}_1$ are defined by the measurement operators M_0, M_1, respectively; that is,

$$\mathcal{E}_i(\rho) = M_i \rho M_i^\dagger$$

for all density operators ρ and $i = 0, 1$. We write $\mathcal{G} = \mathcal{E} \circ \mathcal{E}_1$.

Lemma 5.4.1. *The quantum operation $\mathcal{G} + \mathcal{E}_0$ is trace-preserving:*

$$tr[(\mathcal{G} + \mathcal{E}_0)(\rho)] = tr(\rho) \tag{5.30}$$

for all partial density operators ρ.

Proof. It suffices to see that

$$\sum_i (E_i M_1)^\dagger E_i M_1 + M_0^\dagger M_0 = M_1^\dagger \left(\sum_i E_i^\dagger E_i \right) M_1 + M_0^\dagger M_0$$
$$= M_1^\dagger M_1 + M_0^\dagger M_0 = I.$$

$\square$

The next lemma shows that every complex matrix can be represented by four positive matrices.

Lemma 5.4.2. *For any matrix A, there are positive matrices B_1, B_2, B_3, B_4 such that*

(i) $A = (B_1 - B_2) + i(B_3 - B_4)$; *and*
(ii) $trB_i^2 \le tr(A^{\dagger}A)$ $(i = 1, 2, 3, 4)$.

Proof. We can take Hermitian operators

$$(A + A^{\dagger})/2 = B_1 - B_2, \quad -i(A - A^{\dagger})/2 = B_3 - B_4,$$

where B_1, B_2 are positive operators with orthogonal supports, and B_3, B_4 are also positive operators with orthogonal supports. Then it holds that

$$
\begin{aligned}
\sqrt{trB_1^2} &= \sqrt{tr(B_1{}^{\dagger}B_1)} \\
&\le \sqrt{tr(B_1{}^{\dagger}B_1 + B_2{}^{\dagger}B_2)} \\
&= \|((A + A^{\dagger})/2 \otimes I)|\Phi\rangle\| \\
&\le (\|(A \otimes I)|\Phi\rangle\| + \|(A^{\dagger} \otimes I)|\Phi\rangle\|)/2 \\
&= \sqrt{tr(A^{\dagger}A)}.
\end{aligned}
$$

It is similar to prove that $trB_i^2 \le tr(A^{\dagger}A)$ for $i = 2, 3, 4$. $\qquad\square$

Let R be the matrix representation of quantum operation $\mathcal{G}$; see its defining equation (5.14). Then a bound of the powers of R is given in the following:

Lemma 5.4.3. *For any integer $n \ge 0$, and for any state $|\alpha\rangle$ in $\mathcal{H} \otimes \mathcal{H}$, we have:*

$$\|R^n|\alpha\rangle\| \le 4\sqrt{d}\||\alpha\rangle\|$$

where $d = \dim \mathcal{H}$ is the dimension of Hilbert space $\mathcal{H}$.

Proof. Suppose that $|\alpha\rangle = \sum_{i,j} a_{ij}|ij\rangle$. Then we can write:

$$|\alpha\rangle = (A \otimes I)|\Phi\rangle$$

where $A = (a_{ij})$ is a $d \times d$ matrix. A routine calculation yields:

$$\||\alpha\rangle\| = \sqrt{trA^{\dagger}A}.$$

We write:

$$A = (B_1 - B_2) + i(B_3 - B_4)$$

according to Lemma 5.4.2. The idea behind this decomposition is that the trace-preserving property of equation (5.30) only applies to positive operators. Put

$$|\beta_i\rangle = (B_i \otimes I)|\Phi\rangle$$

for $i = 1, 2, 3, 4$. Using the triangle inequality, we obtain:

$$\|R^n|\alpha\rangle\| \leq \sum_{i=1}^{4} \|R^n|\beta_i\rangle\| = \sum_{i=1}^{4} \|(\mathcal{G}^n(B_i) \otimes I)|\Phi\rangle\|.$$

Note that

$$\|(\mathcal{G}^n(B_i) \otimes I)|\Phi\rangle\| = \sqrt{\mathrm{tr}(\mathcal{G}^n(B_i))^2}, \tag{5.31}$$

$$\mathrm{tr}B_i^2 \leq (\mathrm{tr}B_i)^2. \tag{5.32}$$

Moreover, we know from Lemma 5.4.1 that

$$\mathrm{tr}[\mathcal{G}^n(B_i)] \leq \mathrm{tr}[(\mathcal{G} + \mathcal{E}_0)^n(B_i)] = \mathrm{tr}B_i. \tag{5.33}$$

Combining equations (5.31), (5.32) and (5.33) yields

$$\sqrt{\mathrm{tr}(\mathcal{G}^n(B_i))^2} \leq \sqrt{(\mathrm{tr}\mathcal{G}^n(B_i))^2} \leq \sqrt{(\mathrm{tr}B_i)^2}.$$

Furthermore, by the Cauchy inequality we have

$$(\mathrm{tr}B_i)^2 \leq d \cdot (\mathrm{tr}B_i^2).$$

Therefore, it follows from Lemma 5.4.2 that

$$\|R^n|\alpha\rangle\| \leq \sum_{i=1}^{4} \sqrt{d \cdot \mathrm{tr}B_i^2} \leq 4\sqrt{d \cdot \mathrm{tr}(A^\dagger A)} = 4\sqrt{d}\||\alpha\rangle\|.$$

$\square$

Now we are ready to prove Lemma 5.1.10. We prove part (i) by refutation. If there is some eigenvalue λ of R with $|\lambda| > 1$, suppose the corresponding normalized eigenvector is $|x\rangle$: $R|x\rangle = \lambda|x\rangle$. Choose integer n such that $|\lambda|^n > 4\sqrt{d}$. Then

$$\|R^n|x\rangle\| = \|\lambda^n|x\rangle\| = |\lambda|^n > 4\sqrt{d}\||x\rangle\|.$$

This contradicts Lemma 5.4.3.

Part (ii) can also be proved by refutation. Without any loss of generality, we assume that $|\lambda_1| = 1$ with $k_1 > 1$ in the Jordan decomposition of R: $R = SJ(R)S^{-1}$. Suppose that $\{|i\rangle\}_{i=1}^{d^2}$ is the orthonormal basis of $\mathcal{H} \otimes \mathcal{H}$ compatible with the numbering of the columns and rows of R. Take an unnormalized vector $|y\rangle = S|k_1\rangle$, where $|k_1\rangle$ is the k_1th state in the basis $\{|i\rangle\}_{i=1}^{d^2}$. Since S is nonsingular, there are real numbers $L, r > 0$ such that

$$r \cdot \||x\rangle\| \leq \|S|x\rangle\| \leq L \cdot \||x\rangle\|$$

for any vector $|x\rangle$ in $\mathcal{H} \otimes \mathcal{H}$. By definition, it holds that $\||y\rangle\| \leq L$. We can choose integer n such that $nr > L \cdot 4\sqrt{d}$ because $r > 0$. Then a routine calculation yields:

$$R^n|y\rangle = L \cdot \sum_{t=0}^{k_1-1} \binom{n}{t} \lambda_1{}^{n-t}|k_1 - t\rangle,$$

Consequently, we have:

$$\|R^n|y\rangle\| \geq r \cdot \sum_{t=1}^{k_1} \binom{n}{t} |\lambda_1|^{n-t}$$

$$\geq nr > L \cdot 4\sqrt{d} \geq 4\sqrt{d}\||y\rangle\|.$$

This contradicts Lemma 5.4.3 again, and we complete the proof.

Proof of Lemma 5.1.13. Recall from Subsection 5.1.2 that $J(N)$ is the matrix obtained from the Jordan normal form $J(R)$ of R through replacing the 1-dimensional Jordan blocks corresponding to the eigenvalues with module 1 by number 0. Without any loss of generality, we assume that the eigenvalues of R satisfy:

$$1 = |\lambda_1| = \cdots = |\lambda_s| > |\lambda_{s+1}| \geq \cdots \geq |\lambda_l|.$$

Then

$$J(R) = \begin{pmatrix} U & 0 \\ 0 & J_1 \end{pmatrix}$$

where $U = diag(\lambda_1, \cdots, \lambda_s)$ is an $s \times s$ diagonal unitary, and

$$J_1 = diag\left(J_{k_{s+1}}(\lambda_{s+1}), \cdots, J_{k_l}(\lambda_l)\right).$$

Moreover, we have:

$$J(N) = \begin{pmatrix} 0 & 0 \\ 0 & J_1 \end{pmatrix}.$$

The convergence of

$$\sum_{n=0}^{\infty} (\mathcal{E}_0 \circ \mathcal{G}^n)$$

follows immediately from Lemma 3.3.4, and it in turn implies the convergence of $\sum_{n=0}^{\infty} N_0 R^n$. It is clear that

$$\sum_{n=0}^{\infty} N_0 R^n = \sum_{n=0}^{\infty} N_0 S J(R)^n S^{-1}.$$

Since S is nonsingular, we see that

$$\sum_{n=0}^{\infty} N_0 SJ(R)^n$$

converges. This implies that

$$\lim_{n \to \infty} N_0 SJ(R)^n = 0.$$

Now we write:

$$N_0 S = \begin{pmatrix} Q & P \\ V & T \end{pmatrix},$$

where Q is an $s \times s$ matrix, T is a $(d^2 - s) \times (d^2 - s)$ matrix, and $d = \dim \mathcal{H}$ is the dimension of the state space $\mathcal{H}$. Then

$$N_0 SJ(R)^n = \begin{pmatrix} QU^n & PJ_1^n \\ VU^n & TJ_1^n \end{pmatrix},$$

and it follows that $\lim_{n \to \infty} QU^n = 0$ and $\lim_{n \to \infty} VU^n = 0$. So, we have:

$$tr(Q^{\dagger} Q) = \lim_{n \to \infty} tr(QU^n)^{\dagger} QU^n = 0,$$
$$tr(V^{\dagger} V) = \lim_{n \to \infty} tr(VU^n)^{\dagger} VU^n = 0.$$

This yields $Q = 0$ and $V = 0$, and it follows immediately that $N_0 R^n = N_0 N^n$.

Proof of Lemma 5.2.5 (ii). We are going to show that any two BSCCs X, Y of a quantum Markov chain are orthogonal provided $\dim X \neq \dim Y$. This proof requires a technical preparation. An operator A (not necessarily a partial density operator as in Definition 5.2.12 (i)) in $\mathcal{H}$ is called a fixed point of quantum operation $\mathcal{E}$ if $\mathcal{E}(A) = A$. The following lemma shows that fixed points can be preserved by the positive matrix decomposition given in Lemma 5.4.2.

Lemma 5.4.4. *Let $\mathcal{E}$ be a quantum operation in $\mathcal{H}$ and A a fixed point of $\mathcal{E}$. If we have:*

(i) $A = (X_+ - X_-) + i(Y_+ - Y_-)$;
(ii) X_+, X_-, Y_+, Y_- *are all positive matrices; and*
(iii) $supp(X_+) \perp supp(X_-)$ *and* $supp(Y_+) \perp supp(Y_-)$,

then X_+, X_-, Y_+, Y_- are all fixed points of $\mathcal{E}$.

Exercise 5.4.1. *Prove Lemma 5.4.4.*

Now we are ready to prove Lemma 5.2.5 (ii). Suppose without any loss of generality that $\dim X < \dim Y$. By Theorem 5.2.3, we know that there are two minimal fixed point states ρ and σ with $supp(\rho) = X$ and $supp(\sigma) = Y$. Note that for any $\lambda > 0$, $\rho - \lambda \sigma$ is also a fixed point of $\mathcal{E}$. We can take λ sufficiently large such that

$$\rho - \lambda\sigma = \Delta_+ - \Delta_-$$

with $\Delta_\pm$ being positive, $supp(\Delta_-) = supp(\sigma)$, and $supp(\Delta_+) \perp supp(\Delta_-)$. Let P be the projection onto Y. It follows from Lemma 5.4.4 that both Δ_+ and Δ_- are fixed points of $\mathcal{E}$. Then

$$P\rho P = \lambda P\sigma P + P\Delta_+ P - P\Delta_- P = \lambda\sigma - \Delta_-$$

is a fixed point state of $\mathcal{E}$ too. Note that $supp(P\rho P) \subseteq Y$, σ is the minimal fixed point state and $supp(\sigma) = Y$. Therefore, we have $P\rho P = p\sigma$ for some $p \geq 0$. Now if $p > 0$, then by Proposition 5.2.1 (iii) we obtain:

$$Y = supp(\sigma) = supp(P\rho P) = span\{P|\psi\rangle : |\psi\rangle \in X\}.$$

This implies $\dim Y \leq \dim X$, contradicting our assumption. Thus we have $P\rho P = 0$, which implies $X \perp Y$.

Proof of Lemma 5.2.7. Roughly speaking, this lemma asserts that a fixed point state of $\mathcal{E}$ can be decomposed into two orthogonal fixed point states. The proof technique for Lemma 5.2.5 (ii) showing that two BSCCs are orthogonal can be used in the proof of this lemma. First, we note that for any $\lambda > 0$, $\rho - \lambda\sigma$ is also a fixed point of $\mathcal{E}$, and thus we can take λ sufficiently large such that

$$\rho - \lambda\sigma = \Delta_+ - \Delta_-$$

with $\Delta_\pm$ being positive, $supp(\Delta_-) = supp(\sigma)$, and $supp(\Delta_+)$ is the orthogonal complement of $supp(\Delta_-)$ in $supp(\rho)$. By Lemma 5.4.4, both Δ_+ and Δ_- are fixed points of $\mathcal{E}$. Let $\eta = \Delta_+$. We have:

$$supp(\rho) = supp(\rho - \lambda\sigma) = supp(\Delta_+) \oplus supp(\Delta_-) = supp(\eta) \oplus supp(\sigma).$$

Proof of Lemma 5.2.8. For part (i), we are required to figure out the complexity for computing the asymptotic average $\mathcal{E}_\infty(\rho)$ of a density operator ρ. To this end, we first present a lemma about the matrix representation of the asymptotic average of a quantum operation.

Lemma 5.4.5. *Let $M = SJS^{-1}$ be the Jordan decomposition of M where*

$$J = \bigoplus_{k=1}^{K} J_k(\lambda_k) = diag(J_1(\lambda_1), \ldots, J_K(\lambda_K)),$$

and $J_k(\lambda_k)$ is the Jordan block corresponding to the eigenvalue λ_k. Define

$$J_\infty = \bigoplus_{k \ s.t. \ \lambda_k = 1} J_k(\lambda_k)$$

and $M_\infty = SJ_\infty S^{-1}$. Then M_∞ is the matrix representation of $\mathcal{E}_\infty$.

Exercise 5.4.2. *Prove Lemma 5.4.5.*

Now we can prove part (i) of Lemma 5.2.8. We know from [61] that the time complexity of Jordan decomposition for a $d \times d$ matrix is $O(d^4)$. So, we can compute the matrix representation M_∞ of $\mathcal{E}_\infty$ in time $O(d^8)$. Furthermore, $\mathcal{E}_\infty(\rho)$ can be computed using the correspondence (Lemma 5.1.9):

$$(\mathcal{E}_\infty(\rho) \otimes I_{\mathcal{H}}) |\Psi\rangle = M_\infty(\rho \otimes I_{\mathcal{H}}) |\Psi\rangle$$

where $|\Psi\rangle = \sum_{i=1}^{d} |i\rangle |i\rangle$ is the (unnormalized) maximally entangled state in $\mathcal{H} \otimes \mathcal{H}$. For part (ii), we need to settle the complexity for finding the density operator basis of the set of fixed points of $\mathcal{E}$; i.e., { matrices $A : \mathcal{E}(A) = A$}. We first notice that this density operator basis can be computed in the following three steps:

(a) Compute the matrix representation M of $\mathcal{E}$. The time complexity is $O(md^4)$, where $m \leq d^2$ is the number of operators E_i in the Kraus representation $\mathcal{E} = \sum_i E_i \circ E_i^\dagger$.
(b) Find a basis $\mathcal{B}$ for the null space of the matrix $M - I_{\mathcal{H} \otimes \mathcal{H}}$, and transform them into matrix forms. This can be done by Gaussian elimination with complexity being $O((d^2)^3) = O(d^6)$.
(c) For each basis matrix A in $\mathcal{B}$, compute positive matrices X_+, X_-, Y_+, Y_- such that $supp(X_+) \perp supp(X_-)$, $supp(Y_+) \perp supp(Y_-)$, and

$$A = X_+ - X_- + i(Y_+ - Y_-).$$

Let Q be the set of nonzero elements in $\{X_+, X_-, Y_+, Y_-\}$. Then by Lemma 5.4.4, every element of Q is a fixed point state of $\mathcal{E}$. Replace A by elements of Q after normalization. Then the resultant $\mathcal{B}$ is the required density operator basis. At last, we make the elements in $\mathcal{B}$ linearly independent. This can be done by removing the redundant elements in $\mathcal{B}$ using Gaussian elimination. The computational complexity of this step is $O(d^6)$.

So, we see that the total complexity for computing the density operator basis of { matrices $A : \mathcal{E}(A) = A$} is $O(d^6)$.

Proof of Lemma 5.3.4. We first prove the following technical lemma.

Lemma 5.4.6. *Let S be an invariant subspace of $\mathcal{E}_\infty(\mathcal{H})$ under $\mathcal{E}$. Then for any density operator ρ with $supp(\rho) \subseteq \mathcal{E}_\infty(\mathcal{H})$ and any integer k, we have*

$$tr(P_S \mathcal{E}^k(\rho)) = tr(P_S \rho)$$

where P_S is the projection onto S.

Proof. By Lemma 5.2.7, there exists an invariant subspace T such that $\mathcal{E}_\infty(\mathcal{H}) = S \oplus T$ where S and T are orthogonal. Then by Theorem 5.2.2, we have

$$tr(P_S \mathcal{E}^k(\rho)) \geq tr(P_S \rho) \text{ and } tr(P_T \mathcal{E}^k(\rho)) \geq tr(P_T \rho).$$

Furthermore, it follows that

$$1 \geq tr(P_S \mathcal{E}^k(\rho)) + tr(P_T \mathcal{E}^k(\rho))$$
$$\geq tr(P_S \rho) + tr(P_T \rho) = tr(\rho) = 1.$$

Thus we have:

$$tr(P_S \mathcal{E}^k(\rho)) = tr(P_S \rho).$$

$\square$

Now we can prove Lemma 5.3.4. For any pure state $|\varphi\rangle$, we write the corresponding density operator $\varphi = |\varphi\rangle\langle\varphi|$. First of all, we show that $\mathcal{Y}(X)$ is a subspace. Let $|\psi_i\rangle \in \mathcal{Y}(X)$ and α_i be complex numbers, $i = 1, 2$. Then by the definition of $\mathcal{Y}(X)$ there exists N_i such that for any $j \geq N_i$, $supp\left(\mathcal{E}^j(\psi_i)\right) \subseteq X$. Let

$$|\psi\rangle = \alpha_1|\psi_1\rangle + \alpha_2|\psi_2\rangle \text{ and } \rho = |\psi_1\rangle\langle\psi_1| + |\psi_2\rangle\langle\psi_2|.$$

Then $|\psi\rangle \in supp(\rho)$, and from Propositions 5.2.1 (i), (ii) and (iv) we have

$$supp\left(\mathcal{E}^j(\psi)\right) \subseteq supp\left(\mathcal{E}^j(\rho)\right) = supp\left(\mathcal{E}^j(\psi_1)\right) \vee supp\left(\mathcal{E}^j(\psi_2)\right)$$

for any $j \geq 0$. So, we have $supp\left(\mathcal{E}^j(\psi)\right) \subseteq X$ for all $j \geq N \triangleq \max\{N_1, N_2\}$, and thus $|\psi\rangle \in \mathcal{Y}(X)$.

We divide the rest of the proof into the following six claims:

- Claim 1: $\mathcal{Y}(X) \supseteq \bigvee\{B \subseteq X : B \text{ is a BSCC}\}$.
  For any BSCC $B \subseteq X$, from Lemmas 5.2.6 (ii) and 5.2.4 we have $B \subseteq \mathcal{E}_\infty(\mathcal{H})$. Furthermore, as B is a BSCC, it holds that

$$supp\left(\mathcal{E}^i(\psi)\right) \subseteq B \subseteq X$$

  for any $|\psi\rangle \in B$ and any i. Thus $B \subseteq \mathcal{Y}(X)$, and the claim follows from the fact that $\mathcal{Y}(X)$ is a subspace.
- Claim 2: $\mathcal{Y}(X) \subseteq \bigvee\{B \subseteq X : B \text{ is a BSCC}\}$.

  For any $|\psi\rangle \in \mathcal{Y}(X)$, note that $\rho_\psi \triangleq \mathcal{E}_\infty(\psi)$ is a fixed point state. Let $Z = supp(\rho_\psi)$. We claim that $|\psi\rangle \in Z$. This is obvious if $Z = \mathcal{E}_\infty(\mathcal{H})$. Otherwise, as $\mathcal{E}_\infty\left(\frac{I_\mathcal{H}}{d}\right)$ is a fixed point state and

$$\mathcal{E}_\infty(\mathcal{H}) = supp\left(\mathcal{E}_\infty\left(\frac{I_\mathcal{H}}{d}\right)\right),$$

by Lemma 5.2.7 we have $\mathcal{E}_\infty(\mathcal{H}) = Z \oplus Z^\perp$, where $Z^\perp$, the orthocomplement of Z in $\mathcal{E}_\infty(\mathcal{H})$, is also invariant. As Z is again a direct sum of some orthogonal BSCCs, by Lemma 5.3.1 we have

$$\lim_{i \to \infty} tr\left(P_Z \mathcal{E}^i(\psi)\right) = tr(P_Z \mathcal{E}_\infty(\psi)) = 1;$$

that is,

$$\lim_{i \to \infty} tr\left(P_{Z^\perp} \mathcal{E}^i(\psi)\right) = 0.$$

Together with Theorem 5.2.2, this implies $tr(P_{Z^\perp} \psi) = 0$, and so $|\psi\rangle \in Z$. By the definition of $\mathcal{Y}(X)$, there exists $M \geq 0$, such that $supp\left(\mathcal{E}^i(\psi)\right) \subseteq X$ for all $i \geq M$. Thus

$$Z = supp\left(\lim_{N \to \infty} \frac{1}{N} \sum_{i=1}^N \mathcal{E}^i(\psi)\right)$$

$$= supp\left(\lim_{N \to \infty} \frac{1}{N} \sum_{i=M}^N \mathcal{E}^i(\psi)\right) \subseteq X.$$

Furthermore, since Z can be decomposed into the direct sum of some BSCCs, we have

$$|\psi\rangle \in Z \subseteq \bigvee\{B \subseteq X : B \text{ is a BSCC}\}.$$

Thus, Claim 2 is proved.
- Claim 3: $\mathcal{Y}(X^\perp)^\perp \subseteq \mathcal{X}(X)$.
  First, from Claims 1 and 2 previously we have $\mathcal{Y}(X^\perp) \subseteq X^\perp$, and

$$X' \overset{\triangle}{=} \mathcal{Y}(X^\perp)^\perp$$

is invariant. Thus $X \subseteq \mathcal{Y}(X^\perp)^\perp$, and $\mathcal{E}$ is also a quantum operation in the subspace X'. We now consider the quantum Markov chain $\langle X', \mathcal{E}\rangle$. Claim 1 implies that any BSCC in $X^\perp$ is also contained in $\mathcal{Y}(X^\perp)$. Therefore, there is no BSCC in $X' \cap X^\perp$. By Theorem 5.3.2, for any $|\psi\rangle \in X'$, we obtain:

$$\lim_{i \to \infty} tr\left[(P_{X^\perp} \circ \mathcal{E})^i(\psi)\right] = 0.$$

Thus $|\psi\rangle \in \mathcal{X}(X)$ by definition, and the claim is proved.
- Claim 4: $\mathcal{X}(X) \subseteq \mathcal{Y}(X^\perp)^\perp$.
  Similar to Claim 3, we have $\mathcal{Y}(X^\perp) \subseteq X^\perp$ and $\mathcal{Y}(X^\perp)$ is invariant. Let P be the projection onto $\mathcal{Y}(X^\perp)$. Then $P_{X^\perp} P P_{X^\perp} = P$. For any $|\psi\rangle \in \mathcal{X}(X)$, we have:

$$tr\left(P\left(P_{X^\perp} \circ \mathcal{E}\right)(\psi)\right) = tr\left(P_{X^\perp} P P_{X^\perp} \mathcal{E}(\psi)\right)$$
$$= tr(P\mathcal{E}(\psi)) \geq tr(P\psi),$$

where the last inequality is derived by Theorem 5.2.2. Therefore

$$0 = \lim_{i \to \infty} tr\left(\left(P_{X^\perp} \circ \mathcal{E}\right)^i (\psi)\right)$$
$$\geq \lim_{i \to \infty} tr\left(P\left(P_{X^\perp} \circ \mathcal{E}\right)^i (\psi)\right) \geq tr(P\psi),$$

and so $|\psi\rangle \in \mathcal{Y}(X^\perp)^\perp$.

- Claim 5: $\bigvee\{B \subseteq X : B$ is a BSCC$\} \subseteq \mathcal{E}_\infty(X^\perp)^\perp$.
  Suppose that $B \subseteq X$ is a BSCC. Then we have $tr(P_B I_{X^\perp}) = 0$. It follows from Lemma 5.4.6 that

$$tr\left(P_B \mathcal{E}^i(I_{X^\perp})\right) = 0$$

for any $i \geq 0$. Thus

$$tr(P_B \mathcal{E}_\infty(I_{X^\perp})) = 0.$$

  This implies $B \perp \mathcal{E}_\infty(X^\perp)$. Therefore, $B \subseteq \mathcal{E}_\infty(X^\perp)^\perp$. Then the claim follows from the fact that $\mathcal{E}_\infty(X^\perp)^\perp$ is a subspace.
- Claim 6: $\mathcal{E}_\infty(X^\perp)^\perp \subseteq \bigvee\{B \subseteq X : B$ is a BSCC$\}$.
  We first note that $\mathcal{E}_\infty(X^\perp)^\perp$ can be decomposed into the direct sum of BSCCs B_i. For any B_i, we have

$$tr(P_{B_i} \mathcal{E}_\infty(I_{X^\perp})) = 0.$$

Thus, $tr(P_{B_i} I_{X^\perp}) = 0$ and $B_i \perp X^\perp$. Therefore, $B_i \subseteq X$, and the claim is proved.

Finally, we observe that the invariance of $\mathcal{X}(X)$ and $\mathcal{Y}(X)$ is already included in Claims 1 and 2. This completes the proof.

5.5 BIBLIOGRAPHIC REMARKS

The studies of quantum program analysis presented in this chapter were initiated in [227], where termination of a quantum **while**-loop with a unitary transformation as the loop body was considered. In [234], the verification method for probabilistic programs developed by Sharir, Pnueli and Hart [202] was generalized to the quantum case, termination analysis of quantum programs was carried out using a quantum Markov chain as their semantic model, and thus several major results in [227] was significantly extended. The materials presented in Subsections 5.1.1 and 5.1.2 of this chapter are taken from [227] and [234], respectively. Sections 5.2 and 5.3 are mainly based on S. G. Ying et al. [235], where reachability of quantum Markov chains was thoroughly studied; in particular, the notion of BSCC of a quantum graph was introduced. Lemmas 5.4.4 and 5.4.5 are taken from Wolf [216].

For further reading, I suggest that the reader track the following three lines:

(i) *Perturbation of quantum programs*: Although not discussed in this chapter, perturbation analysis is particularly interesting for quantum programs because of noise in the implementation of quantum logical gates. It was proved in [227] that a small disturbance either on the unitary transformation in the loop body or on the measurement in the loop guard can make a quantum loop (almost) terminate, provided that some obvious dimension restriction is satisfied.

(ii) *Analysis of recursive quantum programs*: In this chapter, we only considered analysis of quantum loop programs. In [87], Feng et al. introduced a quantum generalization of Etessami and Yannakakis's recursive Markov chains [79], namely recursive super-operator-valued Markov chains, and developed some techniques for their reachability analysis. It is obvious that these techniques can be used for analysis of recursive quantum programs defined in Section 3.4. Another class of analysis techniques for classical recursive programs is based on pushdown automata; see for example [78]. The notion of pushdown quantum automata was introduced in [103], but it still is not clear how to use pushdown quantum automata in the analysis of recursive quantum programs.

(iii) *Analysis of nondeterministic and concurrent quantum programs*: An analysis for termination of nondeterministic quantum programs was carried out by Li et al. [152], generalizing several results by Hart, Sharir and Pnueli [113] for probabilistic programs. Termination of concurrent quantum programs with fairness conditions was studied by Yu et al. [238]. It was further discussed by S. G. Ying et al. [236] in terms of reachability of quantum Markov decision processes. On the other hand, only the simplest reachability of quantum programs was examined in this chapter. Several more complicated reachability properties of quantum systems were studied by Li et al. [153].

Except the line of research described in this chapter, several other approaches to quantum program analysis have been proposed in the literature. JavadiAbhari et al. [126] present a scalable framework ScaffCC for compilation and analysis of quantum programs written in Scaffold [3]; in particular they considered timing analysis for path estimation. As already mentioned in Subsection 1.1.3, abstract interpretation was generalized by Jorrand and Perdrix [129] for analysis of quantum programs. It was further extended and refined by Honda [118] to reason about separability of quantum variables in quantum programs.

Quantum programs with quantum control

Quantum case statements

Quantum programs in the superposition-of-data paradigm have been systematically investigated in Chapters 3 to 5. In particular, in Chapter 3, we studied quantum **while**-programs and recursive quantum programs, and showed how some quantum algorithms can be conveniently written as this kind of quantum programs. The control flow of a quantum **while**-program is generated by the case statements and **while**-loops within it, and the control flow of a recursive quantum program is further produced by procedure calls. Since the information that determines the control flow of a quantum **while**-program or a recursive quantum program is classical rather than quantum, such a control flow was properly named a classical control flow (in a quantum program).

The aim of this chapter and the next is to introduce quantum programs in the superposition-of-programs paradigm: in other words, quantum programs with quantum control flows. As we know, the control flow of a program is determined by those program constructs within it such as case statement, loop and recursion. Interestingly, the notions of case statement, loop and recursion in classical programming split into two different versions in the quantum setting:

- **(i)** case statement, loop and recursion with classical control, which have been discussed in detail in Chapters 3 to 5;
- **(ii)** quantum case statement, loop and recursion – case statement, loop and recursion with *quantum control.*

As we will see later, a large class of quantum algorithms can be much more conveniently programmed in a programming language with quantum control. This chapter focuses on quantum case statements. Loop and recursion with quantum control flow will be discussed in the next chapter.

This chapter is organized as follows:

- In Section 6.1, the notion of quantum case statement is carefully motivated through the example of quantum walk on a graph. The control flow of a quantum case statement is then analyzed, and the technical difficulty in defining the semantics of quantum case statement is unveiled.

- A new quantum programming language QuGCL is defined in Section 6.2 to support programming with quantum case statements.
- Section 6.3 prepares several key ingredients needed in defining the denotational semantics of QuGCL, including guarded composition of various quantum operations. The denotational semantics of QuGCL is presented in Section 6.4.
- In Section 6.5, the notion of quantum choice is defined based on quantum case statement.
- A family of algebraic laws for QuGCL programs are presented in Section 6.6. They can be used in verification, transformation and compilation of programs with quantum case statements.
- A series of examples are presented in Section 6.7 to illustrate the expressive power of the language QuGCL.
- The possible variants and generalizations of quantum case statements are discussed in Section 6.8.
- The proofs of some lemmas, propositions and theorems in Sections 6.3 to 6.6 are tedious. For readability, they are deferred to the last section, Section 6.9.

6.1 CASE STATEMENTS: FROM CLASSICAL TO QUANTUM

Let us start with an intuitive discussion about the following questions: Why should we introduce the new notion of quantum case statement? How does it differ from the case statement in the quantum programs considered in Chapter 3? We answer these questions and thus motivate the notion of quantum case statement in three steps:

(i) *Case statement in classical programming:* Recall that a conditional statement in classical programming is written as

$$\textbf{if } b \textbf{ then } S_1 \textbf{ else } S_0 \textbf{ fi} \tag{6.1}$$

where b is a Boolean expression. When b is true, subprogram S_1 will be executed; otherwise, S_0 will be executed. More generally, a case statement in classical programming is a collection of guarded commands written as

$$\textbf{if } (\square i \cdot G_i \rightarrow S_i) \textbf{ fi} \tag{6.2}$$

where for each $1 \leq i \leq n$, the subprogram S_i is guarded by the Boolean expression G_i, and S_i will be executed only when G_i is true.

(ii) *Classical case statement in quantum programming:* A notion of a classical case statement in quantum programming was defined in Chapter 3 based on a quantum measurement. Let $\overline{q}$ be a family of quantum variables and $M = \{M_m\}$ a measurement on $\overline{q}$. For each possible measurement outcome m, let S_m be a quantum program. Then a case statement can be written as follows:

$$\textbf{if } (\square m \cdot M[\overline{q}] = m \rightarrow S_m) \textbf{ fi} \tag{6.3}$$

The statement (6.3) selects a command according to the outcome of measurement M: if the outcome is m, then the corresponding command S_m will be executed. In particular, whenever M is a yes-no measurement, that is, it has only two possible outcomes 1 (yes) and 0 (no), then case statement (6.3) is a generalization of conditional statement (6.1), and it can be appropriately termed as a classical conditional statement in quantum programming. As indicated by Exercise 3.4.1, quantum **while**-loop (3.4) can be seen as a recursive program declared by such a conditional statement.

(iii) *Quantum case statement*: In addition to (6.3), there is actually another kind of case statement, which is very useful in quantum programming. This new notion of case statement can be defined by extending a key idea from the definition of the shift operator of a quantum walk on a graph. Recall from Example 2.3.2 that the shift operator is an operator in $\mathcal{H}_d \otimes \mathcal{H}_p$ defined as follows:

$$S|i, v\rangle = |i, v_i\rangle$$

for each direction $1 \leq i \leq n$ and each vertex $v \in V$, where v_i is the ith neighbor of v, and $\mathcal{H}_d$, $\mathcal{H}_p$ are the direction "coin" space and the position space, respectively.

This shift operator can be viewed in a slightly different way: for each $1 \leq i \leq n$, we define the shift S_i in the direction i as an operator in $\mathcal{H}_p$:

$$S_i|v\rangle = |v_i\rangle$$

for any $v \in V$. Then we are able to combine these operators S_i ($1 \leq i \leq n$) along the "coin" to form the whole shift operator S:

$$S|i, v\rangle = |i\rangle S_i|v\rangle \tag{6.4}$$

for any $1 \leq i \leq n$ and $v \in V$. It is worth noticing that operators S and S_i ($1 \leq i \leq n$) are defined in different Hilbert spaces: S is in $\mathcal{H}_d \otimes \mathcal{H}_p$, whereas all S_i are in $\mathcal{H}_p$.

Let us carefully observe the behavior of shift operator S. The operators $S_1, \ldots, S_n$ can be seen as a collection of programs independent of each other. Then S can be seen as a kind of case statement of $S_1, \ldots, S_n$ because S selects one of them for execution. But equation (6.4) clearly indicates that this case statement is different from (6.3): the selection in equation (6.4) is made according to the basis state $|i\rangle$ of the "coin space," which is quantum information rather than classical information. Thus, we can appropriately call S a *quantum case statement*. At this stage, the reader might still not be convinced that the behaviors of case statement (6.3) and a quantum case statement are really different, despite the fact that measurement outcomes m are classical information, and basis states $|i\rangle$ are quantum information. The essential difference between them will become clearer later, when we consider the control flow of a quantum case statement.

The preceding idea can be significantly extended. Let $S_1, S_2, \ldots, S_n$ be a collection of general quantum programs whose state spaces are the same Hilbert space $\mathcal{H}$. We introduce an external quantum system, called the "coin" system. It is allowed to be a single system or a composite system, so denoted by a quantum register $\overline{q}$ consisting of a family of new quantum variables that do not appear in $S_1, S_2, \ldots, S_n$. Assume that the state space of system $\overline{q}$ is an n-dimensional Hilbert space $\mathcal{H}_{\overline{q}}$ and $\{|i\rangle\}_{i=1}^n$ is an orthonormal basis of it. Then a quantum case statement S can be defined by combining programs $S_1, S_2, \ldots, S_n$ along the basis $\{|i\rangle\}$:

$$
\begin{aligned}
S \equiv \mathbf{qif}\,[\,\overline{q}\,] :\quad & |1\rangle \to S_1 \\
\square \quad & |2\rangle \to S_2 \\
& \ldots\ldots \\
\square \quad & |n\rangle \to S_n \\
\mathbf{fiq}\quad &
\end{aligned}
\tag{6.5}
$$

or more compactly

$$
S \equiv \mathbf{qif}\,[\,\overline{q}\,](\square i \cdot |i\rangle \to S_i)\,\mathbf{fiq}
$$

Quantum Control Flows:

Now let us look at the control flow of quantum case statement (6.5) – the order of its execution. The control flow of S can be clearly seen through its semantics. Following equation (6.4), it is reasonable to conceive that the semantics $[\![S]\!]$ of S should be defined in the tensor product $\mathcal{H}_{\overline{q}} \otimes \mathcal{H}$ by

$$
[\![S]\!](|i\rangle|\varphi\rangle) = |i\rangle([\![S_i]\!]|\varphi\rangle)
\tag{6.6}
$$

for every $1 \leq i \leq n$ and $|\varphi\rangle \in \mathcal{H}$, where $[\![S_i]\!]$ is the semantics of S_i. Then the control flow of program S is determined by "coin" variables $\overline{q}$. For each $1 \leq i \leq n$, S_i is guarded by the basis state $|i\rangle$. In other words, the execution of program (6.5) is controlled by "coin" $\overline{q}$: when $\overline{q}$ is in state $|i\rangle$, subprogram S_i will be executed. The really interesting thing here is that $\overline{q}$ is a quantum "coin" rather than a classical "coin," and thus it can be not only in the basis states $|i\rangle$ but also in a superposition of them. A superposition of these basis states yields a quantum control flow – *superposition of control flows*:

$$
[\![S]\!]\left(\sum_{i=1}^n \alpha_i|i\rangle|\varphi_i\rangle\right) = \sum_{i=1}^n \alpha_i|i\rangle([\![S_i]\!]|\varphi_i\rangle)
\tag{6.7}
$$

for all $|\varphi_i\rangle \in \mathcal{H}$ and complex numbers α_i $(1 \leq i \leq n)$. Intuitively, in equation (6.7), for every $1 \leq i \leq n$, subprogram S_i is executed with probability amplitude α_i. This is very different from the classical case statement (6.3) of quantum programs where different guards " $M[\,\overline{q}\,] = m_1$ ", $\ldots$, " $M[\,\overline{q}\,] = m_n$ " cannot be superposed.

Technical Difficulty in Defining Semantics of Quantum Case Statements:

At first glance, it seems that the defining equation of shift operator in a quantum walk can be smoothly generalized to equation (6.6) to define the denotational semantics of a general quantum case statement. But there is actually a major (and subtle) difficulty in equation (6.6). For the case where no quantum measurements occur in any S_i ($1 \leq i \leq n$), the operational semantics of each S_i is simply given as a sequence of unitary operators, and equation (6.6) is not problematic at all. Whenever some S_i contains quantum measurements, however, its semantic structure becomes a tree of linear operators with branching happening at the points where the measurements are performed. Then equation (6.6) becomes meaningless within the framework of quantum mechanics, and defining the semantics of quantum case statement S requires properly combining a collection of trees of quantum operations such that the relevant quantum mechanical principles are still obeyed. This problem will be circumvented in Sections 6.3 and 6.4 by introducing a semi-classical semantics in terms of operator-valued functions.

Exercise 6.1.1. *Why can equation (6.6) not properly define the semantics of quantum case statement (6.5) when a quantum measurement appears in some of S_i ($1 \leq i \leq n$)? Give some example(s) to illustrate your argument.*

6.2 QuGCL: A LANGUAGE WITH QUANTUM CASE STATEMENT

The notion of a quantum case statement was carefully motivated in the previous section. Now we start to study programming with the quantum case statement. First of all, we formally define a programming language QuGCL with the program construct of quantum case statement. It can be seen as a quantum counterpart of Dijkstra's GCL (Guarded Command Language). The alphabet of QuGCL is given as follows:

- As in Chapter 3, we assume a countable set $qVar$ of quantum variables ranged over by $q, q_1, q_2, \ldots$. For each quantum variable $q \in qVar$, its type is a Hilbert space $\mathcal{H}_q$, which is the state space of the quantum system denoted by q. For a quantum register $\overline{q} = q_1, q_2, \ldots, q_n$ of distinct quantum variables, we write:

$$\mathcal{H}_{\overline{q}} = \bigotimes_{i=1}^{n} \mathcal{H}_{q_i}.$$

- For simplicity of the presentation, QuGCL is designed as a purely quantum programming language, but we include a countably infinite set Var of classical variables ranged over by $x, y, \ldots$ so that we can use them to record the outcomes of quantum measurements. However, classical computation described by, for example, the assignment statement $x := e$ in a classical programming language, is excluded. For each classical variable $x \in Var$, its type is assumed to be a non-empty set D_x; that is, x takes values from D_x. In applications, if x is used to store the outcome of a quantum measurement M, then all possible outcomes of M should be in D_x.

- The sets of classical and quantum variables are required to disjoint: $qVar \cap Var = \emptyset$.

Using the alphabet presented here, we can define programs in QuGCL. For each QuGCL program S, we write $var(S)$ for the set of its classical variables, $qvar(P)$ for its quantum variables and $cvar(P)$ for its "coin" variables.

Definition 6.2.1. *QuGCL programs are inductively defined as follows:*

(i) **abort** *and* **skip** *are programs, and*

$$var(\mathbf{abort}) = var(\mathbf{skip}) = \emptyset,$$
$$qvar(\mathbf{abort}) = qvar(\mathbf{skip}) = \emptyset,$$
$$cvar(\mathbf{abort}) = cvar(\mathbf{skip}) = \emptyset.$$

(ii) *If $\bar{q}$ is a quantum register, and U is a unitary operator in $\mathcal{H}_{\bar{q}}$, then*

$$\bar{q} := U[\bar{q}]$$

is a program, and

$$var(\bar{q} := U[\bar{q}]) = \emptyset, \quad qvar(\bar{q} := U[\bar{q}]) = \bar{q}, \quad cvar(\bar{q} := U[\bar{q}]) = \emptyset.$$

(iii) *If S_1 and S_2 are programs such that $var(S_1) \cap var(S_2) = \emptyset$, then $S_1; S_2$ is a program, and*

$$var(S_1; S_2) = var(S_1) \cup var(S_2),$$
$$qvar(S_1; S_2) = qvar(S_1) \cup qvar(S_2),$$
$$cvar(S_1; S_2) = cvar(S_1) \cup cvar(S_2).$$

(iv) *If $\bar{q}$ is a quantum register, x is a classical variable, $M = \{M_m\}$ is a quantum measurement in $\mathcal{H}_{\bar{q}}$ such that all possible outcomes of M are in D_x, and $\{S_m\}$ is a family of programs indexed by the outcomes m of measurement M such that $x \notin \bigcup_m var(S_m)$, then the classical case statement of S_m's guarded by measurement outcomes m's:*

$$S \equiv \mathbf{if}\ (\square m \cdot M[\bar{q} : x] = m \rightarrow S_m)\ \mathbf{fi} \tag{6.8}$$

is a program, and

$$var(S) = \{x\} \cup \left(\bigcup_m var(S_m) \right),$$
$$qvar(S) = \bar{q} \cup \left(\bigcup_m qvar(S_m) \right),$$
$$cvar(S) = \bigcup_m cvar(S_m).$$

(v) *If $\overline{q}$ is a quantum register, $\{|i\rangle\}$ is an orthonormal basis of $\mathcal{H}_{\overline{q}}$, and $\{S_i\}$ is a family of programs indexed by the basis states $|i\rangle$'s such that*

$$\overline{q} \cap \left(\bigcup_i qvar(S_i) \right) = \emptyset,$$

then the quantum case statement of S_i's guarded by basis states $|i\rangle$'s:

$$S \equiv \mathbf{qif}\,[\,\overline{q}\,]\,(\square i \cdot |i\rangle \rightarrow S_i)\ \mathbf{fiq} \tag{6.9}$$

is a program, and

$$var(S) = \bigcup_i var(S_i),$$

$$qvar(S) = \overline{q} \cup \left(\bigcup_i qvar(S_i) \right),$$

$$cvar(S) = \overline{q} \cup \left(\bigcup_i cvar(S_i) \right).$$

This definition looks quite complicated with quantum programs and their classical, quantum and "coin" variables being defined simultaneously. But the syntax of QuGCL can be simply summarized as follows:

$$
\begin{aligned}
S := \ &\mathbf{abort} \mid \mathbf{skip} \mid \overline{q} := U[\,\overline{q}\,] \mid S_1; S_2 \\
&\mid \mathbf{if}\,(\square m \cdot M[\overline{q}:x] = m \rightarrow S_m)\ \mathbf{fi} \qquad \text{(classical case statement)} \\
&\mid \mathbf{qif}\,[\,\overline{q}\,](\square i \cdot |i\rangle \rightarrow S_i)\ \mathbf{fiq} \qquad \text{(quantum case statement)}
\end{aligned}
$$

For simplicity, we often write $U[\overline{q}]$ for the unitary statement $\overline{q} := U[\overline{q}]$. The meanings of **skip**, unitary transformation and sequential composition in QuGCL are the same as in the quantum **while**-language defined in Chapter 3. As in Dijkstra's GCL, **abort** is the undefined instruction that can do anything and even does not need to terminate. The intuitive meaning of quantum case statement (6.9) was already carefully explained in Section 6.1. But several delicate points in the design of the language QuGCL deserve careful explanations:

- The requirement $var(S_1) \cap var(S_2) = \emptyset$ in the sequential composition $S_1; S_2$ means that the outcomes of measurements performed at different points are stored in different classical variables. Such a requirement is mainly for technical convenience, and it will considerably simplify the presentation.
- The statements (6.8) and (6.3) are essentially the same, and the only difference between them is that a classical variable x is added in (6.8) to record the measurement outcome. It is required in statement (6.8) that $x \notin \bigcup_m var(S_m)$. This means that the classical variables already used to record the outcomes of the measurements in S_m's are not allowed to store the outcome of a new measurement. This technical requirement is cumbersome, but it can significantly

simplify the presentation of the semantics of QuGCL. On the other hand, it is not required that the measured quantum variables $\overline{q}$ do not occur in S_m. So, measurement M can be performed not only on an external system but also on some quantum variables within S_m.

- It should be emphasized that in the quantum case statement (6.9) the variables in $\overline{q}$ are not allowed to appear in any S_i's. This indicates that the "coin system" $\overline{q}$ is *external* to programs S_i's. This requirement is so important that it will be emphasized again and again in this chapter and the next. The reason for this requirement will become clear when we consider the semantics of quantum case statement in the following two sections.
- Obviously, all "coins" are quantum variables: $cvar(S) \subseteq qvar(S)$ for all programs S. It will be needed in defining a kind of equivalence between quantum programs to distinguish the set $cvar(S)$ of "coin" variables from other quantum variables in S.

6.3 GUARDED COMPOSITIONS OF QUANTUM OPERATIONS

The syntax of quantum programming language QuGCL was defined in the last section. Now we consider how to define the semantics of QuGCL. It is clear that the main issue in defining the semantics of QuGCL is the treatment of the quantum case statement, because the semantics of the other program constructs either are trivial or were already well-defined in Chapter 3. As was pointed out in Section 6.1, a major difficulty in defining the semantics of a quantum case statement emerges in the case where quantum measurements occur in some of its branch subprograms. So, in this section, we prepare the key mathematical tool – guarded composition of quantum operations – for overcoming this difficulty.

6.3.1 GUARDED COMPOSITION OF UNITARY OPERATORS

To ease the understanding of a general definition of guarded composition, we start with a special case of the guarded composition of unitary operators, which is a straightforward generalization of the quantum walk shift operator S in equation (6.4). In this easy case, no quantum measurements are involved.

Definition 6.3.1. *For each $1 \leq i \leq n$, let U_i be a unitary operator in Hilbert space $\mathcal{H}$. Let $\mathcal{H}_q$ be an auxiliary Hilbert space, called the "coin space," with $\{|i\rangle\}$ as an orthonormal basis. Then we define a linear operator U in $\mathcal{H}_q \otimes \mathcal{H}$ by*

$$U(|i\rangle|\psi\rangle) = |i\rangle U_i|\psi\rangle \tag{6.10}$$

for any $|\psi\rangle \in \mathcal{H}$ and for any $1 \leq i \leq n$. By linearity we have:

$$U\left(\sum_i \alpha_i|i\rangle|\psi_i\rangle\right) = \sum_i \alpha_i|i\rangle U_i|\psi_i\rangle \tag{6.11}$$

for any $|\psi_i\rangle \in \mathcal{H}$ and complex numbers α_i. The operator U is called the guarded composition of U_i $(1 \leq i \leq n)$ along the basis $\{|i\rangle\}$ and written as

$$U \equiv \bigoplus_{i=1}^{n} (|i\rangle \to U_i) \text{ or simply } U \equiv \bigoplus_{i=1}^{n} U_i$$

It is easy to check that the guarded composition U is a unitary operator in $\mathcal{H}_q \otimes \mathcal{H}$. In particular, quantum " coin" q should be considered as a system external to the principal system that has $\mathcal{H}$ as its state space; otherwise the state space of the system composed by the "coin" and the principal system is not $\mathcal{H}_q \otimes \mathcal{H}$, and defining equations (6.10) and (6.11) are inappropriate.

Actually, the guarded composition of unitary operators is nothing new; it is just a quantum multiplexor (QMUX) introduced in Subsection 2.2.4.

Example 6.3.1. *A QMUX U with k select qubits and d-qubit-wide data bus can be represented by a block-diagonal matrix:*

$$U = diag(U_0, U_1, \ldots, U_{2^k-1}) = \begin{pmatrix} U_0 & & & \\ & U_1 & & \\ & & \ldots & \\ & & & U_{2^k-1} \end{pmatrix}.$$

Multiplexing $U_0, U_1, \ldots, U_{2^k-1}$ with k select qubits is exactly the guarded composition

$$\bigoplus_{i=0}^{2^k-1} (|i\rangle \to U_i)$$

along the computational basis $\{|i\rangle\}$ of k qubits.

The guarded composition U of U_i's in Definition 6.3.1 certainly depends on the chosen orthogonal basis $\{|i\rangle\}$ of the " coin" space $\mathcal{H}_q$. For any two different orthonormal bases $\{|i\rangle\}$ and $\{|\varphi_i\rangle\}$ of the "coin space" $\mathcal{H}_q$, there exists a unitary operator U_q such that $|\varphi_i\rangle = U_q|i\rangle$ for all i. Furthermore, a routine calculation yields:

Lemma 6.3.1. *The two compositions along different bases $\{|i\rangle\}$ and $\{|\varphi_i\rangle\}$ are related to each other by*

$$\bigoplus_{i} (|\varphi_i\rangle \to U_i) = (U_q \otimes I_{\mathcal{H}}) \bigoplus_{i} (|i\rangle \to U_i) (U_q^{\dagger} \otimes I_{\mathcal{H}})$$

where $I_{\mathcal{H}}$ is the identity operator in $\mathcal{H}$.

The preceding lemma shows that the guarded composition along one orthonormal basis $\{|\varphi_i\rangle\}$ can be expressed in terms of the guarded composition along any other orthonormal basis $\{|i\rangle\}$. Therefore, the choice of orthonormal basis of the "coin space" is not essential for the definition of guarded composition.

6.3.2 OPERATOR-VALUED FUNCTIONS

A general form of guarded composition of quantum operations cannot be defined by a straightforward generalization of Definition 6.3.1. Instead, we need an auxiliary notion of operator-valued function. For any Hilbert space $\mathcal{H}$, we write $\mathcal{L}(\mathcal{H})$ for the space of (bounded linear) operators in $\mathcal{H}$.

Definition 6.3.2. *Let Δ be a nonempty set. Then a function $F : \Delta \to \mathcal{L}(\mathcal{H})$ is called an operator-valued function in $\mathcal{H}$ over Δ if*

$$\sum_{\delta \in \Delta} F(\delta)^{\dagger} \cdot F(\delta) \sqsubseteq I_{\mathcal{H}}, \tag{6.12}$$

where $I_{\mathcal{H}}$ is the identity operator in $\mathcal{H}$, and $\sqsubseteq$ stands for the Löwner order (see Definition 2.1.13). In particular, F is said to be full when inequality (6.12) becomes equality.

The simplest examples of operator-valued function are unitary operators and quantum measurements.

Example 6.3.2

(i) *A unitary operator U in Hilbert space $\mathcal{H}$ can be seen as a full operator-valued function over a singleton $\Delta = \{\epsilon\}$. This function maps the only element ϵ of Δ to U.*

(ii) *A quantum measurement $M = \{M_m\}$ in Hilbert space $\mathcal{H}$ can be seen as a full operator-valued function over the set $\Delta = \{m\}$ of its possible outcomes. This function maps each outcome m to the corresponding measurement operator M_m.*

It is interesting to compare part (ii) of the preceding example with Example 2.1.9 (ii) where a quantum operation is induced from a quantum measurement by ignoring the measurement outcomes. However, in the preceding example the measurement outcomes are explicitly recorded in the index set $\Delta = \{m\}$.

More generally than the preceding example, a quantum operation defines a family of operator-valued functions. Let $\mathcal{E}$ be a quantum operation in Hilbert space $\mathcal{H}$. Then $\mathcal{E}$ has the Kraus operator-sum representation:

$$\mathcal{E} = \sum_{i} E_i \circ E_i^{\dagger},$$

meaning:

$$\mathcal{E}(\rho) = \sum_{i} E_i \rho E_i^{\dagger}$$

for all density operators ρ in $\mathcal{H}$ (see Theorem 2.1.1). For such a representation, we set $\Delta = \{i\}$ for the set of indexes, and define an operator-valued function over Δ by

$$F(i) = E_i$$

for every i. Since operator-sum representation of $\mathcal{E}$ is not unique, by the previous procedure $\mathcal{E}$ defines possibly more than a single operator-valued function.

Definition 6.3.3. *The set $\mathbb{F}(\mathcal{E})$ of operator-valued functions generated by a quantum operation $\mathcal{E}$ consists of the operator-valued functions defined by all different Kraus operator-sum representations of $\mathcal{E}$.*

Conversely, an operator-valued function determines uniquely a quantum operation.

Definition 6.3.4. *Let F be an operator-valued function in Hilbert space $\mathcal{H}$ over set Δ. Then F defines a quantum operation $\mathcal{E}(F)$ in $\mathcal{H}$ as follows:*

$$\mathcal{E}(F) = \sum_{\delta \in \Delta} F(\delta) \circ F(\delta)^{\dagger};$$

that is,

$$\mathcal{E}(F)(\rho) = \sum_{\delta \in \Delta} F(\delta) \rho F(\delta)^{\dagger}$$

for every density operator ρ in $\mathcal{H}$.

To further clarify the relationship between operator-valued functions and quantum operations, for a family $\mathbb{F}$ of operator-valued functions, we write:

$$\mathcal{E}(\mathbb{F}) = \{\mathcal{E}(F) : F \in \mathbb{F}\}.$$

It is obvious that $\mathcal{E}(\mathbb{F}(\mathcal{E})) = \{\mathcal{E}\}$ for each quantum operation $\mathcal{E}$. On the other hand, for any operator-valued function F over $\Delta = \{\delta_1, \ldots, \delta_k\}$, it follows from Lemma 4.3.1 (i.e., Theorem 8.2 in [174]) that $\mathbb{F}(\mathcal{E}(F))$ consists of all operator-valued functions G over some set $\Gamma = \{\gamma_1, \ldots, \gamma_l\}$ such that

$$G(\gamma_i) = \sum_{j=1}^{n} u_{ij} \cdot F(\delta_j)$$

for each $1 \leq i \leq n$, where $n = \max(k, l)$, $U = (u_{ij})$ is an $n \times n$ unitary matrix, $F(\delta_i) = G(\gamma_j) = 0_{\mathcal{H}}$ for all $k + 1 \leq i \leq n$ and $l + 1 \leq j \leq n$, and $0_{\mathcal{H}}$ is the zero operator in $\mathcal{H}$.

6.3.3 GUARDED COMPOSITION OF OPERATOR-VALUED FUNCTIONS

Now we are going to define the guarded composition of operator-valued functions. Before doing so, we need to introduce a notation. Let Δ_i be a nonempty set for every $1 \leq i \leq n$. Then we write:

$$\bigoplus_{i=1}^{n} \Delta_i = \left\{\oplus_{i=1}^{n}\delta_i : \delta_i \in \Delta_i \text{ for every } 1 \leq i \leq n\right\}. \tag{6.13}$$

Here, $\oplus_{i=1}^{n}\delta_i$ is simply a notation indicating a formal, syntactic combination of δ_i $(1 \leq i \leq n)$. The intuitive meaning behind this notation will be explained when δ_i are used to denote the states of classical variables in the next section.

Definition 6.3.5. *For each* $1 \leq i \leq n$, *let* F_i *be an operator-valued function in Hilbert space* $\mathcal{H}$ *over set* Δ_i. *Let* $\mathcal{H}_q$ *be a "coin" Hilbert space with* $\{|i\rangle\}$ *as an orthonormal basis. Then the guarded composition*

$$F \triangleq \bigoplus_{i=1}^{n} (|i\rangle \rightarrow F_i) \ \text{ or simply } \ F \triangleq \bigoplus_{i=1}^{n} F_i$$

of F_i $(1 \leq i \leq n)$ *along the basis* $\{|i\rangle\}$ *is an operator-valued function*

$$F : \bigoplus_{i=1}^{n} \Delta_i \rightarrow \mathcal{L}(\mathcal{H}_q \otimes \mathcal{H})$$

in $\mathcal{H}_q \otimes \mathcal{H}$ *over* $\oplus_{i=1}^{n} \Delta_i$. *It is defined in the following three steps:*

(i) *For any* $\delta_i \in \Delta_i$ $(1 \leq i \leq n)$,

$$F(\oplus_{i=1}^{n}\delta_i)$$

is an operator in $\mathcal{H}_q \otimes \mathcal{H}$.

(ii) *For each* $|\Psi\rangle \in \mathcal{H}_q \otimes \mathcal{H}$, *there is a unique tuple* $(|\psi_1\rangle, \ldots, |\psi_n\rangle)$ *such that* $|\psi_1\rangle, \ldots, |\psi_n\rangle \in \mathcal{H}$ *and* $|\Psi\rangle$ *can be written as*

$$|\Psi\rangle = \sum_{i=1}^{n} |i\rangle|\psi_i\rangle,$$

and then we define

$$F(\oplus_{i=1}^{n}\delta_i)|\Psi\rangle = \sum_{i=1}^{n} \left(\prod_{k \neq i} \lambda_{k\delta_k} \right) |i\rangle(F_i(\delta_i)|\psi_i\rangle). \tag{6.14}$$

(iii) *For any* $\delta_k \in \Delta_k$ $(1 \leq k \leq n)$, *the coefficients*

$$\lambda_{k\delta_k} = \sqrt{\frac{trF_k(\delta_k)^{\dagger}F_k(\delta_k)}{\sum_{\tau_k \in \Delta_k} trF_k(\tau_k)^{\dagger}F_k(\tau_k)}}. \tag{6.15}$$

In particular, if F_k *is full and* $d = \dim \mathcal{H} < \infty$, *then*

$$\lambda_{k\delta_k} = \sqrt{\frac{trF_k(\delta_k)^{\dagger}F_k(\delta_k)}{d}}.$$

This definition is very involved. In particular, at first glance it is not easy to see where the product of $\lambda_{k\delta_k}$ in equation (6.14) comes from. A simple answer to this question is that the product is chosen for normalization of probability amplitudes. This point can be clearly seen from the proof of Lemma 6.3.3 (presented in Section 6.9 following). Intuitively, the square $\lambda_{k\delta_k}^2$ of the coefficients defined in equation (6.15) can be understood as a kind of conditional probability. Actually, some different choices of coefficients in equations (6.14) and (6.15) are possible; a further discussion on this issue is given in Subsection 6.8.1.

One thing worthy of a special attention is that the state space of guarded composition F in the preceding definition is $\mathcal{H}_q \otimes \mathcal{H}$, and thus quantum "coin" q must be treated as a system external to the principal system with state space $\mathcal{H}$.

It is easy to see that whenever Δ_i is a singleton for all $1 \leq i \leq n$, then all $\lambda_{k\delta_k} = 1$, and equation (6.14) degenerates to (6.11). So, the preceding definition is a generalization of guarded composition of unitary operators introduced in Definition 6.3.1.

The following lemma shows that the guarded composition of operator-valued functions is well-defined.

Lemma 6.3.2. *The guarded composition $\bigoplus_{i=1}^{n} (|i\rangle \to F_i)$ is an operator-valued function in $\mathcal{H}_q \otimes \mathcal{H}$ over $\bigoplus_{i=1}^{n} \Delta_i$. In particular, if all F_i $(1 \leq i \leq n)$ are full, then so is F.*

For readability, the proof of this lemma is postponed to Section 6.9. The reader is encouraged to work out a proof as an exercise.

Similar to Lemma 6.3.1, the choice of orthonormal basis of the "coin space" in the guarded composition of operator-valued function is not essential. For any two orthonormal bases $\{|i\rangle\}$ and $\{|\varphi_i\rangle\}$ of the "coin space" $\mathcal{H}_q$, let U_q be the unitary operator such that $|\varphi_i\rangle = U_q|i\rangle$ for all i. Then we have:

Lemma 6.3.3. *The two compositions along different bases $\{|i\rangle\}$ and $\{|\varphi_i\rangle\}$ are related to each other by*

$$\bigoplus_{i=1}^{n} (|\varphi_i\rangle \to F_i) = (U_q \otimes I_{\mathcal{H}}) \cdot \bigoplus_{i=1}^{n} (|i\rangle \to F_i) \cdot (U_q^\dagger \otimes I_{\mathcal{H}});$$

that is,

$$\bigoplus_{i=1}^{n} (|\varphi_i\rangle \to F_i)\,(\oplus_{i=1}^{n}\delta_i) = (U_q \otimes I_{\mathcal{H}}) \left[\bigoplus_{i=1}^{n} (|i\rangle \to F_i)\,(\oplus_{i=1}^{n}\delta_i) \right] (U_q^\dagger \otimes I_{\mathcal{H}})$$

for any $\delta_1 \in \Delta_1, \ldots, \delta_n \in \Delta_n$.

We now give an example to illustrate Definition 6.3.5. This example shows how to compose two quantum measurements via a quantum " coin," which is a qubit.

Example 6.3.3. *Consider a guarded composition of two simplest quantum measurements:*

- *$M^{(0)}$ is the measurement on a qubit (the principal qubit) p in the computational basis $|0\rangle, |1\rangle$, i.e. $M^{(0)} = \{M_0^{(0)}, M_1^{(0)}\}$, where*

$$M_0^{(0)} = |0\rangle\langle 0|, \quad M_1^{(0)} = |1\rangle\langle 1|;$$

- $M^{(1)}$ is the measurement of the same qubit but in a different basis:

$$|\pm\rangle = \frac{1}{\sqrt{2}}(|0\rangle \pm |1\rangle),$$

i.e., $M^{(1)} = \{M_+^{(1)}, M_-^{(1)}\}$, where

$$M_+^{(1)} = |+\rangle\langle+|, \quad M_-^{(1)} = |-\rangle\langle-|.$$

Then the guarded composition of $M^{(0)}$ and $M^{(1)}$ along the computational basis of another qubit (the "coin qubit") q is the measurement

$$M = M^{(0)} \oplus M^{(1)} = \{M_{0+}, M_{0-}, M_{1+}, M_{1-}\}$$

on two qubits q and p, where ij is an abbreviation of $i \oplus j$, and

$$M_{ij}(|0\rangle_q|\psi_0\rangle_p + |1\rangle_q|\psi_1\rangle_p) = \frac{1}{\sqrt{2}}\left(|0\rangle_q M_i^{(0)}|\psi_0\rangle_p + |1\rangle_q M_j^{(1)}|\psi_1\rangle_p\right)$$

for any states $|\psi_0\rangle, |\psi_1\rangle$ of the principal qubit p and $i \in \{0,1\}, j \in \{+,-\}$. Furthermore, for each state $|\Psi\rangle$ of two qubits q, p and for any $i \in \{0,1\}, j \in \{+,-\}$, a routine calculation yields that the probability that the outcome is ij when performing the guarded composition M of $M^{(0)}$ and $M^{(1)}$ on the two qubit system q, p in state $|\Psi\rangle$ is

$$p(i,j||\Psi\rangle, M) = \frac{1}{2}\left[p\left(i|_q\langle0|\Psi\rangle, M^{(0)}\right) + p\left(j|_q\langle1|\Psi\rangle, M^{(1)}\right)\right],$$

where:

(i) if $|\Psi\rangle = |0\rangle_q|\psi_0\rangle_p + |1\rangle_q|\psi_1\rangle_p$, then

$$_q\langle k|\Psi\rangle = |\psi_k\rangle$$

is the "conditional" state of the principal qubit p given that the two qubit system q, p is in state $|\Psi\rangle$ and the "coin" qubit q is in the basis state $|k\rangle$ for $k = 0, 1$;

(ii) $p\left(i|_q\langle0|\Psi\rangle, M^{(0)}\right)$ is the probability that the outcome is i when performing measurement $M^{(0)}$ on qubit p in state $_q\langle0|\Psi\rangle$;

(iii) $p\left(j|_q\langle1|\Psi\rangle, M^{(1)}\right)$ is the probability that the outcome is j when performing measurement $M^{(1)}$ on qubit p in state $_q\langle1|\Psi\rangle$.

6.3.4 GUARDED COMPOSITION OF QUANTUM OPERATIONS

In the last subsection, we learned how to compose a family of operator-valued functions employing an external quantum "coin." Now the guarded composition of a family of quantum operations can be defined through the guarded composition of the operator-valued functions generated from them.

Definition 6.3.6. *For each* $1 \leq i \leq n$, *let* $\mathcal{E}_i$ *be a quantum operation (i.e., super-operator) in Hilbert space* $\mathcal{H}$. *Let* $\mathcal{H}_q$ *be a "coin" Hilbert space with* $\{|i\rangle\}$ *as an orthonormal basis. Then the guarded composition of* $\mathcal{E}_i$ $(1 \leq i \leq n)$ *along the basis* $\{|i\rangle\}$ *is defined to be the family of quantum operations in* $\mathcal{H}_q \otimes \mathcal{H}$:

$$\bigoplus_{i=1}^{n} (|i\rangle \to \mathcal{E}_i) = \left\{ \mathcal{E}\left(\bigoplus_{i=1}^{n} (|i\rangle \to F_i) \right) : F_i \in \mathbb{F}(\mathcal{E}_i) \text{ for every } 1 \leq i \leq n \right\},$$

where:

(i) $\mathbb{F}(\mathcal{F})$ *stands for the set of operator-valued functions generated by quantum operation* $\mathcal{F}$ *(see Definition 6.3.3);*
(ii) $\mathcal{E}(F)$ *is the quantum operation defined by an operator-valued function* F *(see Definition 6.3.4).*

Similar to the cases in Definitions 6.3.1 and 6.3.5, the guarded composition $\bigoplus_{i=1}^{n} (|i\rangle \to \mathcal{E}_i)$ is a quantum operation in space $\mathcal{H}_q \otimes \mathcal{H}$, and thus quantum "coin" q is external to the principal system with state space $\mathcal{H}$.

It is easy to see that if $n = 1$ then the preceding guarded composition of quantum operations consists of only $\mathcal{E}_1$. For $n > 1$, however, it is usually not a singleton, as shown by the following example. For any unitary operator U in a Hilbert space $\mathcal{H}$, we write $\mathcal{E}_U = U \circ U^\dagger$ for a quantum operation defined by U, that is, $\mathcal{E}_U(\rho) = U\rho U^\dagger$ for all density operators ρ in $\mathcal{H}$ (see Example 2.1.8).

Example 6.3.4. *Suppose that* U_0 *and* U_1 *are two unitary operators in a Hilbert space* $\mathcal{H}$. *Let* U *be the composition of* U_0 *and* U_1 *guarded by the computational basis* $|0\rangle, |1\rangle$ *of a qubit:*

$$U = U_0 \oplus U_1.$$

Then $\mathcal{E}_U$ *is an element of the guarded composition*

$$\mathcal{E} = \mathcal{E}_{U_0} \oplus \mathcal{E}_{U_1}$$

of super-operators $\mathcal{E}_{U_0}$ *and* $\mathcal{E}_{U_1}$. *But* $\mathcal{E}$ *contains more than one element. Indeed, it holds that*

$$\mathcal{E} = \{\mathcal{E}_{U_\theta} = U_\theta \circ U_\theta^\dagger : 0 \leq \theta < 2\pi\},$$

where

$$U_\theta = U_0 \oplus e^{i\theta} U_1.$$

Note that the non-uniqueness of the members of the guarded composition $\mathcal{E}$ *is caused by the relative phase* θ *between* U_0 *and* U_1.

We now examine the choice of basis of the "coin space" in the guarded composition of quantum operations. To this end, we need the following two notations:

- For any two quantum operations $\mathcal{E}_1$ and $\mathcal{E}_2$ in a Hilbert space $\mathcal{H}$, their sequential composition $\mathcal{E}_2 \circ \mathcal{E}_1$ is the quantum operation in $\mathcal{H}$ defined by

$$(\mathcal{E}_2 \circ \mathcal{E}_1)(\rho) = \mathcal{E}_2(\mathcal{E}_1(\rho))$$

  for any density operator ρ in $\mathcal{H}$. This notation was already introduced in Subsection 5.1.2.
- More generally, for any quantum operation $\mathcal{E}$ and any set Ω of quantum operations in Hilbert space $\mathcal{H}$, we define the sequential compositions of Ω and $\mathcal{E}$ by

$$\mathcal{E} \circ \Omega = \{\mathcal{E} \circ \mathcal{F} : \mathcal{F} \in \Omega\} \quad \text{and} \quad \Omega \circ \mathcal{E} = \{\mathcal{F} \circ \mathcal{E} : \mathcal{F} \in \Omega\}.$$

The following lemma can be easily derived from Lemma 6.3.3, and it shows that the choice of orthonormal basis of the "coin space" is not essential for the guarded composition of quantum operations. For any two orthonormal bases $\{|i\rangle\}$ and $\{|\varphi_i\rangle\}$ of the "coin space" $\mathcal{H}_q$, let U_q be the unitary operator such that $|\varphi_i\rangle = U_q|i\rangle$ for all i. Then we have:

Lemma 6.3.4. *The two compositions along different bases $\{|i\rangle\}$ and $\{|\varphi_i\rangle\}$ are related to each other by*

$$\bigoplus_{i=1}^{n} (|\varphi_i\rangle \to \mathcal{E}_i) = \left[\mathcal{E}_{U_q^\dagger \otimes I_\mathcal{H}} \circ \bigoplus_{i=1}^{n} (|i\rangle \to \mathcal{E}_i) \right] \circ \mathcal{E}_{U_q \otimes I_\mathcal{H}},$$

where $\mathcal{E}_{U_q \otimes I_\mathcal{H}}$ and $\mathcal{E}_{U_q^\dagger \otimes I_\mathcal{H}}$ are the quantum operations in $\mathcal{H}_q \otimes \mathcal{H}$ defined by unitary operators $U_q \otimes I_\mathcal{H}$ and $U_q^\dagger \otimes I_\mathcal{H}$, respectively.

Exercise 6.3.1. *Prove Lemmas 6.3.1, 6.3.3 and 6.3.4.*

6.4 SEMANTICS OF QuGCL PROGRAMS

With the preparation in Section 6.3, we are ready to define the semantics of the quantum programming language QuGCL presented in Section 6.2. Before doing it, we introduce several notations needed in this section.

- Let $\mathcal{H}$ and $\mathcal{H}'$ be two Hilbert spaces, and let E be an operator in $\mathcal{H}$. Then the cylindrical extension of E in $\mathcal{H} \otimes \mathcal{H}'$ is defined to be the operator $E \otimes I_{\mathcal{H}'}$, where $I_{\mathcal{H}'}$ is the identity operator in $\mathcal{H}'$. For simplicity, we will write E for $E \otimes I_{\mathcal{H}'}$ whenever there is no possibility of confusion.
- Let F be an operator-valued function in $\mathcal{H}$ over Δ. Then the cylindrical extension of F in $\mathcal{H} \otimes \mathcal{H}'$ is the operator-valued function $\overline{F}$ in $\mathcal{H} \otimes \mathcal{H}'$ over Δ defined by

$$\overline{F}(\delta) = F(\delta) \otimes I_{\mathcal{H}'}$$

  for every $\delta \in \Delta$. For simplicity, we often write F for $\overline{F}$ whenever the context prevents any confusion.

- Let $\mathcal{E} = \sum_i E_i \circ E_i^\dagger$ be a quantum operation in $\mathcal{H}$. Then the cylindrical extension of $\mathcal{E}$ in $\mathcal{H} \otimes \mathcal{H}'$ is defined to be the quantum operation:

$$\overline{\mathcal{E}} = \sum_i (E_i \otimes I_{\mathcal{H}'}) \circ (E_i^\dagger \otimes I_{\mathcal{H}'}).$$

For simplicity, $\mathcal{E}$ will be used to denote its extension $\overline{\mathcal{E}}$ when no confusion is possible. In particular, if E is an operator in $\mathcal{H}$, and ρ is a density operator in $\mathcal{H} \otimes \mathcal{H}'$, then $E\rho E^\dagger$ should be understood as $(E \otimes I_{\mathcal{H}'})\rho(E^\dagger \otimes I_{\mathcal{H}'})$.

6.4.1 CLASSICAL STATES

The first step in defining the semantics of QuGCL is to define the states of classical variables in QuGCL. As already stated in Section 6.2, classical variables in QuGCL will only be used to record the outcomes of quantum measurements.

Definition 6.4.1. *Classical states and their domains are inductively defined as follows:*

- **(i)** ϵ *is a classical state, called the empty state, and $dom(\epsilon) = \emptyset$;*
- **(ii)** *If $x \in Var$ is a classical variable, and $a \in D_x$ is an element of the domain of x, then $[x \leftarrow a]$ is a classical state, and $dom([x \leftarrow a]) = \{x\}$;*
- **(iii)** *If both δ_1 and δ_2 are classical states, and $dom(\delta_1) \cap dom(\delta_2) = \emptyset$, then $\delta_1\delta_2$ is a classical state, and $dom(\delta_1\delta_2) = dom(\delta_1) \cup dom(\delta_2)$;*
- **(iv)** *If δ_i is a classical state for every $1 \le i \le n$, then $\oplus_{i=1}^n \delta_i$ is a classical state, and*

$$dom\left(\oplus_{i=1}^n \delta_i\right) = \bigcup_{i=1}^n dom(\delta_i).$$

Intuitively, a classical state δ defined by clauses (i) to (iii) in this definition can be seen as a (partial) assignment to classical variables; more precisely, δ is an element of Cartesian product $\prod_{x \in dom(\delta)} D_x$; that is, a choice function:

$$\delta : dom(\delta) \to \bigcup_{x \in dom(\delta)} D_x$$

such that $\delta(x) \in D_x$ for every $x \in dom(\delta)$. The state $\oplus_{i=1}^n \delta_i$ defined by clause (iv) is a formal combination of states δ_i $(1 \le i \le n)$. It will be used in defining the semantics of quantum case statement, which is a guarded composition of operator-valued functions. From equation (6.13) and Definition 6.3.5 we can see why such a combination is required. More concretely, we have:

- The empty state ϵ is the empty function. Since $\prod_{x \in \emptyset} D_x = \{\epsilon\}$, ϵ is the only possible state with an empty domain.
- The state $[x \leftarrow a]$ assigns value a to variable x but the values of the other variables are undefined.

- The composed state $\delta_1\delta_2$ can be seen as the assignment to variables in $dom(\delta_1) \cup dom(\delta_2)$ given by

$$(\delta_1\delta_2)(x) = \begin{cases} \delta_1(x) & \text{if } x \in dom(\delta_1), \\ \delta_2(x) & \text{if } x \in dom(\delta_2). \end{cases} \tag{6.16}$$

Equation (6.16) is well-defined since it is required that $dom(\delta_1) \cap dom(\delta_2) = \emptyset$. In particular, $\epsilon\delta = \delta\epsilon = \delta$ for any state δ, and if $x \notin dom(\delta)$ then $\delta[x \leftarrow a]$ is the assignment to variables in $dom(\delta) \cup \{x\}$ given by

$$\delta[x \leftarrow a](y) = \begin{cases} \delta(y) & \text{if } y \in dom(\delta), \\ a & \text{if } y = x. \end{cases}$$

Hence, $[x_1 \leftarrow a_1] \cdots [x_k \leftarrow a_k]$ is a classical state that assigns value a_i to variable x_i for all $1 \leq j \leq k$. It will be abbreviated to

$$[x_1 \leftarrow a_1, \cdots, x_k \leftarrow a_k]$$

in the sequel.
- The state $\oplus_{i=1}^{n}\delta_i$ can be thought of as a kind of nondeterministic choice of δ_i $(1 \leq i \leq n)$. As will be seen in the next subsection (in particular, clause (v) of Definition 6.4.2), a classical state $\delta = [x_1 \leftarrow a_1, \cdots, x_k \leftarrow a_k]$ is actually generated by a sequence of measurements $M_1, \ldots, M_k$ with their outcomes $a_1, \ldots, a_k$ stored in variables $x_1, \ldots, x_k$, respectively. However, for quantum measurements $M_1, \ldots, M_k$, other outcomes $a'_1, \ldots, a'_k$ are possible, and then we may have many other classical states $\delta' = [x_1 \leftarrow a'_1, \cdots, x_k \leftarrow a'_k]$. So, a state of the form $\oplus_{i=1}^{n}\delta_i$ is needed to record a collection of all different outcomes of measurement sequence $M_1, \ldots, M_k$.

6.4.2 SEMI-CLASSICAL SEMANTICS

Now we can define the semi-classical semantics of QuGCL, which will serve as a stepping stone for defining its purely quantum semantics. For each QuGCL program S, we write $\Delta(S)$ for the set of all possible states of its classical variables.

- The semi-classical denotational semantics $\lVert S \rVert$ of S will be defined as an operator-valued function in $\mathcal{H}_{qvar(S)}$ over $\Delta(S)$, where $\mathcal{H}_{qvar(S)}$ is the state Hilbert space of quantum variables occurring in S.

In particular, if $qvar(S) = \emptyset$, for example $S = \textbf{abort}$ or $\textbf{skip}$, then $\mathcal{H}_{qvar(S)}$ is a one-dimensional space $\mathcal{H}_\emptyset$, and an operator in $\mathcal{H}_\emptyset$ can be identified with a complex number; for instance, the zero operator is number 0 and the identity operator is number 1. For any set $V \subseteq qVar$ of quantum variables, we write I_V for the identity operator in Hilbert space $\mathcal{H}_V = \bigotimes_{q \in V} \mathcal{H}_q$.

Definition 6.4.2. *The classical states $\Delta(S)$ and semi-classical semantic function $\|S\|$ of a QuGCL program S are inductively defined as follows:*

 (i) $\Delta(\mathbf{abort}) = \{\epsilon\}$, *and* $\|\mathbf{abort}\|(\epsilon) = 0$;
 (ii) $\Delta(\mathbf{skip}) = \{\epsilon\}$, *and* $\|\mathbf{skip}\|(\epsilon) = 1$;
(iii) *If* $S \equiv \overline{q} := U[\,\overline{q}\,]$, *then* $\Delta(S) = \{\epsilon\}$, *and* $\|S\|(\epsilon) = U_{\overline{q}}$, *where* $U_{\overline{q}}$ *is the unitary operator U acting in* $\mathcal{H}_{\overline{q}}$;
(iv) *If* $S \equiv S_1; S_2$, *then*

$$\Delta(S) = \Delta(S_1); \Delta(S_2)$$
$$= \{\delta_1\delta_2 : \delta_1 \in \Delta(S_1), \delta_2 \in \Delta(S_2)\}, \tag{6.17}$$

$$\|S\|(\delta_1\delta_2) = (\|S_2\|(\delta_2) \otimes I_{V \backslash qvar(S_2)}) \cdot (\|S_1\|(\delta_1) \otimes I_{V \backslash qvar(S_1)})$$

where $V = qvar(S_1) \cup qvar(S_2)$;
 (v) *If S is a classical case statement:*

$$S \equiv \mathbf{if} \ (\Box m \cdot M[\overline{q} : x] = m \to S_m) \ \mathbf{fi},$$

where quantum measurement $M = \{M_m\}$, *then*

$$\Delta(S) = \bigcup_m \{\delta[x \leftarrow m] : \delta \in \Delta(S_m)\},$$

$$\|S\|(\delta[x \leftarrow m]) = (\|S_m\|(\delta) \otimes I_{V \backslash qvar(S_m)}) \cdot (M_m \otimes I_{V \backslash \overline{q}})$$

for every $\delta \in \Delta(S_m)$ *and for every outcome m, where*

$$V = \overline{q} \cup \left(\bigcup_m qvar(S_m) \right);$$

(vi) *If S is a quantum case statement:*

$$S \equiv \mathbf{qif} \ [\,\overline{q}\,] \ (\Box i \cdot |i\rangle \to S_i) \ \mathbf{fiq},$$

then

$$\Delta(S) = \bigoplus_i \Delta(S_i), \tag{6.18}$$

$$\|S\| = \bigoplus_i (|i\rangle \to \|S_i\|), \tag{6.19}$$

where operation $\bigoplus$ *in equation (6.18) is defined by equation (6.13), and* $\bigoplus$ *in equation (6.19) stands for the guarded composition of operator-valued functions (see Definition 6.3.5).*

Since it is required in Definition 6.2.1 that $var(S_1) \cap var(S_2) = \emptyset$ in the sequential composition $S_1; S_2$, we have $dom(\delta_1) \cap dom(\delta_2) = \emptyset$ for any $\delta_1 \in \Delta(S_1)$ and $\delta_2 \in \Delta(S_2)$. Thus, equation (6.17) is well-defined.

Intuitively, the semi-classical semantics of quantum programs can be imagined as follows:

- If a quantum program S does not contain any quantum case statement, then its semantic structure is a tree with its nodes labelled by basic commands and its edges by linear operators. This tree grows up from the root in the following way:
  - if the current node is labelled by a unitary transformation U, then a single edge stems from the node and it is labelled by U; and
  - if the current node is labelled by a measurement $M = \{M_m\}$, then for each possible outcome m, an edge stems from the node and it is labelled by the corresponding measurement operator M_m.

  Obviously, branching in the semantic tree comes from the different possible outcomes of a measurement in S. Each classical state $\delta \in \Delta(S)$ is corresponding to a branch in the semantic tree of S, and it denotes a possible path of execution. Furthermore, the value of semantic function $\|S\|$ in state δ is the (sequential) composition of the operators labelling the edges of δ. This can be clearly seen from clauses (i) - (v) of the preceding definition.
- The semantic structure of a quantum program S with quantum case statements is much more complicated. It can be seen as a tree with superpositions of nodes that generate superpositions of branches. The value of semantic function $\|S\|$ in a superposition of branches is then defined as the guarded composition of the values in these branches.

6.4.3 PURELY QUANTUM SEMANTICS

The purely quantum semantics of a quantum program written in QuGCL can be naturally defined as the quantum operation induced by its semi-classical semantic function (see Definition 6.3.4).

Definition 6.4.3. *For each QuGCL program S, its purely quantum denotational semantics is the quantum operation $[\![S]\!]$ in $\mathcal{H}_{qvar(S)}$ defined as follows:*

$$[\![S]\!] = \mathcal{E}(\|S\|) = \sum_{\delta \in \Delta(S)} \|S\|(\delta) \circ \|S\|(\delta)^\dagger, \tag{6.20}$$

where $\|S\|$ is the semi-classical semantic function of S.

The following proposition presents an explicit representation of the purely quantum semantics of a program in terms of its subprograms. This representation is easier to use in applications than the preceding abstract definition.

Proposition 6.4.1

(i) $[\![\mathbf{abort}]\!] = 0$;
(ii) $[\![\mathbf{skip}]\!] = 1$;
(iii) $[\![S_1; S_2]\!] = [\![S_2]\!] \circ [\![S_1]\!]$;

(iv) $[\![\bar{q} := U[\bar{q}]]\!] = U_{\bar{q}} \circ U_{\bar{q}}^{\dagger};$
(v)

$$[\![\mathbf{if}\ (\square m \cdot M[\bar{q} : x] = m \to S_m)\ \mathbf{fi}]\!] = \sum_m \left[[\![S_m]\!] \circ (M_m \circ M_m^{\dagger}) \right].$$

Here, $[\![S_m]\!]$ *should be seen as a cylindrical extension in* $\mathcal{H}_V$ *from* $\mathcal{H}_{qvar(S_m)}$, $M_m \circ M_m^{\dagger}$ *is seen as a cylindrical extension in* $\mathcal{H}_V$ *from* $\mathcal{H}_{\bar{q}}$, *and*

$$V = \bar{q} \cup \left(\bigcup_m qvar(S_m) \right);$$

(vi)

$$[\![\mathbf{qif}\ [\bar{q}]\ (\square i \cdot |i\rangle \to S_i)\ \mathbf{fiq}]\!] \in \bigoplus_i \left(|i\rangle \to [\![S_i]\!] \right). \tag{6.21}$$

Here $[\![S_i]\!]$ *should be understood as a cylindrical extension in* $\mathcal{H}_V$ *from* $\mathcal{H}_{qvar(S_i)}$ *for every* $1 \leq i \leq n$, *and*

$$V = \bar{q} \cup \left(\bigcup_i qvar(S_i) \right).$$

It should be mentioned that symbol $\circ$ in clause (iii) and its first occurrence in clause (v) of the preceding proposition stands for composition of quantum operations; that is, $(\mathcal{E}_2 \circ \mathcal{E}_1)(\rho) = \mathcal{E}_2(\mathcal{E}_1(\rho))$ for all density operators ρ. But the symbol $\circ$ in clause (iv) and its second occurrence in clause (v) is used to define a quantum operation from an operator; that is, for an operator A, $A \circ A^{\dagger}$ is the quantum operation $\mathcal{E}_A$ defined by $\mathcal{E}_A(\rho) = A\rho A^{\dagger}$ for every density operator ρ. Essentially, clauses (ii) - (v) in this proposition are the same as the corresponding clauses in Proposition 3.3.1. The proof of this proposition is deferred to Section 6.9. Actually, the proof is not difficult, although it is tedious. The reader is encouraged to try to prove this proposition in order to gain a better understanding of Definitions 6.4.2 and 6.4.3.

The preceding proposition shows that the purely quantum denotational semantics is *almost compositional*, but it is *not completely compositional* because the symbol "$\in$" appears in equation (6.21). The symbol "$\in$" can be understood as a *refinement relation*. It is worth noting that in general the symbol "$\in$" in (6.21) cannot be replaced by equality. This is exactly the reason that the purely quantum semantics of a program has to be derived through its semi-classical semantics but cannot be defined directly by a structural induction.

It should be stressed that the symbol "$\in$" in equation (6.21) does not mean that the purely quantum semantics of the quantum case statement is not well-defined. In fact, it is uniquely defined by equations (6.19) and (6.20) as a quantum operation. The right-hand side of equation (6.21) is not the semantics of any program. It is the guarded composition of the semantics of programs S_i. Since it is the guarded composition of a family of quantum operations, it can be a set consisting of more than one quantum operation, as shown in Example 6.3.4. The semantics of the quantum case statement is one member of the set of quantum operations in the right-hand side of equation (6.21).

Exercise 6.4.1. *Find an example to show that equation (6.21) is not true when the symbol "∈" is replaced by equality.*

Equivalence between quantum programs can be introduced based on their purely quantum denotational semantics. Roughly speaking, two programs are equivalent if the outputs computed by them are the same for the same input. Formally, we have:

Definition 6.4.4. *Let P and Q be two QuGCL programs. Then:*

(i) *We say that P and Q are equivalent and write P = Q if*

$$[\![P]\!] \otimes \mathcal{I}_{Q \setminus P} = [\![Q]\!] \otimes \mathcal{I}_{P \setminus Q},$$

where $\mathcal{I}_{Q \setminus P}$ is the identity quantum operation in $\mathcal{H}_{qvar(Q) \setminus qvar(P)}$ and $\mathcal{I}_{P \setminus Q}$ the identity quantum operation in $\mathcal{H}_{qvar(P) \setminus qvar(Q)}$.

(ii) *The "coin-free" equivalence $P =_{CF} Q$ holds if*

$$tr_{\mathcal{H}_{cvar(P) \cup cvar(Q)}}([\![P]\!] \otimes \mathcal{I}_{Q \setminus P}) = tr_{\mathcal{H}_{cvar(P) \cup cvar(Q)}}([\![Q]\!] \otimes \mathcal{I}_{P \setminus Q}).$$

The symbol "*tr*" in this equation denotes partial trace. The partial trace on density operators was introduced in Definition 2.1.22. Furthermore, the notion of partial trace can be generalized to quantum operations: for any quantum operation $\mathcal{E}$ in $\mathcal{H}_1 \otimes \mathcal{H}_2$, $tr_{\mathcal{H}_1}(\mathcal{E})$ is a quantum operation from $\mathcal{H}_1 \otimes \mathcal{H}_2$ to $\mathcal{H}_2$ defined by

$$tr_{\mathcal{H}_1}(\mathcal{E})(\rho) = tr_{\mathcal{H}_1}(\mathcal{E}(\rho))$$

for all density operators ρ in $\mathcal{H}_1 \otimes \mathcal{H}_2$.

Obviously, $P = Q$ implies $P =_{CF} Q$. The "coin-free" equivalence means that "coin" variables are only used to produce quantum control flows of programs (or to realize superposition of programs, as discussed in the next section). The computational outcome of a program P is stored in the "principal" state space $\mathcal{H}_{qvar(P) \setminus cvar(P)}$. For the special case of $qvar(P) = qvar(Q)$, we have:

- $P = Q$ if and only if $[\![P]\!] = [\![Q]\!]$; and
- $P =_{CF} Q$ if and only if $tr_{\mathcal{H}_{cvar(P)}}[\![P]\!] = tr_{\mathcal{H}_{cvar(P)}}[\![Q]\!]$.

The notions of equivalence given in the previous definition provide a basis for quantum program transformation and optimization where the transformed program is required to be equivalent to the source program. A set of algebraic laws that can help to establish equivalence between QuGCL programs will be presented in Section 6.6.

6.4.4 WEAKEST PRECONDITION SEMANTICS

The notion of quantum weakest precondition was introduced in Subsection 4.1.1, and the weakest precondition semantics of quantum **while**-programs was presented in Subsection 4.2.2. Here, we give the weakest precondition semantics of QuGCL programs, which can be derived from Proposition 6.4.1 together with Proposition 4.1.1.

As in classical programming and in the case of quantum **while**-programs, weakest precondition semantics provides us with a way for analyzing QuGCL programs backwards.

Proposition 6.4.2

(i) $wp.\textbf{abort} = 0$;

(ii) $wp.\textbf{skip} = 1$;

(iii) $wp.(P_1; P_2) = wp.P_2 \circ wp.P_1$;

(iv) $wp.\bar{q} := U[\bar{q}] = U_{\bar{q}}^{\dagger} \circ U_{\bar{q}}$;

(v)

$$wp.\textbf{if} \ (\Box m \cdot M[\bar{q} : x] = m \rightarrow P_m) \ \textbf{fi}$$
$$= \sum_m \left[(M_m^{\dagger} \circ M_m) \circ wp.P_m \right];$$

(vi) $wp.\textbf{qif} \ [\bar{q}] \ (\Box i \cdot |i\rangle \rightarrow P_i) \ \textbf{fiq} \in \Box_i \ (|i\rangle \rightarrow wp.P_i)$.

Some cylindrical extensions of quantum operations are used but unspecified in the preceding proposition because they can be recognized from the context. It should be noticed that the symbol $\circ$ is used in two different ways, as remarked after Proposition 6.4.1. Again, the symbol "$\in$" in the preceding clause (vi) cannot be replaced by equality because the right-hand side of clause (vi) is a set that may contain more than one quantum operation.

We can define the refinement relation between quantum QuGCL programs in terms of their weakest precondition semantics. To this end, we first generalize the Löwner order to the case of quantum operations: for any two quantum operations $\mathcal{E}$ and $\mathcal{F}$ in Hilbert space $\mathcal{H}$,

- $\mathcal{E} \sqsubseteq \mathcal{F}$ if and only if $\mathcal{E}(\rho) \sqsubseteq \mathcal{F}(\rho)$ for all density operators ρ in $\mathcal{H}$.

Definition 6.4.5. *Let P and Q be two QuGCL programs. Then we say that P is refined by Q and write* $P \sqsubseteq Q$ *if*

$$wp.P \otimes \mathcal{I}_{Q \setminus P} \sqsubseteq wp.Q \otimes \mathcal{I}_{P \setminus Q},$$

where $\mathcal{I}_{Q \setminus P}$ *and* $\mathcal{I}_{P \setminus Q}$ *are the same as in Definition 6.4.4.*

Intuitively, $P \sqsubseteq Q$ means that P is improved by Q because the precondition of P is weakened to the precondition of Q. It is easy to see that $P \sqsubseteq Q$ and $Q \sqsubseteq P$ implies $P \equiv Q$. The notion of "coin-free" refinement can be defined in a way similar to Definition 6.4.4 (ii).

The refinement techniques have been successfully developed in classical programming so that specifications (of users' requirements) can be refined step by step using various refinement laws and finally transferred to codes that can be executed on machines; see [27] and [172] for a systematic exposition of refinement techniques. These techniques were also extended to probabilistic programming in [220]. Here, we are not going to further consider how refinement techniques can be used in quantum programming, but leave it as a topic for future research.

6.4.5 AN EXAMPLE

To close out this section, we present a simple example that helps us to understand the semantic notions introduced here.

Example 6.4.1. *Let q be a qubit variable and x, y two classical variables. Consider the QuGCL program*

$$
\begin{aligned}
P \equiv \ &\textbf{qif } |0\rangle \rightarrow H[q]; \\
&\qquad\quad \textbf{if } M^{(0)}[q:x] = 0 \rightarrow X[q]; \\
&\qquad\quad \square \qquad\qquad\quad 1 \rightarrow Y[q] \\
&\qquad\quad \textbf{fi} \\
&\square\ |1\rangle \rightarrow S[q]; \\
&\qquad\quad \textbf{if } M^{(1)}[q:x] = 0 \rightarrow Y[q] \\
&\qquad\quad \square \qquad\qquad\quad 1 \rightarrow Z[q] \\
&\qquad\quad \textbf{fi}; \\
&\qquad\quad X[q]; \\
&\qquad\quad \textbf{if } M^{(0)}[q:y] = 0 \rightarrow Z[q] \\
&\qquad\quad \square \qquad\qquad\quad 1 \rightarrow X[q] \\
&\qquad\quad \textbf{fi} \\
&\textbf{fiq}
\end{aligned}
$$

where $M^{(0)}, M^{(1)}$ are the measurements on a qubit in computational basis $|0\rangle, |1\rangle$ and basis $|\pm\rangle$, respectively (see Example 6.3.3), H is the Hadamard gate, X, Y, Z are the Pauli matrices, and S is the phase gate (see Examples 2.2.1 and 2.2.2). The program P is a quantum case statement between two subprograms P_0 and P_1 with the "coin" omitted. The first subprogram P_0 is the Hadamard gate followed by the measurement in the computational basis, where whenever the outcome is 0, then the gate X follows; whenever the outcome is 1, then the gate Y follows. The second subprogram P_1 is the gate S followed by the measurement in basis $|\pm\rangle$, the gate X, and the measurement in the computational basis.

For simplicity, we write a for classical state $[x \leftarrow a]$ of program P_0 and bc for classical state $[x \leftarrow b, y \leftarrow c]$ of program P_1 for any $a, c \in \{0, 1\}$ and $b \in \{+, -\}$. Then the semi-classical semantic functions of P_0 and P_1 are given as follows:

$$
\begin{cases}
\llbracket P_0 \rrbracket(0) = X \cdot |0\rangle\langle 0| \cdot H = \frac{1}{\sqrt{2}} \begin{pmatrix} 0 & 0 \\ 1 & 1 \end{pmatrix}, \\[2mm]
\llbracket P_0 \rrbracket(1) = Y \cdot |1\rangle\langle 1| \cdot H = \frac{i}{\sqrt{2}} \begin{pmatrix} -1 & 1 \\ 0 & 0 \end{pmatrix}, \\[2mm]
\llbracket P_1 \rrbracket(+0) = Z \cdot |0\rangle\langle 0| \cdot X \cdot Y \cdot |+\rangle\langle +| \cdot S = \frac{1}{2} \begin{pmatrix} i & -1 \\ 0 & 0 \end{pmatrix},
\end{cases}
$$

$$\begin{cases} \llbracket P_1 \rrbracket(+1) = X \cdot |1\rangle\langle 1| \cdot X \cdot Y \cdot |+\rangle\langle +| \cdot S = \frac{1}{2}\begin{pmatrix} -i & 1 \\ 0 & 0 \end{pmatrix}, \\[1.5em] \llbracket P_1 \rrbracket(-0) = Z \cdot |0\rangle\langle 0| \cdot X \cdot Z \cdot |-\rangle\langle -| \cdot S = \frac{1}{2}\begin{pmatrix} 1 & -i \\ 0 & 0 \end{pmatrix}, \\[1.5em] \llbracket P_1 \rrbracket(-1) = X \cdot |1\rangle\langle 1| \cdot X \cdot Z \cdot |-\rangle\langle -| \cdot S = \frac{1}{2}\begin{pmatrix} 1 & -i \\ 0 & 0 \end{pmatrix}. \end{cases}$$

The semi-classical semantic function of P is an operator-valued function in the state space of two qubits over classical states

$$\Delta(P) = \{a \oplus bc : a, c \in \{0, 1\} \text{ and } b \in \{+, -\}\}.$$

It follows from equation (6.14) that

$$\llbracket P \rrbracket(a \oplus bc)(|0\rangle|\varphi\rangle) = \lambda_{1(bc)}|0\rangle(\llbracket P_0 \rrbracket(a)|\varphi\rangle),$$
$$\llbracket P \rrbracket(a \oplus bc)(|1\rangle|\varphi\rangle) = \lambda_{0a}|1\rangle(\llbracket P_1 \rrbracket(bc)|\varphi\rangle),$$

where $\lambda_{0a} = \frac{1}{\sqrt{2}}$ and $\lambda_{1(bc)} = \frac{1}{2}$ for $a, c \in \{0, 1\}$ and $b \in \{+, -\}$. Using

$$\llbracket P \rrbracket(a \oplus bc) = \sum_{i,j \in 0,1} (\llbracket P \rrbracket(a \oplus bc)|ij\rangle)\langle ij|,$$

we can compute:

$$\llbracket P \rrbracket(0 \oplus +0) = \frac{1}{2\sqrt{2}}\begin{pmatrix} 0 & 1 & 0 & 0 \\ 0 & 1 & 0 & 0 \\ 0 & 0 & i & 0 \\ 0 & 0 & -1 & 0 \end{pmatrix},$$

$$\llbracket P \rrbracket(0 \oplus +1) = \frac{1}{2\sqrt{2}}\begin{pmatrix} 0 & 1 & 0 & 0 \\ 0 & 1 & 0 & 0 \\ 0 & 0 & -i & 0 \\ 0 & 0 & 1 & 0 \end{pmatrix},$$

$$\llbracket P \rrbracket(0 \oplus -0) = \llbracket P \rrbracket(0 \oplus -1) = \frac{1}{2\sqrt{2}}\begin{pmatrix} 0 & 1 & 0 & 0 \\ 0 & 1 & 0 & 0 \\ 0 & 0 & 1 & 0 \\ 0 & 0 & -i & 0 \end{pmatrix},$$

$$\llbracket P \rrbracket(1 \oplus +0) = \frac{1}{2\sqrt{2}}\begin{pmatrix} -1 & 0 & 0 & 0 \\ 1 & 0 & 0 & 0 \\ 0 & 0 & i & 0 \\ 0 & 0 & -1 & 0 \end{pmatrix},$$

$$\|P\|(1 \oplus +1) = \frac{1}{2\sqrt{2}} \begin{pmatrix} -1 & 0 & 0 & 0 \\ 1 & 0 & 0 & 0 \\ 0 & 0 & -i & 0 \\ 0 & 0 & 1 & 0 \end{pmatrix},$$

$$\|P\|(1 \oplus -0) = \|P\|(1 \oplus -1) = \frac{1}{2\sqrt{2}} \begin{pmatrix} 1 & 0 & 0 & 0 \\ 1 & 0 & 0 & 0 \\ 0 & 0 & 1 & 0 \\ 0 & 0 & -i & 0 \end{pmatrix}.$$

Then the purely quantum semantics of program P is the quantum operation:

$$[P] = \sum_{a,c \in \{0,1\} \ and \ b \in \{+,-\}} E_{abc} \circ E_{abc}^{\dagger},$$

where $E_{abc} = \|P\|(a \oplus bc)$. Moreover, it follows from Proposition 4.1.1 that the weakest precondition semantics of P is the quantum operation:

$$wp.P = \sum_{a,c \in \{0,1\} \ and \ b \in \{+,-\}} E_{abc}^{\dagger} \circ E_{abc}.$$

Exercise 6.4.2. *Use the preceding example to convince yourself that equation (6.6) is not suitable for defining the semantics of a quantum case statement of which some branch contains measurements.*

6.5 QUANTUM CHOICE

In the previous three sections, we introduced the syntax and semantics of the quantum programming language QuGCL with the new program construct of quantum case statement. A notion of quantum choice can be defined in terms of the quantum case statement. This notion is very useful for simplification of the presentation. But more importantly, it is of independent significance conceptually.

6.5.1 CHOICES: FROM CLASSICAL TO QUANTUM via PROBABILISTIC

The initial idea of quantum choice also comes from the definition of quantum walks. To motivate the notion of quantum choice, let us go through a conceptual transition from nondeterministic choice to probabilistic choice and then to quantum choice.

(i) **Classical Choice**: We first observe that nondeterminism arises from case statement (6.2) as a consequence of the " overlapping" of the guards $G_1, G_2, \ldots, G_n$; that is, if more than one guards G_i are true at the same time, the case statement needs to select one from the corresponding commands S_i for execution. In particular, if $G_1 = G_2 = \cdots = G_n = \textbf{true}$, then the case statement becomes a demonic choice:

$$\square_{i=1}^{n} S_i \tag{6.22}$$

where the alternatives S_i are chosen unpredictably.

(ii) **Probabilistic Choice**: To formalize randomized algorithms, research on probabilistic programming started in the 1980s with the introduction of probabilistic choice:

$$\square_{i=1}^{n} S_i @ p_i \tag{6.23}$$

where $\{p_i\}$ is a probability distribution; that is, $p_i \geq 0$ for all i, and $\sum_{i=1}^{n} p_i = 1$. The probabilistic choice (6.23) randomly chooses the command S_i with probability p_i for every i, and thus it can be seen as a refinement (or resolution) of the demonic choice (6.22).

(iii) **Quantum Choice**: Recall from Examples 2.3.1 and 2.3.2 that the single-step operator of a quantum walk is a " coin tossing operator" followed by a shift operator, which, as indicated in Section 6.1, can be seen as a quantum case statement. Simply following this idea, a general form of quantum choice can be easily defined based on the notion of quantum case statement.

Definition 6.5.1. *Let S be a program such that $\overline{q} = qvar(S)$, and let S_i be programs for all i. Assume that quantum variables $\overline{q}$ are external to all S_i; that is,*

$$\overline{q} \cap \left(\bigcup_i qvar(S_i) \right) = \emptyset.$$

If $\{|i\rangle\}$ is an orthonormal basis of $\mathcal{H}_{\overline{q}}$, the state Hilbert space of the "coin" system denoted by $\overline{q}$, then the quantum choice of S_i's with " coin-tossing" program S along the basis $\{|i\rangle\}$ is defined as

$$[S]\left(\bigoplus_i |i\rangle \to S_i \right) \triangleq S; \mathbf{qif}\,[\,\overline{q}\,]\,(\square i \cdot |i\rangle \to S_i)\,\mathbf{fiq}. \tag{6.24}$$

In particular, if $n = 2$, then the quantum choice will be abbreviated to $S_0\,_S \oplus S1$ or $S_0 \oplus\,_S S_1$.

This definition is not easy to understand in an abstract way. For a better understanding of it, the reader should revisit Examples 2.3.1 and 2.3.2 with the idea of this definition in mind. At this point, she/he can also move to read Example 6.7.1 following.

Since a quantum choice is defined in terms of quantum case statements, the semantics of the former can be directly derived from that of the latter.

Obviously, if the "coin-tossing program" S does nothing, that is, its semantics is the identity operator in $\mathcal{H}_{\overline{q}}$, for example $S = \mathbf{skip}$, then quantum choice "$[S]\left(\bigoplus_i |i\rangle \to S_i \right)$" coincides with quantum case statement "$\mathbf{qif}\,[\,\overline{q}\,]\,(\square i \cdot |i\rangle \to S_i)$ **fiq**". In general, however, we should carefully distinguish a quantum choice from a quantum case statement.

It is interesting to compare quantum choice (6.24) with probabilistic choice (6.23). As said before, a probabilistic choice is a resolution of nondeterminism. In a probabilistic choice, we can simply say that the choice is made according to a certain probability distribution, and do not have necessarily to specify how this distribution is generated. However, when defining a quantum choice, a "device" that can actually perform the choice, namely a "quantum coin," has to be explicitly introduced. So, a quantum choice can be further seen as a resolution of nondeterminism in the choice of (quantum) "devices" that generate the probability distribution of a probabilistic choice. A mathematical formulation of this idea will be given in the next subsection.

A Quantum Programming Paradigm – Superposition-of-Programs:

A *programming paradigm* is a way of building the structure and elements of programs. A programming language with quantum case statement and quantum choice supports a new quantum programming paradigm – *superposition-of-programs*. The basic idea of superposition-of-programs was already briefly discussed in Subsection 1.2.2. Now, after introducing the formal definition of quantum choice, this idea becomes much clearer. Actually, programmers can think of quantum choice (6.24) as a superposition-of-programs. More precisely, quantum choice (6.24) first runs " coin-tossing" program S to create a superposition of the respective execution paths of programs S_i $(1 \leq i \leq n)$, and then enters a quantum case statement of $S_1, \ldots, S_n$. During the execution of the quantum case statement, each S_i is running along its own path within the whole superposition of execution paths of $S_1, \ldots, S_n$.

Superposition-of-programs can be thought of as a higher-level superposition than *superposition-of-data*. The idea of superposition-of-data is well-understood by the quantum computation community, and the studies of quantum programming in the previous chapters have been carried out around this idea. However, the studies of superposition-of-programs are still at the very beginning, and this chapter and the next represent the first step toward this new quantum programming paradigm. Quantum case statement and quantum choice are two important ingredients in the realization of the quantum programming paradigm of superposition-of-programs. But only quantum case statement was introduced as a primitive program construct in the syntax of QuGCL because quantum choice may be easily defined as a derived program construct from quantum case statement. In the next chapter, the notion of quantum recursion with quantum control flow will be introduced in order to further realize the superposition-of-programs paradigm.

6.5.2 QUANTUM IMPLEMENTATION OF PROBABILISTIC CHOICE

The relationship between probabilistic choice and quantum choice was briefly discussed after Definition 6.5.1. Now we examine this relationship in a more precise way. To this end, we first expand the syntax and semantics of QuGCL to include probabilistic choice.

Definition 6.5.2. *Let P_i be a QuGCL program for each $1 \leq i \leq n$, and let $\{p_i\}_{i=1}^{n}$ be a sub-probability distribution; that is, $p_i > 0$ for each $1 \leq i \leq n$ and $\sum_{i=1}^{n} p_i \leq 1$. Then*

(i) *The probabilistic choice of $P_1, \ldots, P_n$ according to $\{p_i\}_{i=1}^{n}$ is*

$$\sum_{i=1}^{n} P_i @ p_i.$$

(ii) *The quantum variables of the choice are:*

$$qvar\left(\sum_{i=1}^{n} P_i@p_i\right) = \bigcup_{i=1}^{n} qvar(P_i).$$

(iii) *The purely quantum denotational semantics of the choice is:*

$$\left[\!\!\left[\sum_{i=1}^{n} P_i@p_i\right]\!\!\right] = \sum_{i=1}^{n} p_i \cdot [\![P_i]\!]. \tag{6.25}$$

Intuitively, program $\sum_{i=1}^{n} P_i@p_i$ chooses P_i to execute with probability p_i for every $1 \leq i \leq n$, and it aborts with probability $1 - \sum_{i=1}^{n} p_i$. The right-hand side of equation (6.25) is the probabilistic combination of quantum operations $[\![P_i]\!]$ according to distribution $\{p_i\}$; that is,

$$\left(\sum_{i=1}^{n} p_i \cdot [\![P_i]\!]\right)(\rho) = \sum_{i=1}^{n} p_i \cdot [\![P_i]\!](\rho)$$

for all density operators ρ. It is obvious that $\sum_{i=1}^{n} p_i \cdot [\![P_i]\!]$ is a quantum operation too.

A clear description about the relationship between probabilistic choice and quantum choice requires us to further expand the syntax and semantics of QuGCL by introducing local quantum variables.

Definition 6.5.3. *Let S be a QuGCL program, $\overline{q}$ a quantum register and ρ a density operator in $\mathcal{H}_{\overline{q}}$. Then*

(i) *The block command defined by S restricted to $\overline{q} = \rho$ is:*

$$\text{\textbf{begin local }} \overline{q} := \rho; S \text{ \textbf{end}}. \tag{6.26}$$

(ii) *The quantum variables of the block command are:*

$$qvar\,(\text{\textbf{begin local }} \overline{q} := \rho; S \text{ \textbf{end}}) = qvar(S) \setminus \overline{q}.$$

(iii) *The purely quantum denotational semantics of the block command is given as follows:*

$$[\![\text{\textbf{begin local }} \overline{q} := \rho; S \text{ \textbf{end}}]\!]\,(\sigma) = tr_{\mathcal{H}_{\overline{q}}}([\![S]\!](\sigma \otimes \rho))$$

for any density operator σ in $\mathcal{H}_{qvar(S) \setminus \overline{q}}$. Here, the symbol "tr" stands for partial trace (see Definition 2.1.22).

This definition is essentially a restatement of Definition 3.3.7. The only difference between them is that in block (6.26), $\overline{q}$ has to be initialized before program S using the statement $\overline{q} := \rho$, since initialization is not included in the syntax of QuGCL.

Let us consider a simple example that can help us to understand the preceding two definitions.

Example 6.5.1. (Continuation of Example 6.3.3; Probabilistic mixture of measurements). *Let $M^{(0)}$ and $M^{(1)}$ be the measurements on a qubit in the computational basis and in the basis $|\pm\rangle$, respectively. We consider a random choice between $M^{(0)}$ and $M^{(1)}$.*

- *If we perform measurement $M^{(0)}$ on qubit p in state $|\psi\rangle$ and discard the outcomes of measurement, then we get*

$$\rho_0 = M_0^{(0)}|\psi\rangle\langle\psi|M_0^{(0)} + M_1^{(0)}|\psi\rangle\langle\psi|M_1^{(0)};$$

- *If we perform measurement $M^{(1)}$ on $|\psi\rangle$ and discard the outcomes, then we get*

$$\rho_1 = M_+^{(1)}|\psi\rangle\langle\psi|M_+^{(1)} + M_-^{(1)}|\psi\rangle\langle\psi|M_-^{(1)}.$$

Here, measurement operators $M_0^{(0)}, M_1^{(0)}, M_+^{(1)}, M_-^{(1)}$ are as in Example 6.3.3. We now take the unitary matrix

$$U = \left(\begin{array}{cc} \sqrt{s} & \sqrt{r} \\ \sqrt{r} & -\sqrt{s} \end{array}\right)$$

where $s, r \geq 0$ and $s + r = 1$, and introduce a "coin" qubit q. Let

$$P_i \equiv \textbf{if } M^{(i)}[p:x] = 0 \rightarrow \textbf{skip}$$
$$\square \qquad\qquad 1 \rightarrow \textbf{skip}$$
$$\textbf{fi}$$

for $i = 0, 1$, and put the quantum choice of P_0 and P_1 according to the "coin tossing operator" U into a block with the "coin" qubit q as a local variable:

$$P \equiv \textbf{begin local } q := |0\rangle; P_0 \; {}_{U[q]}\oplus P_1 \textbf{ end}$$

Then for any $|\psi\rangle \in \mathcal{H}_p$, $i \in \{0, 1\}$ and $j \in \{+, -\}$, we have:

$$[\![P]\!](|\psi\rangle\langle\psi|) = tr_{\mathcal{H}_q}\left(\sum_{i\in\{0,1\} \text{ and } j\in\{+,-\}} |\psi_{ij}\rangle\langle\psi_{ij}|\right)$$

$$= 2\left(\sum_{i\in\{0,1\}} \frac{s}{2}M_i^{(0)}|\psi\rangle\langle\psi|M_i^{(0)} + \sum_{j\in\{+,-\}} \frac{r}{2}M_j^{(1)}|\psi\rangle\langle\psi|M_j^{(1)}\right)$$

$$= s\rho_0 + r\rho_1,$$

where:

$$|\psi_{ij}\rangle \triangleq M_{ij}(U|0\rangle|\psi\rangle) = \sqrt{\frac{s}{2}}|0\rangle M_i^{(0)}|\psi\rangle + \sqrt{\frac{r}{2}}|1\rangle M_j^{(1)}|\psi\rangle,$$

and measurement operators M_{ij} are as in Example 6.3.3. So, program P can be seen as a probabilistic mixture of measurements $M^{(0)}$ and $M^{(1)}$, with respective probabilities s, r.

Now we are ready to precisely characterize the relationship between probabilistic choice and quantum choice. Roughly speaking, if the "coin" variables are immediately treated as local variables, then a quantum choice degenerates to a probabilistic choice.

Theorem 6.5.1. *Let $qvar(S) = \overline{q}$. Then we have:*

$$\textbf{begin local } \overline{q} := \rho; [S] \left(\bigoplus_{i=1}^{n} |i\rangle \to S_i \right) \textbf{ end} = \sum_{i=1}^{n} S_i @ p_i \tag{6.27}$$

where probability $p_i = \langle i| [\![S]\!](\rho)|i\rangle$ for every $1 \le i \le n$.

For readability, the tedious proof of this theorem is deferred to Section 6.9. The inverse of this theorem is also true. For any probability distribution $\{p_i\}_{i=1}^{n}$, we can find an $n \times n$ unitary operator U such that

$$p_i = |U_{i0}|^2 \ (1 \le i \le n).$$

So, it follows immediately from the preceding theorem that a probabilistic choice $\sum_{i=1}^{n} S_i @ p_i$ can always be implemented by a quantum choice:

$$\textbf{begin local } \overline{q} := |0\rangle; [U[\overline{q}]] \left(\bigoplus_{i=1}^{n} |i\rangle \to S_i \right) \textbf{ end}$$

where $\overline{q}$ is a family of new quantum variables with an n-dimensional state space. As said in Subsection 6.5.1, probabilistic choice (6.23) can be thought of as a refinement of nondeterministic choice (6.22). Since for a given probability distribution $\{p_i\}$, there is more than one "coin program" S to implement the probabilistic choice $\sum_{i=1}^{n} S_i @ p_i$ in equation (6.27), a quantum choice can be further seen as a refinement of a probabilistic choice where a specific "device" (quantum "coin") is explicitly given for generating the probability distribution $\{p_i\}$.

6.6 ALGEBRAIC LAWS

The algebraic approach has been employed in classical programming, which establishes various algebraic laws for programs so that calculation of programs becomes possible by using these laws. In particular, algebraic laws are useful for verification, transformation and compilation of programs. In this section, we present a family of basic algebraic laws for quantum case statement and quantum choice. For readability, all of the proofs of these laws are postponed to Section 6.9.

The laws given in the following theorem show that the quantum case statement is idempotent, commutative and associative, and sequential composition is distributive over the quantum case statement from the right.

Theorem 6.6.1 (Laws for Quantum Case Statement).

(i) *Idempotent Law: If $S_i = S$ for all i, then*

$$\textbf{qif } (\square i \cdot |i\rangle \rightarrow S_i) \textbf{ fiq} = S.$$

(ii) *Commutative Law: For any permutation τ of $\{1, \ldots, n\}$, we have:*

$$\textbf{qif } [\,\overline{q}\,] \left(\square_{i=1}^{n} i \cdot |i\rangle \rightarrow S_{\tau(i)} \right) \textbf{ fiq}$$
$$= U_{\tau^{-1}}[\,\overline{q}\,]; \textbf{qif } [\,\overline{q}\,] \left(\square_{i=1}^{n} i \cdot |i\rangle \rightarrow S_i \right) \textbf{ fiq}; U_{\tau}[\,\overline{q}\,],$$

where:
(a) *τ^{-1} is the inverse of τ, i.e., $\tau^{-1}(i) = j$ if and only if $\tau(j) = i$ for $i, j \in \{1, \ldots, n\}$; and*
(b) *U_{τ} (respectively $U_{\tau^{-1}}$) is the unitary operator permutating the basis $\{|i\rangle\}$ of $\mathcal{H}_{\overline{q}}$ with τ (respectively τ^{-1}); that is,*

$$U_{\tau}(|i\rangle) = |\tau(i)\rangle \ (\text{respectively } U_{\tau^{-1}}(|i\rangle) = |\tau^{-1}(i)\rangle)$$

for every $1 \leq i \leq n$.
(iii) *Associative Law:*

$$\textbf{qif } (\square i \cdot |i\rangle \rightarrow \textbf{qif } (\square j_i \cdot |j_i\rangle \rightarrow S_{ij_i}) \textbf{ fiq}) \textbf{ fiq}$$
$$= \textbf{qif } (\overline{\alpha}) \left(\square i, j_i \cdot |i, j_i\rangle \rightarrow S_{ij_i} \right) \textbf{ fiq}$$

for some family $\overline{\alpha}$ of parameters, where the right-hand side is a parameterized quantum case statement that will be defined in Subsection 6.8.1.
(iv) *Distributive Law: If $\overline{q} \cap qvar(Q) = \emptyset$, then*

$$\textbf{qif } [\,\overline{q}\,] (\square i \cdot |i\rangle \rightarrow S_i) \textbf{ fiq}; Q =_{CF} \textbf{qif } (\overline{\alpha})[\,\overline{q}\,] (\square i \cdot |i\rangle \rightarrow (S_i; Q)) \textbf{ fiq}$$

for some family $\overline{\alpha}$ of parameters, where the right-hand side is a parameterized quantum case statement. In particular, if we further assume that Q contains no measurements, then

$$\textbf{qif } [\,\overline{q}\,] (\square i \cdot |i\rangle \rightarrow S_i) \textbf{ fiq}; Q = \textbf{qif } [\,\overline{q}\,] (\square i \cdot |i\rangle \rightarrow (S_i; Q)) \textbf{ fiq}.$$

A quantum choice is defined as a "coin" program followed by a quantum case statement. A natural question would be: is it possible to move the " coin" program to the end of a quantum case statement? The following theorem positively answers this question under the condition that encapsulation in a block with local variables is allowed.

Theorem 6.6.2. *For any programs S_i and unitary operator U, we have:*

$$[U[\bar{q}]]\left(\bigoplus_{i=1}^{n}|i\rangle \to S_i\right) = \mathbf{qif}\ (\square i \cdot U_{\bar{q}}^{\dagger}|i\rangle \to S_i)\ \mathbf{fiq};\ U[\bar{q}].\tag{6.28}$$

More generally, for any programs S_i and S with $\bar{q} = qvar(S)$, there are new quantum variables $\bar{r}$, a pure state $|\varphi_0\rangle \in \mathcal{H}_{\bar{r}}$, an orthonormal basis $\{|\psi_{ij}\rangle\}$ of $\mathcal{H}_{\bar{q}} \otimes \mathcal{H}_{\bar{r}}$, programs Q_{ij}, and a unitary operator U in $\mathcal{H}_{\bar{q}} \otimes \mathcal{H}_{\bar{r}}$ such that

$$[S]\left(\bigoplus_{i=1}^{n}|i\rangle \to S_i\right) = \mathbf{begin\ local}\ \bar{r} := |\varphi_0\rangle;$$
$$\mathbf{qif}\ (\square i,j \cdot |\psi_{ij}\rangle \to Q_{ij})\ \mathbf{fiq};\tag{6.29}$$
$$U[\bar{q},\bar{r}]$$
$$\mathbf{end}.$$

The next theorem is the counterpart of Theorem 6.6.1 for quantum choice, showing that quantum choice is also idempotent, commutative and associative, and sequential composition is distributive over quantum choice from the right.

Theorem 6.6.3 (Laws for Quantum Choice).

(i) *Idempotent Law: If $qvar(Q) = \bar{q}$, $tr[\![Q]\!](\rho) = 1$ and $S_i = S$ for all $1 \le i \le n$, then*

$$\mathbf{begin\ local}\ \bar{q} := \rho; [Q]\left(\bigoplus_{i=1}^{n}|i\rangle \to S_i\right)\ \mathbf{end} = S.$$

(ii) *Commutative Law: For any permutation τ of $\{1,\ldots,n\}$, we have:*

$$[S]\left(\bigoplus_{i=1}^{n}|i\rangle \to S_{\tau(i)}\right) = [S; U_\tau[\bar{q}]]\left(\bigoplus_{i=1}^{n}|i\rangle \to S_i\right); U_{\tau^{-1}}[\bar{q}],$$

where $qvar(S) = \bar{q}$, and U_τ, $U_{\tau^{-1}}$ are the same as in Theorem 6.6.1 (2).

(iii) *Associative Law: Let*

$$\Gamma = \{(i,j_i) : 1 \le i \le m \ and \ 1 \le j_i \le n_i\} = \bigcup_{i=1}^{m}(\{i\} \times \{1,\ldots,n_i\})$$

and

$$R = [S]\left(\bigoplus_{i=1}^{n}|i\rangle \to Q_i\right).$$

Then

$$\left(\bigoplus_{i=1}^{m} |i\rangle \to [Q_i]\left(\bigoplus_{j_i=1}^{n_i} |j_i\rangle \to R_{ij_i}\right)\right) = [R(\overline{\alpha})]\left(\bigoplus_{(i,j_i)\in\Gamma} |i,j_i\rangle \to R_{ij_i}\right),$$

for some family $\overline{\alpha}$ of parameters, where the right-hand side is a parameterized quantum choice defined in Subsection 6.8.1.

(i) *Distributive Law: If qvar(S) $\cap$ qvar(Q) = $\emptyset$, then*

$$[S]\left(\bigoplus_{i=1}^{n} |i\rangle \to S_i\right); Q =_{CF} [S(\overline{\alpha})]\left(\bigoplus_{i=1}^{n} |i\rangle \to (S_i; Q)\right)$$

for some family $\overline{\alpha}$ of parameters, where the right-hand side is a parameterized quantum choice. Here, symbol "$=_{CF}$" stands for "coin-free" equivalence (see Definition 6.4.4). In particular, if we further assume that Q contains no measurements, then

$$[S]\left(\bigoplus_{i=1}^{n} |i\rangle \to S_i\right); Q = [S]\left(\bigoplus_{i=1}^{n} |i\rangle \to (S_i; Q)\right).$$

6.7 ILLUSTRATIVE EXAMPLES

A theory of programming with quantum case statements and quantum choice has been developed in the previous sections, using the quantum programming language QuGCL. In this section, we give some examples to show how some quantum algorithms can be conveniently written as programs in the language QuGCL.

6.7.1 QUANTUM WALKS

The design of the language QuGCL, in particular the definition of quantum case statement and quantum choice, was inspired by the construction of some simplest quantum walks. A large number of variants and generalizations of quantum walks have been introduced in the last decade. Quantum walks have been widely used in the development of quantum algorithms including quantum simulation. Various extended quantum walks in the literature can be easily written as QuGCL programs. Here, we only present several simple examples.

Example 6.7.1. *Recall from Example 2.3.1 that the Hadamard walk is a quantum generalization of a one-dimensional random walk. Let p, c be the quantum variables for position and coin, respectively. The type of variable p is the infinite-dimensional Hilbert space*

$$\mathcal{H}_p = span\{|n\rangle : n \in \mathbb{Z} \ (integers)\} = \left\{ \sum_{n=-\infty}^{\infty} \alpha_n |n\rangle : \sum_{n=-\infty}^{\infty} |\alpha_n|^2 < \infty \right\},$$

and the type of c is the 2-dimensional Hilbert space $\mathcal{H}_c = span\{|L\rangle, |R\rangle\}$, *where* L, R *stand for Left and Right, respectively. The state space of the Hadamard walk is* $\mathcal{H} = \mathcal{H}_c \otimes \mathcal{H}_p$. *Let* $I_{\mathcal{H}_p}$ *be the identity operator in* $\mathcal{H}_p$, H *the* 2×2 *Hadamard matrix and* T_L, T_R *the left- and right-translations, respectively; that is,*

$$T_L|n\rangle = |n-1\rangle, \qquad T_R|n\rangle = |n+1\rangle$$

for every $n \in \mathbb{Z}$. *Then a single step of the Hadamard walk can be described by the unitary operator*

$$W = (|L\rangle\langle L| \otimes T_L + |R\rangle\langle R| \otimes T_R)(H \otimes I_{\mathcal{H}_p}). \tag{6.30}$$

It can also be written as the QuGCL program:

$$T_L[p]_{H[c]} \oplus T_R[p] \equiv H[c]; \ \mathbf{qif} \ [c] \ |L\rangle \to T_L[p]$$
$$\square \qquad |R\rangle \to T_R[p]$$
$$\mathbf{fiq}.$$

This program is the quantum choice of the left-translation T_L *and the right-translation* T_R *according to the "coin" program H[c]. The Hadamard walk repeatedly runs this program.*

The following are several variants of this walk considered in the recent physics literature.

(i) *A simple variant of the Hadamard walk is the unidirectional quantum walk, where the walker either moves to the right or stays in the previous position. So, the left-translation* T_L *should be replaced by the program* **skip** *whose semantics is the identity operator* $I_{\mathcal{H}_p}$, *and a single step of the new quantum walk can be written as the QuGCL program:*

$$\mathbf{skip}_{H[c]} \oplus T_R[p].$$

It is a quantum choice of **skip** *and the right-translation* T_R.

(ii) *A feature of the Hadamard walk and its unidirectional variant is that the "coin tossing operator" H is independent of the position and time. A new kind of quantum walk was proposed, where the "coin tossing" operator depends on both position n and time t:*

$$C(n,t) = \frac{1}{\sqrt{2}} \left(\begin{array}{cc} c(n,t) & s(n,t) \\ s^*(n,t) & -e^{i\theta}c(n,t) \end{array} \right).$$

Then for a given time t, step t of the walk can be written as the QuGCL program:

$$W_t \equiv \textbf{qif } [p](\square n \cdot |n\rangle \to C(n,t)[c]) \textbf{ fiq};$$
$$\textbf{qif } [c] \, |L\rangle \to T_L[p]$$
$$\square \qquad |R\rangle \to T_R[p]$$
$$\textbf{fiq}.$$

The program W_t is a sequential composition of two quantum case statements. In the first quantum case statement, "coin-tossing" program $C(n,t)$ is selected to execute on quantum coin variable c according to position $|n\rangle$, and a superposition of different positions is allowed. Furthermore, since W_t may be different for different time points t, the first T steps can be written as the program:

$$W_1; W_2; \dots; W_T.$$

(iii) *Another simple generalization of the Hadamard walk is the quantum walk with three "coin" states. The "coin" space of this walk is a 3-dimensional Hilbert space $\mathcal{H}_c = span\{|L\rangle, |0\rangle, |R\rangle\}$, where L and R are used to indicate moving to the left and to the right, respectively, as before, but 0 means staying at the previous position. The "coin tossing" operator is the unitary*

$$U = \frac{1}{3} \begin{pmatrix} -1 & 2 & 2 \\ 2 & -1 & 2 \\ 2 & 2 & -1 \end{pmatrix}.$$

Then a single step of the walk can be written as the QuGCL program:

$$[U[c]] \, (|L\rangle \to T_L[p] \oplus |0\rangle \to \textbf{skip} \oplus |R\rangle \to T_R[p]).$$

This is the quantum choice of **skip**, *the left- and right-translations according to the "coin" program $U[c]$.*

The quantum walks in this example have only a single walker as well as a single "coin." In the following two examples, we consider some more complicated quantum walks in which multiple walkers participate and multiple "coins" are equipped to control the walkers.

Example 6.7.2. *We consider a one-dimensional quantum walk driven by multiple "coins." In this walk, there is still a single walker, but it is controlled by M different "coins". Each of these "coins" has its own state space, but the "coin tossing" operator for all of them is the same, namely the 2×2 Hadamard matrix. Now let variable p, Hilbert spaces $\mathcal{H}_p, \mathcal{H}_c$ and operators T_L, T_R, H be the same as in Example 6.7.1, and let $c_1, \dots, c_M$ be the quantum variables for the M "coins." Then the state space of the walk is*

$$\mathcal{H} = \bigotimes_{m=1}^{M} \mathcal{H}_{c_m} \otimes \mathcal{H}_p,$$

where $\mathcal{H}_{c_m} = \mathcal{H}_c$ for all $1 \leq m \leq M$. We write

$$W_m \equiv \left(T_L[p]_{H[c_1]} \oplus T_R[p]\right); \ldots; \left(T_L[p]_{H[c_m]} \oplus T_R[p]\right)$$

for $1 \leq m \leq M$. If we cycle among the M "coins," starting from the "coin" c_1, then the first T steps of the walk can be written in the language QuGCL as follows:

$$W_M; \ldots; W_M; W_r$$

where W_M is iterated for $d = \lfloor T/M \rfloor$ times, and $r = T - Md$ is the remainder of T divided by M. This program is a sequential composition of T quantum choices of the left- and right-translations controlled by different "coins."

Example 6.7.3. We consider a quantum walk consisting of two walkers on a line sharing "coins." The two walkers have different state spaces, and each of them has its own "coin." So, the state Hilbert space of the whole quantum walk is $\mathcal{H}_c \otimes \mathcal{H}_c \otimes \mathcal{H}_p \otimes \mathcal{H}_p$. If the two walkers are completely independent, then the step operator of this walk is $W \otimes W$, where W is defined by equation (6.30). But more interesting is the case where a two-qubit unitary operator U is introduced to entangle the two "coins." This case can be thought of as that the two walkers are sharing "coins." A step of this quantum walk can be written as a QuGCL program as follows:

$$U[c_1, c_2]; \left(T_L[q_1]_{H[c_1]} \oplus T_R[q_1]\right); \left(T_L[q_2]_{H[c_2]} \oplus T_R[q_2]\right)$$

where q_1, q_2 are the position variables and c_1, c_2 the "coin" variables of the two walkers, respectively. Here, the two walkers both use the Hadamard operator H for " coin-tossing."

Obviously, a generalization to the case with more than two walkers can also be easily programmed in QuGCL.

6.7.2 QUANTUM PHASE ESTIMATION

Not only quantum walk-based algorithms can be conveniently programmed in the language QuGCL. In this subsection, we show how to program a quantum phase estimation algorithm in QuGCL. Recall the algorithm from Subsection 2.3.7, given a unitary operator U and its eigenvector $|u\rangle$. The goal of this algorithm is to estimate the phase φ of the eigenvalue $e^{2\pi i\varphi}$ corresponding to $|u\rangle$. The algorithm is described in Figure 6.1. Here, for each $j = 0, 1, \ldots, t-1$, an oracle performs the controlled-U^{2^j} operator, and $FT^\dagger$ stand for the inverse quantum Fourier transform.

- **Procedure:**

$$1.\ |0\rangle^{\otimes t}|u\rangle \xrightarrow{H^{\otimes}\ \text{on the first } t\ \text{qubits}} \frac{1}{\sqrt{2^t}} \sum_{j=0}^{2^t-1} |j\rangle|u\rangle$$

$$2.\ \xrightarrow{\text{oracles}} \frac{1}{\sqrt{2^t}} \sum_{j=0}^{2^t-1} |j\rangle U^j|u\rangle = \frac{1}{\sqrt{2^t}} \sum_{j=0}^{2^t-1} e^{2\pi ij\varphi}|j\rangle|u\rangle$$

$$3.\ \xrightarrow{FT^\dagger} \frac{1}{\sqrt{2^t}} \sum_{j=0}^{2^t-1} e^{2\pi ij\varphi} \left(\frac{1}{\sqrt{2^t}} \sum_{k=0}^{2^t-1} e^{-2\pi ijk/2^t}|k\rangle \right)|u\rangle$$

$$4.\ \xrightarrow{\text{measure the first } t\ \text{qubits}} |m\rangle|u\rangle,$$

FIGURE 6.1

Quantum phase estimation.

Now we use qubit variables $q_1, \ldots, q_t$ as well as a quantum variable p of which the type is the Hilbert space of unitary operator U. We also use a classical variable to record the outcomes of a measurement. Then quantum phase estimation can be written as the QuGCL program in Figure 6.2, where:

- **Program:**

  1. $\mathbf{skip}_{H[c_1]} \oplus S_1$;

     $\ldots\ldots$

  2. $\mathbf{skip}_{H[c_t]} \oplus S_t$;
  3. $q_t := H[q_t]$;
  4. T_t;
  5. $q_{t-1} := H[q_{t-1}]$;
  6. T_{t-1};
  7. $q_{t-2} := H[q_{t-2}]$;

     $\ldots\ldots$

  8. T_2;
  9. $q_1 := H[q_1]$;
  10. $\mathbf{if}\ (\square\ M[q_1, \ldots, q_t : x] = m \to \mathbf{skip})\ \mathbf{fi}$

FIGURE 6.2

Quantum phase estimation program.

- for $1 \leq k \leq t$,

$$S_k \equiv q := U[q]; \ldots; q := U[q]$$

(the sequential composition of 2^{k-1} copies of unitary transformation U);
- for $2 \leq k \leq t$, the subprogram T_k is given in Figure 6.3, and the operator $R_k^\dagger$ in T_k is given by

$$R_k^\dagger = \begin{pmatrix} 1 & 0 \\ 0 & e^{-2\pi i/2^k} \end{pmatrix};$$

1. **qif** $[q_t]$ $|0\rangle \to$ **skip**
2. □ $|1\rangle \to R_k^\dagger[q_{k-1}]$
3. **fiq**;
4. **qif** $[q_{t-1}]$ $|0\rangle \to$ **skip**
5. □ $|1\rangle \to R_{k-1}^\dagger[q_{k-1}]$
6. **fiq**;

        . . . . . .

7. **qif** $[q_{k+1}]$ $|0\rangle \to$ **skip**
9. □ $|1\rangle \to R_2^\dagger[q_{k-1}]$
10. **fiq**

FIGURE 6.3

Subprogram T_k.

- $M = \{M_m : m \in \{0, 1\}^t\}$ is the measurement on t qubits in the computational basis; that is, $M_m = |m\rangle\langle m|$ for every $m \in \{0, 1\}^t$.
- Subprograms $T_2, \ldots T_k$ are displayed in Figure 6.3.

It can be seen from equation (2.24) that the part made up of lines 3-9 in the phase estimation program (Figure 6.2) is actually the inverse quantum Fourier transform. Since the language QuGCL does not include any initialization statement, $|0\rangle^t|u\rangle$ in Figure 6.1 can only be seen as an input to the program.

6.8 DISCUSSIONS

In the previous sections, the two program constructs of quantum case statement and quantum choice have been thoroughly studied, and they were used to program quantum walk-based algorithms and quantum phase estimation. It was mentioned in

Subsection 6.3.3 that a choice of coefficients different from that in Definition 6.3.5 is possible, which implies the possibility of a different semantics of a quantum case statement. This section is devoted to discussing several variants of quantum case statement and quantum choice. These variants can only appear in the quantum setting and have no counterparts in classical programming. They are both conceptually interesting and useful in applications. Indeed, some of these variants were already used in the statements of several algebraic laws in Section 6.6.

6.8.1 COEFFICIENTS IN GUARDED COMPOSITIONS OF QUANTUM OPERATIONS

The coefficients in the right-hand side of the defining equation (6.14) of guarded composition of operator-valued functions are chosen in a very special way, with a physical interpretation in terms of conditional probability. This subsection shows that other choices of these coefficients are possible.

Let us first consider the simplest case: the guarded composition

$$U \triangleq \bigoplus_{k=1}^{n} (|k\rangle \to U_k)$$

of unitary operators U_k ($1 \leq k \leq n$) in a Hilbert space $\mathcal{H}$ along an orthonormal basis $\{|k\rangle\}$ of a "coin" Hilbert space $\mathcal{H}_c$. If for each $1 \leq k \leq n$, we add a relative phase θ_k into the defining equation (6.10) of U:

$$U(|k\rangle|\psi\rangle) = e^{i\theta_k}|k\rangle U_k|\psi\rangle \tag{6.31}$$

for all $|\psi\rangle \in \mathcal{H}$, then equation (6.11) is changed to

$$U\left(\sum_k \alpha_k|k\rangle|\psi_k\rangle\right) = \sum_k \alpha_k e^{i\theta_k}|k\rangle U_k|\psi_k\rangle. \tag{6.32}$$

Note that phases θ_k in equation (6.31) can be different for different basis states $|k\rangle$. It is easy to see that the new operator U defined by equation (6.31) or (6.32) is still unitary.

The idea of adding relative phases also applies to the guarded composition of operator-valued functions. Consider

$$F \triangleq \bigoplus_{k=1}^{n} (|k\rangle \to F_k)$$

where $\{|k\rangle\}$ is an orthonormal basis of $\mathcal{H}_c$, and F_k is an operator-valued function in $\mathcal{H}$ over Δ_k for every $1 \leq k \leq n$. We arbitrarily choose a sequence $\theta_1, \ldots, \theta_n$ of real numbers and change the defining equation (6.14) of F to

$$F(\oplus_{k=1}^n \delta_k)|\Psi\rangle = \sum_{k=1}^n e^{i\theta_k} \left(\prod_{l \neq k} \lambda_{l\delta_l} \right) |k\rangle (F_k(\delta_k)|\psi_k\rangle) \qquad (6.33)$$

for any state

$$|\Psi\rangle = \sum_{k=1}^n |k\rangle|\psi_k\rangle \in \mathcal{H}_c \otimes \mathcal{H},$$

where $\lambda_{l\delta_l}$'s are the same as in Definition 6.3.5. Then it is clear that F defined by equation (6.33) is still an operator-valued function. Indeed, this conclusion is true for a much more general definition of guarded composition of operator-valued functions. Let F_k be an operator-valued function in $\mathcal{H}$ over Δ_k for each $1 \leq k \leq n$, and let

$$\overline{\alpha} = \left\{ \alpha^{(k)}_{\delta_1,\dots,\delta_{k-1},\delta_{k+1},\dots,\delta_n} : 1 \leq k \leq n, \ \delta_l \in \Delta_l \ (l = 1,\dots,k-1,k+1,\dots,n) \right\} \qquad (6.34)$$

be a family of complex numbers satisfying the normalization condition:

$$\sum_{\delta_1 \in \Delta_1,\dots,\delta_{k-1} \in \Delta_{k-1},\delta_{k+1} \in \Delta_{k+1},\dots,\delta_n \in \Delta_n} \left| \alpha^{(k)}_{\delta_1,\dots,\delta_{k-1},\delta_{k+1},\dots,\delta_n} \right|^2 = 1 \qquad (6.35)$$

for every $1 \leq k \leq n$. Then we can define the $\overline{\alpha}$-guarded composition

$$F \overset{\triangle}{=} (\overline{\alpha}) \bigoplus_{k=1}^n (|i\rangle \to F_k)$$

of F_k $(1 \leq k \leq n)$ along an orthonormal basis $\{|k\rangle\}$ of $\mathcal{H}_c$ by

$$F \left(\oplus_{k=1}^n \delta_k \right) \left(\sum_{k=1}^n |k\rangle|\psi_k\rangle \right) = \sum_{k=1}^n \alpha^{(k)}_{\delta_1,\dots,\delta_{k-1},\delta_{k+1},\dots,\delta_n} |k\rangle \, (F_k(\delta_k)|\psi_k\rangle) \qquad (6.36)$$

for any $|\psi_1\rangle,\dots,|\psi_n\rangle \in \mathcal{H}$ and for any $\delta_k \in \Delta_k$ $(1 \leq k \leq n)$. Note that coefficient

$$\alpha^{(k)}_{\delta_1,\dots,\delta_{k-1},\delta_{k+1},\dots,\delta_n}$$

does not contain parameter δ_k. This independence together with condition (6.35) guarantees that the $\overline{\alpha}$-guarded composition is an operator-valued function, as can be seen from the proof of Lemma 6.3.2 presented in Section 6.9.

Example 6.8.1

(i) *Definition 6.3.5 is a special case of $\overline{\alpha}$-guarded composition because if for any* $1 \leq i \leq n$ *and* $\delta_k \in \Delta_k$ $(k = 1,\dots,i-1,i+1,\dots,n)$, *we set*

$$\alpha^i_{\delta_1,\dots,\delta_{i-1},\delta_{i+1},\dots,\delta_n} = \prod_{k \neq i} \lambda_{k\delta_k},$$

where $\lambda_{k\delta_k}$'s are given by equation (6.15), then equation (6.36) degenerates to (6.14).

(ii) *Another possible choice of $\overline{\alpha}$ is*

$$\alpha^i_{\delta_1,\ldots,\delta_{i-1},\delta_{i+1},\ldots,\delta_n} = \frac{1}{\sqrt{\prod_{k\neq i}|\Delta_k|}}$$

for all $1 \le i \le n$ and $\delta_k \in \Delta_k$ $(k = 1,\ldots,i-1,i+1,\ldots,n)$. Obviously, for this family $\overline{\alpha}$ of coefficients, the $\overline{\alpha}$-guarded composition cannot be obtained by modifying Definition 6.3.5 with relative phases.

Now we are able to define parameterized quantum case statement and quantum choice.

Definition 6.8.1

(i) *Let $\overline{q}$, $\{|i\rangle\}$ and $\{S_i\}$ be as in Definition 6.2.1 (iv). Furthermore, let the classical states $\Delta(S_i) = \Delta_i$ for every i, and let $\overline{\alpha}$ be a family of parameters satisfying condition (6.35), as in equation (6.34). Then the $\overline{\alpha}$-quantum case statement of $S_1,\ldots,S_n$ guarded by basis states $|i\rangle$'s is*

$$S \equiv \mathbf{qif}\,(\overline{\alpha})[\,\overline{q}\,]\,(\Box i \cdot |i\rangle \to S_i)\;\mathbf{fiq} \tag{6.37}$$

and its semi-classical semantics is

$$\|S\| = (\overline{\alpha})\bigoplus_{i=1}^{n}\left(|i\rangle \to \|S_i\|\right).$$

(ii) *Let S, $\{|i\rangle\}$ and S_i's be as in Definition 6.5.1, and let $\overline{\alpha}$ be as above. Then the $\overline{\alpha}$-quantum choice of S_i's according to S along the basis $\{|i\rangle\}$ is defined as*

$$[S(\overline{\alpha})]\left(\bigoplus_i |i\rangle \to S_i\right) \equiv S;\mathbf{qif}\,(\overline{\alpha})[\,\overline{q}\,]\,(\Box i \cdot |i\rangle \to S_i)\;\mathbf{fiq}.$$

The symbol $[\,\overline{q}\,]$ in quantum case statement (6.37) can be dropped whenever quantum variables $\overline{q}$ can be recognized from the context. At the first glance, it seems unreasonable that the parameters $\overline{\alpha}$ in the syntax (6.37) of $\overline{\alpha}$-quantum case statement are indexed by the classical states of S_i. But this is not problematic at all because the classical states of S_i are completely determined by the syntax of S_i.

The purely quantum denotational semantics of the $\overline{\alpha}$-quantum case statement can be obtained from its semi-classical semantics according to Definition 6.4.3, and the semantics of $\overline{\alpha}$-quantum choice can be derived from the semantics of the $\overline{\alpha}$-quantum case statement. The notions of parameterized quantum case statement and quantum choice were already used in the presentation of several theorems in Section 6.6.

Problem 6.8.1. *Prove or disprove the following statement: for any $\overline{\alpha}$, there exists a unitary operator U such that*

$$\mathbf{qif}\ (\overline{\alpha})[\,\overline{q}\,]\,(\square i \cdot\ |i\rangle \to S_i)\ \mathbf{fiq} = [U[\,\overline{q}\,]]\left(\bigoplus_i |i\rangle \to S_i\right).$$

What happens when $U[\,\overline{q}\,]$ is replaced by a general quantum program (of which the semantics can be a general quantum operation rather than a unitary)?

6.8.2 QUANTUM CASE STATEMENTS GUARDED BY SUBSPACES

A major difference between case statement (6.2) of classical programs and quantum case statement (6.9) can be revealed by a comparison between their guards: the guards G_i in the former are propositions about the program variables, whereas the guards $|i\rangle$ in the latter are basis states of the "coin" space $\mathcal{H}_c$. However, this difference is not as big as we imagine at first glance. In the Birkhoff-von Neumann quantum logic [42], a proposition about a quantum system is expressed by a closed subspace of the state Hilbert space of the system. This observation leads us to a way to define quantum case statement guarded by propositions about the "coin" system instead of basis states of the " coin" space.

Definition 6.8.2. *Let $\overline{q}$ be a sequence of quantum variables and $\{S_i\}$ be a family of quantum programs such that*

$$\overline{q} \cap \left(\bigcup_i qvar(S_i)\right) = \emptyset.$$

Suppose that $\{X_i\}$ is a family of propositions about the "coin" system $\overline{q}$, i.e., closed subspaces of the " coin" space $\mathcal{H}_{\overline{q}}$, satisfying the following two conditions:

(i) *X_i's are pairwise orthogonal, i.e., $X_{i_1} \perp X_{i_2}$ provided $i_1 \neq i_2$;*
(ii) *$\bigoplus_i X_i \overset{\triangle}{=} span\left(\bigcup_i X_i\right) = \mathcal{H}_{\overline{q}}.$*

Then

(i) *The quantum case statement of S_i's guarded by subspaces X_i's:*

$$S \equiv \mathbf{qif}\,[\,\overline{q}\,]\,(\square i \cdot X_i \to S_i)\ \mathbf{fiq} \tag{6.38}$$

is a program.
(ii) *The quantum variables of S are:*

$$qvar(S) = \overline{q} \cup \left(\bigcup_i qvar(S_i)\right).$$

(iii) *The purely quantum denotational semantics of the quantum case statement is:*

$$[\![S]\!] = \{[\![\mathbf{qif}\,[\,\overline{q}\,]\,(\Box i,j_i \cdot |\varphi_{ij_i}\rangle \to S_{ij_i})\;\mathbf{fiq}]\!] : \{|\varphi_{ij_i}\rangle\}\;\text{is an orthonormal} \tag{6.39}$$
$$\text{basis of } X_i \text{ for each } i,\;\; \text{and } S_{ij_i} = S_i \text{ for every } i,j_i\}.$$

Intuitively, $\{X_i\}$ in quantum case statement (6.38) can be thought of as a partition of the whole state Hilbert space $\mathcal{H}_{\overline{q}}$. For simplicity, the variables $\overline{q}$ in equation (6.38) can be dropped if they can be recognized from the context. It is clear that the (disjoint) union $\bigcup_i\{|\varphi_{ij_i}\rangle\}$ of the bases of subspaces X_i's in equation (6.39) is an orthonormal basis of the whole " coin" space $\mathcal{H}_c$. From the right-hand side of equation (6.39), we note that the purely quantum semantics of program (6.38) guarded by subspaces is a set of quantum operations rather than a single quantum operation. So, quantum case statement (6.38) is a nondeterministic program, and its nondeterminism comes from different choices of the bases of guard subspaces. Furthermore, a quantum case statement guarded by basis states of these subspaces is a refinement of quantum case statement (6.38). On the other hand, if $\{|i\rangle\}$ is an orthonormal basis of $\mathcal{H}_{\overline{q}}$, and for each i, X_i is the one-dimensional subspace $span\{|i\rangle\}$, then the previous definition degenerates to the quantum case statement (6.9) guarded by basis states $|i\rangle$.

The notion of equivalence for quantum programs in Definition 6.4.4 can be easily generalized to the case of nondeterministic quantum programs (i.e., programs with a set of quantum operations rather than a single quantum operation as its semantics) provided we make the following conventions:

- If Ω is a set of quantum operations and $\mathcal{F}$ a quantum operation, then

$$\Omega \otimes \mathcal{F} = \{\mathcal{E} \otimes \mathcal{F} : \mathcal{E} \in \Omega\};$$

- We identify a single quantum operation with the set containing only this quantum operation.

Some basic properties of quantum case statement guarded by subspaces are given in the following:

Proposition 6.8.1

(i) *If for every i, S_i does not contain any measurement, then for any orthonormal basis $\{|\varphi_{ij_i}\rangle\}$ of X_i $(1 \le i \le n)$, we have:*

$$\mathbf{qif}\,(\Box i \cdot X_i \to S_i)\;\mathbf{fiq} = \mathbf{qif}\,\left(\Box i,j_i \cdot |\varphi_{ij_i}\rangle \to S_{ij_i}\right)\;\mathbf{fiq}$$

where $S_{ij_i} = S_i$ for every i,j_i. In particular, if for every i, U_i is a unitary operator in $\mathcal{H}_{\overline{q}}$, then

$$\mathbf{qif}\,[\overline{p}](\Box i \cdot X_i \to U_i[\,\overline{q}\,])\;\mathbf{fiq} = U[\overline{p},\overline{q}]$$

where

$$U = \sum_i (I_{X_i} \otimes U_i)$$

is an unitary operator in $\mathcal{H}_{\overline{p}\cup\overline{q}}$.

(ii) *Let U be a unitary operator in $\mathcal{H}_{\bar{q}}$. If for every i, X_i is an invariant subspace of U, i.e.,*

$$UX_i = \{U|\psi\rangle : |\psi\rangle \in X_i\} \subseteq X_i,$$

then

$$U[\bar{q}]; \textbf{qif}\,[\bar{q}]\,(\square i \cdot X_i \rightarrow S_i) \;\textbf{fiq}; U^{\dagger}[\bar{q}] = \textbf{qif}\,[\bar{q}]\,(\square i \cdot X_i \rightarrow S_i) \;\textbf{fiq}.$$

Exercise 6.8.1. *Prove Proposition 6.8.1.*

We conclude this section by pointing out that a generalized notion of quantum choice can be defined based on either a parameterized quantum case statement or quantum case statement guarded by subspaces, and the algebraic laws established in Section 6.6 can be easily generalized for a parameterized quantum case statement and quantum choice as well as those guarded by subspaces. The details are omitted here, but the reader can try to figure it out as an exercise.

6.9 PROOFS OF LEMMAS, PROPOSITIONS AND THEOREMS

The proofs of the main lemmas, propositions and theorems in this chapter all include tedious calculations. So, for readability, these results have been stated in the previous sections without proofs. To complete this chapter, here we present their detailed proofs.

Proof of Lemma 6.3.2. Let F be the operator-valued function given in Definition 6.3.5. We write:

$$\overline{F} \triangleq \sum_{\delta_1 \in \Delta_1, \ldots, \delta_n \in \Delta_n} F(\oplus_{i=1}^{n}\delta_i)^{\dagger} \cdot F(\oplus_{i=1}^{n}\delta_i).$$

Let us start with an auxiliary equality. For any $|\Phi\rangle, |\Psi\rangle \in \mathcal{H}_c \otimes \mathcal{H}$, we can write

$$|\Phi\rangle = \sum_{i=1}^{n} |i\rangle|\varphi_i\rangle \;\text{ and }\; |\Psi\rangle = \sum_{i=1}^{n} |i\rangle|\psi_i\rangle$$

where $|\varphi_i\rangle, |\psi_i\rangle \in \mathcal{H}$ for each $1 \leq i \leq n$. Then we have:

$$\langle\Phi|\overline{F}|\Psi\rangle = \sum_{\delta_1,\ldots,\delta_n} \langle\Phi|F(\oplus_{i=1}^n \delta_i)^\dagger \cdot F(\oplus_{i=1}^n \delta_i)|\Psi\rangle$$

$$= \sum_{\delta_1,\ldots,\delta_n} \sum_{i,i'=1}^n \left(\prod_{k\neq i}\lambda_{k\delta_k}^*\right)\left(\prod_{k\neq i'}\lambda_{k\delta_k}\right)\langle i|i'\rangle\langle\varphi_i|F_i(\delta_i)^\dagger F_{i'}(\delta_{i'})|\psi_{i'}\rangle$$

$$= \sum_{\delta_1,\ldots,\delta_n} \sum_{i=1}^n \left(\prod_{k\neq i}|\lambda_{k\delta_k}|^2\right)\langle\varphi_i|F_i(\delta_i)^\dagger F_i(\delta_i)|\psi_i\rangle$$

$$= \sum_{i=1}^n \left[\sum_{\delta_1,\ldots,\delta_{i-1},\delta_{i+1},\ldots,\delta_n}\left(\prod_{k\neq i}|\lambda_{k\delta_k}|^2\right)\cdot\sum_{\delta_i}\langle\varphi_i|F_i(\delta_i)^\dagger F_i(\delta_i)|\psi_i\rangle\right] \qquad (6.40)$$

$$= \sum_{i=1}^n \sum_{\delta_i}\langle\varphi_i|F_i(\delta_i)^\dagger F_i(\delta_i)|\psi_i\rangle$$

$$= \sum_{i=1}^n \langle\varphi_i|\sum_{\delta_i} F_i(\delta_i)^\dagger F_i(\delta_i)|\psi_i\rangle$$

because for each k, we have:

$$\sum_{\delta_k}|\lambda_{k\delta_k}|^2 = 1,$$

and thus

$$\sum_{\delta_1,\ldots,\delta_{i-1},\delta_{i+1},\ldots,\delta_n}\left(\prod_{k\neq i}|\lambda_{k\delta_k}|^2\right) = \prod_{k\neq i}\left(\sum_{\delta_k}|\lambda_{k\delta_k}|^2\right) = 1. \qquad (6.41)$$

Now we are ready to prove our conclusions by using equation (6.40).

(i) We first prove that $\overline{F} \sqsubseteq I_{\mathcal{H}_c\otimes\mathcal{H}}$, i.e., F is an operator-valued function in $\mathcal{H}_c \otimes \mathcal{H}$ over $\bigoplus_{i=1}^n \Delta_n$. It suffices to show that

$$\langle\Phi|\overline{F}|\Phi\rangle \leq \langle\Phi|\Phi\rangle$$

for each $|\Phi\rangle \in \mathcal{H}_c \otimes \mathcal{H}$. In fact, for each $1 \leq i \leq n$, since F_i is an operator-valued function, we have:

$$\sum_{\delta_i} F_i(\delta_i)^\dagger F_i(\delta_i) \sqsubseteq I_{\mathcal{H}}.$$

Therefore, it holds that

$$\langle\varphi_i|\sum_{\delta_i} F_i(\delta_i)^\dagger F_i(\delta_i)|\varphi_i\rangle \leq \langle\varphi_i|\varphi_i\rangle.$$

Then it follows immediately from equation (6.40) that

$$\langle\Phi|\overline{F}|\Phi\rangle \leq \sum_{i=1}^{n}\langle\varphi_i|\varphi_i\rangle = \langle\Phi|\Phi\rangle.$$

So, F is an operator-valued function.

(ii) Secondly, we prove that F is full for the case where all F_i $(1 \leq i \leq n)$ are full. It requires us to show that $\overline{F} = I_{\mathcal{H}_c \otimes \mathcal{H}}$. In fact, for every $1 \leq i \leq n$, we have:

$$\sum_{\delta_i} F_i(\delta_i)^{\dagger} F_i(\delta_i) = I_{\mathcal{H}}$$

because F_i is full. Thus, it follows from equation (6.40) that

$$\langle\Phi|\overline{F}|\Psi\rangle = \sum_{i=1}^{n}\langle\varphi_i|\psi_i\rangle = \langle\Phi|\Psi\rangle$$

for any $|\Phi\rangle, |\Psi\rangle \in \mathcal{H}_c \otimes \mathcal{H}$. So, it holds that $\overline{F} = I_{\mathcal{H}_c \otimes \mathcal{H}}$ by arbitrariness of $|\Phi\rangle$ and $\Psi\rangle$, and F is full.

Proof of Proposition 6.4.1. Clauses (i) to (iv) are obvious, and we only prove (v) and (vi).

(1) To prove clause (v), let

$$S \equiv \text{if } (\square m \cdot M[\overline{q} : x] = m \rightarrow S_m) \text{ fi.}$$

Then by Definitions 6.4.2 and 6.4.3, for any partial density operator ρ in $\mathcal{H}_{qvar(S)}$, we have:

$$[\![S]\!](\rho) = \sum_{m} \sum_{\delta \in \Delta(S_m)} [\![S]\!](\delta[x \leftarrow m])\rho[\![S]\!](\delta[x \leftarrow m])^{\dagger}$$

$$= \sum_{m} \sum_{\delta \in \Delta(S_m)} \left([\![S_m]\!](\delta) \otimes I_{qvar(S)\backslash qvar(S_m)}\right)\left(M_m \otimes I_{qvar(S)\backslash\overline{q}}\right)$$

$$\rho\left(M_m^{\dagger} \otimes I_{qvar(S)\backslash\overline{q}}\right)\left([\![S_m]\!](\delta)^{\dagger} \otimes I_{qvar(S)\backslash qvar(S_m)}\right)$$

$$= \sum_{m} \sum_{\delta \in \Delta(S_m)} \left([\![S_m]\!](\delta) \otimes I_{qvar(S)\backslash qvar(S_m)}\right)\left(M_m\rho M_m^{\dagger}\right)$$

$$\left([\![S_m]\!](\delta)^{\dagger} \otimes I_{qvar(S)\backslash qvar(S_m)}\right)$$

$$= \sum_{m}[\![S_m]\!]\left(M_m\rho M_m^{\dagger}\right)$$

$$= \left(\sum_{m}\left[(M_m \circ M_m^{\dagger}); [\![S_m]\!]\right]\right)(\rho).$$

(2) Finally, we prove clause (vi). For simplicity of the presentation, we write:

$$S \equiv \text{qif } [\overline{q}](\square i \cdot |i\rangle \rightarrow S_i) \text{ fiq.}$$

By Definitions 6.4.2, we obtain:

$$\|S\| = \bigoplus_i (|i\rangle \rightarrow \|S_i\|) \,.$$

Note that $\|S_i\| \in \mathbb{F}(\llbracket S_i \rrbracket)$ for every $1 \leq i \leq n$, where $\mathbb{F}(\mathcal{E})$ stands for the set of operator-valued functions generated by quantum operation $\mathcal{E}$ (see Definition 6.3.3). Therefore, it follows from Definition 6.4.3 that

$$\llbracket S \rrbracket = \mathcal{E}(\|S\|) \in \left\{ \mathcal{E} \left(\bigoplus_i (|i\rangle \rightarrow F_i) \right) : F_i \in \mathbb{F}(\llbracket S_i \rrbracket) \text{ for every } i \right\}$$

$$= \bigoplus_i (|i\rangle \rightarrow \llbracket S_i \rrbracket) \,.$$

Proof of Theorem 6.5.1. To simplify the presentation, we write:

$$R \equiv \mathbf{qif} \, [\, \overline{q} \,](\square i \cdot |i\rangle \rightarrow S_i) \, \mathbf{fiq}.$$

To prove the equivalence of two QuGCL programs, we have to show that their purely quantum semantics are the same. However, purely quantum semantics is defined in terms of semi-classical semantics (see Definition 6.4.3). So, we need to work at the level of semi-classical semantics first, and then lift it to the purely quantum semantics. Assume that the semi-classical semantics $\|S_i\|$ is the operator-valued function over Δ_i such that

$$\|S_i\|(\delta_i) = E_{i\delta_i}$$

for each $\delta_i \in \Delta_i$. Let states $|\psi\rangle \in \mathcal{H}_{\bigcup_{i=1}^n qvar(S_i)}$ and $|\varphi\rangle \in \mathcal{H}_{\overline{q}}$. We can write $|\varphi\rangle = \sum_{i=1}^n \alpha_i |i\rangle$ for some complex numbers α_i $(1 \leq i \leq n)$. Then for any $\delta_i \in \Delta_i$ $(1 \leq i \leq n)$, we have:

$$|\Psi_{\delta_1 \ldots \delta_n}\rangle \triangleq \|R\|(\oplus_{i=1}^n \delta_i)(|\varphi\rangle|\psi\rangle)$$

$$= \|R\|(\oplus_{i=1}^n \delta_i) \left(\sum_{i=1}^n \alpha_i |i\rangle |\psi\rangle \right)$$

$$= \sum_{i=1}^n \alpha_i \left(\prod_{k \neq i} \lambda_{k\delta_k} \right) |i\rangle (E_{i\sigma_i} |\psi\rangle)$$

where $\lambda_{i\delta_i}$'s are defined as in equation (6.15). We continue to compute:

$$|\Psi_{\delta_1 \ldots \delta_n}\rangle \langle \Psi_{\delta_1 \ldots \delta_n}| = \sum_{i,j=1}^n \left[\alpha_i \alpha_j^* \left(\prod_{k \neq i} \lambda_{k\delta_k} \right) \left(\prod_{k \neq j} \lambda_{k\delta_k} \right) |i\rangle \langle j| \otimes E_{i\delta_i} |\psi\rangle \langle \psi| E_{j\delta_j}^\dagger \right],$$

and it follows that

$$tr_{\mathcal{H}_{\bar{q}}}|\Psi_{\delta_1\ldots\delta_n}\rangle\langle\Psi_{\delta_1\ldots\delta_n}| = \sum_{i=1}^{n}|\alpha_i|^2\left(\prod_{k\neq i}\lambda_{k\delta_k}\right)^2 E_{i\delta_i}|\psi\rangle\langle\psi|E_{i\delta_i}^{\dagger}.$$

Using equation (6.41), we obtain:

$$
\begin{aligned}
tr_{\mathcal{H}_{\bar{q}}}[\![R]\!](|\varphi\psi\rangle\langle\varphi\psi|) &= tr_{\mathcal{H}_{\bar{q}}}\left(\sum_{\delta_1,\ldots,\delta_n}|\Psi_{\delta_1\ldots\delta_n}\rangle\langle\Psi_{\delta_1\ldots\delta_n}|\right) \\
&= \sum_{\delta_1,\ldots,\delta_n}tr_{\mathcal{H}_{\bar{q}}}|\Psi_{\delta_1\ldots\delta_n}\rangle\langle\Psi_{\delta_1\ldots\delta_n}| \\
&= \sum_{i=1}^{n}|\alpha_i|^2\left[\sum_{\delta_1,\ldots,\delta_{i-1},\delta_{i+1},\ldots,\delta_n}\left(\prod_{k\neq i}\lambda_{k\delta_k}\right)^2\right]\cdot\left[\sum_{\delta_i}E_{i\delta_i}|\psi\rangle\langle\psi|E_{i\delta_i}^{\dagger}\right] \\
&= \sum_{i=1}^{n}|\alpha_i|^2[\![S_i]\!](|\psi\rangle\langle\psi|).
\end{aligned}
$$

(6.42)

Now we do spectral decomposition for $[\![S]\!](\rho)$, which is a density operator, and assume that

$$[\![S]\!](\rho) = \sum_{l}s_l|\varphi_l\rangle\langle\varphi_l|.$$

We further write $|\varphi_l\rangle = \sum_{i}\alpha_{li}|i\rangle$ for every l. For any density operator σ in $\mathcal{H}_{\bigcup_{i=1}^{n}qvar(S_i)}$, we can write σ in the form of $\sigma = \sum_{m}r_m|\psi_m\rangle\langle\psi_m|$. Then using equation (6.42), we get:

$$
\begin{aligned}
[\![\textbf{begin local } \bar{q} := \rho; [S]&\left(\bigoplus_{i=1}^{n}|i\rangle \to S_i\right)\textbf{ end}]\!](\sigma) \\
&= tr_{\mathcal{H}_{\bar{q}}}[\![S;R]\!](\sigma\otimes\rho) = tr_{\mathcal{H}_{\bar{q}}}[\![R]\!](\sigma\otimes[\![S]\!](\rho)) \\
&= tr_{\mathcal{H}_{\bar{q}}}[\![R]\!]\left(\sum_{m,l}r_m s_l|\psi_m\varphi_l\rangle\langle\psi_m\varphi_l|\right) \\
&= \sum_{m,l}r_m s_l tr_{\mathcal{H}_{\bar{q}}}[\![R]\!](|\psi_m\varphi_l\rangle\langle\psi_m\varphi_l|)
\end{aligned}
$$

$$= \sum_{m,l} r_m s_l \sum_{i=1}^{n} |\alpha_{li}|^2 [\![S_i]\!] (|\psi_m\rangle\langle\psi_m|)$$

$$= \sum_{l} \sum_{i=1}^{n} s_l |\alpha_{li}|^2 [\![S_i]\!] \left(\sum_{m} r_m |\psi_m\rangle\langle\psi_m| \right)$$

$$= \sum_{l} \sum_{i=1}^{n} s_l |\alpha_{li}|^2 [\![S_i]\!] (\sigma)$$

$$= \sum_{i=1}^{n} \left(\sum_{l} s_l |\alpha_{li}|^2 \right) [\![S_i]\!] (\sigma) = \left[\!\!\left[\sum_{i=1}^{n} S_i @ p_i \right]\!\!\right] (\sigma),$$

where:

$$p_i = \sum_{l} s_l |\alpha_{li}|^2 = \sum_{l} s_l \langle i|\varphi_l\rangle\langle\varphi_l|i\rangle$$

$$= \langle i| \left(\sum_{l} s_l |\varphi_l\rangle\langle\varphi_l| \right) |i\rangle = \langle i| [\![S]\!] (\rho) |i\rangle.$$

Proof of Theorem 6.6.2. We first prove the easier part, namely equation (6.28). Let *LHS* and *RHS* stand for the left- and right-hand side of equation (6.28), respectively. What we want to prove is $[\![LHS]\!] = [\![RHS]\!]$. But as explained in the proof of Theorem 6.5.1, we need to work with the semi-classical semantics, and show that $\|LHS\| = \|RHS\|$. Assume that $\|S_i\|$ is the operator-valued function over Δ_i such that

$$\|S_i\|(\delta_i) = F_{i\delta_i}$$

for each $\delta_i \in \Delta_i$ $(1 \leq i \leq n)$. We write:

$$S \equiv \mathbf{qif} \, (\square i \cdot U_{\bar{q}}^{\dagger}|i\rangle \rightarrow S_i) \, \mathbf{fiq}.$$

Then for any state $|\psi\rangle = \sum_{i=1}^{n} |i\rangle|\psi_i\rangle$, where $|\psi_i\rangle \in \mathcal{H}_V$ $(1 \leq i \leq n)$, and $V = \bigcup_{i=1}^{n} qvar(S_i)$, we have:

$$\|S\|(\oplus_{i=1}^{n}\delta_i)|\psi\rangle = \|S\|(\oplus_{i=1}^{n}\delta_i) \left[\sum_{i=1}^{n} \left(\sum_{j=1}^{n} U_{ij}(U_{\bar{q}}^{\dagger}|j\rangle) \right) |\psi_i\rangle \right]$$

$$= \|S\|(\oplus_{i=1}^{n}\delta_i) \left[\sum_{j=1}^{n} (U_{\bar{q}}^{\dagger}|j\rangle) \left(\sum_{i=1}^{n} U_{ij}|\psi_i\rangle \right) \right]$$

$$= \sum_{j=1}^{n} \left(\prod_{k \neq j} \lambda_{k\delta_k} \right) (U_{\bar{q}}^{\dagger}|j\rangle) F_{j\delta_j} \left(\sum_{i=1}^{n} U_{ij}|\psi_i\rangle \right),$$

where $\lambda_{k\delta_k}$'s are defined by equation (6.15). Then it holds that

$$
\begin{aligned}
[\![RHS]\!](\oplus_{i=1}^n \delta_i)|\psi\rangle &= U_{\overline{q}}([\![S]\!](\oplus_{i=1}^n \delta_i)|\psi\rangle) \\
&= \sum_{j=1}^n \left(\prod_{k\neq j}\lambda_{k\delta_k}\right)|j\rangle F_{j\delta_j}\left(\sum_{i=1}^n U_{ij}|\psi_i\rangle\right) \\
&= [\![S]\!](\oplus_{i=1}^n \delta_i)\left[\sum_{j=1}^n |j\rangle\left(\sum_{i=1}^n U_{ij}|\psi_i\rangle\right)\right] \\
&= [\![S]\!](\oplus_{i=1}^n \delta_i)\left[\sum_{i=1}^n \left(\sum_{j=1}^n U_{ij}|j\rangle\right)|\psi_i\rangle\right] \\
&= [\![S]\!](\oplus_{i=1}^n \delta_i)\left(\sum_{i=1}^n (U_{\overline{q}}|i\rangle)|\psi_i\rangle\right) \\
&= [\![LHS]\!](\oplus_{i=1}^n \delta_i)|\psi\rangle.
\end{aligned}
$$

So, we complete the proof of equation (6.28).

Now we turn to prove the harder part, namely equation (6.29). The basic idea is to use equation (6.28) that we just proved to prove the more general equation (6.29). What we need to do is to turn the general "coin" program S in equation (6.29) into a special "coin" program, which is a unitary transformation. The technique that we used before to deal with quantum operations is always the Kraus operator-sum representation. Here, however, we have to employ the system-environment model of quantum operations (see Theorem 2.1.1). Since $[\![S]\!]$ is a quantum operation in $\mathcal{H}_{\overline{q}}$, there must be a family of quantum variables $\overline{r}$, a pure state $|\varphi_0\rangle \in \mathcal{H}_{\overline{r}}$, a unitary operator U in $\mathcal{H}_{\overline{q}} \otimes \mathcal{H}_{\overline{r}}$, and a projection operator K onto some closed subspace $\mathcal{K}$ of $\mathcal{H}_{\overline{r}}$ such that

$$
[\![S]\!](\rho) = tr_{\mathcal{H}_{\overline{r}}}(KU(\rho \otimes |\varphi_0\rangle\langle\varphi_0|)U^\dagger K) \tag{6.43}
$$

for all density operators ρ in $\mathcal{H}_{\overline{q}}$. We choose an orthonormal basis of $\mathcal{K}$ and then extend it to an orthonormal basis $\{|j\rangle\}$ of $\mathcal{H}_{\overline{r}}$. Define pure states $|\psi_{ij}\rangle = U^\dagger|ij\rangle$ for all i, j and programs

$$
Q_{ij} \equiv \begin{cases} S_i & \text{if } |j\rangle \in \mathcal{K}, \\ \textbf{abort} & \text{if } |j\rangle \notin \mathcal{K}. \end{cases}
$$

Then by a routine calculation we have:

$$
[\![\textbf{qif }(\square i,j \cdot |ij\rangle \to Q_{ij})\textbf{ fiq}]\!](\sigma) = [\![\textbf{qif }(\square i \cdot |i\rangle \to S_i)\textbf{ fiq}]\!](K\sigma K) \tag{6.44}
$$

for any $\sigma \in \mathcal{H}_{\overline{q} \cup \overline{r} \cup V}$, where

$$V = \bigcup_{i=1}^{n} qvar(S_i).$$

We now write *RHS* for the right-hand side of equation (6.29). Then we have:

$$\llbracket RHS \rrbracket(\rho) = tr_{\mathcal{H}_{\overline{r}}} \left(\llbracket \mathbf{qif} \, (\square i,j \cdot U^{\dagger} |ij\rangle \rightarrow Q_{ij}) \, \mathbf{fiq}; U[\overline{q}, \overline{r}] \rrbracket (\rho \otimes |\varphi_0\rangle \langle \varphi_0|) \right)$$

$$= tr_{\mathcal{H}_{\overline{r}}} \left(\left\llbracket [U[\overline{q}, \overline{r}]] \left(\bigoplus_{i,j} |ij\rangle \rightarrow Q_{ij} \right) \right\rrbracket (\rho \otimes |\varphi_0\rangle \langle \varphi_0|) \right)$$

$$= tr_{\mathcal{H}_{\overline{r}}} \left(\llbracket \mathbf{qif} \, (\square i,j \cdot |ij\rangle \rightarrow Q_{ij}) \, \mathbf{fiq} \rrbracket (U(\rho \otimes |\varphi_0\rangle \langle \varphi_0|)U^{\dagger}) \right)$$

$$= tr_{\mathcal{H}_{\overline{r}}} \llbracket \mathbf{qif} \, (\square i \cdot |i\rangle \rightarrow S_i) \, \mathbf{fiq} \rrbracket (KU(\rho \otimes |\varphi_0\rangle \langle \varphi_0|)U^{\dagger}K)$$

$$= \llbracket \mathbf{qif} \, (\square i \cdot |i\rangle \rightarrow S_i) \, \mathbf{fiq} \rrbracket (tr_{\mathcal{H}_{\overline{r}}}(KU(\rho \otimes |\varphi_0\rangle \langle \varphi_0|)U^{\dagger}K))$$

$$= \llbracket \mathbf{qif} \, (\square i \cdot |i\rangle \rightarrow S_i) \, \mathbf{fiq} \rrbracket (\llbracket S \rrbracket(\rho))$$

$$= \left\llbracket [S] \left(\bigoplus_{i} |i\rangle \rightarrow S_i \right) \right\rrbracket (\rho)$$

for all density operators ρ in $\mathcal{H}_{\overline{q}}$. Here, the second equality is obtained by using equation (6.28), the fourth equality comes from (6.44), the fifth equality holds because

$$\overline{r} \cap qvar(\mathbf{qif} \, (\square i \cdot |i\rangle \rightarrow S_i) \, \mathbf{fiq}) = \emptyset,$$

and the sixth equality follows from equation (6.43). Therefore, equation (6.29) is proved.

Proof of Theorem 6.6.1 and Theorem 6.6.3. The proof of Theorem 6.6.1 is similar to but simpler than the proof of Theorem 6.6.3. So, here we only prove Theorem 6.6.3.

(1) Clause (i) is immediate from Theorem 6.5.1.
(2) To prove clause (ii), we write:

$$Q \equiv \mathbf{qif} \, [\overline{q}](\square i \cdot |i\rangle \rightarrow S_i) \, \mathbf{fiq},$$
$$R \equiv \mathbf{qif} \, [\overline{q}](\square i \cdot |i\rangle \rightarrow S_{\tau(i)}) \, \mathbf{fiq}.$$

By definition, we have $LHS = S; R$ and

$$RHS = S; U_{\tau}[\overline{q}]; Q; U_{\tau^{-1}}[\overline{q}].$$

So, it suffices to show that $R \equiv U_{\tau}[\overline{q}]; Q; U_{\tau^{-1}}[\overline{q}]$. Again, we first need to deal with the semi-classical semantics of the two sides of this equality. Assume that $\lfloor S_i \rfloor$ is the operator-valued function over Δ_i with

$$\lfloor S_i \rfloor(\delta_i) = E_{i\delta_i}$$

for each $\delta_i \in \Delta_i$ $(1 \leq i \leq n)$. For each state $|\Psi\rangle \in \mathcal{H}_{\overline{q} \cup \bigcup_{i=1}^{n} qvar(S_i)}$, we can write

$$|\Psi\rangle = \sum_{i=1}^{n} |i\rangle |\psi_i\rangle$$

for some $|\psi_i\rangle \in \mathcal{H}_{\bigcup_{i=1}^{n} qvar(S_i)}$ $(1 \leq i \leq n)$. Then for any $\delta_1 \in \Delta_{\tau(1)}, \ldots, \delta_n \in \Delta_{\tau(n)}$, it holds that

$$|\Psi_{\delta_1 \ldots \delta_n}\rangle \triangleq \llbracket R \rrbracket (\oplus_{i=1}^{n} \delta_i)(|\Psi\rangle)$$

$$= \sum_{i=1}^{n} \left(\prod_{k \neq i} \mu_{k \delta_k} \right) |i\rangle (E_{\tau(i)\delta_i} |\psi_i\rangle),$$

where:

$$\mu_{k \delta_k} = \sqrt{\frac{tr E_{\tau(k)\delta_k}^{\dagger} E_{\tau(k)\delta_k}}{\sum_{\theta_k \in \Sigma_{\tau(k)}} tr E_{\tau(k)\theta_k}^{\dagger} E_{\tau(k)\theta_k}}} = \lambda_{\tau(k)\delta_k} \qquad (6.45)$$

for every k and δ_k, and $\lambda_{i\sigma_i}$'s are defined by equation (6.15). On the other hand, we first observe:

$$|\Psi'\rangle \triangleq (U_\tau)_{\overline{q}}(|\Psi\rangle) = \sum_{i=1}^{n} |\tau(i)\rangle |\psi_i\rangle = \sum_{j=1}^{n} |j\rangle |\psi_{\tau^{-1}(j)}\rangle.$$

Then for any $\delta_1 \in \Delta_1, \ldots, \delta_n \in \Delta_n$, it holds that

$$|\Psi''_{\delta_1 \ldots \delta_n}\rangle \triangleq \llbracket Q \rrbracket \left(\bigoplus_{i=1}^{n} \delta_i \right) (|\Psi'\rangle)$$

$$= \sum_{j=1}^{n} \left(\prod_{l \neq j} \lambda_{l \delta_{\tau^{-1}(l)}} \right) |j\rangle (E_{j\delta_{\tau^{-1}(j)}} |\psi_{\tau^{-1}(j)}\rangle)$$

$$= \sum_{i=1}^{n} \left(\prod_{k \neq i} \lambda_{\tau(k)\delta_k} \right) |\tau(i)\rangle (E_{\tau(i)\delta_i} |\psi_i\rangle).$$

Furthermore, we have:

$$(U_{\tau^{-1}})_{\overline{q}}(|\Psi''_{\delta_1 \ldots \delta_n}\rangle) = \sum_{i=1}^{n} \left(\prod_{k \neq i} \lambda_{\tau(k)\delta_k} \right) |i\rangle (E_{\tau(i)\delta_i} |\psi_i\rangle).$$

Consequently, we can compute the purely quantum semantics:

$$[\![U_\tau[\,\overline{q}\,];Q;U_{\tau^{-1}}[\,\overline{q}\,]]\!](|\Psi\rangle\langle\Psi|) = [\![Q;U_{\tau^{-1}}[\,\overline{q}\,]]\!](|\Psi'\rangle\langle\Psi'|)]\!]$$

$$= (U_{\tau^{-1}})_{\overline{q}}\left(\sum_{\delta_1,\ldots,\delta_n}|\Psi''_{\delta_1\ldots\delta_n}\rangle\langle\Psi''_{\delta_1\ldots\delta_n}|\right)(U_\tau)_{\overline{q}} \qquad (6.46)$$

$$= \sum_{\delta_1,\ldots,\delta_n}|\Psi_{\delta_1\ldots\delta_n}\rangle\langle\Psi_{\delta_1\ldots\delta_n}| = [\![R]\!](\Psi)\langle\Psi|).$$

Here, the third equality comes from equation (6.45) and the fact that τ is one-onto-one, and thus $\tau^{-1}(j)$ traverses over $1,\ldots,n$ as j does. Therefore, it follows from equation (6.46) and spectral decomposition that

$$[\![R]\!](\rho) = [\![U_\tau[\,\overline{q}\,];Q;U_{\tau^{-1}}[\,\overline{q}\,]]\!](\rho)$$

for any density operator ρ in $\mathcal{H}_{\overline{q}\cup\bigcup_{i=1}^n qvar(S_i)}$, and we complete the proof of clause (ii).

(3) To prove clause (iii), we write:

$$X_i \equiv \mathbf{qif}\,(\square j_i \cdot |j_i\rangle \to R_{ij_i})\,\mathbf{fiq},$$

$$Y_i \equiv [Q_i]\left(\bigoplus_{j_i=1}^{n_i}|j_i\rangle \to R_{ij_i}\right)$$

for every $1 \le i \le m$, and we further put:

$$X \equiv \mathbf{qif}\,(\square i \cdot |i\rangle \to Y_i)\,\mathbf{fiq},$$

$$T \equiv \mathbf{qif}\,(\square i \cdot |i\rangle \to Q_i)\,\mathbf{fiq},$$

$$Z \equiv \mathbf{qif}\,(\overline{\alpha})(\square i,j_i \in \Delta \cdot |i,j_i\rangle \to R_{ij_i})\,\mathbf{fiq}.$$

Then by the definition of quantum choice we have $LHS = S;X$ and $RHS = S;T;Z$. So, it suffices to show that $X \equiv T;Z$. To do this, we consider the semi-classical semantics of the involved programs. For each $1 \le i \le m$, and for each $1 \le j_i \le n_i$, we assume:

- $\lfloor Q_i \rfloor$ is the operator-valued function over Δ_i such that

$$\lfloor Q_i \rfloor(\delta_i) = F_{i\delta_i}$$

  for every $\delta_i \in \Delta_i$; and
- $\lfloor R_{ij_i} \rfloor$ is the operator-valued function over Σ_{ij_i} such that

$$\lfloor R_{ij_i} \rfloor(\sigma_{ij_i}) = E_{(ij_i)\sigma_{ij_i}}$$

  for every $\sigma_{ij_i} \in \Sigma_{ij_i}$.

We also assume that state $|\Psi\rangle = \sum_{i=1}^{m} |i\rangle|\Psi_i\rangle$ where each $|\Psi_i\rangle$ is further decomposed into

$$|\Psi_i\rangle = \sum_{j_i=1}^{n_i} |j_i\rangle|\psi_{ij_i}\rangle$$

with $|\psi_{ij_i}\rangle \in \mathcal{H}_{\bigcup_{j_i=1}^{n_i} qvar(R_{ij_i})}$ for every $1 \le i \le m$ and $1 \le j_i \le n_i$. To simplify the presentation, we use the abbreviation $\overline{\sigma}_i = \oplus_{j_i=1}^{n_i} \sigma_{ij_i}$. Now we compute the semi-classical semantics of program Y_i:

$$
\begin{aligned}
[\![Y_i]\!](\delta_i \overline{\sigma}_i)|\Psi_i\rangle &= [\![X_i]\!](\overline{\sigma}_i)([\![Q_i]\!](\delta_i)|\Psi_i\rangle) \\
&= [\![X_i]\!](\overline{\sigma}_i) \left(\sum_{j_i=1}^{n_i} \left(F_{i\delta_i}|j_i\rangle \right) |\psi_{ij_i}\rangle \right) \\
&= [\![X_i]\!](\overline{\sigma}_i) \left[\sum_{j_i=1}^{n_i} \left(\sum_{l_i=1}^{n_i} \langle l_i|F_{i\delta_i}|j_i\rangle|l_i\rangle \right) |\psi_{ij_i}\rangle \right] \\
&= [\![X_i]\!](\overline{\sigma}_i) \left[\sum_{l_i=1}^{n_i} |l_i\rangle \left(\sum_{j_i=1}^{n_i} \langle l_i|F_{i\delta_i}|j_i\rangle|\psi_{ij_i}\rangle \right) \right] \\
&= \sum_{l_i=1}^{n_i} \left[\Lambda_{il_i} \cdot |l_i\rangle \left(\sum_{j_i=1}^{n_i} \langle l_i|F_{i\delta_i}|j_i\rangle E_{(il_i)\sigma_{il_i}}|\psi_{ij_i}\rangle \right) \right]
\end{aligned}
$$
(6.47)

where the coefficients:

$$\Lambda_{il_i} = \prod_{l \ne l_i} \lambda_{(il)\sigma_{il}},$$

$$\lambda_{(il)\sigma_{il}} = \sqrt{\frac{tr E_{(il)\sigma_{il}}^{\dagger} E_{(il)\sigma_{il}}}{\sum_{k=1}^{n_i} tr E_{(ik)\sigma_{ik}}^{\dagger} E_{(ik)\sigma_{ik}}}}$$

for each $1 \le l \le n_i$. Then using equation (6.47), we can further compute the semi-classical semantics of program X:

$$
\begin{aligned}
[\![X]\!](\oplus_{i=1}^{m}(\delta_i \overline{\sigma}_i))|\Psi\rangle &= \sum_{i=1}^{m} \left(\Gamma_i \cdot |i\rangle [\![Y_i]\!](\delta_i \overline{\sigma}_i)|\Psi_i\rangle \right) \\
&= \sum_{i=1}^{m} \sum_{l_i=1}^{n_i} \left[\Gamma_i \cdot \Lambda_{il_i} \cdot |il_i\rangle \left(\sum_{j_i=1}^{n_i} \langle l_i|F_{i\delta_i}|j_i\rangle E_{(il_i)\sigma_{il_i}}|\psi_{ij_i}\rangle \right) \right]
\end{aligned}
$$
(6.48)

where:

$$\Gamma_i = \prod_{h \neq i} \gamma_{h\overline{\sigma}_h},$$

$$\gamma_{i\overline{\sigma}_i} = \sqrt{\frac{tr\|Y_i\|(\delta_i\overline{\sigma}_i)^\dagger \|Y_i\|(\delta_i\overline{\sigma}_i)}{\sum_{h=1}^{m} tr\|Y_h\|(\delta_h\overline{\sigma}_h)^\dagger \|Y_h\|(\delta_h\overline{\sigma}_h)}} \tag{6.49}$$

for every $1 \leq i \leq m$. On the other hand, we can compute the semi-classical semantics of program T:

$$\|T\|(\oplus_{i=1}^{m}\delta_i)|\Psi\rangle = \|T\|(\oplus_{i=1}^{m}\delta_i)\left(\sum_{i=1}^{m}|i\rangle|\Psi_i\rangle\right)$$

$$= \sum_{i=1}^{m}\left(\Theta_i \cdot |i\rangle F_{i\delta_i}|\Psi_i\rangle\right)$$

$$= \sum_{i=1}^{m}\left[\Theta_i \cdot |i\rangle \left(\sum_{j_i=1}^{n_i}(F_{i\delta_i}|j_i\rangle)|\psi_{ij_i}\rangle\right)\right]$$

$$= \sum_{i=1}^{m}\left[\Theta_i \cdot |i\rangle \left(\sum_{j_i=1}^{n_i}\left(\sum_{l_i=1}^{n_i}\langle l_i|F_{i\delta_i}|j_i\rangle|l_i\rangle\right)|\psi_{ij_i}\rangle\right)\right]$$

$$= \sum_{i=1}^{m}\sum_{l_i=1}^{n_i}\left[\Theta_i \cdot |il_i\rangle \left(\sum_{j_i=1}^{n_i}\langle l_i|F_{i\delta_i}|j_i\rangle|\psi_{ij_i}\rangle\right)\right]$$

where:

$$\Theta_i = \prod_{h \neq i} \theta_{h\delta_h},$$

$$\theta_{i\delta_i} = \sqrt{\frac{trF_{i\delta_i}^\dagger E_{i\delta_i}}{\sum_{h=1}^{m} trF_{h\delta_h}^\dagger F_{h\delta_h}}}$$

for every $1 \leq i \leq m$. Consequently, we obtain the semi-classical semantics of program $T; Z$:

$$\|T;Z\|\left((\oplus_{i=1}^{m}\delta_i)(\oplus_{i=1}^{m}\overline{\sigma}_i)\right)|\Psi\rangle = \|Z\|(\oplus_{i=1}^{m}\overline{\sigma}_i)\left(\|T\|(\oplus_{i=1}^{m}\delta_i)|\Psi\rangle\right)$$

$$= \|Z\|\left(\oplus_{i=1}^{m}\oplus_{l_i=1}^{n_i}\sigma_{ij_i}\right)\left(\sum_{i=1}^{m}\sum_{l_i=1}^{n_i}\left[\Theta_i \cdot |il_i\rangle \left(\sum_{j_i=1}^{n_i}\langle l_i|F_{i\delta_i}|j_i\rangle|\psi_{ij_i}\rangle\right)\right]\right) \tag{6.50}$$

$$= \sum_{i=1}^{m}\sum_{l_i=1}^{n_i}\left[\alpha_{\{\sigma_{jk_j}\}_{(j,k_j)\neq(i,l_i)}}^{il_i} \cdot \Theta_i \cdot |il_i\rangle \left(\sum_{j_i=1}^{n_i}\langle l_i|F_{i\delta_i}|j_i\rangle E_{(il_i)\sigma_{il_i}}|\psi_{ij_i}\rangle\right)\right].$$

By comparing equations (6.48) and (6.50), we see that it suffices to take

$$\alpha^{il_i}_{\{\sigma_{jk_j}\}_{(j,k_j)\neq(i,l_i)}} = \frac{\Gamma_i \cdot \Delta_{il_i}}{\Theta_i} \tag{6.51}$$

for all i, l_i and $\{\sigma_{jk_j}\}_{(j,k_j)\neq(i,l_i)}$. What remains to prove is the normalization condition:

$$\sum_{\{\sigma_{jk_j}\}_{(j,k_j)\neq(i,l_i)}} \left| \alpha^{il_i}_{\{\sigma_{jk_j}\}_{(j,k_j)\neq(i,l_i)}} \right|^2 = 1. \tag{6.52}$$

To do this, we first compute coefficients $\gamma_{i\overline{\sigma}_i}$. Let $\{|\varphi\rangle\}$ be an orthonormal basis of $\mathcal{H}_{\bigcup_{j_i=1}^{n_i} qvar(R_{ij_i})}$. Then we have:

$$G_{\varphi j_i} \triangleq \lfloor Y_i \rfloor (\delta_i \overline{\sigma}_i) |\varphi\rangle |j_i\rangle = \sum_{l_i=1}^{n_i} \Lambda_{il_i} \cdot \langle l_i | F_{i\delta_i} | j_i \rangle E_{(il_i)\sigma_{il_i}} |\varphi\rangle |l_i\rangle.$$

It follows that

$$G^{\dagger}_{\varphi j_i} G_{\varphi j_i} = \sum_{l_i, l'_i = 1}^{n_i} \Lambda_{il_i} \cdot \Lambda_{il'_i} \langle j_i | F^{\dagger}_{i\delta_i} | l_i \rangle \langle l'_i | F_{i\delta_i} | j_i \rangle \langle \varphi | E^{\dagger}_{(il_i)\sigma_{il_i}} E_{(il'_i)\sigma_{il'_i}} |\varphi\rangle \langle l_i | l'_i \rangle$$

$$= \sum_{l_i=1}^{n_i} \Lambda_{il_i}^2 \cdot \langle j_i | F^{\dagger}_{i\delta_i} | l_i \rangle \langle l_i | F_{i\delta_i} | j_i \rangle \langle \varphi | E^{\dagger}_{(il_i)\sigma_{il_i}} E_{(il_i)\sigma_{il_i}} |\varphi\rangle.$$

Furthermore, we obtain:

$$tr\lfloor Y_i \rfloor (\delta_i \overline{\sigma}_i)^{\dagger} \lfloor Y_i \rfloor (\delta_i \overline{\sigma}_i) = \sum_{\varphi j_i} G^{\dagger}_{\varphi j_i} G_{\varphi j_i}$$

$$= \sum_{l_i=1}^{n_i} \Lambda_{il_i}^2 \cdot \left(\sum_{j_i} \langle j_i | F^{\dagger}_{i\delta_i} | l_i \rangle \langle l_i | F_{i\delta_i} | j_i \rangle \right) \left(\sum_{\varphi} \langle \varphi | E^{\dagger}_{(il_i)\sigma_{il_i}} E_{(il_i)\sigma_{il_i}} |\varphi\rangle \right) \tag{6.53}$$

$$= \sum_{l_i=1}^{n_i} \Lambda_{il_i}^2 \cdot tr(F^{\dagger}_{i\delta_i} | l_i \rangle \langle l_i | F_{i\delta_i}) tr(E^{\dagger}_{(il_i)\sigma_{il_i}} E_{(il_i)\sigma_{il_i}}).$$

Now a routine but tedious calculation yields equation (6.52) through substituting equation (6.53) into (6.49) and then substituting equations (6.49) and (6.51) into (6.52).

(4) Finally, we prove clause (iv). To prove the first equality, we write:

$$X \equiv \mathbf{qif}\ (\square i \cdot |i\rangle \to S_i)\ \mathbf{fiq},$$
$$Y \equiv \mathbf{qif}\ (\overline{\alpha})(\square i \cdot |i\rangle \to (S_i; Q))\ \mathbf{fiq}.$$

Then by definition we have $LHS = S; X; Q$ and $RHS = S; Y$. So, it suffices to show that $X; Q =_{CF} Y$. Suppose that

$$\|S_i\|(\sigma_i) = E_{i\sigma_i}$$

for every $\sigma_i \in \Delta(S_i)$ and $\|Q\|(\delta) = F_\delta$ for every $\delta \in \Delta(Q)$, and suppose that

$$|\Psi\rangle = \sum_{i=1}^n |i\rangle|\psi_i\rangle$$

where $|\psi_i\rangle \in \mathcal{H}_{\bigcup_i qvar(S_i)}$ for all i. Then it holds that

$$\|X; Q\|((\oplus_{i=1}^n \sigma_i)\delta)|\Psi\rangle = \|Q\|(\delta)(\|X\|(\oplus_{i=1}^n \sigma_i)|\Psi\rangle)$$

$$= F_\delta \left(\sum_{i=1}^n \Lambda_i |i\rangle (E_{i\sigma_i}|\psi_i\rangle) \right)$$

$$= \sum_{i=1}^n \Lambda_i \cdot |i\rangle (F_\delta E_{i\sigma_i}|\psi_i\rangle)$$

because $qvar(S) \cap qvar(Q) = \emptyset$, where:

$$\Lambda_i = \prod_{k \neq i} \lambda_{k\sigma_k},$$

$$\lambda_{i\sigma_i} = \sqrt{\frac{tr E_{i\sigma_i}^\dagger E_{i\sigma_i}}{\sum_{k=1}^n tr E_{k\sigma_k}^\dagger E_{k\sigma_k}}}. \tag{6.54}$$

Furthermore, we have:

$$tr_{\mathcal{H}_{qvar(S)}} (\|X; Q\|(|\Psi\rangle\langle\Psi|))$$

$$= tr_{\mathcal{H}_{qvar(S)}} \left[\sum_{\{\sigma_i\},\delta} \sum_{i,j} \Lambda_i \Lambda_j \cdot |i\rangle\langle j|(F_\delta E_{i\sigma_i}|\psi_i\rangle\langle\psi_j|E_{j\sigma_j}^\dagger F_\delta^\dagger) \right] \tag{6.55}$$

$$= \sum_{\{\sigma_i\},\delta} \sum_i \Lambda_i^2 \cdot F_\delta E_{i\sigma_i}|\psi_i\rangle\langle\psi_i|E_{i\sigma_i}^\dagger F_\delta^\dagger.$$

On the other hand, we can compute the semi-classical semantics of Y:

$$\|Y\|(\oplus_{i=1}^n \sigma_i\delta_i)|\Psi\rangle = \sum_{i=1}^n \alpha_{\{\sigma_k,\delta_k\}_{k\neq i}}^{(i)} \cdot |i\rangle(\|S_i; Q\|(\sigma_i\delta_i)|\psi_i\rangle)$$

$$= \sum_{i=1}^n \alpha_{\{\sigma_k,\delta_k\}_{k\neq i}}^{(i)} \cdot |i\rangle(F_{\delta_i} E_{\sigma_i}|\psi_i\rangle).$$

Furthermore, we obtain:

$$tr_{\mathcal{H}_{qvar(S)}}(\llbracket Y \rrbracket(|\Psi\rangle\langle\Psi|))$$

$$= tr_{\mathcal{H}_{qvar(S)}}\left[\sum_{\{\sigma_i,\delta_i\}}\sum_{i,j}\alpha^{(i)}_{\{\sigma_k,\delta_k\}_{k\neq i}}(\alpha^{(j)}_{\{\sigma_l,\delta_l\}_{l\neq j}})^* \cdot |i\rangle\langle j|(F_{\delta_i}E_{i\sigma_i}|\psi_i\rangle\langle\psi_j|E^\dagger_{j\sigma_j}F^\dagger_{\delta_j})\right]$$

$$= \sum_{\{\sigma_i\},\delta}\sum_i\left|\alpha^{(i)}_{\{\sigma_k,\delta_k\}_{k\neq i}}\right|^2 \cdot F_{\delta_i}E_{i\sigma_i}|\psi_i\rangle\langle\psi_i|E^\dagger_{i\sigma_i}F^\dagger_{\delta_i}.$$

$$(6.56)$$

Comparing equations (6.55) and (6.56), we see that

$$tr_{\mathcal{H}_{qvar(S)}}(\llbracket X;Q \rrbracket(|\Psi\rangle\langle\Psi|)) = tr_{\mathcal{H}_{qvar(S)}}(\llbracket Y \rrbracket(|\Psi\rangle\langle\Psi|))$$

if we take

$$\alpha^{(i)}_{\{\sigma_k,\delta_k\}_{k\neq i}} = \frac{\Lambda_i}{\sqrt{|\Delta(Q)|}}$$

for all i, $\{\sigma_k\}$ and $\{\delta_k\}$. Since

$$qvar(S) \subseteq cvar(X;Q) \cup cvar(Y),$$

it follows that

$$tr_{\mathcal{H}_{cvar(X;Q)\cup cvar(Y)}}(\llbracket X;Q \rrbracket(|\Psi\rangle\langle\Psi|)) = tr_{\mathcal{H}_{cvar(X;Q)\cup cvar(Y)}}(\llbracket Y \rrbracket(|\Psi\rangle\langle\Psi|)).$$

Therefore, we can assert that

$$tr_{\mathcal{H}_{cvar(X;Q)\cup cvar(Y)}}(\llbracket X;Q \rrbracket(\rho)) = tr_{\mathcal{H}_{cvar(X;Q)\cup cvar(Y)}}(\llbracket Y \rrbracket(\rho))$$

for all density operators ρ by spectral decomposition. Thus, we have $X;Q \equiv_{CF} Y$, and the proof of the first equality of clause (iv) is completed.

For the special case where Q contains no measurements, $\Delta(Q)$ is a singleton, say $\{\delta\}$. We write:

$$Z \equiv \textbf{qif } (\square i \cdot |i\rangle \to (P_i;Q)) \textbf{ fiq}.$$

Then

$$\llbracket Z \rrbracket(\oplus^n_{i=1}\sigma_i\delta)|\Psi\rangle = \sum_{i=1}^n\left(\prod_{k\neq i}\theta_{k\sigma_k}\right) \cdot |i\rangle(F_\delta E_{\sigma_i}|\psi_i\rangle),$$

where:

$$\theta_{i\sigma_i} = \sqrt{\frac{trE^\dagger_{i\sigma_i}F^\dagger_\delta F_\delta E_{i\sigma_i}}{\sum_{k=1}^n trE^\dagger_{k\sigma_k}F^\dagger_\delta F_\delta E_{k\sigma_k}}} = \lambda_{i\sigma_i},$$

and $\lambda_{i\sigma_i}$ is given by equation (6.54), because $F_\delta^\dagger F_\delta$ is the identity operator. Consequently, $\|X; Q\| = \|Z\|$, and we complete the proof of the second equality of clause (iv).

6.10 BIBLIOGRAPHIC REMARKS

This chapter is mainly based on the draft paper [233]; an earlier version of [233] appeared as [232]. The examples presented in Subsection 6.7.1 were taken from recent physics literature: the unidirectional quantum walk was examined in [171]; the quantum walk with "coin tossing operator" depending on time and position was employed in [145] to implement quantum measurement; the quantum walk with three coin states was considered in [122]; the one-dimensional quantum walk driven by multiple coins was defined in [49]; and the quantum walk consisting of two walkers on a line sharing coins was introduced in [217].

- *GCL and its extensions*: The programming language QuGCL studied in this chapter is a quantum counterpart of Dijkstra's GCL (Guarded Command Language). The language GCL was originally defined in [74], but one can find an elegant and systematic presentation of GCL in [172]. The language pGCL for probabilistic programming was defined by introducing probabilistic choice into GCL; for a systematic exposition of probabilistic programming with probabilistic choice, we refer to [166]. A comparison between quantum choice and probabilistic choice was given in Section 6.5.

  Another quantum extension qGCL of GCL was defined in Sanders and Zuliani's pioneering paper [191]; see also [241]. qGCL was obtained by adding three primitives for quantum computation – initialization, unitary transformation, quantum measurement – into the probabilistic language pGCL. Note that the control flows of qGCL programs are always classical. QuGCL can also be seen as an extension of qGCL obtained by adding a quantum case statement (with quantum control flow).

- *Quantum control flow*: Quantum programs with quantum control flow were first considered by Altenkirch and Grattage [14], but the way of defining quantum control flow in this chapter is very different from that used in [14]. A careful discussion about the difference between the approach in [14] and ours can be found in [232,233]. Our approach was mainly inspired by the following line of research: a superposition of evolutions (rather than that of states) of a quantum system was considered by physicists Aharonov et al. [11] as early as 1990, and they proposed to introduce an external system in order to implement the superposition. The idea of using such an external "coin" system was rediscovered by Aharonov et al. and Ambainis et al. in defining quantum walks [9,19]. The fact that the shift operator S of a quantum walk can be seen as a quantum case statement and the single-step operator W as a quantum choice was noticed in [232,233] by introducing the single-direction shift operators S_i's.

It then motivated the design decision of quantum case statement and quantum choice as well as the quantum programming paradigm of superposition-of-programs.

Whenever no measurements are involved, then the semantics of a quantum case statement can be defined in terms of the guarded composition of unitary operators. However, defining the semantics of a quantum case statement in its full generality requires the notion of guarded composition of quantum operations, introduced in [232,233].

- *More related literature*: As pointed out in Subsection 6.3.1, guarded composition of unitary operators is essentially a quantum multiplexor introduced by Shende et al. [201] and discussed in Subsection 2.2.4. It was called a measuring operator by Kitaev et al. in [135].

The quantum programming language Scaffold [3] supports quantum control primitives with the restriction that the code comprising the body of each module must be purely quantum (and unitary). Hence, its semantics only requires guarded composition of unitary operators, defined in Subsection 6.3.1. Recently, some very interesting discussions about quantum case statements were given by Bădescu and Panangaden [28]; in particular, they observed that quantum case statements are not monotone with respect to the Löwner order and thus not compatible with the semantics of recursion defined in [194].

In recent years, there have been quite a few papers concerning superposition of quantum gates or more general quantum operations in the physics literature. Zhou et al. [240] proposed an architecture-independent technique for adding control to arbitrary unknown quantum operations and demonstrated this in a photonic system. This problem was further considered by Araújo et al. [22] and Friis et al. [91].

The interesting idea of superposition of causal structures in quantum computation was first introduced by Chiribella et al. [55]. It was generalized by Araújo et al. [23] and implemented by Procopio et al. [181].

Quantum recursion

Recursion is one of the central ideas of computer science. Most programming languages support recursion or at least a special form of recursion such as the **while**-loop. A quantum extension of the **while**-loop was already introduced in Section 3.1. A more general notion of recursion in quantum programming was defined in Section 3.4. It was appropriately called *classical recursion of quantum programs* because its control flow is determined by the involved case statements of the form (3.3) and **while**-loops of the form (3.4) and thus is doomed to be classical, as discussed in Section 3.1.

In the last chapter, we studied quantum case statements and quantum choices of which the control flows are genuinely quantum because they are governed by quantum "coins." This chapter further defines the notion of quantum recursion based on quantum case statement and quantum choice. The control flow of such a quantum recursive program is then quantum rather than classical. As we will see later, the treatment of quantum recursion with quantum control is much harder than classical recursion in quantum programming.

The chapter is organized as follows.

- The syntax of quantum recursive programs is defined in Section 7.1. Recursive quantum walks are introduced in Section 7.2 as examples for carefully motivating the notion of quantum recursion. Section 7.1 provides us with a language in which a precise formulation of recursive quantum walks is possible.
- It requires mathematical tools from second quantization – a theoretical framework in which we are able to depict quantum systems with a variable number of particles – to define the semantics of quantum recursive programs. Since it is used only in this chapter, second quantization was not included in the preliminaries chapter (Chapter 2). Instead, we introduce the basics of second quantization, in particular Fock spaces and operators in them, in Section 7.3.
- We define the semantics of quantum recursion in two steps. The first step is carried out in Section 7.4 where quantum recursive equations are solved in the free Fock space, which is mathematically convenient to manipulate but does not represent a realistic system in physics. The second step is completed in Section 7.5 where the solutions of recursive equations are symmetrized so that

273

they can apply in the physically meaningful framework, namely the symmetric and antisymmetric Fock spaces of bosons and fermions. Furthermore, the principal system semantics of a quantum recursive program is defined in Section 7.6 by tracing out auxiliary "quantum coins" from its symmetrized semantics.

- Recursive quantum walks are reconsidered in Section 7.7 to illustrate various semantic notions introduced in this chapter. A special class of quantum recursions, namely quantum **while**-loops with quantum control flows are carefully examined in Section 7.8.

7.1 SYNTAX OF QUANTUM RECURSIVE PROGRAMS

In this section, we formally define the syntax of quantum recursive programs. To give the reader a clearer picture, we choose not to include quantum measurements in the declarations of quantum recursions. It is not difficult to add quantum measurements into the theory of quantum recursive programs by combining the ideas used in this chapter and the last one, but the presentation will be much more complicated.

Let us start by exhibiting the alphabet of the language of quantum recursive programs. In the last chapter, any quantum variable can serve as a "coin" in defining a quantum case statement. For convenience, in this chapter we explicitly separate quantum "coins" from other quantum variables; that is, we assume two sets of quantum variables:

- principal system variables, ranged over by $p, q, \ldots$;
- "coin" variables, ranged over by $c, d, \ldots$.

These two sets are required to be disjoint. We also assume a set of procedure identifiers, ranged over by $X, X_1, X_2, \ldots$. A modification of the quantum programming language QuGCL presented in the last chapter is defined by the next:

Definition 7.1.1. *Program schemes are defined by the following syntax:*

$$P ::= X \mid \textbf{abort} \mid \textbf{skip} \mid P_1; P_2 \mid U[\overline{c}, \overline{q}] \mid \textbf{qif} [c](\square i \cdot |i\rangle \rightarrow P_i) \textbf{ fiq}$$

Obviously, this definition is obtained from Definition 6.2.1 by adding procedure identifiers and excluding measurements (and thus classical variables for recording the outcomes of measurements). More explicitly,

- X is a procedure identifier;
- **abort**, **skip**, and sequential composition $P_1; P_2$ are as in Definition 6.2.1.
- Unitary transformation $U[\overline{c}, \overline{q}]$ is the same as before except that "coins" and principal system variables are separated; that is, $\overline{c}$ is a sequence of "coin" variables, $\overline{q}$ is a sequence of principal system variables, and U is a unitary operator in the state Hilbert space of the system consisting of $\overline{c}$ and $\overline{q}$. We will always put "coin" variables before principal system variables. Both $\overline{c}$ and $\overline{q}$ are

allowed to be empty. When $\bar{c}$ is empty, we simply write $U[\bar{q}]$ for $U[\bar{c}, \bar{q}]$ and it describes the evolution of the principal system $\bar{q}$; when $\bar{q}$ is empty, we simply write $U[\bar{c}]$ for $U[\bar{c}, \bar{q}]$ and it describes the evolution of the "coins" $\bar{c}$. If both $\bar{c}$ and $\bar{q}$ are not empty, then $U[\bar{c}, \bar{q}]$ describes the interaction between "coins" $\bar{c}$ and the principal system $\bar{q}$.

- Quantum case statement **qif** $[c](\square i \cdot |i\rangle \rightarrow P_i)$ **fiq** is as in Definition 6.2.1. Here, for simplicity we only use a single "coin" c rather than a sequence of "coins." Once again, we emphasize that "coin" c is required not to occur in any subprogram P_i because, according to its physical interpretation, it is always external to the principal system.

Recall from Section 6.5, quantum choice can be defined in terms of quantum case statement and sequential composition:

$$[P(c)] \bigoplus_i (|i\rangle \rightarrow P_i) \triangleq P; \mathbf{qif}\,[c]\,(\square i \cdot |i\rangle \rightarrow P_i)\ \mathbf{fiq}$$

where P contains only quantum variable c. In particular, if the "coin" is a qubit, then a quantum choice can be abbreviated as

$$P_0 \oplus_P P_1 \text{ or } P_0\ {}_P\oplus P_1.$$

Quantum program schemes without procedure identifiers are actually a special class of quantum programs considered in the last chapter. So, their semantics can be directly derived from Definition 6.4.2. For the convenience of the reader, we explicitly display their semantics in the following definition. The principal system of a quantum program P is the composition of the systems denoted by principal system variables appearing in P. We write $\mathcal{H}$ for the state Hilbert space of the principal system.

Definition 7.1.2. *The semantics $[\![P]\!]$ of a program P (i.e., a program scheme without procedure identifiers) is inductively defined as follows:*

- **(i)** *If $P = $ **abort**, then $[\![P]\!] = 0$ (the zero operator in $\mathcal{H}$), and if $P = $ **skip**, then $[\![P]\!] = I$ (the identity operator in $\mathcal{H}$);*
- **(ii)** *If P is a unitary transformation $U[\bar{c}, \bar{q}]$, then $[\![P]\!]$ is the unitary operator U (in the state Hilbert space of the system consisting of $\bar{c}$ and $\bar{q}$);*
- **(iii)** *If $P = P_1; P_2$, then $[\![P]\!] = [\![P_2]\!] \cdot [\![P_1]\!]$;*
- **(iv)** *If $P = $ **qif** $[c](\square i \cdot |i\rangle \rightarrow P_i)$ **fiq**, then*

$$[\![P]\!] = \square\,(c, |i\rangle \rightarrow [\![P_i]\!]) \triangleq \sum_i \left(|i\rangle_c \langle i| \otimes [\![P_i]\!]\right). \tag{7.1}$$

This definition is a special case of Definition 6.4.2 where the semi-classical semantics of QuGCL programs were defined. However, the reader may have noticed that in the preceding definition we use $[\![P]\!]$ to denote the semantics of a program P, and in the last chapter $\|P\|$ is employed to denote the semi-classical semantics of

P and $[\![P]\!]$ denotes the purely quantum semantics of P. We choose to write $[\![P]\!]$ for the semantics of P in Definition 7.1.2 because in this chapter programs contain no measurements, so their semi-classical semantics and purely quantum semantics are essentially the same. Obviously, $[\![P]\!]$ in the preceding definition is an operator in the state Hilbert space of the system consisting of both the principal system of P and the "coins" in P; i.e., $\mathcal{H}_C \otimes \mathcal{H}$, where $\mathcal{H}_C$ is the state space of the "coins" in P. Since **abort** may appear in P, $[\![P]\!]$ is not necessarily a unitary. Using the terminology from the last chapter, $[\![P]\!]$ can be seen as an operator-valued function in $\mathcal{H}_C \otimes \mathcal{H}$ over a singleton $\Delta = \{\epsilon\}$.

Finally, we can define the syntax of quantum recursive programs. If a program scheme P contains at most the procedure identifiers $X_1, \ldots, X_m$, then we write

$$P = P[X_1, \ldots, X_m].$$

Definition 7.1.3

(i) *Let $X_1, \ldots, X_m$ be different procedure identifiers. A declaration for $X_1, \ldots, X_m$ is a system of equations:*

$$D: \begin{cases} X_1 \Leftarrow P_1, \\ \ldots\ldots \\ X_m \Leftarrow P_m, \end{cases}$$

where for every $1 \leq i \leq m$, $P_i = P_i[X_1, \ldots, X_m]$ is a program scheme containing at most procedure identifiers $X_1, \ldots, X_m$.

(ii) *A recursive program consists of a program scheme $P = P[X_1, \ldots, X_m]$, called the main statement, and a declaration D for $X_1, \ldots, X_m$ such that all "coin" variables in P do not appear in D; that is, they do not appear in the procedure bodies $P_1, \ldots, P_m$.*

The requirement in the preceding definition that the "coins" in the main statement P and those in the declaration D are distinct is obviously necessary because a "coin" used to define a quantum case statement is always considered to be external to its principal system.

Perhaps, the reader already noticed that Definition 7.1.3 looks almost the same as Definitions 3.4.2 and 3.4.3. But there is actually an essential difference between them: in the preceding definition, program schemes $P_1, \ldots, P_m$ in the declaration D and the main statement P can contain quantum case statements, whereas only case statements of the form (3.3) (and **while**-loops of the form (3.4)) are present in Definitions 3.4.2 and 3.4.3. Therefore, as said repeatedly, a recursive program defined here has quantum control flow, but a recursive program considered in Section 3.4 has only classical control flow. For this reason, the former is termed a *quantum recursive program* and the latter a *recursive quantum program*. As we saw in Section 3.4, the techniques in classical programming theory can be straightforwardly generalized to define the semantics of recursive quantum programs. On the other hand, if a quantum program containing quantum case statements is not recursively defined, its semantics can be defined using the techniques developed in the last chapter; in particular, Definition 7.1.2 is a simplified version of Definition 6.4.2. However, new techniques are required in order to define the semantics of quantum recursive programs, as will be clearly seen at the end of the next section.

7.2 MOTIVATING EXAMPLES: RECURSIVE QUANTUM WALKS

The syntax of quantum recursive programs was introduced in the last section. The aim of this section is two-fold:

(i) present a motivating example of quantum recursive program;
(ii) give a hint to answering the question: how to define the semantics of quantum recursive programs?

This aim will be achieved by considering a class of examples, called recursive quantum walks, which are a variant of the quantum walks introduced in Subsection 2.3.4. Actually, recursive quantum walks can only be properly presented with the help of the syntax given in the last section.

7.2.1 SPECIFICATION OF RECURSIVE QUANTUM WALKS

A one-dimensional quantum walk, called a Hadamard walk, was defined in Example 2.3.1. For simplicity, in this section we focus on the recursive Hadamard walk, a modification of the Hadamard walk. Recursive quantum walks on a graph can be defined by modifying Example 2.3.2 in a similar way.

Recall from Examples 2.3.2 and 6.7.1 that the state Hilbert space of the Hadamard walk is $\mathcal{H}_d \otimes \mathcal{H}_p$, where

- $\mathcal{H}_d = \text{span}\{|L\rangle, |R\rangle\}$ is the "direction coin" space, and L, R are used to indicate the directions Left and Right, respectively;
- $\mathcal{H}_p = \text{span}\{|n\rangle : n \in \mathbb{Z}\}$ is the position space, and n indicates the position marked by integer n.

The single-step operator W of the Hadamard walk is a quantum choice, which is the sequential composition of a "coin-tossing" Hadamard operator H on the "direction coin" d and translation operator T on the position variable p. The translation T is a quantum case statement that selects left or right translations according to the basis states $|L\rangle, |R\rangle$ of the "coin" d:

- If d is in state $|L\rangle$ then the walker moves one position left;
- If d is in state $|R\rangle$ then it moves one position right.

Of course, d can also be in a superposition of $|L\rangle$ and $|R\rangle$, and thus a superposition of left and right translations happens, which produces a quantum control flow. Formally,

$$W = T_L[p] \oplus_{H[d]} T_R[p] = H[d]; \text{qif } [d] |L\rangle \to T_L[p]$$
$$\square \quad |R\rangle \to T_R[p]$$
$$\textbf{fiq}$$

where T_L and T_R are the left and right translation operators, respectively, in the position space $\mathcal{H}_p$. The Hadamard walk is then defined in a simple way of recursion with the single-step operator W, namely *repeated applications* of W.

Now we slightly modify the Hadamard walk using a little bit more complicated form of recursion.

Example 7.2.1

(i) *The unidirectionally recursive Hadamard walk first runs the "coin-tossing" Hadamard operator $H[d]$ and then a quantum case statement:*
  - *If the "direction coin" d is in state $|L\rangle$ then the walker moves one position left;*
  - *If d is in state $|R\rangle$ then it moves one position right, followed by **a procedure behaving as the recursive walk itself**.*

  Using the syntax presented in the last section, the unidirectionally recursive Hadamard walk can be precisely defined to be a recursive program X declared by the following equation:

$$X \Leftarrow T_L[p] \oplus_{H[d]} (T_R[p]; X) \tag{7.2}$$

  where d, p are the direction and position variables, respectively.

(ii) *The bidirectionally recursive Hadamard walk first runs the "coin-tossing" Hadamard operator $H[d]$ and then a quantum case statement:*
  - *If the "direction coin" d is in state $|L\rangle$ then the walker moves one position left, followed by **a procedure behaving as the recursive walk itself**;*
  - *If d is in state $|R\rangle$ then it moves one position right, also followed by **a procedure behaving as the recursive walk itself**.*

  More precisely, the walk can be defined to be the program X declared by the following recursive equation:

$$X \Leftarrow (T_L[p]; X) \oplus_{H[d]} (T_R[p]; X). \tag{7.3}$$

(iii) *A variant of the bidirectionally recursive Hadamard walk is the program X (or Y) declared by the following system of recursive equations:*

$$\begin{cases} X \Leftarrow T_L[p] \oplus_{H[d]} (T_R[p]; Y), \\ Y \Leftarrow (T_L[p]; X) \oplus_{H[d]} T_R[p]. \end{cases} \tag{7.4}$$

  The main difference between recursive equations (7.3) and (7.4) is that in the former procedure identifier X is calling itself, but in the latter X is calling Y and at the same time Y is calling X.

(iv) *Note that we used the same "coin" d in the two equations of (7.4). If two different "coins" d and e are used, then we have another variant of the bidirectionally recursive Hadamard walk specified by*

$$\begin{cases} X \Leftarrow T_L[p] \oplus_{H[d]} (T_R[p]; Y), \\ Y \Leftarrow (T_L[p]; X) \oplus_{H[e]} T_R[p]. \end{cases} \tag{7.5}$$

(v) *We can define a recursive quantum walk in another way if a quantum case statement with three branches is employed:*

$$X \Leftarrow U[d]; \mathbf{qif}\ [d]\ |L\rangle \to T_L[p]$$
$$\square \qquad |R\rangle \to T_R[p]$$
$$\square \qquad |I\rangle \to X$$
$$\mathbf{fiq}$$

where d is not a qubit but a qutrit, i.e., a quantum system with 3-dimensional state Hilbert space $\mathcal{H}_d = span\{|L\rangle, |R\rangle, |I\rangle\}$, L, R stand for the directions Left and Right, respectively, and I for Iteration, and U is a 3×3 unitary matrix, e.g. the 3-dimensional Fourier transform:

$$F_3 = \begin{pmatrix} 1 & 1 & 1 \\ 1 & e^{\frac{2}{3}\pi i} & e^{\frac{4}{3}\pi i} \\ 1 & e^{\frac{4}{3}\pi i} & e^{\frac{2}{3}\pi i} \end{pmatrix}.$$

Now let us have a glimpse of the behaviors of recursive quantum walks. We employ an idea similar to that used in Section 3.2. We use E to denote the empty program or termination. A configuration is defined to be a pair

$$\langle S, |\psi\rangle \rangle$$

with S being a program or the empty program E, and $|\psi\rangle$ a pure state of the quantum system. Then the behavior of a program can be visualized by a sequence of transitions between superpositions of configurations. Note that in Section 3.2 the computation of a program is a sequence of transitions between configurations. Here, however, we have to consider transitions between superpositions of configurations. Naturally, these superpositions of configurations are generated by quantum control flow of the program.

We only consider the unidirectionally recursive quantum walk X declared by equation (7.2) as an example. The reader is encouraged to work out the first few transitions of other walks in the preceding example in order to better understand how quantum recursive calls happen. Assume that it is initialized in state $|L\rangle_d|0\rangle_p$; that is, the "coin" is in direction L and the walker is at position 0. Then we have:

$$\langle X, |L\rangle_d |0\rangle_p \rangle \overset{(a)}{\to} \frac{1}{\sqrt{2}} \langle E, |L\rangle_d |-1\rangle_p \rangle + \frac{1}{\sqrt{2}} \langle X, |R\rangle_d |1\rangle_p \rangle$$

$$\overset{(b)}{\to} \frac{1}{\sqrt{2}} \langle E, |L\rangle_d |-1\rangle_p \rangle + \frac{1}{2} \langle E, |R\rangle_d |L\rangle_{d_1} |0\rangle_p \rangle + \frac{1}{2} \langle X, |R\rangle_d |R\rangle_{d_1} |2\rangle_p \rangle$$

$$\to \dots \dots \tag{7.6}$$

$$\to \sum_{i=0}^{n} \frac{1}{\sqrt{2^{i+1}}} \langle E, |R\rangle_{d_0} \dots |R\rangle_{d_{i-1}} |L\rangle_{d_i} |i-1\rangle_p \rangle$$

$$+ \frac{1}{\sqrt{2^{n+1}}} \langle X, |R\rangle_{d_0} \dots |R\rangle_{d_{n-1}} |R\rangle_{d_n} |n+1\rangle_p \rangle$$

Here, $d_0 = d$, and new quantum "coins" $d_1, d_2, \dots$ that are identical to the original "coin" d are introduced in order to avoid the conflict of variables for "coins." To see why these distinct "coins" $d_1, d_2, \dots$ have to be introduced, we recall from Sections 6.1 and 6.2 that the "coins" $\bar{q}$ in a quantum case statement **qif** $[\bar{q}]$ $(\square i \cdot |i\rangle \to S_i)$ **fiq** are required to be external to subprograms S_i. Therefore, in equation (7.2) "coin" d is external to procedure X. Now let us see what happens in equation (7.6). First, the term after the arrow $\overset{(a)}{\to}$ is obtained by replacing the symbol X in the term before $\overset{(a)}{\to}$ with $T_L[p] \oplus_{H[d]} (T_R[p]; X)$. So, in the term after $\overset{(a)}{\to}$, d is external to X. To obtain the term after $\overset{(b)}{\to}$, we replace the symbol X in the term after $\overset{(a)}{\to}$ by $T_L[p] \oplus_{H[d_1]} (T_R[p]; X)$. Here, d_1 must be different from d; otherwise in the term after $\overset{(a)}{\to}$, $d = d_1$ occurs (although implicitly) in X, and thus a contradiction occurs. Repeating this argument illustrates that $d_0 = d, d_1, d_2, \dots$ should be different from each other.

Exercise 7.2.1. *Show the first few steps of recursive quantum walks defined by equations (7.4) and (7.5) initialized in $|L\rangle_d |0\rangle_p$. Observe the difference between the behaviors of the two walks. Notice that such a difference is impossible for classical random walks, where it does not matter if two different "coins" with the same probability distribution are used.*

The preceding recursive quantum walks are good examples of quantum recursion, but their behaviors are not very interesting from the viewpoint of quantum physics. As pointed out in Subsection 2.3.4, the major difference between the behaviors of classical random walks and quantum walks is caused by quantum interference – two separate paths leading to the same point may be out of phase and cancel one another. It is clear from equation (7.6) that quantum interference does not happen in the unidirectionally recursive quantum walk. Similarly, no quantum interference occurs in the other recursive quantum walks defined in the preceding example. The following is a much more interesting recursive quantum walk that shows a new phenomenon of quantum interference. As can be seen in equation (2.19), the paths that are cancelled in a (nonrecursive) quantum walk are finite. However, it is possible that infinite paths are cancelled in a recursive quantum walk.

Example 7.2.2. *Let $n \geq 2$. A variant of a bidirectionally recursive quantum walk can be defined as the program X declared by the following recursive equation:*

$$X \Leftarrow (T_L[p] \oplus_{H[d]} T_R[p])^n; ((T_L[p]; X) \oplus_{H[d]} (T_R[p]; X)) \tag{7.7}$$

Here, we use S^n to denote the sequential composition of n copies of a program S.

Now let us look at the behavior of this walk. We assume that the walk is initialized in state $|L\rangle_d|0\rangle_p$. Then the first three steps of the walk are given as follows:

$$\langle X, |L\rangle_d|0\rangle_p \rangle \rightarrow \frac{1}{\sqrt{2}}[\langle X_1, |L\rangle_d|-1\rangle_p\rangle + \langle X_1, |R\rangle_d|1\rangle_p\rangle]$$

$$\rightarrow \frac{1}{2}[\langle X_2, |L\rangle_d|-2\rangle_p\rangle + \langle X_2, |R\rangle_d|0\rangle_p\rangle + \langle X_2, |L\rangle_d|0\rangle_p\rangle - \langle X_2, |R\rangle_d|2\rangle_p\rangle]$$

$$\rightarrow \frac{1}{2\sqrt{2}}[\langle X_3, |L\rangle_d|-3\rangle_p\rangle + \langle X_3, |R\rangle_d|-1\rangle_p\rangle + \langle X_3, |L\rangle_d|-1\rangle_p\rangle - \langle X_3, |R\rangle_d|1\rangle_p\rangle$$

$$+ \langle X_3, |L\rangle_d|-1\rangle_p\rangle + \langle X_3, |R\rangle_d|1\rangle_p\rangle - \langle X_3, |L\rangle_d|1\rangle_p\rangle + \langle X_3, |R\rangle_d|3\rangle_p\rangle]$$

$$= \frac{1}{2\sqrt{2}}[\langle X_3, |L\rangle_d|-3\rangle_p\rangle + \langle X_3, |R\rangle_d|-1\rangle_p\rangle + 2\langle X_3, |L\rangle_d|-1\rangle_p\rangle$$

$$- \langle X_3, |L\rangle_d|1\rangle_p\rangle + \langle X_3, |R\rangle_d|3\rangle_p\rangle] \tag{7.8}$$

where

$$X_i = (T_L[p] \oplus_{H[d]} T_R[p])^{n-i}; ((T_L[p]; X) \oplus_{H[d]} (T_R[p]; X))$$

for $i = 1, 2, 3$. We observe that in the last step of equation (7.8) two configurations

$$-\langle X_3, |R\rangle_d|1\rangle_p\rangle, \quad \langle X_3, |R\rangle_d|1\rangle_p\rangle$$

cancel one another. It is clear that both of them can generate infinite paths because they contain the recursive walk X itself. Comparing equation (7.8) with (7.6), the reader may wonder why no new "coins" were introduced in (7.8). Actually, only the part $(T_L[p] \oplus_{H[d]} T_R[p])^n$ in the right-hand side of equation (7.7) is executed and no recursive calls happen in the three steps given in equation (7.8). Of course, fresh "coins" will be needed in the later steps where X is recursively called in order to avoid variable conflicts.

The behavior of the recursive program specified by the following equation:

$$X \Leftarrow ((T_L[p]; X) \oplus_{H[d]} (T_R[p]; X)); (T_L[p] \oplus_{H[d]} T_R[p])^n \tag{7.9}$$

is even more puzzling. Note that equation (7.9) is obtained from equation (7.7) by changing the order of the two subprograms on the right-hand side.

Exercise 7.2.2. *Examine the behavior of the walk X declared by equation (7.9) starting at $|L\rangle_d|0\rangle_p$.*

7.2.2 HOW TO SOLVE RECURSIVE QUANTUM EQUATIONS

We have already seen from equations (7.6) and (7.8) the first steps of the recursive quantum walks. But a precise description of their behaviors amounts to solving recursive equations (7.2), (7.3), (7.4), (7.5) and (7.7). In the theory of classical programming languages, syntactic approximation is employed to define the semantics of recursive programs. It was also successfully used in Section 3.4 to define the semantics of recursive quantum programs. Naturally, we would like to see whether syntactic approximation can be applied to quantum recursive programs too. To begin with, let us recall this technique by considering a simple recursive program declared by a single equation

$$X \Leftarrow F(X).$$

Let

$$\begin{cases} X^{(0)} = \textbf{abort}, \\ X^{(n+1)} = F[X^{(n)}/X] \text{ for } n \geq 0. \end{cases}$$

where $F[X^{(n)}/X]$ is the result of substitution of X in $F(X)$ by $X^{(n)}$. The program $X^{(n)}$ is called the nth syntactic approximation of X. Roughly speaking, the syntactic approximations $X^{(n)}$ ($n = 0, 1, 2, \ldots$) describe the initial fragments of the behavior of the recursive program X. Then the semantics $[\![X]\!]$ of X is defined to be the limit of the semantics $[\![X^{(n)}]\!]$ of its syntactic approximations $X^{(n)}$:

$$[\![X]\!] = \lim_{n \to \infty} [\![X^{(n)}]\!].$$

Now we try to apply this method to the unidirectionally recursive Hadamard walk and construct its syntactic approximations as follows:

$$X^{(0)} = \textbf{abort},$$
$$X^{(1)} = T_L[p] \oplus_{H[d]} (T_R[p]; \textbf{abort}),$$
$$X^{(2)} = T_L[p] \oplus_{H[d]} (T_R[p]; T_L[p] \oplus_{H[d_1]} (T_R[p]; \textbf{abort})),$$
$$X^{(3)} = T_L[p] \oplus_{H[d]} (T_R[p]; T_L[p] \oplus_{H[d_1]} (T_R[p]; T_L[p] \oplus_{H[d_2]} (T_R[p]; \textbf{abort}))),$$
$$\cdots\cdots\cdots\cdots \tag{7.10}$$

However, a problem arises in constructing these approximations: we have to continuously introduce new "coin" variables in order to avoid variable conflict; that is, for every $n = 1, 2, \ldots$, we have to introduce a new "coin" variable d_n in the $(n+1)$th syntactic approximation because, as emphasized many times before, "coins" $d, d_1, \ldots, d_{n-1}$ should be considered external to the innermost system that contains d_n. Therefore, variables $d, d_1, d_2, \ldots, d_n, \ldots$ denote distinct "coins." On the other hand, they must be thought of as identical particles in the sense that their physical properties are the same. Moreover, the number of the "coin" particles that are needed in running the recursive Hadamard walk is usually unknown beforehand because we do not know when the walk terminates. Obviously, a solution to this problem requires a mathematical framework in which we can deal with quantum systems where the number of particles of the same type – the "coins" – may vary. It is worth noting that this problem appears only in the quantum case but not in the theory of classical programming languages, because it is caused by employing an external "coin" system in defining a quantum case statement.

7.3 SECOND QUANTIZATION

At the end of the last section, we observed that solving a quantum recursive equation requires a mathematical model of a quantum system consisting of a variable number of identical particles. It is clear that such a model is out of the scope of basic quantum mechanics described in Section 2.1, where we only considered a composite quantum system with a fixed number of subsystems that are not necessarily identical (see the Postulate of quantum mechanics 4 in Subsection 2.1.5). Fortunately, physicists had developed a formalism for describing quantum systems with variable particle number, namely second quantization, more than 80 years ago. For the convenience of the reader, we give a brief introduction to the second quantization method in this section. This introduction focuses on the mathematical formulation of second quantization needed in the sequent sections; for physical interpretations, the reader can consult reference [163].

7.3.1 MULTIPLE-PARTICLE STATES

We first consider a quantum system of a fixed number of particles. It is assumed that these particles have the same state Hilbert space, but they are not necessarily identical particles. Let $\mathcal{H}$ be the state Hilbert space of a single particle. For any $n \geq 1$, we can define the tensor product $\mathcal{H}^{\otimes n}$ of n copies of $\mathcal{H}$ by Definition 2.1.18. For any family $|\psi_1\rangle, \ldots, |\psi_n\rangle$ of single-particle states in $\mathcal{H}$, the Postulate of quantum mechanics 4 asserts that we have a state

$$|\psi_1\rangle \otimes \cdots \otimes |\psi_n\rangle = |\psi_1 \otimes \cdots \otimes \psi_n\rangle$$

of n independent particles, in which the ith particle is in state $|\psi_i\rangle$ for every $1 \leq i \leq n$. Then $\mathcal{H}^{\otimes n}$ consists of the linear combinations of vectors $|\psi_1 \otimes \cdots \otimes \psi_n\rangle$:

$$
\begin{aligned}
\mathcal{H}^{\otimes n} &= span\{|\psi_1 \otimes \cdots \otimes \psi_n\rangle : |\psi_1\rangle, \ldots, |\psi_n\rangle \in \mathcal{H}\} \\
&= \left\{ \sum_{i=1}^{m} \alpha_i |\psi_{i1} \otimes \cdots \otimes \psi_{in}\rangle : m \geq 0, \alpha_i \in \mathbb{C}, |\psi_{i1}\rangle, \ldots, |\psi_{in}\rangle \in \mathcal{H} \right\}.
\end{aligned}
$$

Recall from Subsection 2.1.5 that $\mathcal{H}^{\otimes n}$ is a Hilbert space too. More explicitly, the basic operations of vectors in $\mathcal{H}^{\otimes n}$ are defined by the following equations together with linearity:

(i) Addition:

$$|\psi_1 \otimes \cdots \otimes \psi_i \otimes \cdots \otimes \psi_n\rangle + |\psi_1 \otimes \cdots \otimes \psi_i' \otimes \cdots \otimes \psi_n\rangle$$
$$= |\psi_1 \otimes \cdots \otimes (\psi_i + \psi_i') \otimes \cdots \otimes \psi_n\rangle;$$

(ii) Scalar product:

$$\lambda|\psi_1 \otimes \cdots \otimes \psi_i \otimes \cdots \otimes \psi_n\rangle = |\psi_1 \otimes \cdots \otimes (\lambda\psi_i) \otimes \cdots \otimes \psi_n\rangle;$$

(iii) Inner product:

$$\langle\psi_1 \otimes \cdots \otimes \psi_n|\varphi_1 \otimes \cdots \otimes \varphi_n\rangle = \prod_{i=1}^{n} \langle\psi_i|\varphi_i\rangle.$$

Exercise 7.3.1. *Show that if $\mathcal{B}$ is a basis of $\mathcal{H}$, then*

$$\{|\psi_1 \otimes \cdots \otimes \psi_n\rangle : |\psi_1\rangle, \ldots, |\psi_n\rangle \in \mathcal{B}\}$$

is a basis of $\mathcal{H}^{\otimes n}$.

Permutation Operators:

Now we turn to consider a quantum system of multiple identical particles that possess the same intrinsic properties. Let us start by introducing several operators for describing the symmetry of identical particles. For each permutation π of $1, \ldots, n$, i.e., a bijection from $\{1, \ldots, n\}$ onto itself that maps i to $\pi(i)$ for every $1 \leq i \leq n$, we can define the permutation operator P_π in the space $\mathcal{H}^{\otimes n}$ by

$$P_\pi|\psi_1 \otimes \cdots \otimes \psi_n\rangle = |\psi_{\pi(1)} \otimes \cdots \otimes \psi_{\pi(n)}\rangle$$

together with linearity. Several basic properties of permutation operators are given in the following:

Proposition 7.3.1

(i) P_π *is a unitary operator.*

(ii) $P_{\pi_1}P_{\pi_2} = P_{\pi_1\pi_2}$, $P_\pi^\dagger = P_{\pi^{-1}}$, *where $\pi_1\pi_2$ is the composition of π_1 and π_2, $P_\pi^\dagger$ stands for the conjugate transpose (i.e., inverse) of P_π, and π^{-1} is the inverse of π.*

Furthermore, symmetrization and antisymmetrization operators can be defined in terms of permutation operators:

Definition 7.3.1. *The symmetrization and antisymmetrization operators in $\mathcal{H}^{\otimes n}$ are defined by*

$$S_+ = \frac{1}{n!} \sum_\pi P_\pi,$$

$$S_- = \frac{1}{n!} \sum_\pi (-1)^\pi P_\pi,$$

where π traverses over all permutations of $1, \ldots, n$, and $(-1)^\pi$ is the signature of the permutation π; that is,

$$(-1)^\pi = \begin{cases} 1 & \text{if } \pi \text{ is even,} \\ -1 & \text{if } \pi \text{ is odd.} \end{cases}$$

We list several useful properties of symmetrization and antisymmetrization in the following:

Proposition 7.3.2

(i) $P_\pi S_+ = S_+ P_\pi = S_+$.
(ii) $P_\pi S_- = S_- P_\pi = (-1)^\pi S_-$.
(iii) $S_+^2 = S_+ = S_+^\dagger$.
(iv) $S_-^2 = S_- = S_-^\dagger$.
(v) $S_+ S_- = S_- S_+ = 0$.

Exercise 7.3.2. *Prove Propositions 7.3.1 and 7.3.2.*
Symmetric and Antisymmetric States:
Of course, quantum mechanics described in Section 2.1 can be used to cope with a quantum system of multiple particles. However, it is not complete when these particles are identical, and it must be supplemented by the following:

- **The principle of symmetrization:** The states of n identical particles are either completely symmetric or completely antisymmetric with the permutation of the n particles.
  - The symmetric particles are called *bosons*;
  - The antisymmetric particles are called *fermions*.

At the beginning of this subsection, we saw that $\mathcal{H}^{\otimes n}$ is the state Hilbert space of n particles if all of them have the same state space $\mathcal{H}$. According to the preceding principle, it is not the case that every vector in $\mathcal{H}^{\otimes n}$ can be used to denote a state of n identical particles. However, for each state $|\Psi\rangle$ in $\mathcal{H}^{\otimes n}$, we can construct the following two states by symmetrization or antisymmetrization:

- a symmetric (bosonic) state: $S_+|\Psi\rangle$;
- an antisymmetric (a fermionic) state: $S_-|\Psi\rangle$.

In particular, the symmetric and antisymmetric states corresponding to the product of one-particle states $|\psi_1\rangle, \ldots, |\psi_n\rangle$ are written as

$$|\psi_1, \cdots, \psi_n\rangle_v = S_v|\psi_1 \otimes \cdots \otimes \psi_n\rangle_v$$

where v is $+$ or $-$. With this notation, the principle of symmetrization can be restated as follows:

- For the bosons, the order of states $|\psi_i\rangle$ in $|\psi_1, \cdots, \psi_n\rangle_+$ is insignificant.
- For the fermions, $|\psi_1, \cdots, \psi_n\rangle_-$ changes sign under permutations of two states:

$$|\psi_1, \cdots, \psi_i, \cdots, \psi_j, \cdots, \psi_n\rangle_- = -|\psi_1, \cdots, \psi_j, \cdots, \psi_i, \cdots, \psi_n\rangle_-. \qquad (7.11)$$

An immediate corollary of equation (7.11) is the following:

- **Pauli's exclusion principle:** If two states $|\psi_i\rangle$ and $|\psi_j\rangle$ are identical, then $|\psi_1, \cdots, \psi_i, \cdots, \psi_j, \cdots, \psi_n\rangle_-$ vanishes – two fermions can never be found in the same individual quantum state.

In summary, the principle of symmetrization implies that the state space of a system of n identical particles is not the total of $\mathcal{H}^{\otimes n}$, but rather one of the following two subspaces:

Definition 7.3.2

(i) *The n-fold symmetric tensor product of $\mathcal{H}$:*

$$\mathcal{H}_+^{\otimes n} = S_+\left(\mathcal{H}^{\otimes n}\right)$$

$$= \textit{the closed subspace of } \mathcal{H}^{\otimes n} \textit{ generated by the symmetric}$$
$$\textit{tensor products } |\psi_1, \cdots, \psi_n\rangle_+ \textit{ with } |\psi_1\rangle, \ldots, |\psi_n\rangle \in \mathcal{H}$$

(ii) *The n-fold antisymmetric tensor product of $\mathcal{H}$:*

$$\mathcal{H}_-^{\otimes n} = S_-\left(\mathcal{H}^{\otimes n}\right)$$

$$= \textit{the closed subspace of } \mathcal{H}^{\otimes n} \textit{ generated by the antisymmetric}$$
$$\textit{tensor products } |\psi_1, \cdots, \psi_n\rangle_- \textit{ with } |\psi_1\rangle, \ldots, |\psi_n\rangle \in \mathcal{H}$$

The addition, scalar product and inner product in $\mathcal{H}_\nu^{\otimes n}$ ($\nu = +, -$) are directly inherited from $\mathcal{H}^{\otimes n}$. In particular, the following proposition provides a convenient way to compute the inner products in $\mathcal{H}_\pm^{\otimes n}$:

Proposition 7.3.3. *The inner product of symmetric and antisymmetric tensor products:*

$$+\langle\psi_1, \cdots, \psi_n|\varphi_1, \cdots, \varphi_n\rangle_+ = \frac{1}{n!}per\left(\langle\psi_i|\varphi_j\rangle\right)_{ij},$$

$$-\langle\psi_1, \cdots, \psi_n|\varphi_1, \cdots, \varphi_n\rangle_- = \frac{1}{n!}det\left(\langle\psi_i|\varphi_j\rangle\right)_{ij},$$

where det and per stand for the determinant of matrix and the permutation (i.e., the determinant without the minus signs), respectively.

Exercise 7.3.3

(i) *Compute the dimensions of the symmetric and antisymmetric tensor product spaces $\mathcal{H}_\pm^{\otimes n}$.*

(ii) *Prove Proposition 7.3.3.*

7.3.2 FOCK SPACES

Quantum systems of a fixed number of identical particles were studied in the last subsection. Now let us see how to describe a quantum system with a variable number of particles. A natural idea is that the state Hilbert space of such a system is the direct sum of the state spaces of different numbers of particles. To realize this idea, let us first introduce the notion of direct sum of Hilbert spaces.

Definition 7.3.3. *Let* $\mathcal{H}_1, \mathcal{H}_2, \ldots$ *be an infinite sequence of Hilbert spaces. Then their direct sum is defined to be the vector space:*

$$\bigoplus_{i=1}^{\infty} \mathcal{H}_i = \left\{ (|\psi_1\rangle, |\psi_2\rangle, \ldots) : |\psi_i\rangle \in \mathcal{H}_i \ (i = 1, 2, \ldots) \ \text{with} \ \sum_{i=1}^{\infty} |||\psi_i||^2 < \infty \right\}$$

in which we define:

- *Addition:*

$$(|\psi_1\rangle, |\psi_2\rangle, \ldots) + (|\varphi_1\rangle, |\varphi_2\rangle, \ldots) = (|\psi_1\rangle + |\varphi_1\rangle, |\psi_2\rangle + |\varphi_2\rangle, \ldots);$$

- *Scalar multiplication:*

$$\alpha(|\psi_1\rangle, |\psi_2\rangle, \ldots) = (\alpha|\psi_1\rangle, \alpha|\psi_2\rangle, \ldots);$$

- *Inner product:*

$$\langle (\psi_1, \psi_2, \ldots) | (\varphi_1, \varphi_2, \ldots) \rangle = \sum_{i=1}^{\infty} \langle \psi_i | \varphi_i \rangle.$$

Exercise 7.3.4. *Show that* $\bigoplus_{i=1}^{\infty} \mathcal{H}_i$ *is a Hilbert space.*

Let $\mathcal{H}$ be the state Hilbert space of one particle. If we introduce the vacuum state $|0\rangle$, then the 0-fold tensor product of $\mathcal{H}$ can be defined as the one-dimensional space

$$\mathcal{H}^{\otimes 0} = \mathcal{H}_{\pm}^{\otimes 0} = span\{|0\rangle\}.$$

Now we are ready to describe the state space of a quantum system with a variable number of identical particles.

Definition 7.3.4

(i) *The free Fock space over* $\mathcal{H}$ *is defined to be the direct sum of the n-fold tensor products of* $\mathcal{H}$:

$$\mathcal{F}(\mathcal{H}) = \bigoplus_{n=0}^{\infty} \mathcal{H}^{\otimes n}.$$

(ii) *The symmetric (bosonic) Fock space and the antisymmetric (fermionic) Fock space over* $\mathcal{H}$ *are defined by*

$$\mathcal{F}_v(\mathcal{H}) = \bigoplus_{n=0}^{\infty} \mathcal{H}_v^{\otimes n}$$

where $v = +$ for bosons or $v = -$ for fermions.

The principle of symmetrization tells us that only the symmetric or antisymmetric Fock space is meaningful in physics, but here we also introduce the free Fock space since it is a useful mathematical tool that is sometimes easier to deal with than the symmetric and antisymmetric Fock spaces, as we will see in the next section.

To understand the Fock spaces better, let us look more carefully at the states and operations in them:

(i) A state in $\mathcal{F}_v(\mathcal{H})$ is of the form:

$$|\Psi\rangle = \sum_{n=0}^{\infty} |\Psi(n)\rangle \stackrel{\triangle}{=} (|\Psi(0)\rangle, |\Psi(1)\rangle, \cdots, |\Psi(n)\rangle, \cdots)$$

where $|\Psi(n)\rangle \in \mathcal{H}_v^{\otimes n}$ is a state of n particles for all $n = 0, 1, 2, \ldots$, and

$$\sum_{n=0}^{\infty} \langle \Psi(n)|\Psi(n)\rangle < \infty.$$

(ii) Basic operations in $\mathcal{F}_v(\mathcal{H})$:
- Addition:

$$\left(\sum_{n=0}^{\infty} |\Psi(n)\rangle\right) + \left(\sum_{n=0}^{\infty} |\Phi(n)\rangle\right) = \sum_{n=0}^{\infty} (|\Psi(n)\rangle + |\Phi(n)\rangle);$$

- Scalar product:

$$\alpha \left(\sum_{n=0}^{\infty} |\Psi(n)\rangle\right) = \sum_{n=0}^{\infty} \alpha|\Psi(n)\rangle;$$

- Inner product:

$$\left\langle \sum_{n=0}^{\infty} \Psi(n)\Big| \sum_{n=0}^{\infty} \Phi(n) \right\rangle = \sum_{n=0}^{\infty} \langle \Psi(n)|\Phi(n)\rangle.$$

(iii) Basis of $\mathcal{F}_v(\mathcal{H})$: The symmetric or antisymmetric product states $|\psi_1, \ldots, \psi_n\rangle_v$ ($n \geq 0$ and $|\psi_1\rangle, \ldots, |\psi_n\rangle \in \mathcal{H}$) form a basis of Fock space $\mathcal{F}_v(\mathcal{H})$; that is,

$$\mathcal{F}_v(\mathcal{H}) = span\{|\psi_1, \cdots, \psi_n\rangle_v : n = 0, 1, 2, \ldots \text{ and } |\psi_1\rangle, \ldots, |\psi_n\rangle \in \mathcal{H}\}$$

where $|\psi_1, \cdots, \psi_n\rangle_v$ is the vacuum state $|0\rangle$ if $n = 0$.

(iv) We identify state $(0, \ldots, 0, |\Psi(n)\rangle, 0, \ldots, 0)$ in $\mathcal{F}_v(\mathcal{H})$ with the state $|\Psi(n)\rangle$ in $\mathcal{H}_v^{\otimes n}$. Then $\mathcal{H}_v^{\otimes n}$ can be seen as a subspace of $\mathcal{F}_v(\mathcal{H})$. Moreover, for different particle numbers $m \neq n$, $\mathcal{H}_v^{\otimes m}$ and $\mathcal{H}_v^{\otimes n}$ are orthogonal because $\langle \Psi(m)|\Psi(n)\rangle = 0$.

Operators in Fock Spaces:

We already learned that a state of a quantum system with a variable number of identical particles can be represented by a vector in the Fock spaces. Now we move forward to prepare the mathematical tools for the description of observables and evolution of such a quantum system. We first define operators in the direct sum of Hilbert spaces.

Definition 7.3.5. *For each $i \geq 1$, let A_i be a bounded operator on $\mathcal{H}_i$ such that the sequence $\|A_i\|$ $(i = 1, 2, \ldots)$ of norms (see Definition 2.1.11) is bounded; that is, $\|A_i\| \leq C$ $(i = 1, 2, \ldots)$ for some constant C. Then we define operator*

$$A = (A_1, A_2, \ldots)$$

in $\bigoplus_{i=1}^{\infty} \mathcal{H}_i$ as follows:

$$A(|\psi_1\rangle, |\psi_2\rangle, \ldots) = (A_1|\psi_1\rangle, A_2|\psi_2\rangle, \ldots) \tag{7.12}$$

for every $(|\psi_1\rangle, |\psi_2\rangle, \ldots) \in \bigoplus_{i=1}^{\infty} \mathcal{H}_i$.

Similarly, we can define operator $A = (A_1, \ldots, A_n)$ in the direct sum $\bigoplus_{i=1}^{n} \mathcal{H}_i$ for a finite number n.

We often write:

$$\sum_{i=1}^{\infty} A_i = (A_1, A_2, \ldots) \text{ and } \sum_{i=1}^{n} A_i = (A_1, \ldots, A_n).$$

Exercise 7.3.5. *Show that A defined by equation (7.12) is a bounded operator in $\bigoplus_{i=1}^{\infty} \mathcal{H}_i$ and*

$$\|A\| \leq \sup_{i=1}^{\infty} \|A_i\|.$$

Now we can use this idea to define operators in Fock spaces. For each $n \geq 1$, let $\mathbf{A}(n)$ be an operator in $\mathcal{H}^{\otimes n}$. Then operator

$$\mathbf{A} = \sum_{n=0}^{\infty} \mathbf{A}(n) \tag{7.13}$$

can be defined in the free Fock space $\mathcal{F}(\mathcal{H})$ by Definition 7.3.5:

$$\mathbf{A}|\Psi\rangle = \mathbf{A}\left(\sum_{n=0}^{\infty} |\Psi(n)\rangle\right) = \sum_{n=0}^{\infty} \mathbf{A}(n)|\Psi(n)\rangle$$

for any

$$|\Psi\rangle = \sum_{n=0}^{\infty} |\Psi(n)\rangle$$

in $\mathcal{F}(\mathcal{H})$, where $\mathbf{A}|0\rangle = 0$; that is, the vacuum state is considered to be an eigenvector of operator $\mathbf{A}$ with eigenvalue 0. Obviously, for all $n \geq 0$, $\mathcal{H}_v^{\otimes n}$ is invariant under $\mathbf{A}$; that is, $\mathbf{A}(\mathcal{H}_v^{\otimes n}) \subseteq \mathcal{H}_v^{\otimes n}$.

A general operator in the form of (7.13) does not necessarily preserve symmetry (respectively, antisymmetry) of bosons (respectively, fermions). To define an operator in the bosonic or fermionic Fock space, we need to consider its symmetry.

Definition 7.3.6. *If for each $n \geq 0$ and for each permutation π of $1, \ldots, n$, P_π and $\mathbf{A}(n)$ commute; that is,*

$$P_\pi \mathbf{A}(n) = \mathbf{A}(n) P_\pi,$$

then operator $\mathbf{A} = \sum_{n=0}^{\infty} \mathbf{A}(n)$ is said to be symmetric.

It is easy to see that both the symmetric Fock space $\mathcal{F}_+(\mathcal{H})$ and the antisymmetric Fock space $\mathcal{F}_-(\mathcal{H})$ are closed under a symmetric operator $\mathbf{A} = \sum_{n=0}^{\infty} \mathbf{A}(n)$:

$$\mathbf{A}(\mathcal{F}_v(\mathcal{H})) \subseteq \mathcal{F}_v(\mathcal{H})$$

for $v = +, -$. In other words, a symmetric operator $\mathbf{A}$ maps a bosonic (or fermionic) state $|\Psi\rangle$ to a bosonic (respectively, fermionic) state $\mathbf{A}|\Psi\rangle$.

Exercise 7.3.6. *Is the following statement correct: if an operator $\mathbf{A}$ in $\mathcal{F}(\mathcal{H})$ satisfies that $\mathbf{A}(\mathcal{F}_+(\mathcal{H})) \subseteq \mathcal{F}_+(\mathcal{H})$ (or $\mathbf{A}(\mathcal{F}_-(\mathcal{H})) \subseteq \mathcal{F}_-(\mathcal{H})$), then $\mathbf{A}$ is symmetric? Prove your conclusion.*

We can further introduce the symmetrization functional $\mathbb{S}$ that maps every operator $\mathbf{A} = \sum_{n=0}^{\infty} \mathbf{A}(n)$ to a symmetric operator:

$$\mathbb{S}(\mathbf{A}) = \sum_{n=0}^{\infty} \mathbb{S}(\mathbf{A}(n)) \tag{7.14}$$

where for each $n \geq 0$,

$$\mathbb{S}(\mathbf{A}(n)) = \frac{1}{n!} \sum_{\pi} P_\pi \mathbf{A}(n) P_\pi^{-1} \tag{7.15}$$

with π traversing over all permutations of $1, \ldots, n$, where P_π^{-1} is the inverse of P_π. Thus, each operator $\mathbf{A}$ in the free Fock space can be transformed by the symmetrization functional $\mathbb{S}$ to an operator $\mathbf{S}(\mathbf{A})$ that can be properly applied in the bosonic or fermionic Fock spaces.

7.3.3 OBSERVABLES IN FOCK SPACES

In the last subsection, Fock spaces were introduced as the state Hilbert spaces of quantum systems with variable particle number. We also studied various operators in the Fock spaces. Now we see how to describe the observables of these systems.

Many-Body Observables:

To warm up, let us start with the observables of a fixed number $n \geq 1$ of particles. By the basic postulates of quantum mechanics, in general, an observable of a quantum system with n particles can be expressed by a Hermitian operator in $\mathcal{H}^{\otimes n}$. Here, we like to carefully look at a very special class of observables in $\mathcal{H}^{\otimes n}$.

First, let us consider the simplest case where only one of the n particles is observed. Assume that O is a single-particle observable in $\mathcal{H}$. Then for each $1 \leq i \leq n$, the action $O^{[i]}$ of O on the ith factor of $\mathcal{H}^{\otimes n}$ can be defined by

$$O^{[i]}|\psi_1 \otimes \cdots \psi_i \otimes \cdots \otimes \psi_n\rangle = |\psi_1 \otimes \cdots \otimes (O\psi_i) \otimes \cdots \otimes \psi_n\rangle$$

together with linearity; that is,

$$O^{[i]} = I^{\otimes(i-1)} \otimes O \otimes I^{\otimes(n-i)},$$

where I is the identity operator in $\mathcal{H}$. Obviously, for a fixed i, the operator $O^{[i]}$ is not symmetric. Combining these actions $O^{[i]}$ on different particles i, we have:

Definition 7.3.7. *The one-body observable corresponding to O is*

$$O_1(n) = \sum_{i=1}^{n} O^{[i]}.$$

Secondly, we consider an observable on two of the n particles. Assume that O is an observable in the two-particle space $\mathcal{H} \otimes \mathcal{H}$. Then for any $1 \leq i < j \leq n$, we can define $O^{[ij]}$ in $\mathcal{H}^{\otimes n}$ as the operator that acts as O on the ith and jth factors of $\mathcal{H}^{\otimes n}$ and trivially on others; that is, the cylindrical extension of O in $\mathcal{H}^{\otimes n}$:

$$O^{[ij]} = O[i,j] \otimes \left(I^{\otimes(i-1)} \otimes I^{\otimes(j-i-1)} \otimes I^{\otimes(n-j)} \right).$$

If observable O is allowed to apply to any two of these n particles, we have:

Definition 7.3.8. *The two-body observable for the system of n particles corresponding to O is defined as*

$$O_2(n) = \sum_{1 \leq i < j \leq n} O^{[ij]}.$$

Exercise 7.3.7. *Show that if O is invariant under exchange of two particles: $O^{[ij]} = O^{[ji]}$ for all $1 \leq i, j \leq n$, then*

$$O_2(n) = \frac{1}{2} \sum_{i \neq j} O^{[ij]}.$$

Furthermore, we can define k-body observables $O_k(n)$ for $2 < k \leq n$ in a way similar to Definitions 7.3.7 and 7.3.8.

Observables in Fock Spaces:

The previous preparation enables us to study observables with a variable number of particles. Actually, equation (7.13) provides us with a natural way to define observables in Fock spaces; more precisely, if for each $n \geq 1$, the operator $\mathbf{A}(n)$ in equation (7.13) is an observable of n particles, then

$$\mathbf{A} = \sum_{n=0}^{\infty} \mathbf{A}(n)$$

is called an extensive observable in the free Fock space $\mathcal{F}(\mathcal{H})$. In particular, if $\mathbf{A}$ is symmetric, then it is also an observable in both the symmetric and antisymmetric Fock spaces.

The following proposition gives a convenient method for computing the mean value of an extensive observable.

Proposition 7.3.4. *The mean value of* $\mathbf{A} = \sum_{n=0}^{\infty} \mathbf{A}(n)$ *in state* $|\Psi\rangle = \sum_{n=0}^{\infty} |\Psi(n)\rangle$ *is*

$$\langle \Psi | \mathbf{A} | \Psi \rangle = \sum_{n=0}^{\infty} \langle \Psi(n) | \mathbf{A}(n) | \Psi(n) \rangle$$
$$= \sum_{n=0}^{\infty} \langle \Psi(n) | \Psi(n) \rangle \cdot \frac{\langle \Psi(n) | \mathbf{A}(n) | \Psi(n) \rangle}{\langle \Psi(n) | \Psi(n) \rangle}$$

where:

(i) $\langle \Psi(n) | \Psi(n) \rangle$ *is the probability to find n particles in the state* $|\Psi\rangle$;

(ii)

$$\frac{\langle \Psi(n) | \mathbf{A}(n) | \Psi(n) \rangle}{\langle \Psi(n) | \Psi(n) \rangle}$$

is the mean value of $\mathbf{A}(n)$ *for the system of n particles.*

To conclude this subsection, let us consider two special classes of observables in the Fock spaces. As an application of the previous procedure, for a given $k \geq 1$, the k-body observables in the free Fock space can be defined as follows:

$$\mathbf{O}_k = \sum_{n \geq k} O_k(n),$$

where for all $n \geq k$, $O_k(n)$ is the k-body observable in $\mathcal{H}^{\otimes n}$ (see Definitions 7.3.7 and 7.3.8). Furthermore, note that $\mathbf{O}_k$ is symmetric; for example, one-body observables $O_1(n)$ commute with the permutations:

$$O_1(n)|\psi_1, \ldots, \psi_n\rangle_\pm = \sum_{j=1}^{n} |\psi_1, \ldots, \psi_{j-1}, O\psi_j, \psi_{j+1}, \ldots, \psi_n\rangle_\pm.$$

A similar equation holds for $k \geq 2$. Therefore, $\mathbf{O}_k$ can be directly used in the symmetric and antisymmetric Fock spaces.

Another important observable in Fock spaces is defined in the following:

Definition 7.3.9. *The particle number operator N in $\mathcal{F}_\pm(\mathcal{H})$ is defined by*

$$\mathbf{N}\left(\sum_{n=0}^{\infty} |\Psi(n)\rangle\right) = \sum_{n=0}^{\infty} n|\Psi(n)\rangle.$$

As suggested by its name, for each $n \geq 0$, the particle number operator $\mathbf{N}$ gives the number n explicitly in front of the n-particle component $|\Psi(n)\rangle$ of $|\Psi\rangle$. Several basic properties of the particle number operator are given in the following two propositions:

Proposition 7.3.5

(i) *For each $n = 0, 1, 2 \ldots$, $\mathcal{H}_\pm^{\otimes n}$ is the eigen-subspace of $\mathbf{N}$ with eigenvalue n.*
(ii) *The mean value of $\mathbf{N}$ in state $|\Psi\rangle = \sum_{n=0}^{\infty} |\Psi(n)\rangle$ is*

$$\langle\Psi|\mathbf{N}|\Psi\rangle = \sum_{n=0}^{\infty} n\langle\Psi(n)|\Psi(n)\rangle.$$

Proposition 7.3.6. *Extensive observables* $\mathbf{A}$ *and particle number operator* $\mathbf{N}$ *commute:* $\mathbf{AN} = \mathbf{NA}$.

Exercise 7.3.8. *Prove Propositions 7.3.5 and 7.3.6.*

7.3.4 EVOLUTION IN FOCK SPACES

We now turn to consider the dynamics of a quantum system with a variable particle number. Such a quantum system can evolve in two different ways:

(i) the evolution does not change the number of particles; and
(ii) the evolution changes the number of particles.

In this subsection, we focus on the first kind of evolution, and the second will be discussed in the next subsection. Obviously, equation (7.13) also gives us a method to define an evolution of the first kind. More precisely, if for every $n \geq 0$, the dynamics of n particles is modelled by operator $\mathbf{A}(n)$, then $\mathbf{A} = \sum_{n=0}^{\infty} \mathbf{A}(n)$ describes an evolution in the Fock spaces that does not change the number of particles. Let us more carefully examine a special evolution of this kind. Assume that the (discrete-time) evolution of one particle is represented by unitary operator U. Then the evolution of n particles without mutual interactions can be described by operator

$$\mathbf{U}(n) = U^{\otimes n}$$

in $\mathcal{H}^{\otimes n}$:

$$\mathbf{U}(n)|\psi_1 \otimes \ldots \otimes \psi_n\rangle = |U\psi_1 \otimes \ldots \otimes U\psi_n\rangle \tag{7.16}$$

for all $|\psi_1\rangle, \ldots, |\psi_n\rangle$ in $\mathcal{H}$. Here, the same unitary U applies to all of the n particles simultaneously. It is easy to verify that $\mathbf{U}(n)$ commutes with the permutations:

$$\mathbf{U}(n)|\psi_1, \ldots, \psi_n\rangle_\pm = |U\psi_1, \ldots, U\psi_n\rangle_\pm.$$

Then using equation (7.13), we can define a symmetric operator in the Fock spaces:

$$\mathbf{U} = \sum_{n=0}^{\infty} \mathbf{U}(n). \tag{7.17}$$

Clearly, it depicts the evolution of a quantum system with variable number of particles but without mutual interaction between the particles.

7.3.5 CREATION AND ANNIHILATION OF PARTICLES

In the previous subsection, we learned how to describe the first kind of evolution in the Fock spaces, where the number of particles is not changed; for example, the operator $\mathbf{U}$ defined by equation (7.17) maps the states of n particles to states of particles of the same number. In this subsection, we study the second kind of evolution in the Fock spaces that can change the number of particles. Obviously, this kind of evolution cannot be treated within the basic framework of quantum mechanics presented in Section 2.1. Nevertheless, the transitions between states of different particle numbers can be described by two basic operators: creation and annihilation.

Definition 7.3.10. *For each one-particle state $|\psi\rangle$ in $\mathcal{H}$, the creation operator $a^\dagger(\psi)$ associated with $|\psi\rangle$ in $\mathcal{F}_\pm(\mathcal{H})$ is defined by*

$$a^\dagger(\psi)|\psi_1, \ldots, \psi_n\rangle_\nu = \sqrt{n+1}|\psi, \psi_1, \ldots, \psi_n\rangle_\nu \tag{7.18}$$

for any $n \geq 0$ and all $|\psi_1\rangle, \ldots, |\psi_n\rangle$ in $\mathcal{H}$, together with linearity.

From its defining equation (7.18), we see that the operator $a^\dagger(\psi)$ adds a particle in the individual state $|\psi\rangle$ to the system of n particles without modifying their respective states; in particular, the symmetry or antisymmetry of the state is preserved in this transition. The coefficient $\sqrt{n+1}$ is added in the right-hand side of equation (7.18) mainly for the sake of coefficient normalization.

Definition 7.3.11. *For each one-particle state $|\psi\rangle$ in $\mathcal{H}$, the annihilation operator $a(\psi)$ in $\mathcal{F}_\pm(\mathcal{H})$ is defined to be the Hermitian conjugate of $a^\dagger(\psi)$:*

$$a(\psi) = (a^\dagger(\psi))^\dagger$$

that is,

$$\left(a^\dagger(\psi)|\varphi_1, \ldots, \varphi_n\rangle_\nu, |\psi_1, \ldots, \psi_n\rangle_\nu\right) = (|\varphi_1, \ldots, \varphi_n\rangle_\nu, a(\psi)|\psi_1, \ldots, \psi_n\rangle_\nu) \tag{7.19}$$

for all $|\varphi_1\rangle, \ldots, |\varphi_n\rangle, |\psi_1\rangle, \ldots, |\psi_n\rangle \in \mathcal{H}$ and for every $n \geq 0$.

The following proposition gives a representation of annihilation operators.
Proposition 7.3.7

$$a(\psi)|\mathbf{0}\rangle = 0,$$

$$a(\psi)|\psi_1, \cdots, \psi_n\rangle_\pm = \frac{1}{\sqrt{n}} \sum_{i=1}^{n} (v)^i \langle \psi | \psi_i \rangle |\psi_1, \cdots, \psi_{i-1}, \psi_{i+1}, \cdots, \psi_n\rangle_\pm.$$

It can be clearly seen from this proposition that annihilation operator $a(\psi)$ decreases the number of particles by one unit, while preserving the symmetry of the state.

Exercise 7.3.9. *Prove Proposition 7.3.7. Hint: use the defining equation (7.19) of $a(\psi)$.*

7.4 SOLVING RECURSIVE EQUATIONS IN THE FREE FOCK SPACE

As convinced by an example of a recursive quantum walk at the end of Section 7.2, we have to deal with a quantum system with a variable number of identical particles in order to model the behavior of quantum "coins" employed in the execution of a quantum recursive program. So, a mathematical framework for this purpose, namely second quantization, was introduced in the last section. Indeed, second quantization provides us with all of the necessary tools for defining the semantics of quantum recursion. The purpose of this and the next sections is to carefully define the semantics of quantum recursive programs. This will be done in two steps. In this section, we show how to solve recursive equations in the free Fock spaces without considering symmetry or antisymmetry of the particles that are used to implement the quantum "coins."

7.4.1 A DOMAIN OF OPERATORS IN THE FREE FOCK SPACE

Similar to the cases of recursive classical programs and classical recursion of quantum programs studied in Section 3.4, we first need to set the stage – a domain in which we can accommodate the solutions of quantum recursive equations. In this subsection, we study such a domain as an abstract mathematical object, leaving its applications to semantics of recursive quantum programs aside. This focus can give us a better understanding of the structure of the domain.

Let C be a set of quantum "coins." For each $c \in C$, let $\mathcal{H}_c$ be the state Hilbert space of "coin" c and $\mathcal{F}(\mathcal{H}_c)$ the free Fock space over $\mathcal{H}_c$. We write

$$\mathcal{G}(\mathcal{H}_C) \triangleq \bigotimes_{c \in C} \mathcal{F}(\mathcal{H}_c)$$

for the tensor product of the free Fock spaces of all "coins." We also assume that $\mathcal{H}$ is the state Hilbert space of the principal system. Then the state space of the quantum system combining the principal system with variable numbers of "coins" is $\mathcal{G}(\mathcal{H}_C) \otimes \mathcal{H}$.

Let ω be the set of nonnegative integers. Then ω^C is the set of C-indexed tuples of nonnegative integers: $\bar{n} = \{n_c\}_{c \in C}$ with $n_c \in \omega$ for all $c \in C$. It is clear that

$$\mathcal{G}(\mathcal{H}_C) \otimes \mathcal{H} = \bigoplus_{\bar{n} \in \omega^C} \left[\left(\bigotimes_{c \in C} \mathcal{H}_c^{\otimes n_c} \right) \otimes \mathcal{H} \right]$$

Furthermore, let $\mathcal{O}(\mathcal{G}(\mathcal{H}_C) \otimes \mathcal{H})$ be the set of all operators of the form

$$\mathbf{A} = \sum_{\bar{n} \in \omega^C} \mathbf{A}(\bar{n}),$$

where $\mathbf{A}(\bar{n})$ is an operator in $\left(\bigotimes_{c \in C} \mathcal{H}_c^{\otimes n_c} \right) \otimes \mathcal{H}$ for each $\bar{n} \in \omega^C$. Then $\mathcal{O}(\mathcal{G}(\mathcal{H}_C) \otimes \mathcal{H})$ will serve as the space of the solutions of quantum recursive equations. To present the partial order in $\mathcal{O}(\mathcal{G}(\mathcal{H}_C) \otimes \mathcal{H})$ needed for solving quantum recursive equations, we first define a partial order $\leq$ in ω^C as follows:

- $\bar{n} \leq \bar{m}$ if and only if $n_c \leq m_c$ for all $c \in C$.

A subset $\Omega \subseteq \omega^C$ is said to be *below-closed* if $\bar{n} \in \Omega$ and $\bar{m} \leq \bar{n}$ imply $\bar{m} \in \Omega$.

Definition 7.4.1. *The flat order $\sqsubseteq$ on $\mathcal{O}(\mathcal{G}(\mathcal{H}_C) \otimes \mathcal{H})$ is defined as follows: for any $\mathbf{A} = \sum_{\bar{n} \in \omega^C} \mathbf{A}(\bar{n})$ and $\mathbf{B} = \sum_{\bar{n} \in \omega^C} \mathbf{B}(\bar{n})$ in $\mathcal{O}(\mathcal{G}(\mathcal{H}_C) \otimes \mathcal{H})$,*

- $\mathbf{A} \sqsubseteq \mathbf{B}$ *if and only if there exists a below-closed subset $\Omega \subseteq \omega^C$ such that*
  - $\mathbf{A}(\bar{n}) = \mathbf{B}(\bar{n})$ *for all $\bar{n} \in \Omega$; and*
  - $\mathbf{A}(\bar{n}) = 0$ *for all $\bar{n} \in \omega^C \setminus \Omega$.*

As said previously, the flat order can be simply understood as an abstract mathematical object. But our intention behind it has to be explained along with its application to the semantics of quantum recursive programs. A quantum recursive program P is executed by repeated substitutions, in each of which new "coins" should be added in order to avoid variable conflict, as shown in the example at the end of Section 7.2. For each $\bar{n} \in \omega^C$, n_c is used to record the number of copies of "coin" c employed in the computation of P. So, $\bar{n} \leq \bar{m}$ indicates that the (copies of) "coins" denoted by $\bar{m}$ are more than that denoted by $\bar{n}$. Obviously, the more "coins" are used in the execution of P, the more "content" is computed. Thus, if $\mathbf{A}$ and $\mathbf{B}$ are the partial computational results of P at two different stages of execution, then $\mathbf{A} \sqsubseteq \mathbf{B}$ means that the computed "content" at the stage of $\mathbf{B}$ is more than that at the stage of $\mathbf{A}$. This explanation will become clearer after reading Proposition 7.4.1.

The following is a key lemma in this chapter that unveils the lattice-theoretic structure of operators in the free Fock space.

Lemma 7.4.1. $(\mathcal{O}(\mathcal{G}(\mathcal{H}_C) \otimes \mathcal{H}), \sqsubseteq)$ *is a complete partial order (CPO) (see Definition 3.3.4).*

Proof. First, $\sqsubseteq$ is reflexive because ω^C itself is below-closed. To show that $\sqsubseteq$ is transitive, we assume that $\mathbf{A} \sqsubseteq \mathbf{B}$ and $\mathbf{B} \sqsubseteq \mathbf{C}$. Then there exist below-closed subsets $\Omega, \Gamma \subseteq \omega^C$ such that

(i) $\mathbf{A}(\overline{n}) = \mathbf{B}(\overline{n})$ for all $\overline{n} \in \Omega$ and $\mathbf{A}(\overline{n}) = 0$ for all $\overline{n} \in \omega^C \setminus \Omega$;
(ii) $\mathbf{B}(\overline{n}) = \mathbf{C}(\overline{n})$ for all $\overline{n} \in \Gamma$ and $\mathbf{B}(\overline{n}) = 0$ for all $\overline{n} \in \omega^C \setminus \Gamma$.

Clearly, $\Omega \cap \Gamma$ is below-closed too, and $\mathbf{A}(\overline{n}) = \mathbf{B}(\overline{n}) = \mathbf{C}(\overline{n})$ for all $\overline{n} \in \Omega \cap \Gamma$. On the other hand, if

$$\overline{n} \in \omega^C \setminus (\Omega \cap \Gamma) = (\omega^C \setminus \Omega) \cup [\Omega \cap (\omega^C \setminus \Gamma)],$$

then:

- either $\overline{n} \in \omega^C \setminus \Omega$ and it follows from clause (i) that $\mathbf{A}(\overline{n}) = 0$;
- or $\overline{n} \in \Omega \cap (\omega^C \setminus \Gamma)$ and by combining clauses (i) and (ii) we obtain $\mathbf{A}(\overline{n}) = \mathbf{B}(\overline{n}) = 0$.

Therefore, $\mathbf{A} \sqsubseteq \mathbf{C}$. Similarly, we can prove that $\sqsubseteq$ is antisymmetric. So, $(\mathcal{O}(\mathcal{G}(\mathcal{H}_C) \otimes \mathcal{H}), \sqsubseteq)$ is a partial order.

Obviously, the operator $\mathbf{A} = \sum_{\overline{n} \in \omega^C} \mathbf{A}(\overline{n})$ with $\mathbf{A}(\overline{n}) = 0$ (the zero operator in $\left(\bigotimes_{c \in C} \mathcal{H}_c^{\otimes n_c}\right) \otimes \mathcal{H}$) for all $\overline{n} \in \omega^C$ is the least element of $(\mathcal{O}(\mathcal{G}(\mathcal{H}_C) \otimes \mathcal{H}), \sqsubseteq)$. Now it suffices to show that any chain $\{\mathbf{A}_i\}$ in $(\mathcal{O}(\mathcal{G}(\mathcal{H}_C) \otimes \mathcal{H}), \sqsubseteq)$ has the least upper bound. For each i, we put

$$\Delta_i = \{\overline{n} \in \omega^C : \mathbf{A}_i(\overline{n}) \neq 0\},$$
$$\Delta_i \downarrow = \{\overline{m} \in \omega^C : \overline{m} \leq \overline{n} \text{ for some } \overline{n} \in \Delta_i\}.$$

Here $\Delta_i \downarrow$ is the below-completion of Δ_i. Furthermore, we define operator $\mathbf{A} = \sum_{\overline{n} \in \omega^C} \mathbf{A}(\overline{n})$ as follows:

$$\mathbf{A}(\overline{n}) = \begin{cases} \mathbf{A}_i(\overline{n}) & \text{if } \overline{n} \in \Delta_i \downarrow \text{ for some } i, \\ 0 & \text{if } \overline{n} \notin \bigcup_i (\Delta_i \downarrow). \end{cases}$$

- *Claim* 1: $\mathbf{A}$ is well-defined; that is, if $\overline{n} \in \Delta_i \downarrow$ and $\overline{n} \in \Delta_j \downarrow$, then $\mathbf{A}_i(\overline{n}) = \mathbf{A}_j(\overline{n})$. In fact, since $\{\mathbf{A}_i\}$ is a chain, we have $\mathbf{A}_i \sqsubseteq \mathbf{A}_j$ or $\mathbf{A}_j \sqsubseteq \mathbf{A}_i$. We only consider the case of $\mathbf{A}_i \sqsubseteq \mathbf{A}_j$ (the case of $\mathbf{A}_j \sqsubseteq \mathbf{A}_i$ can be proved by duality). Then there exists a below-closed subset $\Omega \subseteq \omega^C$ such that $\mathbf{A}_i(\overline{n}) = \mathbf{A}_j(\overline{n})$ for all $\overline{n} \in \Omega$ and $\mathbf{A}_i(\overline{n}) = 0$ for all $\overline{n} \in \omega^C \setminus \Omega$. It follows from $\overline{n} \in \Delta_i \downarrow$ that $\overline{n} \leq \overline{m}$ for some $\overline{m}$ with $\mathbf{A}_i(\overline{m}) \neq 0$. Since $\overline{m} \notin \omega^C \setminus \Omega$, i.e. $\overline{m} \in \Omega$, we have $\overline{n} \in \Omega$ because Ω is below-closed. So, $\mathbf{A}_i(\overline{n}) = \mathbf{A}_j(\overline{n})$.
- *Claim* 2: $\mathbf{A} = \bigsqcup_i \mathbf{A}_i$. In fact, for each i, $\Delta_i \downarrow$ is below-closed, and $\mathbf{A}_i(\overline{n}) = \mathbf{A}(\overline{n})$ for all $\overline{n} \in \Delta_i \downarrow$ and $\mathbf{A}_i(\overline{n}) = 0$ for all $\overline{n} \in \omega^C \setminus (\Delta_i \downarrow)$. So, $\mathbf{A}_i \sqsubseteq \mathbf{A}$, and $\mathbf{A}$ is an upper bound of $\{\mathbf{A}_i\}$. Now assume that $\mathbf{B}$ is an upper bound of $\{\mathbf{A}_i\}$: for all i,

$\mathbf{A}_i \sqsubseteq \mathbf{B}$; that is, there exists below-closed $\Omega_i \subseteq \omega^C$ such that $\mathbf{A}_i(\bar{n}) = \mathbf{B}(\bar{n})$ for all $\bar{n} \in \Omega_i$ and $\mathbf{A}_i(\bar{n}) = 0$ for all $\bar{n} \in \omega^C \setminus \Omega_i$. By the definition of Δ_i and below-closeness of Ω_i, we know that $\Delta_i \downarrow \subseteq \Omega_i$. We take

$$\Omega = \bigcup_i (\Delta_i \downarrow) .$$

Clearly, Ω is below-closed, and if $\bar{n} \in \omega^C \setminus \Omega$, then $\mathbf{A}(\bar{n}) = 0$. On the other hand, if $\bar{n} \in \Omega$, then for some i, we have $\bar{n} \in \Delta_i \downarrow$, and it follows that $\bar{n} \in \Omega_i$ and $\mathbf{A}(\bar{n}) = \mathbf{A}_i(\bar{n}) = \mathbf{B}(\bar{n})$. Therefore, $\mathbf{A} \sqsubseteq \mathbf{B}$. $\qquad\square$

The previous lemma presented the lattice-theoretical structure of $\mathcal{O}(\mathcal{G}(\mathcal{H}_C) \otimes \mathcal{H})$. Now we further define two algebraic operations in $\mathcal{O}(\mathcal{G}(\mathcal{H}_C) \otimes \mathcal{H})$, namely product and guarded composition. These two operations will be used to define the semantics of sequential compositions and quantum case statements in quantum program schemes.

Definition 7.4.2. *For any operators* $\mathbf{A} = \sum_{\bar{n} \in \omega^C} \mathbf{A}(\bar{n})$ *and* $\mathbf{B} = \sum_{\bar{n} \in \omega^C} \mathbf{B}(\bar{n})$ *in* $\mathcal{O}(\mathcal{G}(\mathcal{H}_C) \otimes \mathcal{H})$, *their product is defined as*

$$\mathbf{A} \cdot \mathbf{B} = \sum_{\bar{n} \in \omega^C} (\mathbf{A}(\bar{n}) \cdot \mathbf{B}(\bar{n})) , \tag{7.20}$$

which is also in $\mathcal{O}(\mathcal{G}(\mathcal{H}_C) \otimes \mathcal{H})$.

This definition is a component-wise extension of ordinary operator product: for each $\bar{n} \in \omega^C$, $\mathbf{A}(\bar{n}) \cdot \mathbf{B}(\bar{n})$ is the product of operators $\mathbf{A}(\bar{n})$ and $\mathbf{B}(\bar{n})$ in $\left(\bigotimes_{c \in C} \mathcal{H}_c^{n_c} \right) \otimes \mathcal{H}$. The guarded composition of operators in the free Fock space can be defined by simply extending equation (7.1) in the same way.

Definition 7.4.3. *Let* $c \in C$ *and* $\{|i\rangle\}$ *be an orthonormal basis of* $\mathcal{H}_c$, *and let* $\mathbf{A}_i = \sum_{\bar{n} \in \omega^C} \mathbf{A}_i(\bar{n})$ *be an operator in* $\mathcal{O}(\mathcal{G}(\mathcal{H}_C) \otimes \mathcal{H})$ *for each* i. *Then the guarded composition of* $\mathbf{A}_i$'s *along with the basis* $\{|i\rangle\}$ *is*

$$\square (c, |i\rangle \to \mathbf{A}_i) = \sum_{\bar{n} \in \omega^C} \left(\sum_i (|i\rangle_c \langle i| \otimes \mathbf{A}_i(\bar{n})) \right) . \tag{7.21}$$

Note that for each $\bar{n} \in \omega^C$, $\sum_i (|i\rangle_c \langle i| \otimes \mathbf{A}_i(n))$ is an operator in

$$\mathcal{H}_c^{\otimes (n_c + 1)} \otimes \left(\bigotimes_{d \in C \setminus \{c\}} \mathcal{H}_d^{n_d} \right) \otimes \mathcal{H},$$

and thus $\square (c, |i\rangle \to \mathbf{A}_i) \in \mathcal{O}(\mathcal{G}(\mathcal{H}_C) \otimes \mathcal{H})$.

The following lemma shows that both product and guarded composition of operators in the free Fock space are continuous with respect to the flat order (see Definition 3.3.5).

Lemma 7.4.2. *Let* $\{\mathbf{A}_j\}$ *and* $\{\mathbf{B}_j\}$ *be chains in* $(\mathcal{O}(\mathcal{G}(\mathcal{H}_C) \otimes \mathcal{H}), \sqsubseteq)$, *and so are* $\{\mathbf{A}_{ij}\}$ *for each* i. *Then*

(i) $\bigsqcup_j (\mathbf{A}_j \cdot \mathbf{B}_j) = \left(\bigsqcup_j \mathbf{A}_j\right) \cdot \left(\bigsqcup_j \mathbf{B}_j\right).$

(ii) $\bigsqcup_j \square\, (c, |i\rangle \to \mathbf{A}_{ij}) = \square\left(c, |i\rangle \to \left(\bigsqcup_j \mathbf{A}_{ij}\right)\right).$

Proof. We only prove part (ii). The proof of part (i) is similar. For each i, we assume that

$$\bigsqcup_j \mathbf{A}_{ij} = \mathbf{A}_i = \sum_{\bar{n} \in \omega^C} \mathbf{A}_i(\bar{n}).$$

By the construction of least upper bound in $(\mathcal{O}(\mathcal{G}(\mathcal{H}_C) \otimes \mathcal{H}), \sqsubseteq)$ given in the proof of Lemma 7.4.1, we can write

$$\mathbf{A}_{ij} = \sum_{\bar{n} \in \Omega_{ij}} \mathbf{A}_i(\bar{n})$$

for some $\Omega_{ij} \subseteq \omega^C$ with $\bigcup_j \Omega_{ij} = \omega^C$ for every i. By appending zero operators to the end of shorter summations, we may further ensure that index sets Ω_{ij}'s for all i are the same, say Ω_j. Then by the defining equation (7.21) we obtain:

$$\bigsqcup_j \square\, (c, |i\rangle \to \mathbf{A}_{ij}) = \bigsqcup_j \sum_{\bar{n} \in \Omega_j} \left(\sum_i (|i\rangle_c \langle i| \otimes \mathbf{A}_i(\bar{n}))\right)$$

$$= \sum_{\bar{n} \in \omega^C} \left(\sum_i (|i\rangle_c \langle i| \otimes \mathbf{A}_i(\bar{n}))\right) = \square\, (c, |i\rangle \to \mathbf{A}_i).$$

$\square$

7.4.2 SEMANTIC FUNCTIONALS OF PROGRAM SCHEMES

The semantics of quantum programs (i.e., program schemes without procedure identifiers) was already defined in Definition 7.1.2. With the preparation in the last subsection, now we are able to define the semantics of general quantum program schemes.

Let $P = P[X_1, \ldots, X_m]$ be a program scheme with procedure identifiers $X_1, \ldots, X_m$. We write C for the set of "coins" occurring in P. For each $c \in C$, let $\mathcal{H}_c$ be the state Hilbert space of quantum "coin" c. By the principal system of P we mean the composition of the systems denoted by principal variables appearing in P. Let $\mathcal{H}$ be the state Hilbert space of the principal system. Then the semantics of P can be defined as a functional in the domain $\mathcal{O}(\mathcal{G}(\mathcal{H}_C) \otimes \mathcal{H})$ described in the last subsection.

Definition 7.4.4. *The semantic functional of program scheme $P = P[X_1, \ldots, X_m]$ is a mapping*

$$\llbracket P \rrbracket : \mathcal{O}(\mathcal{G}(\mathcal{H}_C) \otimes \mathcal{H})^m \to \mathcal{O}(\mathcal{G}(\mathcal{H}_C) \otimes \mathcal{H}).$$

For any operators $\mathbf{A}_1, \ldots, \mathbf{A}_m \in \mathcal{O}(\mathcal{G}(\mathcal{H}_C) \otimes \mathcal{H})$, $\llbracket P \rrbracket(\mathbf{A}_1, \ldots, \mathcal{A}_m)$ is inductively defined as follows:

(i) *If $P = $ **abort**, then $[\![P]\!](\mathbf{A}_1,\ldots,\mathbf{A}_m)$ is the zero operator*

$$\mathbf{A} = \sum_{\bar{n}\in\omega^C} \mathbf{A}(\bar{n})$$

with $\mathbf{A}(\bar{n}) = 0$ (the zero operator in $\left(\bigotimes_{c\in C} \mathcal{H}_c^{\otimes n_c}\right) \otimes \mathcal{H}$) for all $\bar{n}\in\omega^C$;

(ii) *If $P = $ **skip**, then $[\![P]\!](\mathbf{A}_1,\ldots,\mathbf{A}_m)$ is the identity operator*

$$\mathbf{A} = \sum_{\bar{n}\in\omega^C} \mathbf{A}(\bar{n})$$

with $\mathbf{A}(\bar{n}) = I$ (the identity operator in $\left(\bigotimes_{c\in C} \mathcal{H}_c^{\otimes n_c}\right) \otimes \mathcal{H}$) for all $\bar{n}\in\omega^C$ with $n_c \neq 0$ for every $c\in C$;

(iii) *If $P = U[\bar{c},\bar{q}]$, then $[\![P]\!](\mathbf{A}_1,\ldots,\mathbf{A}_m)$ is the cylindrical extension of U:*

$$\mathbf{A} = \sum_{\bar{n}\in\omega^C} \mathbf{A}(\bar{n})$$

with

$$\mathbf{A}(\bar{n}) = I_1 \otimes I_2(\bar{n}) \otimes U \otimes I_3$$

where:
(a) *I_1 is the identity operator in the state Hilbert space of those "coins" that are not in $\bar{c}$;*
(b) *$I_2(\bar{n})$ is the identity operator in $\bigotimes_{c\in\bar{c}} \mathcal{H}_c^{\otimes(n_c-1)}$; and*
(c) *I_3 is the identity operator in the state Hilbert space of those principal variables that are not in $\bar{q}$ for all $n \geq 1$;*

(iv) *If $P = X_j$ ($1 \leq j \leq m$), then $[\![P]\!](\mathbf{A}_1,\ldots,\mathbf{A}_m) = \mathbf{A}_j$;*

(v) *If $P = P_1; P_2$, then*

$$[\![P]\!](\mathbf{A}_1,\ldots,\mathbf{A}_m) = [\![P_2]\!](\mathbf{A}_1,\ldots,\mathbf{A}_m) \cdot [\![P_1]\!](\mathbf{A}_1,\ldots,\mathbf{A}_m)$$

(see the defining equation (7.20) of the product of operators in the free Fock space);

(vi) *If $P = $ **qif** $[c](\Box i \cdot |i\rangle \to P_i)$ **fiq**, then*

$$[\![P]\!](\mathbf{A}_1,\ldots,\mathbf{A}_m) = \Box\left(c, |i\rangle \to [\![P_i]\!](\mathbf{A}_1,\ldots,\mathbf{A}_m)\right)$$

(see the defining equation (7.21) of guarded composition of operators in the free Fock space).

It is easy to see that whenever $m = 0$, that is, P contains no procedure identifiers, then the previous definition degenerates to Definition 7.1.2.

As we learned from classical programming theory and in Section 3.4, continuity of the functions involved in a recursive equation is usually crucial for the existence of solutions of the equation. So, we now examine continuity of the semantic functionals defined previously. To this end, the Cartesian power $\mathcal{O}(\mathcal{G}(\mathcal{H}_C) \otimes \mathcal{H})^m$ is naturally equipped with the order $\sqsubseteq$ defined component-wise from the flat order in the CPO $\mathcal{O}(\mathcal{G}(\mathcal{H}_C) \otimes \mathcal{H})$: for any $\mathbf{A}_1, \ldots, \mathbf{A}_m, \mathbf{B}_1, \ldots, \mathbf{B}_m \in \mathcal{O}(\mathcal{G}(\mathcal{H}_C) \otimes \mathcal{H})$,

- $(\mathbf{A}_1, \ldots, \mathbf{A}_m) \sqsubseteq (\mathbf{B}_1, \ldots, \mathbf{B}_m)$ if and only if for every $1 \le i \le m$, $\mathbf{A}_i \sqsubseteq \mathbf{B}_i$.

The second occurrence of symbol "$\sqsubseteq$" in the preceding statement stands for the flat order in $\mathcal{O}(\mathcal{G}(\mathcal{H}_C) \otimes \mathcal{H})$. Then $(\mathcal{O}(\mathcal{G}(\mathcal{H}_C) \otimes \mathcal{H})^m, \sqsubseteq)$ is a CPO too. Furthermore, we have:

Theorem 7.4.1 (Continuity of Semantic Functionals). *For any program scheme* $P = P[X_1, \ldots, X_m]$, *the semantic functional*

$$\llbracket P \rrbracket : (\mathcal{O}(\mathcal{G}(\mathcal{H}_C) \otimes \mathcal{H})^m, \sqsubseteq) \to (\mathcal{O}(\mathcal{G}(\mathcal{H}_C) \otimes \mathcal{H}), \sqsubseteq)$$

is continuous.

Proof. It can be easily proved by induction on the structure of P using Lemma 7.4.2. $\square$

There is an essential difference between quantum recursive programs defined in this chapter and recursive quantum programs studied in Section 3.4. The semantics of recursive quantum programs can be defined in a way that is very similar to the way in which we deal with recursion in classical programming theory. More explicitly, it can be properly characterized as a fixed point of semantic functionals. However, semantic functionals are not complete for describing the behavior of quantum recursive programs considered here. They must be combined with the notion of *creation functional* defined in the following:

Definition 7.4.5. *For each "coin" $c \in C$, the creation functional*

$$\mathbb{K}_c : \mathcal{O}(\mathcal{G}(\mathcal{H}_C) \otimes \mathcal{H}) \to \mathcal{O}(\mathcal{G}(\mathcal{H}_C) \otimes \mathcal{H})$$

is defined as follows: for any $\mathbf{A} = \sum_{\bar{n} \in \omega^C} \mathbf{A}(\bar{n}) \in \mathcal{O}(\mathcal{G}(\mathcal{H}_C) \otimes \mathcal{H})$,

$$\mathbb{K}_c(\mathbf{A}) = \sum_{\bar{n} \in \omega^C} (I_c \otimes \mathbf{A}(\bar{n}))$$

where I_c is the identity operator in $\mathcal{H}_c$.

We observe that $\mathbf{A}(\bar{n})$ is an operator in $\left(\bigotimes_{d \in C} \mathcal{H}_d^{\otimes n_d} \right) \otimes \mathcal{H}$, whereas $I_c \otimes \mathbf{A}(\bar{n})$ is an operator in

$$\mathcal{H}_c^{\otimes (n_c+1)} \otimes \left(\bigotimes_{d \in C \setminus \{c\}} \mathcal{H}_d^{\otimes n_d} \right) \otimes \mathcal{H}.$$

In a sense, the creation functional can be seen as a counterpart of creation operator (Definition 7.3.10) in the domain $\mathcal{O}(\mathcal{G}(\mathcal{H}_C) \otimes \mathcal{H})$. Intuitively, the creation functional $\mathbb{K}_c$ moves all copies of $\mathcal{H}_c$ one position to the right so that the ith copy becomes the

$(i + 1)$th copy for all $i = 0, 1, 2, \ldots$. Thus, a new position is created at the left end for a new copy of $\mathcal{H}_c$. For other "coins" d, $\mathbb{K}_c$ does not move any copy of $\mathcal{H}_d$.

It is clear that for any two "coins" c, d, the corresponding creation functionals $\mathbb{K}_c$ and $\mathbb{K}_d$ commute; that is,

$$\mathbb{K}_a \circ \mathbb{K}_d = \mathbb{K}_d \circ \mathbb{K}_c.$$

Note that the set C of "coins" in a program scheme P is finite. Suppose that $C = \{c_1, c_2, \ldots, c_k\}$. Then we can define the creation functional

$$\mathbb{K}_C = \mathbb{K}_{c_1} \circ \mathbb{K}_{c_2} \circ \ldots \circ \mathbb{K}_{c_k}.$$

For the special case where the set C of "coins" is empty, $\mathbb{K}_C$ is the identity functional; that is, $\mathbb{K}_C(\mathbf{A}) = \mathbf{A}$ for all $\mathbf{A}$.

Continuity of the creation functionals with respect to the flat order between operators in the free Fock space is shown in the following:

Lemma 7.4.3 (Continuity of Creation Functionals). *For each $c \in C$, the creation functionals*

$$\mathbb{K}_c \text{ and } \mathbb{K}_C : (\mathcal{O}(\mathcal{G}(\mathcal{H}_C) \otimes \mathcal{H}), \sqsubseteq) \to (\mathcal{O}(\mathcal{G}(\mathcal{H}_C) \otimes \mathcal{H}), \sqsubseteq)$$

are continuous.

Proof. Straightforward by definition. □

Combining continuity of semantic functionals and the creation functionals (Theorem 7.4.1 and Lemma 7.4.3), we obtain:

Corollary 7.4.1. *Let $P = P[X_1, \ldots, X_m]$ be a program scheme and C the set of "coins" occurring in P. We define the functional*

$$\mathbb{K}_C^m \circ [\![P]\!] : (\mathcal{O}(\mathcal{G}(\mathcal{H}_C) \otimes \mathcal{H})^m, \sqsubseteq) \to (\mathcal{O}(\mathcal{G}(\mathcal{H}_C) \otimes \mathcal{H}), \sqsubseteq)$$

by

$$(\mathbb{K}_C^m \circ [\![P]\!])(\mathbf{A}_1, \ldots, \mathbf{A}_m) = [\![P]\!](\mathbb{K}_C(\mathbf{A}_1), \ldots, \mathbb{K}_C(\mathbf{A}_m))$$

for any $\mathbf{A}_1, \ldots, \mathbf{A}_m \in \mathcal{O}(\mathcal{G}(\mathcal{H}_C) \otimes \mathcal{H})$. Then $\mathbb{K}_C^m \circ [\![P]\!]$ is continuous.

7.4.3 FIXED POINT SEMANTICS

Now we have all the ingredients needed to define the denotational semantics of quantum recursive programs using the standard fixed point technique. Let us consider a recursive program P declared by the system of equations:

$$D : \begin{cases} X_1 \Leftarrow P_1, \\ \quad \cdots\cdots \\ X_m \Leftarrow P_m, \end{cases} \tag{7.22}$$

where $P_i = P_i[X_1, \ldots, X_m]$ is a program scheme containing at most procedure identifiers $X_1, \ldots, X_m$ for every $1 \leq i \leq m$. Using the functional $[\![\cdot]\!]$ and $\mathbb{K}_C$ defined in the last subsection, the system D of recursive equations naturally induces a semantic functional:

$$[\![D]\!] : \mathcal{O}(\mathcal{G}(\mathcal{H}_C) \otimes \mathcal{H})^m \to \mathcal{O}(\mathcal{G}(\mathcal{H}_C) \otimes \mathcal{H})^m$$

defined as follows:

$$[\![D]\!](\mathbf{A}_1, \ldots, \mathbf{A}_m) = ((\mathbb{K}_C^m \circ [\![P_1]\!])(\mathbf{A}_1, \ldots, \mathbf{A}_m), \ldots, \\ (\mathbb{K}_C^m \circ [\![P_m]\!])(\mathbf{A}_1, \ldots, \mathbf{A}_m)) \tag{7.23}$$

for all $\mathbf{A}_1, \ldots, \mathbf{A}_m \in \mathcal{O}(\mathcal{G}(\mathcal{H}_C) \otimes \mathcal{H})$, where C is the set of "coins" appearing in D, that is, in one of $P_1, \ldots, P_m$. It follows from Corollary 7.4.1 that

$$[\![D]\!] : (\mathcal{O}(\mathcal{G}(\mathcal{H}_C) \otimes \mathcal{H})^m, \sqsubseteq) \to (\mathcal{O}(\mathcal{G}(\mathcal{H}_C) \otimes \mathcal{H})^m, \sqsubseteq)$$

is continuous. Then the Knaster-Tarski Fixed Point Theorem (see Theorem 3.3.1) asserts that $[\![D]\!]$ has the least fixed point $\mu [\![D]\!]$, which is exactly what we need to define the semantics of P.

Definition 7.4.6. *The fixed point (denotational) semantics of the quantum recursive program P declared by D is*

$$[\![P]\!]_{fix} = [\![P]\!](\mu [\![D]\!]);$$

that is, if $\mu [\![D]\!] = (\mathbf{A}_1^*, \ldots, \mathbf{A}_m^*) \in \mathcal{O}(\mathcal{G}(\mathcal{H}_C) \otimes \mathcal{H})^m$, then

$$[\![P]\!]_{fix} = [\![P]\!](\mathbf{A}_1^*, \ldots, \mathbf{A}_m^*)$$

(see Definition 7.4.4).

7.4.4 SYNTACTIC APPROXIMATION

The fixed point semantics of quantum recursive programs was discussed in the last subsection. We now turn to consider the syntactic approximation technique for defining the semantics of quantum recursive programs. The semantics defined in this subsection will be proved to be equivalent to the fixed point semantics.

As discussed at the end of Section 7.2, a problem that was not present in the classical programming theory is that we have to carefully avoid the conflict of quantum "coin" variables when defining the notion of substitution. To overcome it, we assume that each "coin" variable $c \in C$ has infinitely many copies $c_0, c_1, c_2, \ldots$ with $c_0 = c$. The variables $c_1, c_2, \ldots$ are used to represent a sequence of particles that are all identical to the particle $c_0 = c$. Then the notion of a quantum program scheme defined in Section 7.1 will be used in a slightly broader way: a quantum program scheme may contain not only a "coin" c but also some of its copies $c_1, c_2, \ldots$. Such a quantum program scheme is called a generalized quantum program scheme. If such a generalized quantum program scheme contains no procedure identifiers, then it is called a generalized quantum program. With these assumptions, we can introduce the notion of substitution.

Definition 7.4.7. *Let* $P = P[X_1, \ldots, X_m]$ *be a generalized quantum program scheme that contains at most procedure identifiers* $X_1, \ldots, X_m$, *and let* $Q_1, \ldots, Q_m$ *be generalized quantum programs (without any procedure identifier). Then the simultaneous substitution*

$$P[Q_1/X_1, \ldots, Q_m/X_m]$$

of $X_1, \ldots, X_m$ *by* $Q_1, \ldots, Q_m$ *in* P *is inductively defined as follows:*

(i) *If* $P = $ **abort**, **skip** *or an unitary transformation, then*

$$P[Q_1/X_1, \ldots, Q_m/X_m] = P;$$

(ii) *If* $P = X_i$ $(1 \leq i \leq m)$, *then*

$$P[Q_1/X_1, \ldots, Q_m/X_m] = Q_i;$$

(iii) *If* $P = P_1; P_2$, *then*

$$P[Q_1/X_1, \ldots, Q_m/X_m] = P_1[Q_1/X_1, \ldots, Q_m/X_m];$$
$$P_2[Q_1/X_1, \ldots, Q_m/X_m];$$

(iv) *If* $P = $ **qif** $[c](\Box i \cdot |i\rangle \to P_i)$ **fiq**, *then*

$$P[Q_1/X_1, \ldots, Q_m/X_m] = \textbf{qif } [c](\Box i \cdot |i\rangle \to P_i') \textbf{ fiq}$$

where for every i, P_i' *is obtained through replacing the* j*th copy* c_j *of* c *in* $P_i[Q_1/X_1, \ldots, Q_m/X_m]$ *by the* $(j+1)$*th copy* c_{j+1} *of* c *for all* j.

Note that in Clause (iv) of this definition, since P is a generalized quantum program scheme, the "coin" c may not be an original "coin" but some copy d_k of an original "coin" $d \in C$. In this case, the jth copy of c is actually the $(k+j)$th copy of d: $c_j = (d_k)_j = d_{k+j}$ for $j \geq -d$.

The semantics of a generalized quantum program P can be given using Definition 7.1.2 in such a way that a "coin" c and its copies $c_1, c_2, \ldots$ are treated as distinct variables to each other. For each "coin" c, let n_c be the greatest index n such that the copy c_n appears in P. Then the semantics $[\![P]\!]$ of P is an operator in $\left(\bigotimes_{c \in C} \mathcal{H}_c^{\otimes n_c}\right) \otimes \mathcal{H}$. Furthermore, it can be identified with its cylindrical extension in $\mathcal{O}(\mathcal{G}(\mathcal{H}_C) \otimes \mathcal{H})$:

$$\sum_{\overline{m} \in \omega^C} \left(I(\overline{m}) \otimes [\![P]\!]\right),$$

where for each $\overline{m} \in \omega^C$, $I(\overline{m})$ is the identity operator in $\bigotimes_{c \in C} \mathcal{H}_c^{\otimes m_c}$. Based on this observation, the semantics of substitution defined previously is characterized by the following:

Lemma 7.4.4. *For any (generalized) quantum program scheme* $P = P[X_1, \ldots, X_m]$ *and (generalized) quantum programs* $Q_1, \ldots, Q_m$, *we have:*

$$\llbracket P[Q_1/X_1, \ldots, Q_m/X_m] \rrbracket = (\mathbb{K}_C^m \circ \llbracket P \rrbracket)(\llbracket Q_1 \rrbracket, \ldots, \llbracket Q_m \rrbracket)$$
$$= \llbracket P \rrbracket(\mathbb{K}_C(\llbracket Q_1 \rrbracket), \ldots, \mathbb{K}_C(\llbracket Q_m \rrbracket)),$$

where $\mathbb{K}_C$ *is the creation functional with C being the set of "coins" in P.*

Proof. We prove the lemma by induction on the structure of P.

- Case 1. $P = $ **abort**, **skip** or an unitary transformation. Obvious.
- Case 2. $P = X_j$ $(1 \leq j \leq m)$. Then

$$P[Q_1/X_1, \ldots, Q_m/X_m] = Q_m.$$

On the other hand, since the set of "coins" in P is empty,

$$\mathbb{K}_C(\llbracket Q_i \rrbracket) = \llbracket Q_i \rrbracket$$

for all $1 \leq i \leq m$. Thus, by clause (iv) of Definition 7.4.4 we obtain:

$$\llbracket P[Q_1/X_1, \ldots, Q_m/X_m] \rrbracket = \llbracket Q_m \rrbracket$$
$$= \llbracket P \rrbracket(\llbracket Q_1 \rrbracket, \ldots, \llbracket Q_m \rrbracket)$$
$$= \llbracket P \rrbracket(\mathbb{K}_C(\llbracket Q_1 \rrbracket), \ldots, \mathbb{K}_C(\llbracket Q_m \rrbracket)).$$

- Case 3. $P = P_1; P_2$. Then by clause (iii) of Definition 7.1.2, clause (v) of Definition 7.4.4 and the induction hypothesis, we have:

$$\llbracket P[Q_1/X_1, \ldots, Q_m/X_m] \rrbracket = \llbracket P_1[Q_1/X_1, \ldots, Q_m/X_m]; P_2[Q_1/X_1, \ldots, Q_m/X_m] \rrbracket$$
$$= \llbracket P_2[Q_1/X_1, \ldots, Q_m/X_m] \rrbracket \cdot \llbracket P_1[Q_1/X_1, \ldots, Q_m/X_m] \rrbracket$$
$$= \llbracket P_2 \rrbracket(\mathbb{K}_C(\llbracket Q_1 \rrbracket), \ldots, \mathbb{K}_C(\llbracket Q_m \rrbracket)) \cdot \llbracket P_1 \rrbracket(\mathbb{K}_C(\llbracket Q_1 \rrbracket), \ldots, \mathbb{K}_C(\llbracket Q_m \rrbracket))$$
$$= \llbracket P_1; P_2 \rrbracket(\mathbb{K}_C(\llbracket Q_1 \rrbracket), \ldots, \mathbb{K}_C(\llbracket Q_m \rrbracket))$$
$$= \llbracket P \rrbracket(\mathbb{K}_C(\llbracket Q_1 \rrbracket), \ldots, \mathbb{K}_C(\llbracket Q_m \rrbracket)).$$

- Case 4. $P = $ **qif** $[c](\square i \cdot |i\rangle \rightarrow P_i)$ **fiq**. Then

$$P[Q_1/X_1, \ldots, Q_m/X_m] = \textbf{qif } [c](\square i \cdot |i\rangle \rightarrow P_i') \textbf{ fiq},$$

where P_i' is obtained according to clause (iv) of Definition 7.4.7. For each i, by the induction hypothesis we obtain:

$$\llbracket P_i[Q_1/X_1, \ldots, Q_m/X_m] \rrbracket = \llbracket P_i \rrbracket(\mathbb{K}_{C \setminus \{c\}}(\llbracket Q_1 \rrbracket), \ldots, \mathbb{K}_{C \setminus \{c\}}(\llbracket Q_m \rrbracket))$$

because the "coin" c does not appear in P_i'. Furthermore, it follows that

$$\llbracket P_i' \rrbracket = \mathbb{K}_c(\llbracket P_i[Q_1/X_1, \ldots, Q_m/X_m] \rrbracket)$$
$$= \mathbb{K}_c(\llbracket P_i \rrbracket (\mathbb{K}_{C \setminus \{c\}}(\llbracket Q_1 \rrbracket), \ldots, \mathbb{K}_{C \setminus \{c\}}(\llbracket Q_m \rrbracket)))$$
$$= \llbracket P_i \rrbracket ((\mathbb{K}_c \circ \mathbb{K}_{C \setminus \{c\}})(\llbracket Q_1 \rrbracket), \ldots, (\mathbb{K}_c \circ \mathbb{K}_{C \setminus \{c\}})(\llbracket Q_m \rrbracket))$$
$$= \llbracket P_i \rrbracket (\mathbb{K}_C(\llbracket Q_1 \rrbracket), \ldots, \mathbb{K}_C(\llbracket Q_m \rrbracket)).$$

Therefore, by clause (iv) of Definition 7.1.2, clause (vi) of Definition 7.4.4 and equation (7.21), we have:

$$\llbracket P[Q_1/X_1, \ldots, Q_m/X_m] \rrbracket = \sum_i \left(|i\rangle \langle i| \otimes \llbracket P_i' \rrbracket \right)$$
$$= \square(c, |i\rangle) \to \llbracket P_i \rrbracket (\mathbb{K}_C(\llbracket Q_1 \rrbracket), \ldots, \mathbb{K}_C(\llbracket Q_m \rrbracket))$$
$$= \llbracket P \rrbracket (\mathbb{K}_C(\llbracket Q_1 \rrbracket), \ldots, \mathbb{K}_C(\llbracket Q_m \rrbracket)).$$

$\square$

Essentially, the previous lemma shows that the semantic functional of a generalized quantum program scheme is compositional modulo the creation functional.

Now the notion of syntactic approximation can be properly defined based on Definition 7.4.7.

Definition 7.4.8

(i) *Let $X_1, \ldots, X_m$ be procedure identifiers declared by the system D of recursive equations (7.22). Then for each $1 \le k \le m$, the nth syntactic approximation $X_k^{(n)}$ of X_k is inductively defined as follows:*

$$\begin{cases} X_k^{(0)} = \textbf{abort}, \\ X_k^{(n+1)} = P_k[X_1^{(n)}/X_1, \ldots, X_m^{(n)}/X_m] \ for \ n \ge 0. \end{cases}$$

(ii) *Let $P = P[X_1, \ldots, X_m]$ be a quantum recursive program declared by the system D of equations (7.22). Then for each $n \ge 0$, its nth syntactic approximation $P^{(n)}$ is inductively defined as follows:*

$$\begin{cases} P^{(0)} = \textbf{abort}, \\ P^{(n+1)} = P[X_1^{(n)}/X_1, \ldots, X_m^{(n)}/X_m] \ for \ n \ge 0. \end{cases}$$

Syntactic approximation actually gives an operational semantics of quantum recursive programs. As in the theory of classical programming, substitution represents an application of the so-called *copy rule*:

• At runtime, a procedure call is treated like the procedure body inserted at the place of call.

Of course, simplifications may happen within $X_k^{(n)}$ by operations of linear operators; for example,

$$CNOT[q_1, q_2]; X[q_2]; CNOT[q_1, q_2]$$

can be replaced by $X[q_2]$, where q_1, q_2 are principal system variables, *CNOT* is the controlled-NOT gate and X is the NOT gate. To simplify the presentation, we choose not to explicitly describe these simplifications.

The major difference between the classical case and the quantum case is that in the latter we need to continuously introduce new "coin" variables to avoid variable conflict when we unfold a quantum recursive program using its syntactic approximations: for each $n \geq 0$, a new copy of each "coin" in P_k is created in the substitution

$$X_k^{(n+1)} = P_k[X_1^{(n)}/X_1, \ldots, X_m^{(n)}/X_m]$$

(see clause (iv) of Definition 7.4.7). Thus, a quantum recursive program should be understood as a quantum system with variable particle number and described in the second quantization formalism.

Note that for all $1 \leq k \leq m$ and $n \geq 0$, the syntactic approximation $X_k^{(n)}$ is a generalized quantum program containing no procedure identifiers. Thus, its semantics $[\![X_k^{(n)}]\!]$ can be given by a slightly extended version of Definition 7.1.2: a "coin" c and its copies $c_1, c_2, \ldots$ are allowed to appear in the same (generalized) program and they are considered as distinct variables. As before, the principal system is the composite system of the subsystems denoted by principal variables appearing in $P_1, \ldots, P_m$ and its state Hilbert space is denoted by $\mathcal{H}$. Assume that C is the set of "coin" variables appearing in $P_1, \ldots, P_m$. For each $c \in C$, we write $\mathcal{H}_c$ for the state Hilbert space of quantum "coin" c. Then it is easy to see that $[\![X_k^{(n)}]\!]$ is an operator in

$$\bigoplus_{j=0}^{n} \left(\mathcal{H}_C^{\otimes n_j} \otimes \mathcal{H} \right)$$

where $\mathcal{H}_C = \bigotimes_{c \in C} \mathcal{H}_c$. So, we can imagine that $[\![X_k^{(n)}]\!] \in \mathcal{O}(\mathcal{G}(\mathcal{H}_C) \otimes \mathcal{H})$. Furthermore, we have:

Lemma 7.4.5. *For each $1 \leq k \leq m$, $\left\{ [\![X_k^{(n)}]\!] \right\}_{n=0}^{\infty}$ is an increasing chain with respect to the flat order, and thus*

$$[\![X_k^{(\infty)}]\!] = \lim_{n \to \infty} [\![X_k^{(n)}]\!] \triangleq \bigsqcup_{n=0}^{\infty} [\![X_k^{(n)}]\!] \tag{7.24}$$

exists in $(\mathcal{O}(\mathcal{G}(\mathcal{H}_C) \otimes \mathcal{H}), \sqsubseteq)$.

Proof. We show that

$$[\![X_k^{(n)}]\!] \sqsubseteq [\![X_k^{(n+1)}]\!]$$

by induction on n. The case of $n = 0$ is trivial because

$$[\![X_k^{(0)}]\!] = [\![\mathbf{abort}]\!] = 0.$$

In general, by the induction hypothesis on $n-1$ and Corollary 7.4.1, we have:

$$
\begin{aligned}
\llbracket X_k^{(n)} \rrbracket &= \llbracket P_k \rrbracket (\mathbb{K}_C(\llbracket X_1^{(n-1)} \rrbracket), \ldots, \mathbb{K}_C(\llbracket X_m^{(n-1)} \rrbracket)) \\
&\sqsubseteq \llbracket P_k \rrbracket (\mathbb{K}_C(\llbracket X_1^{(n)} \rrbracket), \ldots, \mathbb{K}_C(\llbracket X_m^{(n)} \rrbracket)) \\
&= \llbracket X_k^{(n+1)} \rrbracket,
\end{aligned}
$$

where C is the set of "coins" in D. Then existence of the least upper bound (7.24) follows immediately from Lemma 7.4.1. $\qquad\square$

We now are ready to define the operational semantics of quantum recursive programs.

Definition 7.4.9. *Let P be a quantum recursive program declared by the system D of equations (7.22). Then its operational semantics is*

$$
\llbracket P \rrbracket_{op} = \llbracket P \rrbracket \left(\llbracket X_1^{(\infty)} \rrbracket, \ldots, \llbracket X_m^{(\infty)} \rrbracket \right).
$$

The operator $\llbracket P \rrbracket_{op}$ is called the operational semantics for the reason that it is defined based on the copy rule. But it is actually not an operational semantics in the strict sense because the notion of limit is involved in $\llbracket X_i^{(\infty)} \rrbracket$ ($1 \le i \le m$).

The operational semantics of quantum recursive program P can be characterized by the limit of its syntactic approximations (with respect to its declaration D).

Proposition 7.4.1. *It holds in the domain $(\mathcal{O}(\mathcal{G}(\mathcal{H}_C) \otimes \mathcal{H}), \sqsubseteq)$ that*

$$
\llbracket P \rrbracket_{op} = \bigsqcup_{n=0}^{\infty} \llbracket P^{(n)} \rrbracket.
$$

Proof. It follows from Lemma 7.4.4 that

$$
\begin{aligned}
\bigsqcup_{n=0}^{\infty} \llbracket P^{(n)} \rrbracket &= \bigsqcup_{n=0}^{\infty} \llbracket P[X_1^{(n)}/X_1, \ldots, X_m^{(n)}/X_m] \rrbracket \\
&= \bigsqcup_{n=0}^{\infty} \llbracket P \rrbracket \left(\mathbb{K}_C(\llbracket X_1^{(n)} \rrbracket), \ldots, \mathbb{K}_C(\llbracket X_m^{(n)} \rrbracket) \right)
\end{aligned}
$$

where $\mathbb{K}_C$ is the creation functional with respect to the "coins" C in P. However, all the "coin" C in P do not appear in $X_1^{(n)}, \ldots, X_m^{(n)}$ (see the condition in Definition 7.1.3). So,

$$
\mathbb{K}_C \left(\llbracket X_k^{(n)} \rrbracket \right) = \llbracket X_k^{(n)} \rrbracket
$$

for every $1 \leq k \leq m$, and by Theorem 7.4.1 we obtain:

$$\bigsqcup_{n=0}^{\infty} \llbracket P^{(n)} \rrbracket = \bigsqcup_{n=0}^{\infty} \llbracket P \rrbracket \left(\llbracket X_1^{(n)} \rrbracket, \ldots, \llbracket X_m^{(n)} \rrbracket \right)$$

$$= \llbracket P \rrbracket \left(\bigsqcup_{n=0}^{\infty} \llbracket X_1^{(n)} \rrbracket, \ldots, \bigsqcup_{n=0}^{\infty} \llbracket X_m^{(n)} \rrbracket \right)$$

$$= \llbracket P \rrbracket \left(\llbracket X_1^{\infty} \rrbracket, \ldots, \llbracket X_m^{\infty} \rrbracket \right)$$

$$= \llbracket P \rrbracket_{op}.$$

$\square$

Intuitively, for each $n \geq 0$, $\llbracket P^{(n)} \rrbracket$ denotes the partial computational result of recursive program P up to the nth step. Thus, the preceding proposition shows that the complete computational result can be approximated by partial computational results.

Finally, the equivalence between denotational and operational semantics of recursive programs is established in the following:

Theorem 7.4.2 (Equivalence of Denotational Semantics and Operational Semantics). *For any quantum recursive program P, we have:*

$$\llbracket P \rrbracket_{fix} = \llbracket P \rrbracket_{op}.$$

Proof. By Definitions 7.4.6 and 7.4.9, it suffices to show that $\left(\llbracket X_1^{(\infty)} \rrbracket, \ldots, \right.$ $\left. \llbracket X_m^{(\infty)} \rrbracket \right)$ is the least fixed point of semantic functional $\llbracket D \rrbracket$, where D is the declaration of procedure identifiers in P. With Theorem 7.4.1 and Lemmas 7.4.3 and 7.4.4, we obtain:

$$\llbracket X_k^{(\infty)} \rrbracket = \bigsqcup_{n=0}^{\infty} \llbracket X_k^{(n)} \rrbracket$$

$$= \bigsqcup_{n=0}^{\infty} \llbracket P_k[X_1^{(n)}/X_1, \ldots, X_m^{(n)}/X_m] \rrbracket$$

$$= \bigsqcup_{n=0}^{\infty} \llbracket P_k \rrbracket \left(\mathbb{K}_C(\llbracket X_1^{(n)} \rrbracket), \ldots, \mathbb{K}_C(\llbracket X_m^{(n)} \rrbracket) \right)$$

$$= \llbracket P_k \rrbracket \left(\mathbb{K}_C \left(\bigsqcup_{n=0}^{\infty} \llbracket X_1^{(n)} \rrbracket \right), \ldots, \mathbb{K}_C \left(\bigsqcup_{n=0}^{\infty} \llbracket X_m^{(n)} \rrbracket \right) \right)$$

$$= \llbracket P_k \rrbracket (\mathbb{K}_C(\llbracket X_1^{(\infty)} \rrbracket), \ldots, \mathbb{K}_C(\llbracket X_m^{(\infty)} \rrbracket))$$

for every $1 \leq k \leq m$, where C is the set of "coins" in D. So, $\left(\llbracket X_1^{(\infty)} \rrbracket, \ldots, \llbracket X_m^{(\infty)} \rrbracket \right)$ is a fixed point of $\llbracket D \rrbracket$. On the other hand, if $(\mathbf{A}_1, \ldots, \mathbf{A}_m) \in \mathcal{O}(\mathcal{G}(\mathcal{H}_C) \otimes \mathcal{H})^m$ is a fixed point of $\llbracket D \rrbracket$, then we can prove that for every $n \geq 0$,

$$\left([\![X_1^{(n)}]\!], \ldots, [\![X_m^{(n)}]\!] \right) \sqsubseteq (\mathbf{A}_1, \ldots, \mathbf{A}_m)$$

by induction on n. Indeed, the case of $n = 0$ is obvious. In general, using the induction hypothesis on $n - 1$, Corollary 7.4.1 and Lemma 7.4.4 we obtain:

$$
\begin{aligned}
(\mathbf{A}_1, \ldots, \mathbf{A}_m) &= [\![D]\!](\mathbf{A}_1, \ldots, \mathbf{A}_m) \\
&= \left(\left(\mathbb{K}_C^m \circ [\![P_1]\!] \right)(\mathbf{A}_1, \ldots, \mathbf{A}_m), \ldots, \left(\mathbb{K}_C^m \circ [\![P_m]\!] \right)(\mathbf{A}_1, \ldots, \mathbf{A}_m) \right) \\
&\sqsupseteq \left(\left(\mathbb{K}_C^m \circ [\![P_1]\!] \right)\left([\![X_1^{(n-1)}]\!], \ldots, [\![X_m^{(n-1)}]\!] \right), \ldots, \right. \\
&\qquad\qquad \left. \left(\mathbb{K}_C^m \circ [\![P_m]\!] \right)\left([\![X_1^{(n-1)}]\!], \ldots, [\![X_m^{(n-1)}]\!] \right) \right) \\
&= \left([\![X_1^{(n)}]\!], \ldots, [\![X_m^{(n)}]\!] \right).
\end{aligned}
$$

Therefore, it holds that

$$\left([\![X_1^{(\infty)}]\!], \ldots, [\![X_m^{(\infty)}]\!] \right) = \bigsqcup_{n=0}^{\infty} \left([\![X_1^{(n)}]\!], \ldots, [\![X_m^{(n)}]\!] \right) \sqsubseteq (\mathbf{A}_1, \ldots, \mathbf{A}_m),$$

and $\left([\![X_1^{(\infty)}]\!], \ldots, [\![X_m^{(\infty)}]\!] \right)$ is the least fixed point of $[\![D]\!]$. $\qquad\square$

In light of this theorem, we will simply write $[\![P]\!]$ for both the denotational (fixed point) and operational semantics of a recursive program P. But we should carefully distinguish the semantics $[\![P]\!] \in \mathcal{O}(\mathcal{G}(\mathcal{H}_C) \otimes \mathcal{H})$ of a recursive program $P = P[X_1, \ldots, X_m]$ declared by a system of equations about $X_1, \ldots, X_m$ from the semantic functional

$$[\![P]\!] : \mathcal{O}(\mathcal{G}(\mathcal{H}_C) \otimes \mathcal{H})^m \to \mathcal{O}(\mathcal{G}(\mathcal{H}_C) \otimes \mathcal{H})$$

of program scheme $P = P[X_1, \ldots, X_m]$. Usually, such a difference can be recognized from the context.

7.5 RECOVERING SYMMETRY AND ANTISYMMETRY

The last section developed the techniques for solving quantum recursive equations in the free Fock space. However, the solutions found in the free Fock space are still not what we really need because they may not preserve symmetry or antisymmetry and thus cannot directly apply to the symmetric Fock space for bosons or the antisymmetric Fock space for fermions. In this section, we introduce the technique of symmetrization that allows us to transform every solution in the free Fock space to a solution in the bosonic or fermionic Fock spaces.

7.5.1 **SYMMETRIZATION FUNCTIONAL**

Let us first isolate a special subdomain of $\mathcal{O}(\mathcal{G}(\mathcal{H}_C) \otimes \mathcal{H})$, namely the domain of symmetric operators. As in Subsection 7.4.1, let $\mathcal{H}$ be the state Hilbert space of the principal system and C the set of "coins," and

$$\mathcal{G}(\mathcal{H}_C) \otimes \mathcal{H} = \left(\bigotimes_{c \in C} \mathcal{F}(\mathcal{H}_c) \right) \otimes \mathcal{H} = \bigoplus_{\bar{n} \in \omega^C} \left[\left(\bigotimes_{c \in C} \mathcal{H}_c^{\otimes n_c} \right) \otimes \mathcal{H} \right],$$

where ω is the set of nonnegative integers, and for each $c \in C$, $\mathcal{F}(\mathcal{H}_c)$ is the free Fock space over the state Hilbert space $\mathcal{H}_c$ of "coin" c. As a simple generalization of Definition 7.3.6, we have:

Definition 7.5.1. *For any operator* $\mathbf{A} = \sum_{\bar{n} \in \omega^C} \mathbf{A}(\bar{n}) \in \mathcal{O}(\mathcal{G}(\mathcal{H}_C) \otimes \mathcal{H})$, *we say that* $\mathbf{A}$ *is symmetric if for each* $\bar{n} \in \omega^C$, *for each* $c \in C$ *and for each permutation* π *of* $0, 1, \ldots, n_c - 1$, P_π *and* $\mathbf{A}(\bar{n})$ *commute; that is,*

$$P_\pi \mathbf{A}(\bar{n}) = \mathbf{A}(\bar{n}) P_\pi .$$

Note that in this definition P_π actually stands for its cylindrical extension

$$P_\pi \otimes \left(\bigotimes_{d \in C \setminus \{c\}} I_d \right) \otimes I$$

in $\left(\bigotimes_{d \in C} \mathcal{H}_d^{\otimes n_d} \right) \otimes \mathcal{H}$, where I_d is the identity operator in $\mathcal{H}_d^{\otimes n_d}$ for every $d \in C \setminus \{c\}$, and I is the identity operator in $\mathcal{H}$.

We write $\mathcal{SO}(\mathcal{G}(\mathcal{H}_C) \otimes \mathcal{H})$ for the set of all symmetric operators $\mathbf{A} \in \mathcal{O}(\mathcal{G}(\mathcal{H}_C) \otimes \mathcal{H})$. Its lattice-theoretic structure is presented in the following:

Lemma 7.5.1. $(\mathcal{SO}(\mathcal{G}(\mathcal{H}_C) \otimes \mathcal{H}), \sqsubseteq)$ *is a complete sub-partial order of CPO* $(\mathcal{O}(\mathcal{G}(\mathcal{H}_C) \otimes \mathcal{H}), \sqsubseteq)$.

Proof. It suffices to observe that symmetry of operators is preserved by the least upper bound in $(\mathcal{O}(\mathcal{G}(\mathcal{H}_C) \otimes \mathcal{H}), \sqsubseteq)$; that is, if $\mathbf{A}_i$ is symmetric, so is $\bigsqcup_i \mathbf{A}_i$, as constructed in the proof of Lemma 7.4.1. $\square$

Now we can generalize the symmetrization functional defined by equations (7.14) and (7.15) into the space $\mathcal{O}(\mathcal{G}(\mathcal{H}_C) \otimes \mathcal{H})$.

Definition 7.5.2

(i) *For each* $\bar{n} \in \omega^C$, *the symmetrization functional* $\mathbb{S}$ *over operators in the space* $\left(\bigotimes_{c \in C} \mathcal{H}_c^{\otimes n_c} \right) \otimes \mathcal{H}$ *is defined by*

$$\mathbb{S}(\mathbf{A}) = \left(\prod_{c \in C} \frac{1}{n_c!} \right) \cdot \sum_{\{\pi_c\}} \left[\left(\bigotimes_{c \in C} P_{\pi_c} \right) \mathbf{A} \left(\bigotimes_{c \in C} P_{\pi_c}^{-1} \right) \right]$$

for every operator $\mathbf{A}$ *in* $\left(\bigotimes_{c \in C} \mathcal{H}_c^{\otimes n_c}\right) \otimes \mathcal{H}$, *where* $\{\pi_c\}$ *traverses over all* C-*indexed families with* π_c *being a permutation of* $0, 1, \ldots, n_c - 1$ *for every* $c \in C$.

(ii) *The symmetrization functional can be extended to* $\mathcal{O}(\mathcal{G}(\mathcal{H}_C) \otimes \mathcal{H})$ *in a natural way:*

$$\mathbb{S}(\mathbf{A}) = \sum_{\overline{n} \in \omega^C} \mathbb{S}(\mathbf{A}(\overline{n}))$$

for any $\mathbf{A} = \sum_{\overline{n} \in \omega^C} \mathbf{A}(\overline{n}) \in \mathcal{O}(\mathcal{G}(\mathcal{H}_C) \otimes \mathcal{H})$.

Obviously, $\mathbb{S}(\mathbf{A}) \in \mathcal{SO}(\mathcal{G}(\mathcal{H}_C) \otimes \mathcal{H})$. Clause (i) of the preceding definition is essentially the same as equation (7.15) but applied to a more complicated space $\left(\bigotimes_{c \in C} \mathcal{H}_c^{\otimes n_c}\right) \otimes \mathcal{H}$. Clause (ii) is then a component-wise generalization of clause (i). Furthermore, the following lemma establishes continuity of the symmetrization functional with respect to the flat order.

Lemma 7.5.2. *The symmetrization functional*

$$\mathbb{S} : (\mathcal{O}(\mathcal{G}(\mathcal{H}_C) \otimes \mathcal{H}), \sqsubseteq) \to (\mathcal{SO}(\mathcal{G}(\mathcal{H}_C) \otimes \mathcal{H}), \sqsubseteq)$$

is continuous.

Proof. What we need to prove is that

$$\mathbb{S}\left(\bigsqcup_i \mathbf{A}_i\right) = \bigsqcup_i \mathbb{S}(\mathbf{A}_i)$$

for any chain $\{\mathbf{A}_i\}$ in $(\mathcal{O}(\mathcal{G}(\mathcal{H}_C) \otimes \mathcal{H}), \sqsubseteq)$. Assume that $\mathbf{A} = \bigsqcup_i \mathbf{A}_i$. Then by the proof of Lemma 7.4.1, we can write

$$\mathbf{A} = \sum_{\overline{n} \in \omega} \mathbf{A}(\overline{n}) \text{ and } \mathbf{A}_i = \sum_{\overline{n} \in \Omega_i} \mathbf{A}(\overline{n})$$

for some Ω_i with $\bigcup_i \Omega_i = \omega^C$. So, it holds that

$$\bigsqcup_i \mathbb{S}(\mathbf{A}_i) = \bigsqcup_i \sum_{\overline{n} \in \Omega_i} \mathbb{S}(\mathbf{A}(\overline{n})) = \sum_{\overline{n} \in \omega^C} \mathbb{S}(\mathbf{A}(\overline{n})) = \mathbb{S}(\mathbf{A}).$$

$\square$

7.5.2 SYMMETRIZATION OF THE SEMANTICS OF QUANTUM RECURSIVE PROGRAMS

With the preparation in the previous subsection, now we can directly apply the symmetrization functional to the solutions of quantum recursive equations in the free Fock space to give the semantics of quantum recursive programs in the symmetric or antisymmetric Fock space.

Definition 7.5.3. *Let* $P = P[X_1, \ldots, X_m]$ *be a quantum recursive program declared by the system* D *of equations (7.22). Then its symmetric semantics* $[\![P]\!]_{sym}$ *is the symmetrization of its semantics* $[\![P]\!]$ *in the free Fock space:*

$$[\![P]\!]_{sym} = \mathbb{S}([\![P]\!])$$

where $\mathbb{S}$ *is the symmetrization functional,*

$$[\![P]\!] = [\![P]\!]_{fix} = [\![P]\!]_{op} \in \mathcal{O}(\mathcal{G}(\mathcal{H}_C) \otimes \mathcal{H})$$

(see Theorem 7.4.2), C *is the set of "coins" in* D, *and* $\mathcal{H}$ *is the state Hilbert space of the principal system of* D.

Intuitively, for each "coin" $c \in C$, we use $v_c = +$ or $-$ to indicate that c is a boson or a fermion, respectively. Moreover, we write v for the sequence $\{v_c\}_{c \in C}$. Then

$$\mathcal{G}_v(\mathcal{H}_C) \triangleq \bigotimes_{c \in C} \mathcal{F}_{v_c}(\mathcal{H}_c) \subsetneq \mathcal{G}(\mathcal{H}_C).$$

According to the principle of symmetrization, a physically meaningful input to program P should be a state $|\Psi\rangle$ in $\mathcal{G}_v(\mathcal{H}_C) \otimes \mathcal{H}$. However, the output $[\![P]\!](|\Psi\rangle)$ is not necessarily in $\mathcal{G}_v(\mathcal{H}_C) \otimes \mathcal{H}$ and thus might not be meaningful. Nevertheless, it holds that

$$[\![P]\!]_{sym}(|\Psi\rangle) = \mathbb{S}([\![P]\!])(|\Psi\rangle) \in \mathcal{G}_v(\mathcal{H}_C) \otimes \mathcal{H}.$$

As a symmetrization of Proposition 7.4.1, we have a characterisation of symmetric semantics in terms of syntactic approximations:

Proposition 7.5.1. $[\![P]\!]_{sym} = \bigsqcup_{n=0}^{\infty} \mathbb{S}([\![P^{(n)}]\!])$.

Proof. It follows from Proposition 7.4.1 and Lemma 7.5.2 (continuity of the symmetrization functional) that

$$[\![P]\!]_{sym} = \mathbb{S}([\![P]\!]) = \mathbb{S}\left(\bigsqcup_{n=0}^{\infty} [\![P^{(n)}]\!]\right) = \bigsqcup_{n=0}^{\infty} \mathbb{S}([\![P^{(n)}]\!]).$$

$\square$

7.6 PRINCIPAL SYSTEM SEMANTICS OF QUANTUM RECURSION

In the last section, the symmetric semantics of quantum recursive programs was defined by symmetrizing their semantics in the free Fock space. Let P be a quantum recursive program with $\mathcal{H}$ being the state Hilbert space of its principal variables and C being the set of its "coin." Then semantics $[\![P]\!]$ is an operator in space $\mathcal{G}(\mathcal{H}_C) \otimes \mathcal{H}$, where $\mathcal{G}(\mathcal{H}_C) = \bigotimes_{c \in C} \mathcal{F}(\mathcal{H}_c)$, and for each $c \in C$, $\mathcal{H}_c$ is the state Hilbert space of "coin" c, $\mathcal{F}(\mathcal{H}_c)$ is the free Fock space over $\mathcal{H}_c$. Furthermore, we put

$$\mathcal{G}_v(\mathcal{H}_C) = \bigotimes_{c \in C} \mathcal{F}_{v_c}(\mathcal{H}_c)$$

where v is the sequence $\{v_c\}_{c \in C}$, and for each $c \in C$, $v_c = +$ or $-$ if "coin" c is implemented by a boson or a fermion, respectively. Then symmetric semantics $[\![P]\!]_{sym}$ is an operator in $\mathcal{G}_v(\mathcal{H}_C) \otimes \mathcal{H}$. As we know from the discussions in the previous sections, quantum "coins" in C (and their copies) are only introduced to help the execution of program P but do not actually participate in the computation. What really concerns us is the computation done by the principal system. More precisely, we consider the computation of P with input $|\psi\rangle \in \mathcal{H}$ of principal variables. Assume that the "coins" are initialized in state $|\Psi\rangle \in \mathcal{G}_v(\mathcal{H}_C)$. Then the computation of the program P starts in state $|\Psi\rangle \otimes |\psi\rangle$. At the end, the computational result of P will be stored in the Hilbert space $\mathcal{H}$ of the principal system. This observation leads to the following:

Definition 7.6.1. *Given a state $|\Psi\rangle \in \mathcal{G}_v(\mathcal{H}_C)$. The principal system semantics of program P with respect to "coin" initialization $|\Psi\rangle$ is the mapping $[\![P, \Psi]\!]$ from pure states in $\mathcal{H}$ to partial density operators, i.e., positive operators with trace ≤ 1 (see Section 3.2), in $\mathcal{H}$:*

$$[\![P, \Psi]\!](|\psi\rangle) = tr_{\mathcal{G}_v(\mathcal{H}_C)}(|\Phi\rangle\langle\Phi|)$$

for each pure state $|\psi\rangle$ in $\mathcal{H}$, where

$$|\Phi\rangle = [\![P]\!]_{sym}(|\Psi\rangle \otimes |\psi\rangle),$$

$[\![P]\!]_{sym}$ is the symmetric semantics of P, and $tr_{\mathcal{G}_v(\mathcal{H}_C)}$ is the partial trace over $\mathcal{G}_v(\mathcal{H}_C)$ (see Definition 2.1.22).

As a corollary of Proposition 7.5.1, we have the following characterization of the principal system semantics in terms of syntactic approximation:

Proposition 7.6.1. *For any quantum recursive program P, any initial "coin" state $|\Psi\rangle$ and any principal system state $|\psi\rangle$,*

$$[\![P, \Psi]\!](|\psi\rangle) = \bigsqcup_{n=0}^{\infty} tr_{\bigotimes_{c \in C} \mathcal{H}_{v_c}^{\otimes n}}(|\Phi_n\rangle\langle\Phi_n|)$$

where C is the set of "coins" in P,

$$|\Phi_n\rangle = \mathbb{S}([\![P^{(n)}]\!](|\Psi\rangle \otimes |\psi\rangle))$$

and $P^{(n)}$ is the nth syntactic approximation of P for every $n \geq 0$.

Exercise 7.6.1. *Prove the above proposition.*

7.7 ILLUSTRATIVE EXAMPLES: REVISIT RECURSIVE QUANTUM WALKS

A general theory of quantum recursive programs has been developed in the previous sections. To illustrate the ideas proposed there, let us reconsider two simple recursive quantum walks defined in Section 7.2.

Example 7.7.1 (Unidirectionally recursive Hadamard walk). *Recall from Example 7.2.1 that the unidirectionally recursive Hadamard walk is defined as quantum recursive program X declared by*

$$X \Leftarrow T_L[p] \oplus_{H[d]} (T_R[p]; X).$$

(i) *For each $n \geq 0$, the semantics of the nth approximation of the walk is*

$$[\![X^{(n)}]\!] = \sum_{i=0}^{n-1} \left[\left(\bigotimes_{j=0}^{i-1} |R\rangle_{d_j}\langle R| \otimes |L\rangle_{d_i}\langle L| \right) \mathbf{H}(i) \otimes T_L T_R^i \right] \tag{7.25}$$

where $d_0 = d$, $\mathbf{H}(i)$ is the operator in $\mathcal{H}_d^{\otimes i}$ defined from the Hadamard operator H by equation (7.16). This can be easily shown by induction on n, starting from the first three approximations displayed in equation (7.10). Therefore, the semantics of the unidirectionally recursive Hadamard walk in the free Fock space $\mathcal{F}(\mathcal{H}_d) \otimes \mathcal{H}_p$ is the operator:

$$\begin{aligned}
[\![X]\!] &= \lim_{n \to \infty} [\![X^{(n)}]\!] \\
&= \sum_{i=0}^{\infty} \left[\left(\bigotimes_{j=0}^{i-1} |R\rangle_{d_j}\langle R| \otimes |L\rangle_{d_i}\langle L| \right) \mathbf{H}(i) \otimes T_L T_R^i \right] \\
&= \left[\sum_{i=0}^{\infty} \left(\bigotimes_{j=0}^{i-1} |R\rangle_{d_j}\langle R| \otimes |L\rangle_{d_i}\langle L| \right) \otimes T_L T_R^i \right] (\mathbf{H} \otimes I)
\end{aligned} \tag{7.26}$$

where $\mathcal{H}_d = span\{|L\rangle, |R\rangle\}$, $\mathcal{H}_p = span\{|n\rangle : n \in \mathbb{Z}\}$, I is the identity operator in the position Hilbert space $\mathcal{H}_p$, $\mathbf{H}(i)$ is as in equation (7.25), and

$$\mathbf{H} = \sum_{i=0}^{\infty} \mathbf{H}(i)$$

is the extension of H in the free Fock space $\mathcal{F}(\mathcal{H}_d)$ over the direction Hilbert space $\mathcal{H}_d$.

(ii) *For each $i \geq 0$, we compute the symmetrization:*

$$\mathbb{S}\left(\bigotimes_{j=0}^{i-1} |R\rangle_{d_j}\langle R| \otimes |L\rangle_{d_i}\langle L|\right)$$

$$= \frac{1}{(i+1)!} \sum_{\pi} P_{\pi}\left(\bigotimes_{j=0}^{i-1} |R\rangle_{d_j}\langle R| \otimes |L\rangle_{d_i}\langle L|\right) P_{\pi}^{-1}$$

(where π traverses over all permutations of $0, 1, \ldots, i$)

$$= \frac{1}{i+1} \sum_{j=0}^{i} (|R\rangle_{d_0}\langle R| \otimes \ldots \otimes |R\rangle_{d_{j-1}}\langle R| \otimes |L\rangle_{d_j}\langle L|$$

$$\otimes |R\rangle_{d_{j+1}}\langle R| \otimes \ldots \otimes |R\rangle_{d_i}\langle R|)$$

$$\triangleq G_i.$$

Therefore, the symmetric semantics of the unidirectionally recursive Hadamard walk is

$$\mathbb{S}(\llbracket X \rrbracket) = \left(\sum_{i=0}^{\infty} G_i \otimes T_L T_R^i\right)(\mathbf{H} \otimes I).$$

Example 7.7.2 (Bidirectionally recursive Hadamard walk). *Let us consider the semantics of the bidirectionally recursive Hadamard walk. Recall from Example 7.2.1 that it is declared by equations:*

$$\begin{cases} X \Leftarrow T_L[p] \oplus_{H[d]} (T_R[p]; Y), \\ Y \Leftarrow (T_L[p]; X) \oplus_{H[d]} T_R[p]. \end{cases} \tag{7.27}$$

To simplify the presentation, we first introduce several notations. For any string $\Sigma = \sigma_0\sigma_1 \ldots \sigma_{n-1}$ of symbols L and R, its dual is defined to be

$$\overline{\Sigma} = \overline{\sigma_0}\overline{\sigma_1} \ldots \overline{\sigma_{n-1}}$$

where $\overline{L} = R$ and $\overline{R} = L$. We write the pure state

$$|\Sigma\rangle = |\sigma_0\rangle_{d_0} \otimes |\sigma_1\rangle_{d_1} \otimes \ldots \otimes |\sigma_{n-1}\rangle_{d_{n-1}}$$

in the space $\mathcal{H}_d^{\otimes n}$. Then its density operator representation is

$$\rho_{\Sigma} = |\Sigma\rangle\langle\Sigma| = \bigotimes_{j=0}^{n-1} |\sigma_j\rangle_{d_j}\langle\sigma_j|.$$

Moreover, we write the composition of left and right translations:

$$T_{\Sigma} = T_{\sigma_{n-1}} \ldots T_{\sigma_1} T_{\sigma_0}.$$

(i) *The semantics of procedures X and Y in the free Fock space are*

$$[\![X]\!] = \left[\sum_{n=0}^{\infty} \left(\rho_{\Sigma_n} \otimes T_n \right) \right] (\mathbf{H} \otimes I_p),$$

$$[\![Y]\!] = \left[\sum_{n=0}^{\infty} \left(\rho_{\overline{\Sigma_n}} \otimes T_n' \right) \right] (\mathbf{H} \otimes I_p),$$

(7.28)

where $\mathbf{H}$ *is as in Example 7.7.1, and*

$$\Sigma_n = \begin{cases} (RL)^k L & \text{if } n = 2k+1, \\ (RL)^k RR & \text{if } n = 2k+2, \end{cases}$$

$$T_n = T_{\Sigma_n} = \begin{cases} T_L & \text{if } n \text{ is odd,} \\ T_R^2 & \text{if } n \text{ is even,} \end{cases}$$

$$T_n' = T_{\overline{\Sigma_n}} = \begin{cases} T_R & \text{if } n \text{ is odd,} \\ T_L^2 & \text{if } n \text{ is even.} \end{cases}$$

It is clear from equations (7.26) and (7.28) that the behaviors of unidirectionally and bidirectionally recursive Hadamard walks are very different: the former can go to any one of the positions $-1, 0, 1, 2, \ldots,$ *but in the latter walk X can only go to the positions* -1 *and* 2, *and Y can only go to the positions* 1 *and* -2.

(ii) *The symmetric semantics of the bidirectionally recursive Hadamard walk specified by equaltion (7.27) is:*

$$[\![X]\!] = \left[\sum_{n=0}^{\infty} (\gamma_n \otimes T_n) \right] (\mathbf{H} \otimes I_p),$$

$$[\![Y]\!] = \left[\sum_{n=0}^{\infty} (\delta_n \otimes T_n) \right] (\mathbf{H} \otimes I_p)$$

where:

$$\gamma_{2k+1} = \frac{1}{\binom{2k+1}{k}} \sum_{\Gamma} \rho_{\Gamma},$$

$$\delta_{2k+1} = \frac{1}{\binom{2k+1}{k}} \sum_{\Delta} \rho_{\Delta}$$

with Γ ranging over all strings of $(k+1)$ Ls and k Rs and Δ ranging over all strings of k Ls and $(k+1)$ Rs, and

$$\gamma_{2k+2} = \frac{1}{\binom{2k+2}{k}} \sum_{\Gamma} \rho_{\Gamma},$$

$$\sigma_{2k+2} = \frac{1}{\binom{2k+2}{k}} \sum_{\Delta} \rho_{\Delta}$$

with Γ ranging over all strings of k Ls and $(k+2)$ Rs and Δ ranging over all strings of $(k+2)$ Ls and k Rs.

(iii) *Finally, we consider the principal system semantics of the bidirectionally recursive Hadamard walk. Suppose that it starts from the position 0.*

(a) *If the "coins" are bosons initialized in state*

$$|\Psi\rangle = |L, L, \ldots, L\rangle_+ = |L\rangle_{d_0} \otimes |L\rangle_{d_1} \otimes \ldots \otimes |L\rangle_{d_{n-1}},$$

then we have

$$[\![X]\!]_{sym}(|\Psi\rangle \otimes |0\rangle) = \begin{cases} \dfrac{1}{\sqrt{2^n}\binom{2k+1}{k}} \sum_{\Gamma} |\Gamma\rangle \otimes |-1\rangle \\ \qquad\qquad\qquad\qquad if\, n = 2k+1, \\[2mm] \dfrac{1}{\sqrt{2^n}\binom{2k+2}{k}} \sum_{\Delta} |\Delta\rangle \otimes |2\rangle \\ \qquad\qquad\qquad\qquad if\, n = 2k+2, \end{cases}$$

where Γ traverses over all strings of $(k+1)$ L's and k R's, and Δ traverses over all strings of k L's and $(k+2)$ R's. Therefore, the principal system semantics with the "coin" initialisation $|\Psi\rangle$ is:

$$[\![X, \Psi]\!](|0\rangle) = \begin{cases} \frac{1}{2^n}|-1\rangle\langle-1| & if\, n\ is\ odd, \\ \frac{1}{2^n}|2\rangle\langle2| & if\, n\ is\ even. \end{cases}$$

(b) *For each single-particle state $|\psi\rangle$ in $\mathcal{H}_d$, the corresponding coherent state of bosons in the symmetric Fock space $\mathcal{F}_+(\mathcal{H}_d)$ over $\mathcal{H}_d$ is defined as*

$$|\psi\rangle_{coh} = \exp\left(-\frac{1}{2}\langle\psi|\psi\rangle\right) \sum_{n=0}^{\infty} \frac{[a^{\dagger}(\psi)]^n}{n!} |0\rangle$$

where $|0\rangle$ is the vacuum state and $a^{\dagger}(\cdot)$ the creation operator. If the "coins" are initialized in the coherent state $|L\rangle_{coh}$ of bosons corresponding to $|L\rangle$, then we have:

$$[\![X]\!]_{sym}(|L\rangle_{coh} \otimes |0\rangle)$$

$$= \frac{1}{\sqrt{e}} \left(\sum_{k=0}^{\infty} \frac{1}{\sqrt{2^{2k+1}} \binom{2k+1}{k}} \sum_{\Gamma_k} |\Gamma_k\rangle \right) \otimes |-1\rangle$$

$$+ \frac{1}{\sqrt{e}} \sum_{k=0}^{\infty} \left(\frac{1}{\sqrt{2^{2k+2}} \binom{2k+2}{k}} \sum_{\Delta_k} |\Delta_k\rangle \right) \otimes |2\rangle,$$

where Γ_k ranges over all strings of $(k+1)$ Ls and k Rs, and Δ_k ranges over all strings of k Ls and $(k+2)$ Rs. So, the principal system semantics with "coin" initialization $|L\rangle_{coh}$ is:

$$[\![X, L_{coh}]\!](|0\rangle) = \frac{1}{\sqrt{e}} \left(\sum_{k=0}^{\infty} \frac{1}{2^{2k+1}} |-1\rangle\langle -1| + \sum_{k=0}^{\infty} \frac{1}{2^{2k+2}} |2\rangle\langle 2| \right)$$

$$= \frac{1}{\sqrt{e}} \left(\frac{2}{3} |-1\rangle\langle -1| + \frac{1}{3} |2\rangle\langle 2| \right).$$

It is interesting to compare termination in subclauses (a) and (b) of clause (iii) in this example. In case (a), the "coins" start in an n-particle state, so the quantum recursive program X terminates within n steps; that is, termination probability within n steps is $p_T^{(\leq n)} = 1$. But in case (b), the "coins" start in a coherent state, and program X does not terminate within a finite number of steps although it almost surely terminates; that is, $p_T^{(\leq n)} < 1$ for all n and $\lim_{n\to\infty} p_T^{(\leq n)} = 1$.

To conclude this section, we point out that only the behavior of the two simplest among the recursive quantum walks defined in Section 7.2 were examined here. The analysis of the others, in particular the recursive quantum walks defined by equations (7.7) and (7.9), seems very difficult, and is left as a topic for further studies.

7.8 QUANTUM WHILE-LOOPS (WITH QUANTUM CONTROL)

The general form of quantum recursion was carefully studied in previous sections. In this section, as an application of the theory developed before, we consider a special class of quantum recursive programs, namely quantum loops with quantum control flows.

Arguably, the **while**-loop is the simplest and most popular form of recursion used in various programming languages. Recall that in classical programming, the **while**-loop:

$$\textbf{while } b \textbf{ do } S \textbf{ od} \tag{7.29}$$

can be seen as the recursive program X declared by the equation:

$$X \Leftarrow \textbf{if } b \textbf{ then } S; X \textbf{ else skip fi} \tag{7.30}$$

where b is a Boolean expression. In Chapter 3, we defined a measurement-based **while**-loop:

$$\textbf{while } M[\overline{q}] = 1 \textbf{ do } P \textbf{ od} \tag{7.31}$$

as a quantum extension of loop (7.29), where M is a quantum measurement. As pointed out before, the control flow of this loop is classical before it is determined by the outcomes of measurement M.

It was shown that loop (7.31) is the solution of the recursive equation with classical case statement in quantum programming:

$$
\begin{aligned}
X \Leftarrow \ \textbf{if } M[\overline{q}] &= 0 \rightarrow \ \textbf{skip} \\
\square \qquad & 1 \rightarrow P; X \\
\textbf{fi} \qquad &
\end{aligned}
\tag{7.32}
$$

In Chapter 6, we pointed out that, in the quantum setting, the notion of case statement splits into two different versions: (a) the one used in equation (7.32), and (b) the quantum case statement with quantum control. Furthermore, the notion of quantum choice was defined based on the quantum case statement. Now we can define a kind of quantum **while**-loop by using quantum case statement and quantum choice in the place of the classical case statement **if** ... **then** ... **else** ... **fi** in equation (7.30) or (7.32). Inherited from the quantum case statement and quantum choice, the control flow of this new quantum loop is genuinely quantum.

Example 7.8.1 (Quantum **while**-loops with quantum control).

(i) *The first form of quantum **while**-loop with quantum control:*

$$\textbf{qwhile } [c] = |1\rangle \textbf{ do } U[q] \textbf{ od} \tag{7.33}$$

is defined to be the quantum recursive program X declared by

$$
\begin{aligned}
X \Leftarrow \ \textbf{qif}[c] \ |0\rangle &\rightarrow \ \textbf{skip} \\
\square \qquad |1\rangle &\rightarrow U[q]; X \\
\textbf{fiq} \qquad &
\end{aligned}
\tag{7.34}
$$

where c is a quantum "coin" variable denoting a qubit, q is a principal quantum variable, and U is a unitary operator in the state Hilbert space $\mathcal{H}_q$ of system q.

(ii) *The second form of quantum **while**-loop with quantum control:*

$$\textbf{qwhile } V[c] = |1\rangle \textbf{ do } U[q] \textbf{ od} \tag{7.35}$$

is defined to be the quantum recursive program X declared by

$$X \Leftarrow \mathbf{skip} \oplus_{V[c]} (U[q]; X)$$
$$\equiv V[c]; \mathbf{qif}[c] \; |0\rangle \to \mathbf{skip}$$
$$\square \quad |1\rangle \to U[q]; X \qquad (7.36)$$
$$\mathbf{fiq}$$

Note that the quantum recursive equation (7.36) is obtained by replacing the quantum case statement **qif** . . . **fiq** *in equation (7.34) with the quantum choice* $\oplus_{V[c]}$.

(iii) *Actually, quantum loops (7.33) and (7.35) are not very interesting because there is not any interaction in them between the quantum "coin" c and the principal quantum system q. This situation corresponds to the trivial case of classical loop (7.30) where the loop guard b is irrelevant to the loop body S. The classical loop (7.30) becomes truly interesting only when the loop guard b and the loop body S share some program variables. Likewise, a much more interesting form of quantum* **while***-loop with quantum control is*

$$\mathbf{qwhile} \; W[c; q] = |1\rangle \; \mathbf{do} \; U[q] \; \mathbf{od} \qquad (7.37)$$

which is defined to be the program X declared by the quantum recursive equation

$$X \Leftarrow W[c, q]; \mathbf{qif}[c] \; |0\rangle \to \mathbf{skip}$$
$$\square \quad |1\rangle \to U[q]; X$$
$$\mathbf{fiq}$$

where W is a unitary operator in the state Hilbert space $\mathcal{H}_c \otimes \mathcal{H}_q$ *of the composed system of the quantum "coin" c and the principal system q. The operator W describes the interaction between the "coin" c and the principal system q. It is obvious that the loop (7.37) degenerates to the loop (7.35) whenever* $W = V \otimes I$, *where I is the identity operator in* $\mathcal{H}_q$.

It is very interesting to compare quantum loops in the preceding example with the measurement-based **while**-loop (7.31). First of all, we stress once again that the control flow of the former is defined by a quantum "coin" and thus it is quantum; in contrast, the control flow of the latter is determined by the outcomes of a measurement and thus it is classical. In order to further understand the difference between loops (7.31) and (7.37), let us have a close look at the semantics of loop (7.37).

• A routine calculation shows that the semantics of the loop (7.37) in the free Fock space is the operator:

$$\llbracket X \rrbracket = \sum_{k=1}^{\infty} (|1\rangle_{c_0} \langle 1| \otimes (|1\rangle_{c_1} \langle 1| \otimes \ldots (|1\rangle_{c_{k-2}} \langle 1| \otimes (|0\rangle_{c_{k-1}} \langle 0| \otimes U^{k-1}[q])$$

$$W[c_{k-1}, q]) W[c_{k-2}, q] \ldots) W[c_1, q]) W[c_0, q]$$

$$= \sum_{k=1}^{\infty} \left[\left(\bigotimes_{j=0}^{k-2} |1\rangle_{c_j} \langle 1| \otimes |0\rangle_{c_{k-1}} \langle 0| \otimes U^{k-1}[q] \right) \prod_{j=0}^{k-1} W[c_j, q] \right].$$

- Furthermore, the symmetric semantics of the loop is:

$$\llbracket X \rrbracket_{sym} = \sum_{k=1}^{\infty} \left[\left(\mathbf{A}(k) \otimes U^{k-1}[q] \right) \prod_{j=0}^{k-1} W[c_j, q] \right],$$

where:

$$\mathbf{A}(k) = \frac{1}{k} \sum_{j=0}^{k-1} |1\rangle_{c_0} \langle 1| \otimes \ldots \otimes |1\rangle_{c_{j-1}} \langle 1| \otimes |0\rangle_{c_j} \langle 0|$$

$$\otimes |1\rangle_{c_{j+1}} \langle 1| \otimes \ldots \otimes |1\rangle_{c_{k-1}} \langle 1|.$$

- Now we consider the principal semantics of loop (7.37) in a special case. Let q be a qubit, $U = H$ (the Hadamard gate) and $W = CNOT$ (the controlled-NOT). If the "coins" are initialized in the n-boson state

$$|\Psi_n\rangle = |0, 1, \ldots, 1\rangle_+ = \frac{1}{n} \sum_{j=0}^{n-1} |1\rangle_{c_0} \ldots |1\rangle_{c_{j-1}} |0\rangle_{c_j} |1\rangle_{c_{j+1}} \ldots |1\rangle_{c_{n-1}}$$

and the principal system q starts in state $|-\rangle = \frac{1}{\sqrt{2}} (|0\rangle - |1\rangle)$, then we have:

$$|\Phi_n\rangle \overset{\Delta}{=} \llbracket X \rrbracket_{sym}(|\Psi_n\rangle \otimes |-\rangle) = (-1)^n \frac{1}{n} |\Psi_n\rangle \otimes |\psi_n\rangle$$

where

$$|\psi_n\rangle = \begin{cases} |+\rangle & \text{if } n \text{ is even,} \\ |-\rangle & \text{if } n \text{ is odd.} \end{cases}$$

Consequently, the principal system semantics is

$$\llbracket X, \Psi_n \rrbracket(|-\rangle) = tr_{\mathcal{F}_T(\mathcal{H}_v)}(|\Phi_n\rangle \langle \Phi_n|) = \frac{1}{n^3} |\psi_n\rangle \langle \psi_n|.$$

We conclude this chapter by leaving a series of problems for further studies.

Problem 7.8.1. *Although in this chapter we presented several examples of quantum recursion, it is still not well understood what kind of computational problems can be solved more conveniently by using quantum recursion. Another* *important question is: what kind of physical systems can be used to implement quantum recursion where new "coins" must be continuously created?*

Problem 7.8.2. *We do not even fully understand how should a quantum recursion use its "coins" in its computational process. In the definition of the principal system semantics of a recursive program (Definition 7.6.1), a state $|\Psi\rangle$ in the Fock space of "coin" is given a priori. This means that the states of a "coin" and its copies are given once for all. Another possibility is that the states of the copies of a "coin" are created step by step. As an example, let us consider the recursive program X declared by*

$$X \Leftarrow a_c^\dagger(|0\rangle); R_y[c,p]; \textbf{qif } [c] \; |0\rangle \rightarrow \textbf{skip}$$
$$\square \; |1\rangle \rightarrow T_R[p]; X$$
$$\textbf{fiq}$$

where $a^\dagger$ is the creation operator, c is a "coin" variable with state space $\mathcal{H}_c = span\{|0\rangle, |1\rangle\}$, the variable p and operator T_R are as in the Hadamard walk,

$$R_y[c,p] = \sum_{n=0}^{\infty} \left[R_y \left(\frac{\pi}{2^{n+1}} \right) \otimes |n\rangle_p \langle n| \right]$$

and $R_y(\theta)$ is the rotation of a qubit about the y-axis in the Bloch sphere (see Example 2.2.3). Intuitively, $R_y[c,p]$ is a controlled rotation where the position of p is used to determine the rotated angle. It is worth noting that this program X is a quantum loop defined in equation (7.37) but modified by adding a creation operator at the beginning. Its initial behavior starting at position 0 with the "coin" c being in the vacuum state $|0\rangle$ is visualized by the following transitions:

$$|\textbf{0}\rangle|0\rangle_p \xrightarrow{a_d^\dagger(|0\rangle)} |0\rangle|0\rangle_p \xrightarrow{R_x[d,p]} \frac{1}{\sqrt{2}} (|0\rangle + |1\rangle) |0\rangle_p$$
$$\xrightarrow{\textbf{qif...fiq}} \frac{1}{\sqrt{2}} \left[\langle E, |0\rangle|0\rangle_p \rangle + \langle X, |1\rangle|1\rangle_p \rangle \right].$$

The first configuration at the end of the preceding equation terminates, but the second continues the computation as follows:

$$|1\rangle|1\rangle_p \xrightarrow{a_d^\dagger(|0\rangle)} |0, 1\rangle_v|0\rangle_p \xrightarrow{R_x[d,p]} \cdots .$$

It is clear from this example that the computation of a recursive program with the creation operator is very different from that without it. A careful study of quantum recursions that allow the creation operator to appear in their syntax is certainly interesting.

Problem 7.8.3. *The theory of quantum recursive programs in this chapter was developed in the language of Fock spaces. The second quantization method* *can be equivalently presented using the occupation number representation (see [163], Section 2.1.7; also see Definition 7.3.9 for a related notion – the particle number operator). Give an occupation number restatement of the theory of quantum recursion.*

Problem 7.8.4. *Floyd-Hoare logic for quantum programs with classical control flows was presented in Chapter 4. How can you develop a Floyd-Hoare logic for quantum programs with quantum control flows defined in the last and this chapter?*

7.9 BIBLIOGRAPHIC REMARKS

Quantum recursion with classical control flow (in the superposition-of-data paradigm) was discussed in Section 3.4. This chapter can be seen as the counterpart of Section 3.4 in the superposition-of-programs paradigm, dealing with quantum recursion with quantum control flow. The exposition of this chapter is based on the draft paper [222].

Quantum recursion studied both in Section 3.4 and in this chapter is quantum generalization of classical recursion in imperative programming. Two good references for the theory of classical recursive programs are [21] (Chapters 4 and 5) and [158] (Chapter 5). The book [162] contains many examples of recursive programs. It is very interesting to examine the quantum counterparts of these examples.

The lambda calculus is a suitable formalism for coping with recursion and high-order computation, and it provides a solid basis for functional programming. Both the lambda calculus and functional programming have been extended into the quantum setting; see Section 8.3 and the references cited there. But so far, only quantum recursion with classical control has been considered in functional quantum programming.

The main mathematical tool employed in this chapter is the second quantization method. The materials about second quantization in Section 7.3 are standard and can be found in many textbooks of advanced quantum mechanics. Our presentation in Section 7.3 largely follows [163].

Prospects

PART

IV

Prospects

In the previous chapters, we have systematically studied foundations of quantum programming along the line from superposition-of-data to superposition-of-programs. We saw from the previous chapters that various methodologies and techniques in classical programming can be extended or adapted to program quantum computers. On the other hand, the subject of quantum programming is not a simple and straightforward generalization of its classical counterpart, and we have to deal with many completely new phenomena that arise in the quantum realm but would not arise in classical programming. These problems come from the " weird" nature of quantum systems: for example, no-cloning of quantum data, non-commutativity of observables, coexistence of classical and quantum control flows. They make quantum programming a rich and exciting subject.

This final chapter presents an overview of further developments in and prospects for quantum programming. More explicitly, its aim is two-fold:

- We briefly discuss some important approaches to quantum programming or related issues that are not treated in the main body of this book.
- We point out some topics for future research that are, as I believe, important for further development of the subject, but are not mentioned in the previous chapters.

8.1 QUANTUM PROGRAMS AND QUANTUM MACHINES

Understanding the notions of algorithm, program and computational machine and their relationship was the starting point of computer science. All of these fundamental notions have been generalized into the framework of quantum computation. We already studied quantum circuits in Section 2.2. The studies of quantum programming presented in this book are mainly based on the circuit model of quantum computation. In this section, we consider the relationship between quantum programs and other quantum computational models.

Quantum Programs and Quantum Turing Machines:

Benioff [35] constructed a quantum mechanical model of a Turing machine. His construction is the first quantum mechanical description of a computer, but it is not a real quantum computer, because the machine may exist in an intrinsically quantum state between computation steps, but at the end of each computation step the tape of the machine always goes back to one of its classical states. The first truly quantum Turing machine was described by Deutsch [69] in 1985. In his machine, the tape is able to exist in quantum states too. A thorough exposition of the quantum Turing machine is given in [38]. Yao [218] showed that a quantum circuit model is equivalent to a quantum Turing machine in the sense that they can simulate each other in polynomial time.

The relationship between programs and Turing machines is well understood; see for example [41,127]. But up to now, not much research on the relationship between quantum programs and quantum Turing machines has been done, except some interesting discussions by Bernstein and Vazirani in [38]. For example, a fundamental issue that is still not properly understood is *programs as data* in quantum computation. It seems that this issue has very different implications in the paradigm of superposition-of-data studied in Part II of this book and in the paradigm of superposition-of-programs studied in Part III.

Quantum Programs and Nonstandard Models of Quantum Computation:

Quantum circuits and quantum Turing machines are quantum generalizations of their classical counterparts. However, several novel models of quantum computation that have no evident classical analogs have been proposed too:

(i) *Adiabatic Quantum Computation*: This model was proposed by Farhi et al. [80]. It is a continuous-time model of quantum computation in which the evolution of the quantum register is governed by a Hamiltonian that varies slowly. The state of the system is prepared at the beginning in the ground state of the initial Hamiltonian. The solution of a computational problem is then encoded in the ground state of the final Hamiltonian. The adiabatic theorem in quantum physics guarantees that the final state of the system will differ from the ground state of the final Hamiltonian by a negligible amount, provided the Hamiltonian of the system evolves slowly enough. Thus, the solution can be obtained with a high probability by measuring the final state. Adiabatic computing was shown by Aharonov et al. [10] to be polynomially equivalent to conventional quantum computing in the circuit model, and it can be seen as a special form of quantum annealing [136].

(ii) *Measurement-Based Quantum Computation*: In the quantum Turing machine and quantum circuits, measurements are mainly used at the end to extract computational outcomes from quantum states. However, Raussendorf and Briegel [183] proposed a one-way quantum computer and Nielsen [175] and Leung [151] introduced teleportation quantum computation, both of them suggesting that measurements can play a much more important role in quantum computation. In a one-way quantum computer, universal computation can be realized by one-qubit measurements together with a special entangled state, called a cluster state, of a large number of qubits. Teleportation quantum computation is based on Gottesman and Chuang's idea of teleporting quantum gates [104] and allows us to realize universal quantum computation using only projective measurement, quantum memory, and preparation of the $|0\rangle$ state.

(iii) *Topological Quantum Computation*: A crucial challenge in constructing large quantum computers is quantum decoherence. Topological quantum computation was proposed by Kitaev [134] as a model of quantum computation in which a revolutionary strategy is adopted to build significantly more stable quantum computers. This model employs two-dimensional quasi-particles, called anyons, whose world lines form braids, which are used to construct logic gates of quantum computers. The key point is that small perturbations do not change the topological properties of these braids. This makes quantum decoherence simply irrelevant for topological quantum computers.

Only very few papers have been devoted to studies of programming in these nonstandard models of quantum computation. Rieffel et al. [187] developed some techniques for programming quantum annealers. Danos et al. [63] proposed a calculus for formally reasoning about (programs in) measurement-based quantum computation. Compilation for topological quantum computation was considered by Kliuchnikov et al. [138].

Research in this direction will be vital once the physical implementation of some of these models becomes possible. On the other hand, it will be challenging due to the fundamental differences between these nonstandard models and quantum circuits. For example, the mathematical description of topological quantum computation is given in terms of topological quantum field theory, knot theory and lower-dimensional topology. The studies of programming methodology for topological quantum computers (e.g., fixed point semantics of recursive programs) might even bring exciting open problems to these mainstream areas of mathematics.

8.2 IMPLEMENTATION OF QUANTUM PROGRAMMING LANGUAGES

This book is devoted to the exposition of high-level concepts and models of quantum programming. From a practical viewpoint, implementing quantum programming languages and designing quantum compilers are very important. Some research in this direction had already been reported in the early literature; for example, Svore et al. [207] proposed a layered quantum software architecture which is a four-phase design flow mapping a high-level language quantum program onto a quantum device through an intermediate quantum assembly language. Zuliani [242] designed a compiler for the language qGCL in which compilation is realized by algebraic transformation from a qGCL program into a normal form that can be directly executed by a target machine. Nagarajan et al. [176] defined a hybrid classical-quantum computer architecture – the Sequential Quantum Random Access Memory machine (SQRAM) – based on Knill's QRAM, presented a set of templates for quantum assembly code, and developed a compiler for a subset of Selinger's QPL.

A translation between the quantum extension of the **while**-language defined in Chapter 3 and a quantum extension of classical flowchart language was given in [228]. All of these studies are based on the popular circuit model of quantum computation. Nevertheless, as mentioned in the last section, Danos et al. [63] presented an elegant low-level language based on a novel and promising physical implementation model of quantum computation, namely the measurement-based one-way quantum computer.

Recently, quantum compilation including optimization of quantum circuits has been intensively researched. A series of compilation techniques has been developed through the recent projects of languages Quipper [106], LIQUi|> [215], Scaffold [3,126] and QuaFL [150]. In particular, significant progress in synthesis and optimization of quantum circuits has been made in the last few years; see for examples [20,44,45,99,137,188,237,239].

At this moment, the majority of research on quantum language implementation is devoted to quantum circuit optimization. No work except [242] has been reported in the literature on transformations and optimization of high-level language constructs like quantum loops, which is obviously an important issue (see, for example, [13], Chapter 9). In particular, we need to examine whether the techniques successfully applied in classical compiler optimization, e.g., loop fusion and loop interchange, can be used for quantum programs. On the other hand, the analysis techniques developed in Chapter 5 may help in, for example, data-flow analysis and redundancy elimination of quantum programs.

Another important topic for future research is the compilation of quantum programs with quantum control, defined in Chapters 6 and 7.

8.3 FUNCTIONAL QUANTUM PROGRAMMING

This book focuses on imperative quantum programming, but functional quantum programming has been an active research area in the last decade.

The lambda calculus is a formalism of high-order functions and it is a logical basis of some important classical functional programming languages, such as LISP, Scheme, ML and Haskell. The research on functional quantum programming started with an attempt to define a quantum extension of lambda calculus made by Maymin [165] and van Tonder [212]. In a series of papers [196,197,199], Selinger and Valiron systematically developed quantum lambda calculus with well-defined operational semantics, a strong type system and a practical type inference algorithm. As already mentioned in Subsection 1.1.1, a denotational semantics of quantum lambda calculus was recently properly defined by Hasuo and Hoshino [115] and Pagani et al. [178]. The no-cloning property of quantum data makes quantum lambda calculus closely related to linear lambda calculus developed by the linear logic community. Quantum lambda calculus was used by Selinger and Valiron [198] to provide a fully abstract model for the linear fragment of a quantum functional programming language, which is obtained by adding higher-order functions into Selinger's quantum flowchart language QFC [194].

One of the earliest proposals for functional quantum programming was made by Mu and Bird [173]. They introduced a monadic style of quantum programming and coded the Deutsch-Josza algorithm in Haskell. A line of systematic research on functional quantum programming had been pursued by Altenkirch and Grattage [14]. As mentioned in Subsection 1.1.1, they proposed a functional language QML for quantum computation. An implementation of QML in Haskell was presented by Grattage [105] as a compiler. An equational theory for QML was developed by Altenkirch et al. [15]. Notably, QML is the first quantum programming language with quantum control, but it was defined in a way very different from that presented in Chapters 6 and 7. The recent highlight of functional quantum programming is the implementation of languages Quipper [106,107] and LIQUi|> [215]: the former is an embedded language using Haskell as its host language, and the latter is embedded in F#.

The control flow of all quantum lambda calculus defined in the literature as well as functional quantum programming languages (except QML) is classical. So, an interesting topic for further research is to incorporate quantum control (case statement, choice and recursion) introduced in Chapters 6 and 7 into quantum lambda calculus and functional quantum programming.

8.4 CATEGORICAL SEMANTICS OF QUANTUM PROGRAMS

In this book, the semantics of quantum programming languages has been defined in the standard Hilbert space formalism of quantum mechanics. Abramsky and Coecke [5] proposed a category-theoretic axiomatization of quantum mechanics. This novel axiomatization has been successfully used to address a series of problems in quantum foundations and quantum information. In particular, it provides effective methods for high-level description and verification of quantum communication protocols, including teleportation, logic-gate teleportation, and entanglement swapping. Furthermore, a logic of strongly compact closed categories with biproducts in the form of proof-net calculus was developed by Abramsky and Duncan [6] as a categorical quantum logic. It is particularly suitable for high-level reasoning about quantum processes.

Heunen and Jacobs [117] investigated quantum logic from the perspective of categorical logic, and they showed that kernel subobjects in dagger kernel categories precisely capture orthomodular structure. Jacobs [123] introduced the block construct for quantum programming languages in a categorical manner. More recently, he [124] proposed a categorical axiomatization of quantitative logic for quantum systems where quantum measurements are defined in terms of instruments that may have a side-effect on the observed system. He further used it to define a dynamic logic with test operators that is very useful for reasoning about quantum programs and protocols.

Further applications of category-theoretic techniques to quantum programming will certainly be a fruitful direction of research. In particular, it is desirable to have a categorical characterization of quantum case statement and quantum choice defined in Chapter 6 and quantum recursion based on second quantization defined in Chapter 7.

8.5 FROM CONCURRENT QUANTUM PROGRAMS TO QUANTUM CONCURRENCY

This book only considers sequential quantum programs, but concurrent and distributed quantum computing has already been extensively studied in the literature.

Quantum Process Algebras:

Process algebras are popular formal models of concurrent systems. They provide mathematical tools for the description of interactions, communications and synchronization between processes, and they also provide formal methods for reasoning about behavior equivalence between processes by proving various algebraic laws. Quantum generalization of process algebras has been proposed by several researchers. To provide formal techniques for modelling, analysis and verification of quantum communication protocols, Gay and Nagarajan [93,94] defined the CQP language by adding primitives for measurements and transformations of quantum states and allowing transmission of quantum data in the pi-calculus. To model concurrent quantum computation, Jorrand and Lalire [128,147] defined the QPAlg language by adding primitives expressing unitary transformations and quantum measurements, as well as communications of quantum states, to a classical process algebra, which is similar to CCS. Feng et al. [83,84,229] proposed a model qCCS for concurrent quantum computation, which is a natural quantum extension of classical value-passing CCS and can deal with input and output of quantum states, and unitary transformations and measurements on quantum systems. In particular, the notion of bisimulation between quantum processes was introduced, and their congruence properties were established. Furthermore, symbolic bisimulations and approximate bisimulations (bisimulation metrics) for quantum process algebras are proposed in [81,85,229], respectively. Approximate bisimulation can be used to describe implementation of a quantum process by some (usually finitely many) special quantum gates. One of the most spectacular results in fault-tolerant quantum computation is the threshold theorem, which means that it is possible to efficiently perform an arbitrarily large quantum computation provided the noise in individual quantum gates is below a certain constant. This theorem considers only the case of sequential quantum computation. Its generalization in concurrent quantum computation would be a challenge. The notion of approximate bisimulation provides us with a formal tool for observing robustness of concurrent quantum computation against inaccuracy in the implementation of its elementary gates, and I guess that it can be used to establish a concurrent generalization of the (fault-tolerance) threshold theorem.

Quantum process algebras have already been used in verification of correctness and security of quantum cryptographic protocols, quantum error-correction codes and linear optical quantum computing [24,25,67,68,89,90,98,141,143,219].

Quantum Concurrency:

Research on quantum process algebras was mainly motivated by applications in specification and verification of quantum communication protocols. Actually, concurrency in quantum programming has another special importance: Despite convincing demonstration of quantum computing devices, it is still beyond the ability of the current technology to scale them. So, it was conceived to use the physical resources of two or more small capacity quantum computers to form a large capacity quantum computing system, and various experiments in the physical implementation of distributed quantum computing have been reported in recent years. Concurrency is then an unavoidable issue in programming such distributed quantum computing systems.

Understanding the combined bizarre behavior of concurrent and quantum systems is extremely hard. Almost all existing work in this direction can be appropriately termed as *concurrent quantum programming* but not *quantum concurrent programming*; for example, a *concurrent quantum program* is defined by Yu et al. [238] as a collection of quantum processes together with a kind of *classical* fairness that is used to schedule the execution of the involved processes. However, the behavior of a *quantum concurrent program* is much more complicated. We need to very carefully define its execution model because a series of new problems arises in the quantum setting:

(i) *Interleaving* abstraction has been widely used in the analysis of classical concurrent programs. But entanglement between different quantum processes forces us to restrict its applications. Superposition-of-programs defined in Chapters 6 and 7 adds another dimension of difficulty to this problem; for example, how can the summation operator in quantum process algebras be replaced by a quantum choice?

(ii) Research in physics reveals that certain new *synchronization* mechanisms are possible in the quantum regime; for example, entanglement can be used to overcome certain classical limits in synchronisation [100]. An interesting question is: how to incorporate such new synchronisation mechanisms into quantum concurrent programming?

(iii) We still do not know how to define a notion of fairness that can better embody both the quantum feature of the participating processes and the entanglement between them. A possible way to do this is further generalizing the idea of "quantum coins" and employing some ideas from quantum games [77,168] to control the processes in a quantum concurrent program.

8.6 ENTANGLEMENT IN QUANTUM PROGRAMMING

It has been realized from the very beginning of quantum computing research that entanglement is one of the most important resources that enable a quantum computer to outperform its classical counterpart. However, entanglement in quantum programming has not been discussed at all in the previous chapters. The reason is that research in this direction is almost nonexistent up to now. Here, we introduce the existing several pieces of work on entanglement that have direct or potential connections to quantum programming.

The role of entanglement in sequential quantum computation has been carefully analyzed by several researchers; see for example [130]. Abstract interpretation techniques were employed by Jorrand and Perdrix [129] and Honda [118] to analyze entanglement evolution in quantum programming written in a language similar to the quantum **while**-language defined in Chapter 3. The compiler [126] of quantum programming language Scaffold [3] facilitates a conservative analysis of entanglement. It was observed in [230] that information leakage can be caused by an entanglement, and thus the Trojan Horse may exploit an entanglement between itself and a user with sensitive information as a covert channel. This presents a challenge to programming language-based information-flow security in quantum computing.

It seems that entanglement is more essential in concurrent and distributed quantum computation than in sequential quantum computation [51,58]. An algebraic language for specifying distributed quantum computing circuits and entanglement resources was defined in [226]. It was also noticed in [83–85,229] that entanglement brings extra difficulties to defining bisimulations preserved by parallel composition in quantum process algebras. Conversely, quantum process algebras provide us with a formal framework for examining the role of entanglement in concurrent quantum computation. In the last section, we already mentioned the possible influence of entanglement on interleaving abstraction in the execution models of quantum concurrent programs.

I expect that research on entanglement in quantum programming, especially in the mode of concurrent and distributed computing, will be fruitful.

8.7 MODEL-CHECKING QUANTUM SYSTEMS

Analysis and verification techniques for quantum programs (with classical control) were studied in Chapters 4 and 5. A natural extension of this line of research is model-checking quantum programs and communication protocols. Actually, several model-checking techniques have been developed in the last decade, not only for quantum programs but also for general quantum systems.

The earlier work was mainly targeted at checking quantum communication protocols. Gay et al. [95] used the probabilistic model-checker PRISM [146] to verify the correctness of several quantum protocols including BB84 [36]. Furthermore, they [97] developed an automatic tool QMC (Quantum Model-Checker). QMC uses the stabilizer formalism [174] for the modelling of systems, and the properties to be checked by QMC are expressed in Baltazar et al. quantum computation tree logic [31].

However, to develop model-checking techniques for general quantum systems, including quantum programs, at least the following two problems must be carefully addressed:

- We need to clearly define a conceptual framework in which we can properly reason about quantum systems, including (1) *formal models of quantum systems*, and (2) *specification languages suited to formalise the properties of quantum systems to be checked*.
- The state spaces of the classical systems that model-checking techniques can be applied to are usually finite or countably infinite. But the state spaces of quantum systems are inherently continuous even when they are finite-dimensional, so we have to explore mathematical structures of the state spaces so that it suffices to examine only a finite number of (or at most, countably infinitely many) representative elements, e.g., those in an orthonormal basis.

The models of quantum systems considered in the current literature on quantum model-checking are either quantum automata or quantum Markov chains and Markov decision processes. The actions in a quantum automaton are described by unitary transformations. Quantum Markov models can be seen as a generalization of quantum automata where actions are depicted by general quantum operations (or super-operators).

Since some key issues in model-checking can be reduced to the reachability problem, reachability analysis of quantum Markov chains presented in Section 5.3 provides a basis of quantum model-checking. The issue of checking linear-time properties of quantum systems was considered in [231], where linear-time properties are defined to be an infinite sequence of sets of atomic propositions modelled by closed subspaces of the state Hilbert spaces. But model-checking more general temporal properties is still totally untouched. Indeed, we do not even know how to properly define a general temporal logic for quantum systems, although this problem has been studied by physicists for quite a long time (see [125] for example).

Another kind of quantum Markov chains were introduced by Gudder [111] and Feng et al. [88], which can be more appropriately termed as super-operator valued Markov chains because they are defined by replacing transition probabilities in a classical Markov chain with super-operators. Feng et al. [88] further noticed that super-operator valued Markov chains are especially convenient for a higher-level description of quantum programs and protocols and developed model-checking techniques for them, where a logic called QCTL (quantum computation tree logic, different from that in [31]) was defined by replacing probabilities in PCTL (probabilistic computation tree logic) with super-operators. A model-checker based on [88] was implemented by Feng, Hahn, Turrini and Zhang [86]. Furthermore, the reachability problem for recursive super-operator valued Markov chains was studied by Feng et al. [87].

8.8 QUANTUM PROGRAMMING APPLIED TO PHYSICS

Of course, the subject of quantum programming has been developed mainly with the purpose of programming future quantum computers. However, some ideas, methodologies and techniques in quantum programming may also be applied to quantum physics and quantum engineering.

The hypothesis that *the universe is a quantum computer* has been proposed by several leading physicists [155,211]. If you agree with this view, I would like to argue that *God (or nature) is a quantum programmer*. Furthermore, I believe that translating various ideas from programming theory to quantum physics will produce some novel insights. For example, the notion of quantum weakest precondition defined in Subsection 4.1.1 provides with us a new way for backward analysis of physical systems. Recently, Floyd-Hoare logic has been extended to reason about dynamical systems with continuous evolution described by differential equations [46,180]. It is interesting to develop a logic based on this work and quantum Floyd-Hoare logic presented in Section 4.2 that can be used to reason about continuous-time quantum systems governed by the Schrödinger equation.

As pointed out by Dowling and Milburn [71], we are currently in the midst of a second quantum revolution: transition from quantum theory to quantum engineering. The aim of quantum theory is to find fundamental rules that govern the physical systems already existing in the nature. Instead, quantum engineering intends to design and implement new systems (machines, devices, etc.) that did not exist before to accomplish some desirable tasks, based on quantum theory.

Experiences in today's engineering indicate that it is not guaranteed that a human designer completely understands the behaviors of the systems she/he designed, and a bug in her/his design may cause some serious problems and even disasters. So, correctness, safety and reliability of complex engineering systems have been a key issue in various engineering fields. Certainly, it will be even more serious in quantum engineering than in today's engineering, because it is much harder for a system designer to understand the behaviours of quantum systems. The verification and analysis techniques for quantum programs may be adapted to design and implement automatic tools for correctness and safety verification of quantum engineering systems. Moreover, (a continuous-time extension of) model-checking techniques for quantum systems discussed in the last section are obviously useful in quantum engineering. It is sure that this line of research combined with quantum simulation [59,154] will be fruitful.

Bibliography

[1] S. Aaronson, Quantum lower bound for recursive Fourier sampling, *arXiv:quant-ph*/0209060.

[2] S. Aaronson, Read the fine print, *Nature Physics*, 11(2015)291-293.

[3] A. J. Abhari, A. Faruque, M. Dousti, L. Svec, O. Catu, A. Chakrabati, C.-F. Chiang, S. Vanderwilt, J. Black, F. Chong, M. Martonosi, M. Suchara, K. Brown, M. Pedram and T.Brun, *Scaffold: Quantum Programming Language*, Technical Report TR-934-12, Dept. of Computer Science, Princeton University, 2012.

[4] S. Abramsky, High-Level Methods for Quantum Computation and Information. In: *Proceedings of the 19th Annual IEEE Symposium on Logic in Computer Science (LICS)*, 2004, IEEE Computer Society, 410–414, 2004.

[5] S. Abramsky and B. Coecke, A categorical semantics of quantum protocols. In: *Proceedings of the 19th Annual IEEE Symposium on Logic in Computer Science (LICS)*, 2004, pp. 415-425.

[6] S. Abramsky and R. Duncan, A categorical quantum logic, *Mathematical Structures in Computer Science*, 16(2006)469-489.

[7] S. Abramsky, E. Haghverdi and P. Scott, Geometry of interaction and linear combinatory algebras, *Mathematical Structures in Computer Science*, 12(2002)625-665.

[8] R. Adams, QPEL: Quantum program and effect language. In: *Proceedings of the 11th workshop on Quantum Physics and Logic (QPL)*, EPTCS 172, 2014, pp. 133-153.

[9] D. Aharonov, A. Ambainis, J. Kempe and U. Vazirani, Quantum walks on graphs. In: *Proceedings of the 33rd ACM Symposium on Theory of Computing (STOC)*, 2001, pp. 50-59.

[10] D. Aharonov, W. van Dam, J. Kempe, Z. Landau, S. Lloyd and O. Regev, Adiabatic quantum computation is equivalent to standard quantum computation. In: *Proceedings of the 45th Symposium on Foundations of Computer Science (FOCS)*, 2004, pp. 42-51.

[11] Y. Aharonov, J. Anandan, S. Popescu and L. Vaidman, Superpositions of time evolutions of a quantum system and quantum time-translation machine, *Plysical Review Letters*, 64 (1990) 2965-2968.

[12] Y. Aharonov, L. Davidovich and N. Zagury, Quantum random walks, *Physical Review A*, 48(1993), 1687-1690.

[13] A. V. Aho, M. S. Lam, R. Sethi and J. D. Ullman, *Compilers: Principles, Techniques, and Tools* (second edition), Addison-Wesley, 2007.

[14] T. Altenkirch and J. Grattage, A functional quantum programming language. In: *Proc. of the 20th Annual IEEE Symposium on Logic in Computer Science (LICS)*, 2005, pp. 249-258.

[15] T. Altenkirch, J. Grattage, J. K. Vizzotto and A. Sabry, An algebra of pure quantum programming, *Electronic Notes in Theoretical Computer Science*, 170(2007)23-47.

[16] T. Altenkirch and A. S. Green, The quantum IO monad. In: *Semantic Techniques in Quantum Computation* I. Mackie and S. Gay, eds., Cambridge University Press 2010, pp. 173-205.

[17] A. Ambainis, Quantum walk algorithm for Element Distinctness, *SIAM Journal on Computing*, 37(2007)210-239.

[18] A. Ambainis, Quantum walks and their algorithmic applications, *International Journal of Quantum Information*, 1(2004)507-518.

[19] A. Ambainis, E. Bach, A. Nayak, A. Vishwanath and J. Watrous, One-dimensional quantum walks. In: *Proceedings of the 33rd ACM Symposium on Theory of Computing (STOC)*, 2001, pp. 37-49.

[20] M. Amy, D. Maslov, M. Mosca and M. Rötteler, A meet-in-the-middle algorithm for fast synthesis of depth-optimal quantum circuits, *IEEE Transactions on Computer-Aided Design of Integrated Circuits and Systems*, 32(2013)818-830.

[21] K. R. Apt, F. S. de Boer and E. -R. Olderog, *Verification of Sequential and Concurrent Programs*, Springer, London 2009.

[22] M. Araújo, A. Feix, F. Costa and C. Brukner, Quantum circuits cannot control unknown operations, *New Journal of Physics*, 16(2004) art. no. 093026.

[23] M. Araújo, F. Costa and C. Brukner, Computational advantage from quantum-controlled ordering of gates, *Physical Review Letters*, 113(2014) art. no. 250402.

[24] E. Ardeshir-Larijani, S. J. Gay and R. Nagarajan, Equivalence checking of quantum protocols, *TACAS, 2013*, pp. 478-492.

[25] E. Ardeshir-Larijani, S. J. Gay and R. Nagarajan, Verification of concurrent quantum protocols by equivalence checking. In: *Proceedings of the 20th International Conference on Tools and Algorithms for the Construction and Analysis of Systems (TACAS)*, 2014, pp. 500-514.

[26] S. Attal, Fock spaces, http://math.univ-lyon1.fr/~attal/Mescours/fock.pdf.

[27] R. -J. Back and J. von Wright, *Refinement Calculus: A Systematic Introduction*, Springer, New York, 1998.

[28] C. Bǎdescu and P. Panangaden, Quantum alternation: prospects and problems. In: *Proceedings of the 12th International Workshop on Quantum Physics and Logic (QPL)*, 2015.

[29] C. Baier and J. -P. Katoen, *Principles of Model Checking*, MIT Press, Cambridge, Massachusetts, 2008.

[30] A. Baltag and S. Smets, LQP: the dynamic logic of quantum information, *Mathematical Structures in Computer Science*, 16(2006)491-525.

[31] P. Baltazar, R. Chadha and P. Mateus, Quantum computation tree logic – model checking and complete calculus, *International Journal of Quantum Information*, 6(2008)219-236.

[32] P. Baltazar, R. Chadha, P. Mateus and A. Sernadas, Towards model-checking quantum security protocols. In: P. Dini et al. (eds.), *Proceedings of the 1st Workshop on Quantum Security (QSec07)*, IEEE Press, 2007.

[33] J. Bang-Jensen and G. Gutin, *Digraphs: Theory, Algorithms and Applications*, Springer, Berlin, 2007.

[34] A. Barenco, C. H. Bennett, R. Cleve, D. P. DiVincenzo, N. Margolus, P. Shor, T. Sleator, J. A. Smolin and H. Weinfurter, Elementary gates for quantum computation, *Physical Review A*, 52(1995)3457-3467.

[35] P. A. Benioff, The computer as a physical system: a microscopic quantum mechanical Hamiltonian model of computers as represented by Turing machines, *Journal of Statistical Physics*, 22(1980)563-591.

[36] C. H. Bennett and G. Brassard, Quantum cryptography: public key distribution and coin tossing. In: *Proceedings of International Conference on Computers, Systems and Signal Processing*, 1984.

[37] E. Bernstein and U. Vazirani, Quantum complexity theory. In: *Proc. of the 25th Annual ACM Symposium on Theory of Computing (STOC)*, 1993, pp. 11-20.

[38] E. Bernstein and U. Vazirani, Quantum complexity theory, *SIAM Journal on Computing*, 26(1997)1411-1473.

[39] S. Bettelli, T. Calarco and L. Serafini, Toward an architecture for quantum programming, *The European Physical Journal D*, 25(2003)181-200.

[40] R. Bhatia, *Matrix Analysis*, Springer Verlag, Berlin, 1991.

[41] R. Bird, *Programs and Machines: An Introduction to the Theory of Computation*, John Wiley & Sons, 1976.

[42] G. Birkhoff and J. von Neumann, The logic of quantum mechanics, *Annals of Mathematics*, 37(1936)823-843.

[43] R. F. Blute, P. Panangaden and R. A. G. Seely, Holomorphic models of exponential types in linear logic. In: *Proceedings of the 9th Conference on Mathematical Foundations of Programming Semantics (MFPS)*, Springer LNCS 802, 1994, pp. 474-512.

[44] A. Bocharov, M. Rötteler and K. M. Svore, Efficient synthesis of universal Repeat-Until-Success circuits, *Physical Review Letters*, 114(2015) art. no. 080502.

[45] A. Bocharov and K. M. Svore, Resource-optimal single-qubit quantum circuits, *Physical Review Letters*, 109(2012) art. no. 190501.

[46] R. J. Boulton, R. Hardy and U. Martin, Hoare logic for single-input single-output continuous-time control systems. In: *Proceeding of the 6th International Workshop on Hybrid Systems: Computation and Control (HSCC 2003)*, Springer LNCS 2623, pp. 113-125.

[47] H. -P. Breuer and F. Petruccione, *The Theory of Open Quantum Systems*, Oxford University Press, Oxford, 2002.

[48] T. Brun, A simple model of quantum trajectories, *American Journal of Physics*, 70(2002)719-737.

[49] T. A. Brun, H. A. Carteret and A. Ambainis, Quantum walks driven by many coins, *Physical Review A*, 67 (2003) art. no. 052317.

[50] O. Brunet and P. Jorrand, Dynamic quantum logic for quantum programs, *International Journal of Quantum Information*, 2(2004)45-54.

[51] H. Buhrman and H. Röhrig, Distributed quantum computing. In: *Proceedings of the 28th International Symposium on Mathematical Foundations of Computer Science (MFCS)*, 2003, Springer LNCS 2747, pp 1-20.

[52] R. Chadha, P. Mateus and A. Sernadas, Reasoning about imperative quantum programs, *Electronic Notes in Theoretical Computer Science*, 158(2006)19-39.

[53] A. M. Childs, R. Cleve, E. Deotto, E. Farhi, S. Gutmann and D. A. Spielman, Exponential algorithmic speedup by quantum walk. In: *Proceedings of the 35th ACM Symposium on Theory of Computing (STOC)*, 2003, pp. 59-68.

[54] A. M. Childs, Universal computation by quantum walk, *Physical Review Letters*, 102(2009) art. no. 180501.

[55] G. Chiribella, Perfect discrimination of no-signalling channels via quantum superposition of causal structures, *Physical Review A*, 86(2012) art. no. 040301.

[56] G. Chiribella, G. M. D'Ariano, P. Perinotti and B. Valiron, Quantum computations without definite causal structure, *Physical Review A*, 88(2013), art. no. 022318.

[57] K. Cho, Semantics for a quantum programming language by operator algebras. In: *Proceedings 11th workshop on Quantum Physics and Logic (QPL)*, EPTCS 172, 2014, pp. 165-190.

[58] J.I. Cirac, A.K. Ekert, S.F. Huelga and C. Macchiavello, Distributed quantum computation over noisy channels, *Physical Review A*, 59(1999)4249-4254.

[59] J. I. Cirac and P. Zoller, Goals and opportunities in quantum simulation, *Nature Physics*, 8(2012)264-266.

[60] D. Copsey, M. Oskin, F. Impens, T. Metodiev, A. Cross, F. T. Chong, I. L. Chuang and J. Kubiatowicz, Toward a Scalable, Silicon-Based Quantum Computing Architecture (invited paper), *IEEE Journal of Selected Topics in Quantum Electronics*, 9(2003)1552-1569.

[61] T. H. Cormen, C. E. Leiserson, R. L. Rivest and C. Stein, *Introduction to Algorithms*, The MIT Press, 2009 (Third Edition).

[62] M. Dalla Chiara, R. Giuntini and R. Greechie, *Reasoning in Quantum Theory: Sharp and Unsharp Quantum Logics*, Kluwer, Dordrecht, 2004.

[63] V. Danos, E. Kashefi and P. Panangaden, The measurement calculus, *Journal of the ACM*, 54(2007)8.

[64] V. Danos, E. Kashefi, P. Panangaden and S. Perdrix, Extended measurement calculus. In: *Semantic Techniques in Quantum Computation* I. Mackie and S. Gay, eds., Cambridge University Press 2010, pp. 235-310.

[65] T. A. S. Davidson, *Formal Verification Techniques Using Quantum Process Calculus*, PhD Thesis, University of Warwick, 2012.

[66] T. A. S. Davidson, S. J. Gay, H. Mlnarik, R. Nagarajan and N. Papanikolaou, Model checking for communicating quantum processes, *International Journal of Unconventional Computing*, 8(2012)73-98.

[67] T. A. S. Davidson, S. J. Gay and R. Nagarajan, Formal analysis of quantum systems using process calculus, *Electronic Proceedings in Theoretical Computer Science 59 (ICE 2011)*, pp. 104-110.

[68] T. A. S. Davidson, S. J. Gay, R. Nagarajan and I. V. Puthoor, Analysis of a quantum error correcting code using quantum process calculus, *Electronic Proceedings in Theoretical Computer Science* 95, pp. 67-80.

[69] D. Deutsch, Quantum theory, the Church-Turing principle and the universal quantum computer, *Proceedings of The Royal Society of London* A400(1985)97-117.

[70] E. D'Hondt and P. Panangaden, Quantum weakest preconditions. *Mathematical Structures in Computer Science*, 16(2006)429-451.

[71] J. P. Dowling and G. J. Milburn, Quantum technology: the second quantum revolution, *Philosophical Transactions of the Royal Society London A*, 361(2003) 1655-1674.

[72] Y. X. Deng and Y. Feng, Open bisimulation for quantum processes. In: *Proceedings of IFIP Theoretical Computer Science*, Springer Lecture Notes in Computer Science 7604, pp. 119-133.

[73] D. Deutsch and R. Jozsa, Rapid solutions of problems by quantum computation, *Proceedings of the Royal Society of London A439* (1992) 553-558.

[74] E. W. Dijkstra, Guarded commands, nondeterminacy and formal derivation of programs, *Communications of the ACM*, *18* (1975) 453-457.

[75] E. W. Dijkstra, *A Discipline of Programming*, Prentice-Hall, 1976.

[76] R. Y. Duan, S Severini and A Winter, Zero-error communication via quantum channels, noncommutative graphs, and a quantum Lovasz theta function, *IEEE Transactions on Information Theory*, 59 (2013)1164-1174.

[77] J. Eisert, M. Wilkens and M. Lewenstein, Quantum games and quantum strategies, *Physical Review Letters*, 83(1999)3077-3080.

[78] J. Esparza and S. Schwoon, A BDD-based model checker for recursive programs. In: *Proceedings of the 13th International Conference on Computer Aided Verification (CAV)*, 2001, Springer LNCS 2102, pp. 324-336.

[79] K. Etessami and M. Yannakakis, Recursive Markov chains, stochastic grammars, and monotone systems of nonlinear equations, *Journal of the ACM*, 56(2009) art. no. 1.

[80] E. Farhi, J. Goldstone, S. Gutmann, and M. Sipser, Quantum computation by adiabatic evolution, *arXiv: quant-ph/0001106.*

[81] Y. Feng, Y. X. Deng and M. S. Ying, Symbolic bisimulation for quantum processes, *ACM Transactions on Computational Logic*, 15(2014) art. no. 14.

[82] Y. Feng, R. Y. Duan, Z. F. Ji and M. S. Ying, Proof rules for the correctness of quantum programs, *Theoretical Computer Science, 386* (2007), 151-166.

[83] Y. Feng, R. Y. Duan, Z. F. Ji and M. S. Ying, Probabilistic bisimulations for quantum processes, *Information and Computation*, 205(2007)1608-1639.

[84] Y. Feng, R. Y. Duan and M. S. Ying, Bisimulation for quantum processes. In: *Proceedings of the 38th ACM Symposium on Principles of Programming Languages (POPL)*, 2011, pp. 523-534.

[85] Y. Feng, R. Y. Duan and M. S. Ying, Bisimulation for quantum processes, *ACM Transactions on Programming Languages and Systems*, 34(2012) art. no: 17.

[86] Y. Feng, E. M. Hahn, A. Turrini and L. J. Zhang, QPMC: a model checker for quantum programs and protocols. In: *Proceedings of the 20th International Symposium on Formal Methods (FM 2015)*, Springer LNCS 9109, pp. 265-272.

[87] Y. Feng, N. K. Yu and M. S. Ying, Reachability analysis of recursive quantum Markov chains. In: *Proceedings of the 38th International Symposium on Mathematical Foundations of Computer Science (MFCS)*, 2013, pp. 385-396.

[88] Y. Feng, N. K. Yu and M. S. Ying, Model checking quantum Markov chains, *Journal of Computer and System Sciences*, 79(2013)1181-1198.

[89] S. Franke-Arnold, S. J. Gay and I. V. Puthoor, Quantum process calculus for linear optical quantum computing. In: *Proceedings of the 5th International Conference on Reversible Computation (RC)*, 2013, Proceedings. Lecture Notes in Computer Science 7948, Springer, pp. 234-246.

[90] S. Franke-Arnold, S. J. Gay and I. V. Puthoor, Verification of linear optical quantum computing using quantum process calculus, *Electronic Proceedings in Theoretical Computer Science 160 (EXPRESS/SOS 2014)*, pp. 111-129.

[91] N. Friis, V. Dunjko, W. Dür and H. J. Briegel, Implementing quantum control for unknown subroutines, *Physical Review A*, 89 (2014), art. no. 030303.

[92] S. J. Gay, Quantum programming languages: survey and bibliography, *Mathematical Structures in Computer Science* 16(2006)581-600.

[93] S. J. Gay and R. Nagarajan, Communicating Quantum Processes. In: *Proceedings of the 32nd ACM Symposium on Principles of Programming Languages (POPL)*, 2005, pp. 145-157.

[94] S. J. Gay and R. Nagarajan, Types and typechecking for communicating quantum processes, *Mathematical Structures in Computer Science*, 16(2006)375-406.

[95] S. J. Gay, R. Nagarajan and N. Papanikolaou, Probabilistic model-checking of quantum protocols. In: *Proceedings of the 2nd International Workshop on Developments in Computational Models (DCMÕ06)*, 2006.

[96] S. J. Gay, R. Nagarajan and N. Papanikolaou, Specification and verification of quantum protocols, *Semantic Techniques in Quantum Computation* (S. J. Gay and I. Mackie, eds.), Cambridge University Press, 2010, pp. 414-472.

[97] S. J. Gay, N. Papanikolaou and R. Nagarajan, QMC: a model checker for quantum systems. In: *Proceedings of the 20th International Conference on Computer Aided Verification (CAV)*, 2008, Springer LNCS 5123, pp. 543-547.

[98] S. J. Gay and I. V. Puthoor, Application of quantum process calculus to higher dimensional quantum protocols, *Electronic Proceedings in Theoretical Computer Science 158 (QPL 2014)*, pp. 15-28.

[99] B. Giles and P. Selinger, Exact synthesis of multiqubit Clifford+T circuits, *Physical Review A*, 87(2013), art. no. 032332.

[100] V. Giovannetti, S. Lloyd and L. Maccone, Quantum-enhanced positioning and clock synchronisation, *Nature*, 412(2001)417-419.

[101] J.-Y. Girard, Geometry of interaction I: Interpretation of system F. In: *Logic Colloquium 88*, North Holland, 1989, pp. 221-260.

[102] A. M. Gleason, Measures on the closed subspaces of a Hilbert space, *Journal of Mathematics and Mechanics*, 6(1957)885-893.

[103] M. Golovkins, Quantum pushdown automata. In: *Proceedings of the 27th Conference on Current Trends in Theory and Practice of Informatics (SOFSEM)*, 2000, Springer LNCS 1963, pp. 336-346.

[104] D. Gottesman and I. Chuang, Quantum teleportation as a universal computational primitive, *Nature*, 402(1999)390-393.

[105] J. Grattage, An overview of QML with a concrete implementation in Haskell, *Electronic Notes in Theoretical Computer Science*, 270(2011)165-174.

[106] A. S. Green, P. L. Lumsdaine, N. J. Ross, P. Selinger and B. Valiron, Quipper: A scalable quantum programming language. In: *Proceedings of the 34th ACM Conference on Programming Language Design and Implementation (PLDI)*, 2013, pp. 333-342.

[107] A. S. Green, P. L. Lumsdaine, N. J. Ross, P. Selinger and B. Valiron, An introduction to quantum programming in Quipper, *arXiv: 1304.5485*.

[108] R. B. Griffiths, Consistent histories and quantum reasoning, *Physical Review A*, 54(1996)2759-2774.

[109] L. K. Grover, Fixed-point quantum search, *Physical Review Letters*, 95 (2005), art. no. 150501.

[110] S. Gudder, Lattice properties of quantum effects, *Journal of Mathematical Physics*, 37(1996)2637-2642.

[111] S. Gudder, Quantum Markov chains, *Journal of Mathematical Physics*, 49(2008), art. no. 072105.

[112] A. W. Harrow, A. Hassidim and S. Lloyd, Quantum algorithm for linear systems of equations, *Physical Review Letters*, 103 (2009) art. no. 150502.

[113] S. Hart, M. Sharir and A. Pnueli, Termination of probabilistic concurrent programs, *ACM Transactions on Programming Languages and Systems*, 5(1983)356-380.

[114] J. D. Hartog and E. P. de Vink, Verifying probabilistic programs using a Hoare like logic, *International Journal of Foundations of Computer Science*, 13 (2003)315-340.

[115] I. Hasuo and N. Hoshino, Semantics of higher-order quantum computation via Geometry of Interaction. In: *Proceedings of the 26th Annual IEEE Symposium on Logic in Computer Science (LICS)*, 2011, pp. 237-246.

[116] B. Hayes, Programming your quantum computer, *American Scientist*, 102(2014) 22-25.

[117] C. Heunen and B. Jacobs, Quantum logic in dagger kernel categories. In: *Proceedings of Quantum Physics and Logic 2009*.

[118] K. Honda, Analysis of quantum entanglement in quantum programs using stabiliser formalism. In: *Proceedings of the 12th International Workshop on Quantum Physics and Logic (QPL)*, 2015. arXiv:1511.01181.

[119] C. A. R. Hoare, Procedures and parameters: an axiomatic approach. In: *Symposium on Semantics of Algorithmic Languages*, Springer Lecture Notes in Mathematics 188, 1971, pp 102-116.

[120] T. Hoare and R. Milner (eds.), *Grand Challenges in Computing Research* (organised by BCS, CPHC, EPSRC, IEE, etc.), 2004, http://www.ukcrc.org.uk/grand-challenges/index.cfm.

[121] P. Hoyer, J. Neerbek and Y. Shi, Quantum complexities of ordered searching, sorting and element distinctness. In: *Proceedings of the 28th International Colloquium on Automata, Languages, and Programming (ICALP)*, 2001, pp. 62-73.

[122] N. Inui, N. Konno and E. Segawa, One-dimensional three-state quantum walk, *Physical Review E*, 72 (2005) art. no. 056112.

[123] B. Jacobs, On block structures in quantum computation, *Electronic Notes in Theoretical Computer Science*, 298(2013)233-255.

[124] B. Jacobs, New directions in categorical logic, for classical, probabilistic and quantum Logic, *Logical Methods in Computer Science*, 2015.

[125] C. J. Isham and N. Linden, Quantum temporal logic and decoherence functionals in the histories approach to generalized quantum theory, *Journal of Mathematical Physics*, 35(1994)5452-

[126] A. JavadiAbhari, S. Patil, D. Kudrow, J. Heckey, A. Lvov, F. T. Chong and M. Martonosi, ScaffCC: Scalable compilation and analysis of quantum programs, *Parallel Computing*, 45(2015)2-17.

[127] N. D. Jones, *Computability and Complexity: From a Programming Perspective*, The MIT Press, 1997.

[128] P. Jorrand and M. Lalire, Toward a quantum process algebra. In: *Proceedings of the 1st ACM Conference on Computing Frontier*, 2004, pp. 111-119.

[129] P. Jorrand and S. Perdrix, Abstract interpretation techniques for quantum computation. In: *Semantic Techniques in Quantum Computation* I. Mackie and S. Gay, eds., Cambridge University Press 2010, pp. 206-234.

[130] R. Jozsa and N. Linden, On the role of entanglement in quantum computational speed-up, *Proceedings of the Royal Society of London, Series A Mathematical, Physical and Engineering Sciences*, 459 (2003)2011-2032.

[131] R. Kadison, Order properties of bounded self-adjoint operators, *Proceedings of American Mathematical Society*, 34(1951)505-510.

[132] Y. Kakutani, A logic for formal verification of quantum programs. In: *Proceedings of the 13th Asian Computing Science Conference (ASIAN)*, 2009, Springer LNCS 5913, pp. 79-93.

[133] E. Kashefi, Quantum domain theory – Definitions and applications, *arXiv:quant-ph/0306077*.

[134] A. Kitaev, Fault-tolerant quantum computation by anyons, *ArXiv: quantph/9707021*.

[135] A. Kitaev, A. H. Shen and M. N. Vyalyi, *Classical and Quantum Computation*, American Mathematical Society, Providence 2002.

[136] T. Kadowaki and H. Nishimori, Quantum annealing in the transverse Ising model, *Physical Review E*, 58(1998)5355.

[137] V. Kliuchnikov, D. Maslov and M. Mosca, Fast and efficient exact synthesis of single qubit unitaries generated by Clifford and T gates, *Quantum Information & Computation*, 13(2013)607-630.

[138] V. Kliuchnikov, A. Bocharov and K. M. Svore, Asymptotically optimal topological quantum compiling, *Physical Review Letters*, 112(2014) art. no. 140504.

[139] E.H. Knill, *Conventions for Quantum Pseudo-code*, Technical Report, Los Alamos National Laboratory, 1996.

[140] A. Kondacs and J. Watrous, On the power of quantum finite state automata. In: *Proc. 38th Symposium on Foundation of Computer Science*, 1997, pp. 66-75.

[141] T. Kubota, *Verification of Quantum Cryptographic Protocols using Quantum Process Algebras*, PhD Thesis, Department of Computer Science, University of Tokyo, 2014.

[142] T. Kubota, Y. Kakutani, G. Kato, Y. Kawano and H. Sakurada, Application of a process calculus to security proofs of quantum protocols. In: *Proceedings of Foundations of Computer Science in WORLDCOMP*, 2012, pp. 141-147.

[143] T. Kubota, Y. Kakutani, G. Kato, Y. Kawano and H. Sakurada, Semi-automated verification of security proofs of quantum cryptographic protocols, *Journal of Symbolic Computation*, 2015.

[144] D. Kudrow, K. Bier, Z. Deng, D. Franklin, Y. Tomita, K. R. Brown and F. T. Chong, Quantum rotation: A case study in static and dynamic machine-code generation for quantum computer. In: *Proceedings of the 40th ACM/IEEE International Symposium on Computer Architecture (ISCA)*, 2013, pp. 166-176.

[145] P. Kurzyński and A. Wójcik, Quantum walk as a generalized measure device, *Physical Review Letters*, *110* (2013) art. no. 200404.

[146] M. Kwiatkowska, G. Norman and P. Parker, Probabilistic symbolic model-checking with PRISM: a hybrid approach, *International Journal on Software Tools for Technology Transfer*, 6(2004)128-142.

[147] M. Lalire, Relations among quantum processes: bisimilarity and congruence, *Mathematical Structures in Computer Science*, 16(2006)407-428.

[148] M. Lampis, K. G. Ginis, M. A. Papakyriakou and N. S. Papaspyrou, Quantum data and control made easier, *Electronic Notes in Theoretical Computer Science* 210(2008) 85-105.

[149] A. Lapets and M. Rötteler, Abstract resource cost derivation for logical quantum circuit description. In: *Proceedings of the ACM Workshop on Functional Programming Concepts in Domain-Specific Languages (FPCDSL)*, 2013, pp. 35-42.

[150] A. Lapets, M. P. da Silva, M. Thome, A. Adler, J. Beal and M. Rötteler, QuaFL: A typed DSL for quantum programming. In: *Proceedings of the ACM Workshop on Functional Programming Concepts in Domain-Specific Languages (FPCDSL)*, 2013, pp. 19-27.

[151] D. W. Leung, Quantum computation by measurements, *International Journal of Quantum Information*, 2(2004)33-43.

[152] Y. J. Li, N. K. Yu and M. S. Ying, Termination of nondeterministic quantum programs, *Acta Informatica*, 51(2014)1-24.

[153] Y. J. Li and M. S. Ying, (Un)decidable problems about reachability of quantum systems. In: *Proceedings of the 25th International Conference on Concurrency Theory (CONCUR)*, 2014, pp. 482-496.

[154] S. Lloyd, Universal quantum simulators, *Science*, 273(1996)1073-1078.

[155] S. Lloyd, A theory of quantum gravity based on quantum computation, *arXiv:quant-ph/0501135*.

[156] S. Lloyd, M. Mohseni and P. Rebentrost, Quantum principal component analysis, *Nature Physics*, 10(2014)631-633.

[157] S. Lloyd, M. Mohseni and P. Rebentrost, Quantum algorithms for supervised and unsupervised machine learning, *arXiv:1307.0411v2*.

[158] J. Loeckx and K. Sieber, *The Foundations of Program Verification* (second edition), John Wiley & Sons, Chichester, 1987.

[159] N. B. Lovett, S. Cooper, M. Everitt, M. Trevers and V. Kendon, Universal quantum computation using the discrete-time quantum walk, *Physicl Review A, 81* (2010) art. no. 042330.

[160] I. Mackie and S. Gay (eds.), *Semantic Techniques in Quantum Computation*, Cambridge University Press, 2010.

[161] F. Magniez, M. Santha and M. Szegedy, Quantum algorithms for the triangle problem, *SIAM Journal of Computing*, 37(2007)413-427.

[162] Z. Manna, *Mathematical Theory of Computation*, McGraw-Hill, 1974.

[163] Ph. A. Martin and F. Rothen, *Many-Body Problems and Quantum Field Theory: An Introduction*, Springer, Berlin, 2004.

[164] P. Mateus, J. Ramos, A. Sernadas and C. Sernadas, Temporal logics for reasoning about quantum systems. In: *Semantic Techniques in Quantum Computation* I. Mackie and S. Gay, eds., Cambridge University Press 2010, pp. 389-413.

[165] P. Maymin, Extending the lambda calculus to express randomized and quantumized algorithms, *arXiv:quant-ph/9612052*.

[166] A. McIver and C. Morgan, *Abstraction, Refinement and Proof for Probabilistic Systems*, Springer, New York, 2005.

[167] T. S. Metodi and F. T. Chong, Quantum Computing for Computer Architects, Synthesis Lectures in Computer Architecture # 1, Morgan & Claypool Publishers, 2011 (Second Edition).

[168] D. A. Meyer, Quantum strategies, *Physical Review Letters*, 82 (1999)1052-1055.

[169] J. A. Miszczak, Models of quantum computation and quantum programming languages, *Bulletion of the Polish Academy of Science: Technical Sciences*, 59(2011) 305-324.

[170] J. A. Miszczak, *High-level Structures for Quantum Computing*, Morgan & Claypool Publishers, 2012.

[171] M. Montero, Unidirectional quantum walks: Evolution and exit times, *Physical Review A*, 88 (2013) art. no. 012333.

[172] C. Morgan, *Programming from Specifications*, Prentice Hall, Hertfordshire, 1988.

[173] S. -C. Mu and R. Bird, Functional quantum programming. In: *Proceedings of the 2nd Asian Workshop on Programming Languages and Systems (APLAS)*, 2001, pp. 75-88.

[174] M. A. Nielsen and I. L. Chuang, *Quantum Computation and Quantum Information*, Cambridge University Press, 2000.

[175] M. A. Nielsen, Quantum computation by measurement and quantum memory, *Physical Letters A*, 308(2003)96-100.

[176] R. Nagarajan, N. Papanikolaou and D. Williams, Simulating and compiling code for the Sequential Quantum Random Access Machine, *Electronic Notes in Theoretical Computer Science*, 170(2007)101-124.

[177] B. Ömer, *Structured Quantum Programming*, Ph.D thesis, Technical University of Vienna, 2003.

[178] M. Pagani, P. Selinger and B. Valiron, Applying quantitative semantics to higher-order quantum computing. In: *Proceedings of the 41st ACM Symposium on Principles of Programming Languages (POPL)*, 2014, pp. 647-658.

[179] N. K. Papanikolaou, *Model Checking Quantum Protocols*, PhD Thesis, Department of Computer Science, University of Warwick, 2008.

[180] A. Platzer, Differential dynamic logic for hybrid systems, *Journal of Automated Reasoning*, 41(2008)143-189, 2008.

[181] L. M. Procopio, A. Moqanaki, M. Araújo, F. Costa, I. A. Calafell, E. G. Dowd, D. R. Hamel, L. A. Rozema, C. Brukner and P. Walther, Experimental superposition of orders of quantum gates, *Nature Communications*, 2015, Art. no. 7913.

[182] E. Prugovečki, *Quantum Mechanics in Hilbert Space*, Academic Press, New York, 1981.

[183] R. Raussendorf and H. J. Briegel, A one-way quantum computer, *Physical Review Letters*, 86(2001)5188-5191.

[184] P. Rebentrost, M. Mohseni and S. Lloyd, Quantum support vector machine for big data classification, *Physical Review Letters*, 113(2014) art. no. 130501.

[185] M. Rennela, Towards a quantum domain theory: order-enrichment and fixpoints in W*-algebras. In: *Proceedings of the 30th Conference on the Mathematical Foundations of Programming Semantics (MFPS)*, 2014.

[186] T. Reps, S. Horwitz and M. Sagiv, Precise interprocedural dataflow analysis via graph reachability. In: *Proceedings of the 22nd ACM Symposium on Principles of Programming Languages (POPL)*, 1995, pp. 49-61.

[187] E. G. Rieffel, D. Venturelli, B. O'Gorman, M. B. Do, E. M. Prystay and V. N. Smelyanskiy, A case study in programming a quantum annealer for hard operational planning problems, *Quantum Information Processing*, 14(2015)1-36.

[188] N. J. Ross and P. Selinger, Optimal ancilla-free Clifford+T approximation of z-rotations, *arXiv:1403.2975*

[189] Y. Rouselakis, N. S. Papaspyrou, Y. Tsiouris and E. N. Todoran, Compilation to quantum circuits for a language with quantum data and control. In: *Proceedings of the 2013 Federated Conference on Computer Science and Information Systems (FedCSIS)* 2013, pp. 1537-1544.

[190] R. Rüdiger, Quantum programming languages: an introductory overview, *The Computer Journal*, 50(2007)134-150.

[191] J. W. Sanders and P. Zuliani, Quantum programming. In: *Proceedings of 5th International Conference on Mathematics of Program Construction (MPC)*, Springer LNCS 1837, Springer 2000, pp. 88-99.

[192] M. Santha, Quantum walk based search algorithms. In: *Proceedings of the 5th International Conference on Theory and Applications of Models of Computation (TAMC 2008)*, Springer LNCS 4978, pp 31-46.

[193] F. Schwabl, *Advanced Quantum Mechanics* (Fourth edition), Springer, 2008.

[194] P. Selinger, Towards a quantum programming language, *Mathematical Structures in Computer Science 14* (2004), 527-586.

[195] P. Selinger, A brief survey of quantum programming languages. In: *Proceedings of the 7th International Symposium on Functional and Logic Programming*, LNCS 2998, Springer, 2004, pp. 1-6.

[196] P. Selinger, Toward a semantics for higher-order quantum computation. In: *Proceedings of QPL'2004*, TUCS General Publications No. 33, pp. 127-143.

[197] P. Selinger and B. Valiron, A lambda calculus for quantum computation with classical control, *Mathematical Structures in Computer Science*, 16(2006)527-55.

[198] P. Selinger and B. Valiron, On a fully abstract model for a quantum linear functional language, *Electronic Notes in Theoretical Computer Science* 210(2008) 123-137.

[199] P. Selinger and B. Valiron, Quantum lambda calculus, in: S. Gay and I. Mackie (eds.), *Semantic Techniques in Quantum Computation*, Cambridge University Press 2010, pp. 135-172.

[200] R. Sethi, *Programming Languages: Concepts and Constructs*, Addison-Wesley (2002).

[201] V. V. Shende, S. S. Bullock and I. L. Markov, Synthesis of quantum-logic circuits, *IEEE Transactions on CAD of Integrated Circuits and Systems* 25(2006) 1000-1010.

[202] M. Sharir, A. Pnueli and S. Hart, Verification of probabilistic programs, *SIAM Journal of Computing*, 13 (1984)292-314.

[203] N. Shenvi, J. Kempe and K. B. Whaley, Quantum random-walk search algorithm, *Physical Review A*, 67(2003) art. no. 052307.

[204] P. W. Shor, Algorithms for quantum computation: discrete logarithms and factoring. In: *Proceedings of the 35th IEEE Annual Symposium on Foundations of Computer Science (FOCS)*, 1994, 124-134.

[205] P. W. Shor, Why haven't more quantum algorithms been discovered? *Journal of the ACM*, 50(2003)87-90.

[206] S. Staton, Algebraic effects, linearity, and quantum programming languages. In: *Proceedings of the 42nd ACM Symposium on Principles of Programming Languages (POPL)*, 2015, pp. 395-406.

[207] K. M. Svore, A. V. Aho, A. W. Cross, I. L. Chuang and I. L. Markov, A layered software architecture for quantum computing design tools, *IEEE Computer*, 39(2006) 74-83.

[208] A. Tafliovich and E. C. R. Hehner, Quantum predicative programming. In: *Proceedings of the 8th International Conference on Mathematics of Program Construction (MPC)*, LNCS 4014, Springer, pp. 433-454.

[209] A.Tafliovich and E.C.R.Hehner, Programming with quantum communication, *Electronic Notes in Theoretical Computer Science*, 253(2009)99-118.

[210] G. Takeuti, Quantum set theory, in: E. Beltrametti and B. C. van Fraassen (eds.), *Current Issues in Quantum Logics*, Plenum, New Rork, 1981, pp. 303-322.

[211] G. 't Hooft, The cellular automaton interpretation of quantum mechanics – A view on the quantum nature of our universe, compulsory or impossible?, *arXiv:1405.1548v2*.

[212] A. van Tonder, A lambda calculus for quantum computation, *SIAM Journal on Computing*, 33(2004)1109-1135.

[213] V. S. Varadarajan, *Geometry of Quantum Theory*, Springer-Verlag, New York, 1985.

[214] S. E. Venegas-Andraca, Quantum walks: a comprehensive review, *Quantum Information Processing*, 11(2012)1015-1106.

[215] D. Wecker and K. M. Svore, LIQUi|>: A software design architecture and domain-specific language for quantum computing, http://research.microsoft.com/pubs/209634/1402.4467.pdf.

[216] M. M. Wolf, *Quantum Channels and Operators: Guided Tour*, unpublished lecture notes (2012).

[217] P. Xue and B. C. Sanders, Two quantum walkers sharing coins, *Physical Review A*, 85 (2011) art. no. 022307.

[218] A. C. Yao, Quantum circuit complexity. In: *Proceedings of the 34th Annual IEEE Symposium on Foundations of Computer Science (FOCS)*, 1993, pp. 352-361.

[219] K. Yasuda, T. Kubota and Y. Kakutani, Observational equivalence using schedulers for quantum processes, *Electronic Proceedings in Theoretical Computer Science 172 (QPL 2014)*, pp. 191-203.

[220] M. S. Ying, Reasoning about probabilistic sequential programs in a probabilistic logic, *Acta Informatica*, 39(2003) 315-389.

[221] M. S. Ying, Floyd-Hoare logic for quantum programs, *ACM Transactions on Programming Languages and Systems, 39* (2011), art. no. 19.

[222] M. S. Ying, Quantum recursion and second quantisation, (2014) arXiv:1405.4443.

[223] M. S. Ying, Foundations of quantum programming. In: Kazunori Ueda (Ed.), *Proc. of the 8th Asian Symposium on Programming Languages and Systems (APLAS 2010)*, Lecture Notes in Computer Science 6461, Springer 2010, pp. 16-20.

[224] M. S. Ying, J. X. Chen, Y. Feng and R. Y. Duan, Commutativity of quantum weakest preconditions, *Information Processing Letters*, 104(2007)152-158.

[225] M. S. Ying, R. Y. Duan, Y. Feng and Z. F. Ji, Predicate transformer semantics of quantum programs. In: *Semantic Techniques in Quantum Computation*, I. Mackie and S. Gay, eds., Cambridge University Press 2010, 311-360.

[226] M. S. Ying and Y. Feng, An algebraic language for distributed quantum computing, *IEEE Transactions on Computers* 58(2009)728-743.

[227] M. S. Ying and Y. Feng, Quantum loop programs, *Acta Informatica, 47* (2010), 221-250.

[228] M. S. Ying and Y. Feng, A flowchart language for quantum programming, *IEEE Transactions on Software Engineering*, 37(2011)466-485.

[229] M. S. Ying, Y. Feng, R. Y. Duan and Z. F. Ji, An algebra of quantum processes, *ACM Transactions on Computational Logic*, 10(2009), art. no. 19.

[230] M. S. Ying, Y. Feng and N. K. Yu, Quantum information-flow security: Noninterference and access control. In: *Proceedings of the IEEE 26th Computer Security Foundations Symposium (CSF'2013)*, pp. 130-144.

[231] M. S. Ying, Y. J. Li, N. K. Yu and Y. Feng, Model-checking linear-time properties of quantum systems, *ACM Transactions on Computational Logic*, 15(2014), art. no. 22.

[232] M. S. Ying, N. K. Yu and Y. Feng, Defining quantum control flows of programs, *arXiv:1209.4379*.

[233] M. S. Ying, N. K. Yu and Y. Feng, Alternation in quantum programming: from superposition of data to superposition of programs, *arXiv: 1402.5172*. http://xxx.lanl.gov/abs/1402.5172.

[234] M. S. Ying, N. K. Yu, Y. Feng and R. Y. Duan, Verification of quantum programs, *Science of Computer Programming*, 78(2013)1679-1700.

[235] S. G. Ying, Y. Feng, N. K. Yu and M. S. Ying, Reachability analysis of quantum Markov chains. In: *Proceedings of the 24th International Conference on Concurrency Theory (CONCUR)*, 2013, pp. 334-348.

[236] S. G. Ying and M. S. Ying, Reachability analysis of quantum Markov decision processes, *arXiv:1406.6146*.

[237] N. K. Yu, R. Y. Duan and M. S. Ying, Five two-qubit gates are necessary for implementing Toffoli gate, *Physical Review A*, 88(2013) art. no. 010304.

[238] N. K. Yu and M. S. Ying, Reachability and termination analysis of concurrent quantum programs. In: *Proceedings of the 23th International Conference on Concurrency Theory (CONCUR)*, 2012, pp. 69-83.

[239] N. K. Yu and M. S. Ying, Optimal simulation of Deutsch gates and the Fredkin gate, *Physical Review A*, 91(2015) art. no. 032302.

[240] X. Q. Zhou, T. C. Ralph, P. Kalasuwan, M. Zhang, A. Peruzzo, B. P. Lanyon and J. L. O'Brien, Adding control to arbitrary unknown quantum operations, *Nature Communications, 2* (2011) 413.1-8.

[241] P. Zuliani, *Quantum Programming*, D.Phil. Thesis, University of Oxford, 2001.

[242] P. Zuliani, Compiling quantum programs, *Acta Informatica*, 41(2005)435-473.

[243] P. Zuliani, Quantum programming with mixed states. In: *Proceedings of the 3rd International Workshop on Quantum Programming Languages*, 2005.

[244] P. Zuliani, Reasoning about faulty quantum programs, *Acta Informatica*, 46(2009) 403-432.

Index

Printed in the United States
By Bookmasters